PAINTING HISTORY

THE MURALS OF NORTHERN IRELAND 1908–2024

PAINTING HISTORY

THE MURALS OF NORTHERN IRELAND 1908–2024

TONY CROWLEY

Amherst College Press

The complete manuscript of this work was subjected to a partly closed ("single-anonymous") review process. For more information, visit https://acpress.amherst.edu/peerreview/.

Published in the United States of America by Amherst College Press Manufactured in the United States of America

Library of Congress Control Number: 2024944033
DOI: https://doi.org/10.3998/mpub.14527058

ISBN 979-8-89506-006-3 (paper)
ISBN 979-8-89506-007-0 (open access)
ISBN 979-8-89506-008-7 (hardcover)

For Michael and Geneviève Cuming

Contents

Acknowledgments ix
Acknowledgments for Permissions xi
List of Abbreviations and Acronyms xiii
Maps xv
A Brief Note on Spellings, Grammar, and Punctuation xix
A Note on the Images in the Book xxi

Introduction. Paint and Power: A Personal Journey Through a Political Landscape 1
1 Hegemony: Loyalist Muralism from the Home Rule Crisis to the Troubles 25
2 Counter-Hegemony: The Emergence and Consolidation of Republican Muralism 1981–1993 57
3 Renewal of a tradition: The Re-emergence of Loyalist Muralism 1982–1993 93
4 Ending the War, Negotiating the Peace: The Evolution of Republican Muralism 1994–2006 125
5 Facing Out, Facing In: Peace Negotiation and Internecine Strife: Loyalist Murals 1994–2006 177
6 Managing History: Politics, Legacy, and Dissidence: Republican Murals 2007–2024 227
7 The Problem of Change: Settlement, Uncertainty, and Fragmentation: Loyalist Murals 2007–2024 273
8 The End of Muralism? 323

Notes 333
Bibliography 349

Acknowledgments

I started this research (though it wasn't research when it began) more than forty years ago. It has been a long journey and along the way I have been fortunate to encounter very many people who have helped me in all sorts of ways. They have given me their time, their kindness, their generosity; they have opened doors for me, shared their knowledge, provided me with insights, taken an interest in what I was doing, and offered encouragement. Some of them have also harangued me, warned me when I was making mistakes, and set me straight when I mistook intricacy for simplicity; "Tony, wise up, for fuck's sake" is a phrase that has been addressed to me (deservedly) on more occasions than I care to remember. I cannot name a great number of the people who have given me help, either because, even after all this time, they still do not want to be publicly acknowledged, or because I have only ever known them by their first name. Those who can and can't be named range from muralists to librarians and tech geeks, from paramilitaries to peacemakers (sometimes the same person), from senior politicians to school caretakers, from "ordinary people" (a ridiculous category I know) to members of the police force, from victims to those who were engaged in violence. And then of course there have been the friends that I have been lucky enough to meet and keep… In any case, to adapt a line from Yeats, I number as many as I can in my song. I am grateful to them all; this book, and the research that underpins it, would not have been possible without them.

I would like to express my gratitude to the following people who have helped me one way and another over the years (a number of whom have died—I mark this with an (*) after their name): Joe Baker, Glen Barr (*), David Beresford (*), William Blair, May Blood (*), Stuart Borthwick, Nigel Boyle, Suzanne Breen, Mark Buchholz, Gale Burrow, Ciaran Carson (*), Kevin Carson, Lesley Cherry, Joe Cleary, Karen Corrigan, Kenneth Cotich, Dee Craig, Lisa Crane, Helen Croft (Kerr), Seamus Deane (*), Danny Devenny, Deborah Devenny, Paud Devenny, Mickey Doherty, Enda Duffy, Terry Eagleton, Aaron Edwards, Marianne Elliott, Ciara Ennis, Kai Ernstberger, David Ervine (*), Mark Ervine, Mick Fealty, Tadhg Foley, Rosa Gonzalez, Jessica Davila Greene, Mary Griffiths, Johnny Haddock, Stella Halkyard, Tom Hartley, Erin Hinson, Paddy Hoey, Eamonn Hughes, John Hume (*), Billy Hutchinson, Yeisi Ileczko, Chris Jones, Frances Kane, TJ Kao, Gerard "Mo Chara" Kelly, John Kerrigan, Bobby Lavery (*), Belinda Loftus, Catalina Lopez, Rebecca Lubas, Marty Lyons, Seán Mac Aindreasa (*), Séimí Mac Aindreasa, Seosamh Mac Coille, Paddy McManus (*), Jake Mac Siacais, Pat Magee, Jim McCann, Bríg McClenaghan (*), Dermie McClenaghan (*), Pauline McClenaghan, Henry McDonald (*), Jackie McDonald,

Marissa McGlinchey, Noel McGuigan, Martin McGuinness (*), Anthony McIntyre, Ann McKee, Peter McKee, Pat McGeown (*), John McMichael (*), Ron McMurray, Seany McVeigh (*), Ian Maguire, Martin Melaugh, Alain Miossec, William Mitchell, Danny Morrison, Janet Muller, Kevin Mulroy, Máiréad Nic Craith, Emer Nolan, Gearóid Ó Tuathaigh, Conal Parr, Tom Paulin, Andrea Redmond, Jackie Redpath, Darren Richardson, Warren Roberts, Bill Rolston, Adam Rosenkranz, Ray Ryan, Angela Scullion, Gerry Scullion, Ian Shanks, Dave Simpson, Tony Smith, William Plum Smith (*), Jim Smyth, Allegra Swift, Sabine Troendle, Pat Vince, Micí Walsh, Jacqueline Wernimont, John Williamson, Fr. Des Wilson (*), Cahal Woods.

I have been fortunate to receive institutional support in the writing of this work and I gratefully acknowledge it here. The Leverhulme Trust awarded me a Major Research Fellowship ("The uses of the past: history and social memory in Northern Ireland 1980–2020" ref: 118797) and extended the grant in the light of the difficulties caused by Covid. The School of English and the Faculty of Arts, Humanities and Cultures at the University of Leeds also contributed to the funding of the extension. Without the support of the Trust and the university, the book could not have been written. I also acknowledge a debt to the various libraries in which I have worked; their staff have frequently gone above and beyond in their helpfulness and enthusiasm. I thank in particular Belfast Central Library and the Newspaper Library at Belfast Central Library (where Catherine Morrow and the staff were extraordinarily generous with their time, knowledge, and energy), the Linen Hall Library (specifically the Northern Ireland Political Collection), the Public Record Office of Northern Ireland, the Eileen Hickey Irish Republican History Museum, and the ACT Initiative museum; we are lucky to have the resources that they afford. I also express my gratitude to my colleagues in the School of English at Leeds. To the wonderful staff, past and present, at the Claremont Colleges Library I owe an enormous obligation; their commitment to the Murals of Northern Ireland project has been unfailing, and I thank them for their professional and personal support. I also express my gratitude to the faculty and staff at Scripps College, where the murals archive was first conceived—they were consistently helpful. Finally, it would not have been possible to take this text forward without the know-how of my editor Beth Bouloukos and her team at Amherst, and the technical genius of Katie Rokakis at Michigan; I thank them too.

I am lucky in my friends and I wish to thank the following for their support: Fazia Aitel, Bridget Bennett, Jim Clifford, Chris Connery, Rachael Gilmour, Sudhir Hazareesingh, Gail Hershatter, Hao Huang, John Kerrigan, Grace Laurencin, Andrew Long, Andrew McNeillie, Tom and Susan Mulhearn, Bernard O'Donoghue, Heather O'Donoghue, Mark Ord, John Peacock, Angela Poingdestre, Cathy Rosario, Mary Scott, Dion and Meghan Scott-Kakures, Stephen Sheedy, Julia Snell, Kate Spowage, Jane Taylor (*), Sheila Walker, Bernard and Mary Weston, John Whale, Paul Young. I am also fortunate in my family—the Crowleys—Nicky, Colette, Terry, Jacky (together with all my nephews and nieces). Biggest debts last of course: to Emily, Joseph, and Louise for the best questions, the sense of perspective, the fun and the love.

The book is dedicated to Michael and Geneviève Cuming; I deeply appreciate their unstinting support, generosity, kindness, and love.

Acknowledgments for Permissions

I am deeply grateful to the editors of the *Belfast Telegraph*, *The Newsletter* (*Belfast Newsletter* as was), and the *Londonderry Sentinel*, as well as the librarian at the Linen Hall Library, for their permission to reproduce early images of murals from their publications (details below).

Chapter one: fig. 4: Sir Henry Wilson, Pittsburg Street, North Belfast, *Belfast Telegraph*, July 8 1922.

Chapter one: fig. 5: Sir Henry Wilson, Limestone Road, North Belfast, *Belfast Weekly News*, July 13 1922.

Chapter one: fig. 6: Nurse Edith Cavell, Primitive Street, South Belfast, *Belfast Newsletter*, July 10 1929.

Chapter one: fig. 7: 36th Ulster Regiment, Fortingale Street, West Belfast, *Belfast Telegraph*, July 10 1933.

Chapter one: fig. 8: 1690 1914–1918, Clifford Street, South Belfast, *Northern Whig*, July 6 1934.

Chapter one: fig. 9: Battle of the Somme, Coolfin Street, South Belfast, *Belfast Telegraph*, July 10 1935.

Chapter one: fig. 10: Silver Jubilee, Snugville Street, West Belfast, *Belfast Telegraph*, May 2 1935.

Chapter one: fig. 11: Coronation George VII, Marine Street, North Belfast, *Belfast Newsletter*, May 11 1937.

Chapter one: fig. 12: Royal Family, Snugville Street, West Belfast, *Belfast Telegraph*, July 9 1938.

Chapter one: fig. 13: King Billy with Tommy Henderson, location unknown, postcard in the Northern Ireland Political Collection, Linen Hall library, c.1912.

Chapter one: fig. 14: King Billy Prince of Wales Lord Carson, Maria Place, West Belfast, *Belfast Newsletter*, July 12 1933.

Chapter one: fig. 15: Their only crime was loyalty, Earl Lane, North Belfast, *Belfast Telegraph*, July 7 1939

Chapter one: fig. 16: King Billy, Roslyn Street/Louisa Street, North Belfast *Belfast Telegraph*, July 11 1933.

Chapter one: fig. 17: King Billy, Tierney Street, South Belfast, *Belfast Telegraph*, July 11 1936.

Chapter one: fig. 18: King Billy, Templemore Street, East Belfast, *Belfast Newsletter*, July 12 1937.

Chapter one: fig. 20: Colonel Adam Murray, Clarence Place, Londonderry, *Londonderry Sentinel*, August 13 1958.

Chapter one: fig. 21: King Billy, Earl Place, North Belfast, *Belfast Telegraph*, July 9 1965.

Chapter 3: fig. 7: The blue skies of Ulster, Orkney Drive, Ballymena, *Ballymena Observer*, 1984.

A number of newspapers in this list—the *Belfast Weekly News*, *Northern Whig* and *Ballymena Observer*—have long since ceased publication; despite my best efforts, it has not been possible to trace the erstwhile publishers.

List of Abbreviations and Acronyms

Listed below are the principal acronyms either used in this text or found on the images of the murals. The best (searchable) glossary of terms related to the war and the conflict in Northern Ireland can be found at https://cain.ulster.ac.uk/glossary.php. The CAIN Archive—"Conflict and Politics in Northern Ireland" https://cain.ulster.ac.uk/index.html—is a comprehensive set of resources both for beginners and experienced researchers alike.

32CSM:	32 County Sovereignty Movement
CIRA:	Continuity Irish Republican Army
CnamB:	Cumann na mBan
DUP:	Democratic Unionist Party
GAA:	Gaelic Athletic Association (Cumann Lúthchleas Gael)
GPO:	General Post Office
INLA:	Irish National Liberation Army
IPLO:	Irish People's Liberation Organisation
IRA/PIRA:	Irish Republican Army (Provisional IRA, Provisionals)
IRPWA:	Irish Republican Prisoners Welfare Association
IRSP:	Irish Republican Socialist Party
LVF:	Loyalist Volunteer Force
MP:	Member of Parliament (Westminster)
OIRA:	Official Irish Republican Army
ONH:	Óglaigh na hÉireann
OUP:	Official Unionist Party (now Ulster Unionist Party)
PAF:	Protestant Action Force
POW:	Prisoner of War
PSNI:	Police Service of Northern Ireland
PUP:	Progressive Unionist Party

RHC:	Red Hand Commando
RIR:	Royal Irish Regiment
RIRA:	Real IRA
RNU:	Republican Network for Unity
RSF:	Republican Sinn Féin
RUC:	Royal Ulster Constabulary
SAS:	Special Air Service
SDLP:	Social Democratic and Labour Party
SF:	Sinn Féin
TD:	Teachta Dalá (member of Irish parliament Dáil Éireann)
UDA:	Ulster Defence Association
UDF:	Ulster Defence Fighters
UDP:	Ulster Democratic Party
UDR:	Ulster Defence Regiment
UFF:	Ulster Freedom Fighters
USC:	Ulster Special Constabulary (B Specials)
UUP:	Ulster Unionist Party (formerly Official Unionist Party, OUP)
UVF:	Ulster Volunteer Force
UWC:	Ulster Workers' Council
YCV:	Young Citizen Volunteers

Maps

The best freely available maps of Northern Ireland can be found at googlemaps and the Public Record Office of Northern Ireland (PRONI). On the PRONI historical maps viewer a range of historical six-inch Ordnance Survey maps can be found together with the most detailed contemporary map: https://www.nidirect.gov.uk/services/search-proni-historical-maps-viewer. The maps provided below, taken with permission from the Ireland Story website—https://www.wesleyjohnston.com/users/ireland/geography/index.htm—are rudimentary and offered as no more than preliminary guides; for more precise mapping, see the resources above.

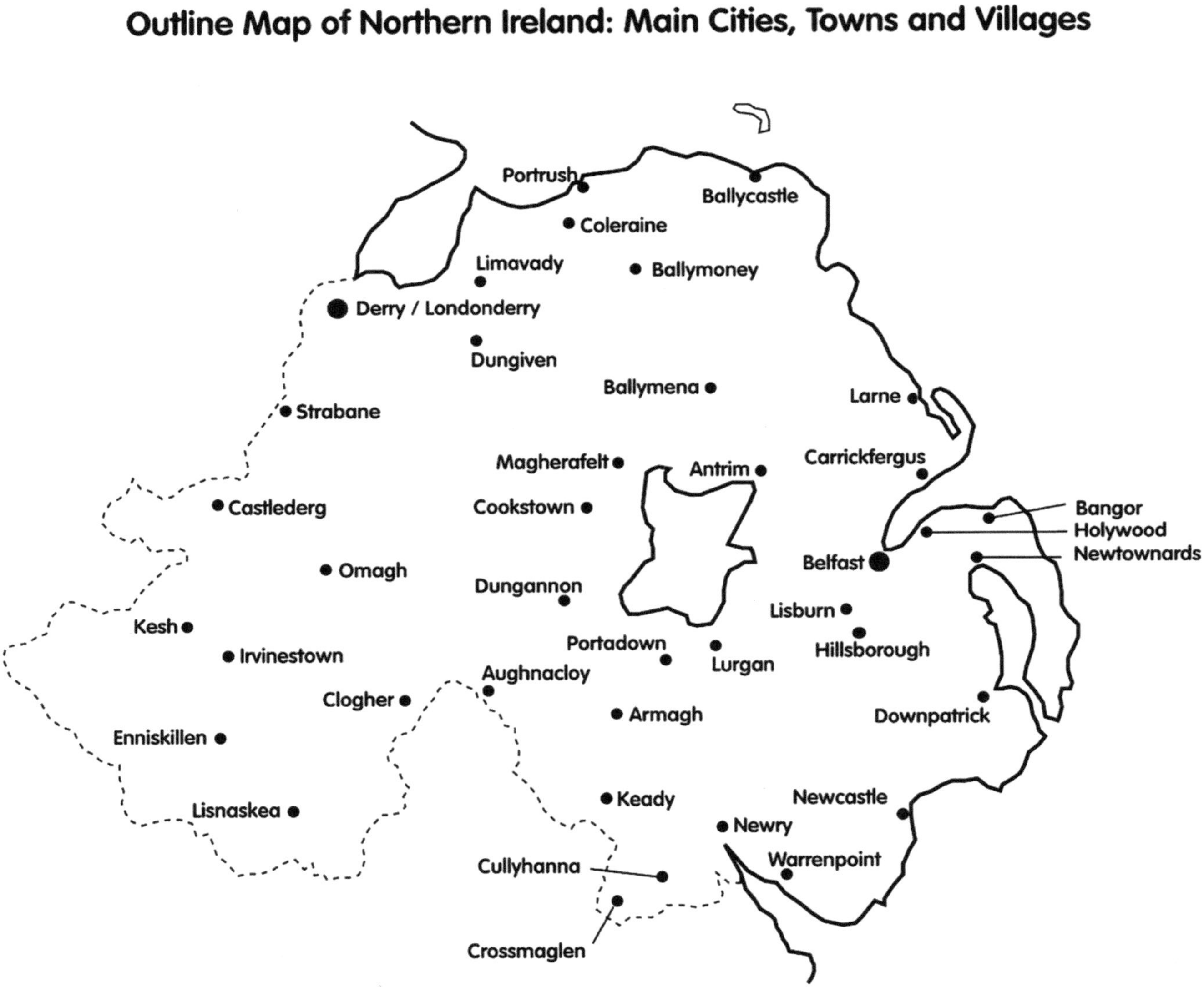

FIGURE 1 Outline map of Northern Ireland: main cities, towns and villages.

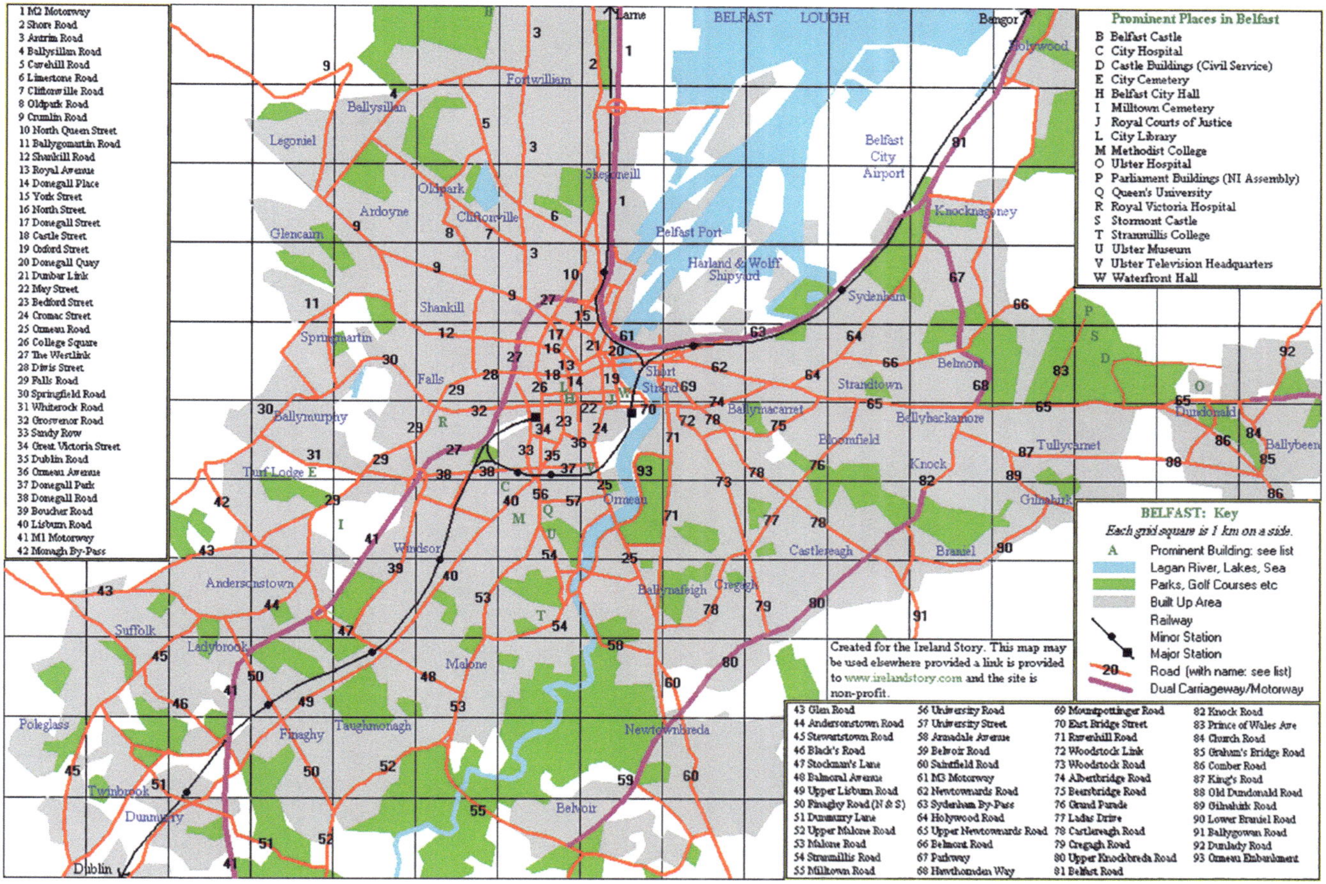

FIGURE 2 Map of Belfast.

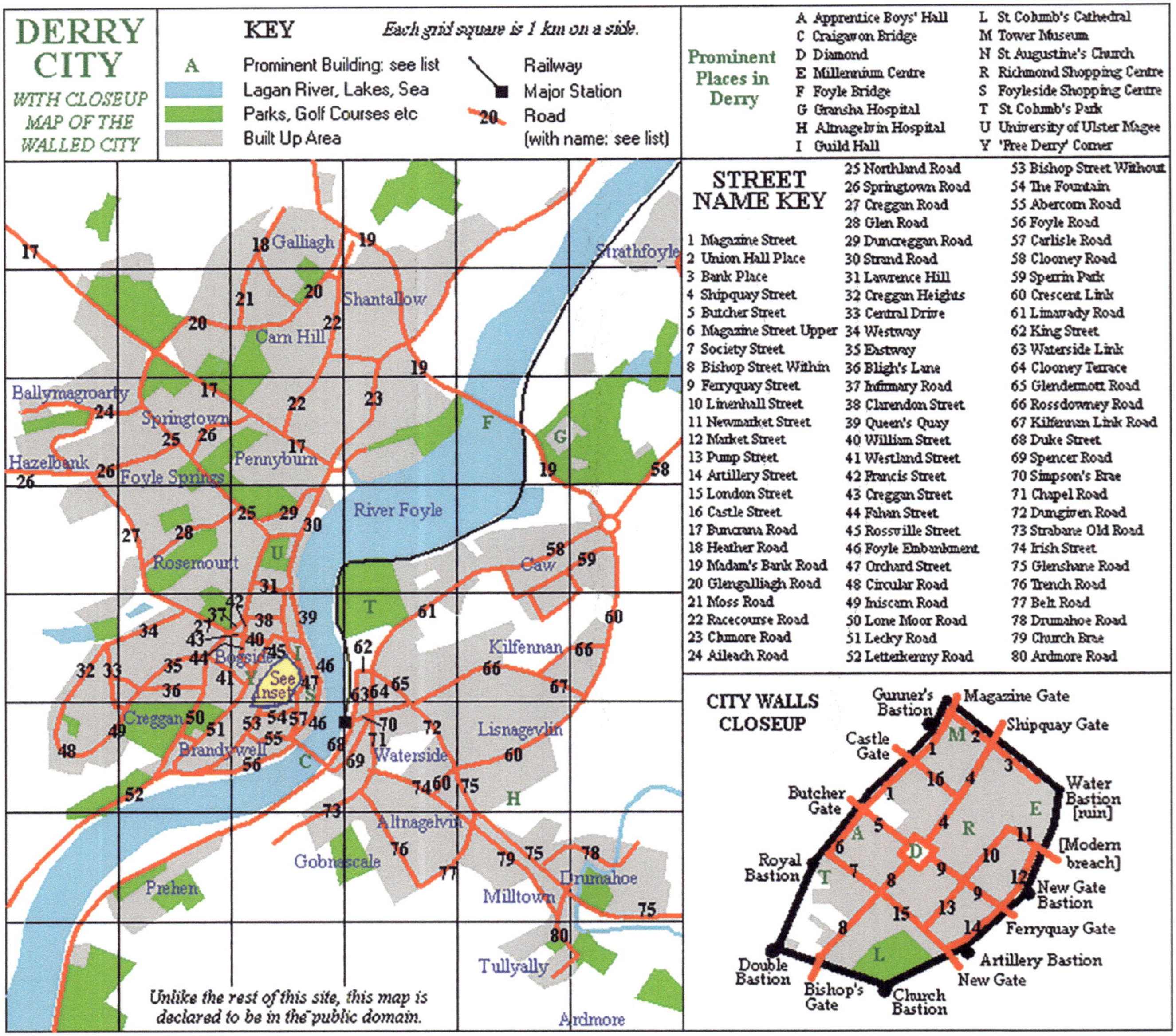

FIGURE 3 Map of Londonderry/Derry.

A Brief Note on Spellings, Grammar, and Punctuation

In graffiti and murals in Northern Ireland, spelling, grammar, and punctuation, in both English and Irish, can occasionally be creative. Throughout this text (and indeed in the murals archive on which it is based) I have treated the murals and graffiti as historical documents: I have therefore neither corrected mistakes nor drawn attention to them.

Erratum

The caption for Figure 100 Chapter 6 should read:

Martin McGuinness meets the Queen, Beechmount Avenue, Beechmount, West Belfast, 2016. Photo by Seosamh Mac Coille/Extramural Activity.

A Note on the Images in the Book

All of the images in this book feature in the Murals of Northern Ireland archive (a collection of almost 23,000 of my photographs over the past forty-odd years). The open-access collection is available at https://ccdl.claremont.edu/digital/collection/mni (or google Claremont Murals of Northern Ireland). To access all the images referenced specifically in this book, please visit the open access version on Fulcrum at https://doi.org/10.3998/mpub.14527058.

INTRODUCTION

Paint and Power: A Personal Journey Through a Political Landscape

To access all images referenced in this chapter, please visit the open access version on Fulcrum at https://doi.org/10.3998/mpub.14527058.

> Toute la Presse est toxique. Lisez les tracts, les affiches, le journal mural. (The entire Press is toxic. Read the pamphlets, the posters, the newspaper on the wall; slogan, Paris 1968)[1]

1. QUESTIONS: THEORETICAL AND PRACTICAL, GENERAL AND SPECIFIC

The application of paint to a wall in public space may appear to be an innocuous undertaking; what could be more innocent than taking a paint brush and a tin of paint to alter the appearance of a blank surface? In truth, public painting is a political act and necessarily raises a host of complex issues related to power. Consider, for example, two apparently simple questions. First, can anyone paint on a public wall? And second, can anyone paint anything on a public wall? In order to answer such questions, and others like them, it is necessary to reflect on power, not simply in the physical sense of the capacity to use a brush and paint (and not everyone can do this), but in the social sense of the right to apply that capacity in a specific place at a particular time. A moment's consideration will reveal the type of issues involved in determining the right in question, ranging from property rights to the right to free expression. For example, does ownership of a wall (say the gable end of a house, or commercial premises, or State property) confer the right to paint, to grant permission to another to paint, or to prevent someone from painting? And if it does entail that right, how and by whom is that right to be enforced? Of course, it could be argued that painting on a wall—be it a slogan or a large-scale mural—without the permission of the owner, constitutes criminal damage, and is therefore open to prosecution. Yet what if the mural is painted on the side of a house whose occupant is happy to host the work, but which nonetheless belongs to a housing agency that is an institution of the State? Where does the prerogative lie in this case—with the householder, or the State? And moving from the practice of painting to the form and content of the work, does ownership give the right to censor? So, if the State, for example, can allow (and indeed commission) the painting of a mural on its property that suits its political purposes, does it also have the right to prevent, deface or remove a mural of which it disapproves? An additional complexity arises if the question of ownership is broadened beyond that of the individual or the State to include the community. In a particular place, can the social interests of a local community override legal proprietorship in order to decide who can paint what? If so, how are these interests to be ascertained, and who is to decide what constitutes the "local community"? Finally, does wall painting require that the painter be skilled aesthetically? Or is it simply the case that anyone can paint anything, anyhow, on a public wall?

These are intricate questions and they raise political issues shaped by the specific historical circumstances in which they are posed. This is true in both general and particular terms. In a general sense, the type of rights conferred by proprietorship only apply in a society in which ownership is protected by law and the machinery of the State. But in a particular sense, such issues are also inflected by the prevailing historical and political circumstances in a given society. For example, in a context in which the very legitimacy of the State itself is at stake, say through an armed insurrection, then questions around the politics of painting are framed necessarily in a distinct way. And if that State has a history of repression and the curtailment of free expression (including the right to express a political viewpoint or a sense of identity) through its laws or accepted practices, then questions around the right to paint become yet more complicated. In such a situation, are those who want to paint against the State bound by its rules? Or is the painting of a slogan or a mural a justifiable act of free expression, or political rebellion, in and of itself? Whose interests prevail in this context? Is it the painter—who may be working on behalf of a political organization (possibly even an illegal paramilitary group), that belongs to a particular social constituency? Is it "the community"—which may be opposed to another community within a fractured political entity (and may itself be divided internally)? Or is it the State—in its guise as a neutral body (despite the fact that it maintains its own political interests with violent force if necessary)?

I came back to these complex legal, political, social, and historical questions repeatedly, one way or another, during what became more than forty years of research in Northern Ireland. But they were hardly at the forefront of my mind when I first went to work in 1979 as a community volunteer on a playscheme for local kids during the summer vacation from university. At that time, the violence of the war in Northern Ireland was a daily reality that came in a variety of forms—from paramilitary bombings and shootings to the repressive apparatus of the "security state" and all its paraphernalia—and it structured the quotidian experience of anyone and everyone in Northern Ireland. It was a dangerous place, and it was necessary to pay attention to cultural and political semiotics in order to try to avoid potential risks (though even then that was not always possible). Being an outsider was a clear disadvantage in this regard, for as Jarman notes: "geographical knowledge of Belfast [is] political knowledge, and physical movement a political enactment of that knowledge. Understanding the spatial configurations of the city is a knowledge that is internalized as an essential part of growing up" (Jarman 1992: 149). Northern Ireland was replete with wrong places and wrong times. In Belfast in particular (Londonderry/Derry was much more segregated by dint of its geography), it was possible for the non-local to cross the boundaries that separated specific socio-cultural areas without realizing it. And that could be a dangerous thing to do. Those with the geo-political knowledge knew, if at all possible, not to cross from one particular place to another directly, not to be seen to be moving from one locale to another by a given route on a regular basis, and not to transgress communally recognized spatial and cultural limits, since doing so might indicate to someone that you "belonged" to a particular identity. Indeed, often enough, the sectarian politics of space were such that you were where you walked. And that could entail horrible consequences—as with the victims of the Shankill butchers (a loyalist assassination squad) who were bundled late at night into cars on "Catholic" or "nationalist" streets (or streets that led to "Catholic" or "nationalist" streets, or streets that might lead to "Catholic" or "nationalist" streets…) and then discovered, tortured, and brutally murdered, in an alley the next morning.[2] The fact that some of the victims of these atrocities were in actuality Protestant simply proves the point: space and identity (whereness and whatness) in Northern Ireland were aligned in the most crude and brutal ways.

The war in Northern Ireland that lasted from 1969–1998 took a very particular and often intimate form. The dangers were ubiquitous and in consequence people became extremely adept at reading the signs. Some signs were recognizably contentious, since as Beresford noted with reference to the process of naming, "there is no neutrality in Northern Ireland" (Beresford 1987: 7). Even the terms used to refer to the place itself signify politically: is it "Northern Ireland"/"Ulster"/"the North"/"the Six Counties"? Is the second city "Londonderry"/"Derry"/"Doire" (or even "stroke city," from the habit of saying "Derry stroke Londonderry")? Was the prison, the site of so much bitterness, strife, and suffering (as well as education, political thinking, and resistance) "Long Kesh" or "the Maze"? Was Ireland "Éire"/"the South"/"the Twenty-Six Counties"/"the Free State," "the Republic"/"Ireland"? And so on. As Carroll has recently observed, "in Northern Ireland, terminology is treacherous, denoting bias, real or perceived" (this was not always an easy distinction to make) (Carroll 2023: xii). Names mattered since the choice of terms carried political weight and could be used to "place" their user; mistakes could be uncomfortable at best and dangerous at worst—blunders taken for signs. I have often witnessed (and participated in) the semiotic dance whereby strangers in Northern Ireland (I am using the "official" name for the place—which is of course a political choice, since "there is no neutrality"…) establish the identity of their interlocutor. Scrutinizing someone's name, address, job, clothes, accent, school, sporting preference, newspaper, holiday destination, and practices of naming (among other things) was and remains a social skill. Other signs were non-linguistic. Along with everyone else, I noticed (and gradually learned) the habit of being constantly on the look-out for indications of trouble: an awareness of overt and subtle changes in spatial demarcation and a sense of any disturbance in the patterns of significance that counted as "normal" in the conflict areas in particular. One result of this tendency was a form of what might be termed "semiotic paranoia," which is to say the propensity to interpret/over-interpret (this was another hard line to draw) signs for the admonitory, fearful meanings that they might contain.

The exemplars of this practice were British soldiers, since one of the functions of their regular foot patrols in the war zones was precisely to monitor and record signs for the purposes of analysis. "Intel," as the Army called it, was nothing but the gathering of information in the form of signs, or, more accurately, "clues": a new car at a particular house, the disruption of regular activity in an area, the disappearance of a specific person, the sudden emptiness of a street. All such phenomena were decoded for their hidden significance, with the soldiers being but the most obvious players of an interpretation game which in reality involved everyone at some level or other.[3]

If some of the signs that needed to be read were hard to identify (to say nothing of the difficulty of understanding their nuances), there were others that stared you in the face since they were written on the walls in letters six-feet high. Indeed, if there is a starting point for the longitudinal research that underpins this work, it lies in my fascination with the walls of working-class areas of Belfast in 1979 which were covered in personal, political, and war-related graffiti (bold, challenging, funny, brutal, crude, simplistic, complicated, incomprehensible, sardonic, pleading, and surreal). For as the poet Ciaran Carson put it in *Belfast Confetti*:

> At times it seems as though every inch of Belfast has been written-on, erased, and written-on again: messages, curses, political imperatives, but mostly names, or nicknames—Robbo, Mackers, Scoot, Fra—sometimes litanized obsessively on every brick of a gable wall, as high as the hand will reach, and sometimes higher, these snakes and ladders cancelling each other out in their bid to be remembered. *Remember 1690. Remember 1916.* Most of all, *Remember me. I was here.* (Carson 1989: 52)

Carson is right to draw attention to the ubiquity of wall-writing and the imperative to remember in Belfast, though I think his emphasis on personal graffiti is over-stated. In any case, having been raised in working-class Liverpool, wall-art, including political graffiti, was hardly unfamiliar to me, and some of it was sectarian. For example, an early BBC documentary on Liverpool (*Morning in the Streets* 1959) shows "God Save the Queen E:R" carefully painted on a gable end (BBC 1959). And two murals of King Billy from the early 1960s are captured in *Seaport: Architecture and Townscape in Liverpool* (Hughes 1964: 127, 128). The two most prominent examples of graffiti in the area in which I was brought up in the 1960s, however, were: "All coppers are bastards" and "God Bless Our Popeye 1967." The former was a reflection on relations between the local population and the police. The latter began as a commemoration of the opening of Liverpool's Catholic Metropolitan Cathedral of Christ the King in 1967, but the area in which we lived was divided along sectarian lines and "God Bless Our Pope" was amended after a day or so to the irreverent message that stayed on the wall for years. Yet although there was political graffiti and some artwork in Liverpool, the amount and extent of it in Belfast in 1979 was both striking and puzzling and it raised many questions. Why was there so much of it? Who did it and how (given that many of the streets were under constant surveillance, often in the form of British Army foot-patrols)? Was it organized and controlled by local people? By the paramilitaries? By local people who were the paramilitaries? By political organizations? And who or what was the intended audience? "The other side" (nationalists/republicans and unionists/loyalists– depending on the area)? State forces ("the Brits" and "peelers," as the British Army and Royal Ulster Constabulary [RUC] were known)? Local residents? The media? The British government? Why did it appear and disappear so rapidly (and who had the power to change it)? Why was it placed in particular locations? And, of course, the central question (though I wouldn't have framed it in this way in 1979): what did it signify as a historically specific genre? One way and another, these questions lead back to the types of more abstract legal and political questions with which this introduction began. But simply by dint of the fact that the graffiti (and some images) existed, with their particular political content and form, they ultimately drew attention—implicitly if not necessarily directly—to the fundamental questions that haunted Northern Ireland during the long war and that still dominate the post-war period. These questions are abstract yet compelling and they underpin the war and its aftermath. They include: what are the social roots of violence? Who has the right to use violence, why and how? How can the legacy of violence (whomever the perpetrator) be addressed? And how can a non-violent and peaceful (these are not quite the same thing), just and legitimate (again, not the same thing) social order be achieved? Whatever can be said for *The Belfast Agreement* (1998) and the Peace Process that it produced, it is evident that these crucial questions have not, as yet, been answered fully. It is also clear that such questions are not confined to the relatively narrow confines of Northern Ireland; they carry much broader significance in the contemporary world.

2. THE SIGNS ON THE WALLS

This work is not a history of the thirty-year war that took place in Northern Ireland, nor the post-war period that has followed it; there are any number of good historical accounts of Northern Ireland's war and peace.[4] Rather, this text will offer a history and an analysis of murals—a mode of cultural production intimately tied to the conflict and its aftermath. Focusing mainly on murals, and to a lesser extent graffiti, street, art and memorials, and undertaken across what is now forty-five years, the research will address the notable fact that a variety of actors—individuals, communities, paramilitary organizations, political and non-political agencies, and the State itself—took to the walls of Northern Ireland in order to intervene in both the war and the consequent Peace Process. Using a range of generic devices, from crude slogans to aesthetically accomplished murals that filled spaces which included gable-ends and walls hundreds of feet long, these actors used paint to represent history, to voice political views, to articulate community concerns and demands, to foster ideology, to create modes of identity, and to shape collective memory. The result is a complex, changing, fascinating body of public art that adds significantly to our understanding of the history of Northern Ireland. Indeed in my own experience, given that the majority of the press coverage of Northern Ireland was indeed consistently "toxic"—often ill-informed, reductive, willfully ignorant, and sometimes simply irresponsible—the signs on the walls were frequently a reliable (if coded) source of information for what was really going on.

The range of the artwork is striking. There were brutally monologic interventions in the war, such as the mural on Rockville Road in West Belfast that gloated over the republican attack at Warrenpoint in 1979 in which the Irish Republican Army (IRA) inflicted its most damaging attack on the British Army (eighteen British soldiers were killed) (Figure 1), or the mural in the loyalist Village, South Belfast, that saluted Michael Stone, the perpetrator of a gun and grenade attack on an IRA funeral in which three were killed and sixty injured (Figure 2).[5] But there are also examples of dialogism, as in the use of Patrick Galvin's poem "Letter to a British soldier on Irish soil" (first

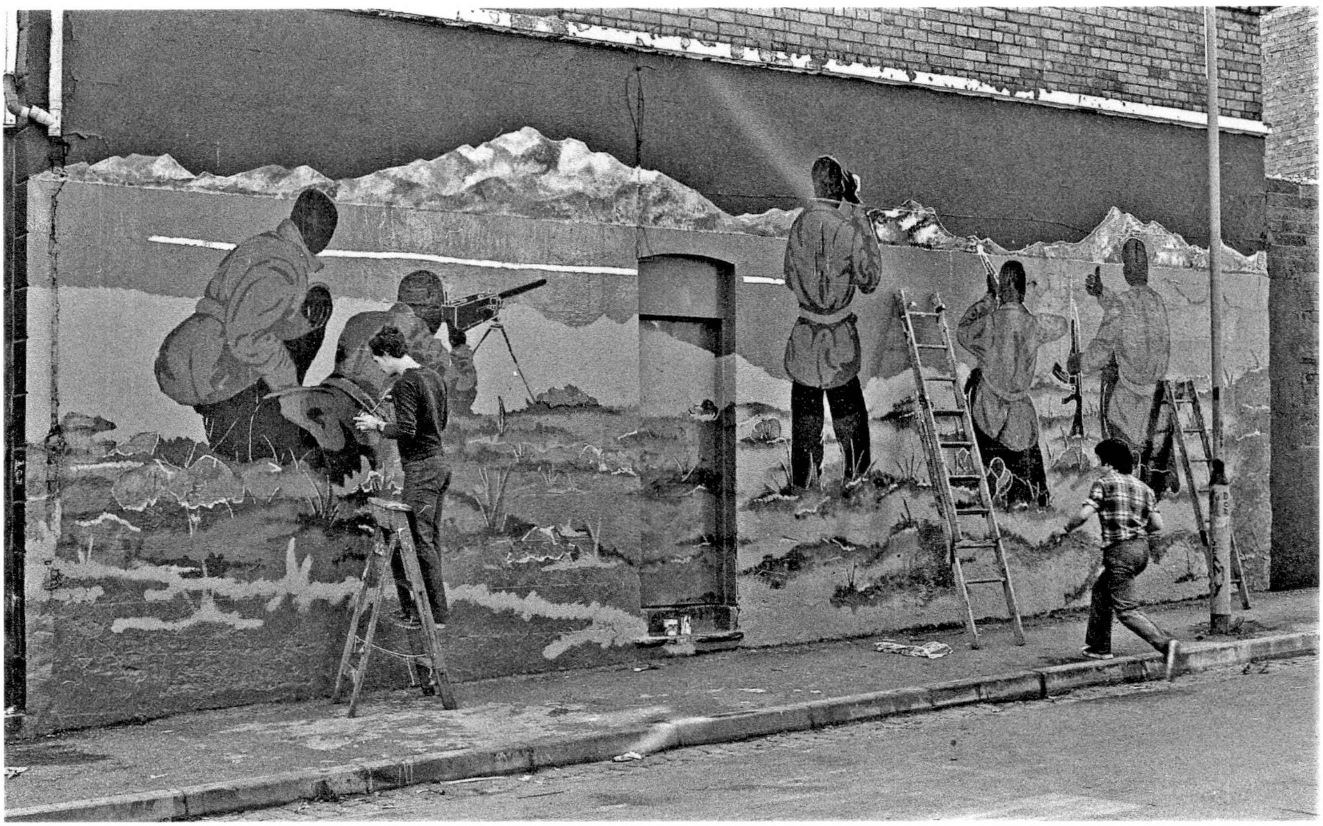

FIGURE 1 Warrenpoint, republican mural, Rockville Street, Falls Road, West Belfast, 1981. Photo by Tony Crowley.

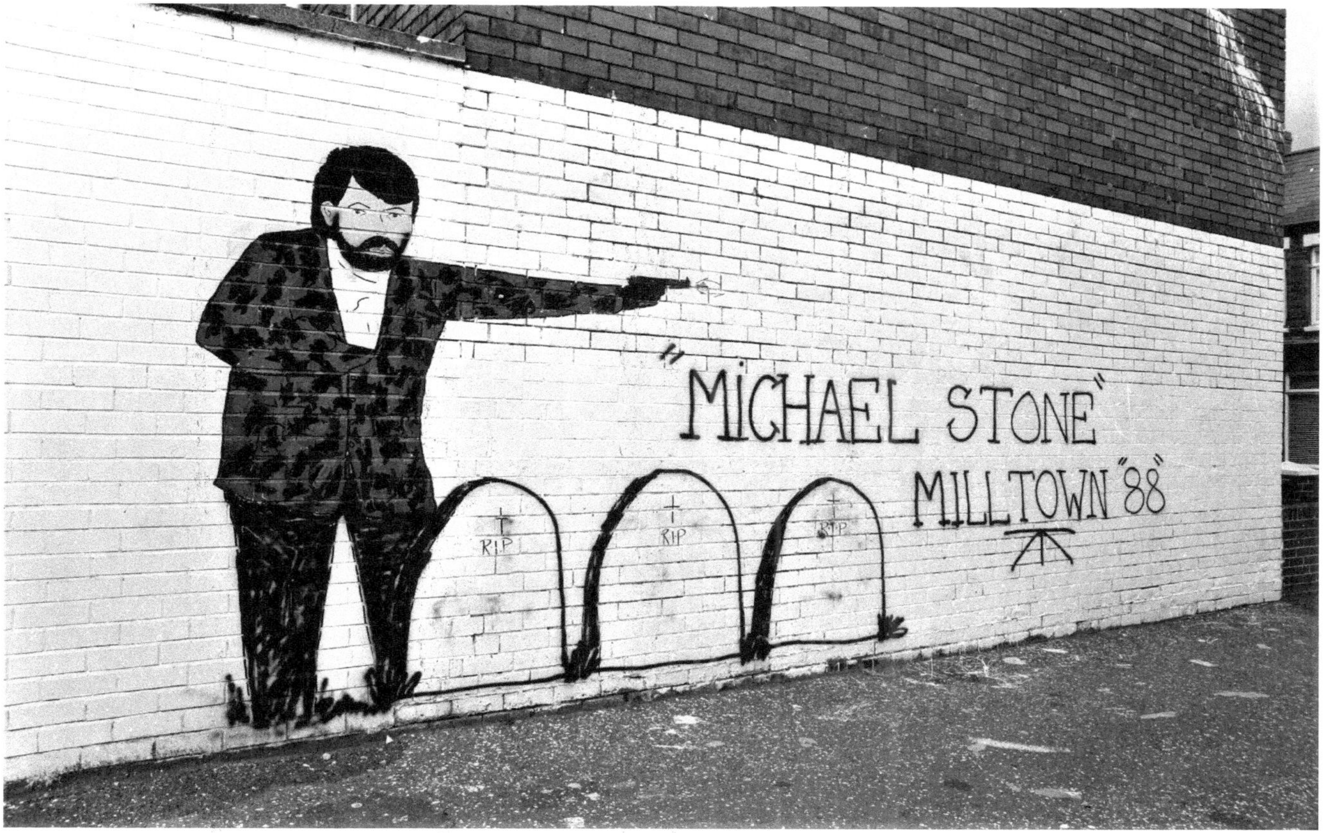

FIGURE 2 Michael Stone, loyalist mural, Tavanagh Street, The Village, South Belfast, 1989. Photo by Tony Crowley.

published in 1972) on a wall in Lenadoon, West Belfast, in 1981 (Galvin 1972) (Figure 3), or competing graffiti of the IRA and British Army on one site in republican Ballymurphy (Figure 4, see Fulcrum). There are also some surprising and complex images which require contextualization. In relation to language politics, for example, there are predictable claims and counter-claims, with Irish/an Gaeilge featuring from the early 1980s as a medium of Irish nationalism and republicanism (Figure 5), and Ulster-Scots as a cipher for unionism and loyalism from the early 1990s (Figure 6). And yet on a loyalist paramilitary mural dedicated to the Red Hand Commando (RHC), the Gaelic slogan "Lamh Dearg Abu" (Victory to the Red Hand) appeared, along with the (loose) translation "Ulster to Victory" (Figure 7, see Fulcrum). Likewise Cú Chulainn, traditionally conceived as a mythological hero of Irish nationalism (his statue stands in the Dublin G.P.O.), has featured, predictably, in republican areas (Figure 8). But on the basis of his role in

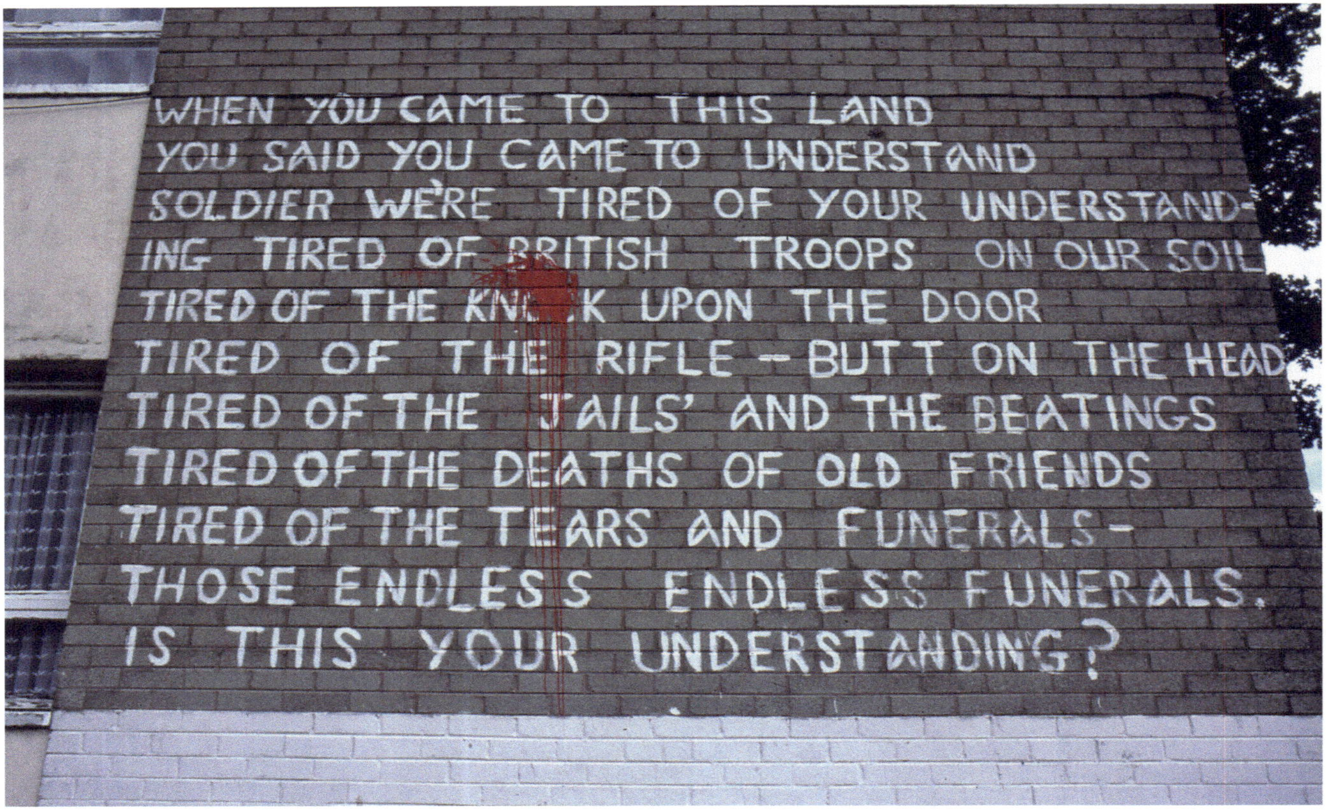

FIGURE 3 "Letter to a British soldier," republican mural, Lenadoon Avenue, Lenadoon, West Belfast, 1981. Photo by Tony Crowley.

the defense of Ulster in *Táin Bó Cúailnge*, one of the central narratives of the Ulster Cycle of Gaelic myths, he has also been deployed as a re-claimed heroic figure in the loyalist re-vision of history (Figure 9).

Such historical re-making has even appeared, somewhat self-reflexively, as a topic for the walls. Thus, challenging the debates within Irish historiography that date from the 1970s, one mural depicted the figure of truth in front of the book of Irish history, while the mask of revisionism was placed aside. The image was framed by a quote from the socialist republican and professional historian Miriam Daly (executed by a loyalist assassination squad): "History is written by the winner" (Figure 10). In fact, Northern Ireland has witnessed a lot of re-historicizing, and much of it has appeared on the walls. There are republican murals, for example, which have made it appear that the war against the British State was fought with the aim of delivering civil rights for Northern Irish

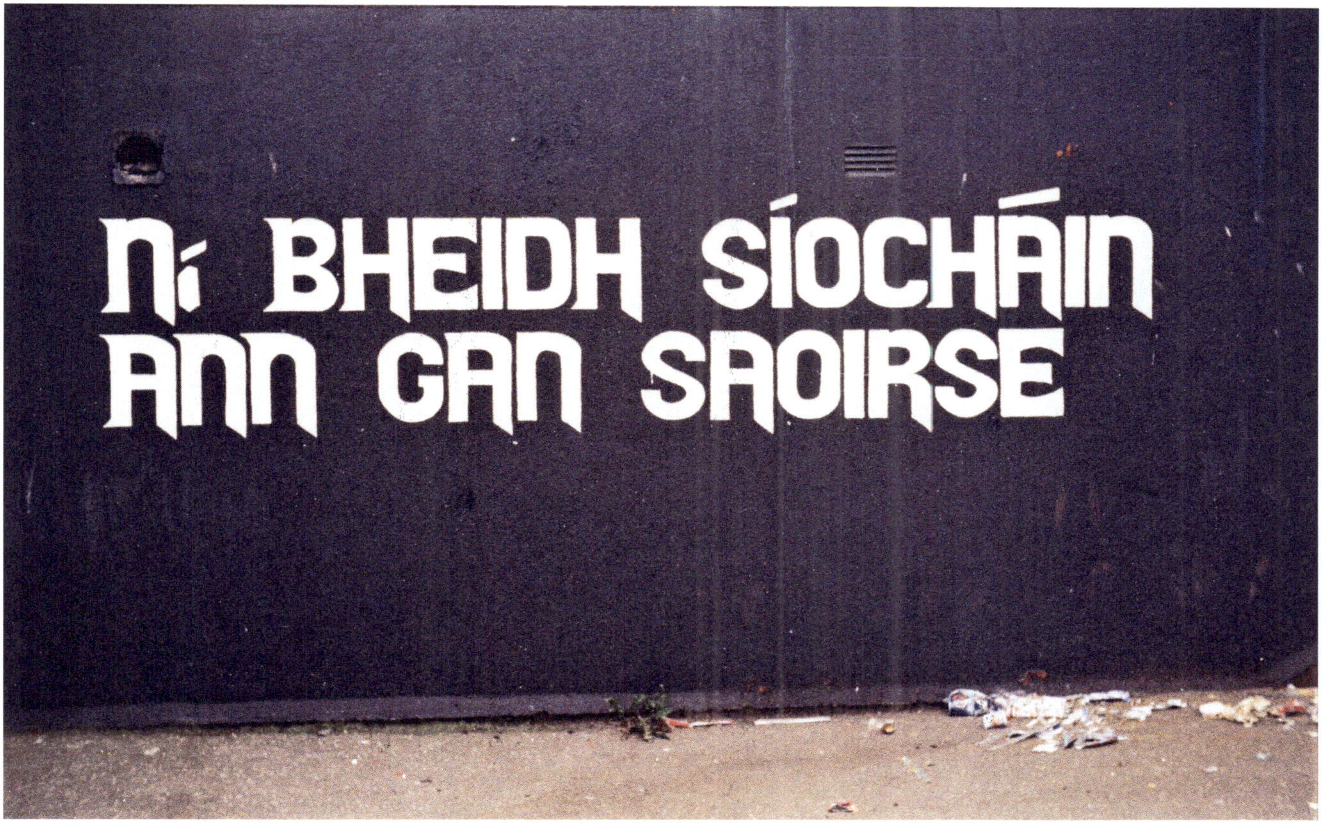

FIGURE 5 Republican mural, Irish language, Ní Bheidh Síocháin Ann Gan Saoirse, Shaws Road, West Belfast, 1983. Photo by Tony Crowley.

nationalists (as opposed to the republican goal—frequently stated during the war—of destroying the Northern Irish State and achieving Irish unity) (Figure 11, see Fulcrum). And there are loyalist murals that depict their community as the undeserving victim of history. Thus the events of the summer of 1969 (usually conceived in terms of State repression and State-facilitated loyalist intimidation of nationalists), are re-cast as bringing devastation to the loyalists of the Shankill, the start of a one-sided sectarian campaign of injustice and violence that lasted for some thirty years (Figure 12, see Fulcrum).

Perhaps the most notable re-historicizing force, however, though there would be competition for the title, is that of the State itself through the "Re-imaging Communities Programme" (2006–2009) and the "Building

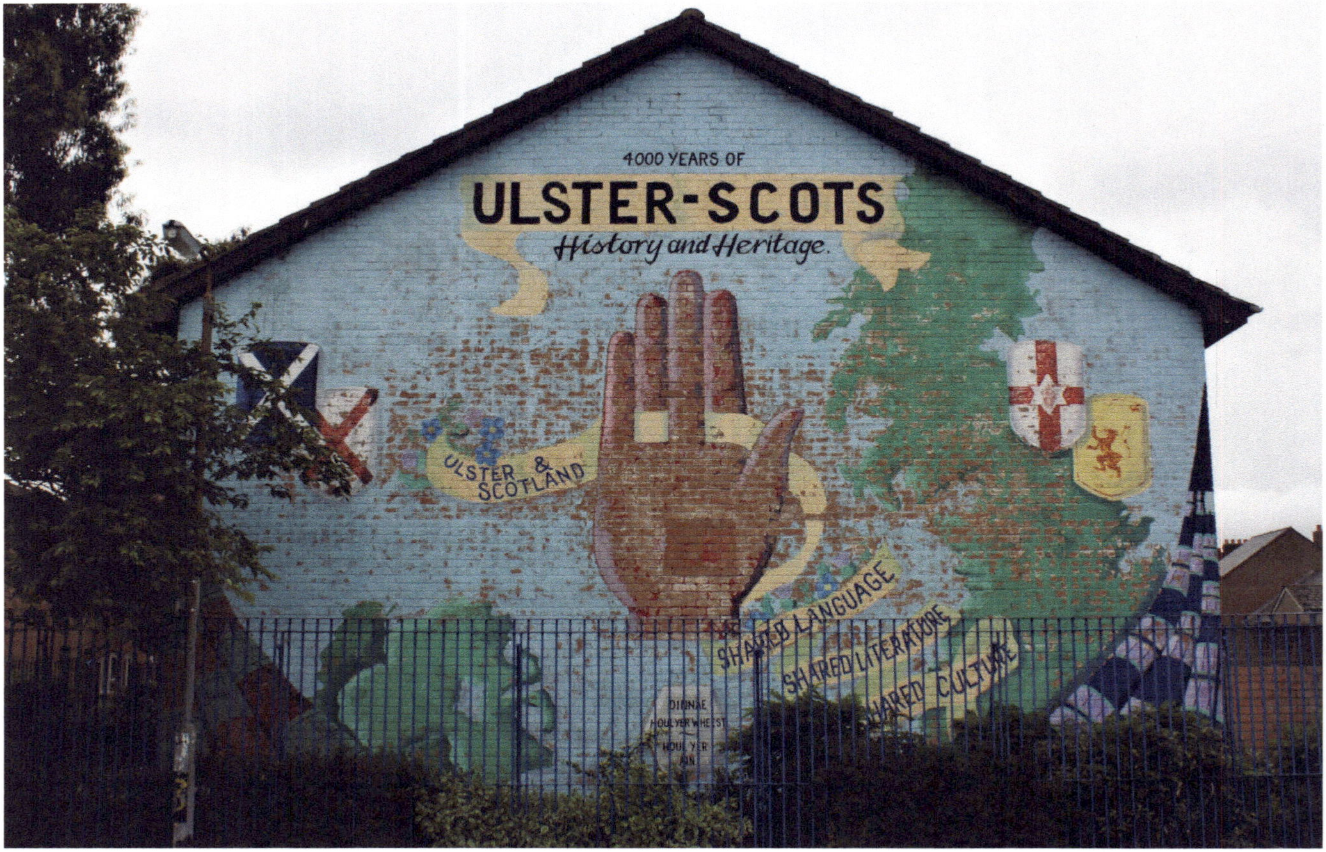

FIGURE 6 Ulster-Scots Loyalist mural, Templemore Street, East Belfast, 1999. Photo by Tony Crowley.

Peace through the Arts: Re-imaging Communities Programme" (2013–2015). Underpinned by millions from the State's coffers, the "re-imaging" schemes sought to eradicate images of the conflict and its related paraphernalia from the walls of loyalist and republican communities (Figure 13) (Figure 14, see Fulcrum) (Figure 15) (Figure 16, see Fulcrum). The overall effect, however, was somewhat undermined by the fact that in most cases, the new "re-images," depicting scenes from communal or local history, were surrounded by other representations of the past: murals that saluted dead paramilitaries, celebrated acts of violence, and articulated forcefully still unreconciled cultural and political divisions (Figure 17) (Figure 18). One muralist somewhat wryly passed comment on this phenomenon in the summer of 2013. Noting that "the Re-imaging Programme cost millions and lasted a few years," he observed that

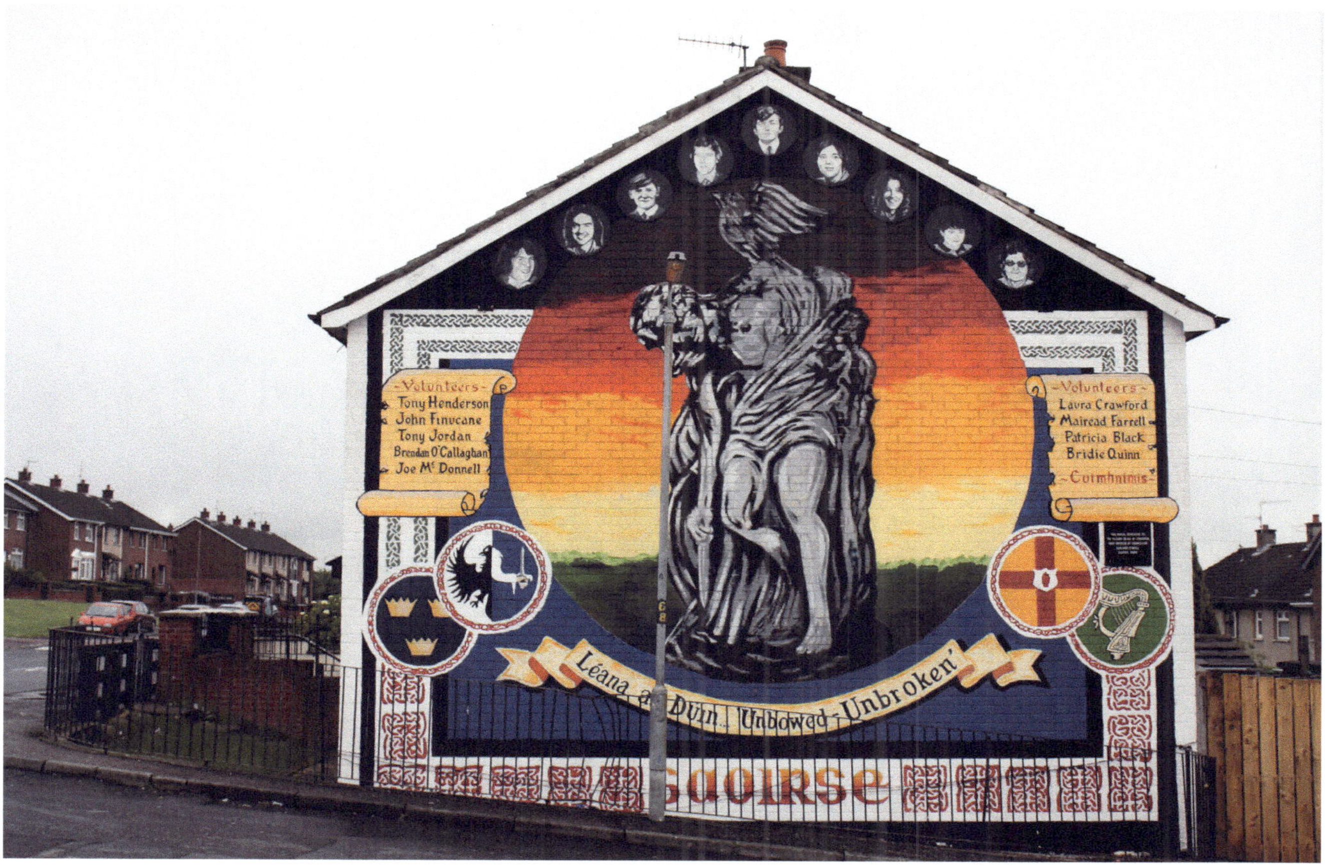

FIGURE 8 Cú Chulainn republican mural, Lenadoon Avenue, Lenadoon, West Belfast, 2009. Photo by Tony Crowley.

"all you need for a new paramilitary mural is some paint, a ladder, a couple of days, a bit of a sense of history and a few quid."[6]

As will be shown in chapter one, muralism is a cultural and political phenomenon which has deep roots in Northern Ireland's history, beginning in the early twentieth century. More recently, it is a practice which has encapsulated, and indeed played a role in, many of the twists and turns of the war and post-war periods, and—in a development that few predicted—it has become one of the mainstays of the Northern Ireland tourist industry over the past twenty years or so (Figure 19, see Fulcrum). But it may be useful before beginning the history and analysis of the

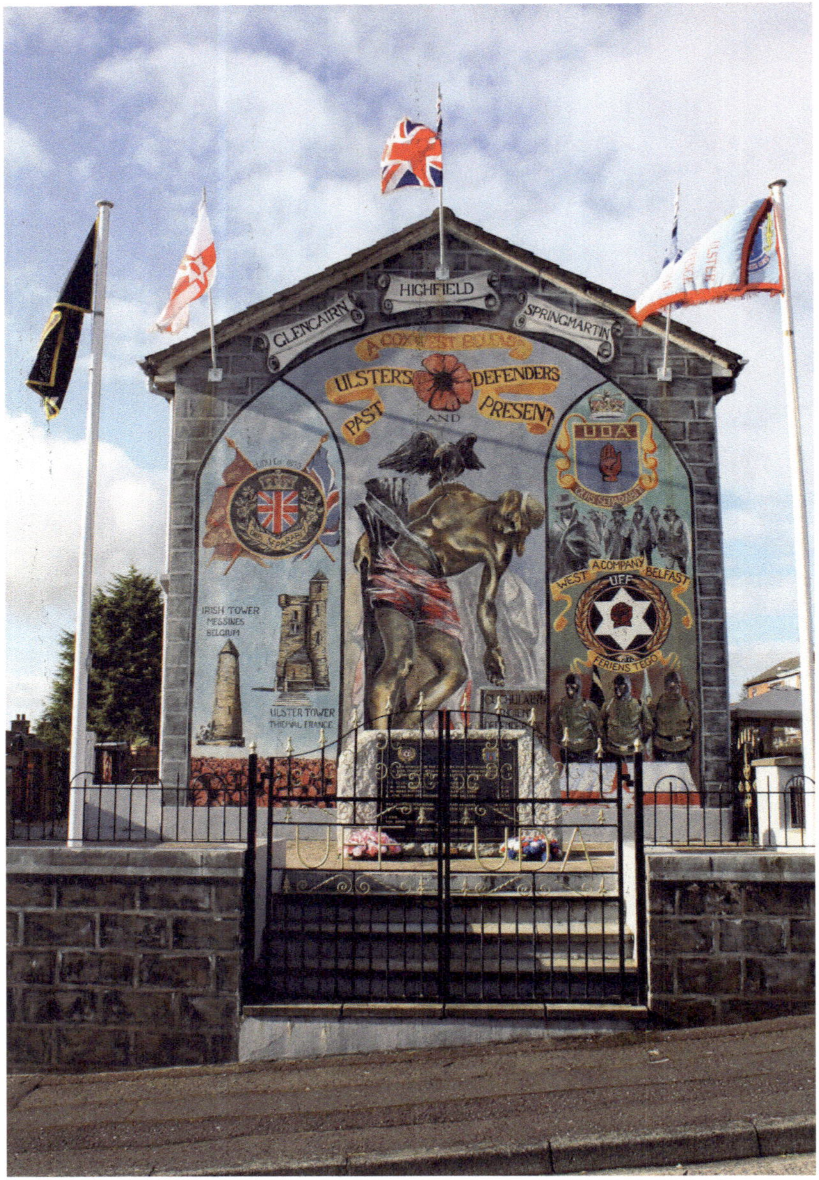

FIGURE 9 Ulster's Defenders loyalist mural, High Green, Highfield, West Belfast, 2000. Photo by Tony Crowley.

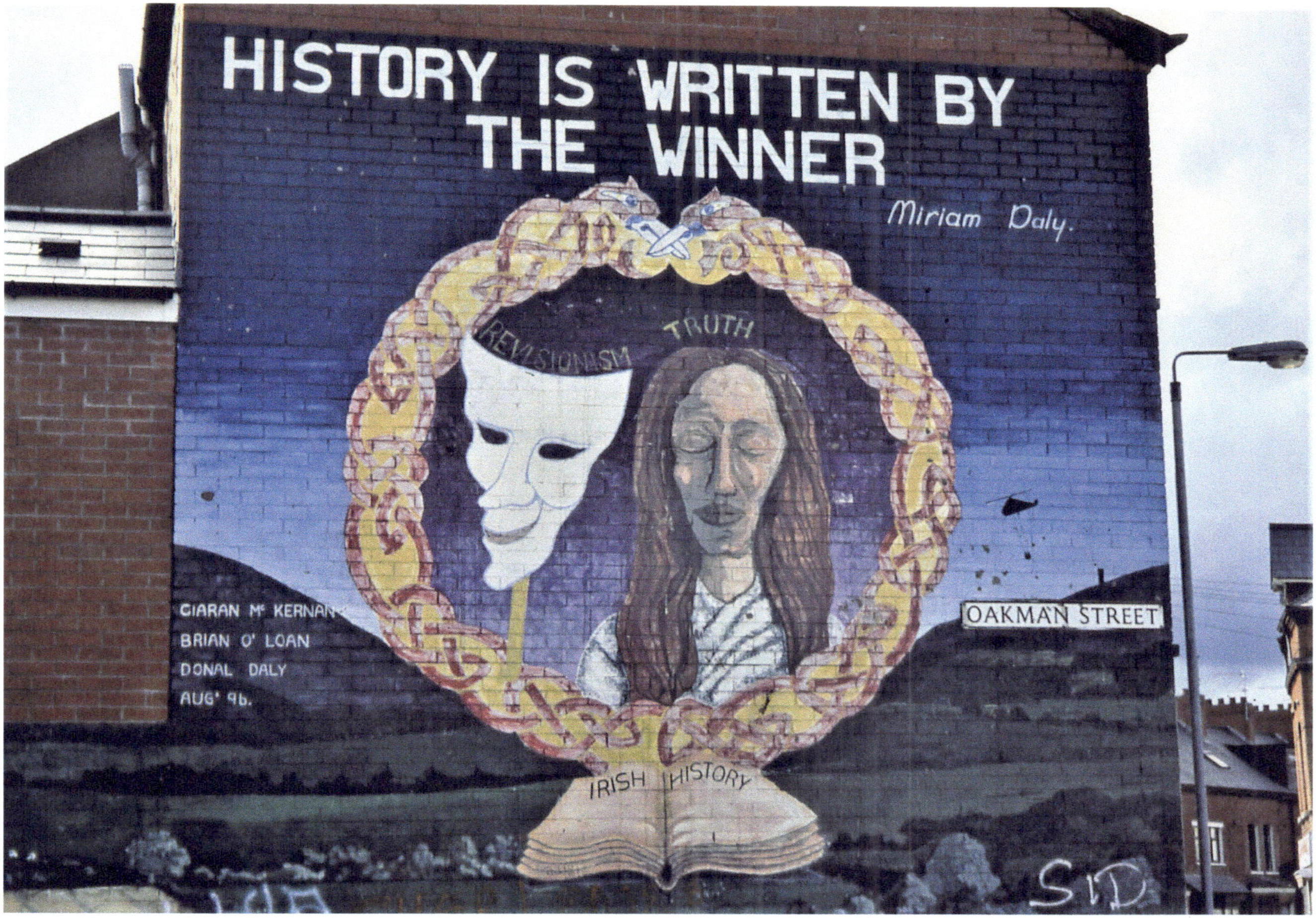

FIGURE 10 Revisionism republican mural, Oakman Street, Falls, West Belfast, 1996. Photo by Tony Crowley.

murals proper, to return again to 1979 and my first experience of the politics of painting in Belfast, as a way of contextualizing what became an academic lifetime's research.

As noted above, there was graffiti everywhere in the working-class areas in which the war was predominantly fought out, and I was interested enough in the walls to take pictures (with a small, poor-quality camera) as a personal record (Figure 20, see Fulcrum). The graffiti was variable; it offered support to paramilitary groups ("Provos are the People and the People are the Provos"), proclaimed violent antagonism ("Death to Thatcher and the R.U.C."),

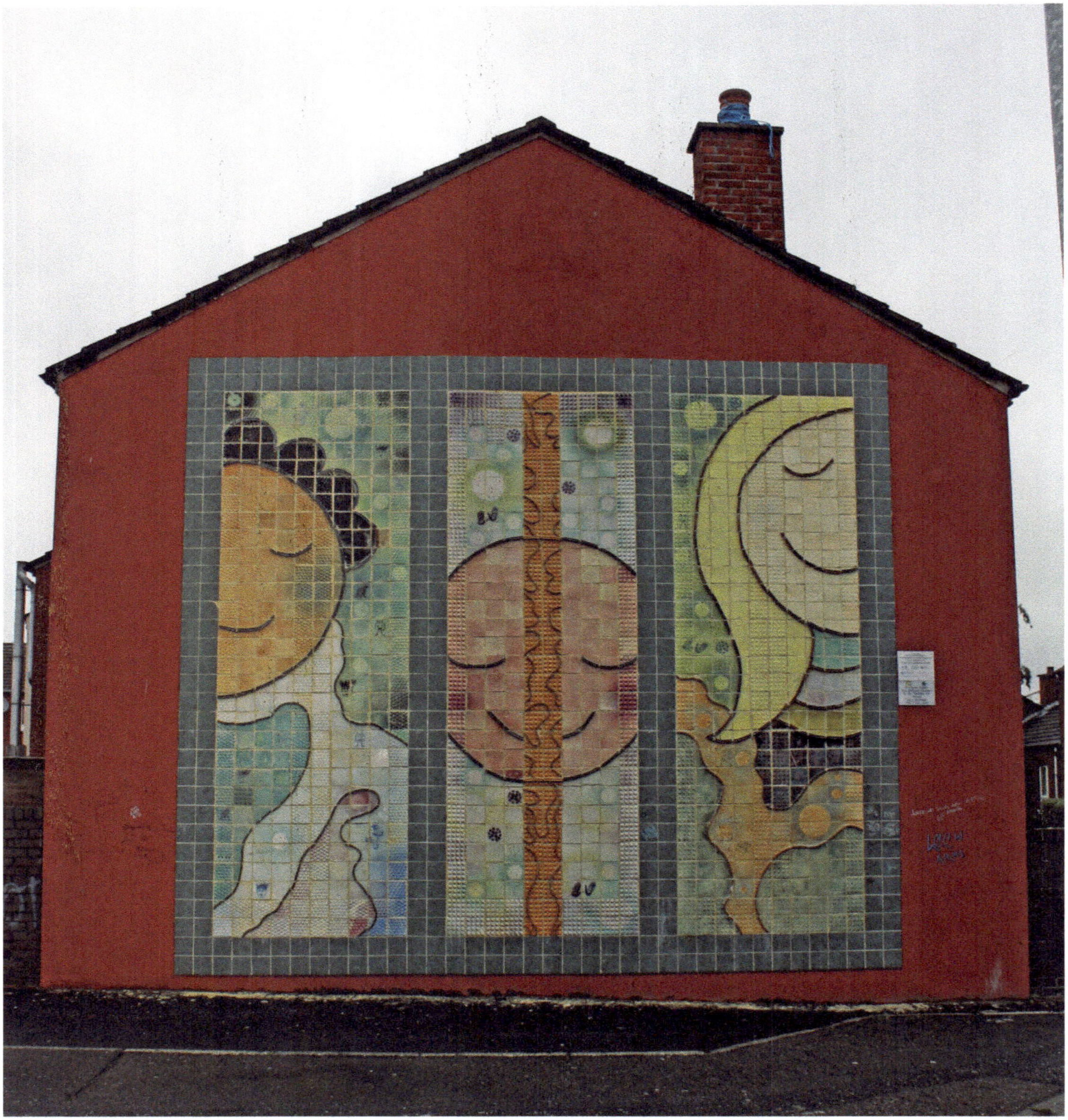

FIGURE 13 Re-imaging non-aligned mural, Brompton Park, Ardoyne, North Belfast, 2009. Photo by Tony Crowley.

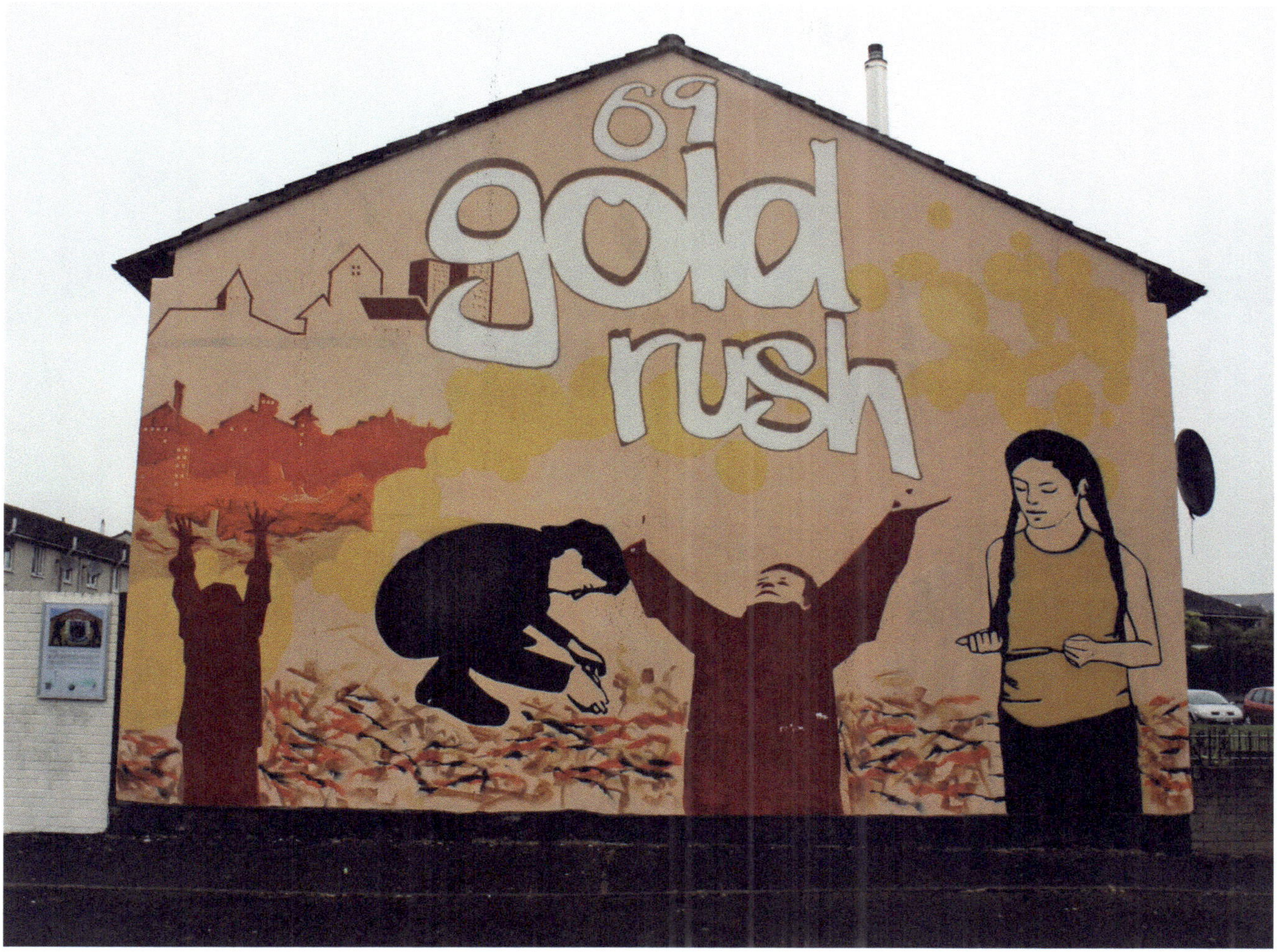

FIGURE 15 Gold rush, non-aligned mural, Hopewell Crescent, Lower Shankill, West Belfast, 2009. Photo by Tony Crowley.

and heralded specific political issues ("Boycott E.E.C"—a Sinn Féin policy in the 1979 European Elections). But while taking photos of this material, a friend took me to see my first mural—a loyalist work in Donegall Pass (Figure 21). It invoked loyalist prisoners, commemorated the Silver Jubilee of Queen Elizabeth II (1952–1977), and featured a variety of symbols (whose significance was largely lost on me at the time): the Crown (the object of loyalty); the red, white and blue of the Union Jack (the expression of political unity); the flags of Northern Ireland

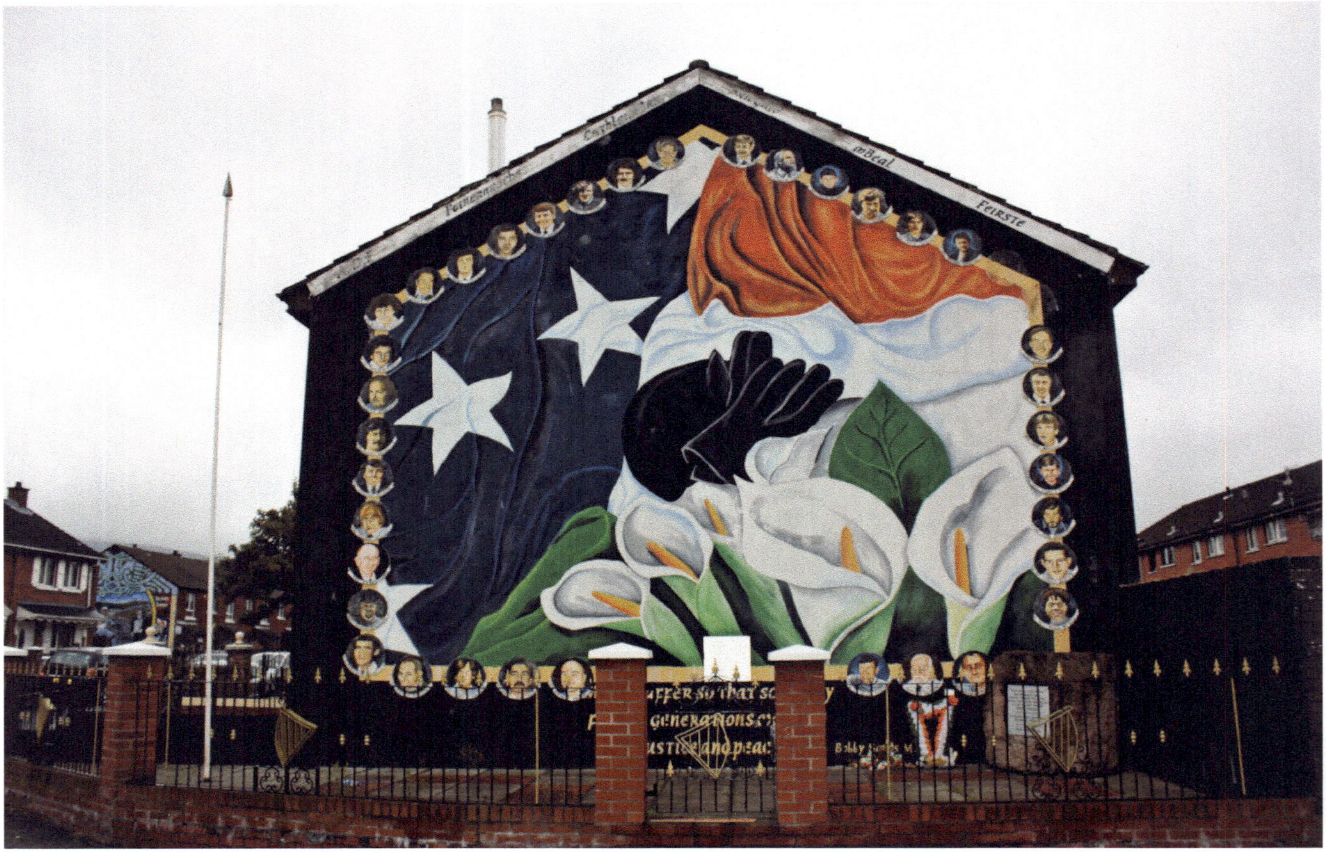

FIGURE 17 Republican memorial mural to IRA Volunteers, Ardoyne Avenue, Ardoyne, North Belfast, 2003. Photo by Tony Crowley.

and Scotland (the postulation of a common Protestant heritage); and the motto of one of the loyalist paramilitary organizations—the Ulster Defence Association (UDA)—"Quis separabit" (Who shall separate us?). This mural belonged to a tradition of which I knew little. Only later did I discover that the history of mural painting in Northern Ireland had been predominantly loyalist from its inception up to the 1970s and belonged to a set of triumphalist aesthetic practices that celebrated the "Protestant State." These ranged from civic statuary to the arches erected over working-class streets in loyalist areas in the run-up to the Twelfth of July celebrations of the anniversary of King William the Third's victory at the Battle of the Boyne in 1690, the bonfires on the "Eleventh Night," Orange Order marches, and of course murals—not least depictions of King Billy on his white charger. And yet,

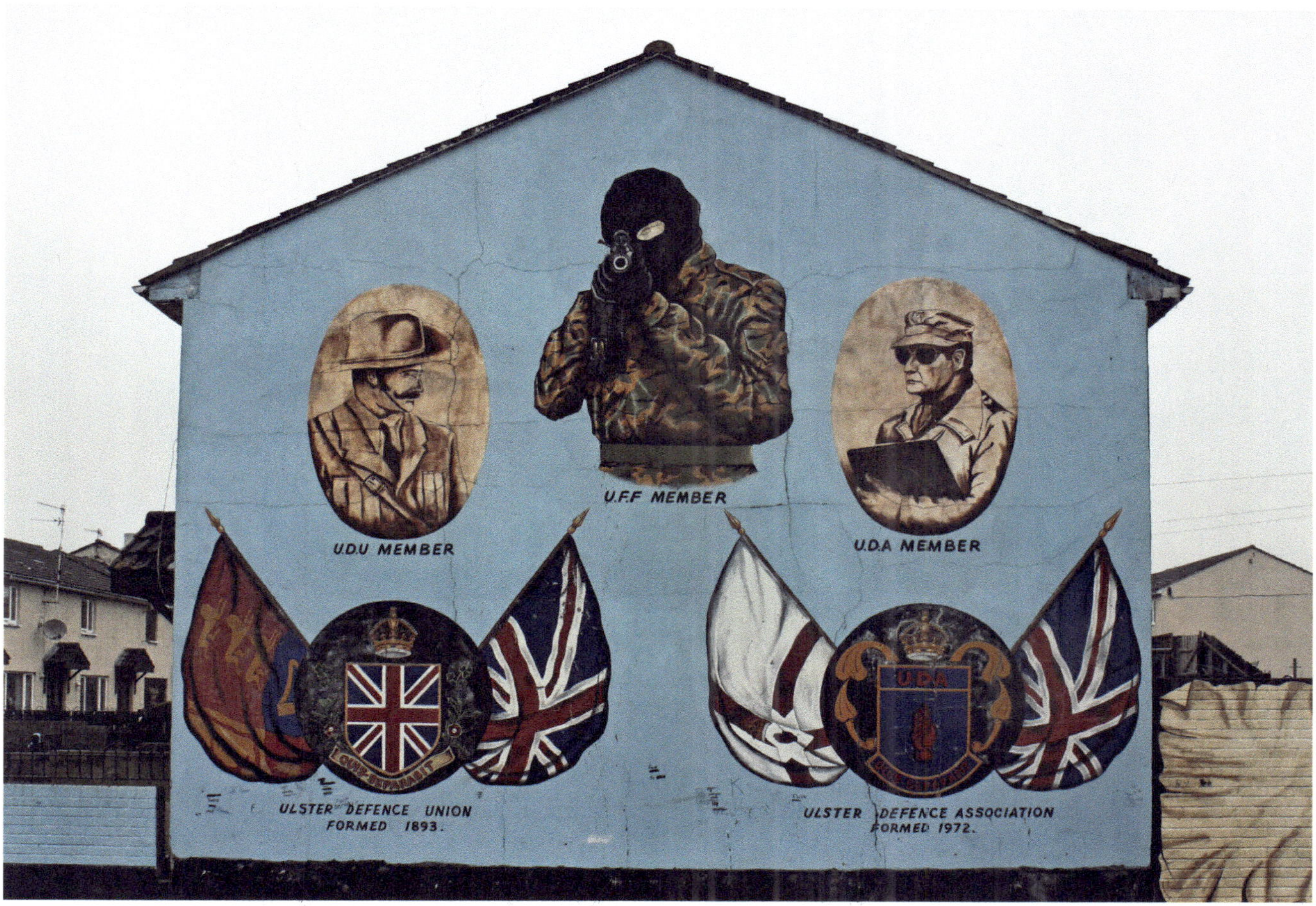

FIGURE 18 Loyalist mural depicting history of armed loyalism, Hopewell Crescent, Lower Shankill, West Belfast, 2000. Photo by Tony Crowley.

in truth, there were relatively few loyalist murals of the traditional kind in the late 1970s and very early 1980s, and the significant development, which marks the beginning of modern muralism in Northern Ireland, was the appearance of republican murals in 1980–1981. This is not to say that nationalist and/or republican murals didn't exist before that period, but they were very few and far between. At just that historical conjuncture, however, republican murals started to appear in large numbers; striking and often powerful, they were in many cases

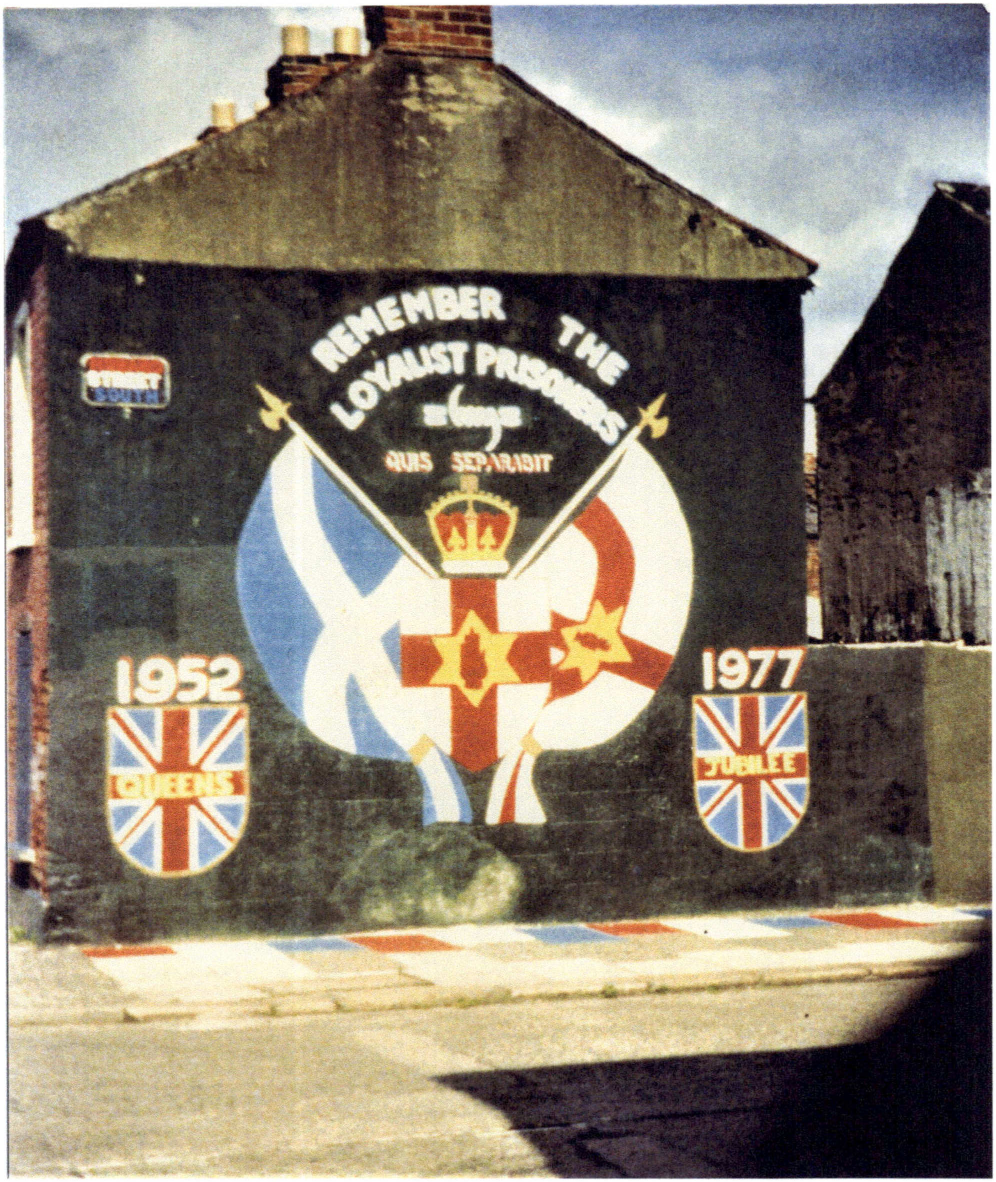

FIGURE 21 Loyalist mural dedicated to the Loyalist prisoners, Howard Street, South Donegall Pass, South Belfast. 1978. Photo Tony Crowley.

semiotically complex and figuratively skilful. This was the beginning of a renewed practice of political painting in contemporary Northern Ireland which has proved to be astonishingly durable and socially significant.

3. PHOTOGRAPHY AND POLITICS

I began photographing the graffiti and murals of Northern Ireland in 1979, which meant that at least while the war was continuing (for the next nineteen years or so), I spent a good amount of time walking the conflict zones with a camera and little or no justification other than a desire to record what I took to be important historical and cultural materials. It was (and remains) a personal journey in the literal and metaphorical senses of the term. I have criss-crossed Northern Ireland for half a lifetime in search of murals and graffiti and found them in a remarkable variety of locations—in cities, towns, small villages, on boards in the middle of the countryside, and sometimes inscribed on the road itself. And during the long voyage I have experienced and witnessed much that has led me to think hard about my own political views and values. As might be imagined, the journey was often complicated, sometimes heart-breaking, and very occasionally dangerous. One constant, at least in the cities during the war, was the surveillance of British soldiers and RUC police officers, and the same scenario was played out repeatedly (usually in republican areas).[7] Like everyone else in those districts, I was liable to being stopped and checked with a series of routine questions—where I'd been, where I was going, what I was doing there. Soldiers could be hostile and a number of times they took the film out of the back of the camera (these were the days before digital technology). On no occasion was I informed why they wanted to stop me from taking photographs. It may simply be that their actions amounted to a recognition of, and resentment towards, the cultural and political importance of the republican murals in particular. This would certainly explain both the soldiers' attempts to destroy these works by paint-bombing them (by throwing balloons full of paint, often during the dawn patrols) and the fact that soldiers and the police largely ignored me when I was taking pictures of loyalist murals (Figure 22, see Fulcrum). But in spite of complaining to squaddies on the street, officers in their barracks, the R.U.C., British Army H.Q. (N.I.), and my MP, nobody ever quite explained to me why it was forbidden to take photographs of paintings on walls in areas that were, according to the British Prime Minister Mrs Thatcher, as British as Finchley.[8]

Once my identity as an outsider (and an academic) had been established, State force personnel usually lost interest in me. The same could be said of encounters in republican and loyalist areas, which were, usually, amicable enough. People were, of course, wary of someone wandering round with a camera (understandably so given the level of overt and covert surveillance to which they were subject), but again, once I'd explained what I was doing, the local response was friendly, generous and, more often than not, helpful. In addition to which, I walked (and walked, and walked…) or used public transport, almost exclusively, which presumably made my presence less suspicious.[9] The only properly threatening experiences arose in particular places when I ran into self-appointed vigilantes who were antagonistic or hostile simply because I was a stranger with a camera. They were usually young men who took it on themselves to act as "defenders" of their locality. Though I could understand their concerns (people were, after all, "scouted" for assassination—intelligence gathering by all sides was constant), this was a different sort of difficulty altogether, since the people involved were unlikely to be allied to any paramilitary or political organization, and they were all the more unpredictable for it. Over time, of course, familiarity bred recognition, and simply by going back to places repeatedly, I got to know people and they recognized me, and the difficulties became fewer. That also meant that I developed an invaluable network of people—mostly, though not exclusively, "ordinary" working-class people—ranging from caretakers to political representatives, from community activists to (ex)-paramilitaries. I am glad to have been able to talk and listen to all of them.

Having spent a lot of time in Northern Ireland, I am under no illusions about the brutality of the war and its horrors, specifically the long-lasting effects of the intimate and specific nature of the violence (as one memorial puts it, quoting the father of a child killed in a sectarian attack, "Bullets do not only travel distance but also through time") (Figure 23). There can also be no over-estimation of the manifold, complex, and horrible impact of a war in which 3,720 people were killed and 47,541 wounded (the majority of whom, in both categories, were civilians). Those numbers, which may appear small by the standards of major conflicts, have to be seen in the context of an overall population at the time of approximately 1.5 million. For on the basis of data gathered by the Northern Ireland Statistics and Research Agency, the statutory Commission for Victims and Survivors has estimated that the war resulted in 500,000 "victims" in Northern Ireland alone—one in three of the population ("victims" in this definition are those directly affected by "death," "bereavement," "physical injury," or "trauma" as a result of the conflict) (Commission for Victims and Survivors 2019). The miserable truth is that in Northern Ireland, every day is someone's anniversary.[10] Given that, evidently, I profoundly disagree with the views and actions of some of the people I have met over the past forty years. But I have also been struck repeatedly by the courage, creativity, and resilience, of individuals and communities who survived overwhelming, sometimes unimaginable, events and circumstances. I have wept listening to people describing their losses and their griefs, and I have laughed with them too since laughter is never far away in Northern Ireland (jokes, slagging, mockery, and self-deprecation are part of a shared way of life). And there were, retrospectively at least, some amusing moments. Sitting in the front of a very expensive BMW driven by a loyalist paramilitary in North Antrim, my explanation of the murals project was interrupted by his casual observation that "your car is rolling down the hill." Given that it was rolling towards his shiny new car, I leapt out and held up my car by pushing against it and digging my feet in, while he strolled up leisurely to put the handbrake on. On another occasion, being pursued down Rossnareen Road onto the Shaws Road in Belfast by a drunk intent on taking my camera, we both came

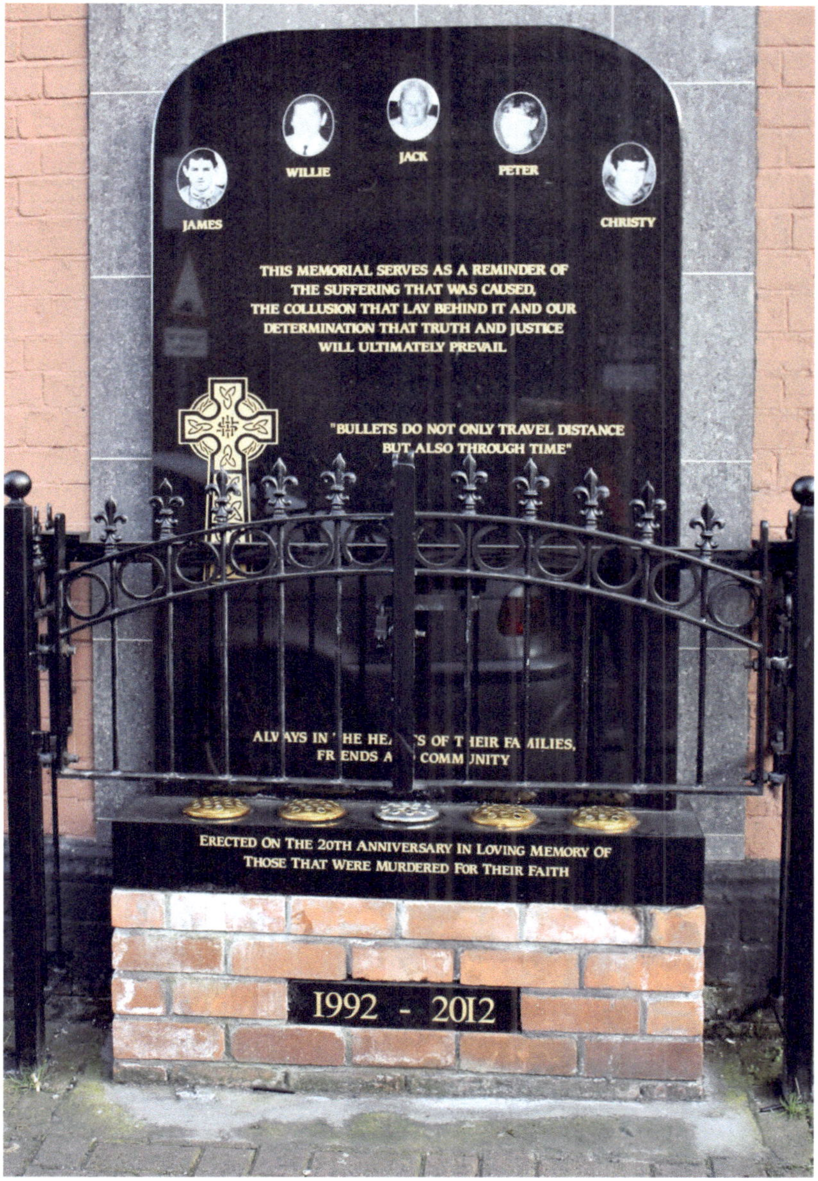

FIGURE 23 Republican memorial, Hatfield Street, Lower Ormeau, South Belfast, 2012. Photo by Tony Crowley.

to an abrupt halt as we were ordered to "stop!" by a British Army foot patrol and a prominent member of the republican movement at the same time (they hadn't seen each other). Everyone froze; I looked at my pursuer, who looked at the republican, who looked at the soldiers, who looked at me… whereupon we all, relatively slowly and carefully, turned away and went about our business. The war was anything but straightforward.

4. READING THE MURALS

I have been taking photographs of the murals one way and another for a long time, and, evidently, I believe that the materials gathered during that period are historically important. In 2005 I began the creation of an online, open-access archive—*The Murals of Northern Ireland* hosted at the Claremont Colleges Digital Library (https://ccdl.claremont.edu/digital/collection/mni)—consisting of more than 22,000 images (each image is given full historical annotation, including location, affiliation, date, and detailed description). A result of sustained international collaboration, and updated on a regular basis, the archive has logged more than 600,000 users, and images have been reproduced in a variety of academic textbooks, critical monographs, TV documentaries and films, numerous doctoral dissertations, and the British GCSE history examination. It stands centrally among the other mural collections that form an invaluable repository of visual materials from Northern Ireland's war and peace: the material gathered in the five volumes of Bill Rolston's *Drawing Support* (1992, 1995, 2003, 2013, 2022); Jonathan McCormick's photographs in the Conflict Archive on the Internet (1996–2006) (McCormick 2019); the work of "Extramural Activity," a site dedicated to hosting images of, and commentary on, contemporary murals (2011–the present); and Alain Miossec's collection "Murals Irlande du nord" (2006–the present).[11] And yet, notwithstanding the appearance of this important documentary work, and the growth of a range of critical and theoretical studies on the murals, it is striking that this form of street art has been, and to a large extent still is, treated antagonistically by the cultural establishment. The dominant attitude veers between hostility and studious indifference. The novelist Glenn Patterson, for example, has dismissed the murals as distasteful "kitsch" (Patterson 2006: 60). Similarly, a collection of twelve pamphlets—"Troubles Archive Essays"—published by the Arts Council of Northern Ireland as a companion to a "Troubles Archive" exhibition at the Ulster Museum—claimed to be "reflective of the relevant work of all parts of the arts community" (Arts Council 2009: 1). The essays addressed topics such as "The impact of the conflict on public space and architecture," "Prison art and the Conflict in Northern Ireland," and "A fusillade of question marks: some reflections on the art of the Troubles." And yet within the essays there was little or no mention of the thousands of murals that have been painted in public spaces since the late 1970s.[12] It was a curious and perplexing response to a form that has not only combined aesthetics and politics over an extended period, but also created an audience for art beyond traditional limits, as evinced by the burgeoning popular-cultural interest over the past fifteen years or so (not least among the large numbers of tourists who visit Northern Ireland to look at and photograph the murals). Clearly, I do not share the cultural establishment's dismissive attitude to the murals; rather, I think that they are both significant historical texts and, at their best, highly wrought artworks of notable aesthetic quality.

CONCLUSION: THE HISTORICITY OF MURALS

My aim in this work is to facilitate an understanding of the murals in Northern Ireland from their inception in the early twentieth century to the present. Before embarking on that task, however, it is necessary to attempt to clarify this study's central complicated keyword—"mural." "Mural" is a broad term which covers a multitude of practices ranging over a long history, and yet the word is a relatively recent coinage in English. Defined as "a decorative painting on a wall or ceiling," and derived from the Latin "mūrālis," "pertaining to or growing on a wall" (from "mūrus," "wall"), the noun "mural" is first recorded in the early twentieth century.[13] The earlier English term for wall paintings, most often used within art history, was "fresco," which dated to the late sixteenth century. The term meant specifically "a kind of water-color painting on a wall or ceiling whose plaster is not quite dry"; the root is the Italian "fresco," "fresh, newly made" (with reference to the plaster). Whatever their origins, however, words often carry dominant and associative meanings, which sometimes obscure the history from which they derived. Thus for most of the twentieth century, "mural" was probably most commonly linked with the work of the Mexican wall artists Diego Rivera, Fernando Leal, David Siqueiros, and José Orozco (while "fresco" evokes Italian Renaissance painting and the art of Giotto, Piero della Francesca, and Michelangelo among others). Yet with both "mural" and "fresco," the contemporary connotations elide a more complex, long-standing, and geographically widespread historical process. The earliest frescoes proper, for example, are Egyptian and more than five thousand years old; frescoes were also found in a number of civilizations ranging from Ancient Greece and Rome to India (Case and Crowfoot Payne 1962; Davis 1992; Sharma 2007). Murals, in the general sense of wall paintings, are even older. A recently discovered figurative representation of a Sulawesi warty pig is some 45,000 years old, while the oldest non-figurative painting is a stencil of a red hand made by a Neanderthal in Maltravieso cave, Cáceres, Spain, around 64,000 years ago (Brumm et al. 2021).[14]

The aims and functions of the earliest wall paintings are unclear, and interpretations range from their use within hunting, to shamanic rituals, to the claim that the paintings were made by ordinary people, including children.[15] Whatever the truth of the various accounts, it is clear that the paintings themselves—be they a simple handprint or a complex image—are intended to represent and communicate. But throughout the history of wall painting, if that implicit desire has been constant, it has been shaped by a variety of other factors, ranging from the skill of the artists, to the available materials, to the social context in which the images are made. In that sense at least, paintings on walls—whether they be Egyptian tomb art, Renaissance church decoration, or contemporary Los Angeles tagging—reflect and refract the history from which they are born and in which they are borne.[16] And given that they are shaped by, and shape, that history, they require interpretation and understanding. For while a Giotto fresco or a Rivera mural may be simply stunning visually, careful historical research into the form and function of the work is needed in order to comprehend its social origins and its deployment, and indeed the full extent of its complex aesthetic achievement. That same historical approach has guided the analysis of the particular type of wall paintings with which this study engages—the murals of Northern Ireland. For like their predecessors, these social and political artworks derive from a specific history and embody and distort it in intricate ways. In consequence, understanding the murals of Northern Ireland demands that they are placed within the complicated, power-laden, conflict-ridden, and often violent history from which they emerged. The analysis that follows is based on this fundamental tenet.

CHAPTER 1

Hegemony: Loyalist Muralism From the Home Rule Crisis to the Troubles

To access all images referenced in this chapter, please visit the open access version on Fulcrum at https://doi.org/10.3998/mpub.14527058.

> I fancy the like of it is not to be seen elsewhere. Endless scribblings on blank walls you will find. But where else have whole gables been covered, turning the streets into a sort of al fresco art gallery? (Joseph William Carey, *Northern Whig* July 14 1924: 6)

1. PUBLIC SPACE AND IDENTITY

The first murals in Northern Ireland were not painted in Northern Ireland (since it did not exist at the time), nor were they called "murals." Known commonly as "gable paintings," or "gable-end paintings," until the 1960s, the first examples of what we now call "murals" were painted in the context of the bitter struggle around Irish independence ("Home Rule"). This was the principal issue in British and Irish history in the late nineteenth and early twentieth centuries, with the decisive period running from the passing of the third Home Rule Bill (1912) to the partition of Ireland (1921), and the consequent creation of the separate states of Northern Ireland (1921) and the Irish Free State/Saorstát Éireann (1922) (the Saorstát eventually became the Republic of Ireland in 1948). It was a time of bitter and divisive conflict, involving a unionist revolt against the British government, a British Army mutiny, the Great War (in which unionists and nationalists fought and died for Britain), the Easter Rising, war between Irish republicans and the British, a Civil War among Irish republicans, and prolonged sectarian strife in Belfast and beyond. The final constitution of both Northern Ireland, composed of six of the nine counties of the province of Ulster, and the Irish Saorstát (made up of the remaining twenty-six counties), reflected the political interests and desires of their majority of their populations. In Northern Ireland the Protestant/unionist/loyalist majority wanted to remain within the United Kingdom; in the Free State the Catholic/nationalist/republican majority wanted to break the link forged by the Acts of Union of 1800 (enforced in 1801) and to create a sovereign, independent nation state (Bew 2007; Lynch 2019; Townsend 2021).[1] The sectarian and majoritarian legacy of the settlement was described by the Prime Minister of Northern Ireland, James

Craig (Lord Craigavon), in a parliamentary debate in 1934: "in the South they boasted of a Catholic State. They still boast of Southern Ireland being a Catholic State. All I boast of is that we are a Protestant Parliament and a Protestant State" (Craigavon 1934: 1095).

Lefebvre has argued that with regard to the lived experience of those who inhabit it, "space is neither a mere 'frame', after the fashion of a frame of a painting, nor a form or container of a virtually neutral kind, designed simply to receive whatever is poured into it" (Lefebvre 1991: 93–94). In other words, the space we live in "has been shaped and molded from historical and natural elements, but this has been a political process. Space is political and ideological. It is a product literally filled with ideologies" (Lefebvre, cited in Soja 1980: 210). Two things follow for Lefebvre: first, "if space is produced, if there is a productive process, then we are dealing with *history*" (Lefebvre 1991: 46, emphasis in original), and second, "space is never empty: it always embodies a meaning" (154). Given the violent and conflictual nature of the history that produced Northern Ireland, it is no surprise that its meaningful spaces were constructed politically and ideologically. This is a process that can take place in a variety of structured and profound ways, including features such as the geographic characteristics of a town, the locations of work and leisure, the demarcation of electoral boundaries, the gendered division of labor, and the delineation of forms of identity. But the everyday production of space is a crucial element in the construction of what the Italian political theorist Antonio Gramsci called political and cultural hegemony—the means by which relations of domination and consent are forged within a specific society. Never absolute or uncontested, and therefore always unfinished and in process, hegemony is nonetheless central to the legitimation of the social order. It is the means by which historically constituted subjects come to know their place both literally and metaphorically—how and where they (and others) belong.[2]

Developing this point in relation to Northern Ireland, Jarman has observed that "space as an ideological product remains unstable in its meaning, while actors may seek to impose meaning on it, to anchor it within a particular ideology" (Jarman 1992: 147). "Unstable" here is ambiguous and refers both to the fact that ideological victory is never complete, and therefore needs to be consistently reinforced, and to the fact that ideology is malleable and historically variable (as will be seen in the analysis of the murals, both republicanism and loyalism have changed significantly over time). Jarman continues: "there is no (en)closure of power over space so total that it precludes the possibility of resistance" (147), and this is an important point in relation to one site of contestation: the walls of Northern Ireland. For it is a striking fact that from the very inception of the conflict that created the State, walls have been a crucial locus of ideological formation; they have been used and re-used, contested and appropriated, won and lost, through historical practice—institutional, communal, and individual. One mode of such practice is the use of graffiti. In 1909, for example, the *Northern Whig* reported sectarian disorder in Banbridge related to the July 12th commemoration. The cause of the disturbance was the erection of a unionist arch and the writing of "No Pope" "in large letters… painted on the gable of a house opposite the post office, where people of the locality went to transact business and old-age pensioners to receive their pension" (*Northern Whig* July 31 1909: 9). In this case, the attempt to inscribe public space as unionist was challenged by counter protestors singing "The Boys of Wexford" and "God Save Ireland," and cursing King William; a violent fracas ensued. Judging the case, the magistrates fined the nationalists and bound them over to keep the peace; the "Protestant men" were instructed to "get that objectionable lettering on the house obliterated at once" (9). A similar case arose in Pettigo, a small town that straddled the Donegal-Fermanagh border, in 1922. In May–June Pettigo had been the site of a major battle between republican and British forces during the Anglo-Irish War, though by December it had been ceded to the Irish Free State and separated from its unionist hinterland by the border which ran along the River Termon (the Irish "termonn," "sanctuary, boundary," derives from the Latin "terminus," "boundary, limit," from Terminus, the Roman god of boundaries). During the military confrontation, the *Northern Whig* reported that "the gable of the house of another Loyalist, on which were printed the words 'Fear God, Honour the King,' was daubed with tar by the Sinn Feiners, and the inscription 'Up De Valera' put up instead." After British re-occupation of the village, it was noted, "these three words in turn disappeared, and today in large white letters upon that black tarred background are the lines—Thee, God, we praise June 4th 1922 Fear God and Honour the King" (*Northern Whig* December 8 1922: 8).[3]

Given its salience, it is worth noting at this point a number of essential characteristics of wall writing as a medium of communication: it is public, cheap, ephemeral, easily replaceable, and requires little skill other than literacy. It is also, as the examples given above demonstrate, dialogically effective in terms of provoking a response. But it is worth reflecting on the turn to the walls in Northern Ireland at just this point in history in relation to both graffiti and murals. For example, an extraordinary, brief film, made in 1920 in Belfast during the war between British and republican forces, offers an important insight in this regard. *The Agony of Belfast*, a two-minute silent work made by Irish Events (an independent film-maker based in Dublin), renders an astonishing snapshot of the war-torn, sectarian city (https://player.bfi.org.uk/free/film/watch-the-agony-of-belfast-1920-online). Framed by a Shakespearean epigraph—"where civil blood makes civil hands unclean"—the film opens with a street scene featuring a corner shop, a broken cobbled street with the cobbles piled as a makeshift barricade, a flag flying from a lamp-post, graffiti that reads "No Pope here" with an accompanying faded message "Police beware," and a group of impoverished women and children (few of the children are wearing shoes).[4] Moving to the opposite side of the street, the film focuses on a different group of children and offers a glimpse of a mural before cutting to show soldiers at a military emplacement outside the Cooperative store on York Street in the north of the city. Returning to the working-class unionist street depicted earlier (unidentified, but from the landscape at the rear, again probably North Belfast), the film presents an extended view of the terraced housing and various flags (Union Jacks of course, though the flag on the lamp-post is the Star Spangled banner—in all likelihood a reference to the involvement of US forces in the First World War). The camera then pans to a slow and detailed view of the mural glimpsed earlier, with adults and children gathered in front of the image and the cobbled street barricades before it. It is an astonishing first filmed recording of a mural: a full gable-end representation of King William and supporters crossing the Boyne, topped with a crest bearing the Red Hand of Ulster, flanked by two Union Jacks. It is an impressive rendering both in terms of scale and detail and was probably copied from one of the many versions circulating in popular culture of the ur-text of unionist murals: Benjamin West's "The Battle of the Boyne" (1778) (Loftus 1990 24–25). The mural does omit, however, an important detail of West's painting—the death of William's Commander, General Schomberg (which features on the bottom right of the original).[5] From the depiction of what popularly became known as "King Billy," the film shifts to a miserable scene of eviction, with a police presence and a family's belongings piled on a cart and on the street. Described by the British Film Institute in its short gloss as "people forced from their homes," the inference is that the eviction may be sectarian (the BFI also mentions "Unionist/Loyalist attacks on Catholics," though the reference is unclear), but alternatively, given that poverty affected working- class nationalist and loyalist communities alike, it may simply be related to the inability to pay the rent. The final sequence of the film features a heavily fortified and well-staffed military post at the end of Henry Street (which confirms the north city location—Henry Street abutted York Street).

The representation of the unionist mural is historically fascinating in various ways, but it may also offer an incidental insight into the non-political use of the walls (at least in the sense of not referring to the politics of the day) in the early twentieth century. Watson has argued that although the trope of King William "may have been derived from existing loyalist imagery, it is still a source of wonder that these murals appear to have developed completely independently, without any contact with other forms of wall-painting" (Watson 1983: 4). Yet at the very beginning of *The Agony of Belfast*, as the camera turns from the corner shop to the children and the street barricade (and thus the political graffiti), it captures a number of advertisements—no less than seven of various sizes for three everyday products—fixed to the wall. In point of fact, by 1920 the advertisement of national products was already governed by guidelines that ensured the reproduction of the brand, but as photographs of late Victorian and early twentieth-century cities show repeatedly, a common form of advertising for local manufacturers and shops was the wall painted by a signwriter. And as Nevett has argued, this was an extension of the early nineteenth-century practice of wall-chalking or the use of whitewash, as evinced by an article in the *London Magazine* in 1825:

> Colburn and Warren surprise you with the variety, brilliancy and country-circulation of their advertisements. The former of the two has not yet, I believe, like the other, had his name whitewashed in letters twice as long as his Magazine upon the walls of the Metropolis and the Park-palings of the country. This is, however, a popular and striking method of advertising. (Nevett 1982: 56)

Indeed such was the ubiquity of this method, that it was prohibited (ineffectively as it turned out) by the Metropolitan Police Act of 1839 (127). By the mid-to-late twentieth century, such techniques had been displaced by the more familiar means of advertising, which were to dominate until the digital age (print, radio, television, and the use of dedicated public spaces). But in that crucial period towards the end of the nineteenth and the beginning of the twentieth centuries, urban space had already become saturated by the signs of commodified modernity. And wall painting, in particular, was a relatively cheap but significant medium through which advertisers could cajole, enjoin, persuade, and convince at scale. It was a lesson evidently not lost on the early loyalist muralists and graffiti writers. Often trained as shipyard painters, housepainters, or sign-writers, these working-class men were "skilled craftsmen with a strong sense of their independent status" (Loftus 1990: 34). They easily turned their hand to the task of filling the blank canvasses of gable ends to advertise important political messages of allegiance and unity, together with their counterparts, difference and division.

2. WALLS AS POLITICAL TEXTS: THE FIRST MURALS

As Jarman has shown, however, the dominant mode of the "visible sectarianisation of public space" in Northern Ireland for most of the twentieth century was not muralism but the arch-building that took place around the July 12th celebrations (Jarman 2001: 3). Dating from the early nineteenth century, arches were originally relatively simple in form. In 1812 in Tandragee, for example, John Gamble noted "a lofty arch, which was thrown across the entire street. The Orange was gracefully blended with oak leaves, laurels and roses. Bits of gilded paper, suited to the solemnity, were interwoven with the flowers" (cited in Loftus 1994: 31). Yet the form and function of the arches developed historically, and by the early twentieth century they featured centrally in intra-communal competitions for the most extravagant celebrations of the Twelfth. Rolston describes such rivalry among working-class unionist areas as founded on the perception of what amounts to "a civic duty"—a duty ordained by the cultural hegemony that played a central role in the formation of the cross-class alliance that underpinned the political hegemony of unionism.

In the 1930s, the local newspaper coverage of the Twelfth included numerous photographs of complex designs that incorporated technology for enhanced effect. In 1935, for example, declaring that "Belfast never looked better than it does this year" (a rhetorical motif that recurred), the *Belfast Telegraph* reported that,

> Arches are all over the city in hundreds, some of them elaborate structures with electrical fittings for illumination at night, all of them outward expressions of the innate loyalty of the inhabitants. A tram ride along the main thoroughfares like the Shankill Road, Crumlin Road, Newtownards Road, Albertbridge Road, Shore Road, indeed, in any part of the city, shows street after street vying with each other in friendly rivalry as to which will make the gayest show. The

> loyalty of a people welded to Britain is shown in mile after mile of bunting and Union Jacks. (*Belfast Telegraph* July 11 1935: 13)

Likewise, the *Belfast News-Letter* observed that unionists used the new forms of street decoration to proclaim "their loyalty to the King and Empire and their faith in cherishing the memory of William of Orange." It continued to note that "the application of electric light for night-time illumination and the installation of loud-speakers are original and pleasing features of all the major arches such as those Sandy Row, Berlin Street, Shankill Road, Fortuna Street, Donegall Road, and Wolff Street, Newtownards Road" (*Belfast News-Letter* July 12 1935: 9). Such innovations promoted a celebratory atmosphere:

> Throughout the afternoon and evening crowds toured the city by motor and tramcar to view the decorations, and by ten o'clock the streets were thronged with eager sight-seers. With bonfires alight, arches illuminated and loudspeakers providing music, the spirit of carnival was awakened and impromptu dances added still further to the gaiety of the gatherings. In several areas crowds paraded from arch to arch till well past midnight, and on the Shankill Road shops remained open till the early hours of the morning, the sellers' flags and favours doing a particularly brisk business (9).

Evidently such reports reflect the political partiality of both newspapers, not least in the tendency to presume that unionist culture was civic culture per se, and that public space belonged without question to the unionist majority. For it simply wasn't the case that unionist street decorations could be seen "in any part of the city"; they were of course conspicuous by their absence in nationalist areas. And despite the invocation of the carnivalesque, it is worth recalling that the 12th July parade of 1935 was followed by some of the most savage sectarian violence of the pre-Troubles history of Northern Ireland (Hepburn 1990).

Though the tradition has declined considerably, arches are still erected in both urban and rural areas of Northern Ireland (Figure 1), but the main focus of the Twelfth celebrations is now Orange parades and enormous bonfires (Figure 2). The relative demise of the arches is explicable by a number of factors. Overhead electricity lines forced them off main thoroughfares in the early twentieth century, but more importantly, the communal labor required, and the economic costs involved, gradually proved prohibitive. In 1935, for example, the *Northern Whig* reported that the Wolff Street arch cost £80 to erect (a sum that would translate today to more than £7,000), a demanding sum for a working-class area to raise (*Northern Whig* July 11 1935: 8). Murals, by contrast, were relatively cheap, tended to rely on the labor of one person (often with a small team of helpers), and, importantly, they endured. Arches were usually erected in the week before the Twelfth and were taken down almost immediately afterwards; murals, with annual re-touching, could last for decades. As a durable public medium, they came to play a central role in the narration of a mode of collective memory that underpinned unionist ascendancy.

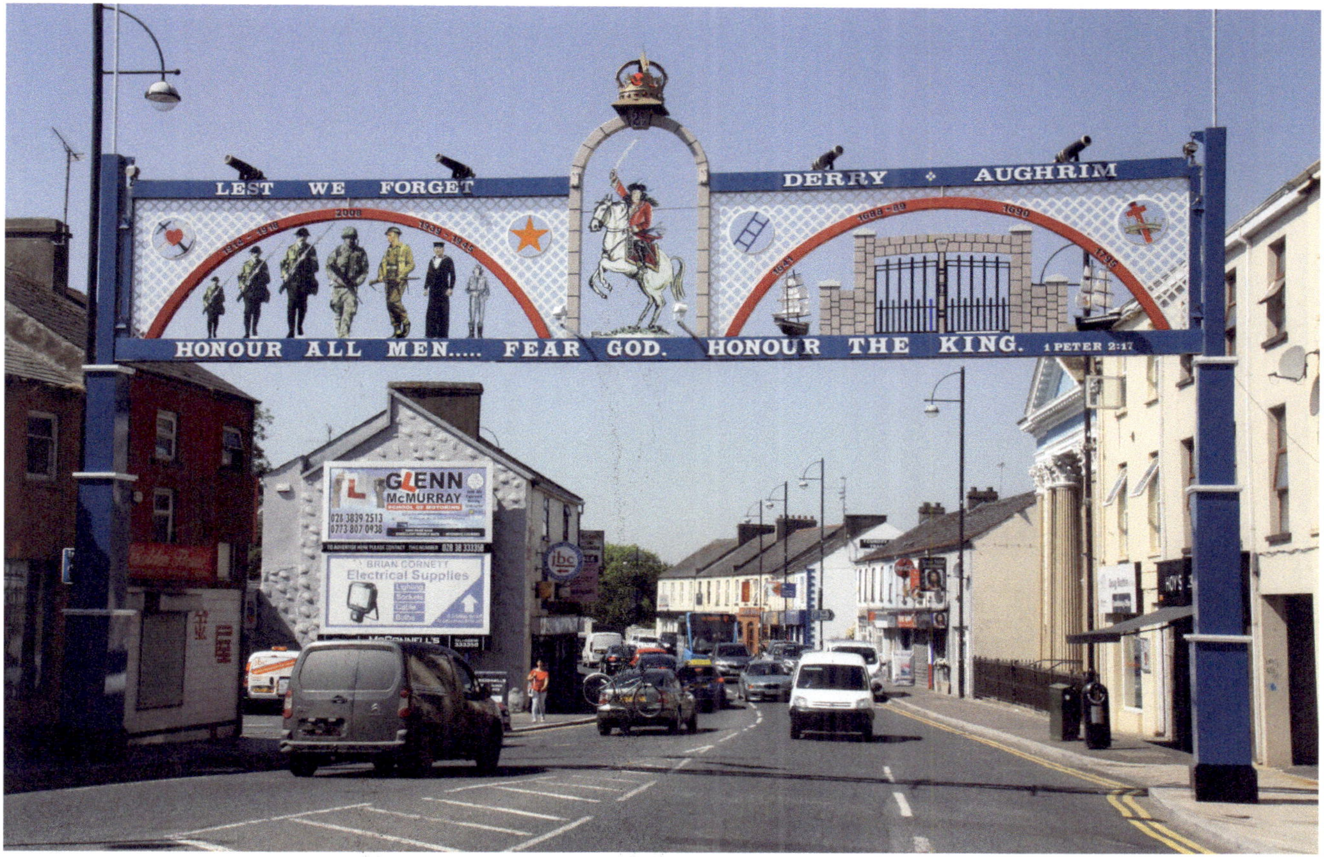

FIGURE 1 Loyalist arch, Bridge Street, Portadown, 2018. Photo by Tony Crowley.

In short, given their everyday visibility, with their familiar tropes and easily recognizable symbols, they became crucial lieux de mémoire (Nora 1989).

If *The Agony of Belfast* shows the first unionist mural on film, the date for the earliest example of unionist muralism is proposed by Loftus as 1908 (Loftus 1983: 11). The claim, which is repeated in various sources as established fact, appears to rest on an article published in 1958 in *Ireland's Saturday Night* (a sports paper published by the *Belfast Telegraph* company). A feature piece, entitled "An Old Craftsman Turns Up," was a follow-up to an earlier article, prompted by a request from a curator at Ulster Museum, which initiated a "search for William III gable-end paintings." Seeking to answer the question "who was the first of these mural artists?," the

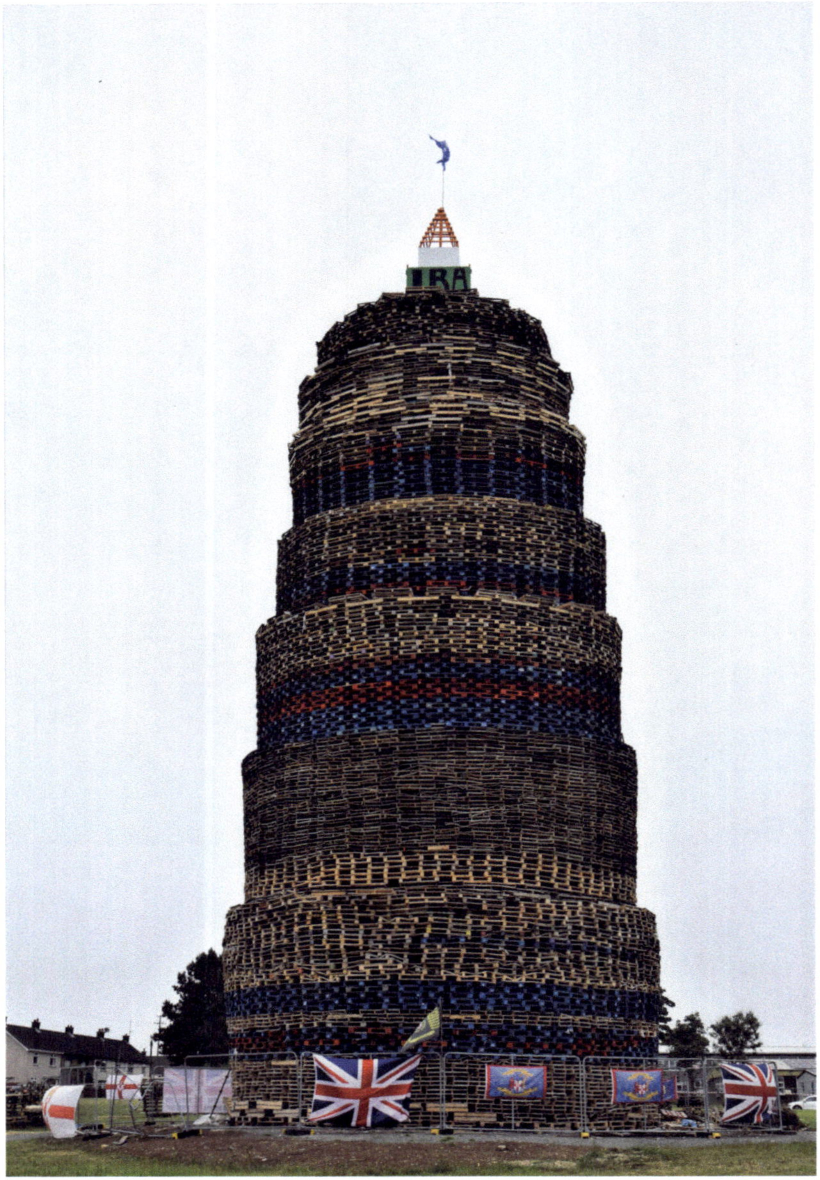

FIGURE 2 Craigyhill loyalist bonfire, Linn Road, Larne, 2021. Photo by Tony Crowley.

writer reports that "a Belfast shipyard watchman, Mr. John McClean, claims that he was responsible for the first of these huge studies in vivid colour of William crossing the Boyne mounted on the traditional white horse... on a gable at Beersbridge Road, Belfast... carried out in 1908" (*Ireland's Saturday Night* July 5 1958: 4). Noting that he had also painted King William in 1910 and 1914, McClean also took credit for "a remarkable mural on the theme of victory" in 1919 and "another one depicting the Battle of the Somme" in 1920. There was, however, an earlier claim for the title of the first muralist. An article in the *Belfast Telegraph* in November 1956 asserted that the redoubtable Tommy Henderson, house-painter and Independent Unionist MP for the Belfast Shankill constituency, "painted the first King Billy in Belfast on the gable end of a grocer's and confectioner's shop he once had in Weir Street" (off the Shankill) (*Belfast Telegraph* November 16 1956: 3).[6] Whatever the truth of these claims, the more important question is why the murals appeared at this juncture. Again, there are a number of contributory elements. As suggested earlier, the indicative use of walls for advertising may have been one factor, the pool of talent experienced in painting in unionist working-class areas another, and the technological development of commercial paints a third (the shipyards were a "source of free and superior quality paint," Loftus 1990: 31). Above all, however, the most important factor is the set of historical circumstances in which the first murals were painted. For 1908–1914 were crucial years in the Home Rule Crisis, particularly after 1910 when the Irish Parliamentary Party held the balance of power at Westminster. Once the Parliament Act (1911) had curtailed the power of the Lords to block legislation, the introduction of the Third Home Rule Bill and the formation of the Ulster Volunteers in 1912 set the stage for the bitter struggle that ended in Partition. Given the other factors cited above, it is no coincidence that loyalist muralism emerged from that history.

3. RESPONDING TO HISTORY

The emphasis on the historical context in which murals were painted is important because muralism was a response, often local in origins but broader in significance, to particular developments at specific times. For this reason, rather than being "timeless" (Cook 2000: 44), the painting of the same image—say King William crossing the Boyne—carried different meanings at distinct historical moments. Thus although it became a recurrent trope, painting the image of King William in 1911 (during the bitter Home Rule struggle) was not the same as painting it in 1922 (post-Partition), nor in the late 1930s (after the sectarian disturbances of 1935), nor in 1945 (after VE Day), nor in the late 1950s (when the practice was thought to be dying out), nor in the 1980s (during the Troubles), nor today (in the post-war period). For despite the fact that the motif was reiterated (with varying execution—some murals were highly artistic, others very poorly executed)—the when, why, and where of its setting shaped its historical significance. Indeed, even the same image in the same place could signify differently over time. King William painted on a wall in a thriving working-class area could look very different as one of the last remnants of the area during a "redevelopment" scheme twenty years later. And a King William that had been allowed to fade without maintenance, or one that had been re-framed by the juxtaposition of a paramilitary mural, might signal important shifts within the pan-class hegemony of unionism.

The first contemporary record of loyalist murals appears in the *Belfast News-Letter* in its account of the 1911 Twelfth celebrations ("The Street Decorations. Imposing Display"). The decorations, the paper opined, demonstrated "the fact that the Orangemen in the present generation are even more strong in their opposition to Home Rule in any shape or form than their predecessors, and that under no circumstances will they submit to be ruled by an Irish Parliament sitting in College Green, Dublin" (*Belfast News-Letter* July 13 1911: 7). As well as "the arches spanning the streets, flags and streamers floated gaily in the breeze… and huge masses of Orange lilies, sweet-william and other flowers now in full bloom, filled numerous windows with gorgeous colour," the report noted, portraits of the King and Queen were in evidence, and slogans hung everywhere: "Remember the deeds of our forefathers," "Derry, Aughrim, Enniskillen and the Boyne," "God save the King." And then, towards the end of the piece, the article also remarked that "splendid paintings of King William crossing the Boyne were to be seen on the gables of houses in Clara Street, off the Beersbridge Road, and in Malcolm Street. These portraits were some eight feet in height and were skillfully and artistically created" (7). The murals may have been those to which McClean was referring in 1958, but as the *Belfast Weekly News* made clear in 1913, this was an innovative and striking development. Describing the "veritable works of art" that featured in the street decorations for Belfast's July Twelfth celebrations, the paper reported that,

> The attention of passers-by was frequently arrested by beautiful examples of the painter's handicraft in the form of representations of King William crossing the Boyne depicted on the gables. This is to a large extent a new departure in the decorations and it is one that commended itself to those who had the pleasure of seeing it. There were numerous expressions of commendation and congratulations to those who were responsible for the appropriate mural ornaments (*Belfast Weekly News* July 17 1913: 9).

Ballymacarrett, in the East of the city, was singled out for particular approbation, and, it was observed, "passers-by could not fail to be struck with the pictorial illustration of King William, mounted on a white charger, painted on the gable of one of the houses in Central Street, and additional distinction was lent to the production by the inclusion of representations of the Royal Standard and the Union Jack" (9).

In one sense it is clear that the motif of William crossing the Boyne was intended to send the same overt message as the cartoon printed on the front page of the same issue of the *Belfast Weekly News* with the title "1690–1913—NO CHANGE" (Figure 3). And yet as the cartoon illustrated, the "no change" message was rhetorical more than real, for this was a crucial historical moment replete with a number of political possibilities. Thus

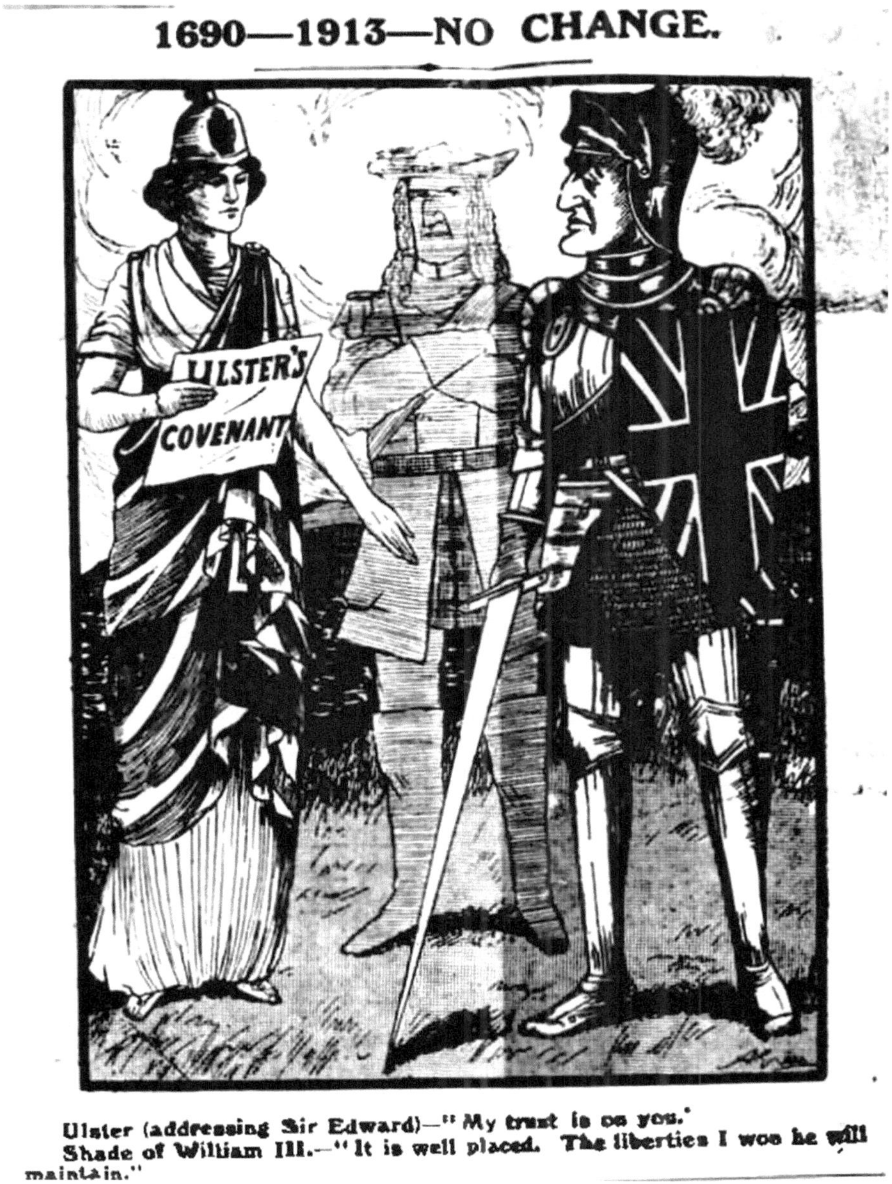

FIGURE 3 No change, *Belfast Weekly News*, July 17 1913.

standing between the female figure of Ulster (draped in the Union Jack, with Red Hand pith helmet and "Ulster's Covenant" in hand), and Edward Carson (dressed as a medieval knight with full armor, over-sized sword and Union Jack shield), King William, arms crossed and eyes fixed on Carson, responds to Ulster's plaint to Carson—"My trust is on you"—with the declaration: "It is well placed. The liberties I won he will maintain" (*Belfast Weekly News* July 17 1913: 1). This is an intriguing cartoon, not least because of the implicit anxiety, rather than confidence, that it conveys. Since for all the assertion of the importance of the "civil and religious liberty" that the Williamite triumph had delivered—as manifested in those new gable paintings of the Boyne scene—it is clear from Ulster's beseeching stance, and William's ghostly stare, that the Protestant Ascendancy was at stake in 1913 rather than assured. And trust in politicians was in short supply. A report in the *Belfast News-Letter* ("The West's awake, and will not have Home Rule"), noted that during a visit to West Belfast by Carson in late July 1913, effigies of Asquith, Redmond, and "Churchill the traitor" were suspended from arches in the Shankill and burned at night (*Belfast News-Letter* July 28 1913: 7). Carson's reception was of course different, and in 1914, "in several districts there were pictorial representations on the gable ends of houses of King William crossing the Boyne, as well as cleverly painted portraits of Edward Carson" (*Belfast News-Letter* July 14 1914: 7). One of those portraits was painted in Carnan Street, by Tommy Henderson (*Belfast Telegraph* August 24 1914: 5). Interestingly, and prophetically, when campaigning electorally in 1923 for the Belfast North constituency, which he lost narrowly to the official unionist candidate, Henderson drew a distinction between his unionism (which was unflinching) and the economic interests of his working-class constituents. A ditty in support of his election contained the lines: "Painting Kings upon a gable/Brings but little bread and cheese" (*Northern Whig* November 23 1923: 7). It was a rare if noteworthy ideological crack in the cross-class unionist monolith.

As the fateful decade 1912–1922 developed, Williamite murals continued to appear. In Londonderry, it was reported that "in the loyal district of Fountain Street life-size paintings of King William III on his charger were on the side-walls of four houses" (*Belfast News-Letter* July 14 1919: 11). These were the first works of Bobby Jackson (Snr), later to become the area's most famous muralist. Two years later, Jackson had added a further piece: "a magnificent picture of King William III crossing the Boyne had been painted on the gable of a house in Clarence Place" (*Belfast News-Letter* August 13 1921: 6). Back in Belfast, as recorded in the *Belfast Telegraph Weekly*—"'Victory'—Twelfth July Demonstrations 1690 1919"—King William appeared in Victoria Park, the *Mountjoy* was depicted breaking the boom during the Siege of Derry in Hornby Street (both in East Belfast), and in Carnan Street, off the Shankill in West Belfast, the "Carnan Roll of Honour" was listed in full (*Belfast Telegraph Weekly* July 19 1919).[7] A couple of years later, "Dromore Street" (probably a mistake for Dromara Street) and Balfour Avenue, off the Ormeau Road, carried "admirable gable wall paintings" of King William crossing the Boyne (*Northern Whig* July 12 1921: 7). In the north of the city, George Hannah, the Unionist MP for Belfast Duncairn, presided over the unveiling of another iteration of the theme, before running into a skirmish between an Orange parade and "hooligans" trying to steal a newly unfurled Orange banner (*Northern Whig* July 13 1921: 10). Yet although William on his charger was the dominant motif, there were other murals that revealed the walls to be the locus of distinctive attempts to record and shape collective memory. As noted, Carson featured in murals as early as 1914, while the events of the First World War, specifically the role of the 36th Ulster Division at the Somme, also started to emerge as a significant topic. The *Belfast Telegraph* reported a memorial service in Ballymacarrett on the first anniversary of the Somme held in front of "a painting of a military subject of a patriotic type not unknown to Belfast"; the service commemorated the artist, who had been killed in the war (*Belfast Telegraph* July 2 1917: 7). Also in Ballymacarrett, "noted for the sturdy character of its working-class population and its unswerving loyalty" (it was built around the shipyards of Harland and Wolff), another mural appeared on Montrose Street dedicated to "the hero of the Revolution" (King William), with inscriptions: "No Home Rule," "No surrender," and "Success to the Ulster Division" (*Belfast News-Letter* July 13 1917: 5).

The emergence of a historical narrative linking past and present is evident in the first report of a post-Partition mural in Willowfield (again in East Belfast). Noting that "the painting of pictures of historic interest… has become a feature of the Orange Order in recent years," the *Belfast Telegraph* recorded the unveiling of a triptych before a crowd of some two thousand: "in the centre panel is William of Orange crossing the Boyne, and on either side of him are Oliver Cromwell and William Johnson of Ballykilbeg" (*Belfast Telegraph* July 5 1922: 2). Such events took a familiar course: music by a Lodge band, the unveiling, an address by a local dignitary (often a Unionist MP), prayers led by the area's clergy, a vote of thanks, and the National Anthem. It was an important concatenation of popular culture, politics, and religion that bolstered the cultural and political hegemony of unionism across classes and in case the message was unclear, it was, as in this example, made explicit. Mrs T. Moles (wife of the MP for Belfast South) advised the working-class crowd that:

> They could all derive valuable lessons from contemplation of the life and character of Oliver Cromwell, with its sturdy Puritanism, its high patriotism, and its great courage and devotion to his native land. In William of Orange they had another great character who, feeble in body but strong in mind, established freedom of conscience and liberty in these lands, and gave to Britain a place she had never lost. In William Johnson they had one whose name would always be revered for a simple faith, single-mindedness and true patriotism. (2)

The link was made across the centuries—from Cromwell, to King William, to Johnson (Johnson was a folk-hero to the Orange Order for defying the ban on Orange Parades in 1867 and being sent to prison as a result; he later became a Unionist MP). The mural would thus play an important role and "serve to remind them of those three men"—guarantors of the historical continuity of Protestant liberties.

The shift of focus to the present continued with the unveiling of a mural of Sir Henry Wilson in Pittsburg Street, North Belfast, and another in loyalist Tigers Bay, in 1922. Wilson had been centrally involved in the Curragh Mutiny and later became Chief of the Imperial General Staff (until 1921), a Unionist MP, and security advisor to the Northern Ireland government; the murals were painted a month after his assassination in London by the IRA. Wilson's importance to contemporary unionism was signaled by the presence, at the unveiling of the Pittsburg Street mural, of the Northern Ireland Prime Minister, who noted Wilson's role in securing "our small but Imperial State" (*Belfast Telegraph* July 10 1922: 7). Recalling another mural elsewhere in Belfast that featured his own image, Lord Craigavon declared that there could be "no greater compliment" than a wall painting paid for by local subscription in a unionist working-class areas. Yet, as well as their historical significance, the Wilson murals are also notable in that they appear to be the first for which a photographic record exists. The Pittsburg mural showed an image of Wilson in Field-Marshall's uniform, Union Jack flying at his side, a decorative border in the form of curtains, "with the Red Hand of Ulster and a laurel wreath below" (7) (Figure 4, see Fulcrum). The more complex and interesting Limestone Road mural featured a framing epigraph—"We mourn our loss"—with a downcast Britannia folding back the curtain on a portrait of Wilson saluted by a soldier with a fallen Union Jack at his feet (Figure 5). The mural also included lines from Rudyard Kipling's "Recessional" (written for Queen Victoria's Diamond Jubilee in 1897):

> The tumult and the shouting dies;
> The Captains and the Kings depart:
> Still stands Thine ancient sacrifice,
> An humble and a contrite heart.
> Lord God of Hosts, be with us yet,
> Lest we forget—lest we forget!
> (Kipling 1994: 340)[8]

Such was the popularity of Wilson among unionists that his image was the subject of a fund-raising fraud; two men were prosecuted for raising money by false pretenses "in aid of the painting of Sir Henry Wilson on a gable in City Street" (*Northern Whig* September 7 1922: 6).

A mural dedicated to Edith Cavell in 1929 in Primitive Street on the Donegall Road in South Belfast again marked a turn to the events of the First World War (Cavell was a British nurse in Belgium executed by the German Army for her role in helping Allied prisoners escape). The image figured Cavell in nurse's uniform reading the Bible against a red Cross and flanked by the Union Jack and Belgian national flag (Figure 6). Importantly, to left and right, the painting included memorials with Kipling's "Lest we Forget" and a scroll with the inscription

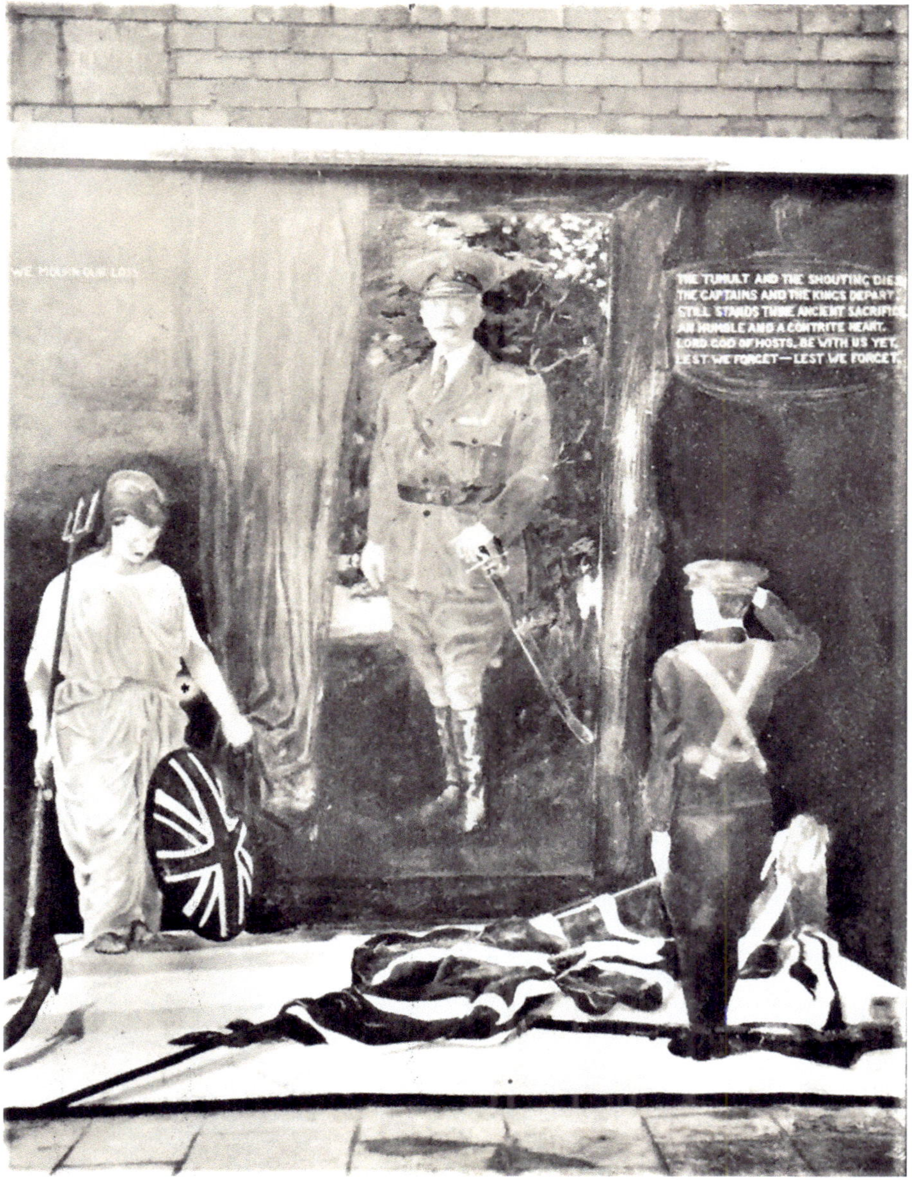

FIGURE 5 The Captains and the Kings, Limestone Road, North Belfast, July 1922.

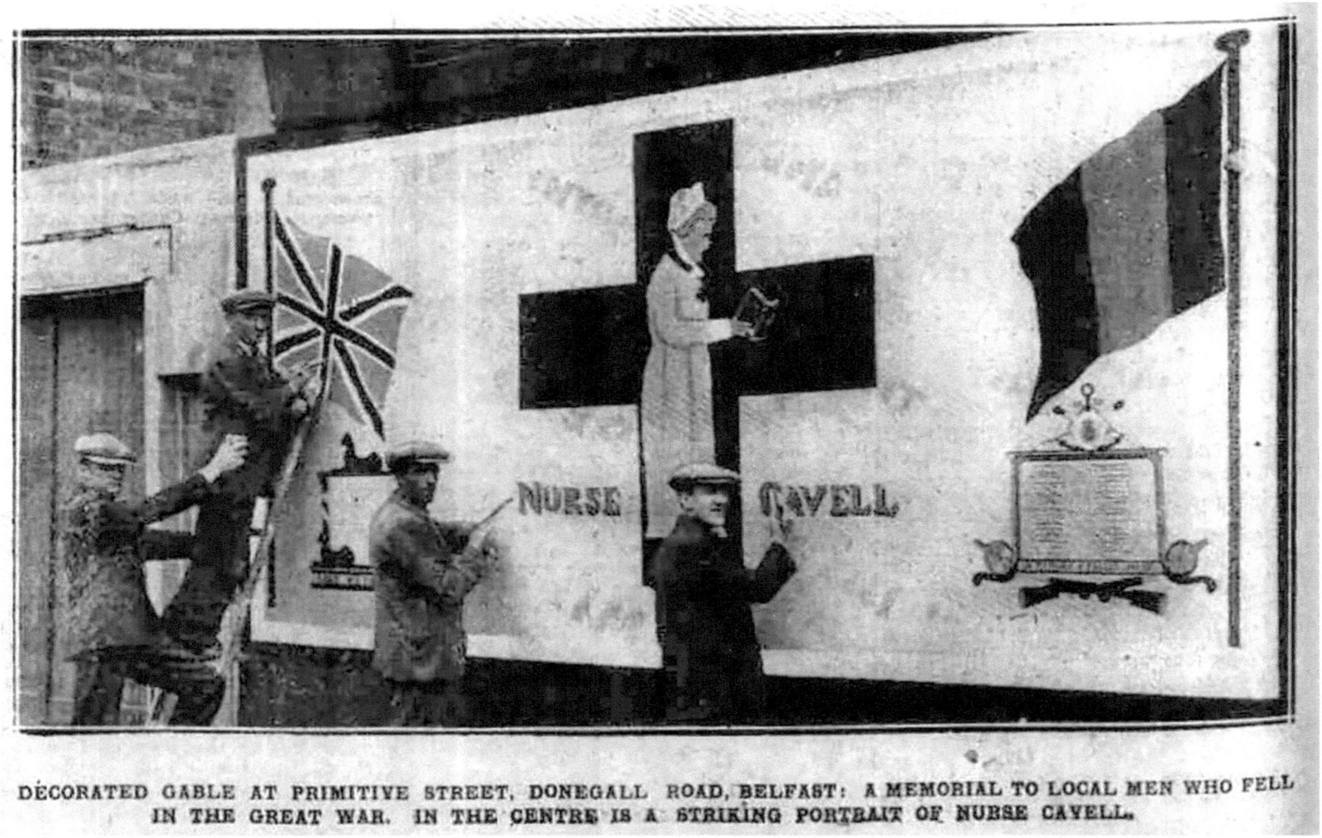

FIGURE 6 Edith Cavell, Primitive Street, South Belfast 1929.

"In memory of Fallen Loyalists" (*Belfast News-Letter* July 10 1929: 8). In 1933 a memorial mural appeared on Fortingale Street, North Belfast, dedicated to the 36th Ulster Division, an infantry division that bore significant losses at the Somme and came to take on mythic status in the unionist cultural imagination (Figure 7). The mural took the form of a harp and crown set against a star (the purple star on an orange background is an Orange Order flag, originally taken from the Williamite forces) with the motto "Quis separabit" ("Who shall separate us?"—used by various British Army regiments in Ireland, the government of Northern Ireland, and, later, the UDA).[9] The crest was encircled in a wreath, on which was inscribed: "In remembrance of the Officers, NCOs & men of the 36th Ulster' (*Belfast Telegraph* July 10 1933: 12). More complex memorial murals followed. The *Belfast News-Letter* noted that in "many striking mural paintings," "an added significance has attached to Ulster's day

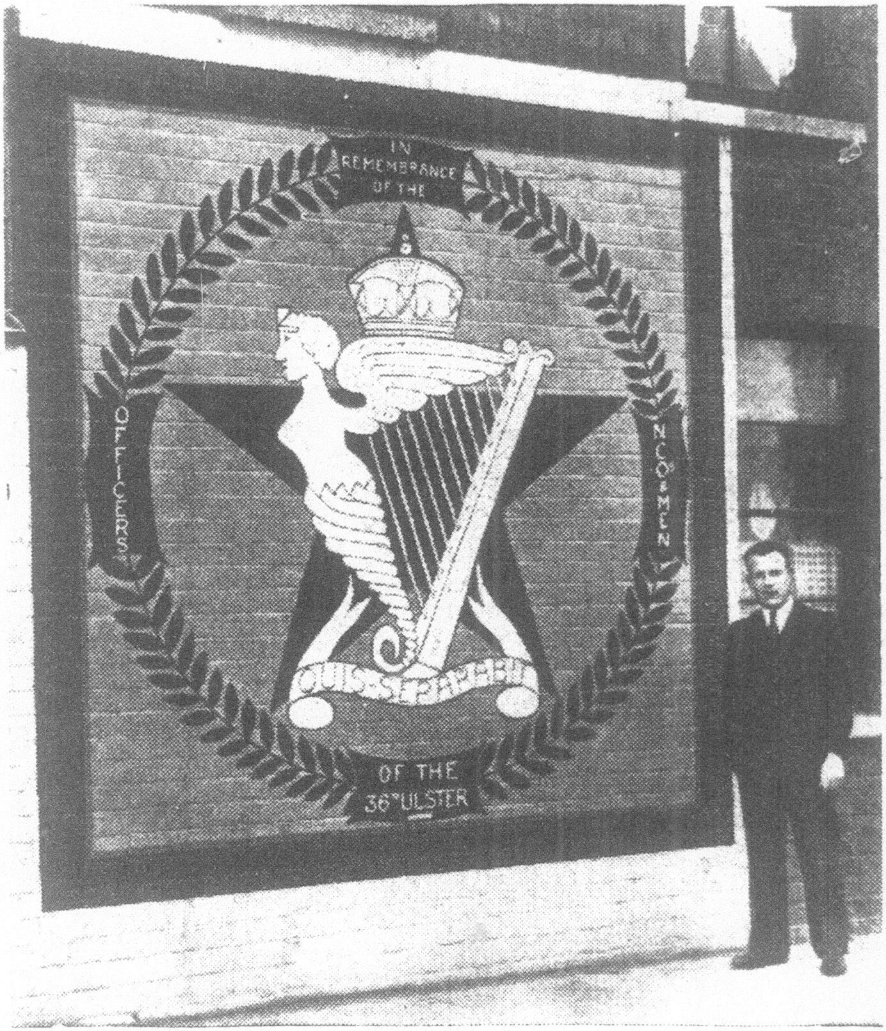

The memorial painting to the officers and N.C.O.'s of the 36th (Ulster) Division at the corner of Fortingale Street (Agnes Street), Belfast, by Mr. John M'Ilroy, Fortingale Street, seen in the picture. It was unveiled by Lady Hungerford.

FIGURE 7 36th Ulster Division, Fortingale Street, West Belfast, July 1933.

of memories, and the Battle of the Somme ranks with Derry, Aughrim and the Boyne as dearly-bought victories which Ulster remembers with gratitude and with honourable pride" (*Belfast Newsletter* July 12 1935: 9). The linkage between "Ulster's recent sacrifices in the Great War… [and] her more ancient struggles" (9) was made explicit in a mural at Clifford Street in South Belfast in 1934 (Figure 8, see Fulcrum). Topped by an image of King William crossing the Boyne against an Orange star with the dates 1690 1914–1918, and flanked by symbols of the Orange Order—compass and square and ladder—with Union Jacks and flags of the Allies, the mural centered on a representation of a Cenotaph (also draped by a Union Jack) over an open Bible. Framed by the inscription "In glorious memory lest we forget," the Bible was placed over a motto—"Their names liveth for evermore"—and to left and right, scrolls commemorated the names of the dead. To the right of the main mural stood a representation of the Relief of Derry. Similarly complex, a mural in Coolfin Street in 1935 also had King William atop, with the same Orange Lodge symbols, though the flags in this case were the Union Jack and the Star-Spangled Banner (signaling, as in the image from 1920 analyzed earlier, gratitude to the United States for its role in the First World War) (Figure 9, see Fulcrum). The center-piece in this mural, however, was a striking, large-scale reproduction of James Prinsep Beadle's iconic painting, "Attack of the Ulster Division, 1 July 1916" (1917), a work now housed in Belfast City Hall.

4. THE SIGNIFICANCE OF KING BILLY AND THE DECLINE OF UNIONIST MURALISM

Loftus asserts that the early unionist murals covered an eclectic range of topics, including the *Mountjoy* breaking the boom during the Siege of Derry, Lord Roberts flanked by two Boer War soldiers, the Angel of Mons, *The Titanic*, and VE Day (Loftus 1983: 11–12). Coronations and Royal Jubilees are also represented in the murals (Figure 10, see Fulcrum) (Figure 11, see Fulcrum) (Figure 12), but as Rolston has observed, "the most common theme was a depiction of King Billy" (Rolston 1991: 21). In fact, apart from one image of William landing at Carrickfergus, painted by Bobby Jackson at Clarence Place in Londonderry around 1950 (Cooper and Sargent 1979: 39), the recurrent image was William crossing the Boyne on his white charger. Perhaps the most striking example is Tommy Henderson's early portrait (specific date unknown), but there were variations on the theme (Figure 13). The King was accompanied by the Prince of Wales and Lord Carson at Maria Place in 1933 (Figure 14, see Fulcrum), while at the junction of Charleville/Snugville Streets in the same year, "one of the most striking decorations ever seen in the city" (*Northern Whig* July 13 1933: 5) featured William front and center, with the Duke of Abercorn against Hillsborough Castle to the left, Lord Carson against the Stormont Parliament to the right, images of the King and Queen, and a representation of the Prince of Wales playing a Lambeg drum (which also carried his image). And in 1939 a complex image of the Siege of Derry and William crossing the Boyne served as a memorial to men jailed for their part in sectarian riots in 1935 (Figure 15, see Fulcrum). But in general, William rode in splendid isolation on murals that were sometimes striking and occasionally not quite so well achieved (horses were, and continued

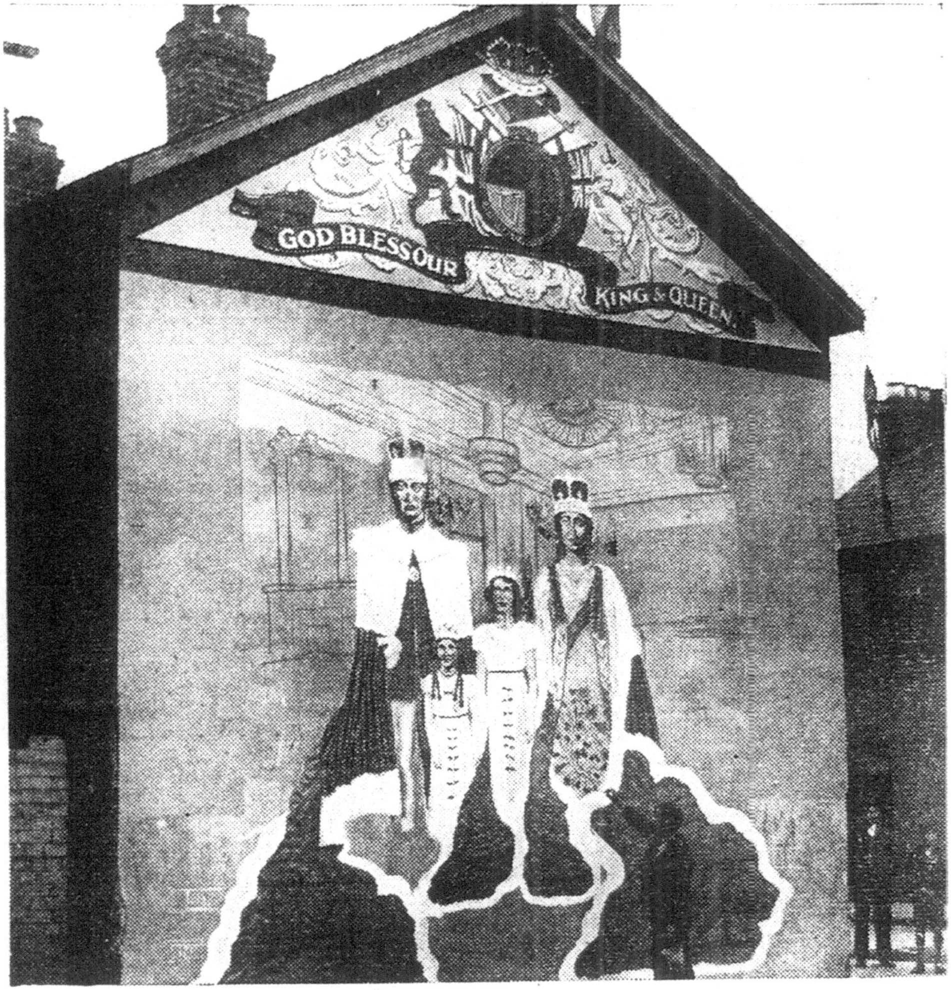

TWELFTH JULY DECORATIONS.—Painting of their Majesties King George VI., Queen Elizabeth, and their Royal Highnesses Princess Elizabeth and Princess Margaret Rose on the gable of a house at corner of Snugville and Charleville Streets, Belfast. The painting was executed by Mr. George F. Wilgaus for Charleville Social Club.

FIGURE 12 God Bless our King and Queen, Snugville Street, West Belfast, July 1938.

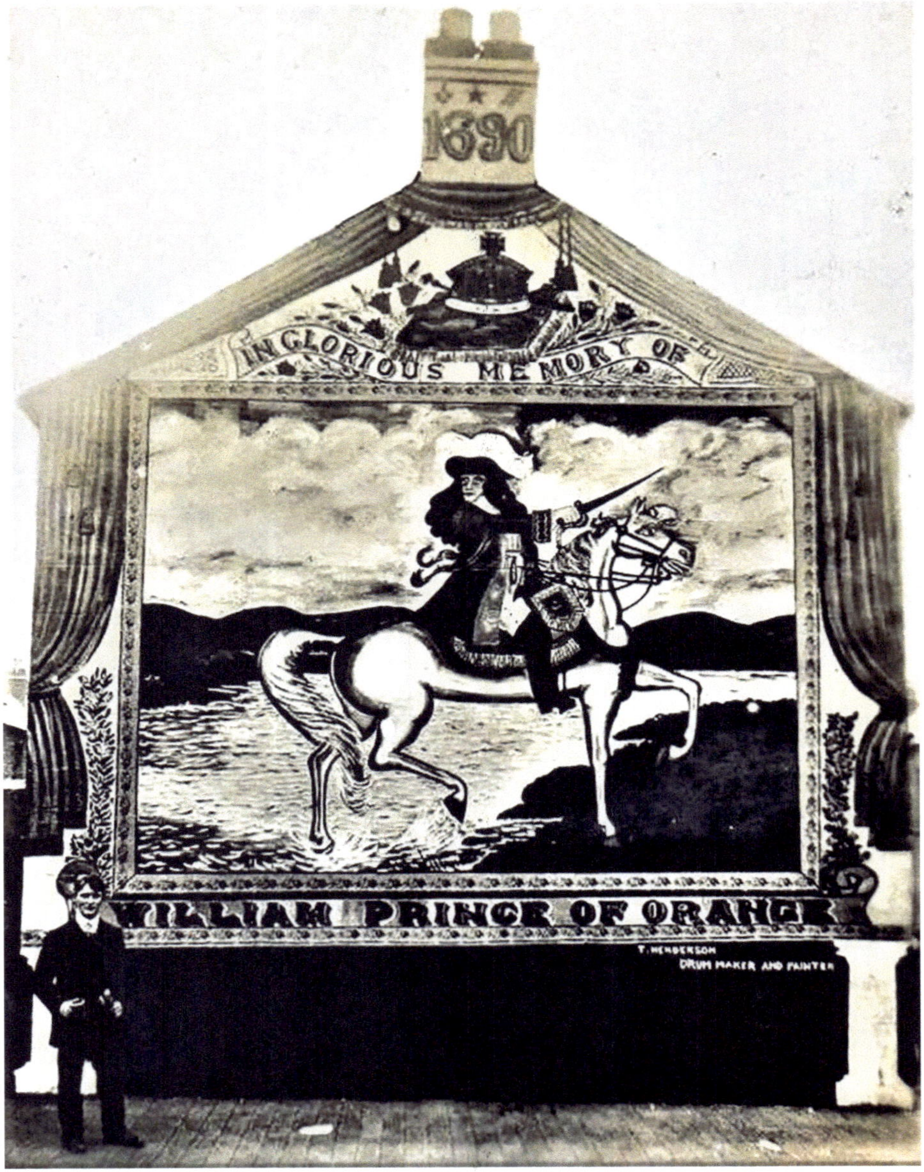

FIGURE 13 In glorious memory, loyalist West Belfast, date unknown ?1912.

to be, the weak spot) (Figure 16, see Fulcrum) (Figure 17) (Figure 18). They were also impressively long-lasting: the Jackson family's murals in Londonderry (re-touched annually) lasted from the 1920s to the 1990s in various locations in The Fountain, while the Rockland Street mural, in South Belfast, endured for a similar period before finally succumbing to demolition in the 1990s (Rolston 1991: 24).

The painting of "King Billy on the wall" was usually prompted by the communal desire to decorate an area for the Twelfth celebrations, although it could also be a reaction to events in a larger context. Thus there was an increased number of murals in the 1930s, some of which were responses to cultural and political events on the other side of the border: the decorations erected for the Catholic Eucharistic Congress in Dublin in 1932, for example, or the Dublin government's adoption of the new *Bunreacht na hÉireann (Constitution of Ireland)* in 1937, with its declaration of the whole island as the national territory. But there was an underlying reason why King William appeared on the walls over and over again. The *Northern Whig* made the point in an article entitled "What 'The Twelfth' means to Ulster":

> The Battle of the Boyne was fought nearly two and half centuries ago, and there are the soundest reasons why the victory of William the Third over James the Second should still be commemorated. For the observance of the anniversary is not a symptom of "excessive preoccupation with the past." It is equally concerned with the events of the present and the possibilities of the future. Vital issues are at stake, involving the rights and liberties of those whose unwavering Protestantism is allied with an unswerving loyalty to King and Constitution. (*Northern Whig* July 12 1938: 6)

In other words, the Twelfth celebrations, in which mural painting played a central role, were not part of an obsession with the past, but a crucial element in the consolidation of a social and political order in the present in which the Protestant and unionist community benefited legally, culturally, and politically at the expense of the Catholic and nationalist community. Not that this made a lot of economic difference to the loyalist working class, and it took a very long time for Henderson's warning cited earlier ("Painting Kings upon a gable/Brings but little bread and cheese"), to be heeded. In 1984 the UDA leader, Andy Tyrie, reflected that during sixty years of unionist rule in Northern Ireland, "the English were first-class citizens, the Ulster Protestants second-class and the Ulster Catholics third-class" (McDonald and Cusack 2004: 84). A more precise analysis eventually found its way on to a loyalist mural in 2014 in the words of one-time Belfast Mayor Hugh Smyth of the Progressive Unionist Party (PUP, allied to the Ulster Volunteer Force, UVF) (Figure 19):

> Historically, Unionist politicians fed their electorate the myth that they were first class citizens... and without question people believed them. Historically, Republican/Nationalist politicians fed their electorate the myth that they were second class citizens... and without question the people believed them. In reality, the truth of the matter was that we all, Protestant and Catholic, were third class citizens, and none of us realised it!

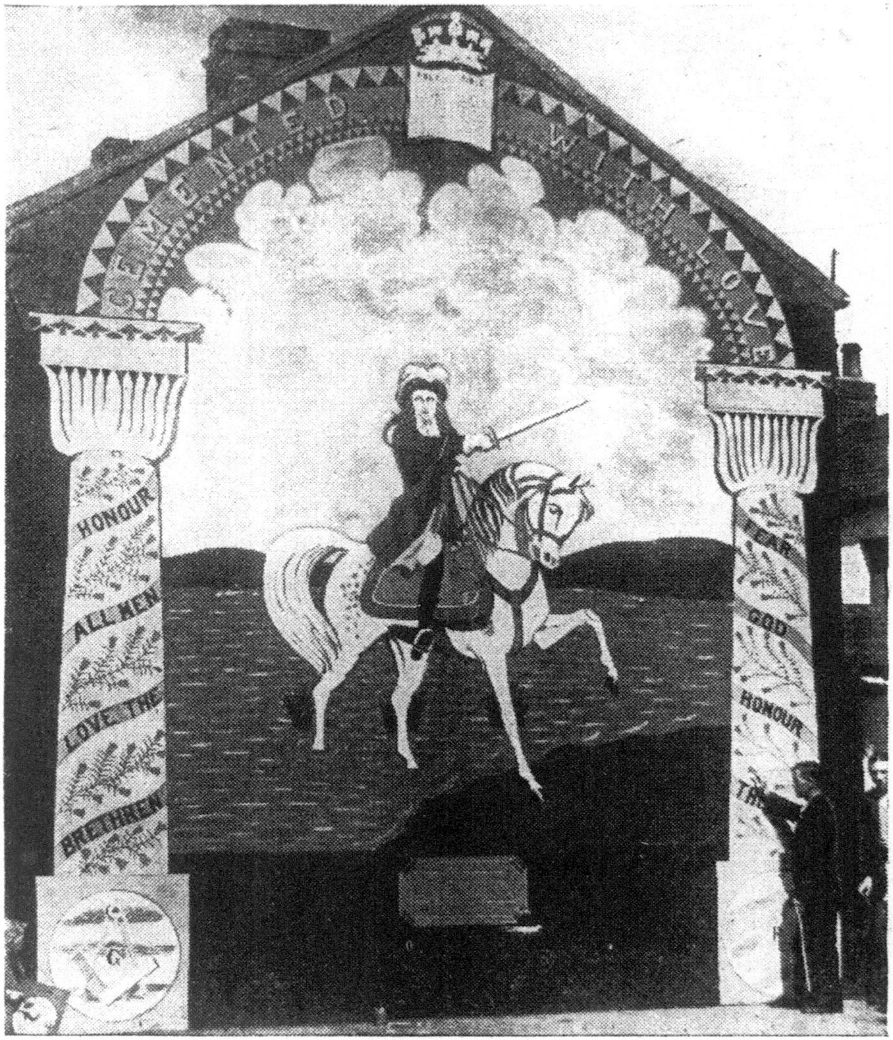

WALL PAINTING OF KING WILLIAM IN TIERNEY STREET, OFF DONEGALL ROAD, BELFAST, EXECUTED BY MR. HOWARD KELLY, WHO IS SEEN ON RIGHT PUTTING FINISHING TOUCHES. HE WAS ASSISTED BY MR, FRED CRONE.

FIGURE 17 Cemented with love, Tierney Street, off Donegall Road, South Belfast, 1936.

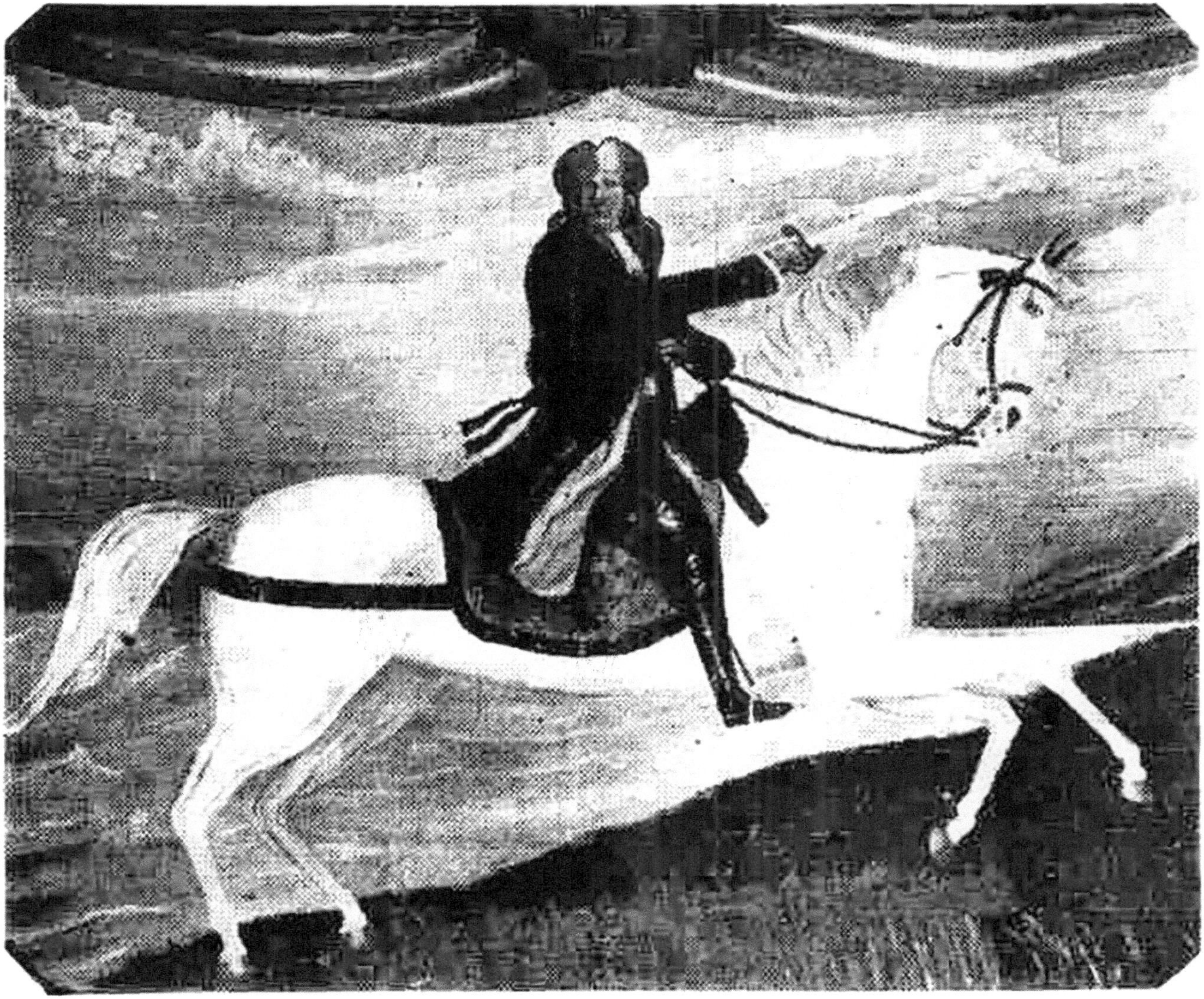

FIGURE 18 King William on a white charger, Templemore Street, East Belfast, 1937.

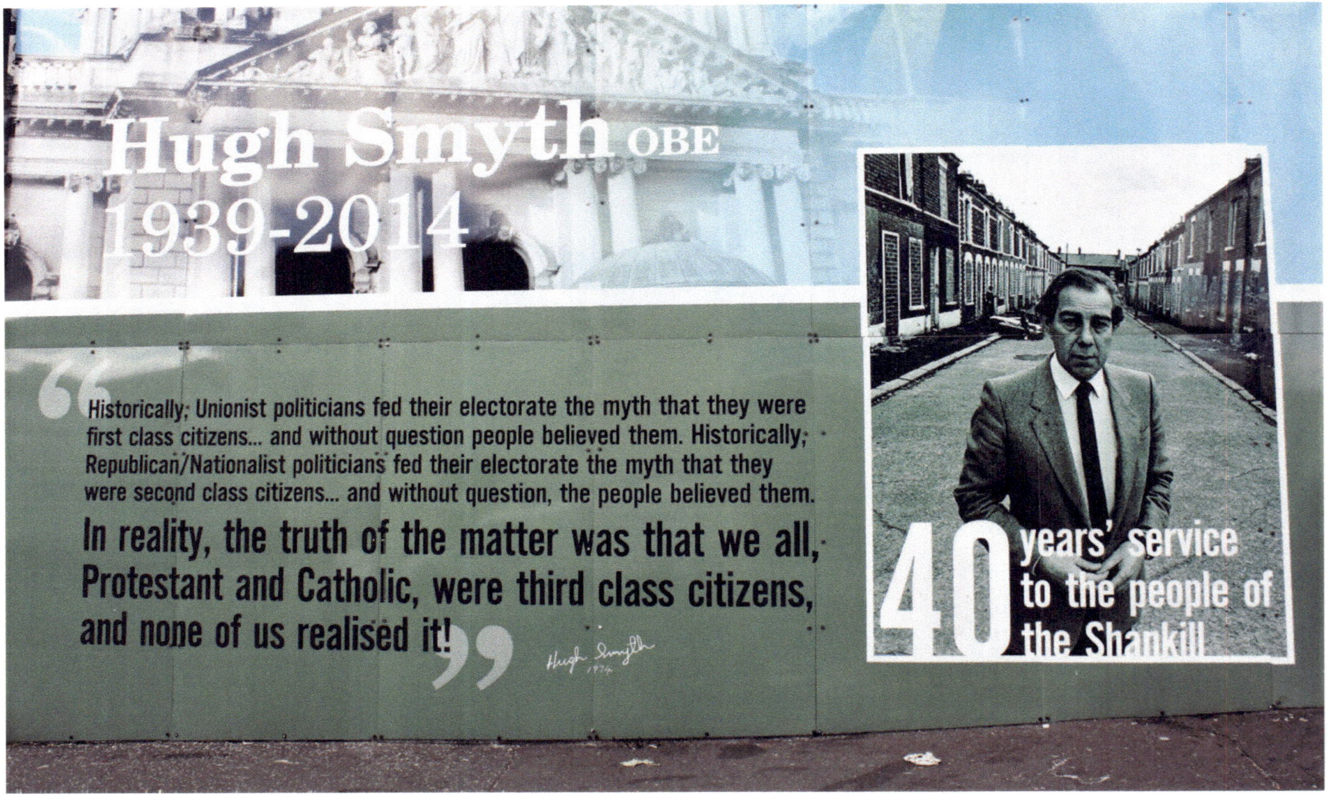

FIGURE 19 Hugh Smyth, Canmore Street, Shankill, 2014. Photo by Tony Crowley.

But marginal gains are marginal gains, and in the social and economic order of Northern Ireland, the Protestant and unionist community was structurally privileged. As the *Northern Whig* piece noted in its discussion of "what 'the Twelfth' means for Ulster" (by which it meant the majority in Northern Ireland), what was at stake in the cultural and political celebration of the Twelfth, were "the rights and liberties" of unwaveringly loyal Protestants. King Billy, staring loftily down from the many walls that he occupied, reminded them of that important lesson.

It is interesting to note that after the Second World War, loyalist muralism declined considerably. There is no consensus as to why this happened. Rolston, for example, suggests "increasing cost, lack of interest, selfishness, consumerism, and something as nebulous as 'the modern age'" (Rolston 1991: 27). But this raises as many questions as it answers (why was there a lack of interest?), and a more significant claim is that "the beginnings of unionist uncertainty were reflected in the decline of traditional cultural expression… a harbinger of impending explosive rifts in the unionist state" (27). This analysis may be slightly proleptic, however, since the splits within unionist hegemony did not really appear until the early-to-mid-1960s. An alternative explanation is that after the Second World War unionist rule was effectively consolidated and under little internal or external pressure (the only significant threat, the IRA's Border Campaign, began in 1956 but petered out and was called off in 1962). As a result, the unionist domination of public space was complete and, in reality, almost uncontested. This would fit with the claim made earlier that unionist muralism arose as part of a response to crisis. For in a period of relative stability (Elliott 2017), it would be more likely that muralism would not play quite as central a role as during periods of real or perceived danger. There was of course some maintenance of the tradition in this period. In Londonderry Bobby Jackson painted a new mural dedicated to Colonel Adam Murray, one of the heroes of the Siege of Derry, in Clarence Place in 1958, and the artist continued with the annual re-touching of the Williamite wall in the same location (Figure 20, see Fulcrum).[10] In Belfast, the Rockland Street mural was one of the few to be re-furbished around the Twelfth celebrations, while "a door-to-door whip around in the Conway Street area" paid for a new mural of William in Eighth Street at a cost of £4 (*Belfast Telegraph* July 8 1965: 3). Also in 1965, in the north of the city, "extra police were on duty… when the Reverend Ian K. Paisley spoke at an unveiling of a painting of King William on the gable end of a house in Earl Place" (*Belfast Telegraph* July 9 1965: 2) (Figure 21, see Fulcrum). The new murals were, however, exceptions. The 1958 article in *Ireland's Saturday Night*, mentioned earlier, relayed the request of an Ulster Museum curator for information that would allow him "to photograph the best of the gable-end paintings before this time-honoured form of craftmanship dies out." It mentioned that a competition to reward "the most attractive specimens might stimulate interest in these fading walls" (*Ireland's Saturday Night* July 5 1958: 4). A little later, in 1963, the *Belfast Newsletter* reported that "the practice of painting King William murals on gables at the corners of Belfast streets is slowly dying" (*Belfast Newsletter* July 9 1963: 7), a claim supported by articles in the *Sunday Press*—"the dying art of gable-painting" (*Sunday Press* January 26 1964: 6)—and the *Belfast Telegraph*—"one of the last examples of a dying art—the colourfully decorated 'gable-end'" (*Belfast Telegraph* August 7 1964: 6). The tradition, it was clearly perceived, was in decline.

5. CRITICAL RESPONSES

It is remarkable that despite the durability of this form of public art, from the early twentieth century to the eve of the Troubles, little attention has been paid to it within the field of cultural criticism. This is puzzling, not least since loyalist muralism took place within a wider practice of muralism in Northern Ireland. Thus in 1908, the very year that the first King William was purportedly painted in working-class East Belfast, the artist James Ward, head of the Dublin Metropolitan School of Art and already an established figure, delivered an important lecture on the topic of "Mural decoration and fresco painting" at the Belfast Municipal Technical Institute (McBrinn 1997: 39). Ward was born on the Shankill Road, the son of a house-painter (James Ward ARCA), but it is doubtful that King Billy was mentioned in his address. The tenor of the talk is more likely reflected in *Fresco Painting: Its Art and Technique*, published a year later, in which "the subject of mural painting" is related to "the laws and principles of good architecture" (Ward 1909: 1):

> The arrangement and composition of line, restfulness of the masses of form, and the harmonic balance and purity of colour are among the primary essentials of mural painting, and all these indispensable requisites of this form of art are due to its contact with architecture. While bearing this in mind, we must not forget that painting has its special functions apart from those of architecture, which include a controlling power over form and colour, and the faculty of illustrating ideas, by means of the representation of a theme or an incident, a subject or a story. (Ward 1909: 2).

The recently completed Belfast City Hall (1906) might have been a good canvas on which to illustrate Ward's theory and practical skills, but the city fathers had already engaged another local artist, Robert Ponsonby Staples, for the task. As it turned out, Staples's projected murals commemorating shipbuilding and linen-making were cancelled in 1913. But Ward, having played a role in the revival of mural art in Britain (he collaborated with Leighton on the *Peace* and *War* murals at the Victoria and Albert Museum), went on to decorate the rotunda of Dublin City Hall with a series of frescoes depicting the city's early history, together with the emblems of Ireland's four provinces.

In his 1908 lecture, Ward asserted that Belfast had little decorative art, but as McBrinn has argued, the claim was "unfounded and misleading" since the city had witnessed "a progressive use of mural decoration in its architecture": "the earliest known murals in Belfast date from the mid-nineteenth century and herald a century and a half of decorative art remarkable for its variety and range" (McBrinn 1997: 40).[11] Within the city center, for example, St Malachy's (1844), a monument to Tudor revivalism, carries three major murals by the Italian artist Piccione behind the Gothic altar. Also in the town center, St George's is decorated with a magnificent set of Pre-Raphaelite murals of New Testament scenes in 1883–1884. And Holy Cross, Ardoyne (1903), has a beautiful collection of murals depicting the Crucifixion, together with a choir of angels on the ceiling. Muralism was not, however, confined to churches (Catholic or Protestant) but was also seen in secular buildings. The Ulster Hall bore extensive mural decoration when it opened in 1862, and in 1902 Joseph Carey was commissioned to produce thirteen new murals for the hall illustrating Belfast history ("the Carey paintings"). The ceiling of the Belfast Opera House (1895) also included decorative painting, as did various business premises across the city. The tradition continued in the early twentieth century: Belfast-born John Lavery and Edwin Lutyens gave *The Madonna of the Lakes* to St Patrick's in 1919, while Anne Marjorie Robinson donated scenes from the life of St

Bridgit to her native city's Museum and Art Gallery (now the Ulster Museum) in 1926. In the 1930s, Staples donated *Shipbuilding*, one of the murals for the abortive City Hall project, to the gallery; the same establishment commissioned the local artist William Conor's *Ulster Past and Present* in 1932 (it was not one of his best works), and Gordon and Hunter's *The Bronze Age in Ulster* in 1934. The use of murals also extended beyond civic institutions; artists such as Sidney Smith and George McCann undertook commercial work for local businesses. Civic muralism was boosted, however, by State subvention in the guise of the Committee for the Encouragement of Music and the Arts (CEMA, later the Arts Council). Looking for a work to celebrate the Festival of Britain in 1951, CEMA, at the behest of the poet, critic, and curator, John Hewitt, commissioned John Luke to paint a mural in Belfast City Hall. Standing at the head of the main staircase, *The Founding of Belfast, 1613* features Sir James Chichester reading James the First's Royal Charter, with Cave Hill to the rear, and representations of linen-making and shipbuilding to either side.[12] In a less parochial mode, Transport House, constructed in 1959 in the International Style and influenced by Dublin's Busáras (built in 1953), carried a five-storey tiled mural representing industry and workers. The style of the mural (which still stands) mimicked Soviet Constructivism, a style widely used in London during the Festival of Britain.

McBrinn asserts that there were "logical but ambiguous connections between gable murals and civic work" and it is clear there were direct links too. Hewitt records that the artist Romeo Toogood painted a mural "on a house gable in Mervue Street, of King William crossing the Boyne about 1920" (Hewitt 1978: 4), and George Wilgaus "painted many of the murals in the Shankill area between the wars" (Loftus 1983: 11). In 1947, John Luke, having turned down a commission from the Jesuits in Dublin (they weren't offering enough), reflected that "it is a far cry from painting (when only a lad) a King Billy crossing the Boyne on a gable wall at the Protestant end of North Queen Street and Lewis Street" (Hewitt 1978: 66). It is, then, as noted above, both striking and curious that the early history of loyalist muralism has remained relatively unexplored in recent criticism (with the notable exceptions of the relatively brief treatments in Loftus 1983 and Rolston 1991). If it is mentioned, it is often dismissed, which is odd, given that it was a significant early mode of a practice that is now recognized the world over—the painting of walls for political purposes. The critical silence is all the more perplexing given that early loyalist muralism was evaluated appreciatively by a number of important artistic and critical figures. In 1924, for example, a piece appeared in the *Northern Whig*—"Belfast's Wall Paintings An Al-fresco Art Gallery"—signed by "J.W.C." (none other than Joseph William Carey, painter of the Ulster Hall murals). Holding the origins of art to be at least in part "the outflow of overcharged feelings" (art as expression), the writer sought to analyze the murals as a "pictorial phenomenon" on "many of Belfast's working-class streets": "al fresco mural decorations in oils, executed upon the unprepared surfaces of gable walls. In size they are but a few yards square, sometimes they occupy a whole end wall from corner to corner, ground to eaves. The subject is usually some or other of the traditional symbols of Ulster loyalism" (*Northern Whig* July 14 1924: 6). "Judged as mural paintings alone," he continued, "it cannot be claimed for these works that they attain any high standard of artistic merit. But as the spontaneous artistic effort of working-class people they are at least remarkable" (6). Reinforcing the point, he noted that although the painters are "hard-toiling members of an industrial community, prosaic, practical people" who "in general care little about as art," "yet for their own pleasure, and on their own initiative, they have been moved to this artistic enterprise" (6). What, then, he pondered, was the origin of the wall painting? His conclusion was that the painters of Orange Lodge banners "had established a tradition" by painting certain subjects in particular ways repeatedly, thus creating "a sort of traditional symbolism" in which a portrait of William III on a horse, for example, is not simply a representation of the king, but a "symbol of Ulster loyalism" (6). The problem with "those really gorgeous emblems" (the banners) was that they were displayed only on the Twelfth rather than permanently, "and so when political feeling became a thing so intense in the lives of the people that it had to be expressed, visualized in some objective form, the convention of the banner painters was there ready-made, waiting to be seized upon, to be transferred to the gable walls by the people themselves" (6). The art therefore "was for the unburdening of over-charged feelings... an example of political enthusiasm flowing over into pictorial expression" (6). And this, he claimed, "is the unique and novel thing":

> Of course custom has staled the interest of it for us. But I fancy the like of it is not to be seen elsewhere. Endless scribblings on blank walls you will find. But where else have whole gables been covered, turning the streets into a sort of al fresco art gallery? I do not, of course, wish to exaggerate the importance of the thing in any way. No new Giotto has emerged. But if such a one had emerged I think he might have found himself provided with tradition and subject as capable of artistic exploitation as any painter who would use those adventitious aids need desire. (6)

The piece ended with a defense of artistic failings in the gable paintings as the writer asked the reader to imagine being a workman with no artistic training (save that of your trade as a house-painter), standing in front of an area of several hundred square feet of rough brick, to be covered by a conventional composition, with materials no better than a few pots of paint. Imagine that, he demanded, and then "think what sort of attempt you should yourself make to draw a prancing horse life-size or any size—and you should be better able to appreciate the relative merit of what these amateurs have achieved" (6).

Another approbatory review was given a decade later by William Conor, one of Northern Ireland's most accomplished artists, perhaps best known for his portrayals of Belfast working-class life.[13] Writing in the *Belfast Telegraph* in 1933, Conor reported being "amazed at the amount of high artistic merit displayed on many of the mural decorations painted on various gables representing King William of Orange crossing the Boyne, the Siege of Derry and other important incidents of this historic period" (*Belfast Telegraph* July 10 1933: 7). Recalling the origins of muralism, Conor described the Belfast work as "a revival of that very ancient art of decorating wall spaces, remains of which are being found in Egypt, India and Mexico, painted four or five thousand years before Christ" (7), and cited artists ranging from Raphael and Leonardo da Vinci to Conor's English contemporaries Frank Brangwyn and Elbert Spencer. "Perhaps," he mused, it was "such humble beginnings as seen in Belfast that gave birth to these past masters in mural decoration" (7).

Praising the work of his working-class contemporaries, Conor, like Carey, drew attention to their conditions of work: "a certain rough wall surface of large dimensions has to be filled and the painter has to submit to the limitations set down by his cheap and rough and ready materials" (7). Such difficulties, he recognized, effect variable quality in the product: "I am fully aware that many of these paintings possess all the inevitable crudities of the amateur, and are gaudy in colour, smudged, and, on the whole, messy" (7). Nevertheless, he maintained, there are some,

> that unquestionably show a certain affinity with primitive art, and those who produced them appear to have had in common with the primitives, who were men simply driven by the strong necessity of expressing what they feel, and having something to say, their one and only object is to say it, and that as completely and as deliberately as possible, leaving no doubt on the mind of the spectator as to the precise meaning of their expression. (7)

Echoing Carey's account of art as the expression of feeling, Conor articulated his own views as to the originality of the muralists:

> these wall decorations have been produced by men whose expression has not been impeded by a diligently studied technique of past generations, nor has there been a cramping over difficult technicalities or art theories. They have set down or omitted nothing, because of rule or precept, seem to know instinctively that the starting point lies beyond them in art, and therein is found their chief appeal—their work is three parts instinctive. (7)

Notwithstanding John Hewitt's evaluation of Conor as "worthy of respect" as Ulster's "most representative" painter (Hewitt 1951: 88), the terms of Conor's positive critical judgment of the muralists echo ironically those that Hewitt used negatively in relation to Conor's own work (not least its "lack of intellectual rigour" and aesthetic naivety Hewitt 1981: 112–114). Nonetheless, Conor defended the early unionist murals against what he termed "high-brow" criticism:

> I know many people will say that these decorations are faulty in drawing, because of a certain distortion and attenuation found in many of them, but this only serves to give greater emphasis and strength to line and color. Wrongly some people who dominate the intellectual life in Belfast frown on these paintings, but a great deal of this narrow-mindedness or

> indifference might be brushed aside if more sympathetic curiosity were aroused as to what these unknown and obscure painters are trying to do in our midst, and the manner in which they have given themselves up with enthusiasm to the embellishment of our city streets. (7)

Taken together, the judgments made by Carey and Conor constitute a striking defense of the unionist working-class artists and their work. Even Hewitt himself, later to become one of Northern Ireland's most important poets and critics, was hardly unsympathetic to the murals: "the only expression of Folk Art [in Ulster], a diminishing one and less and less likely to be encountered by the visitor, has been the ceremonial mural painting practised in the Protestant working-class districts of Belfast and our country towns" (Hewitt 1951: 93). These images, Hewitt noted, "highly conventionalized representations," "usually executed on the gables of houses in house painters' pigments," are "normally restored or newly painted each summer before the general holiday, 'the Twelfth of July'." His judgment of the work was precise:

> The limits within which the anonymous artists worked were rigorously defined by tradition; but often a bold sense of pattern carried out with a naïve sincerity may still be discovered at street-end or alley; roundels and insets frequently achieve a surprising quality which wavers between medieval and Douanier-like conceptions. (94)

Overall, however, Hewitt's perception of a decline in the number of murals and arches, together with replacement of hand-painted banners by "commercial work," led to a negative conclusion: "in the vestiges of these at one time vigorous and strongly indigenous forms of Folk Art there now seems no possibility of finding any basis for the re-creation or development of an Ulster decorative tradition" (94).

The dominant trends in the art-criticism of the period undoubtedly influenced the evaluation of the murals by these three artists/critics. And evidently there is an approbatory tone to terms such as "spontaneous," "instinctive," and "naïve sincerity" ("Douanier-like" is a reference to the work of Henri Rousseau). Yet there is something curiously amiss in this evaluation of the murals. For the account of the muralists as "driven by the strong necessity of expressing what they feel, and having something to say," and the works themselves as the products of "the unburdening of over-charged feelings" and "political enthusiasm flowing over," is elliptical to say the least. Even Hewitt's use of the term "Folk Art" is odd, at least in its opposition to "commercial work," since the dominant figure in the murals was King William, whose image, as Loftus has shown was "handed down" (the etymological meaning of "tradition") over more than a century in commercial form (Loftus 1990). Indeed, it might be said of the accounts of all three critics that they exhibit what Seamus Deane once described as the "peculiar peacefulness" of Conor's paintings (Deane 1983: 46). What is missing from their critical judgment, however, is any specific analysis of the social function of the murals, their political form and content, their historical role, and their stance towards both sides of a public deeply divided by structural sectarianism. In other words, there is no recognition of the significance of the work of the working-class artists in the construction of unionist cultural and political hegemony in Northern Ireland.

6. CONCLUSION

The hegemony of loyalist muralism was not of course uncontested. At times of crisis, murals became the focus of social discontent. In Ballymena in 1933, for example, a painting of King William was vandalized (daubed with "Up Dublin") a day after its unveiling (*Northern Whig* September 19 1933: 7).[14] More ominously, in a challenge to the unionist domination of social space, the monarch's portrait painted on Beverly Street in the Lower Shankill had to be re-done after it was vandalized in 1967 by four boys from the Falls Road: "this morning King Billy looked as fresh as he did when he was first painted six years ago—apart from a few streaks of blue and yellow—but the people of Beverly Street are angry" (*Belfast Telegraph* August 10 1967: 4). It was a symbolic indicator of the emergence of a conflict which was by then in its earliest stages, but which was to engulf Northern Ireland shortly thereafter. The relatively untroubled dominance of unionist muralism was over. Indeed the decline that was first recorded in the late 1950s and 1960s continued. In 1970, one commentator noted that "recent years have witnessed a decline in wall paintings and the competitive spirit in arch design between neighbouring loyalist streets" (Johnston 1970: 206). Even as late as 1983, a community worker on the Shankill Road was moved to proclaim that "the significance of gable wall art in loyalist areas is that it is a dying art, it virtually no longer exists" (Redpath 1983: 20). As will become clear, however, reports of its death were greatly exaggerated.

CHAPTER 2
Counter-Hegemony: The Emergence and Consolidation of Republican Muralism 1981–1993

To access all images referenced in this chapter, please visit the open access version on Fulcrum at https://doi.org/10.3998/mpub.14527058.

> We must create our own mass media. (Bobby Sands, cited in O'Hearn 2006: 237)

1. A VARIETY OF MURALS

John Luke's Belfast City Hall mural, *The Founding of Belfast, 1613* (1951), marked a turning point in civic muralism and "by the late 1960s and 70s decorative commissions declined in Belfast" (McBrinn 1997: 43). McBrinn identifies the cause of this falling off as a shift in sensibility: "images and allegories of the city's past in public places were felt to be anachronistic and obsolete and much decorative art was forgotten, neglected and in certain cases lost" (43). Despite McBrinn's rather coy account of the decline of State-sponsored muralism (Belfast's happy and glorious past was indeed "anachronistic and obsolete" in the war-torn city of the 1970s—but it had rarely been anything else for one section of the population), his summation is nonetheless noteworthy:

> Decorative painting is an important and integral element in our local history, illuminating so many fascinating links between Belfast and other cities in Ireland, Britain and Europe. With so many prominent figures from the local art scene producing major monuments of decorative art, any understanding of our artistic past is surely incomplete without a consideration of them. (43)

Whether it be in the realm of high culture and the accomplished work of established artists, or in the field of popular culture and the productions of working-class housepainters, one thing is clear: muralism was an established feature of Belfast public life.

An exemplification of the perceived power and legitimacy of muralism was evinced in the late 1970s. For if the State had withdrawn from the sponsorship of civic murals by the late 1960s, it was back in the field a decade later. As Rolston has shown, the Northern Office funded a Community Murals scheme in Belfast (by way of Belfast City Council's Community Services Department) between 1977 and1981. Using students from Belfast College of Art and Design, the daunting brief was to consult with local community groups, to liaise with an oversight committee (representing the Community Services department, the Northern Ireland Office's Department of the Environment, the Arts Council, and the College of Art and Design), and "not to paint anything political" (Rolston 1991: 57). Given the fact that Northern Ireland was being torn apart by violent political strife, the order to render only apolitical topics was self-evidently a political choice. What this meant in practice for the production of murals was a predictable if variable practice both in terms of content and reception (Watson 1983; Rolston 1991: 50–68). Topics included jungle scenes (a common trope), rural life (a contrast with the urban landscape), local history and local people (some of whom were identifiable), sports (football, boxing, skateboarding), workers (usually in the shipyards), and fairy tales. The murals were placed across the city but specifically in: Ardoyne, Ballysillan, the Bone, Dee Street, Divis Flats, Highfield, Lord Street, North Queen Street, Shankill, Short Strand, Springhill, St James, Unity Flats, The Village, Whiterock, and Woodvale. Which is to say that they were found in working-class areas that had been ravaged by the war and endemic poverty; none were located in affluent areas.

Remaining apolitical was a complex issue. Representing football and boxing may have been relatively unproblematic, in that they featured centrally in the cultural life of both nationalist/republican and loyalist working-class communities (skateboarding was similarly uncomplicated, though for the opposite reason), but there were no images of hurlers, Gaelic footballers, or indeed rugby players.[1] Murals of workers (almost always male) also resonated across the communities, though they were controversial in areas of high unemployment. For example, Rolston notes the amendment of a mural in loyalist Ainsworth Street featuring welders at Harland and Wolff shipyard: local people carefully painted out the welders as a protest against the loss of "traditional" jobs (Rolston 1991: 61–62). And in nationalist/republican areas, where mass unemployment was simply a fact of life, representations of workers were notably nostalgic, as in an accomplished mural in Divis Flats that featured children and old men (Figure 1, see Fulcrum). More striking perhaps is the effect of the "apolitical" stipulation in terms of what the murals did not depict; there was no conflict, no violence, and no sectarianism. In this respect at least, although they were called "community murals," it is accurate to say that they were in communities but not of them.

The local reception of the murals varied considerably. Watson notes that a triptych in the loyalist Woodvale area, "forming a sort of three ages of man" (consisting of images of children, the welders mentioned above, and older women), "went some way towards fulfilling the apparent desires of the community to have their history and their traditions represented." Accordingly, "the artists all commented on the great hospitality, generosity and cooperation that was given to them" (Watson 1983: 8). Rolston, too, notes that "although they had no opportunity to be involved in the artistic process, except perhaps in discussing the theme, helping with the painting in minor ways, and generally supporting the artists, local people genuinely identified closely with murals that depicted local people, activities and scenes" (Rolston 1991: 61). Yet, despite the successes, there were intrinsic problems, which is hardly surprising given that the muralists were Art College students tasked with liaising with strife-torn communities to which they often did not belong, with a difficult brief, and variable skills with which to execute it. One of the clearest attacks on the mural scheme came from the community priest (and resident of Springhill), Des Wilson, in relation to a jungle mural on republican Springhill Avenue more than 100 yards long. Wilson noted that "the public authorities, impressed by the need to brighten up the city, encouraged and employed artists to paint murals here and there" (Wilson 1983: 19). Such works, he contended, were simply condescending, and invited the viewer "to look on the broken citizens as victims we can do nothing about except escape with them into a world of fantasy which someone has created for us" (20). Wilson's judgment was fierce, but it wasn't quite as harsh as that delivered by a teenage resident of Unity Flats, an impoverished, besieged, nationalist/republican enclave at the bottom of the Shankill. Commenting on a dragon mural on Unity Walk, she addressed the muralists directly: "Is this supposed to brighten the place up? Who are you trying to kid—sure we live in shit" (Watson 1983: 10). Given the depth of the social, political, and economic privation imposed on working-class communities in Northern Ireland in the 1970s and 1980s, this fair comment prompts the obvious question: what were these murals supposed to achieve? The answer is unclear, perhaps known only to those who devised the project. But the community mural scheme does make evident two things. First, murals were an available genre in Northern Ireland. And second, murals were seen as a response to particular types of problem—social, political, communicative.

This point is important when it comes to considering the appearance of a large number of republican murals in 1981. One of the community murals scheme participants, Raymond McCullough, argued for a direct link between their work and that of republican muralists:

> Graffiti was the message on the wall before the (state-sponsored) murals came along. You had the written word on the walls. Then when the (political) murals came along came the visual image. I don't think it's just a coincidence. I think the fact that we were producing the (state-sponsored) murals before that, people could see the impact; they turned from the written word to the visual image (Rolston 1991: 68).

One objection to McCullough's claim is that it decouples the community murals from the long tradition of muralism in Northern Ireland. Rolston, however, noting that "it seems far-fetched to see a close link between both sets of murals" (68), objects to the claim on several other grounds. First, he asserts, "there is little evidence of a link at the personnel level between the council murals and the later political murals" (68). Second, he contends that when the "political mural explosion" arrived, it was not confined to Belfast but appeared in "many areas that had not seen state-sponsored murals" such as Derry, Armagh, Newry, and Lurgan (68). And third, he asserts that the community murals scheme was "spread across the sectarian divide," yet the political murals of 1981–1982 were "confined to nationalist working-class-areas" (68). All of these points are correct (although the Department of the Environment sponsored two murals in Derry—including one in the courtyard of Rossville Flats that featured circus figures and animals) (Figure 2, see Fulcrum). Yet it is not quite clear what relevance these points have with regard to McCullough's claim—which is essentially that the impact of the community murals influenced the shift from the verbal to the visual in republican murals.

Given the available evidence, it seems implausible to suggest that there is a direct link between the community murals scheme and the republican murals of 1981. On the other hand, it seems unlikely that there was no link at all. As will be clear from the history given in this and the previous chapter, "the visual image," in various forms, had gained a prominent place on all sorts of walls in Northern Ireland in the twentieth century. And nationalists and republicans could hardly have been unaware of muralism as a practice. If they were churchgoers (as the overwhelming majority were), they would have seen murals in specific churches during the regular institutional rituals of mass, confession, benediction, baptisms, weddings (and through the Church they might have had access to the medieval Catholic cultural tradition in which murals had an important place). In their everyday lives they may have seen civic murals in public buildings, or King William murals on loyalist walls (such images were hardly hidden away, not least because working-class areas were much less segregated than was later to become the case). And in the late 1970s, they may have been exposed to the community murals. They would then surely have been aware of the mural tradition, even if they played little role in forging it.

2. THE QUESTION OF REPUBLICAN MURALS PRE-1981

There were exceptions to the claim that there was no nationalist or republican tradition of muralism. For example, in Abbey Street, Derry, in 1920, a large mural on Watt's distillery featured a Tricolor, with a harp, a Star-Spangled banner, "IRA" and "Ireland over all" to the top (Cooper 2015: 35). As recorded by Liam Brady, the Officer Commanding of Fianna Eireann in Derry, the mural infuriated the Dorsets, a British Army regiment stationed in the city: "the Dorset Patrol became very annoyed. They went to a nearby yard and procured a ladder and a pot of tar and proceeded to disfigure the two flags." In response, local republicans re-painted the image and added a poem on the incident.

> This is the flag the Dorsets hate it drives them all insane
> But every time they wiped it out it blossomed forth again

The English failed to tame us with their guns and armoured car
So of course they sent the Dorsets with their little tin of tar

But let the Dorsets understand it sure would give us pain
To waste an Irish bullet, on such dirty English swine
Our flag shall wave forever in spite of threat or scar
For we defy the Dorsets and their little tin of tar
Another little verse we add to this rhyme of ours
To let you know the Dorsets work here each night for hours
They gained another victory without scratch or scar
For they wiped out this rhyme of ours with their little tin of tar

Our flag shall wave above us as in the days of old
Not a stain upon its green nor a blot upon its gold
It will blaze over men of Derry and the lightnings of war
When the Dorsets run before us with their little tin of tar
(Brady 1922: 64–65).

The poem was accompanied by two slogans: "Bun eaters lie down" and "Easter 1916 Derry 1920."[2]

This mural was painted pre-Partition in 1920, and the dispute in which it played a role was thus a sign of contested space. After Partition, however, such public displays of nationalist (not to mention republican) sentiment were few and far between in Northern Ireland. This is not to say that confessional affiliation was not occasionally exhibited. During the 1932 Eucharistic Congress, for example, side streets off the Falls were festooned with banners, and the visit of Cardinal D'Alton to Derry in 1955 provoked "a display of flags and bunting, banerettes and scrolls that formed an unbroken canopy… over the whole public highway in every Catholic area of the city" (*Derry Journal* July 4 1955: 4). But political protestation in mural form before the Troubles appears to have been limited to a few instances, such as a commemoration of the 150th anniversary of the execution of Robert Emmet in 1953 in Crumlin Street, North Belfast (Rolston 1991: 73).[3] The 50th anniversary of 1916 was also marked in Ardoyne, though as local resident Davy Wasson confirms, such displays were rare:

> The streets of Ardoyne were decorated with tricolours and the kerbstones were painted. All kinds of bunting and banners were put up to celebrate the Rising. I was amazed at this because I had always associated this type of celebration with the Orange marches, when the Loyalists had their flags and banners up. (McKee 2020: 127)

Once the Troubles had begun, graffiti was at first the dominant mode of protest on the walls in nationalist and republican areas, though there were a number of rudimentary murals. One example, in Fairfield Street, Ardoyne, in the early 1970s, featured a Tricolor, a Starry Plough, and an image of James Connolly (Rolston 1991: 73).[4] Another, in Lenadoon Avenue, Andersonstown, in the late 1970s, included a Tricolor and the slogan "Free Andersonstown" (Figure 3, see Fulcrum). Interestingly, there appear to have been more republican murals in Derry than Belfast in the 1970s, though the most famous—"You are now entering Free Derry"—on what was to become the Free Derry Wall, dates from 1969. Thus the imperative "Resist British Bully Boys!," with accompanying crude representation of a larger-than-life British soldier, appeared in Stanley's Walk in 1971 (Melaugh 2018: 169). In the same location, "Support the Provisionals" (the Provisional IRA) and a large Tricolor appeared around the same time, and a similar slogan—"Provisionals for freedom"—accompanied a Tricolor and "Easter 1916–72" in The Wells. And at Easter 1975 the Lecky flyover carried a Tricolor and superimposed rifle, an Easter lily interspersed between "7" and "5," and "IRA."[5] The victims of Bloody Sunday were remembered in a mural on the bottom of Rossville Flats in 1976 (Figure 4), and in the late 1970s Westland Street bore an image of an IRA volunteer, a Tricolor, "Easter 1916," and an invitation to join the republican movement youth wing—"Na Fianna Eireann"—set against the organization's Sunburst flag (Figure 5, see Fulcrum).

There were, then, at least some republican murals in both Belfast and Derry during the 1970s. But they were limited in number and the "explosion" of republican murals took place only in and after 1981. Which prompts the obvious question: "why did they appear then?" This a complex issue, but in order to address it adequately, it is helpful to pose another question: "why didn't republican murals appear in large numbers before 1981?" After all, as has been shown above, muralism in various modes (loyalist, civic, state-sponsored, and, occasionally, nationalist/republican) was well established as a public art-form in Northern Ireland. So why was muralism not deployed by republicans to any great extent before 1981?

One factor, as Rolston points out, was that after Partition, public space belonged to the unionist/loyalist tradition.

> Nationalists traditionally did not paint murals. This fact alone is indicative of their relationship to the unionist state. Confined to lower status, greater poverty and higher unemployment, their culture became as ghettoised as they were. A vibrant culture existed, especially in relation to Gaelic sports, and Irish dancing, language and music, but it took place in the private space of church halls and sports grounds owned by the Gaelic Athletic Association. It was much more contained than the expansionist unionist culture of the Twelfth of July. (Rolston 1992: iii)

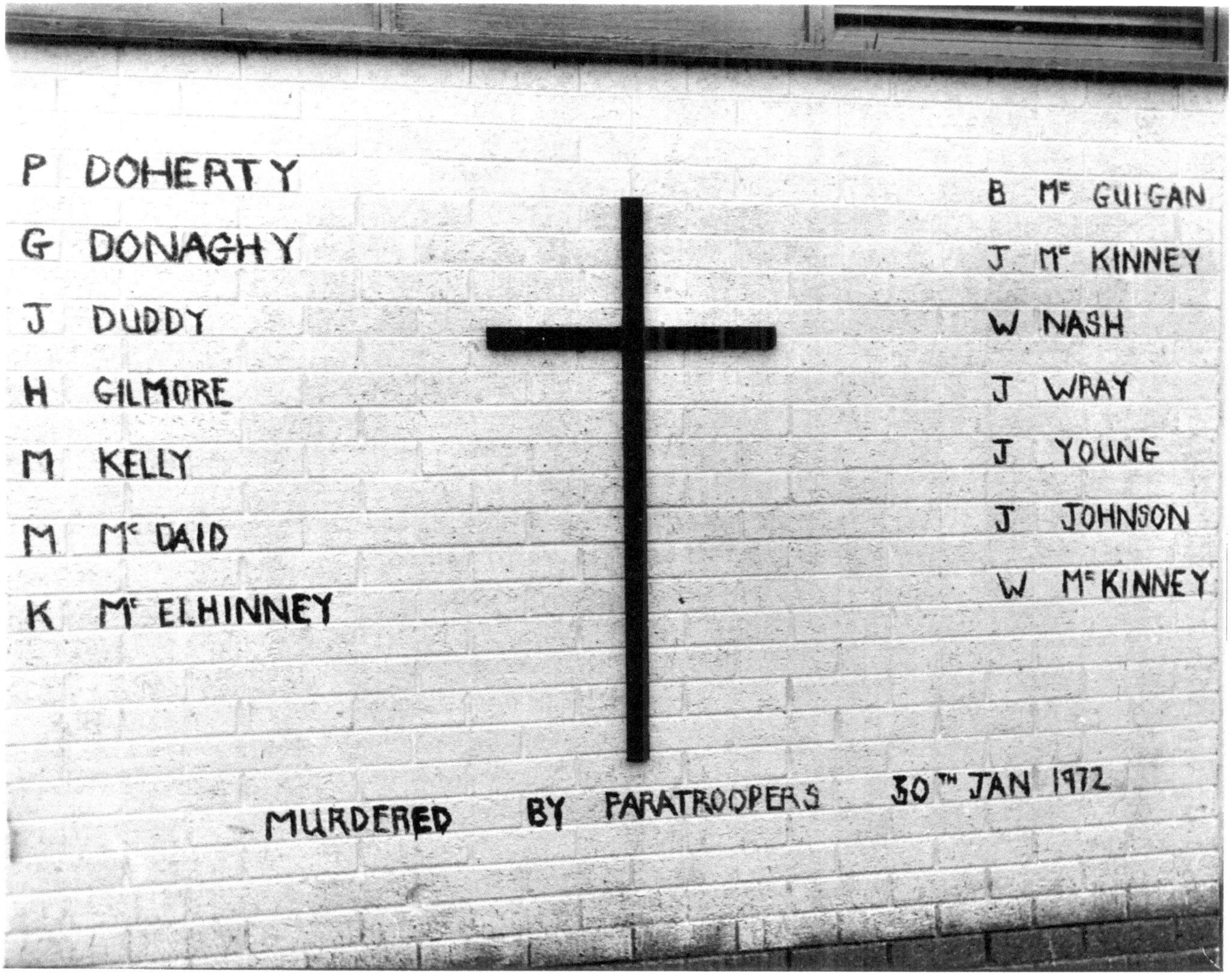

FIGURE 4 Bloody Sunday, Rossville Flats, Derry, 1978. Photo by Tony Crowley.

This geo-cultural hegemony was enforced by law, not least in the Flags and Emblems (Display) Act (Northern Ireland), enacted in 1954. The Act consisted of two main clauses governing the right to the "display of [the] Union flag" and the "removal of provocative emblems":

1. Any person who prevents or threatens to interfere by force with the display of a Union flag (usually known as the Union Jack) by another person on or in any lands or premises lawfully occupied by that other person shall be guilty of an offence against this Act.
2. Where any police officer, having regard to the time or place at which and the circumstances in which any emblem is being displayed, apprehends that the display of such emblem may occasion a breach of the peace, he may require the person displaying or responsible for the display of such emblem to discontinue such display or cause it to be discontinued; and any person who refuses or fails to comply with such a requirement shall be guilty of an offence against this Act. (HMSO 1954: 2)

The provocations in question were nationalist emblems and flags (particularly the Tricolor), and the Act, with its stipulation of a fine up to £500 and imprisonment for a maximum of five years, did not lay dormant on the statute book. In 1964, for example, a Tricolor in the window of the Sinn Féin offices on Divis Street during the General Election campaign led to a police raid to seize the flag, and days of serious rioting; it was a harbinger of the conflict that began in earnest in 1969 (Boyd 1969: ch.11). And during the Troubles, other instances indicated the dangers of infringing the unionist dominance of public space. In 1970 two men were imprisoned for six months for painting a Tricolor and a slogan (from Padraig Pearse's oration at the burial of the Fenian O'Donovan Rossa in 1915)—"Ireland unfree shall never be at peace"—in Annadale Street, Belfast (Jarman 1997: 232). And in 1980, sixteen-year-old Michael McCartan, from the Lower Ormeau area in Belfast, was shot dead by RUC Officer McKeown while painting "Provos" on a wall; the policeman testified that he believed the boy was holding a gun and was acquitted. Murals commemorated McCartan's death in Oakman Street, Beechmount, and the Ormeau Road, South Belfast (Rolston 1991: 102–103). Later again, a leading republican muralist recalled being abused and threatened by British soldiers in the late 1980s (Saleeby-Mulligan 2009: 176–177).

Painting on walls, then, could be dangerous. But this hardly answers the question as to why murals did not appear extensively in working-class nationalist/republican areas before 1981. After all, from the onset of the violence in 1969, these areas were covered in graffiti that abused, mocked, and rejected unionism, loyalism, and the British State (and its uniformed representatives), in no uncertain terms. And as noted above, there were a few murals in nationalist/republican areas (particularly in Derry). In fact, the answer to the question as to why there were so few murals in working-class nationalist/republican areas before 1981, is also the answer to the question as to why there were so many during and after 1981. Which is to say, that before 1981, the republican movement was not ostensibly engaged in a political struggle to attract the support of the republican base, nationalists more generally, and indeed the allegiance of international bodies of various kinds (ranging from Irish America to radical organizations across the world). During and after 1981, however, Irish republicanism was engaged in such a struggle, and the murals played an important role in it. The turning point was the 1981 Hunger Strike (launched after the confused ending of a first Hunger Strike in 1980), during which republicans were able to mobilize mass support domestically and internationally. Though the Hunger Strike itself ended with ten dead republican prisoners, its success lay in the revelation that under the right circumstances, republicanism could command significant support, not least in the realm of electoral politics. It was an important lesson and one that was not lost in republicanism's long and complex internal argument concerning the merits of militarism and/or engagement in democratic politics (Moloney 2007).

3. THE HUNGER STRIKE IMPERATIVE

The origins of the 1981 murals lie directly in the campaign for political status that began in 1976 with Ciarán Nugent's refusal to wear a prison uniform, thus signaling the republican rejection of the British government's new policy of "criminalization" (from Internment to 1976 paramilitary prisoners had been given "Special Status" and were in effect treated as political prisoners). Progressing from the Blanket Protest (in which the prisoners wore only blankets) to the no wash protest (in which they refused to slop out their cells), the bitter struggle of republican prisoners within the H-Blocks became a dispute over legitimacy per se—rather than the relatively limited "five demands"—and was a central focus of republican campaigning in the late 1970s.[6] As Bobby Sands realized, however, by 1979 the prison protest was increasingly ineffective. Sands, the Blanketmen's public relations officer, was a talented writer, thinker, and political strategist and he articulated his critique and plan in a secret communication ("comm") smuggled out to the external republican leadership. He observed primarily that "we have failed to reach a broader base of support" and "therefore we have failed to engage any active support outside of our immediate hard-core" (O'Malley 1990: 54). Such a strategy, Sands argued, could not achieve the prisoners' aims, and therefore it was necessary to "broaden the battle-field—nationally and internationally." Two things needed to be done: "one, we must make more people aware and engage their help. Two, to get these other people, we must organise our own people effectively and massively on the ground" (54). This required new tactics, including the preparation of "an army of propagandists" geared towards "a massive co-ordinated attack" by means of "a massive Paint and Poster Campaign" with the goal of conveying a simple message: "Smash H-Block." The aim would be to have an H-Block poster in "every window in a nationalist area" and a painting campaign to "cover the countryside" with the slogan in such a way as "to make it impossible for people to forget it" (54). In short, Sands proposed to the republican leadership outside the prison that "we must create our own mass media" (O'Hearn 2006: 237). Not long after the comm had been received, the National H-Block Committee was formed in October 1979.

Sands's proposal was put into practice: from 1979 nationalist and republican areas were covered in graffiti with consistent themes—"Smash H-Block," "Don't let the Blanket Men die," "Victory to the POWs" (Figure 6, see Fulcrum), and then, as the Hunger Strikes developed, there were a variety of other messages, ranging from the simple "Don't let them die," to the presentation of the "five demands" (Figure 7, see Fulcrum), or the transcription of Patrick Galvin's poem "Letter to a British Soldier on British Soil" (see **Introduction, fig. 3**). When the first murals relating to the Hunger Strikes began to appear, they were initially little more than enhanced forms of graffiti (with, for example, barbed wire or a coffin added) (Figure 8, see Fulcrum), in the style of some of the Derry murals from the mid-to-late 1970s. Rolston describes these as "quasi-murals" (Rolston 1991: 76), but more sophisticated murals appeared soon after: some involved complex designs, some were crudely figurative, and some were innovative (in an unknowing nod to one of the influences on the origin of muralism in Northern Ireland, republicans commandeered commercial advertising space) (Figure 9, see Fulcrum). In relation to the development of the form, Rolston asserts that there was "a logical step from the ornate graffiti to the first murals," but it is not clear why this should be the case. It was certainly a political step, in that the murals appeared as part of a large-scale republican attempt to forge a counter-hegemony to the dominant social and cultural order. But how and why did "ornate graffiti" evolve to become complex murals?

Again the answer is complicated. As noted above, muralism was an available tradition in Northern Ireland. Dominated by working-class loyalism as the genre was, there were other forms—civic and religious—that offered examples of graphic and effective story-telling (and indeed political story-telling) in Belfast and beyond. And the use of murals as a form of radical political protest had become an established practice elsewhere in the world—from Mexico in the 1920s to New York and Los Angeles in the 1970s (Folgarait 1998; Braun-Reinitz and Weissman 2009). So there was a general availability of the form. But in order to exploit its cultural possibilities, republicans had to take it up on the grand scale envisaged by Bobby Sands. Of course, they did have the few examples from Belfast and Derry to inspire them. And crucially, muralism was part of the general cultural revival that took place among republican prisoners from the early 1970s, as they engaged in, and often proved adept at, various types of artwork in the prison: wood-carving, leather-work, handkerchief embroidery and design, and painting (Loftus 1982 vol. 3: 517–24; Rolston 2014).[7] Within the prison, Cage 11 had an important role in that it housed a number of important republican thinkers (Bobby Sands and Gerry Adams among them). It also held an untrained artist, Danny Devenny (later to become the most important republican muralist), who practiced on the walls, as Jake MacSiacais recalled:

> As soon as you walked into our recreation hut there were murals, it was just an ordinary portacabin with a lot of desks and chairs and a blackboard, and on the left-hand side of the blackboard was a massive proclamation, the Proclamation of the Irish Republic with the heads of the signatories drawn around it, and on the opposite side was a big portrait, the red face, black beret, and star of Che Guevara. So you had Che Guevara and 1916. (O'Malley 1990: 45)[8]

Nevertheless, the appearance of murals during the Hunger Strikes can only be explained as a political choice made possible by a combination of factors: an available artistic convention (muralism); limited but exemplary practice (by republican graffiti-writers and muralists, both earlier in the history of Northern Ireland and within the prison); artists and artistic laborers (some of whom were ex-prisoners, but most of whom were young people with little or no experience of "art"); and perhaps most important of all, political desperation (the need to communicate the political realities of the H-Blocks and the Hunger Strike). No one individual decided to initiate republican muralism outside the prison; it arose as a collective response by small groups of local people to a particularly pressing set of circumstances at a specific political conjuncture. And in this sense, at least, the nascent republican tradition was akin to its loyalist predecessor (in that loyalist muralism began as a response to the Home Rule Crisis). For as loyalist practice since 1908 had demonstrated, walls offered an important place on which a striking, visible, and clear political intervention could be made in the public sphere. This was particularly significant given the informal and formal censorship of republican views that existed across the social field. But once started, the practice of republican muralism caught on rapidly; Rolston has calculated that more than 150 murals were painted in Belfast and Derry alone in the first few months after the death of Bobby Sands (the first Hunger Striker to die) in May 1981 (Rolston 1991: 79).

The first murals proper were, unsurprisingly, painted in republican heartlands in West Belfast—Andersonstown, Ballymurphy, the "Rock" streets in St James's, and Beechmount—and the Bogside in Derry. Yet their form indicates that the muralists had understood Sands's message about the need to "broaden the battle-field—nationally and internationally" in order "to reach a broader base of support." Thus the Hunger Strikers are depicted repeatedly in combinations of word and image drawn from Catholic iconography and designed to appeal to the wider nationalist constituency and to Irish America. In an image in Westland Street, Derry, for example, the link between the Hunger Strikers and the crucified Christ was made explicit (Figure 10, see Fulcrum), and in Beechmount, West Belfast, Ireland itself was depicted carrying a Cross "made in Britain" (Figure 11, see Fulcrum) and crucified on a Union Jack (Figure 12, see Fulcrum). In the same area, a Blanketman was featured with the Catholic image of the Sacred Heart of Jesus (Figure 13, see Fulcrum), and nearby, a Hunger Striker was depicted saying the Rosary overlooked by the Virgin Mary and framed by the often-repeated slogan "Blessed are those who hunger for justice" (Figure 14, see Fulcrum). The aesthetic quality of the early murals was variable. In Rockmore Road, a mural evoked the Christian and republican trope of triumph through sacrifice with a central figure posed ambiguously as either a Blanketman (on his knees but arms aloft in victory), or Christ (about to be scourged), set against an "H" in the form of a barb of prison wire (Figure 15). Superimposed on the image was the injunction "Break Thatcher's back" with the metonymic appeal for "Status now," while to the sides, coils of barbed wire sat atop Tricolors. To the bottom, in an implicit invocation of republican tradition (the Easter Rising (1916), the formation of the Irish Citizen Army (1913), and the United Irishmen (1798)), republican flags, the Tricolor and the Starry Plough, fly on pikestaffs. The image was accompanied by a scroll inscribed, in green, white, and gold lettering, with a declamation by the playwright Sean O'Casey on the death of Thomas Ashe, the first Irish republican Hunger Striker to die in 1917: "You cannot put a rope around the neck of an idea You cannot put an idea against a barrack wall and riddle it with bullets You cannot confine it in the strongest prison cell that your slaves could ever build."[9] The relative sophistication of this image contrasts with the simplicity of one of the oldest and still extant murals at Clowney Street, originally painted by "Beechmount Youth against H Block & Armagh" (Figure 16, see Fulcrum). In this image, a republican phoenix was flanked by crests of the four provinces of Ireland and the rhyming tags: "The people arose in 69 They will do it again at any time" and "Maggie Thatcher think again Don't let our brave men die in vain." The competence of the muralists in figures 14 and 15 contrasts with a work on Lenadoon Avenue in 1981 addressed to British soldiers. Featuring a crude figure of an IRA volunteer (in uniform, mask, and beret) holding a pistol, the mural declared: "Soldier, do you think that you have got away with the murder's of our political prisoner's and innocent children on the street's? Well, think again for your name is engraved on the freedom-fighter's bullet" (Figure 17, see Fulcrum).

Evidently many of the Hunger Strike murals were intended to evoke humanitarian sympathy for the suffering of the prisoners within a broad audience (Figure 18, see Fulcrum).[10] But it would be a mistake to think that the appeal to a wider public was made at the expense of censoring references to the republican campaign of violence. A number of murals to the dead Hunger Strikers represented a traditional republican firing party rendering "The final salute" (Figure 19, see Fulcrum), an implicit reference to Michael Collins' words at Thomas Ashe's funeral: "that volley which we have just heard is the only speech which it is proper to make above the grave of a dead Fenian" (O'Connor 1975: 109). Other references were more explicit. Rockville Street featured a mural of the IRA's attack at Warrenpoint in 1979 that inflicted the British Army's heaviest losses during the conflict (see **Introduction, fig. 1**). Rockdale Street presented a revolutionary, in socialist realist style, with combat fatigues, armalite, Tricolor, and pikestaff, together with a quotation from the Black Panther, Fred Hampton: "You may kill the revolutionary but never the revolution" (Figure 20, see Fulcrum).[11] And on Rossnareen Road (Shaws Road), three IRA volunteers were depicted with RPG7 rocket launchers and a rifle (Figure 21, see Fulcrum). As if to encapsulate the dual stance of humanitarian appeal and commitment to war, two murals in Derry's Bogside featured a lark caught in barbed wire (a figuration of Bobby Sands's story "The lark and the freedom fighter," Sands 1981: 33), alongside a representation of an iconic photograph, taken during the early Troubles by Ciaran Donnelly, of Joe McCann, Staff Captain in the Official IRA, on active service (Figure 22, see Fulcrum).[12] Another image in the same location referenced previous republican figures involved in armed insurrection: Pearse and Connolly, leaders of the 1916 Rising (Figure 23, see Fulcrum).

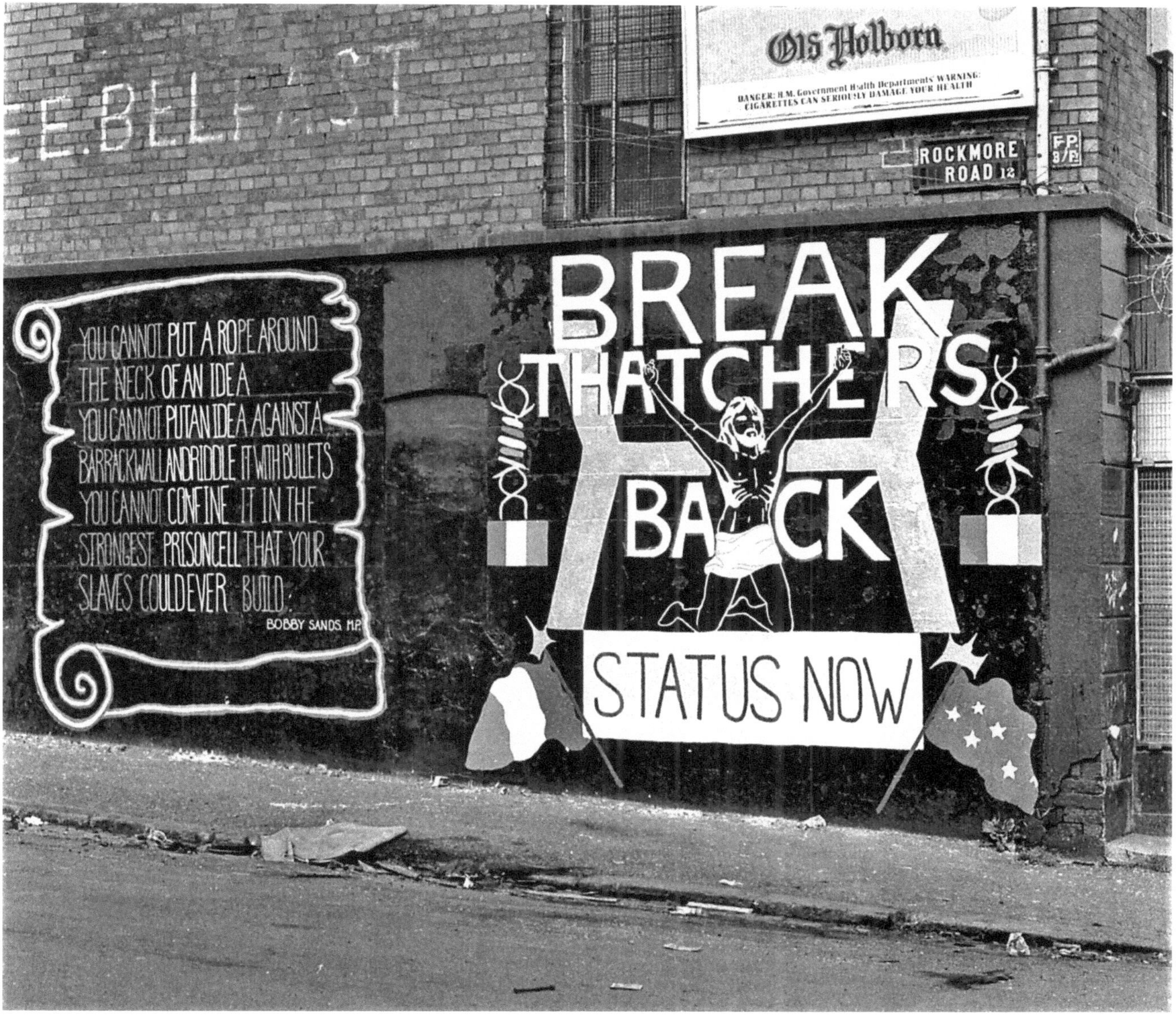

FIGURE 15 Break Thatcher's Back, Rockmore Street, Falls, West Belfast, 1981. Photo by Tony Crowley.

4. EXTENDING THE SCOPE

As well as the emphasis on the commitment to armed struggle, however, there were other early murals that were creative representations of the republican understanding of the historical causes of the conflict. An extensive and accomplished mural in Beechmount Avenue, for example, based on Jeff Perks's cover for a British Committee for Withdrawal pamphlet (Rolston 1991: 88), featured British torture and repression in Ireland over centuries, culminating in the "conveyor belt" system of justice at work in Northern Ireland (Figure 24, see Fulcrum) (Figure 25, see Fulcrum) (Figure 26, see Fulcrum). On the same wall, Ireland was represented in the squeezing grip of a Fascist hand (signified by the Swastika cufflink) (Figure 27). And in Derry, Britain, in the form of the republican bête noire, Prime Minister Margaret Thatcher, was figured as chewing up Ireland (together with the injunction "Get the Brits out!") (Figure 28). Another significant trend in republican muralism that began in this early period was memorialization. The Hunger Strikers were of course remembered by name and image throughout nationalist and republican areas, but the reach of memory work extended further. Irish National Liberation Army (INLA) volunteers Matt McLarnon and Danny Loughran were commemorated by a mural in Divis Flats that bore their names and images (Figure 29, see Fulcrum). And again in Derry, a republican roll of honor commemorating the IRA Derry Brigade (1970–1981) was painted in the gallery at the bottom of Rossville Flats. This mural is interesting not simply for its memory function, but for the fact that it contains a depiction of "the death of Cú Chulainn" copied from Oliver Sheppard's statue of the same title in the Dublin General Post Office (GPO) (Figure 30). It was not the last time that this ideologically flexible mythological figure was to be seen on the walls.

The post-Hunger Strike period saw a decline in the number of murals, which is unsurprising given the energy that had been spent on the prison campaign during the spring and summer of 1981. Murals commemorating the ten dead men still appeared, often in the form of a simple listing of the names with pertinent symbols (Tricolor, Starry Plough, and rifles for example) (Figure 31, see Fulcrum). And on the Shaws Road, the remarkable fact that Bobby Sands had been elected to Westminster was remembered with the assertion that he had been murdered by his fellow members of parliament (Figure 32). But the murals also began to reflect other issues. The putative historical continuity of the IRA campaign was marked by a mural in Islandbawn Street, Beechmount, that linked a rural IRA volunteer in 1916 with an urban fighter in 1982 and the message "We are here to stay"; figuring Bobby Sands's lark against a Tricolor, the image was significant for the early use of Irish on a wall—"Oglaigh na hEireann" (literally, "Volunteers of Ireland," but usually translated as "the IRA") and "Saoirse" ("Freedom") (Figure 33). The resonance of 1916 was also conveyed by a mural of Pádraig Mac Piarais (Patrick Pearse) with a quotation from his eulogy at the funeral of O'Donovan Rossa in 1915: "From the graves of patriot men and women spring living nations" (Figure 34, see Fulcrum). Yet the focus was not simply on the past; links to contemporary national liberation struggles also began to appear, as in the mural on "RPG Avenue" (Beechmount Avenue), that

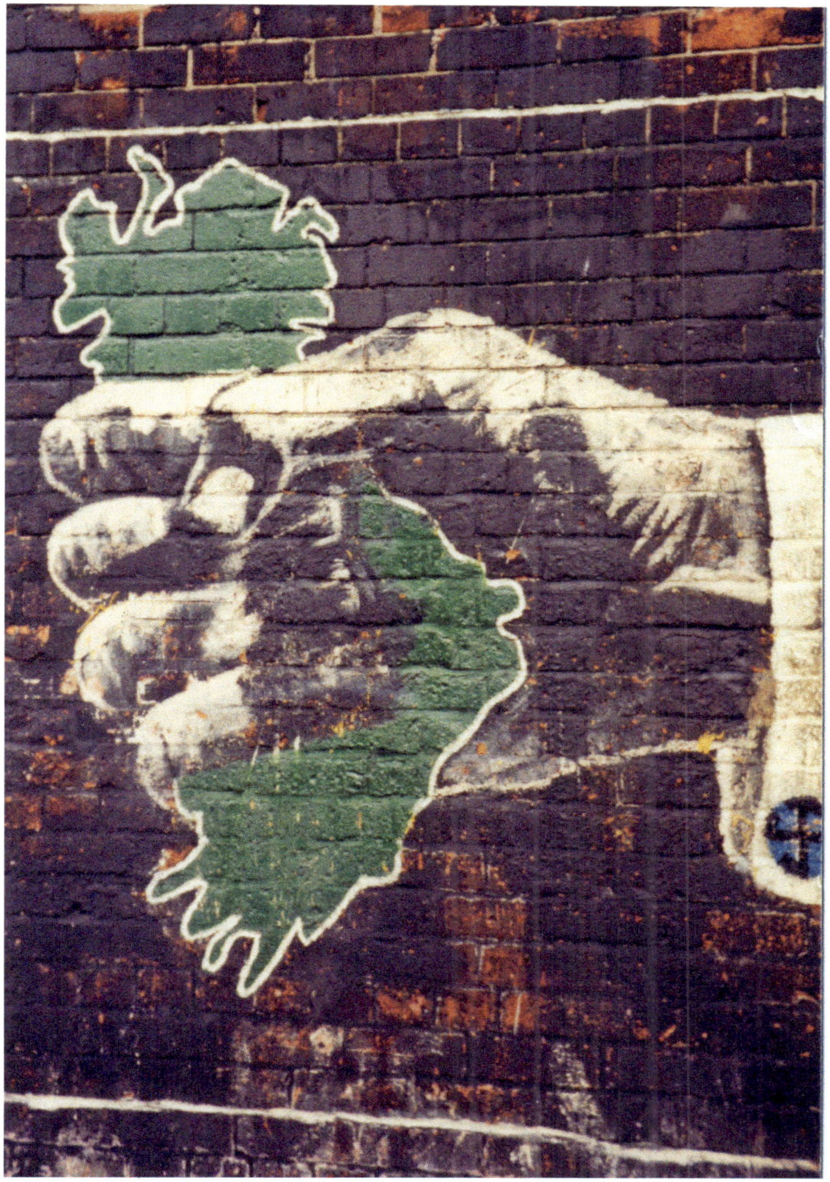

FIGURE 27 Ireland in the grip, Beechmount Avenue, Beechmount, West Belfast, 1982. Photo by Tony Crowley.

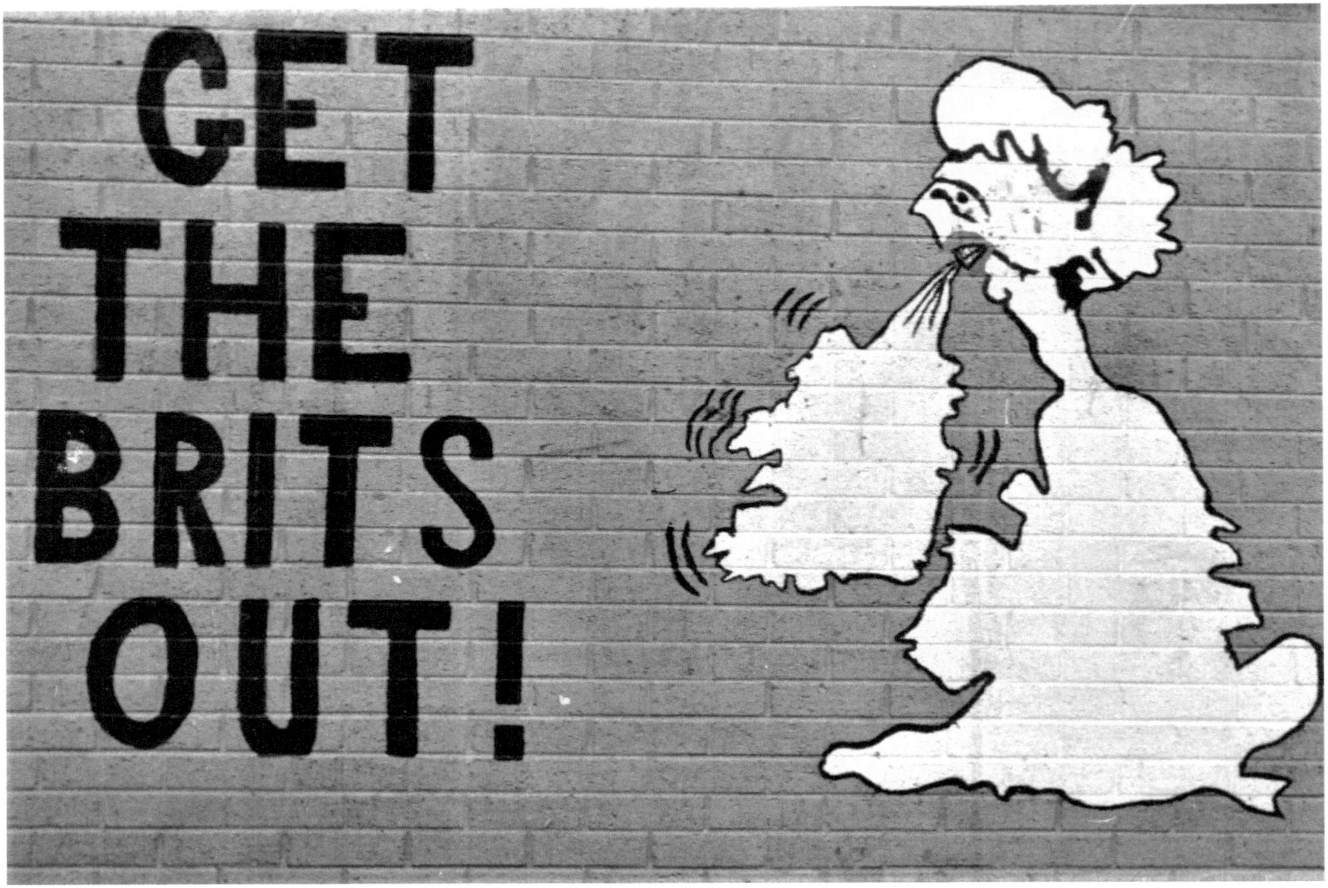

FIGURE 28 Get the Brits out! Rossville Street, Bogside, Derry, 1981. Photo by Tony Crowley.

depicted PLO and IRA volunteers, clutching rifles and a shared rocket launcher, posed against the Palestinian flag and the Tricolor, with the slogan "PLO IRA One struggle" (Figure 35). The turn towards contemporary politics, enabled by the electoral successes of the Hunger Strikers, was also evinced by a mural on the side of the fortified offices of Sinn Féin on the Falls Road. Effectively an advertisement for the republican weekly newspaper *An Phoblacht/Republican News*, the collage of images again linked past and present (Figure 36). The crest of the United Irishmen (a harp, "Equality," "It is new strung and shall be heard," with a liberty cap) was linked to 1916 (the Proclamation of the Republic), which connected to the present (an IRA volunteer, whose activities are read

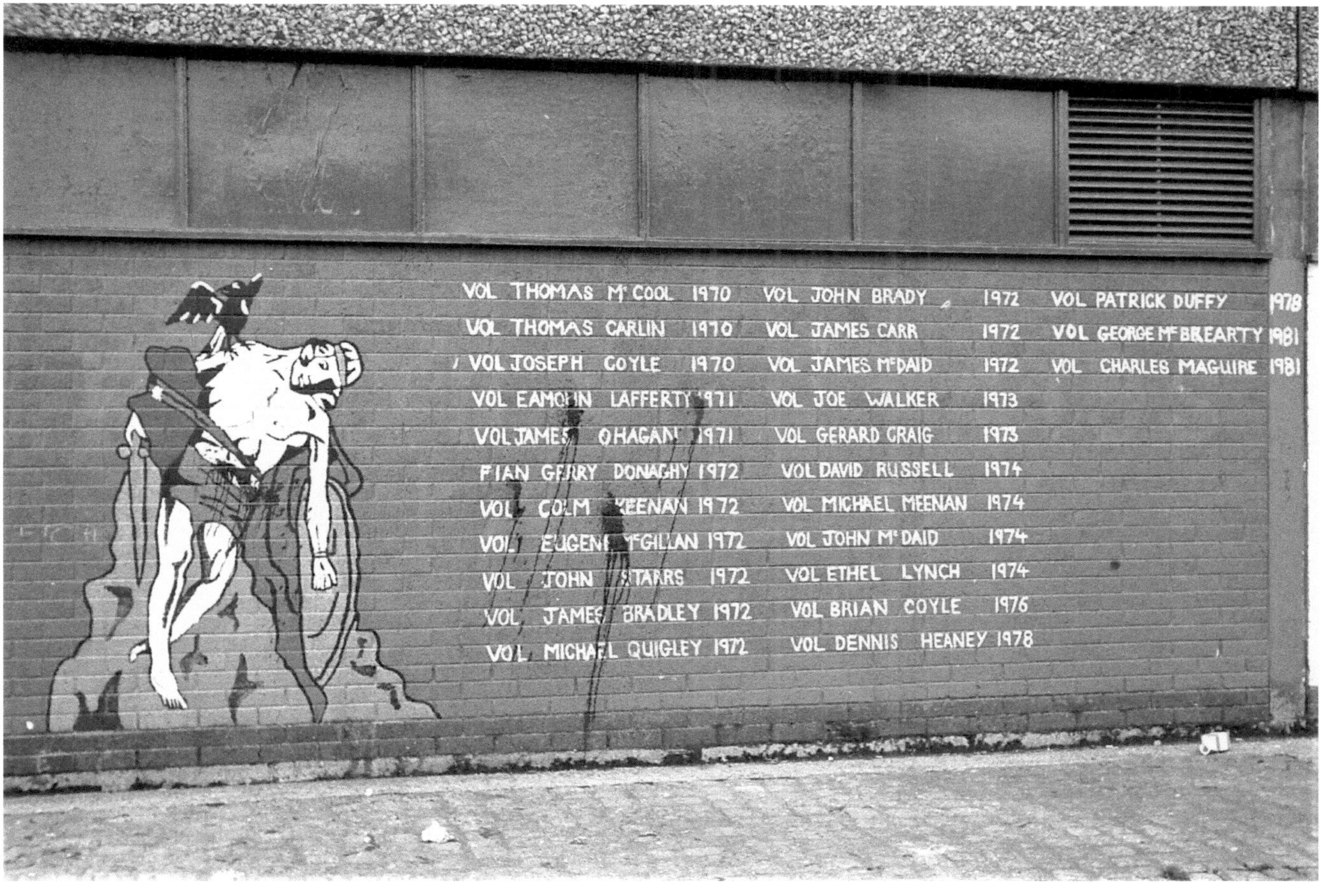

FIGURE 30 Republican roll of honor, Rossville Street, Derry, 1981. Photo by Tony Crowley.

about by two working-class men). In addition, the contents page ranged across topics addressed to different audiences: local (war news), national (prison news), and international (solidarity news). Perhaps most significantly, the *AP/RN*, "Here to stay," "PLO-IRA," and "Graves of patriot men and women" murals, were painted by "Sinn Féin Youth," a clear indication of the mobilizing effect of the Hunger Strikes on young people in republican and nationalist areas. In Derry, meanwhile, British Army violence provoked a response from republican muralists: an image on Rossville Street marked the death of eleven-year-old Stephen McConomy, killed by a plastic bullet fired by a soldier: "They call the killing of Stephen McConomy civil order" (Figure 37, see Fulcrum).

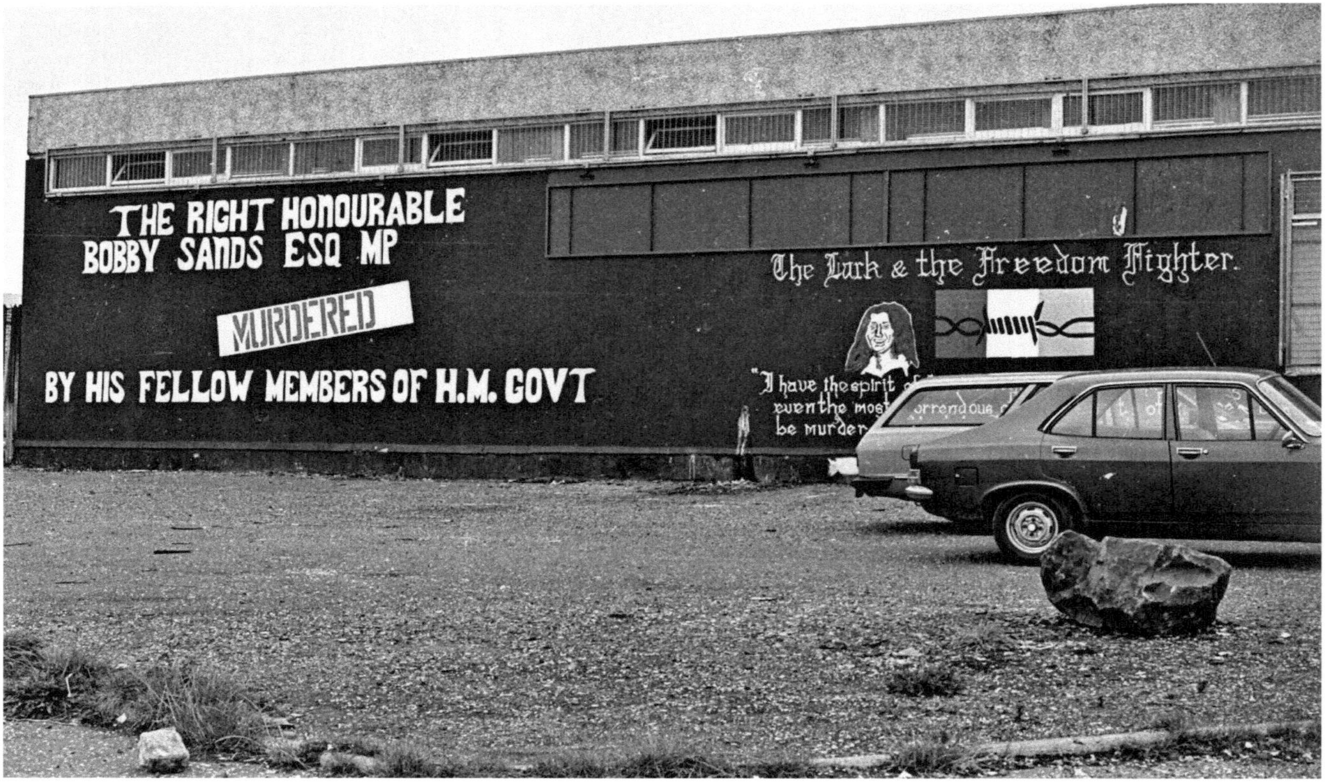

FIGURE 32 Bobby Sands MP, Shaws Road, West Belfast, 1981. Photo by Tony Crowley.

From a historical perspective, the most important political outcome of the Hunger Strikes was the adoption of the "Armalite and ballot box" strategy by the Provisional Republican Movement (Sinn Féin and the IRA)—which is to say, the dual track of armed struggle and electoral politics.[13] Though contentious within republicanism (whose traditional position was to abstain from reformist institutions), this initiative led, eventually and somewhat torturously, to the political settlement embodied in 1998 in *The Belfast Agreement* (also known as *The Good Friday Agreement*). Progress towards that point was by no means as inexorable as some commentators suggest (Moloney 2007), and in the early 1980s any such prospect seemed unlikely. Sinn Féin's initial embrace of electoralism was, however, marked by several important murals. Seán McKnight's unsuccessful campaign in South Belfast in the 1983 General Election, for example, was supported by murals that drew attention to republican tradition (in the figures of James Connolly and Bobby Sands—both of whom stood for office), but

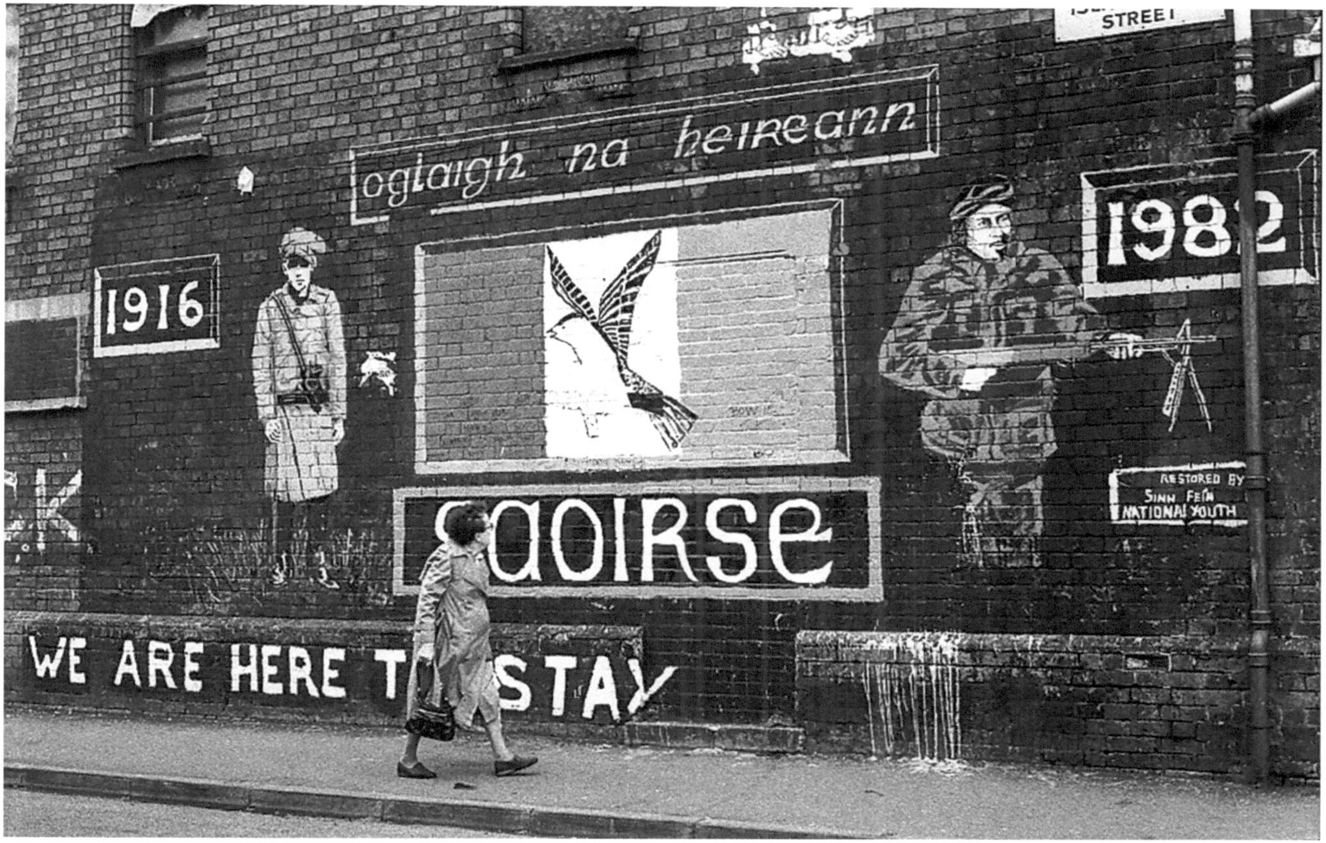

FIGURE 33 We are here to stay, Islandbawn Street, West Belfast, 1982. Photo by Tony Crowley.

also made clear that this was a new departure in a changed historical situation (by way of allusion to the Hunger Strikers) (Figure 38) (Figure 39, see Fulcrum). The real breakthrough, however, was the victory of Gerry Adams in West Belfast in the same poll, and in a carefully calibrated election mural in Beechmount Avenue, sponsored by *An Phoblacht/Republican News*, a woman in heroic mode was represented unfurling a Tricolor, while against a red background, young protesters highlighted social issues (youth, culture, houses, jobs, education for all) (Figure 40, see Fulcrum). The electoral message was "For a New Ireland vote Sinn Féin" (though the other means advocated as a way of achieving the goal was clear—if understated—by its location on "RPG Avenue" and the "Brits out" placard held by one of the protesters). Facing this image, in an ironic reversal of the tenet that Sinn Féin were the political wing of the IRA, a mural proclaimed that "Parliament is the political wing of the

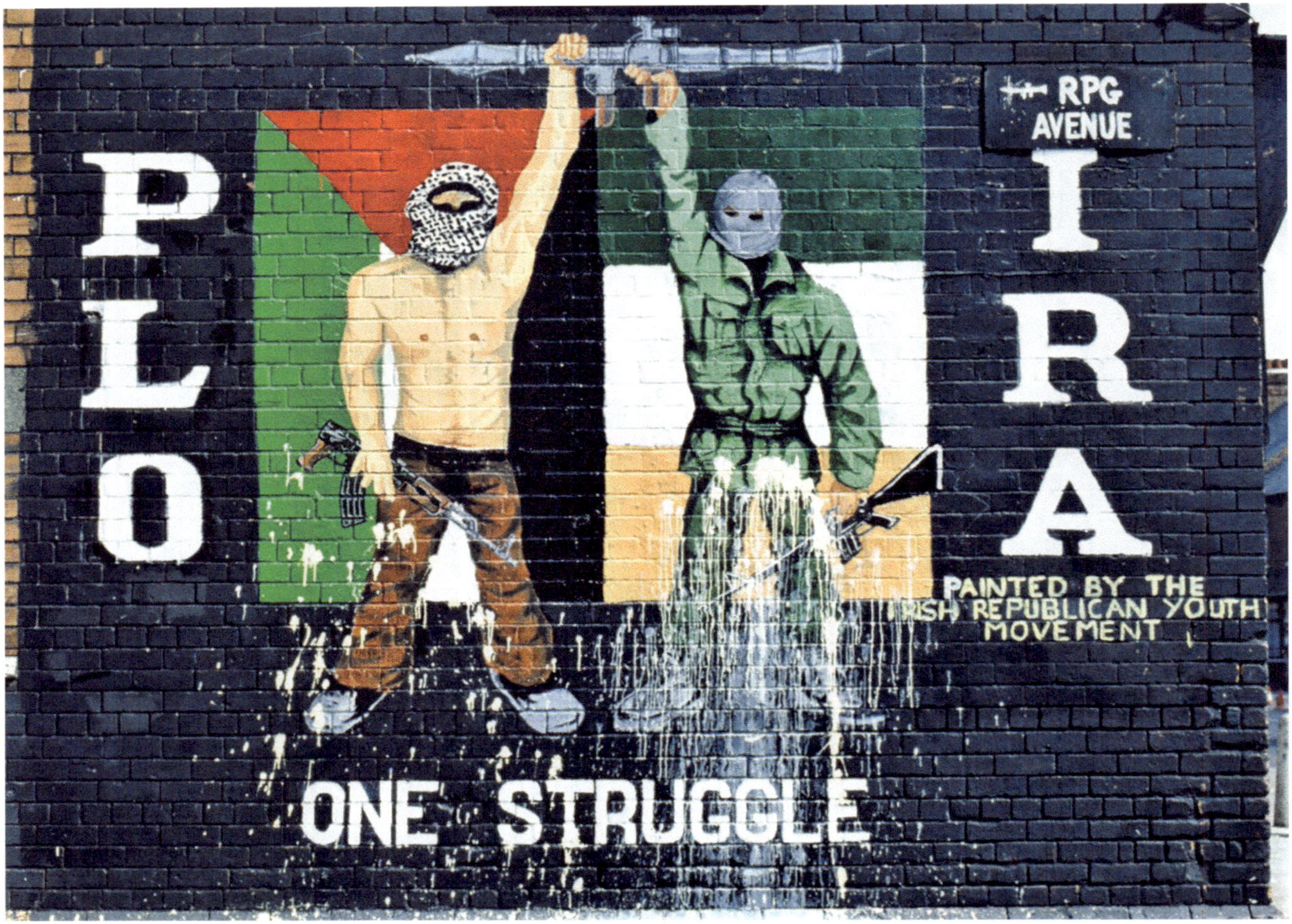

FIGURE 35 One struggle, Beechmount Avenue, West Belfast, 1982. Photo by Tony Crowley.

British Army" (Figure 41, see Fulcrum). Further evidence of a political left-turn was indicated by the appearance of a feminist-republican mural on the Falls Road in 1983 (Sinn Féin's Women's Department had been established in 1980). A slightly earlier mural on the same wall figured women reading, armed, and protesting, with the background of a Tricolor; it was captioned "We must grow tough but without ever losing our tenderness Resistance." Though the quote is from Che Guevara, its use in a gender-specific context was discordant, and the 1983 mural was clearer in its focus on "Solidarity between women in armed struggle" (Figure 42). Framed by

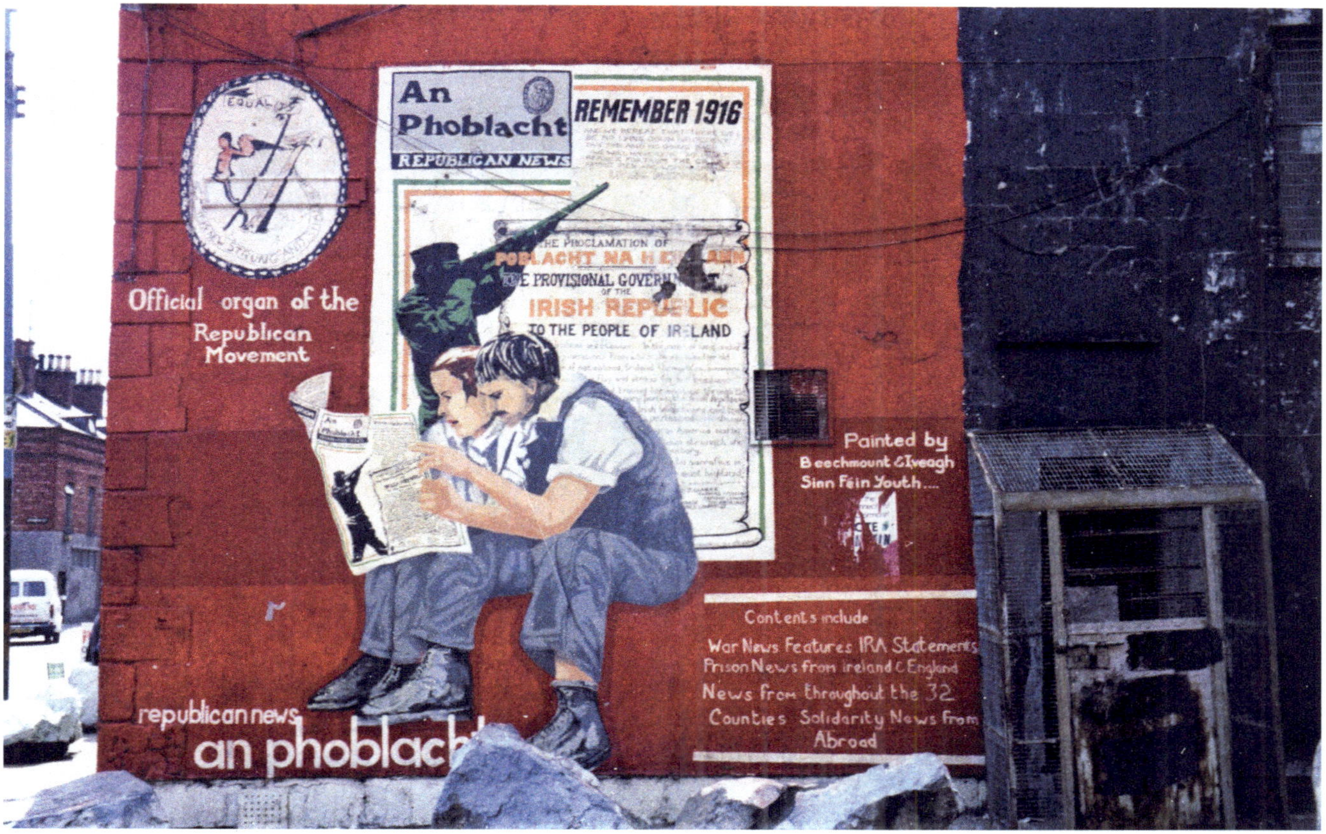

FIGURE 36 *An Phoblacht/Republican News*, Sevastopol Street, West Belfast, 1982. Photo by Tony Crowley.

the universal symbol of women, the mural featured detailed portraits of armed volunteers from the IRA, PLO, and the Southwest African People's Organisation (SWAPO).[14]

As noted earlier, after the successful political impact of murals generated in response to the 1981 Hunger Strike and Sinn Féin's electoral strategy, the pace of republican muralism slowed (Rolston 1991: 104). It was not, after all, a long-standing tradition in nationalist areas and had arisen in relation to very specific events. But it is important not to overstate the level of decline; the 1980s–early 1990s saw republican murals take up a number of themes that were to be consolidated and developed later. The republican war against the British State continued to be represented (significantly, there were very few murals that addressed loyalism directly). Occasionally this was rendered concisely, as in the slogan "The spirit of freedom will never die," with the tag "IRA," painted on

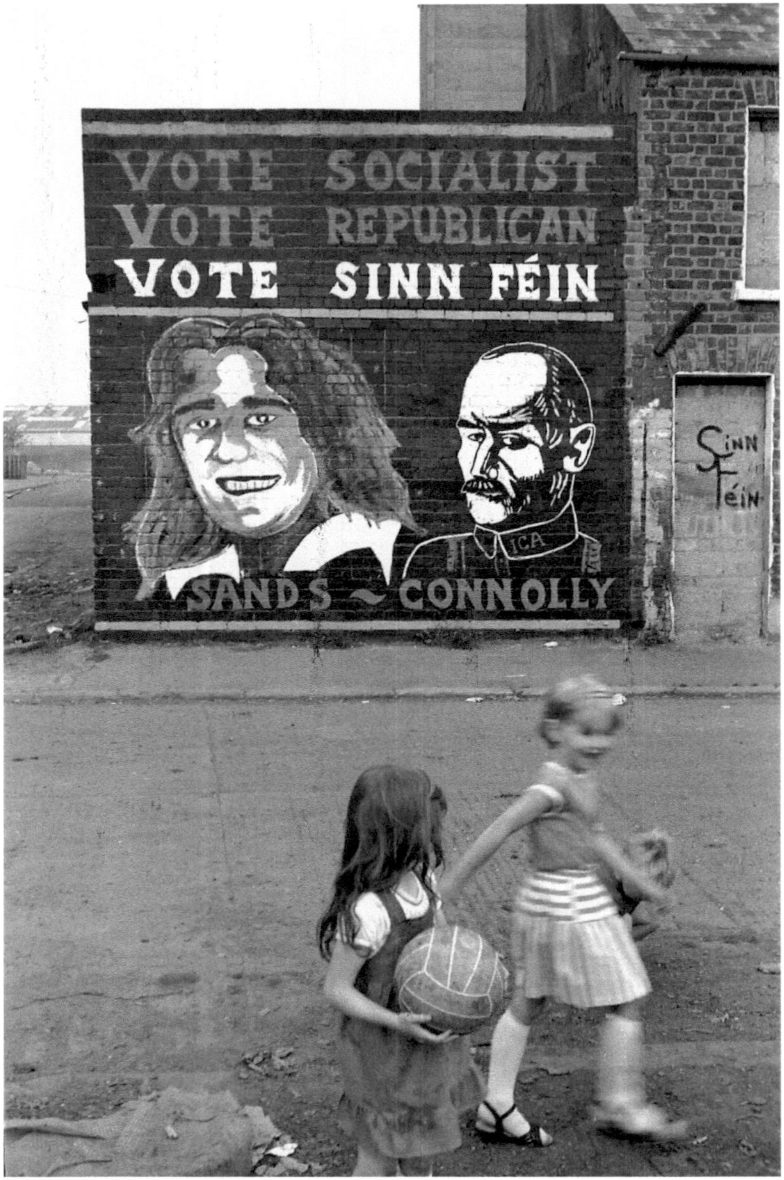

FIGURE 38 Vote Sinn Féin, Bond Street, Markets area, South Belfast, 1983. Photo by Tony Crowley.

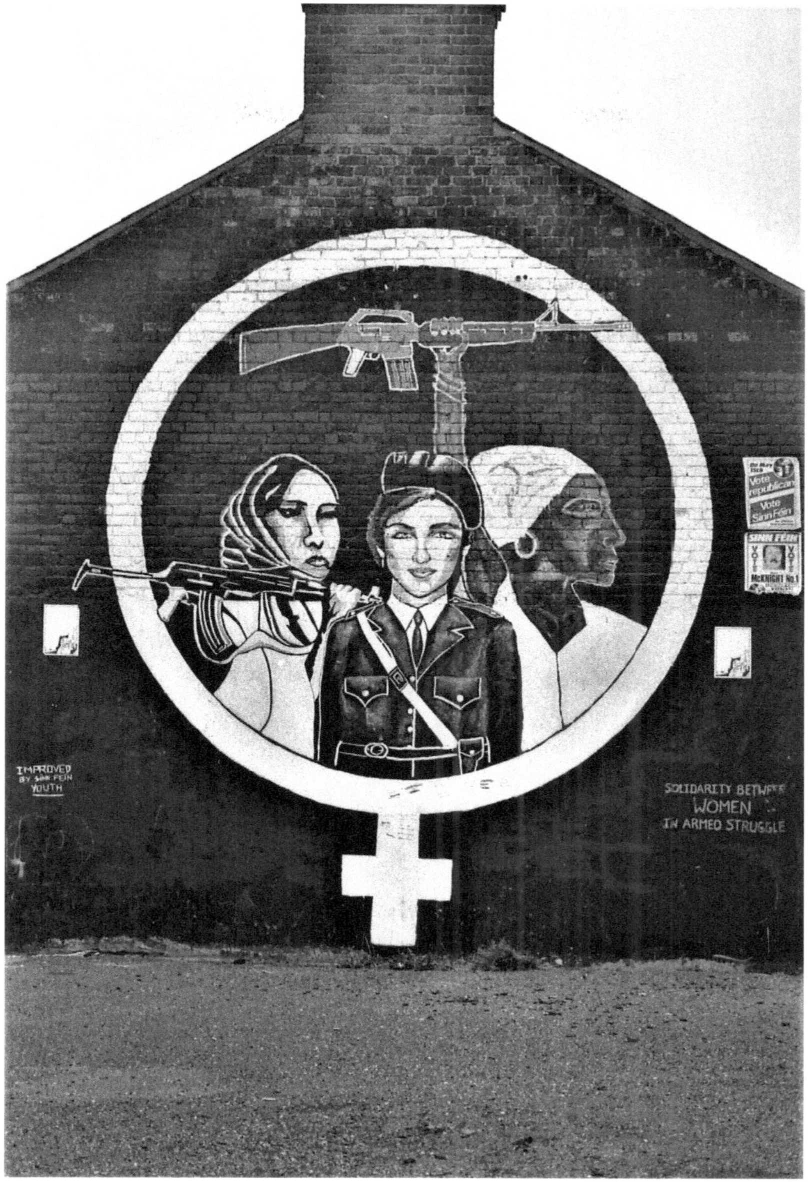

FIGURE 42 Women in armed struggle, Fallswater Road, West Belfast, 1983. Photo by Tony Crowley.

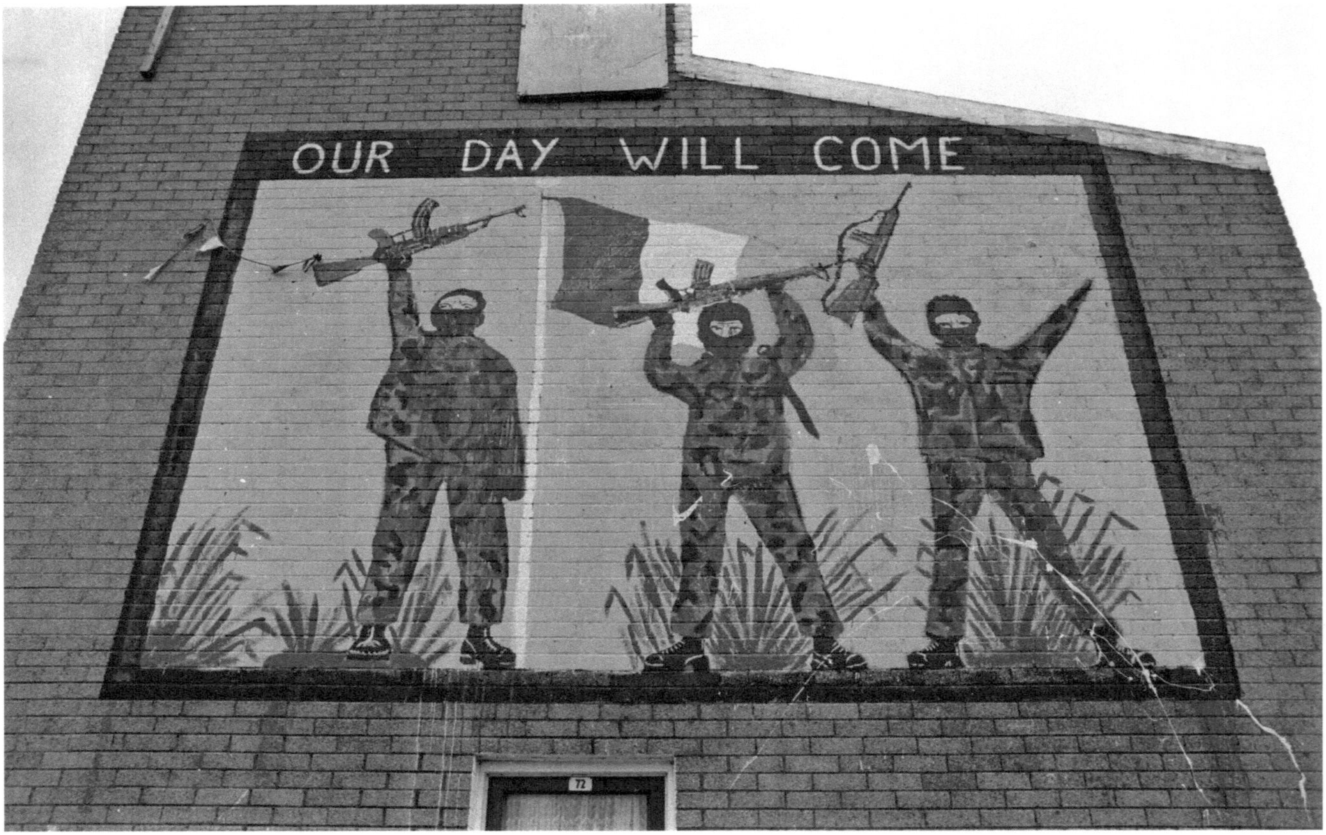

FIGURE 45 Our day will come, Springhill Avenue, Ballymurphy, West Belfast, 1987. Photo by Tony Crowley.

Beechmount Avenue in 1991. But the message could also be delivered brutally, as in the 1988 mural declaring that "Semtex kills more germs than Vortex That's the RA's verdict" (Figure 43, see Fulcrum), or the 20-meter-long piece of graffiti in Regent Street, next to the republican Unity Flats, which proclaimed: "If you want the RUC in Newry ring 999 ask for—9" (a reference to an IRA mortar attack on Newry RUC station in which nine police officers were killed—the largest loss of life suffered by the police service during the Troubles). Armed volunteers were also depicted on the walls. A mural in 1987 in Edlingham Street, New Lodge, heavily paint-bombed by British soldiers, portrayed an IRA volunteer with rifle against a Tricolor and Starry Plough, with "Saoirse" and a quotation from Bobby Sands: "I believe and stand by the God-given right of the Irish nation to sovereign independence, and the right of any Irishman or woman to assert this right in armed revolution" (Figure 44, see Fulcrum). In Springhill in the same year, three IRA volunteers, in camouflage and in a rural setting, posed with weapons against a Tricolor, and underneath the slogan "Our day will come" (an English rendering of Sands's "Tiocfaidh ár lá") (Figure 45).[15] This image sat alongside an even clearer representation of armed force: a mural consisting simply of heavy weaponry, with a Tricolor and Sunburst (the flag of the republican youth movement Na Fianna Éireann) and "IRA" (Rolston 1991: 93).

5. MEMORY, MYTH, LANGUAGE

The art of memory became an important medium for republican muralists in the 1980s. This took two forms. The first was the continued commemoration of key events in the collective memory of republicanism. Anniversaries are key to this process, and they have the singular advantage of being regular (always on the same day), recurrent (the same day each year) and predictable (they can be planned in advance). Thus the 70th anniversary of the 1916 Rising was duly recorded by an apparently simple mural on Paráid An Ardghleanna (Berwick Road), Ardoyne (Figure 46). The mural commemorated the Easter Rising through direct reference—"1916 Easter 1986"—and the quotation of the words of James Larkin in 1913 ("The great appear great because we are on our knees, Let us rise"—taken from the masthead of Connolly's *Worker's Republic*) and Pearse (in an essay on "symbols"—"As long as Ireland is unfree the only attitude of Irishmen and Irishwomen is an attitude of revolt" Pearse 2013: 81). But the mural also linked to the present in the figure of an IRA volunteer with rocket launcher and a reference to the 5th anniversary of the Hunger Strikes, through the prison scene at the top. This scene, however, evinced layered historical reference in that the image—a prostrate prisoner in a cell, looked over by a mother figure to right and Mother Ireland figure to left—was taken from a republican postcard produced in 1972 (Loftus 1990: 45), probably to mark the Hunger Strike undertaken by the IRA commander Billy McKee to gain "Special Status." Another mural on the Whiterock Road, Ballymurphy, by the prolific and influential republican muralist Gerard "Mo Chara" Kelly, also commemorated Cáisc (Easter) 1916 with a design inspired by Robert Ballagh's *1916 Rising 75th Anniversary, The Provisional Government* (Figure 47, see Fulcrum). The same topic was treated on Beechmount ("RPG") Avenue (Figure 48). Adapted from an earlier version, this mural depicted the GPO during the Rising with a republican phoenix rising from the flames. The central image, flanked by the emblems of the four provinces of Ireland and framed by "Free Ireland," represented a manacled hand (restraints "Made in Britain"), holding an Easter lily. Above the image, with Tricolors on either side, a plaque bore the "Roll of Honour A Coy 2nd Batt Bel Brig Óglaigh na hÉireann" ("A" Company 2nd Battalion Belfast Brigade IRA), featuring those who had died since 1970, with the Irish inscription "Fuair siad bás ar son na hÉireann" (They died for Ireland) and Pearse's familiar "Ireland unfree will never be at peace." A slightly fuller extract of Pearse's speech was reproduced at the side of the mural: "The fools The fools They have left us our Fenian dead And while Ireland holds these graves Ireland unfree will never be at peace." The linkage of past and present was and remains an important trope, but significantly, this mural embodied the second form of the art of memory. For what the image and text summoned is the mnemonic power of the dead, a conjuration that was to become central to both republican and loyalist muralism. Evidently, the dead included those who died long ago (1916), but also those who were recently buried—as indicated by the insertion of the dead from the 1970s and 1980s into the republican pantheon, united—whatever their age, gender, role, circumstances of death—by the governing principle that they died for Ireland. Notably, the communal memory forged in such representations is grounded very specifically; these are the local dead. Indeed, as a number of wall plaques raised in the 1980s ordained, the

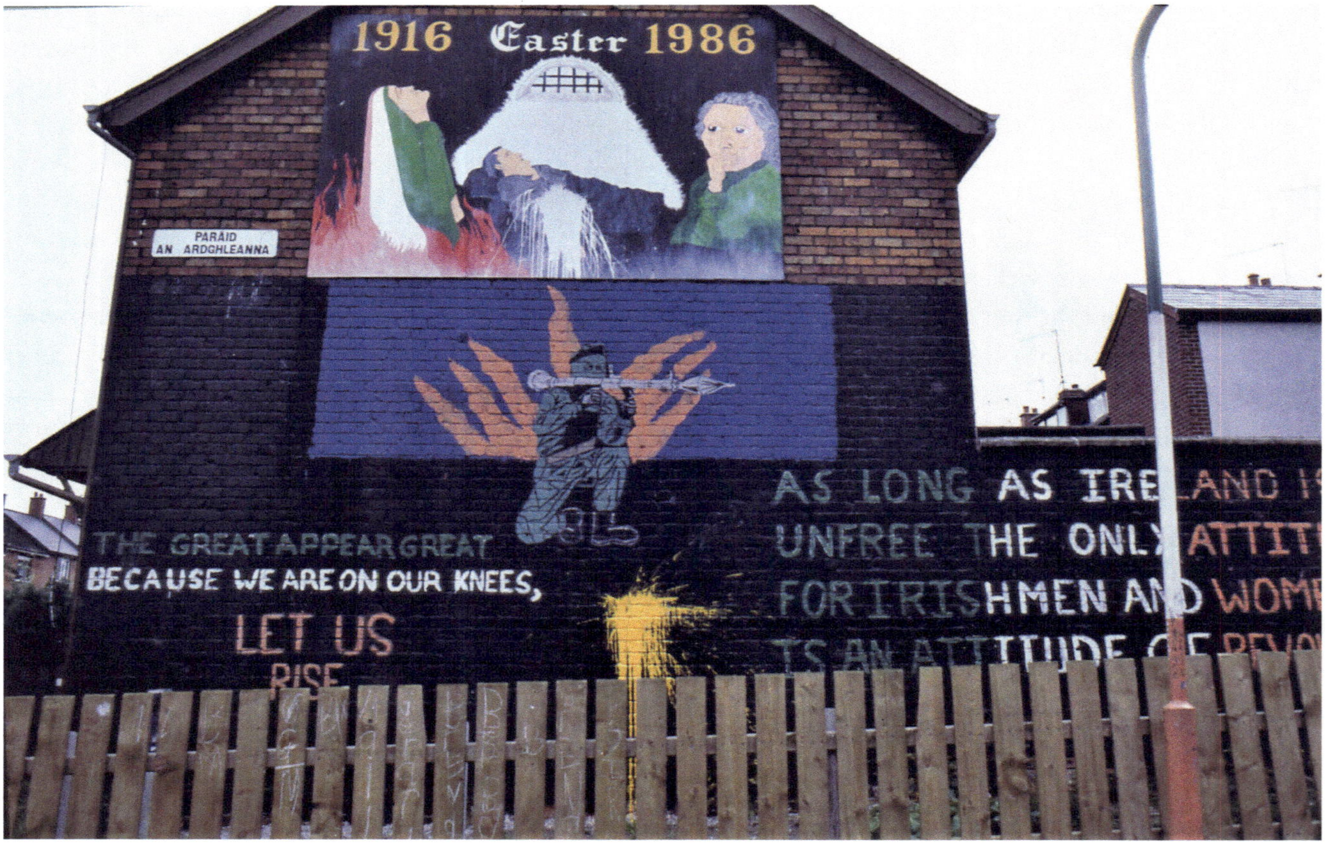

FIGURE 46 Easter 1986, Berwick Road/Paráid An Ardghleanna, Ardoyne, North Belfast, 1986. Photo by Tony Crowley.

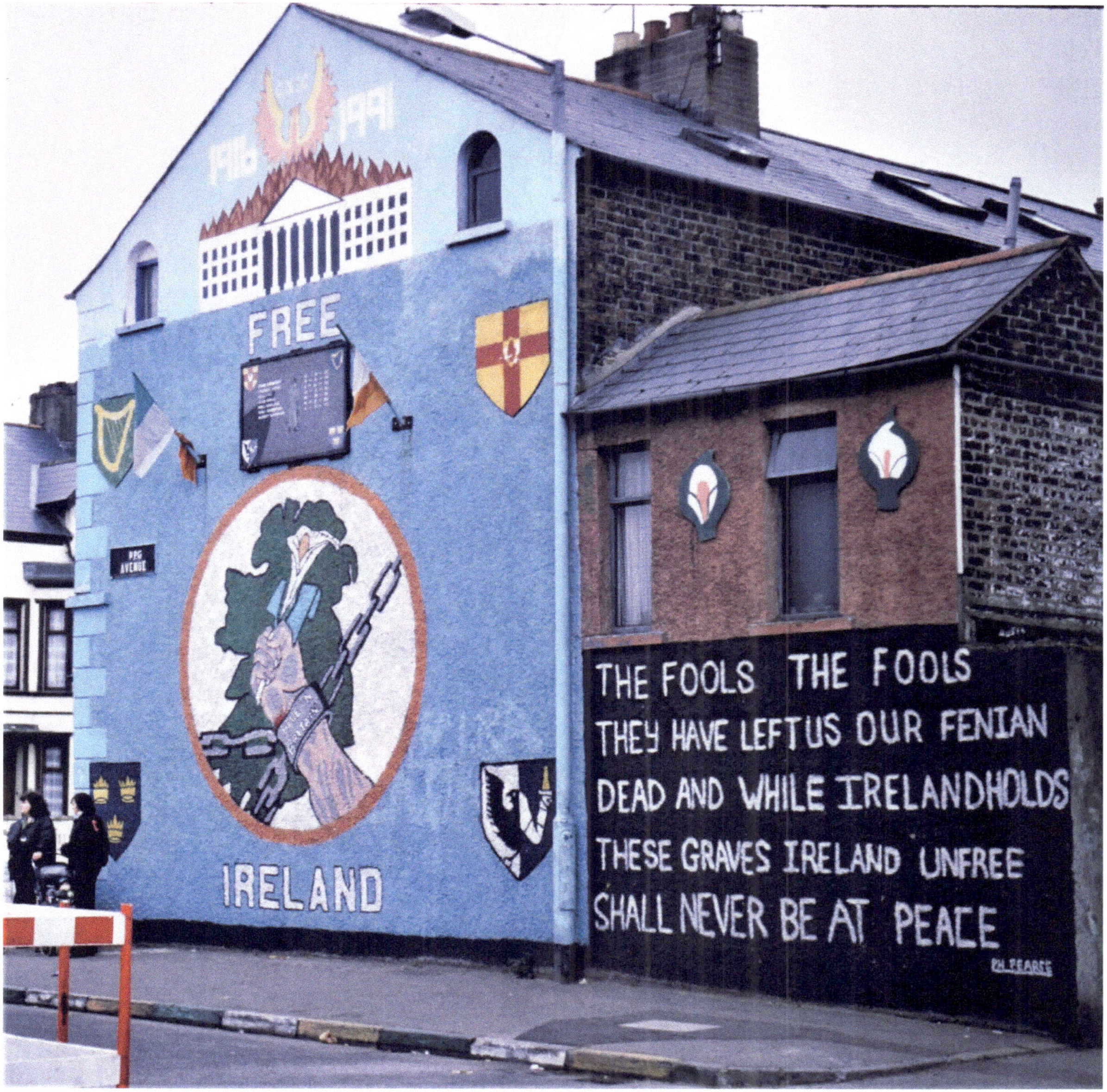

FIGURE 48 The fools, Beechmount Avenue, Beechmount, West Belfast, 1991. Photo by Tony Crowley.

locally remembered dead extended to include not simply republican volunteers, but "civilians who died at the hands of the British Army, RUC, UDR and loyalist extremists" (Figure 49, see Fulcrum).

First among equals in the index of republican memory were the Hunger Strikers, whose commemoration continued apace during the 1980s and 1990s. The 10th anniversary was marked by a mural on the New Lodge Road that featured the image of a prisoner foregrounded against the H-Blocks with the names of the ten dead men and a reminder-cum injunction: "You stood by them then Remember them now." This was a noteworthy example of the implicit mode of memory in which memory itself is invoked, rather than memory as a direct prompt ("remember them and then do X"), a lack of specificity that suggests republican political confidence. But if the Hunger Strikers were the primary focus of remembrance in republican murals, there was a striking shift in the late 1980s to the commemoration of IRA volunteers killed on active service. The heaviest defeat inflicted on the IRA in a single action was the ambush at Loughall in May 1987 in which British Special Forces killed eight members of the IRA's formidable East Tyrone Brigade who were intent on destroying the village police station. A mural on Queen's Parade, New Lodge, duly recorded the event; the traditional republican flags framed a list of the Óglaigh (Volunteers), names in Irish, with a central inscription: "Óglaigh na hÉireann Loch gCál" (IRA Loughgall). The form of this image was interesting in that it revealed the nature of the audience to which it is addressed; there was no reference to the fate of the volunteers (no life dates, or even date of death), indicating that the mural was secure in its presupposition of informed viewers (Figure 50, see Fulcrum). Another mural addressing the same event was more explicit; an early work of "Mo Chara" on Springhill Avenue, Ballymurphy (one of the poorest parts of West Belfast, and thus one of the very poorest parts of the United Kingdom), this was a vibrant and complex memorial image (Figure 51, see Fulcrum). Set in a rural setting, to indicate the provenance of the East Tyrone Brigade, the mural was inscribed entirely in Irish and centered on a Celtic Cross decorated with interlace, with portraits of a number of IRA volunteers flanked by emblems of the four provinces of Ireland. Underneath the Cross stood a roll of honor, "I ndíl cuimhne" (In loving memory), naming "An ochtar óglach de oglaigh na h-Éireann dúnmharú ag Lochgal ar an ochtú lá Bealtaine 1987" (The eight IRA volunteers murdered at Loughgall on the May 8 1987). The same Celtic Cross motif appeared in Unity Flats on another memorial to the three IRA volunteers on a bombing mission who were killed without warning by undercover Special Forces in Gibraltar 1988 (Figure 52, see Fulcrum). Again the four crests appeared, as did the decorated Celtic Cross, here with the inscription "Remember the Gibraltar Martyrs," set against three republican flags—the Tricolor, Sunburst, and, slightly unusually, the flag of the province of Ulster.

Though originally features of "Insular art" (c.600–1300), Celtic crosses and complex interlace decoration were popularized as features of the late nineteenth- and early twentieth-century Gaelic Revival. And many of the tales of Gaelic mythology were published in accessible format for the first time during the flourishing of cultural nationalism that accompanied the political struggle for Irish independence. It is striking therefore that at a time when republicans were attempting to reach a broader nationalist electoral constituency, aspects of traditional Irish culture began to appear in murals. In Tullagh Park, Shaws Road, for example, "An slabhra gan briseadh" (The unbroken chain) depicted in mythological mode a phoenix passing the republican flame through history (signified by pike and sword) to a contemporary torchbearer with automatic rifle (Figure 53, see Fulcrum). Past, present, and future are united in a Burkean invocation of the community of the dead, living, and yet to be born: "We owe it to them… To those who have died, To those whose youth lies battered against a prison wall, To our unborn children!" In this case, the artwork was not particularly sophisticated, but the same cannot be said of Mo Chara's complex and intricate renderings of Jim Fitzpatrick's neo-Celtic reworking of Gaelic myths, which took republican muralism to a different level (Saleeby-Mulligan 2009: 164–170). One ambitious and achieved example, which sat alongside the Loughgall mural on Springhill, was "Is é seo Nuadha Rí Tuatha Dé Danann" (This is Nuadha, King of the Tuatha Dé Danann); it was a serious departure and announced Mo Chara as an important republican community artist (Figure 54, see Fulcrum). Yet if Gaelic mythology was one aspect of traditional Irish culture, another living form began to appear more frequently on the walls: the Irish language. The language had been associated with Irish nationalism since the late nineteenth century, but in the Belfast Shaws Road urban Gaeltacht from the late 1960s, and then within the prison system in the 1970s and 1980s, Irish became an important cultural and political marker for nationalism and republicanism within Northern Ireland (Crowley 2005: 192–196; Mac Giolla Chriost 2012). The medium was, at least in part, the message in slogans such as "Ní bheidh síocháin ann gan saoirse" (There will be no peace without freedom) (1983) (see **Introduction, fig. 6**), "Stad Maggie anois" (Stop Maggie now) (1985) (Figure 55, see Fulcrum), "Beidh an lá Venceremos" (Our day will come—[Spanish] We will win) (1988) (Figure 56, see Fulcrum), and "Saor agus Sóisialach" (Free and Socialist) (1988)—a play on Pearse's goal of an Ireland "not free merely, but Gaelic as well" ("Saor agus Gaelach") (Figure 57).[16] And in 1989 a mural on the side of the Sinn Féin offices on the Falls Road illustrated the role that Irish occupied within republican strategy. Painted across the length of two houses, the left section of the mural was an advertisement for *An Phoblacht/Republican News*—"Ireland's best-selling political weekly"—with the figure of a British soldier leaving republican Ireland. To the right, the image depicted an engagement in 1988 in which IRA volunteers used a heavy machine gun to bring down a Lynx helicopter in South Armagh, underneath which was the slogan "Fiche Blian ag Streachailt Bua do mhuintir na h-Eireann" (Twenty Years of Struggle Victory to the People of Ireland) (Figure 58). The mural thus represented a struggle on three fronts: politics, war, and culture.

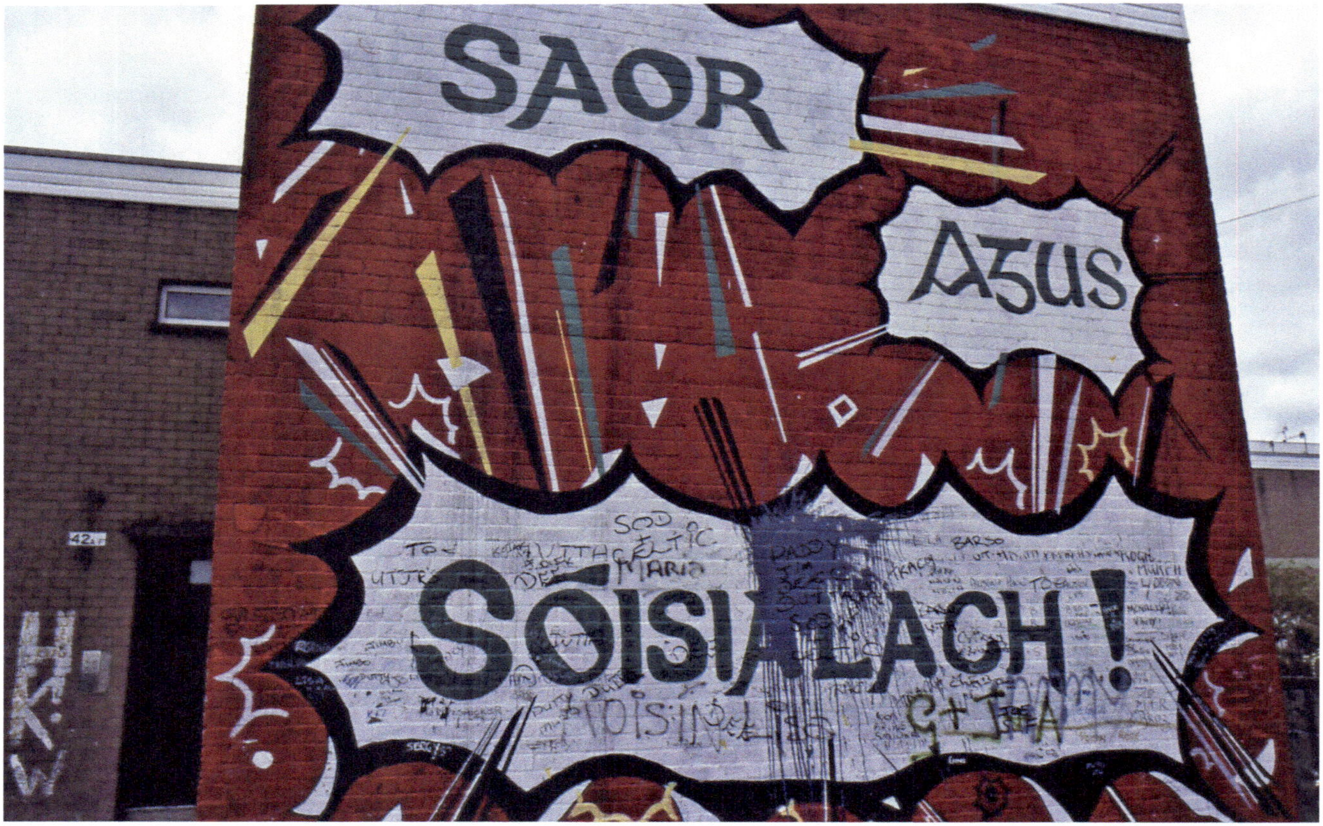

FIGURE 57 Saor agus Sóisialach, Rosnareen Avenue, Anderstown, West Belfast, 1988. Photo by Tony Crowley.

6. INTERNAL AND EXTERNAL DIALOGUE

Republicanism maintained its dialogue with its own supporters and the nationalist community at large (a dialogue that included the threat and practice of violent communal policing) (Rolston 1991: 92), and it used murals to focus on specific events. For example, the killing of Sean Downes by a plastic bullet fired at close range by a policeman during an anti-internment rally in Belfast in 1984 provoked a mural in Derry's Bogside—"Plastic death Who next?"—with images of the perpetrator and victim (Figure 59, see Fulcrum). Other issues included the use of "supergrasses" by the security forces in order to effect mass arrests of alleged republican volunteers (the policy was also used against loyalists—it failed in both cases). An Irish Republican Socialist Party (IRSP) mural drew

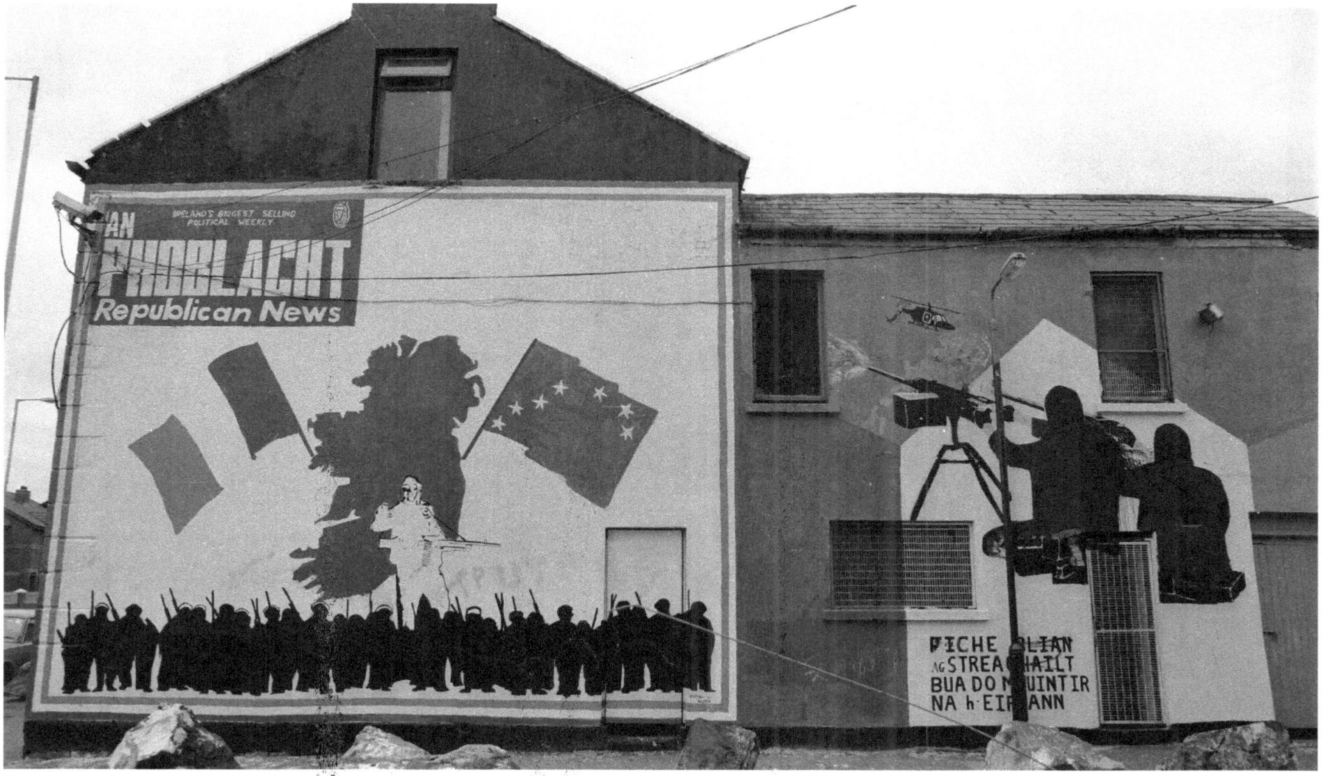

FIGURE 58 Fiche Blian ag Streaghailt, Sevastopol Street, West Belfast, 1989. Photo by Tony Crowley.

similarities between this tactic and that of internment in 1971: "1971 No Trials 1984 Show Trials" (Figure 60, see Fulcrum). And the fate of Joe Doherty, IRA volunteer and prison escapee who was arrested in the United States, featured in a 1988 New Lodge Road mural. Alongside a portrait of Doherty, the mural protested against his proposed extradition back to Northern Ireland: "Would the U.S. Att. General Edwin Meese have deported George Washington? Don't handover Joe Doherty to British Warlords!" (Figure 61, see Fulcrum). Republican murals did not, however, solely address an audience within Northern Ireland; their awareness of global media attention led them to attempt to internationalize the conflict by representing similarities with national-liberation, or civil rights, struggles elsewhere. The IRA-PLO mural (see **chapter two, fig. 35**) is one example, but there were others. Solidarity with the ANC was emphasized with a mural on Beechmount Avenue in 1986 featuring they symbol of uMkhonto we Sizwe (the ANC's armed wing), a rifle, and a Sands quote—"We aim to be free"—while above Sinn Féin declared

West Belfast to be a "Ceantar saor ó apartheid" (Apartheid free zone) (Figure 62). And the seventieth birthday of Nelson Mandela (still in prison at the time) was celebrated by Mo Chara's large portrait on Ross Road, Lower Falls, with the message "Mandela Happy Birthday Comrade Father of—freedom—The future belongs to you!" (Figure 63, see Fulcrum). The same artist also painted two murals that represented the cause of Native Americans (delegations from the American Indian Movement visited nationalist Belfast in 1985 and 1988) (De Baroid 2000: 278;

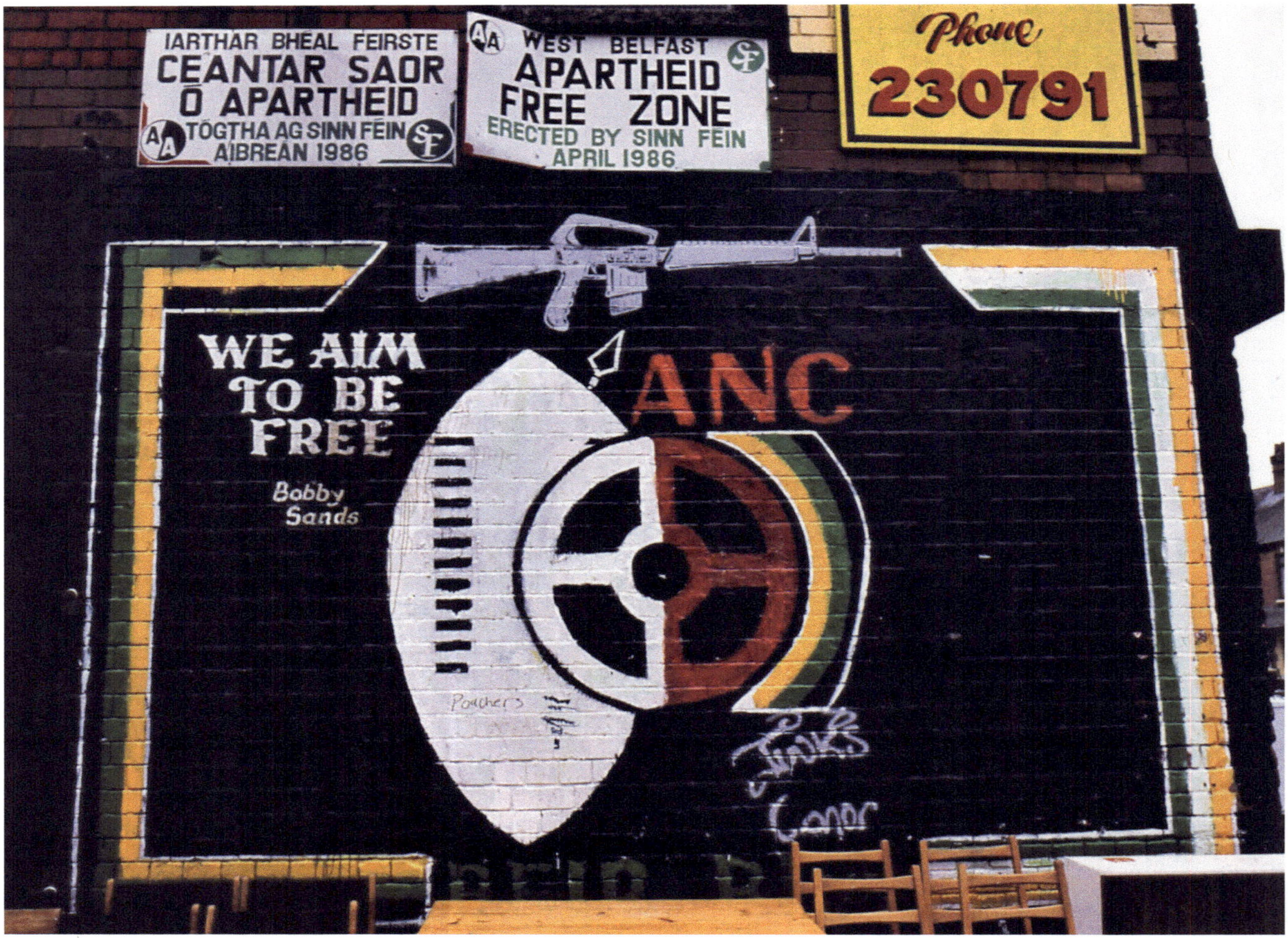

FIGURE 62 We aim to be free, Beechmount Avenue, Beechmount, West Belfast, 1988. Photo by Tony Crowley.

Saleeby-Mulligan 2009: 186). The first, on Springhill Avenue, Ballymurphy, highlighted the case of AIM activist Leonard Peltier (imprisoned since 1977 for his role in the killing of two FBI agents). Featuring a Native American design, the message of the mural was: "Free Leonard Peltier Framed by the FBI" (Figure 64, see Fulcrum). On a grander scale, two years later on the Whiterock Road, Ballymurphy, a Native American figure was set against a Star-Spangled Banner with republican lark and Indian eagle to left and right and the central slogan "Our struggle Your struggle" (Rolston 1992: 59). The international links continued with a collaborative mural project between Mo Chara and the Mexican artist Rubén Ortiz Torres. Commissioned by the West Belfast Community Festival in 1992, the painting featured representations of Connolly, Emiliano Zapata (leader of the 1910 Mexican revolution), an IRA volunteer, and a Latino youth, together with the now familiar refrain "You can kill the revolutionary but not the revolution" (Figure 65, see Fulcrum). As in all of Mo Chara's murals, this work contained significant artistic detail: the figures and faces were well drawn, the colors signified (green, white, and gold combined with Mexican green, white, and red), and symbols encoded the message (the republican phoenix was combined with the eagle of the United Farmworkers logo). Not all republican murals expressing international solidarity, however, were of such high quality. An IRSP/INLA mural in 1989 in the Divis area of West Belfast consisted of a badly drawn star with hammer and sickle, together with the acronyms "IRSP," "INLA," and "FSLN" (Frente Sandinista de Liberación Nacional—the Nicaraguan Sandinistas) (Figure 66, see Fulcrum).

If connections with radical struggles in other locations were important for various strands of republicanism (not least to counter the British media characterization of the war in Northern Ireland as simply a "sectarian conflict" or "civil war" rather than a conflict between republicans and the British State), it remains the case that the most significant strategic policy for Sinn Féin in the 1980s was building electoral support. And again, as noted above, the walls played a role. The continuation of the armalite and ballot box policy was illustrated by a mural in Short Strand that cited Pearse's prescription about the proper attitude of Irishmen and Irishwomen (revolt) and was topped with posters for the local elections in 1985 (Figure 67, see Fulcrum). Sinn Féin's political advance was supported by murals that attempted to mobilize and organize and again Mo Chara played a key role in the party's stronghold of West Belfast. Inspired by the political cartoons of Brian Moore (Cormac) in *An Phoblacht/Republican News*, "So I always looked the other way" appeared on the Whiterock Road in 1988 (Figure 68). Beginning with a representation of the media (a TV) spewing forth bile, the bildung-cartoon depicted the protagonist's journey from indifference to State violence and injustice, and on to a willingness to make a difference by joining Sinn Féin ("622112 Hallo Is that the Sinn Féin office?"). A similar popular cultural motif was also used in the 1989 local election mural "Fight back," in which a ballot box fell on the head of a British paratrooper ("Vote Sinn Fein") (Figure 69, see Fulcrum). But after the dropping of abstentionism in 1986 (initially in relation to the Dublin parliament), the dual policy of electoralism and war was under pressure as electoral support for Sinn Féin depended at least in part on IRA activity (Moloney 2007: 389–390). The electoral results in 1989, for example, were disastrous for Sinn Féin, partly as a result of concern in their constituency about the level and nature of IRA violence (including the Enniskillen bombing in 1987 and "the killing of the corporals" in 1988). Combined with which, tangible political progress appeared to be minimal for republicans, indeed the British government passed a draconian broadcasting ban in 1988 which effectively censored their point of view (Figure 70, see Fulcrum). Yet behind the scenes, even at this desperate, low point in the war, there were significant moves, including (from 1987) meetings between Sinn Féin's Gerry Adams and John Hume, the leader of the Social Democratic and Labour Party (SDLP, the largest constitutional nationalist party) (Moloney 2007: 277–283). And as later became clear, despite their public proclamations, republicans and the British government were also engaged in secret negotiations (English 2003: 267–269). This was the beginning of the long, complex, and often torturous process towards peace, which was eventually

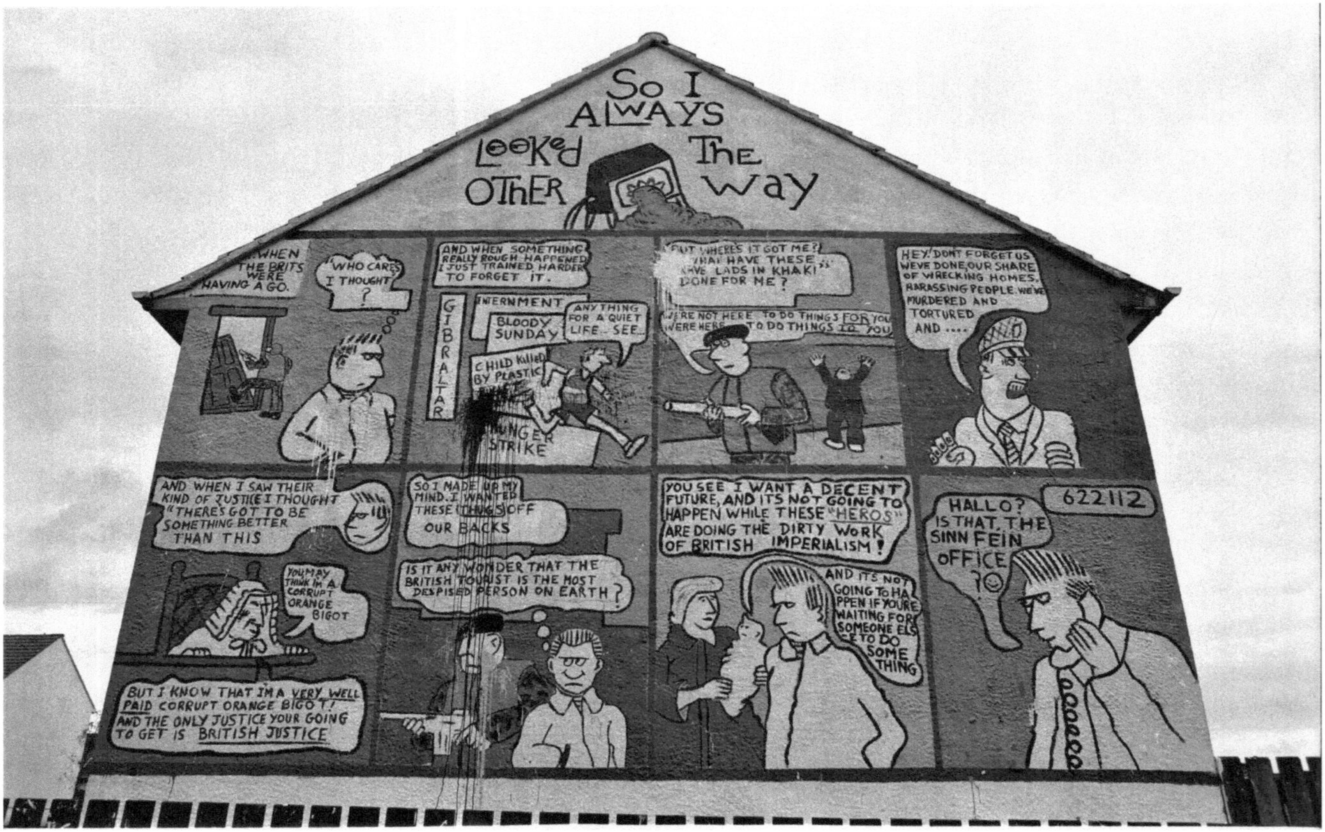

FIGURE 68 I always looked the other way, Whiterock Road, Ballymurphy, West Belfast, 1988. Photo by Tony Crowley.

to stretch out over decades. And as ever, the walls indicated the shift in the structure of feeling that was taking place.[17] In a mural initially painted in Springhill in 1989, but reproduced on the Whiterock Road, and again inspired by a Cormac cartoon (which in turn derived from an image taken from Paris 68), Mo Chara encouraged his audience to "Oppose censorship' by voting for the Sinn Féin candidate in the local elections (Figure 71). The form of the mural signified a new message; a republican head, censored by a Union Jack gag, takes the gag off and is allowed to speak; its message is peace (in the form of a dove rather than Bobby Sands's lark). But it took a while to get there; the momentous first ceasefire took place in 1994 when peace, at least temporarily, broke out.

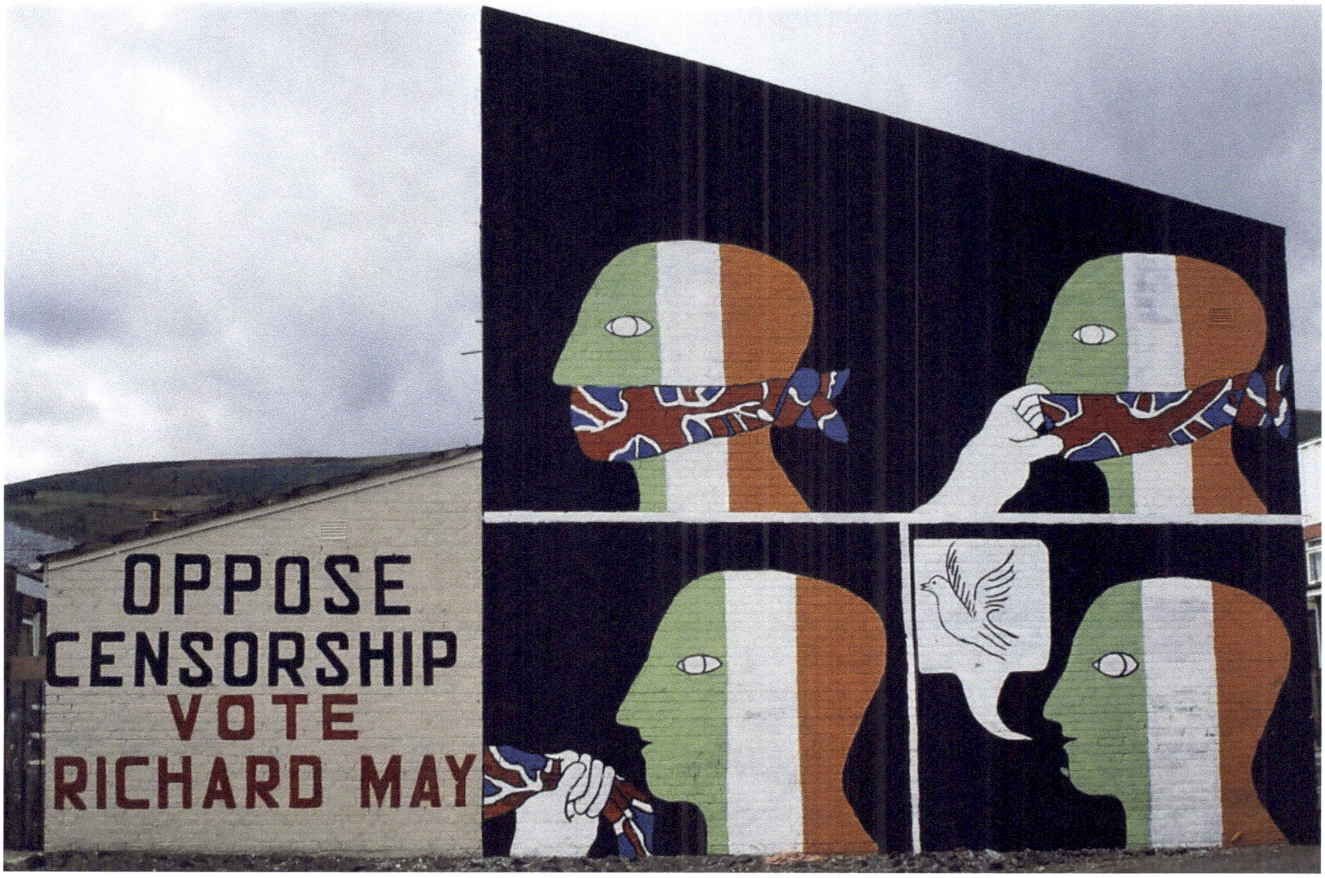

FIGURE 71 Oppose censorship, Springhill Drive, Ballymurphy, West Belfast, 1988. Photo by Tony Crowley.

CHAPTER 3

Renewal of a Tradition: The Re-emergence of Loyalist Muralism 1982–1993

To access all images referenced in this chapter, please visit the open access version on Fulcrum at https://doi.org/10.3998/mpub.14527058.

> Some of these ex-prisoners are painting new Orange Order banners and it is now only a matter of time before their efforts begin to appear on gable walls on behalf of loyalist prisoners. (Redpath 1983: 21)

1. A NEW IMPETUS

It was argued in chapter one that loyalist muralism declined during the 1970s; indeed, as noted earlier, by the early 1980s, one loyalist community worker described it as "a dying art" (Redpath 1983: 20). "Gone," he asserted,

> are the days when a venerable member of the neighbourhood would stretch himself to paint King Billy on his white horse at the end of the street. Gone even are the days when the painting would be touched up as every 12th July approached. A few such painters still exist in Derry and the Donegall Road, but they are the exception. Any genuine wall painting of the last ten years, around the Shankill for example, have tended to be simply Ulster flags or Union Jacks and have not contained any of the details or visual impact of their predecessors. (20)

Claims as to the death of loyalist muralism were, however, over-played and as Redpath observed, the practice persisted in specific areas. In Londonderry, for example, the tradition of loyalist muralism in The Fountain area that began with Bobby Jackson (Sr) in 1919 (*Belfast News-Letter* July 14 1919: 11), was maintained in the family across three generations. Central to local identity (The Fountain is a loyalist enclave on the predominantly nationalist west bank of the Foyle), the Jackson mural of King Billy was relocated in the 1970s by the Northern Ireland Housing Executive during redevelopment of the area (this involved the re-building of the wall on which the mural was painted). Later, in the 1990s, when that wall itself became dilapidated, a "Bobby Jackson Memorial" was instituted, on which, during the loyalist parade season, a version of the original image of King Billy and the lifting of the Siege of Derry was exhibited (Rolston 1998: ii), a practice that continues today (Figure 1, see Fulcrum). Likewise, Belfast's oldest extant mural, also an image of King Billy, stood on the Donegall Road/ Rockland Street; first painted in the 1920s, though re-designed in the 1960s, the mural was retouched annually before being destroyed by fire in the 1980s (Rolston 1991: 24) (Figure 2).

The image of King Billy remained as an icon that served as a reminder of the historical events of 1688–1691 and functioned as a metonym for Protestant Ascendancy; it was central to the cultural and political hegemony of unionism. But if, as Edmund Burke somewhat inaccurately observed, "the [Glorious] Revolution was made to preserve our *antient* indisputable laws and liberties, and that *antient* constitution of government which is our only security for law and liberty" (Burke 2009: 31, emphasis in original), confidence in the religio-social order that had

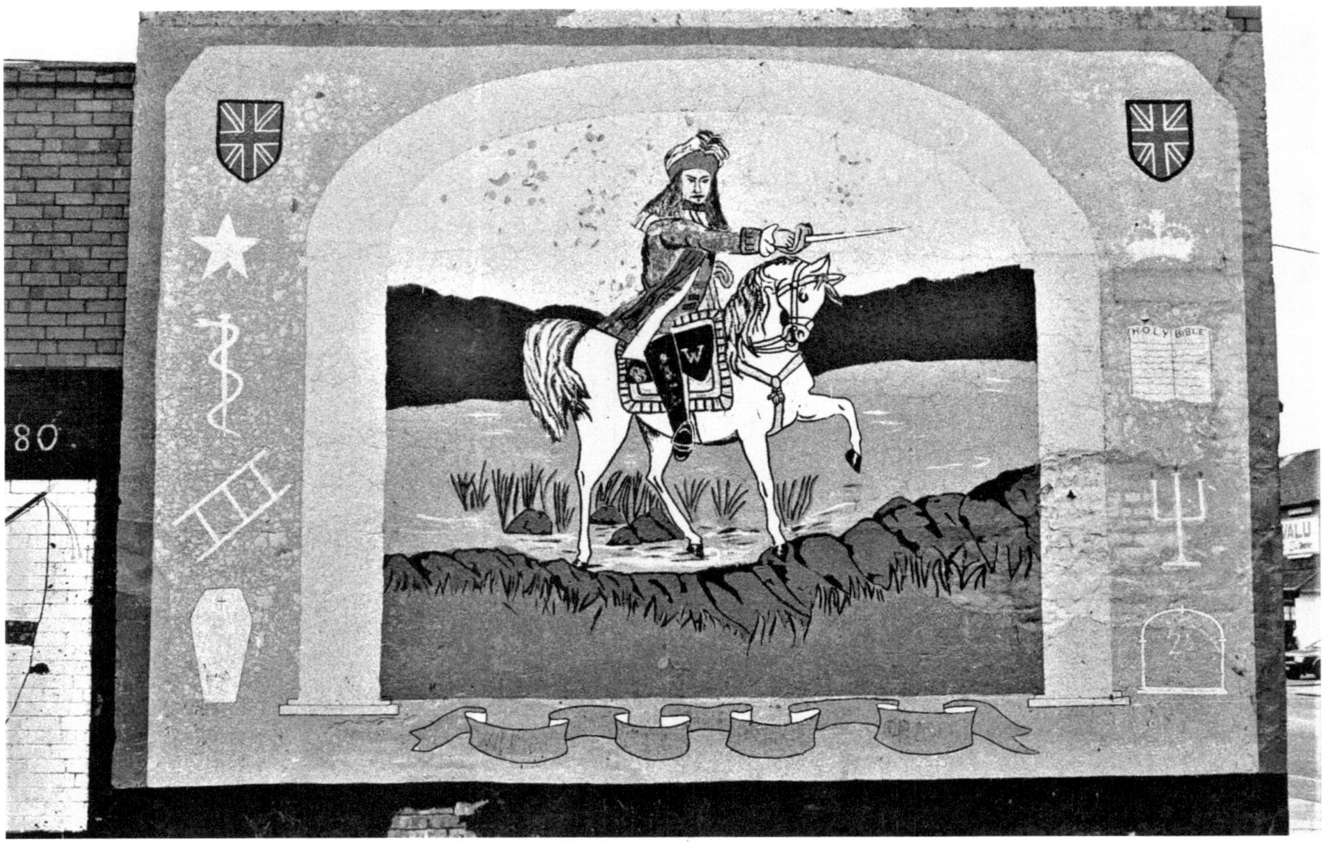

FIGURE 2 King Billy on the wall, Rockland Street, The Village, South Belfast, 1980. Photo by Tony Crowley.

been facilitated by the Revolution, and imposed in Northern Ireland since Partition, waned among unionists and loyalists in the 1980s.[1] What amounts effectively to a cultural and political shift was captured on the walls, a point made by Redpath in his observation that the focus of loyalist muralism had changed from King Billy to "Ulster flags or Union Jacks" that lacked the visual impact of earlier gable paintings (Redpath 1983: 20).[2] The causes of unionist and loyalist anxiety will be considered later in this chapter, but notwithstanding Redpath's sober assessment of the current state of affairs, it is worth citing Redpath's prediction for the future of loyalist street art:

> A new impetus for genuine loyalist art has come from the Kesh. Social clubs and many people's homes proudly display the efforts of their members or relatives who are "inside". Sometimes as framed painting, and often on mirrors these efforts generally reflect the troubles, with statements of support for various paramilitary organisations and paintings of weapons, loyalist symbols or loyalist paramilitary leaders, sometimes "in memorium". This expression is now being felt in the community as prisoners having served their sentences are released. Already some of these ex-prisoners are painting new Orange Order banners and it is now only a matter of time before their efforts begin to appear on gable walls on behalf of loyalist prisoners (21).

To illustrate the point, the article included a photograph of a UVF painting made in the prison, which featured a paramilitary with pistol facing the viewer, eagles either side (though the eagles were more commonly associated with the UVF-affiliated RHC), "1975" and a sash marked with "Ulster Volunteer Force." The bottom of the image features the oval UVF crest dating from 1912—"UVF For God and Ulster" around a Red Hand—flanked by the Union Jack, the Northern Ireland flag, and two rifles.

As noted in the previous chapter, murals were a feature of prison life for republicans in the 1970s, and the same is true of their loyalist counterparts. In two fascinating accounts, based on visits to the prison in 1997, Rolston gives an important insight into prison murals at that time (Rolston 2013; Rolston 2014). But he also comments on the first generation of murals within Long Kesh (before its reconstitution as the Maze prison), specifically UVF murals:

> During the 1970s, before the H Blocks were built, prisoners were held in "cages", Nissen huts from World War II. Each of the groups painted murals, usually on boards, which were displayed in the "cages". Most of these murals were not photographed or the photographs seem not to have survived. The exception is the murals of the UVF. They differ markedly from the UVF murals of the 1990s in the H Blocks. There are references to World War I and the role of the 36th Ulster Division and to the prior Home Rule crisis. There are also memorials to dead comrades. But among the other themes are images which would not have been out of place in a Northern Ireland Tourist Board or even an Irish Tourist Board brochure. (Rolston 2019)[3]

Rolston's photographs of the UVF prison murals record images such as the insignia of the UVF and the 36th Ulster Regiment, a scene from the trenches, a memorial to Edward Carson, the motorized division of the UVF in 1914, a memorial to a UVF member who died in prison, Belfast City Hall (with Northern Ireland flag), a woman spinning outside a traditional cottage (possibly a representation of Dan Winter's cottage near Loughall—the birthplace of the Orange Order), and a snowy prison scene.[4]

A more detailed "insider" account of loyalist prison murals is rendered in *Transcendental Art: A Troubles Archive Essay* (2011) by Billy Hutchinson, a UVF prisoner and one-time leader of the PUP (the political party often associated with the UVF).[5] In the essay, Hutchinson draws attention to the political and cultural leadership of Gusty Spence, Officer Commanding of the UVF in the prison and later an important figure within political loyalism (Spence was originally jailed in 1966 for one of the first murders committed by the newly formed UVF) (Cusack and McDonald 1997: 9–14). Spence imposed a disciplinary regime on UVF prisoners which included an educational component with an emphasis on various types of cultural activity, ranging from handicrafts to creative writing and, crucially, murals.

> Spence's notion of cultural expression through art was rooted in the work of the famous Shankill Road artist, William Conor. Conor, who was known as the "People's Artist" for his expression of life in Ulster society, lived for a long time in the area of Crumlin Road Gaol. Spence was inspired by the works of Conor and by the artistic elite who revered his work for the artistic expression of life in our society in peace and war. Consequently, he had murals painted on the cubicle walls inside the huts in each of the Ulster Volunteer Force (UVF)/Red Hand Commando (RHC) compounds, as a matter of pride in our heritage, not just decoration. These murals were designed to represent our past, present and future, as well as our political expression about our country. Many represented the reality of life within the loyalist community: the poverty; the smudge-face labourers in their cloth caps who trudged home from the factories; a pawn shop on the Old Lodge Road, close to the birthplace of Conor. Even power and ambition found their way onto our walls: Stormont and City Hall; Belfast City Centre with the old red double-decker buses from the '60s, also adorned the walls of our illustrious Art Gallery. (Hutchinson 2011: 1–2)[6]

Evidently the pride in heritage also extended to military and paramilitary history:

> Our military history and traditions provided additional inspiration. All the huts housing UVF/RHC volunteers were named after Battle Honours of the 36th Ulster Division. When I moved to St Quentin in compound 21, the mural was a 1913 UVF depiction of opposition to Home Rule. We were surrounded by art telling the stories of our culture and these influences formed the art gallery in which we lived. (2)

Hutchinson's preferred image bore political significance and revealed an important stance towards history:

> My favourite mural was one inspired by the British anti-war poet, Siegfried Sassoon. *Suicide in the Trenches* depicts a UVF volunteer split down the middle by a bolt of lightning. Half of him depicts a 36th Ulster Division soldier under heavy fire in a rainsoaked WW1 trench. The other half shows a '70s volunteer incarcerated behind barbed wire and over-shadowed by watch towers. Sassoon's poem was emblazoned underneath.
>
> You smug-faced crowds with kindling eye
> Who cheer when soldier lads march by
> Sneak home and pray you'll never know
> The hell where youth and laughter go. (2)[7]

The forging of cultural memory through the everyday linkage of past and present (Conor's mural with that title, held at the Ulster Museum, appears on the cover of Hutchinson's pamphlet) was an important element in UVF prison life. Indeed the past as present trope was central to the political project of working-class loyalism espoused by Spence and his followers in the PUP. For Spence, as Hutchinson concludes,

> taught us to argue our story by using any methods of expression possible, which included narratives in writing and painting in the same way that William Conor expressed working-class life in his drawings and paintings. It was Conor's influence on Spence that paved the way for our depiction of the life of Ulster Society in a country not just divided by class but also by religion and the politics of identity. All of the aforementioned was captured in the paintings in Long Kesh, not primarily for the aesthetics but for the narrative of the loyalist place in history. (3)

Hutchinson's account of the centrality of the prison murals to the loyalist historical narrative is central to an understanding of the development of muralism in general. For as with republican muralism, it is clear that prison experience shaped and influenced both the nature and function of the loyalist works. Indeed in some instances, murals that had appeared within the prison were reproduced on the walls of loyalist areas. A version of Hutchinson's favourite "lightning" mural, for example, with its representation of the past and present of loyalism, was painted on the wall of the Orange Cross Club on Craven Street, Lower Shankill, to commemorate the 70th anniversary of the Battle of the Somme in 1986 (Rolston 1991: 33). And the prison mural of the motorized division of the UVF (probably the work in compound 21 to which Hutchinson refers above), appeared on Spier's Place, the Lower Shankill, in 1987, to commemorate the 75th anniversary of the founding of the UVF (Figure 3). Spence's interest in Conor was also marked much later, in a symbolic act of effacement, when a large UVF mural, at the corner of Northumberland Street and the Shankill Road (Figure 4, see Fulcrum), was replaced by an artwork, "Conor's Corner," celebrating the artist (Figure 5, see Fulcrum) (Figure 6, see Fulcrum). From one perspective, this act of erasure is an example of intra-loyalist (UVF) dialogue, though it is also intended to demonstrate political change to an external audience. But the location of the original mural was politically symbolic and thus also an example of inter-loyalist discourse. Northumberland Street roughly demarcated UVF territory (Mid and Upper Shankill) from that of its rival loyalist paramilitary organization, the UDA (whose provenance is the Lower Shankill). Though that border is now less significant than it was, it was violently policed during the loyalist feud of 2000.

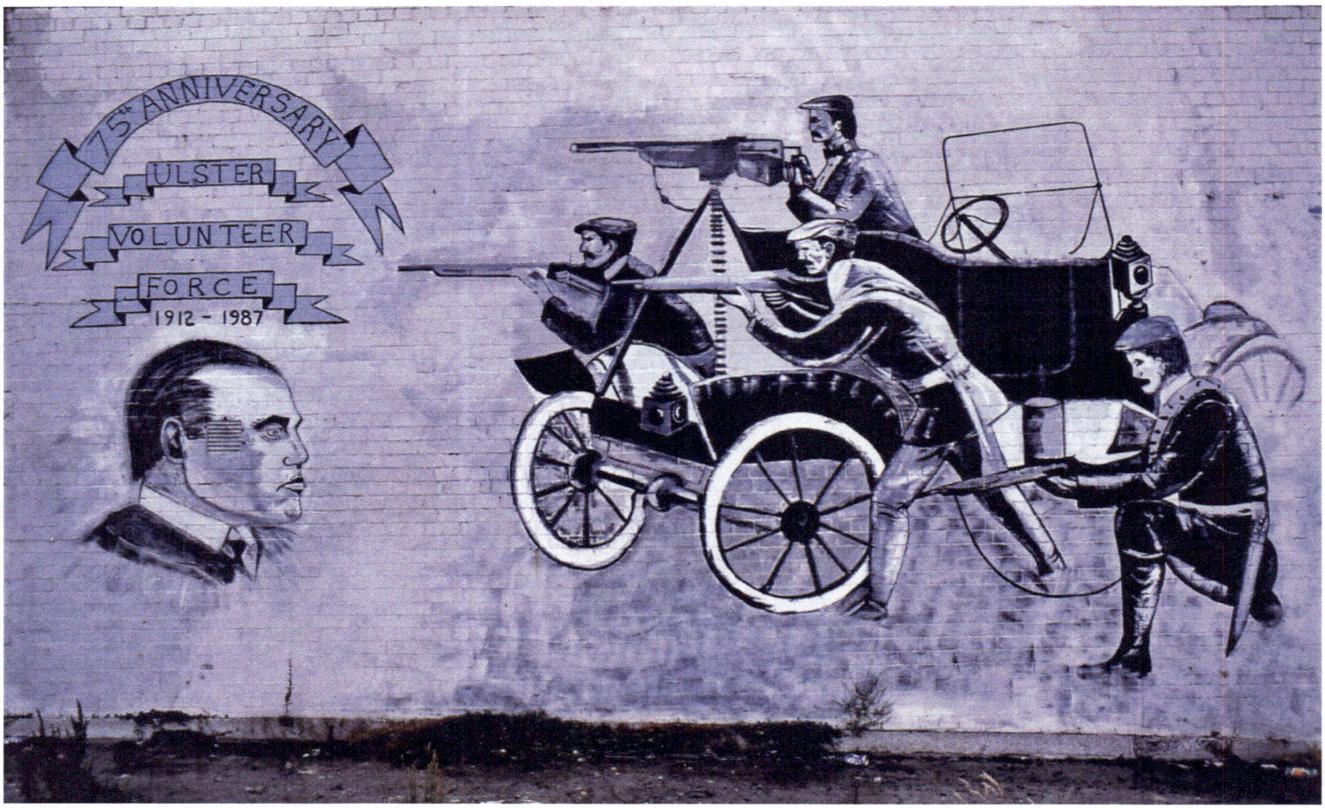

FIGURE 3 75th anniversary UVF, Spiers Place, Shankill, West Belfast, 1987. Photo by Tony Crowley.

As noted earlier, on the basis of his experience working in the loyalist Shankill area, Redpath observed in 1983 that newly released prisoners were painting new Orange Order banners, and he predicted that the artists would soon be working "on gable walls on behalf of loyalist prisoners" (Redpath 1983: 21). Redpath was right about a resurgence in loyalist muralism, but he was wrong about its focus. For rather than limiting itself solely to the plight of prisoners, the new murals reflected the interests and concerns of working-class loyalism more generally. And, responding to the ingenuity and craft of the republican murals during and after the Hunger Strike, loyalist works moved beyond traditional images (while retaining specific icons such as King Billy). In July 1984, for example, a mural appeared on Orkney Drive, in the Ballykeel I estate in Ballymena (Figure 7, see Fulcrum). Unveiled by Eileen Paisley, the wife of Ian Paisley, the local Unionist MP, and Jim Allister, DUP representative in the doomed Northern Ireland Assembly, the mural consisted of a central shield, with a St Andrews Cross and Red Hand of Ulster, flanked by Northern Ireland flags, underpinned by a banner identifying "Ballykeel." Below the main image was a proclamation: "We will not forsake the blue skies of Ulster, For the grey mists of an Irish Republic" (*Ballymena Observer* July 11 1984: 2).[8]

In his comment on the decline of loyalist muralism in the 1970s, Redpath claimed that Ulster flags and Union Jacks tended to predominate. As is clear from the text-image Ballymena mural, however, the Union Jack itself was not an omnipresent symbol, and this indicates a significant shift within loyalism. For although the iconic date of 1690 is featured in the image, the two flags represented in the mural are those of Scotland and Northern Ireland. The Union Jack is conspicuous by its absence, and it is worth analyzing its omission in this and a number of other murals. The Union Jack in its current form dates from the Act of Union (1801) and the creation of the United Kingdom of Great Britain and Ireland; its form was the red cross of St George (England), bordered in white, on the cross of St Patrick (Ireland), both of which are imposed on the Saltire of St Andrew (Scotland). Before 1801, however, the first form of the Union Jack ("jack" originally meant "a ship's flag"), created in 1606 by order of King James the First of England and Sixth of Scotland, consisted solely of the white-edged cross of St George, with the white cross and blue background of the Scottish Saltire (Wales, as part of the kingdom of England at the time, was not represented). In one sense, then, the absence of the Union Jack can be read as suggesting a symbolic harking back to the pre-Union State, in which the Kingdom of Ireland (constituted in 1542) was subject to "personal union" (which is to say, united with England and Scotland under the person of the British monarch) rather than the formal political union of 1801. After all, the Plantation of Ulster, in which many (though not all) of the Protestant settlers arrived from Scotland, began as a Jacobean project. Thus the absence of the post-1801 Union Jack, and the presence of the Scotland and Northern Ireland flags, invokes the historical links between the Protestant people of both countries (and, implicitly, the conquest of the native Irish under colonial rule). In a more immediate, if not unrelated, sense, however, the exclusion of the Union Jack also serves to signal a deeper though related political concern: loyalist distrust of the British government. The anxiety was expressed at the unveiling of the Ballykeel mural in an attack by Jim Allister on "the enemies of Ulster." Rebuking the IRA and the Dublin government, Allister reserved his fiercest ire for the London executive:

> there is another threat—that is the threat of the British Government which tells us that all is well, but which is working to undermine our constitution. We know of these threats and we know our enemy... Ulster is safe—not because of Government guarantees—but because of the spirit of the Ulster people. (2)

Other "enemies" were more local. "There are those in this estate who do not like the red, white and blue," Allister opined, and "to those people and to everyone else who would betray us, the Ulster loyalists say: no surrender" (2). Political discourse can have practical effects in Northern Ireland (Ian Paisley made an art of it during the Troubles); the painting and unveiling of the Ballykeel mural coincided with the violent eviction of a Catholic family from the estate.[9]

Unionist and loyalist preoccupation with the treacherous tendencies of the British government ran deep and was easily summoned. Dating to the Home Rule Crisis, unionists and loyalists professed loyalty to the Crown, while perennially mistrusting the intentions and actions of Her Majesty's ministers (particularly since the imposition of Direct Rule in 1972). London, so the fear ran, was always liable and indeed eager to sell-out Northern Ireland and its Protestant majority, in order to placate republicans and the government in Dublin. There was little hard evidence for such apprehension, but loyalist anxiety was heightened in the early 1980s by the effects of the republican dual strategy of armed struggle and electoralism after the Hunger Strikes.[10] And again, the murals registered the shifting sentiment in working-class areas. In Percy Street on the Lower Shankill, Belfast, in particular, a miniature art gallery of murals appeared immediately before the July 12th celebrations in 1984 (Figure 8). Paid for by residents, and the work of local man Alan Skillen, the eleven "Shankill murals" (seven large, four small) exemplified a riposte to republican muralism and embodied the political (and military) tendencies of the loyalist working class.

One of the striking features of the "Shankill murals" is their location: Percy Place is a small cul-de-sac off the Shankill Road (the main arterial route through loyalist West Belfast); it is not directly visible from the Shankill, nor from republican West Belfast (no more than 400 yards away). Given their "invisibility" to outsiders, it is clear that the Percy Place murals were not "border markers" (a term often inaccurately used to categorize murals in general), but part of an internal dialogue within unionism and loyalism at this specific historical conjuncture. Unsurprisingly, the set of murals featured the most familiar of loyalist icons, King Billy, seated on his white charger, alone, with the inscription "King William III July 1690" (Figure 9); the inclusion of this image places

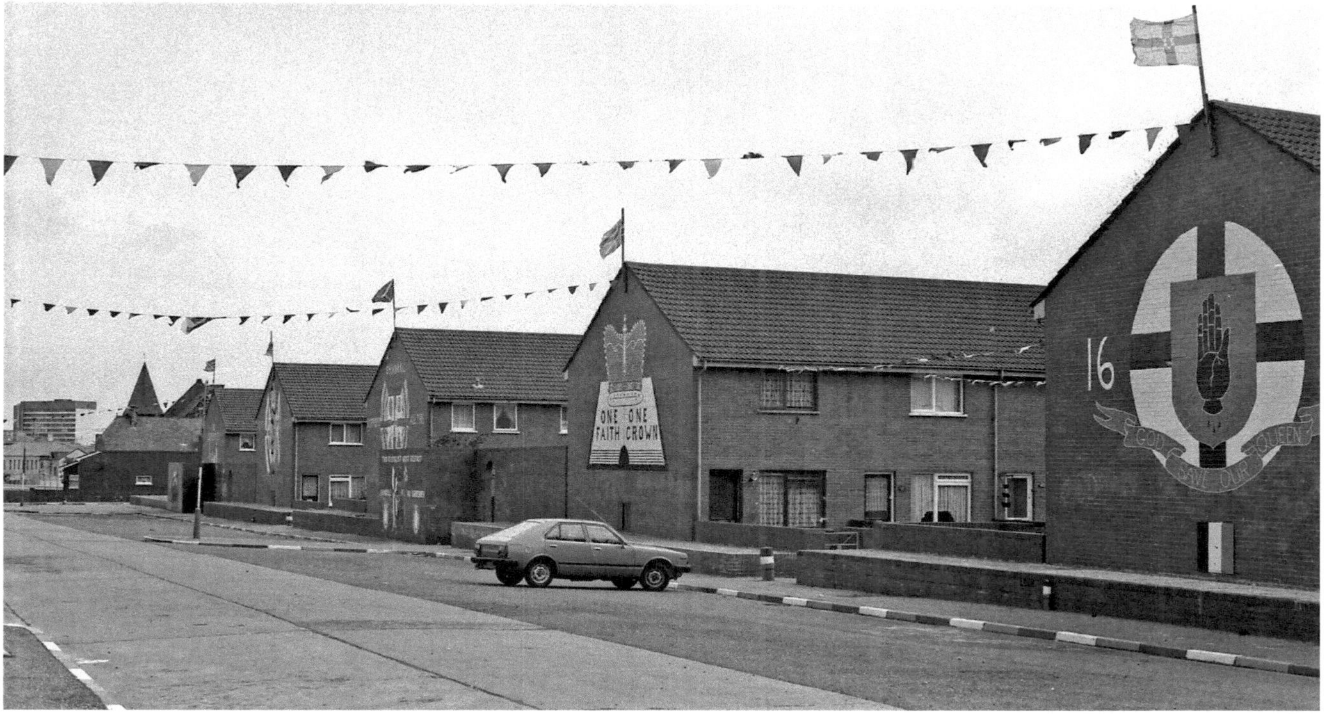

FIGURE 8 The Percy Street gallery, Percy Street, Lower Shankill, West Belfast, 1984. Photo by Tony Crowley.

the murals clearly within unionist tradition. Likewise, the mural that stood next to King Billy featured a Union Jack, in the form of a map of Northern Ireland, with a Red Hand at the center (an allusion to the flag of Northern Ireland), and "Shankill No surrender" atop and below (Figure 10). The geographic indicators in this mural are important; despite the Union Jack, the focus is on Northern Ireland itself, together with the local area (as in the Ballykeel mural, naming the place suggests the right to speak for all). The historical reference, however, in the form of the "No surrender" tag (the words reportedly used to answer King James's demand for the submission of Londonderry in 1689) reiterated the mainstream unionist emphasis of the mural. There is, however, one feature of this mural that made it highly unusual for its time: it contained a reference to the painter's identity—"Skilly" (Alan Skillen).[11] Given the dangers, muralists (republican and loyalist) were reluctant to sign their work until around the mid-1990s.

The other "Shankill murals" were painted on gables across the street and consisted of a number of images that were unionist in allegiance but signaled implicit discontent with the perceived failure of the British State and

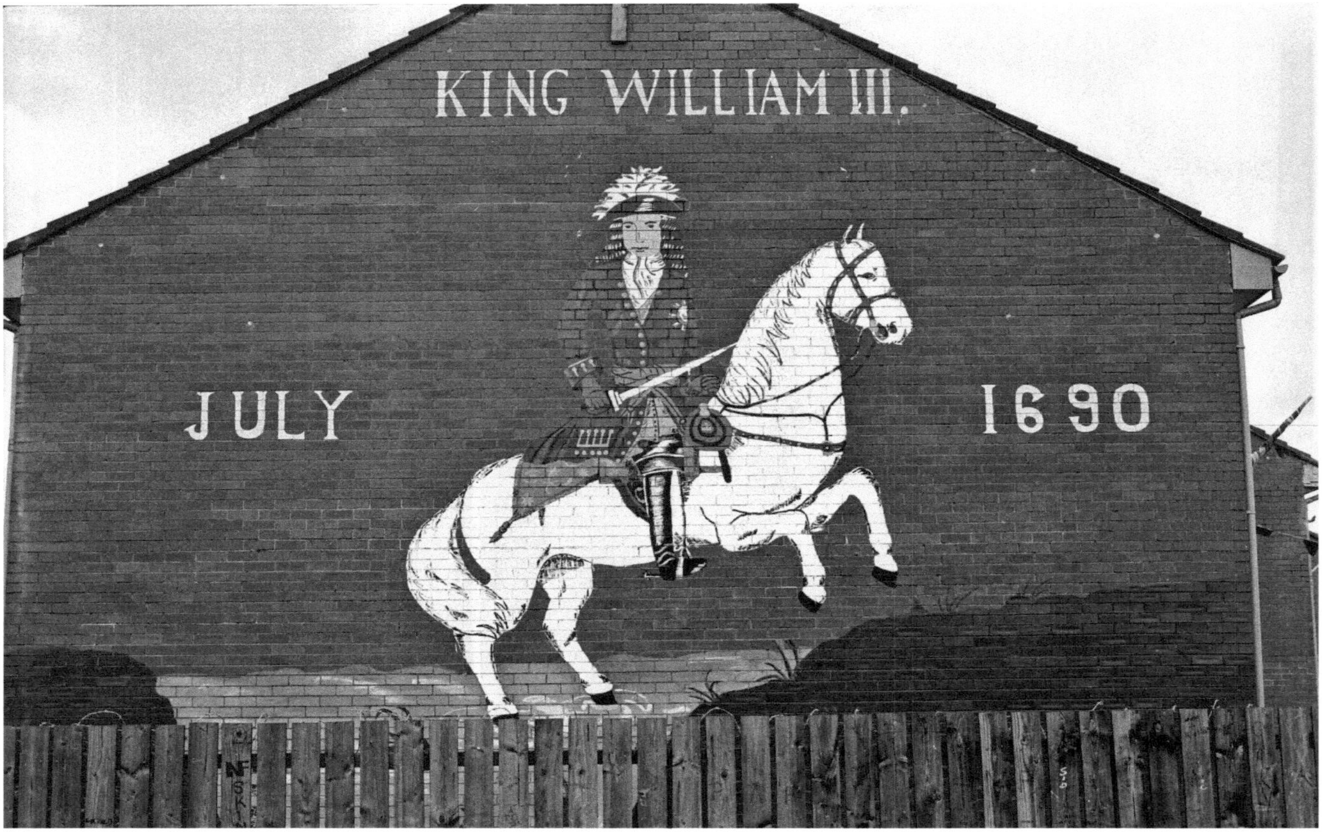

FIGURE 9 King William July 1690, Percy Place, Lower Shankill, West Belfast, 1984, Photo by Tony Crowley.

unionist politicians to address the concerns of the Queen's most loyal subjects. The Union was the focus of the first of these murals, with the Union Jack and Northern Ireland flag flying together, along with "No surrender" and the metonymic "1690." At the center of the mural, however, sat a crest with the Scotland flag and the Red Hand, topped with the Crown (Figure 11, see Fulcrum). The link to Scotland, with its connotation of a common Protestant heritage, is also clear in the next mural in the row (Figure 12, see Fulcrum). Here a Red Hand on a star (the star was a symbol of William's forces) formed the centerpiece; it was set against the flags of Scotland and Northern Ireland, and to dispel any doubt, the message was punctuated for emphasis: "Ulster. Scotland. Together. We. Stand." Notably, the Union Jack was absent and the focus of loyalty was the Crown (depicted here, as in most representations, as the King Edward Crown, worn during the coronation of the British monarch). The same

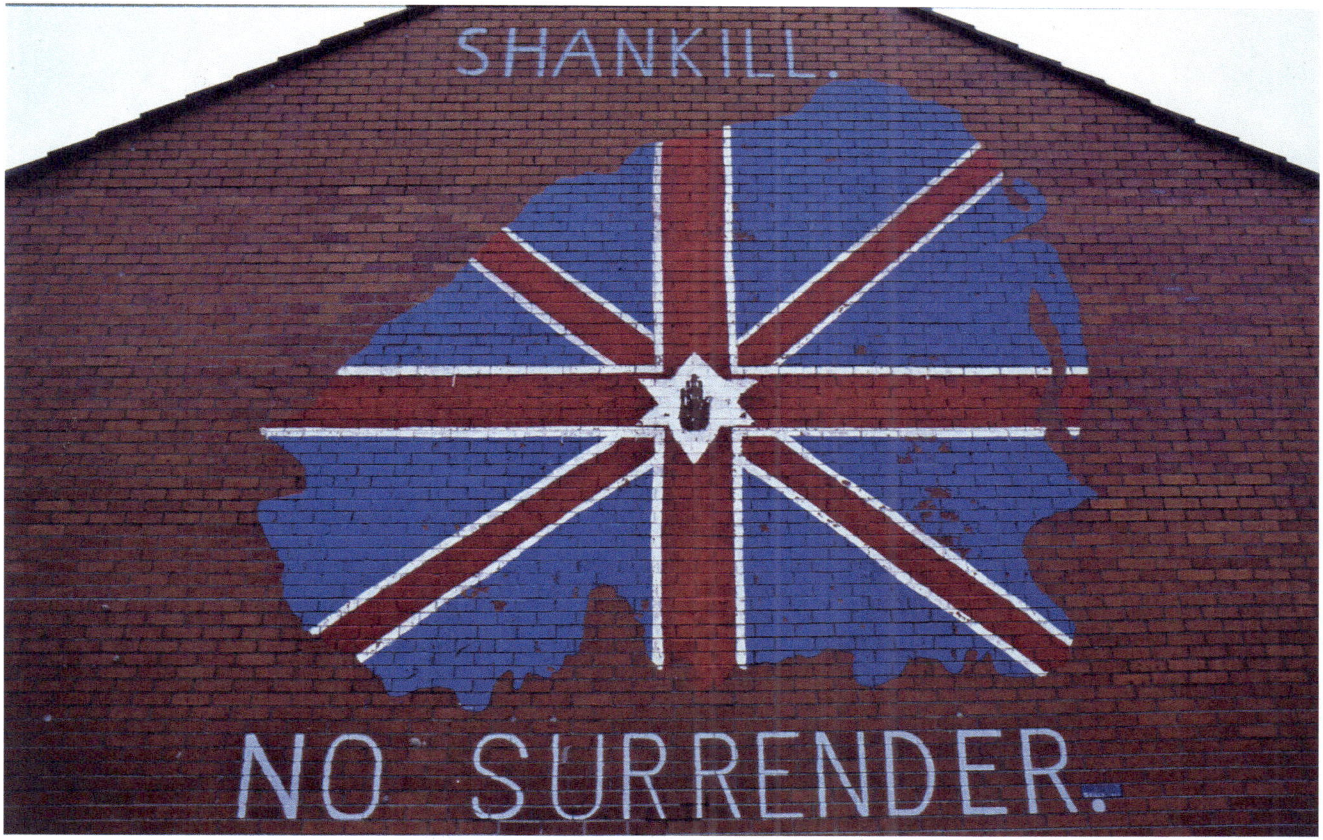

FIGURE 10 Shankill No Surrender, Percy Place, Lower Shankill, West Belfast, 1984. Photo by Tony Crowley.

crown features in another mural—"One Faith One Crown"—sitting atop an open Bible (signifying the importance of Bible study to Protestantism) (Figure 13).[12] There is an interesting distinction in this image between the right to individual understanding (the book is open to interpretation), and the unchallengeable communal allegiance to the Crown—a contrast which highlights the implicit definition of "Protestantism" as in effect simply "not-Catholicism."[13] The allegiance to the Crown was reiterated by "God Save our Queen," a mural incorporating "1690," together with a large Red Hand against a blue shield and the flag of Northern Ireland; the Red Hand in this case was unique among the larger Percy Place murals in featuring dripping blood (Figure 14). Though ostensibly a reference to the Gaelic myth of the Red Hand (in which a chieftain cuts his hand off to reach the Ulster shore first and thus claim it as his own), the blood also inevitably signals the violence of contemporary history, and the

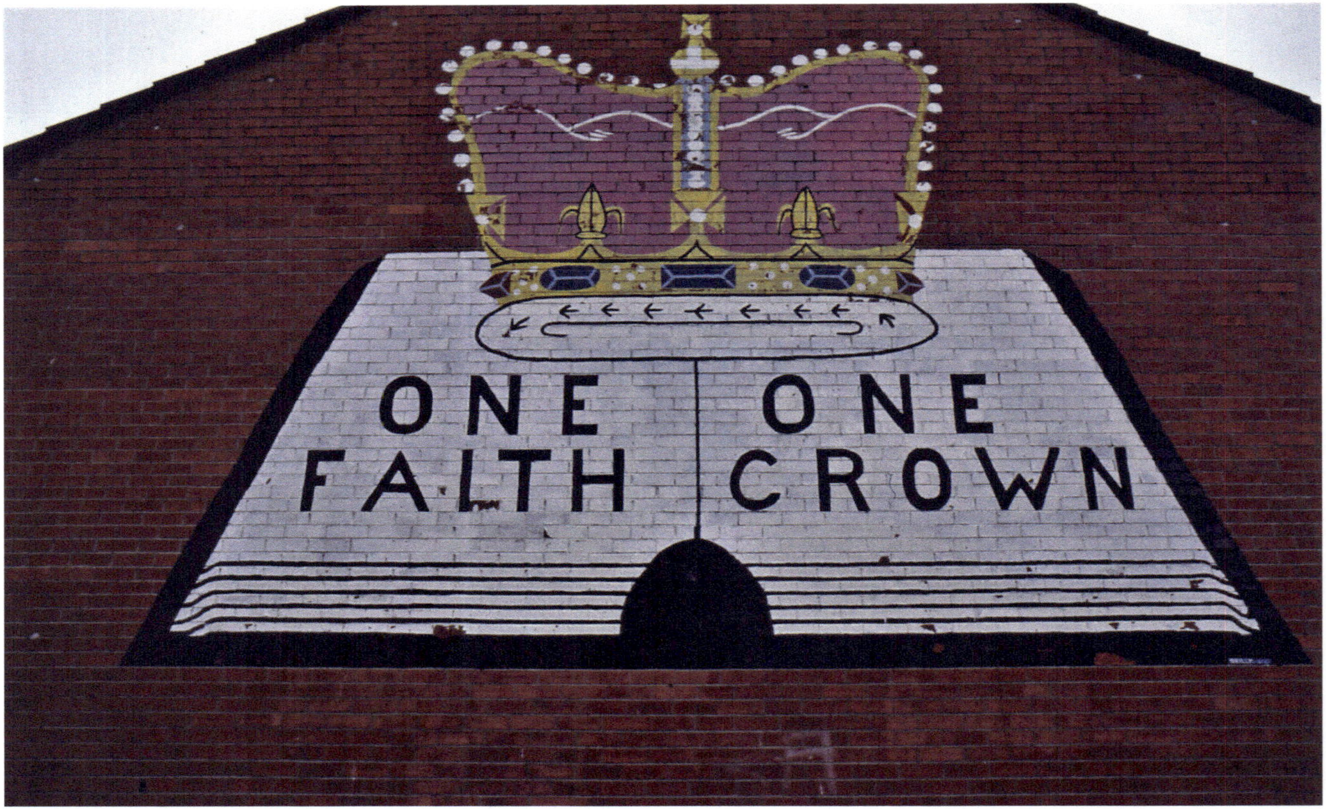

FIGURE 13 One Faith One Crown, Percy Place, Lower Shankill, West Belfast, 1984. Photo by Tony Crowley.

willingness of loyalist paramilitarism to engage in it.[14] This theme was continued in the final large mural of the set, dedicated to loyalist prisoners (Figure 15). Again claiming to speak univocally for the area, "Shankill supports all the loyalist prisoners," this mural included two Union Jacks flanking a central crest that incorporated the insignia of a number of loyalist paramilitary groups, set against the Northern Ireland flag, at the heart of which lies the Red Hand and an outline map of Northern Ireland (the barbed wire above referenced the prison). There were a number of significant features to this mural. Strikingly, it offered support for "all" loyalist prisoners by yoking together the UVF and UDA, as well as the Protestant Action Force (PAF—a cover name for the UVF) and the Young Citizen Volunteers (YCV—the youth organisation of the UVF). This was and remained highly unusual as the different groupings coveted their own identities (and indeed were sometimes engaged in violent feuds).

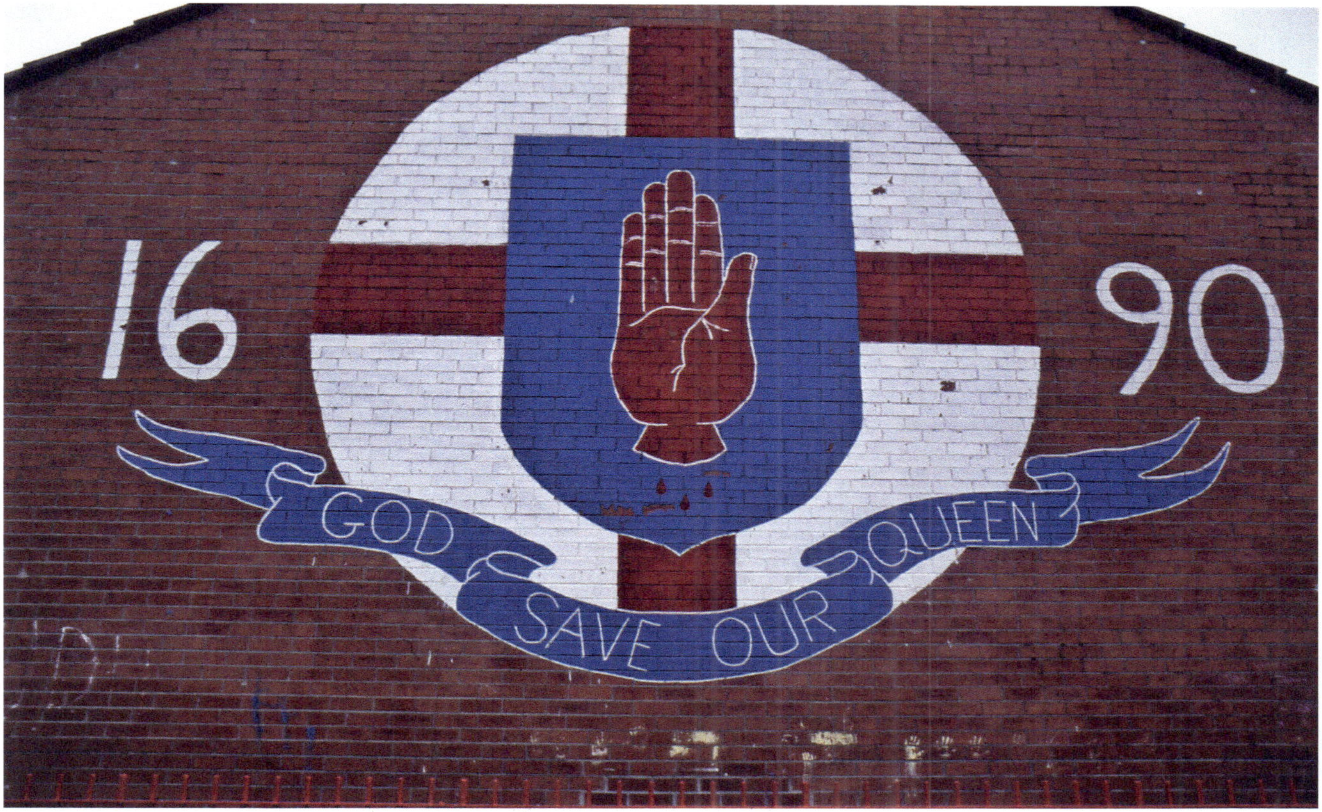

FIGURE 14 God Save our Queen, Percy Place, Lower Shankill, West Belfast, 1984. Photo by Tony Crowley.

More importantly, perhaps, this image addressed directly the issue that the other murals raise only obliquely. For through its composition, the mural at once identified with the British State (through the Union Jacks) but challenged it in asserting the right to use violence (constitutionally the sole prerogative of the State). It thus drew attention to that central conundrum of loyalism (as opposed to unionism more broadly) which centers on the object to which loyalty should be accorded. Evidently, if the State, in the form of its governing executive, imprisons loyalists for their use of violence, then for loyalism the legitimacy of the State is called into question. In which case, as the other murals indicate, loyalty has to be proffered to the Crown itself, rather than the government.

A discussion of the Shankill murals brings to the fore a larger question about the interpretation of the murals of Northern Ireland in general. Which is this: given a set of murals in close proximity, there is a danger that the analysis of any one example will fail to acknowledge the effects achieved by juxtaposition, specifically

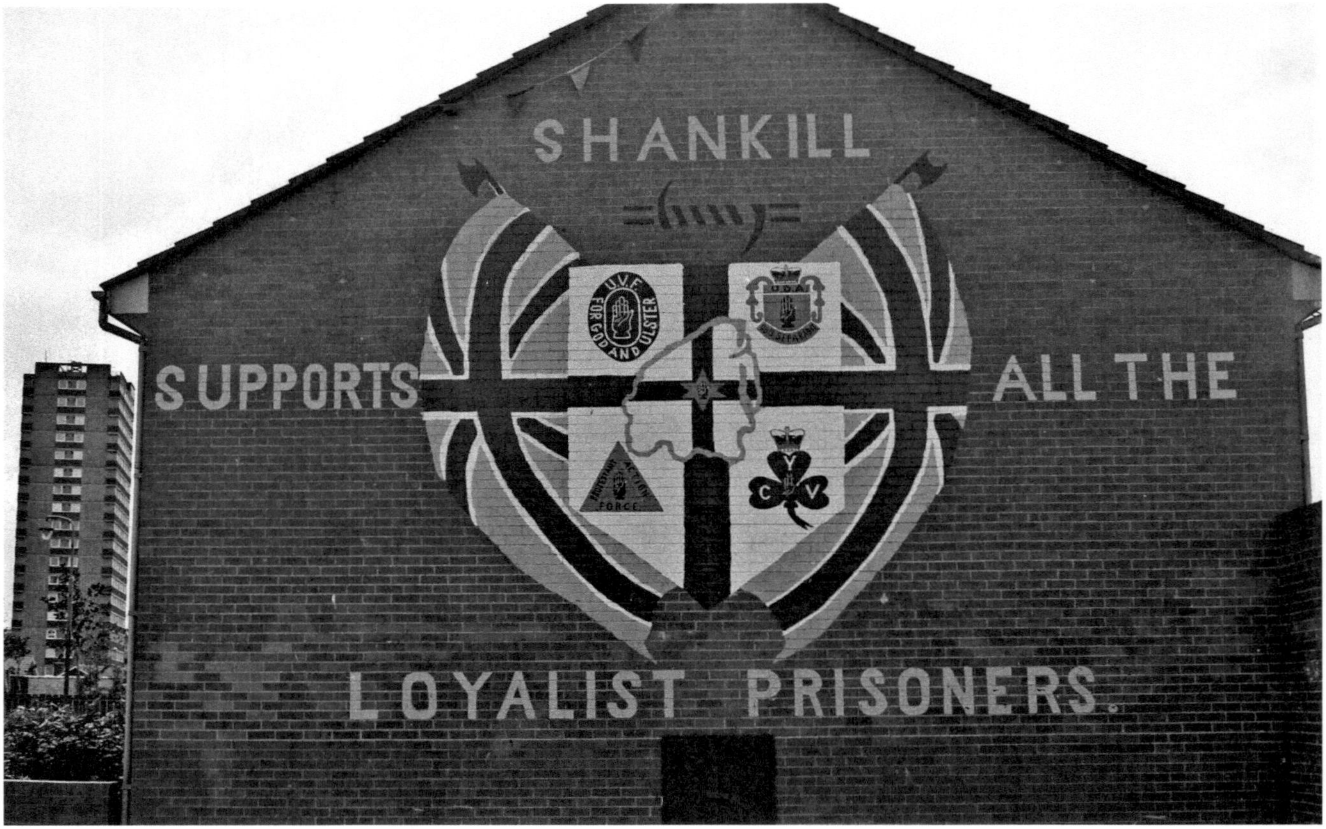

FIGURE 15 Shankill supports all the loyalist prisoners, Percy Place, Lower Shankill, West Belfast, 1984. Photo by Tony Crowley.

the ways in which murals can play off each other. This is in addition to all of the usual caveats about photography—framing, composition, contextualization—that also apply (in my photographs of the Shankill murals, for example, only one includes the tower of Divis Flats—a republican stronghold a short distance away that is clearly visible from Percy Place). But it is the question of juxtaposition that is particularly pertinent in relation to the Shankill murals, since not only were there seven gable murals, there were also four smaller murals that framed the larger murals on one side of the street. Thus "No surrender 1690" sat next to a side-wall image of an armed paramilitary (in full UVF garb), holding a Northern Ireland flag, and set against a representation of Ulster (Figure 16, see Fulcrum). "Ulster. Scotland. United. We. Stand" was accompanied by a UDA "'C' Company" mural, consisting of a UDA crest, "Quis separabit" ("Who shall separate us?"), and the insignia of the Ulster Defence Fighters (UDF) and the Ulster Freedom Fighters (UFF)—cover names for the UDA, together with winged Red Hands (and a misspelled motto—"Sans pure" for "sans peur"—"fearless") (Figure 17, see Fulcrum). By contrast, the loyalist prisoners' mural stood next to a UVF image that proclaimed "This is loyalist West Belfast Shankill No surrender" and focused on an armed paramilitary, with UVF crests ("For God and Ulster"), together with the Ulster banner and a UVF flag (Figure 18). And finally, "God save our Queen" was juxtaposed with a UDA crest, flanked by the flags of Northern Ireland and Scotland, with the Crown (Figure 19, see Fulcrum). The problem is that images of single murals elide the intertextuality of these wall paintings, thereby obscuring the significant fact that this gallery space for the renewed tradition of modern loyalist muralism was the preserve of both of the main loyalist paramilitary organizations.

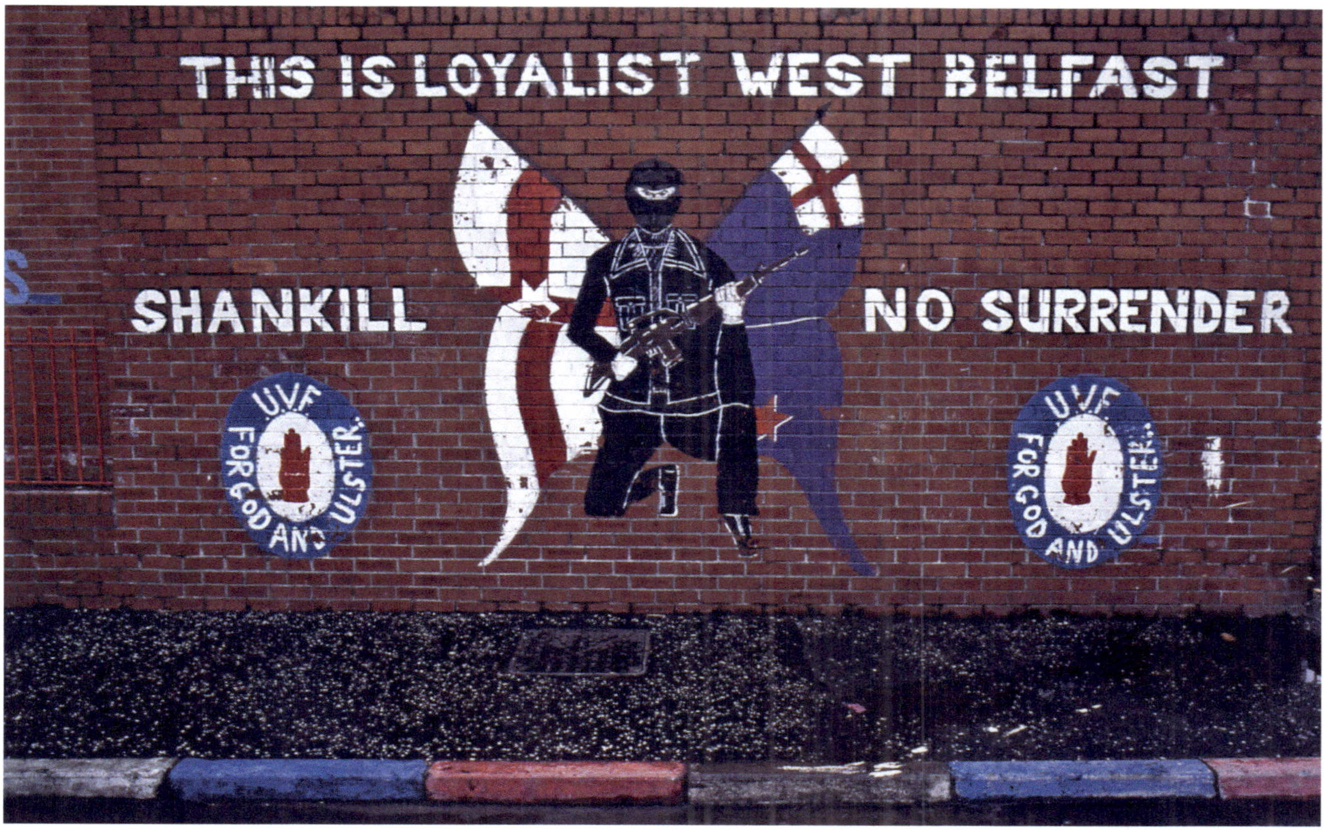

FIGURE 18 This is loyalist West Belfast, Percy Place, Lower Shankill, West Belfast, 1984. Photo by Tony Crowley.

If **figure 19** captures the loyalist paramilitary stance—loyalty to the Crown, but not the government, and Protestant unity—the murals taken together constitute a remarkable collection and point to important social and political developments. Rolston rightly describes them as "an intense representation of loyalist armed struggle that had not been witnessed previously" (Rolston 1991: 40). But they are more than that. As noted above, they capture the paradoxical stance of working-class loyalism in relation to the British State. And, perhaps as importantly, they also "challenge the middle-class values of the political order of Unionism" (Jarman 1997: 220). For the focus here is on the Shankill, and "loyalist West Belfast" more generally (a predominantly working-class area). There are no references to the political parties of unionism—neither the Official Unionist Party (OUP), nor Ian Paisley's DUP—indeed there is no allusion to establishment politics at all. For despite the fact that unionist political parties could rely on the votes of working-class loyalists during elections, those voters were often almost as disillusioned with their own politicians as they were with the treacherous British government. Of course this was not true of all residents of the Shankill and loyalist West Belfast (the murals' claim to speak monologically for all is rhetorical), but for many, the salient political issues of the day were loyalty to the Crown, Protestantism, the fight against the IRA, and prisoners.[15] In addition to remembering the prisoners, however, there was also, as with republicans, the urge to commemorate the dead. A naïve mural on the Crumlin Road, for example, consisting of a Cross topped with a beret (to signal paramilitarism), a Union Jack and Northern Ireland flag, and a Bible and Crown, bore the tag "In memory of those who died 1969–1984." The nature of loyalism, the status of Protestantism, the question of violence, the issue of prisoners, and the memory of the dead were not topics that went away—neither in the murals, nor in the political reality that the murals represented.

1985 was a crucial year in Northern Ireland, not least in the relation to two developments that caused anxiety and provoked an organized response in the unionist and loyalist communities. Both events were taken as signals that the British government had decided to favour nationalism and republicanism over and against those who professed loyalty to the Union. The first was the violent conflict that ensued as a result of the refusal by the police to allow Orange marchers to march down the nationalist Obins Street in Portadown on July 12th. As a result of the police action, the Orange Order finally agreed to re-route the march and in future to return from Drumcree church by way of the nationalist Garvaghy Road (a fateful decision since the new route became the site of bitter conflict between State forces and loyalism in the 1990s). The second and more important development was the *Anglo-Irish Agreement*, signed in November 1985, between the British and Irish governments. The concordat was designed to boost the nationalist Social and Democratic Labour Party (in order to counter the rise of Sinn Féin after the Hunger Strikes), but Article one declared that with regard to the status of Northern Ireland:

The two Governments

(a) affirm that any change in the status of Northern Ireland would only come about with the consent of a majority of "the people of" Northern Ireland;
(b) recognise that the present wish of a majority of "the people of" Northern Ireland is for no change in the status of Northern Ireland;
(c) declare that, if in the future a majority of "the people of" Northern Ireland clearly wish for and formally consent to the establishment of a united Ireland, they will introduce and support in the respective Parliaments legislation to give effect to that wish. (HMSO 1985: 2)

The Union was, for all intents and purposes, copper-bottomed, but crucially, the Agreement also provided for "an Intergovernmental Conference… concerned with Northern Ireland and with relations between the two parts of 'the island of Ireland'," specifically to deal with "political matters; security and related matters; legal matters, including the administration of justice; the promotion of cross-border co-operation" (HMSO 1985: 3). In other words, through the intergovernmental conference, and the establishment of a permanent office at Maryfield, the Irish government was given a direct, albeit limited, say in the affairs of Northern Ireland. The response of the unionist and loyalist community was immediate; within a week more than 100,000 gathered in front of Belfast City Hall to hear Ian Paisley reflect the dominant sentiment of the crowd with the words "Never!-Never!-Never!" (Taylor 2000: 182).

The unionist/loyalist reaction to the *Anglo-Irish Agreement* (an accord which was in retrospect an important step in the search to end the war in Northern Ireland) took many forms. One of the most significant (because of the message it sent rather than its political effectiveness) was the formation of Ulster Resistance in November 1986 at a mass meeting at the Ulster Hall attended by constitutional politicians. The thinking behind the new grouping was explained by Gregory Campbell, a DUP councillor on Londonderry council and later a Westminster MP. He noted that "the logic of the British Government's intentions and their actions, over a period of years, would inevitably lead us into some form of quasi-united Ireland and that what had brought that about was the IRA's military actions." Therefore "the way to stop it would be defensive military actions to try to ensure that the IRA didn't gain the upper hand politically or tactically, but with this moral reservation that they would not resort to the killing of innocent Catholics or murder for the sake of murder" (Taylor 2000: 186–187). In other words, Ulster Resistance would be "a sort of clean-living paramilitary group that would be purely defensive and wouldn't single out innocent Catholics for murder" (186). Campbell's words are striking: an elected representative supported the formation of an armed paramilitary group to take "defensive actions" against the IRA (including, with caveats, murder). Yet his position followed logically from a radical distrust of the British government and the loyalist refusal to recognize the State as the sole legitimate wielder of violence.

A mural that appeared in Redcliffe Parade in East Belfast conveyed the dominant loyalist attitude. It featured a woman in a rural setting with the Union Jack flying behind her; the caption declared "Deserted! Well—I can stand alone" (Figure 20). The provenance of the image is given in the top right corner—"Ulster 1914"—a clue to the fact that the mural is a reproduction of an anti-Home Rule postcard published that year.[16] The invocation of a decisive moment in unionist history is significant, and it draws an implicit parallel between past and present (just as loyalism defied the British government in the past, so it will do the same today). And yet there is a revealing difficulty with the image. For if Ulster (embodied as a countrywoman) has been deserted yet again by the treachery of the British government, then what is to be her fate? She may stand alone, as she did in 1914, and force the government of the United Kingdom to stand by its union with her. Or, in an alternative interpretation, Ulster could "stand alone" by opting for independent status (a policy which the UDA espoused for a time Woods 2006: 69–72). Nevertheless, leaving this important ambiguity aside, perhaps the most important detail of the image is that the woman is armed; rifle in hand, she is prepared to resort to violence to achieve her aims. Given that there had been, up to that point, relatively few representations of women in loyalist murals (and not that many in their republican counterparts), the message was clear: all sections of the community (women and men, rural and urban) will fight for the cause.

To pursue the struggle, it was clear that the new formation of Ulster loyalism would need arms, and to that end Ulster Resistance teamed up with the UVF and the UDA (neither of which could be described as a "clean-living paramilitary group" that would act only defensively and not engage in the killing of innocent Catholics) to arrange a major arms shipment using a Lebanese arms dealer (McDonald and Cusack 2004: 157). The shipment included sophisticated weaponry such as assault rifles, Browning pistols, RPG7 rockets, and fragmentation grenades, to which loyalists previously had restricted access. Though some of this material was lost almost immediately, the remainder meant that loyalist paramilitaries were well equipped for the next phase of their campaign, and they were not shy of advertising the fact on the walls. In Ohio Street, in loyalist West Belfast, for example, a number of murals communicated the threat posed by the newly armed UVF. One mural featured two UVF volunteers in military outfits (including the ubiquitous balaclavas) equipped with a high-powered rifle and a sub-machine gun (Figure 21). Organized by the local UVF unit, "1st Battalion B/Company" (the paramilitary organizations on both sides traditionally adopted the military structures of the British Army), the mural referenced the PAF (a cover name for elements within the UVF), as well as the UVF itself (through crest and flag) and the YCV (founded in 1912 but later the youth wing of the UVF). The YCV flag was notable in this mural in that it carried the names of senior loyalists—Lenny Murphy (the lead figure in the gang of sectarian serial killers, the Shankill butchers), John Bingham, and William (Frenchie) Marchant—all of whom were assassinated by the IRA in the 1980s. The mural thus functions at once as a threat of future action and as a memorial to the dead.

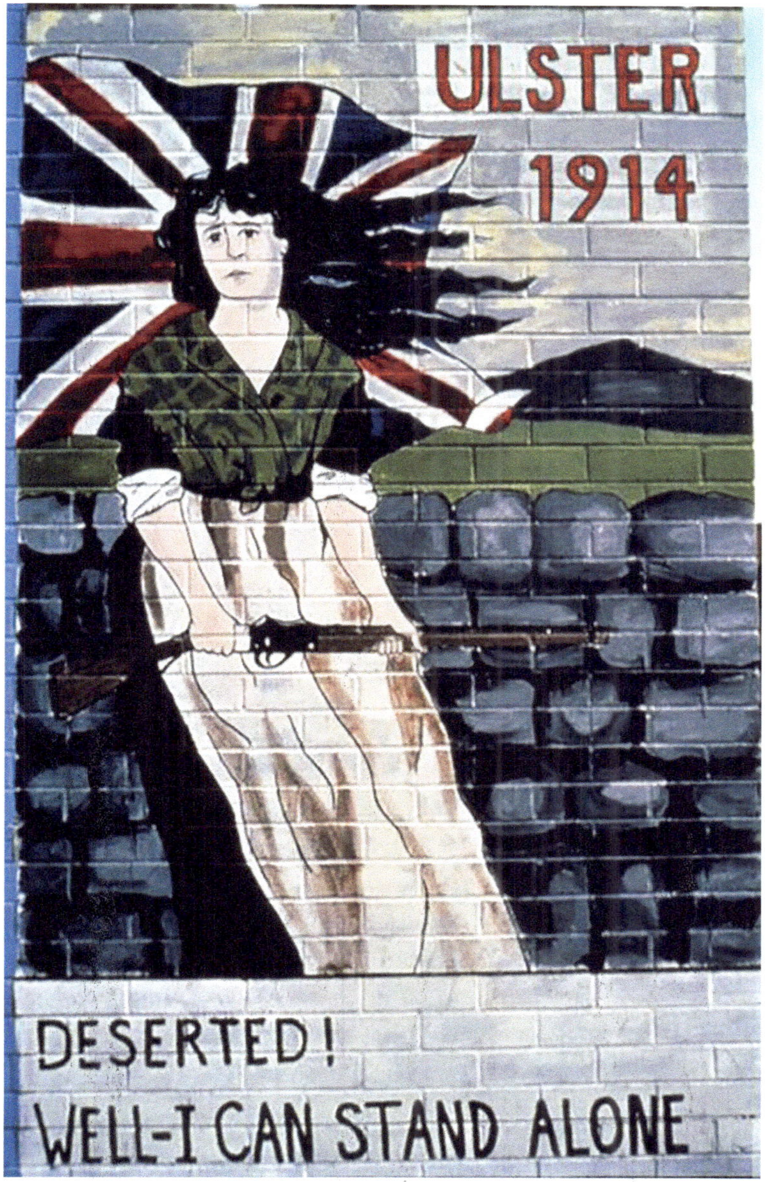

FIGURE 20 Deserted! Redcliffe Parade, East Belfast, 1988. Photo by Tony Crowley.

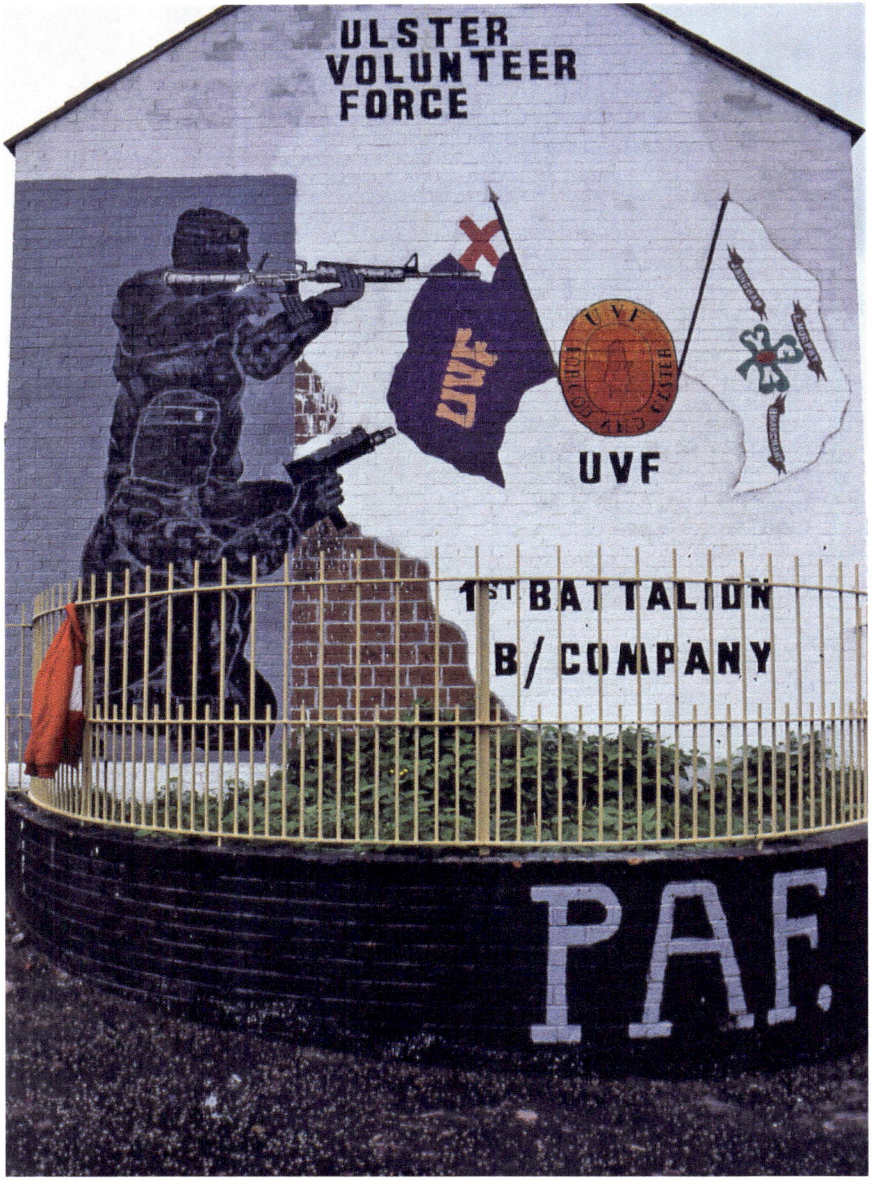

FIGURE 21 UVF PAF, Ohio Street, Woodvale, North Belfast, 1987. Photo by Tony Crowley.

The menace is reinforced by the side-wall mural accompanying the main image. Again using the PAF cover-name, the mural declared that "The UVF reserve the right to strike at republican targets where and when the opportunity arises" (Figure 22, see Fulcrum). A later mural on the same street re-emphasized the significance of the new weaponry that the loyalist paramilitaries had acquired. Set in an urban scene, the image depicted two UVF volunteers with assault rifle and RPG7 rocket launcher and announced " 'The New Era' UVF Active Service Unit Ardoyne 89" (Figure 23, see Fulcrum). Yet the UVF was not the only loyalist paramilitary organization that re-armed and re-structured itself in the 1980s. As a result of a number of internal and external factors (ranging from power struggles to police intelligence successes), the UDA also re-constituted itself in this period as a far more militant organization, and this was reflected in a number of murals (McDonald and Cusack 2004: 171). In Woodvale, North Belfast, for example, the area in which the organization had its origins, a mural sponsored by the William "Bucky" McCullough Memorial Flute Band focused on an automatic rifle with the letters "UFF" (a cover-name for the UDA), barbed wire (to represent prisoners) and a Red Hand, together with paramilitary figures from the UDA and WDA (Woodvale Defence Association—one of the earliest of a number of groups that united to form the UDA); to right and left there were the latest Uzi machine guns (Figure 24, see Fulcrum).

The violence implicit in such murals was realized on the streets as loyalists engaged with the threat posed by republicanism—or specific IRA attacks—by targeting IRA volunteers and Sinn Féin activists. As these attacks became more difficult in the segregated and security-conscious enclaves of Belfast, in particular, the focus turned to rural areas, as a UVF intelligence officer commented: "In Belfast it would have taken a JCB digger to break into certain Provo homes. But in the country it was easier, their houses were larger, harder to protect, and some of them lived in isolated communities" (Cusack and McDonald 1997: 249). This change of tactics explains an otherwise incongruous feature of several loyalist murals in west and north Belfast in the late 1980s: the depiction of loyalist paramilitaries storming across the countryside in full uniform with automatic weapons (Figure 25, see Fulcrum). Such representations were, however, deceptive. Loyalist assassinations in rural areas did not typically involve fire-fights with well-defended redoubts—they were more often than not attacks on unarmed targets (as were republican killings of off-duty police or army reservists). In addition to which, although loyalists did indeed "bring the war to the IRA" in the late 1980s and early 1990s (Taylor 2000: 210), largely in and around Belfast, it remained the case that in the absence of active republicans as accessible targets, loyalists resorted to the tactic of random sectarian assassination as a way of terrorizing the Catholic, nationalist, and republican community.[17] And as the walls indicated, sectarian sentiment was never far from the surface in loyalist areas. In Rathcoole, just north of Belfast, for example, a mural at the bottom of the flats declared the political allegiance of the area—"Loyalist Rathcoole"—and featured a UVF crest, flanked by the Union Jack and Northern Ireland flag; it also depicted a pair of red devils, bearing the flags of Scotland and Northern Ireland, with "KAI" between them ("KAI" stood for "Kill All Irish") (Figure 26, see Fulcrum). In Belfast itself, the Peace Line, dividing the Lower Shankill from the Lower Falls, bore a similar message: "UVF Kill all Taigs" ("Taig" is an offensive term for a Catholic derived from the Irish name "Tadhg") (Figure 27, see Fulcrum). One notable incident that illustrated the easy slippage from republican to nationalist/Catholic in loyalist discourse and paramilitary activity, was the attack by the UDA gunman Michael Stone on the funeral of the IRA volunteers killed at Gibraltar in 1988. Though his ostensible targets were senior republicans, Stone, using a semi-automatic pistol and fragmentation grenades, killed three people (one of whom was an IRA volunteer) at the cemetery. Stone's single-handed assault on the IRA funeral won him heroic status within loyalism (Figure 28); hailed on the walls, one muralist facetiously awarded him some of the highest honors recognized by the British State by giving him an MBE, OBE, and VC (Figure 29, see Fulcrum).

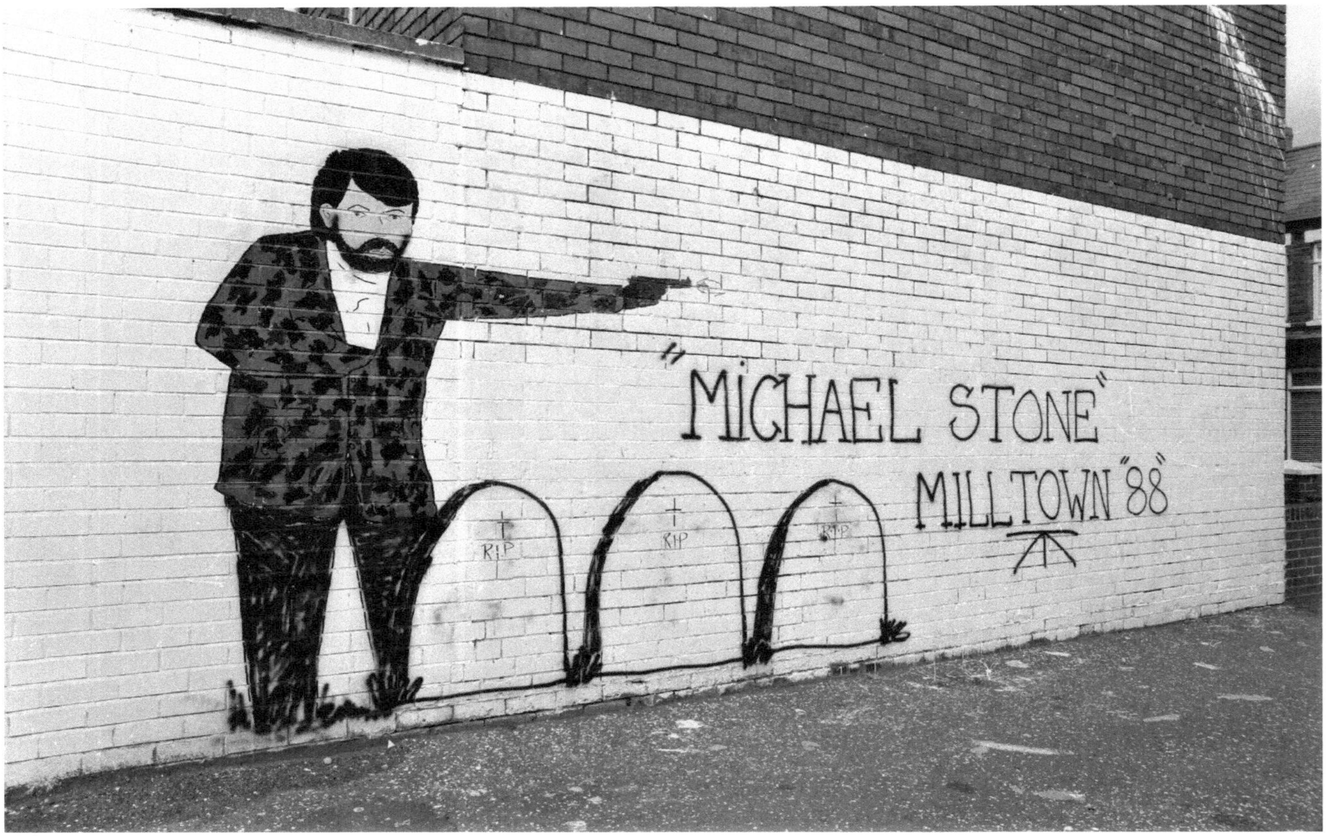

FIGURE 28 Michael Stone, Tavanagh Street, The Village, South Belfast, 1988. Photo by Tony Crowley.

Given the proliferation of loyalist murals in the late 1980s, it is unsurprising that several were of inferior quality. For example, a cartoon-like image of UVF paramilitaries appeared on Rosebank Street, Woodvale, North Belfast, in 1989. Featuring two "blacknecks" (the nickname for UVF volunteers in uniform), the mural was poorly drawn and left apparently unfinished (the right foot of the second figure was missing) (Figure 30, see Fulcrum). Likewise, a mural supporting loyalist prisoners in Stroud Street, Sandy Row, South Belfast, in 1989, was badly executed (it is off-center—a previous attempt alongside it has been scrubbed out) (Figure 31, see Fulcrum). Even in such basic work, however, there was still an element of semiotic complexity. Thus despite the lack of overt identification, the Rosebank image's allegiance to the UVF was clear in the uniform worn by the figures and the use of the slogan "For God and Ulster." And likewise, the Stroud Street mural requires decoding: "LPA" stands for "Loyalist Prisoners' Aid," a prisoners' welfare organization allied with the UDA (unsurprisingly, given that Sandy Row is a UDA stronghold). Not all cartoon murals were poorly achieved. In 1990 Stroud Street also saw an amiable-looking British bulldog (in so far as bulldogs can look amiable) set in an Ulster pith helmet against a Union Jack (Rolston 1992: 21). A more threatening version of the bulldog was found in Granton Park, Tullycarnet, South Belfast, a couple of years later. Dressed in the full regalia of the Tullycarnet Flute Band, the bulldog in this image took the form of Spike, the dog from the Tom and Jerry cartoon series, grabbing hold of a bemused-looking Tom (Figure 32). Again the code has to be unpicked: Tom was dressed in the colors of Celtic Football Club (the Scottish team traditionally supported by Irish nationalists), while Spike, claws at the ready, wore the insignia not simply of the flute band, but also that of the UFF (the clenched red fist on the epaulette). The joke was extended in a mural in the Lower Shankill estate, West Belfast, which appeared in 2000, in which Spike, with Union Jack tee shirt, automatic rifle, and UFF tattoo, chased Jerry (Gerry Adams) in Celtic kit away from Belfast and towards Dublin. Set in the Shankill estate itself, the mural features the local landmarks of the Diamond Jubilee bar (a UDA haunt) and the Divis Tower, and includes intertextual references to other murals (Figure 33, see Fulcrum).[18]

One development that occurred in the late 1980s was the marking of territory by loyalist paramilitary organizations, often within relatively small local areas. Though this was in part directed towards an external audience (residents, people traveling through, and State forces), it was again also part of inter loyalist dialogue. One example of this division of space occurred in the contiguous Village and Sandy Row areas of South Belfast (in total no more than a mile long and half a mile wide). Thus in 1989, in Tavanagh Street, The Village, a mural appeared that featured a number of organizations linked, in one way or another, with the UVF—YCV, PAF, RHC.[19] It was composed in the standard format: paramilitaries and the crests of the relevant organizations, with details of the local group (4th Battalion, South Belfast Brigade) (Figure 34). On Frenchpark Street, another generic mural reiterated the message: "Victory to the UVF," with the flags of Ulster and Scotland, "Rem 1690" and "Loyalist South Belfast" (Figure 35, see Fulcrum). By contrast, on the other side of The Village, the UDA marked the demise of one of its commanders, John McMichael (killed by the IRA in 1987), with a mural on Roden Street, very similar

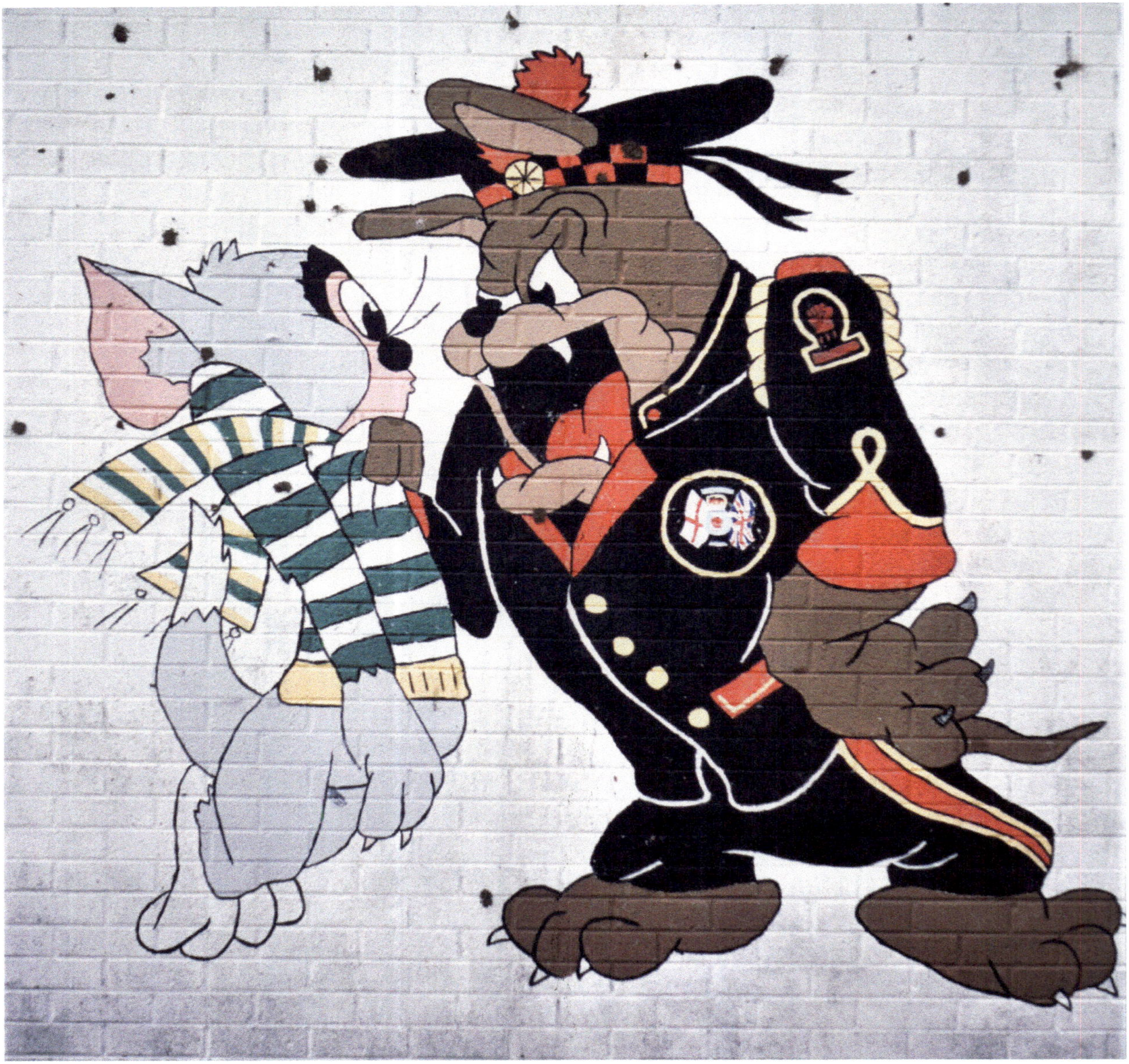

FIGURE 32 Tom and Spike, Granton Park, Tullycarnet, South Belfast, 1992. Photo by Tony Crowley.

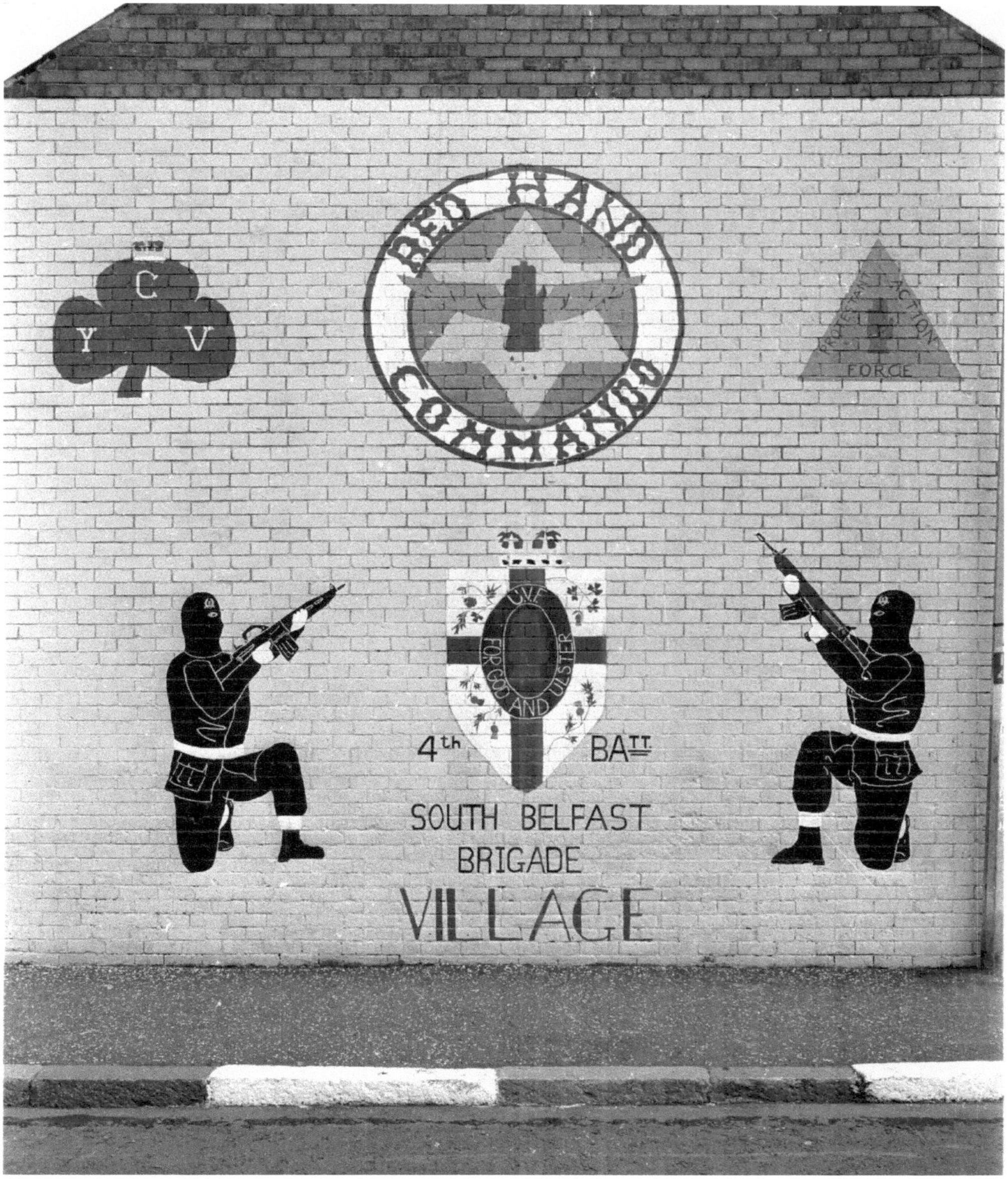

FIGURE 34 Red Hand Commando, Frenchpark Street, South Belfast, 1989. Photo by Tony Crowley.

in composition to the first Village UVF mural discussed above. That is, a UDA crest, with the flags of Scotland and the Union Jack, and the insignia of various organizations linked (again, in one way or another) with the UDA: the Roden Street Defenders flute band, LPA, UFF, and UDF.[20] Dedicated "In memory of John McMichael," the image also referenced the local UDA group ("A" Battalion South Belfast) (Figure 36). It is notable that none of these murals claimed exclusivity within the area (indeed one signaled explicitly that the locale is loyalist rather than the domain of any one paramilitary group). But they did all attempt to stake out control for reasons of recruitment, political status, and financial benefit (primarily through racketeering). There was also a cultural aspect to this specific function of the murals: they often signaled allegiance to a particular flute band (whose provenance might be a matter of a few streets) (Jarman 1997: 222). Thus the Roden Street Defenders image on the McMichael mural lay no more than five streets away from a mural supporting the Pride of The Village flute band (and the RHC) (Figure 37, see Fulcrum), while both stood approximately a mile from another mural that supported the South Belfast Young Conquerors band (and the UVF) on Donegall Pass (Figure 38, see Fulcrum).[21]

Towards the end of the 1980s, loyalist commemoration began to appear on the walls and like its republican counterpart, it took two forms: social and individual. Social memory tended to focus on anniversaries such as the 70th anniversary of the Somme in 1986, the 75th anniversary of the formation of the UVF in 1987 (see **chapter three, figure 3**) or the 36th Ulster Division (Figure 39, see Fulcrum) (which had been commemorated in loyalist murals since just after the First World War). But as ever, memory stretched a long way into the past. For example, the 300th anniversary of the shutting of the gates in the Siege of Derry in 1688 was commemorated in a mural on the Shankill Road (Figure 40). This was a relatively unusual image in the history of loyalist muralism, though it was frequently remembered on Orange Order banners and on loyalist arches that appeared around the 12th of July. Another tricentennial occurred in 1990, and given the iconic status attached to the Williamite victory at the Battle of the Boyne, it was predictably marked in a number of locations with the standard representation of King Billy on a white horse (with or without the death of Schomberg). Again, the quality of these images was variable. Among the best was the mural at Oak Street, Donegall Pass (Figure 41), which featured William, Schomberg, and the blue skies of County Meath.[22] An image on Sandy Row (next to the UDA/UFF mural discussed in the previous paragraph) was similarly impressive; framed as a gallery painting, William sat center-stage, flanked by musketeers (who, interestingly, broke the frame of the work) (Rolston 1998: 1). If this rupture signified the way that the past continues to intrude onto the present, the theme was reiterated in a figurative commemoration of 1690 on Sandy Row that featured the Londonderry coat of arms surrounded by the flags of Ulster and Scotland (the Union Jack was notably absent), with the tag "Londonderry/Under siege No surrender 1690 1990" (Figure 42, see Fulcrum). Other images were not quite so well achieved; on York Road, Tigers Bay, North Belfast, a cartoonish King Billy sat underneath the imperative "Rem 1690" (Figure 43, see Fulcrum).

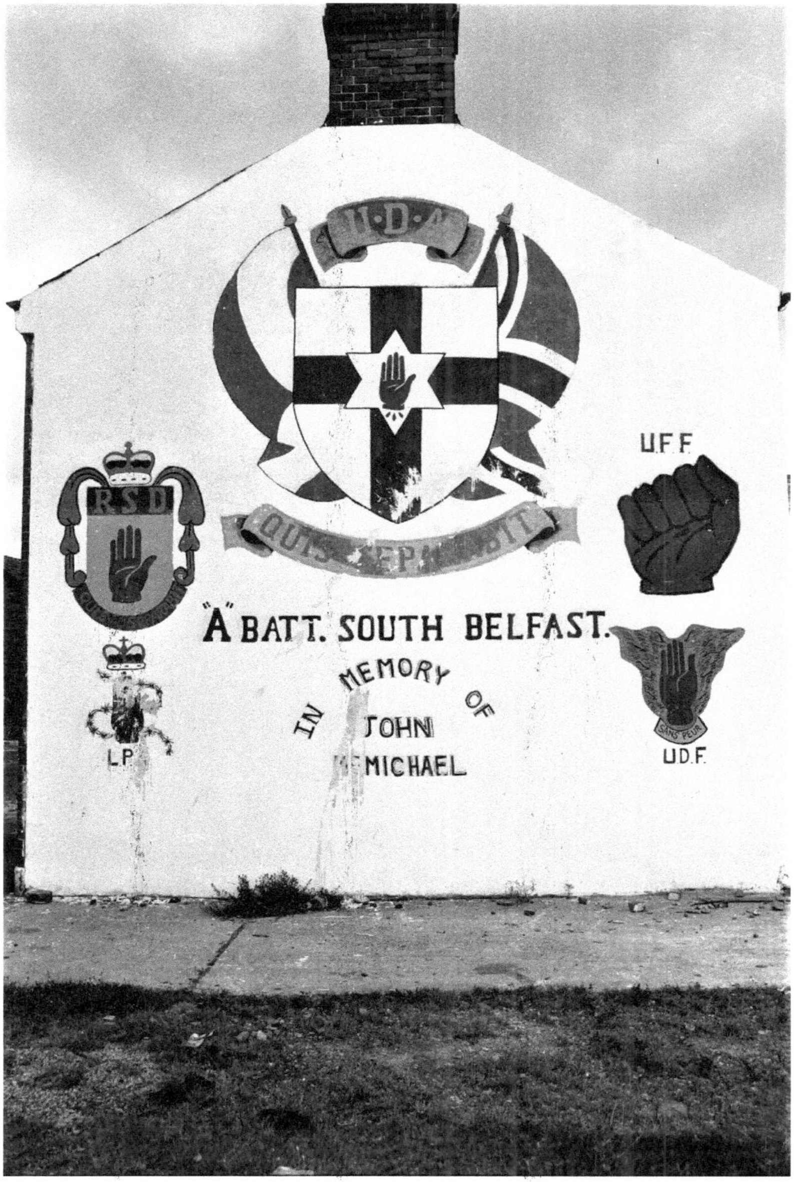

FIGURE 36 John McMichael, Roden Street, The Village, South Belfast, 1989. Photo by Tony Crowley.

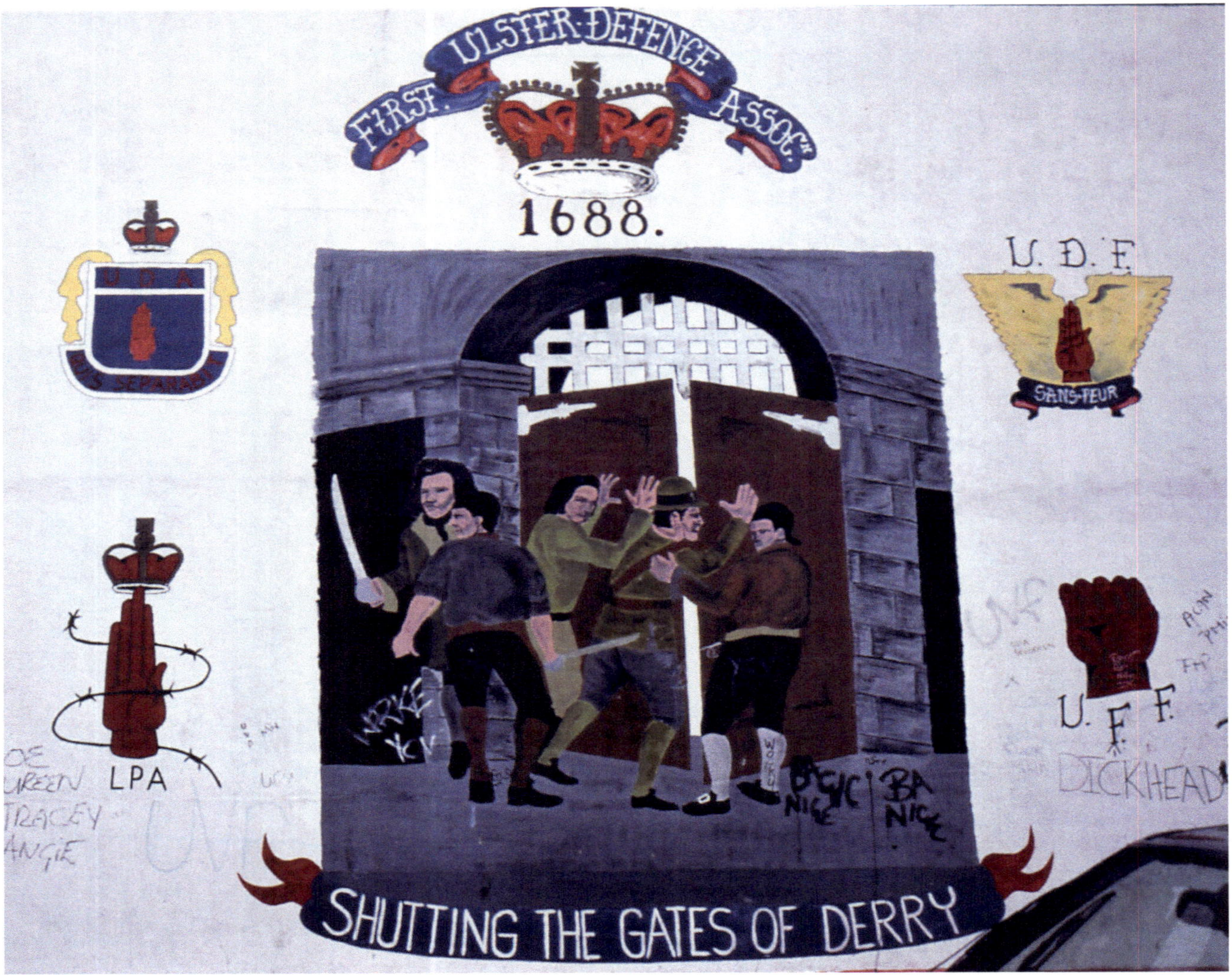

FIGURE 40 First Ulster Defence Association, Shankill Road, West Belfast, 1988. Photo by Tony Crowley.

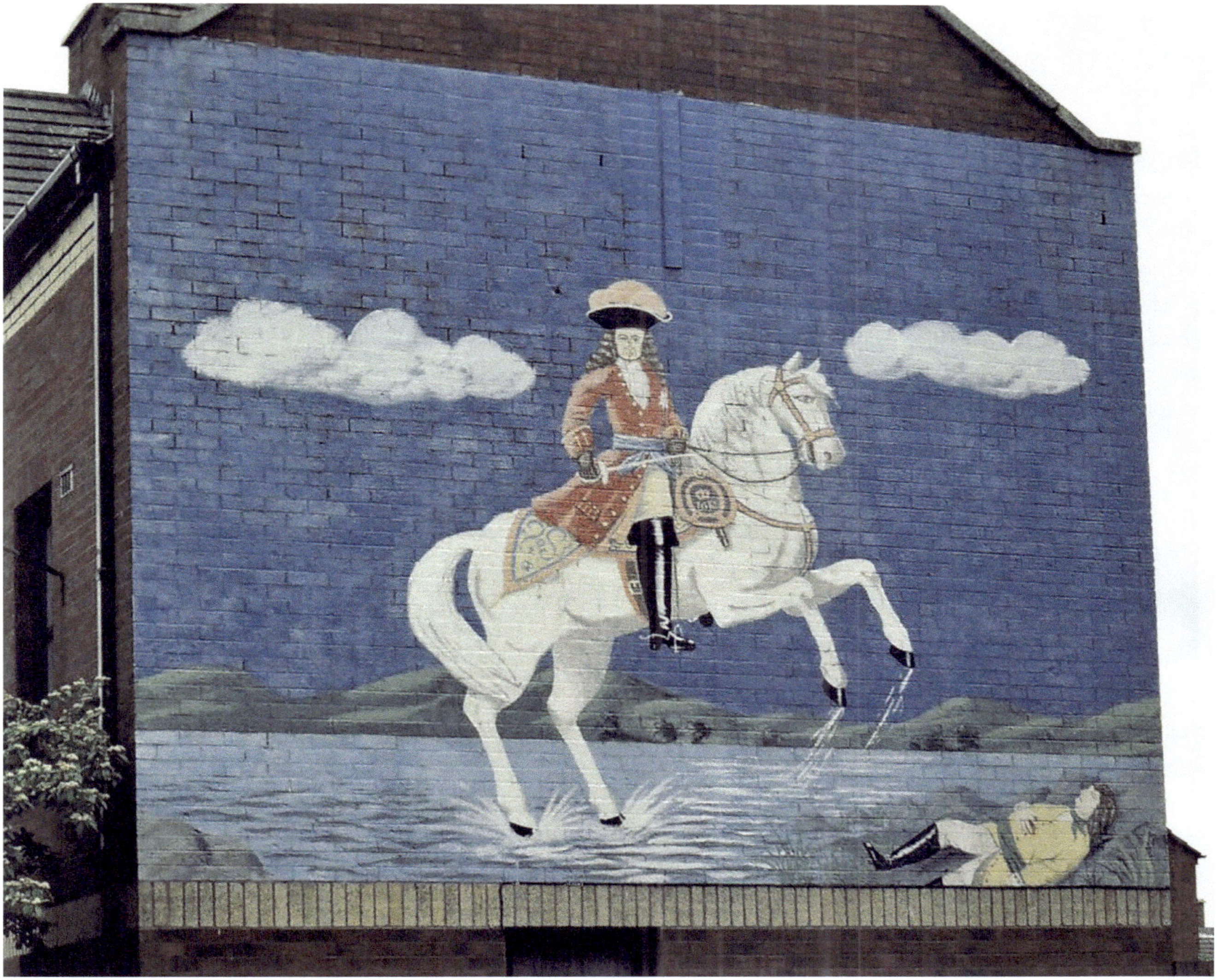

FIGURE 41 King William and Schomberg, Oak Street/Donegall Pass, South Belfast, 1989. Photo by Tony Crowley.

The celebration of centenaries is a somewhat arbitrary phenomenon (why would it matter that it is the 300th anniversary rather than the 299th?). Nevertheless, 1990 was evidently an important date for the unionist and loyalist community and the reproduction of iconic images was perhaps predictable. And yet, as noted in chapter one, mural images are located in history and their significance varies according to the context in which they are deployed. Or as the opinion previously quoted from the *Northern Whig* in 1938 put it: "the observance of the anniversary is not a symptom of 'excessive preoccupation with the past.' It is equally concerned with the events of the present and the possibilities of the future" (*Northern Whig* July 12 1938: 6). In other words, the painting of King William in 1990 is related to but distinct from its earlier instantiations. The issue of "the rights and liberties of those whose unwavering Protestantism is allied with an unswerving loyalty to King and Constitution" (6) may have remained the same (notwithstanding the change of monarch), but the events of the present and the future possibilities that they heralded were very different in 1938 and 1990. After the *Anglo-Irish Agreement* (1985), both constitutional unionism and paramilitary loyalism were disturbed, concerned, and anxious; whatever Westminster proclaimed, the suspicion was that treachery was afoot.

As illustrated earlier, loyalist paramilitary violence was unabashedly on display in murals in the late 1980s. Yet it is worth noting that violence was pretty much absent from depictions of King Billy on the walls in this period. Thus the images discussed earlier in this chapter, from 1980, 1982, 1984, 1989, and 1990, lacked any reference to the fact that William was engaged in warfare, other than the depiction of his sword. Only the images on the Jackson wall (1980), Donegall Pass (1989) (in the dying figure of Schomberg—though even that mural figures William and his Duke alone), and Sandy Row (1990) (with the musketeers), give an inkling that this was one of the most decisive battles in modern European history. It is almost as if the Protestant Ascendancy in Ireland had been established by fiat, rather than a violent and sustained struggle over a two-year period. The negation of violence in these images was an element in the construction of a narrative that suggested that the violence of those loyal to the Crown—past and present—was defensive in nature (an interpretation which, given the historical record, was simply unsustainable). And this helps to explain the second form of loyalist commemoration that appeared in the late 1980s: the remembrance of individual deaths rather than the events of social history. For if loyalists were seen as justified defenders of their rights, then their dead could be framed as the victims of the unjustified violence of their enemies. One example of this form of memory-making was a mural painted in 1987 and dedicated to the memory of Robert Bradford, a Methodist minister and the Ulster Unionist MP for Belfast South who was killed by the IRA in November 1981 (Figure 44, see Fulcrum). Bradford was identified with the right wing of unionism and accused by republicans of contributing to the "loyalist paramilitary sectarian machine" (McKittrick et al. 1999: 886); he was also a democratically elected representative and his killing, at a surgery for his constituents, caused outrage.[23] The mural itself, "In memory Rev. Robert Bradford," topped with Crown and Cross, yoked his death to the Siege of Derry through the depiction of the cannon ("Roaring Meg"), and oddly inaccurate renderings of the city's coat of arms (the London city crest is missing and the figure of death has been displaced by the *Mountjoy*) and motto ("vita veritas victa" rather than "vita veritas victoria").[24] Nevertheless, the analogical point was evident: just as the defenders of Derry fought and died to uphold their rights, likewise Robert Bradford.

If Robert Bradford fitted in with the emerging loyalist narrative about loyalist and republican violence, there were others whose profile was more problematic, but who were, nonetheless, remembered on the walls. The mural to John McMichael, a UFF commander, was one example (see **chapter three, fig. 36**). Another was the 1992 UVF memorial mural in West Belfast on Canmore Street, off the Shankill Road, which consisted of images of paramilitaries—armed or holding the Union Jack and the flag of the USSF (Ulster Special Service Force—a Shankill unit in the 1912 Ulster Volunteers)—together with the UVF crest and a plinth. The inscription read "This mural is a memorial to the volunteers of A Coy B Batt who served the Shankill community so bravely during the years of conflict Gone but not forgotten Here lies a soldier" (Figure 45, see Fulcrum). There is an evident equation here, created by the use of the historically non-specific term "conflict," between the anti-Home Rule volunteers (represented by the flags) and the contemporary UVF (in paramilitary garb)—they are also conjoined by "Here lies a soldier" (a line from the loyalist ballad "Here lies a soldier of the UVF"). The analogy was also clear in another 1992 memorial mural on Derry Hill, Rathcoole Estate, Newtownabbey, dedicated "in loving memory" to "vol. C. Caldwell" (a UVF member killed in an IRA attack on Crumlin Road prison in 1991) (Figure 46, see Fulcrum). Again the melding of past and present is achieved by the depiction of the 1912 volunteer in uniform, the use of the flags of the 1912 UVF and the 14th Battalion Irish Rifles, and the names of First World War battles, together with the representation of the contemporary volunteer and the insignia of modern organizations linked to the UVF (PAF, YCV, RHC). The link is reinforced by the central crest (shared by both UVFs) and the poppy wreath (traditionally used to remember the dead of the World Wars but extended here to include those in the current conflict).

The story of loyalist defensive violence, and the seamless connection between past and present, was presented in a 1992 mural on the Newtownards Road. Featuring images of "Ulster's past defenders'—the "B" Specials and the Ulster Defence Regiment (UDR, locally recruited police and army forces which were phased out in 1970 and 1992 respectively)—the mural posed the question: "who will defend Ulster now?" The answer, which reached back to the long distant past with a depiction of Cú Chulainn—"Ancient defender of Ulster from Irish attacks over 2000 years ago"—was the UDA, "Ulster's present-day defenders" (Figure 47). And yet, although it seems categorical, the mural's message was somewhat confused. The use of Cú Chulainn was certainly a bold appropriation of a Gaelic mythological figure long used by republicans, but the depiction of the UDA member in a uniform of combat gear and army boots was simply inaccurate. More important, perhaps, was the appearance of the crest of independent Ulster at the side of the fighting men, together with the Union Jack underfoot. It raised again significant questions: is the struggle for independence or for the maintenance of the Union? And is this strategy defensive or offensive? The wall that connected the "defender" murals together embodied this ambiguity in a slogan that managed to combine self-protectiveness with aggression. "Our message to the Irish is simple," it declared: "Hands off Ulster Irish out The Ulster conflict is about nationality."

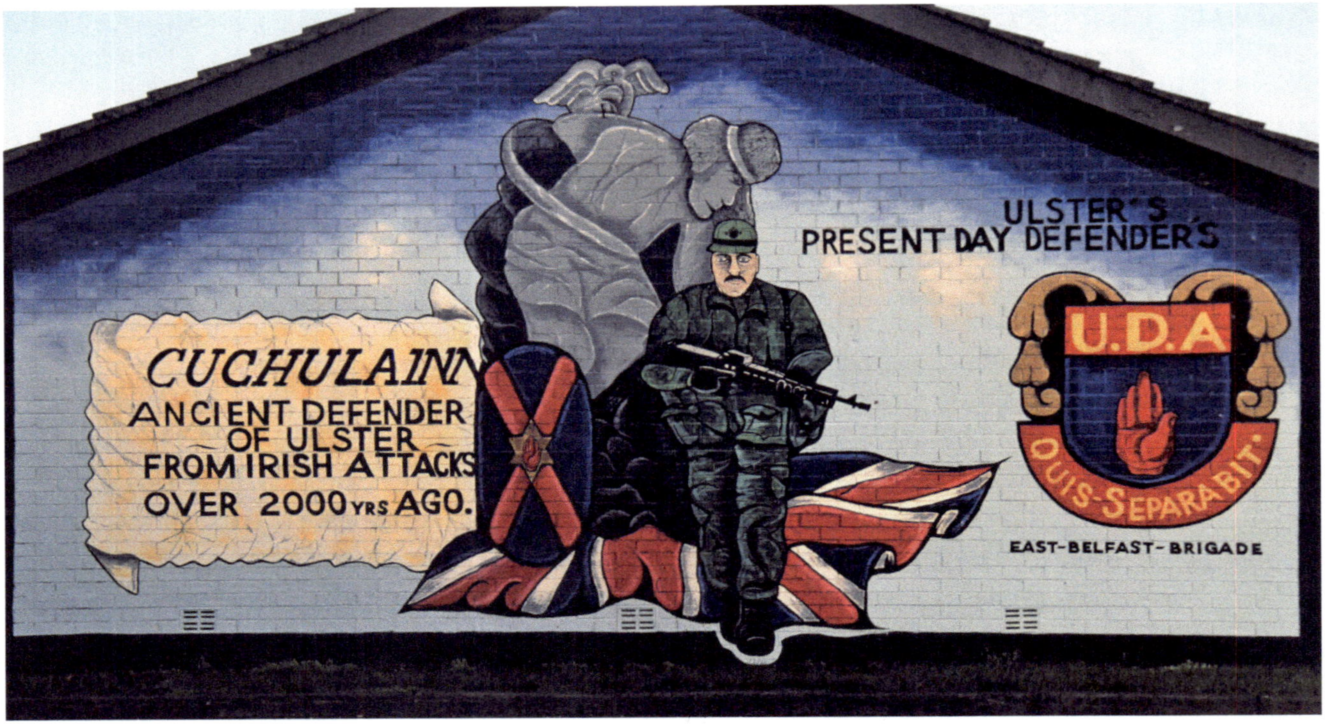

FIGURE 47 Ulster's present-day defenders, Lower Newtownards Road, East Belfast, 1992. Photo by Tony Crowley.

By 1993, then, loyalist murals were marked by both confidence and a sense of anxiety. The trepidation was caused by the recurrent fear that a sell-out would be forged by the British and Irish governments in order to appease republicanism (the joint British and Irish *Downing Street Declaration* in December 1993 was taken as evidence of this, despite the fact that it guaranteed to uphold "the principle of consent"—the unionist veto on constitutional change). But the confidence centered upon the certainty that whatever happened, loyalism would fight to preserve Ulster's identity (though in what form was unclear), not least through the violence with which loyalist paramilitaries would match if not surpass their republican counterparts. Such was the political situation upon which the murals commented and in which they intervened. As ever, the past loomed large—as evinced by the growing importance of specific forms of memorialization of the recent and more distant dead—but at that point, few were prepared for the momentous events that were to take place in the near future. For everyone in Northern Ireland, Ireland, and the rest of the United Kingdom, the world was about to be turned upside down by the declaration of the first IRA ceasefire on August 31 1994 (some twenty-five years after the first outbreak of widespread social violence in Northern Ireland). It was not the end of the conflict, or even the war, but it was the beginning of what has since become known (for better or worse) as the Peace Process.

CHAPTER 4

Ending the War, Negotiating the Peace: The Evolution of Republican Muralism 1994–2006

To access all images referenced in this chapter, please visit the open access version on Fulcrum at https://doi.org/10.3998/mpub.14527058.

Peace or war? (Republican graffiti, Racecourse Road, Derry, 1996 (Figure 1, see Fulcrum))

1. PEACE BREAKS OUT

In 1993 it became known that the leader of constitutional nationalism, John Hume, and the leader of Sinn Féin, Gerry Adams, had been meeting secretly in a series of talks with the goal of "the creation of a peace process which would involve all parties' (Sinn Féin 1993). More importantly, perhaps, it was also confirmed that representatives of republicanism had met with the British and Irish governments. In December 1993, the British Prime Minister and the Irish Taoiseach issued the joint *Downing Street Declaration*. It was a carefully phrased (and punctuated) document, which contained a crucial articulation of principles for the Peace Process. Thus John Major, the British Prime Minister, declared that,

> the Prime Minister, on behalf of the British Government, reaffirms that they will uphold the democratic wish of the greater number of the people of Northern Ireland on the issue of whether they prefer to support the Union or a sovereign united Ireland... The British Government agree that it is for the people of the island of Ireland alone, by agreement between the two parts respectively, to exercise their right of self-determination on the basis of consent, freely and concurrently given, North and South, to bring about a united Ireland, if that is their wish.

While Albert Reynolds, the Taoiseach, on behalf of the Irish Government, asserted that,

> the lessons of Irish history, and especially of Northern Ireland, show that stability and well-being will not be found under any political system which is refused allegiance or rejected on grounds of identity by a significant minority of those governed by it. For this reason, it would be wrong to attempt to impose a united Ireland, in the absence of the freely given consent of the majority of the people of Northern Ireland. [I accept], on behalf of the Irish Government,

> that the democratic right of self-determination by the people of Ireland as a whole must be achieved and exercised with and subject to the agreement and consent of a majority of the people of Northern Ireland.

For both governments, there was a necessary if not sufficient condition for the development of an inclusive political process: "the achievement of peace must involve a permanent end to the use of, or support for, paramilitary violence" (*Downing Street Declaration* 1993: np).

If peace was in the air, on the ground the war continued with a series of ferocious attacks. Between the spring of 1993 and the summer of 1994, in a series of major operations, the IRA bombed prestige targets in London (including the mortaring of Heathrow airport) and killed a number of senior figures within loyalist paramilitarism. And on October 23 1993, an IRA attack that aimed at wiping out the leadership of the UDA/UFF blew up a fish shop on the Shankill Road, causing the deaths of nine civilians (four women, three girls, two men) and one of the bombers. The loyalist response was equally savage. On October 30, the UDA/UFF attacked a bar in Greysteel, a small village outside Derry, killing eight civilians (including an 81-year-old). While in June 1994, in reaction to the INLA assassination of three senior loyalist paramilitaries on the Shankill, the UVF attacked a rural pub in Loughinisland, County Down, killing six civilians as they watched football on TV (including an 87-year-old, the oldest victim of the war). Political representatives may have been laying the groundwork for peace, but the reality was that in the period which covered the end of 1993 and the first half of 1994, "many genuinely feared that Northern Ireland was on the brink of civil war" (Taylor 1997: 340).

Thus it was something of a surprise to the general public (though rumors had been circulating in informed circles) in the late summer of 1994 when the IRA declared that "as of Wednesday, 31st August there will be a complete cessation of military operations." The declaration was justified by the assertion that the republican movement was "entering into a new situation in a spirit of determination and confidence: determined that the injustices which created the conflict will be removed and confident in the strength and justice of our struggle to achieve this" (Irish Republican Army 1994: np). Given the suspension of the armed struggle, it followed that a new political imperative was required, as an internal republican discussion document produced in the summer of 1994 set out: "it is vital that activists realise that the struggle is not over. Another front has opened up and we should have the confidence and put in the effort to succeed on that front" (Cox et al. 2000: 334).

Reactions to the ceasefire varied, of course, ranging from outright dismissal to ecstatic welcome and the response of the nationalist and republican heartlands was significant. Writing from the West Belfast republican stronghold of Ballymurphy, de Baróid, for example, notes that "when it finally came, it took everyone by surprise," adding that "up in Ballymurphy, nobody knew what to think" (de Baróid 2000: 336). While McGlinchey, in an important study of the origins and development of "dissident" republicanism, recalls witnessing "a cavalcade of cars, including black taxis with Tricolors hanging out of their windows, driving up and down the Falls Road, beeping their horns as an atmosphere of celebration and jubilation prevailed" (McGlinchey 2019: x).

This jubilant reaction was prompted by "a feeling that a deal of sorts must have been done" (de Baróid 2000: 352), a sentiment that provoked nationalist and republican optimism and unionist and loyalist fear alike. On both sides, the same question arose: would the IRA really have ended its armed struggle if it had not achieved an agreement incorporating at least some of its goals? It soon became clear, however, that "the ceasefire was a republican act of faith" (353), or at least a calculation that more could be gained by political rather than violent means at that point. There was no deal, other than that outlined in the *Downing Street Declaration*, which was in effect that republicans would be invited to the negotiating table as long as they put down their arms.

2. WIDENING THE FOCUS

The issue of raised expectations, combined with an absence of any immediate concessions, posed a serious problem for the leaders of republicanism, not only, but not least, with their own activists (and indeed a significant section of the leadership itself Moloney 2007: 426). It was clear, therefore, that as well as pressurizing the other parties (unionists, the British and the Irish government), there was a need to persuade their own constituency that serious political change was in the offing. Murals, as a now well-established medium of political discourse, were significant in attempting to achieve this task. Thus not long after the IRA's ceasefire declaration, a mural at the strategically important location of Beechmount Avenue, in the heart of republican West Belfast, asserted republican demands within a framework of "A just and lasting settlement": "British troops out—permanently End unionist veto—permanently Stop collusion permanently Disband RUC and RIR—permanently POWs released—permanently All roads opened—permanently" (Figure 2). Similar demands were made in an impressive mural on the Whiterock Road in Ballymurphy that featured centrally a British soldier set against the local housing estate (including a self-reflexive representation of the "Who fears to speak of Easter Week" mural (see **chapter three, fig. 47**), framed by injunctions in Irish: "Slán abhaile" (Safe journey home) and "Fag ár sraideanna" (Get off our streets) (Figure 3). The mural also bore four smaller images, again carrying calls for an end to collusion and the unionist veto, as well as the disbandment of the RUC and Royal Irish Regiment (RIR) and the release of the prisoners. Another mural in the same year, in Creggan, a stronghold of the Derry Brigade of the IRA, embodied a slogan that soon became familiar: "25 years Time for Peace Time to Go" (Figure 4, see Fulcrum).

It is important to recall that at the start of the Troubles, nationalists and republicans could not have painted murals proclaiming their political intentions for fear of the repercussions that might follow. After twenty-five years of war, however, the situation had changed and the first major murals painted after the ceasefire were important indicators of the message that republicans wanted to convey (almost all were painted by muralists who supported Sinn Féin at the time). And some of the demands that republicanism was making of the British were serious (not least in the broad political and legal consequences implied by the release of prisoners convicted of the most serious offences on the statute book). But the demands set out in the murals bear analysis in order

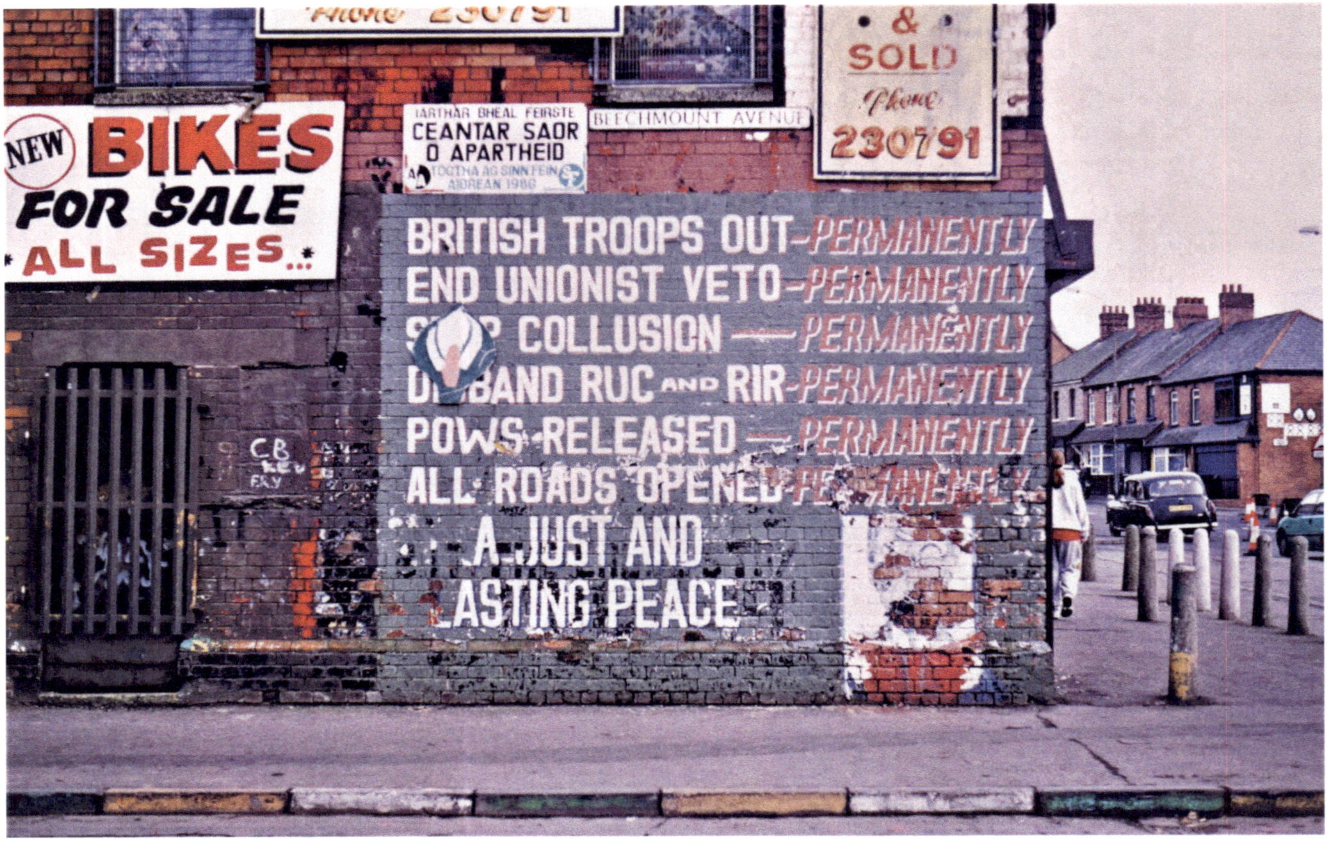

FIGURE 2 Republican demands, Beechmount Avenue, Beechmount, West Belfast, 1994. Photo by Tony Crowley.

to consider exactly what was being communicated. For example, if it was "time to go," to whom did that refer to exactly (in other words, who or what was required to leave)? In and of itself, the demand that British troops leave Northern Ireland permanently was significant, but it was hardly tantamount to the withdrawal of the British State. Likewise, the call to end the unionist veto was also important, but the question was, veto over what? Did it refer to the power of the unionist majority to reject a United Ireland, or was it in effect an appeal for the curtailment of the right of unionists to say "no" to everything (including an "internal" power-sharing settlement)? And again, the demand for an end to collusion between the British State and loyalist paramilitaries meant a lot to those who were threatened by, or had been victims of, such illicit cooperation. But in the end, was this any more than a call for the re-establishment of the minimal expectations that a citizen might have in a liberal democracy

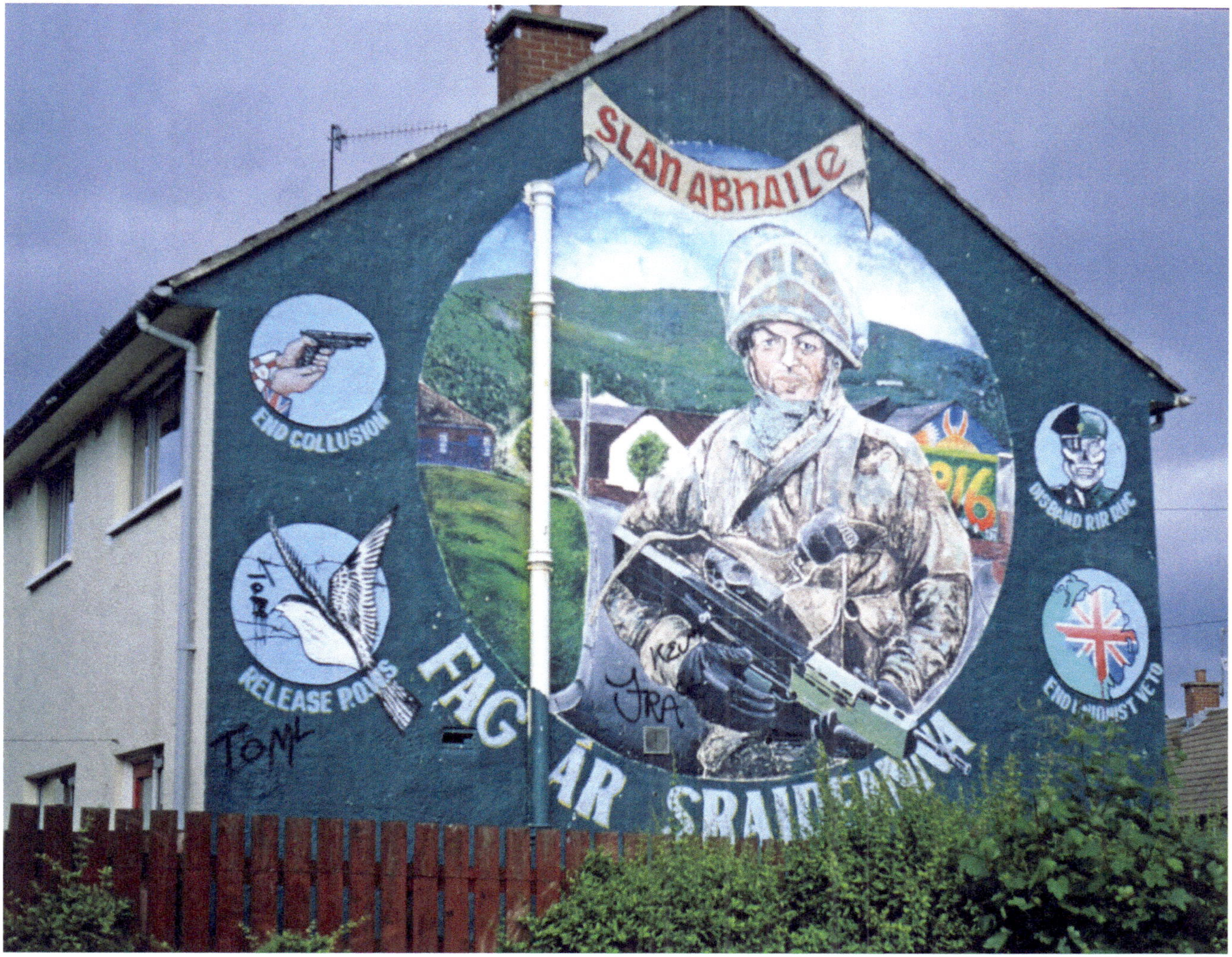

FIGURE 3 Slán abhaile, Whiterock Road, Ballymurphy, West Belfast, 1994. Photo by Tony Crowley.

(specifically, that the State should fulfill its basic role of protection of its citizens through the impartial rule of law)? Even the undoubtedly radical demands to scrap the RUC and RIR (a police force and army regiment which recruited overwhelmingly from the unionist population), and to release prisoners jailed during the conflict, were addressed to the British State (in whose hands rested the power to disband its agencies and close some of its prisons—which it duly did). In sum, the Beechmount, Whiterock, and Derry murals were all important assertions of republican positions after the ceasefire in 1994. But in that regard, they marked a significant shift away from the traditional republican goal that had been articulated repeatedly on the walls in the 1980s: the achievement of a United Ireland in the form of a socialist republic (see **chapter two, fig. 57**). In this sense, then, the murals played an important role in changing the terms of the argument at a crucial conjuncture in the political process, and in persuading the republican movement to follow the leadership as it did so.

Yet if the murals, at least implicitly, marked the developing political stance of republicanism, in other ways they conveyed a renewed sense of confidence in the traditional and thoroughly politicized arena of cultural identity. The historical significance of this concept in Northern Ireland had been asserted in Albert Reynolds' section of the *Downing Street Agreement*, in which he referred to the acceptance or rejection of the political order "on grounds of identity." This was in effect a recognition, though not necessarily an endorsement, of the powerful relationship between political and cultural identity enshrined in differing forms of cultural nationalism—a politico-philosophical doctrine that had its modern origins in the work of the late eighteenth-century German thinker J.G. Herder (Crowley 2020). The formation of unionist/loyalist cultural identity through murals was examined earlier in chapters one and three, but in republican and nationalist murals in the mid-1990s, there was a renewed emphasis on cultural elements that had first appeared in Mo Chara's "neo-Celtic" works of the late 1980s. The post-ceasefire works were distinctive, however, in their overt deployment of themes and images that were reminiscent in terms of style and content of those that had appeared in the late nineteenth-century Gaelic Revival.

Gaelic sports, for example, revived and codified after the formation of the Gaelic Athletic Association (GAA, Cumann Lúthchleas Gael) in 1884, were depicted in a mural painted in Ardoyne in the fall of 1994 (Figure 5). Under "Fáilte go dti Ardeoin" (Welcome to Ardoyne), and surrounded by the crests of the four provinces of Ireland and Celtic latticework, the image represented Gaelic footballers, hurlers, and camogie (women's hurling) players, together with the crest of the local club (Ardoyne Kickham's). From one point of view, the mural appeared to be saying no more than that "Gaelic sports" are part of the heritage of the local community, though the indeterminate "our" points to the larger community of Irish nationalism itself. But the Gaelic slogan—"Is treise dúchas ná oiliúint" (heritage is stronger than upbringing)—sent a more robust and apparently essentialist message.[1] For not only does the use of Gaelic point towards a local audience of Irish speakers, the content of the slogan reinforces the link to cultural nationalism (Herder had made language the key to nationality Crowley 2020), by suggesting that heritage—in the form of traditional cultural practices—can overcome the banal mundanities of upbringing. Another way of putting this might be that traditional cultural identity, such as the Irish language and Gaelic sports, will persist, even within a context in which the dominant culture is Anglicized and Anglo-centric.

The cultural nationalist focus on sport was reflected in a number of murals from this period (Figure 6, see Fulcrum), and there was a clear attempt to involve the young in traditional culture, as evinced by two later murals.

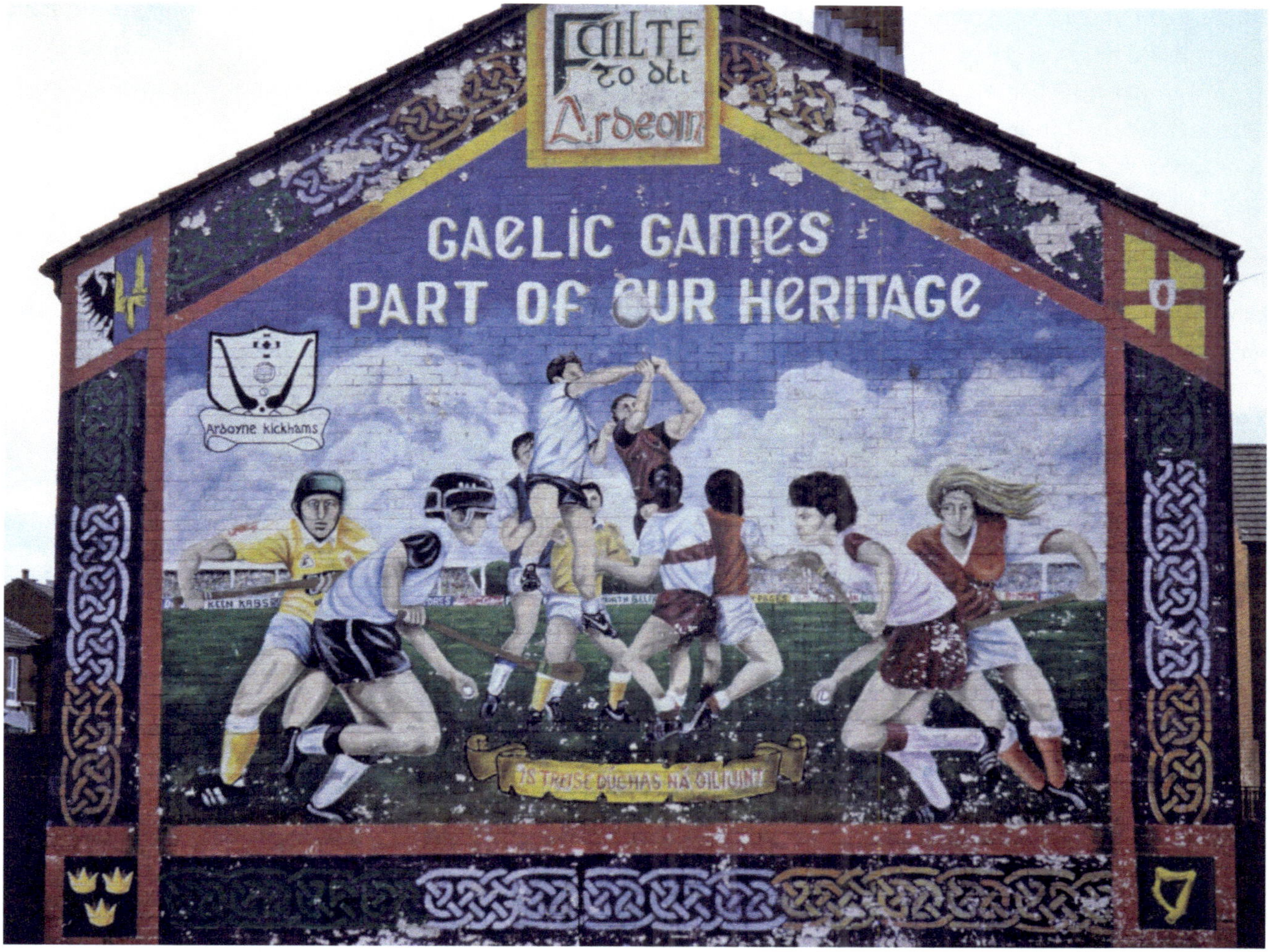

FIGURE 5 Gaelic games, Flax Street, Ardoyne, North Belfast, 1994. Photo by Tony Crowley.

"Óige na bhFál" (Youth of the Falls) heralded "Our youth Our culture Our community Our future" (Figure 7, see Fulcrum). While a mural advertising the "Joe Cahill Perpetual Cup" on Beechview Park (opposite Cardinal O'Donnells GAC, on the site of a former British Army base, Fort Pegasus), united republicanism (Cahill was a founder member and Chief of Staff of the Provisional IRA, and the mural contained a plaque to those who gave their lives to the republican cause), the local community (represented by various figures), and cultural nationalism (the use of the Irish language, Celtic designs, and Gaelic sports). Centrally, it contained the injunction "Mol an óige agus tiocfaidh sí" (Praise the young and they will flourish) (Figure 8).

Cultural nationalism was also represented in several murals with Gaelic mythological themes. Again in Ardoyne, Queen Ériu was represented sitting by a river, dolmen to the rear, with Celtic surround and inscription: "Eire (Eiru) A queen of the Tuatha Dé Danann slain at the battle of Tailtean (Telltown, Co. Meath) 698 BC" (Figure 9). The linkage of the past and present (cultural nationalism enacts a form of seamless history) was reiterated by the Irish inscriptions advertising the "Ardoyne Fleadh Cheoil" (Ardoyne music festival—there are musical figures to bottom left and right) and the central message: "Meon an Phobail a Thógail Tríd an Chultúr" (The people's spirit is raised through culture). In a similar vein, images based on episodes in the early Irish epic *Táin Bó Cúailnge* (The

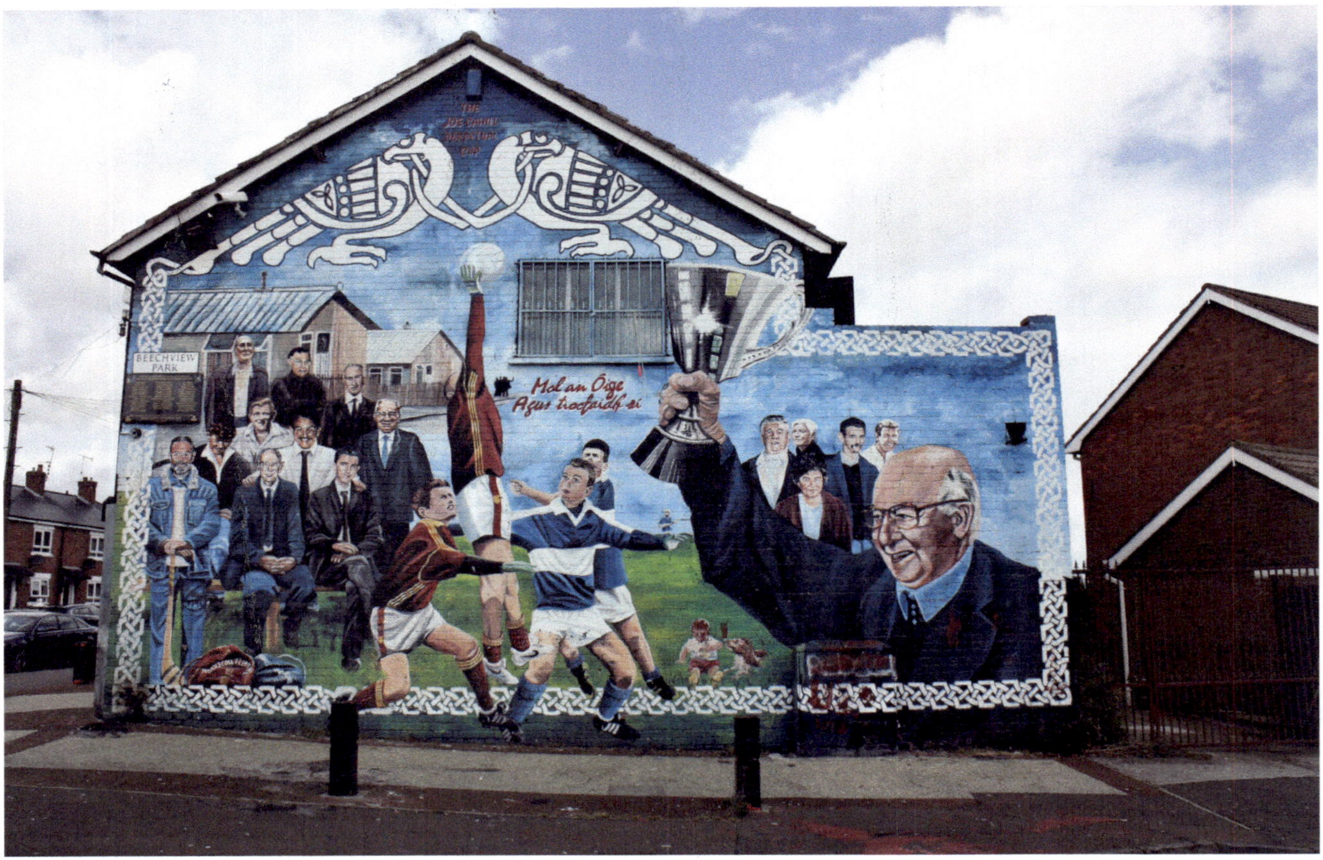

FIGURE 8 Mol an Óige agus tiocfaidh si, Beechview Park, Falls, West Belfast, 2014. Photo by Tony Crowley.

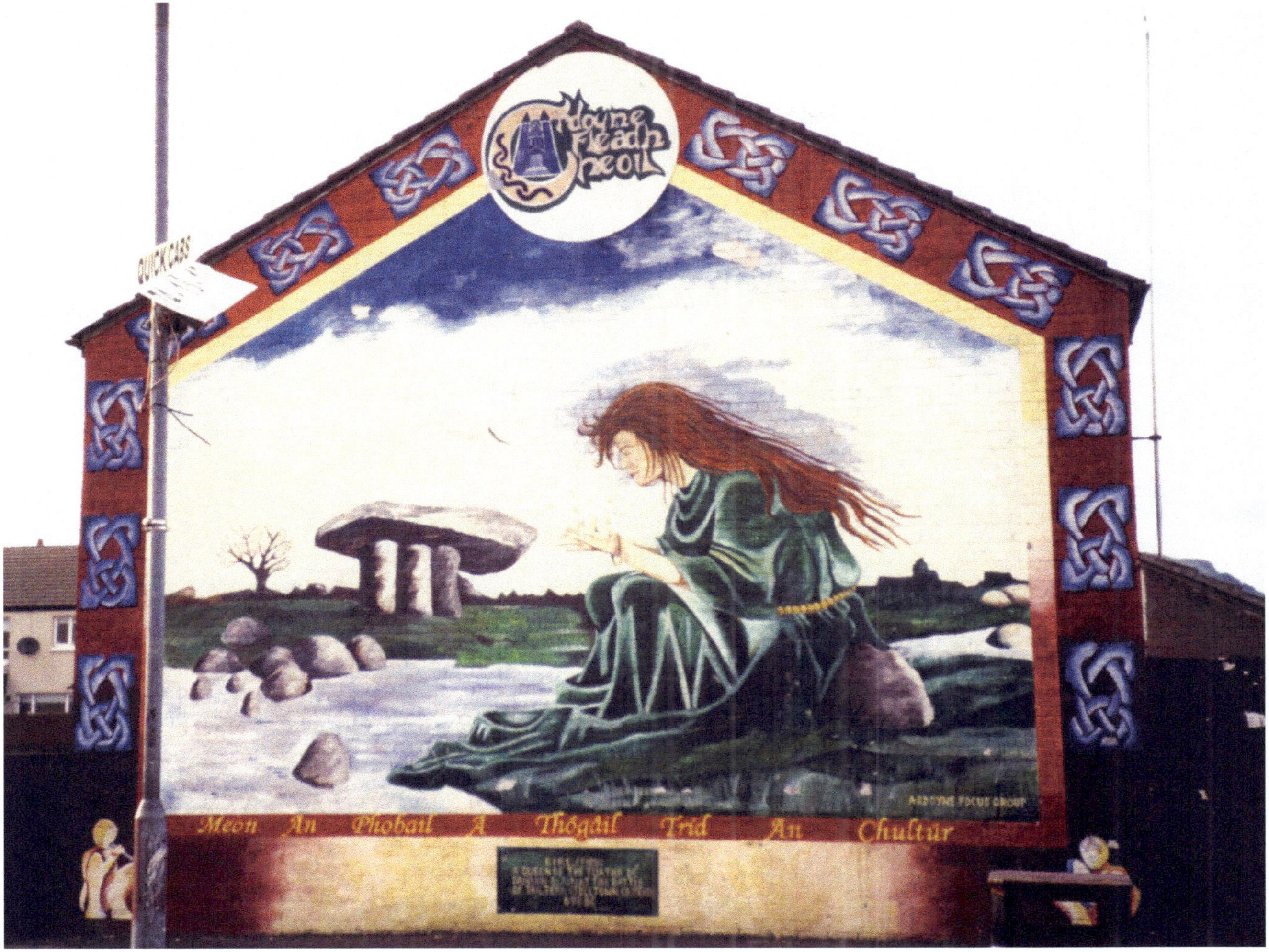

FIGURE 9 Ériu, Brompton Park, Ardoyne, North Belfast, 1995. Photo by Tony Crowley.

Cattle Raid of Cooley), included Cú Chulainn (Figure 10, see Fulcrum), and the draoichláirseoirí an chinn bhaile (the Druid harpers of Cainbile) (Figure 11, see Fulcrum). The dying Cú Chulainn, that much-contested figure, also became the central focus of a significant piece of republican memorialization on Lenadoon Avenue in 1996, again linking past and present through a roll of honor and portraits of the local IRA dead (see **Introduction, fig. 8**). Another aspect of nationalist (rather than republican) culture that also appeared in the murals, was Catholicism.

Statues of the Virgin Mary were a feature of everyday life in nationalist areas and there were, to name but a few, Marian grottoes in Derry, the New Lodge in Belfast, and Kilwikie estate in Lurgan. But the murals were a notable development and the religious themes included the Virgin and child, the apparition of the Virgin Mary at Lourdes and Medjugorje (Figure 12), the Sacred Heart of Jesus (Figure 13, see Fulcrum), and the Clonard Novena (1943–1993) (Figure 14, see Fulcrum). In short, as Mo Chara's mural on Springhill declared, as it yoked language, landscape, and Celtic imagery to the island and people of Ireland: "Tá ár gCultúr Beo" (Our culture is alive) (Figure 15).

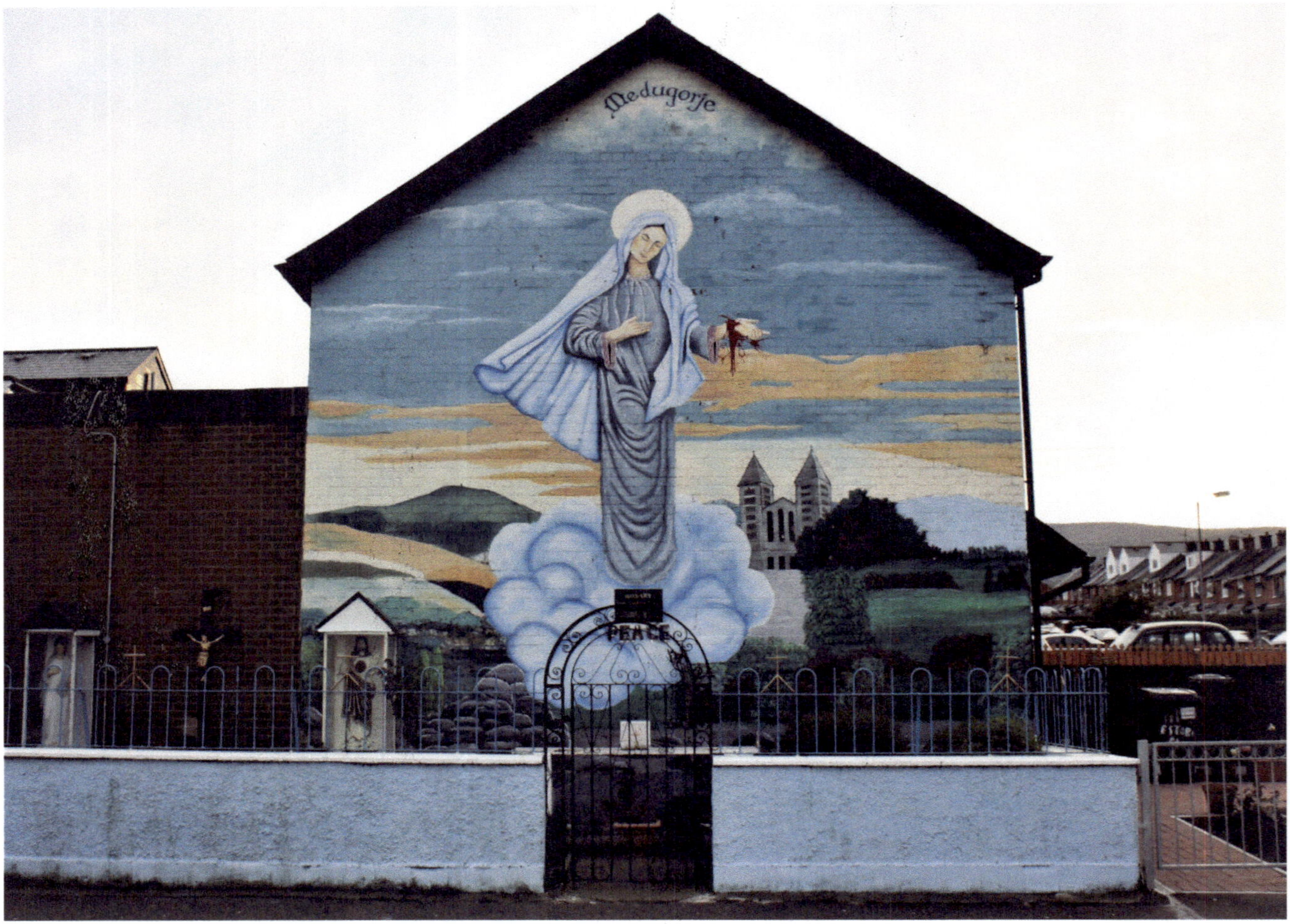

FIGURE 12 Medjugorje, Berwick Road, Ardoyne, North Belfast, 2014. Photo by Tony Crowley.

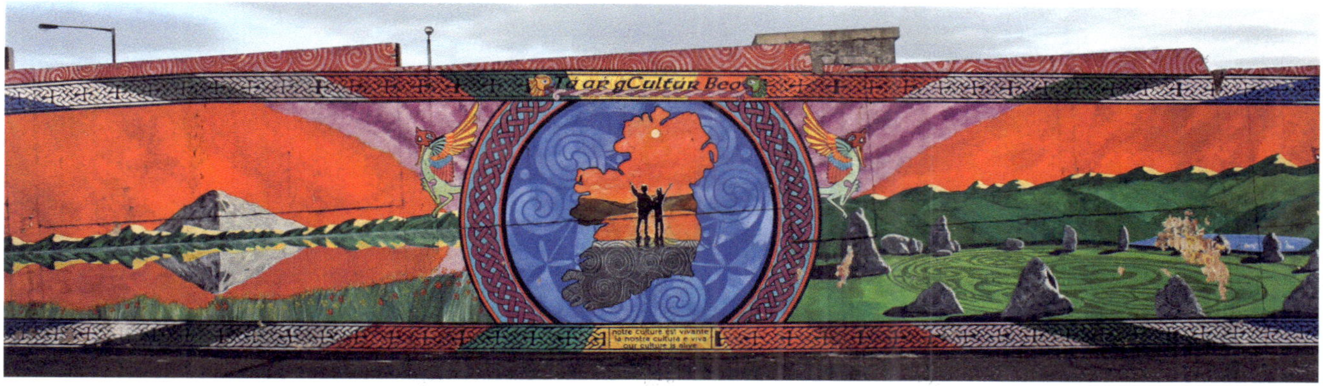

FIGURE 15 Tá ar gCultúr Beo, Springhill Avenue Ballymurphy, West Belfast, 2002. Photo by Tony Crowley.

After the first ceasefire, then, and indeed throughout the rest of the 1990s, the murals helped to shape the collective memory of nationalists and republicans by emphasizing distinctive cultural features such as Gaelic sports, music, the Irish language, mythology, and religion.[2] Above all, however, the murals emphasized a shared history, and they did so by concentrating on indicative and indeed constitutive historical moments. For example, an ambitious and well-executed Ardoyne mural depicted an early nineteenth-century hedge school (a native, vernacular, and successful system of education set up in response to one of the provisions of the Penal Code, which imposed legal and cultural restrictions on the Catholic and Presbyterian population Dowling 1968) (Figure 16). Teacher and students were represented in the image in a rural setting (a "Penal Law Education" notice is mailed to the tree); above, the message in Irish read: "labhair an teanga Gaeilge liom" (speak Irish with me). The invocation of a memory of the systematic disadvantage imposed on the Irish through the Penal Code was reinforced by a slightly later mural in the same area representing a Mass Rock (a secret location where Catholic Mass was celebrated in defiance of legal prohibition) (Figure 17, see Fulcrum). Here the image (originally a postcard) represented a priest saying Mass, surrounded by kneeling parishioners, while in the distance lookouts warned of the approach of British soldiers. Above the image, an inscription in Irish declared: "is í an charraig seo ionad adhartha ar náithreacha áit ar cothaiodh an creideamh do na glúnta a bhí le teacht" (this rock was our ancestors' center of worship, where religion was preserved for the generations that were to come).[3]

If there is one event in Irish history that serves as a metonym for the catastrophic effects of colonial rule within Irish nationalist cultural memory, it is the Great Famine of 1845–1852. And the 150th anniversary was marked in a series of striking murals across West Belfast in particular. In the Ardoyne Avenue gallery, for example, two versions of "An Gorta Mór" (The Great Famine), appeared, the first of which reproduced a contemporary sketch, "Funeral at Skibbereen" (from the *Illustrated London News*, January 30 1847), headed by a quotation from Seamus Heaney's "Requiem for the Croppies": "They buried us without shroud or coffin" (Figure 18).[4] Another representation of the

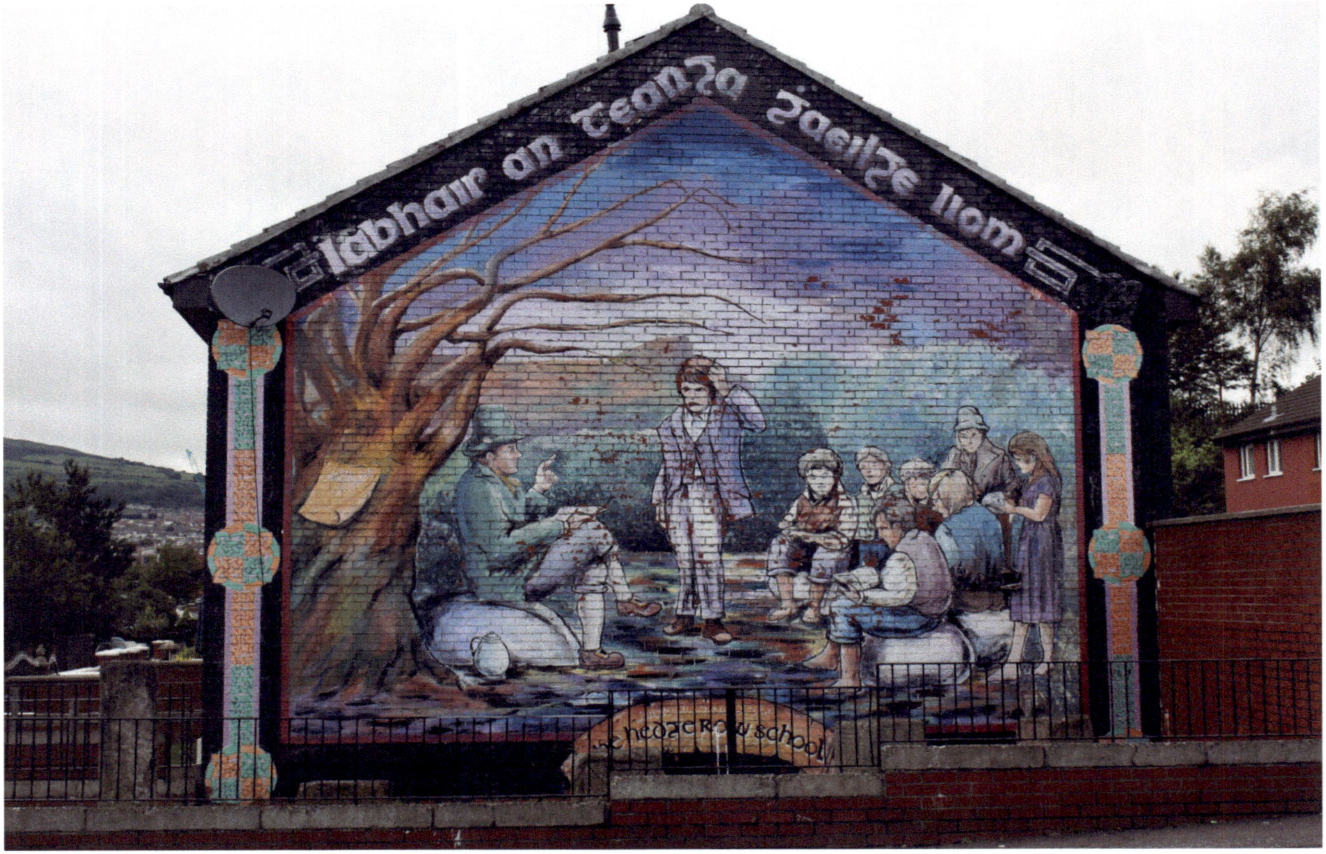

FIGURE 16 Labhair an teanga Gaeilge liom, Ardoyne Avenue, Ardoyne, North Belfast, 1996. Photo by Tony Crowley.

misery of the times appeared in "An tOcrais Mór The Great Hunger," on the New Lodge Road, North Belfast; it featured a painting of a woman, with her two daughters and son, working a potato field, with ruined cottages in the coastal background (Figure 19, see Fulcrum). Other figurative representations included emigrant ships, and "Britain's genocide by starvation—Ireland's holocaust 1845–1849" (Figure 20, see Fulcrum). But there were also more abstract images, such as a mural in Andersonstown, West Belfast, "dedicated to those who died in the Great Hunger," and another on Donegall Road, West Belfast, that carried a verse by "Speranza" (Lady Wilde): "Weary men, what reap ye?—Golden corn for the stranger./ What sow ye?—Human corses that wait for the avenger./ Fainting forms, hunger-stricken, what see you in the offing?/ Stately ships to bear our food away, amid the stranger's scoffing./ There's a proud array of soldiers—what do they round your door?/ They guard our masters' granaries

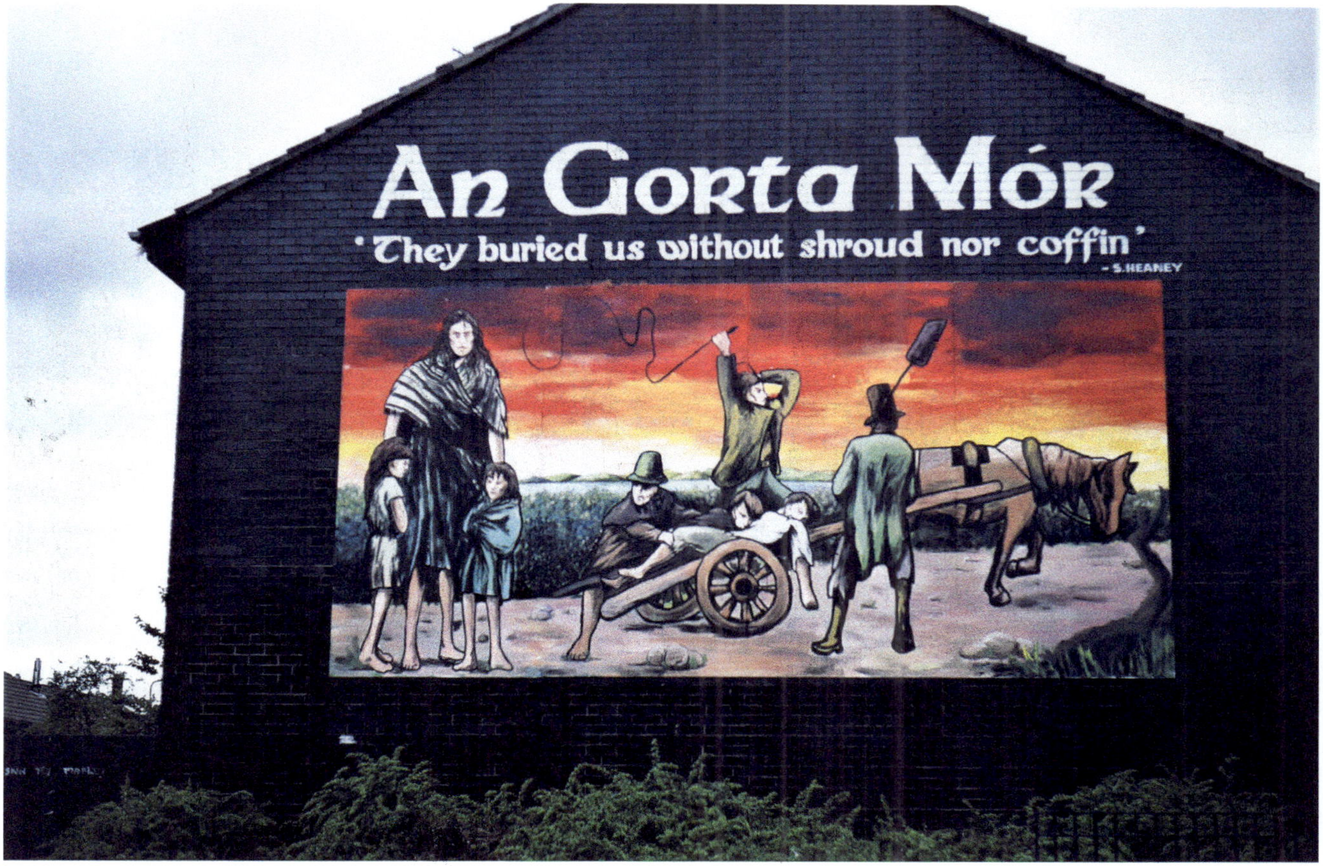

FIGURE 18 An Gorta Mór, Ardoyne Avenue Ardoyne, North Belfast, 1997. Photo by Tony Crowley.

from the thin hands of the poor" (Rolston 1998: 58). A section from Heaney's "At a potato digging," appeared in Lenadoon and conveyed the bitter history of the Famine—"The new potato, sound as stone,/ putrefied when it had lain/ three days in the long clay pit./ Millions rotted along with it." And the murals were clear in the ascription of responsibility for the catastrophe. The artist Rosie McGurran composed a mural on Linden Street, off the Falls, in which "The Famine Queen" (Victoria) held a bushel of corn as she walked among her distressed and dying Irish subjects (Figure 21, see Fulcrum). Other paintings made the point more pointedly. A mural on the Falls declared sardonically that "There was no Famine" (Rolston 1998: 57), while a stark image on Lenadoon Avenue, bore the message—inscribed on tombstones—"Nature sent the potato blight," "Government and Landlords created the Famine" (Figure 22). Dating from 1996, but still in relatively good repair, this is one of the oldest republican murals.

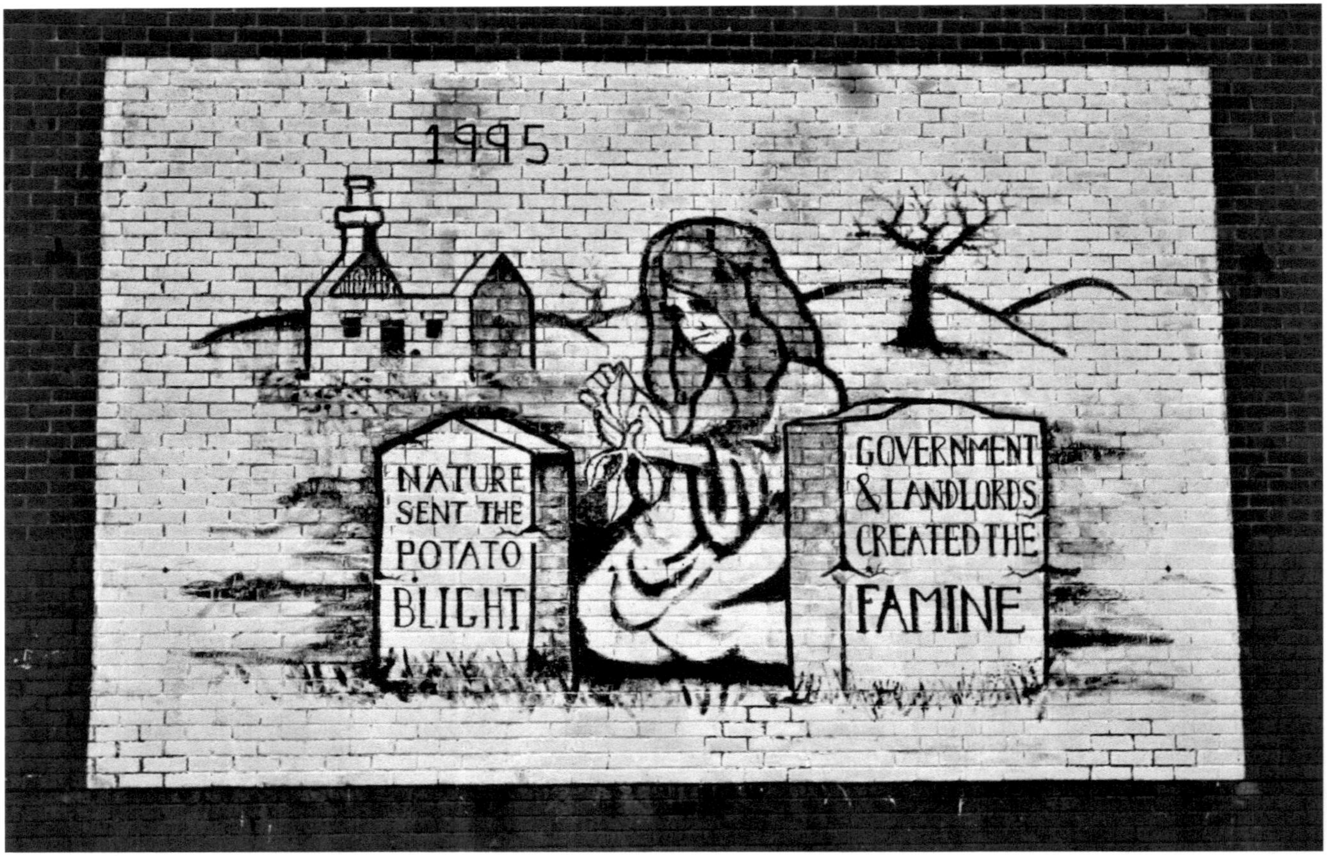

FIGURE 22 Government and landlords created the Famine, Lenadoon Avenue Lenadoon, West Belfast, 1995. Photo by Tony Crowley.

Republicans were acutely aware of the importance of the formation of collective memory, and the murals reflected this in their use of a variety of representational modes—figurative, abstract, and poetic. Republicans were also conscious of the contentious nature of the recording of history, and one fascinating mural on Oakman Street, in the republican heartland of Beechmount, West Belfast, illustrates the point. The mural is dedicated to Miriam Daly, an active republican (and lecturer in history at Queen's University Belfast), who was assassinated by the UDA in 1980. Addressing the revisionism debates in Irish historiography (Brady 1994), the mural depicted the figure of truth, the mask of revisionism, and the book of Irish history, with the warning, in Daly's words, that "History is written by the winner" (Figure 23). It is interesting in this regard to reflect

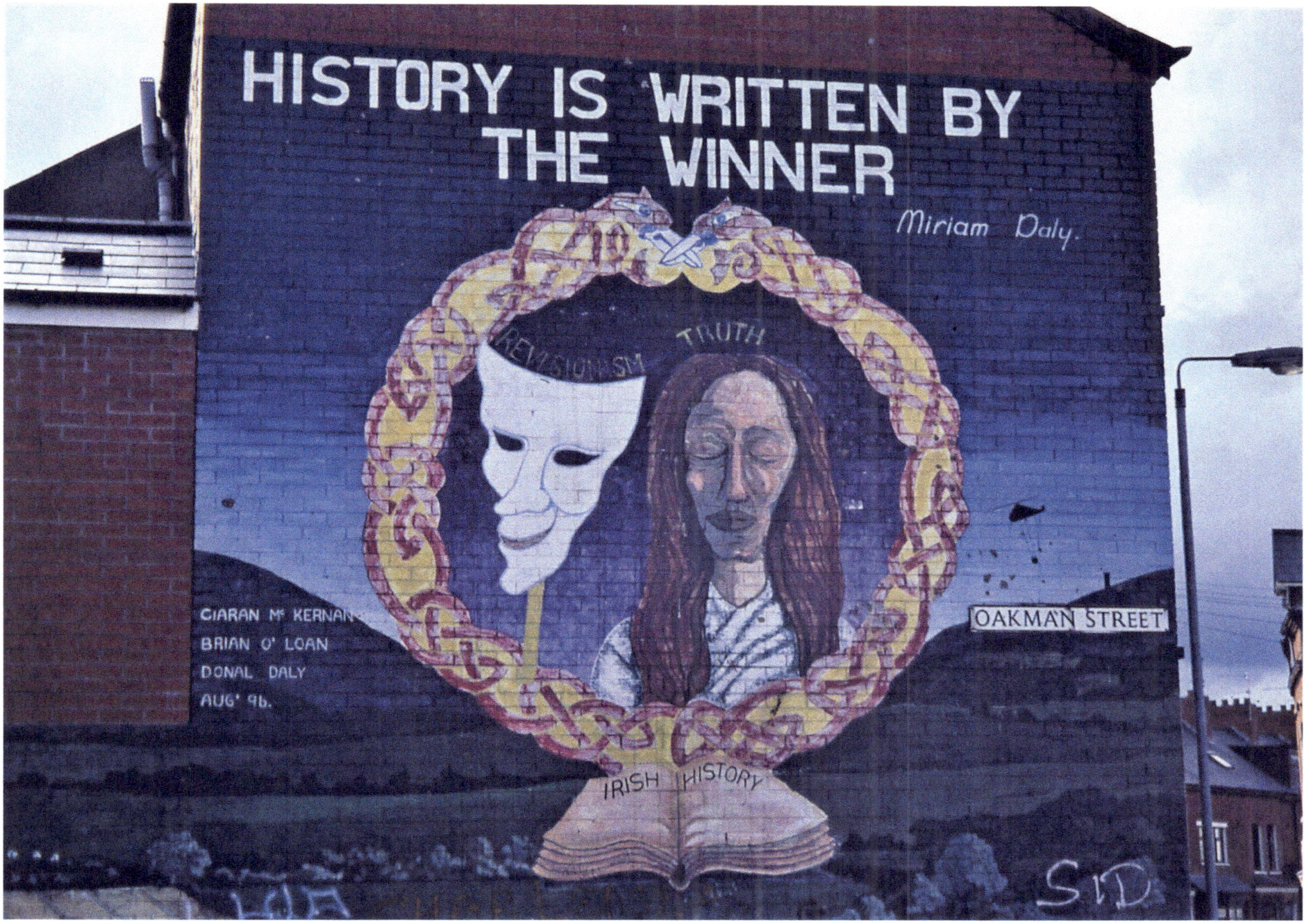

FIGURE 23 History is written by the winner, Oakman Street, Falls, West Belfast, 1996. Photo by Tony Crowley.

on the representation of history featured in the cultural nationalist murals described above. For what this republican writing of history suggests is a post-ceasefire broadening of the narrative focus of what became known as "mainstream republicanism" towards concerns more frequently associated with the discourse of Irish nationalism (indeed it can be read as an indication of the direction of travel of Sinn Féin towards constitutional nationalism).

3. REMEMBERING THE REPUBLICAN PAST

There was one mode of the recording of history, however, in which republicans stuck firmly to their traditional agenda: the memorialization of their past. This was not entirely a new development, since as noted in chapter two, republicans represented their own history frequently. But this practice certainly became more evident post-1994. For example, the founding moment of Irish republicanism, the formation of the United Irishmen and the 1798 Rebellion, was commemorated in a series of murals, of which the most important appeared at South Link in West Belfast. Incorporating the insignia of the United Irishmen—a harp with the motto "It is new strung and shall be heard"—the mural depicted the rebels, with pikestaffs, marching against a background of lakes and mountains, with Celtic surround and dates recording the bicentenary (1798–1998); at the bottom lies an inscription in Irish—"Na hÉireannaigh Aontaithe" (the United Irishmen). To the right, marking the influence of the French Revolution on the rebels, a smaller mural heralded "Liberté Egalité Fraternité" (Figure 24, see Fulcrum). Other murals depicted leading figures of 1798 such as William Drennan (Figure 25, see Fulcrum), Henry Joy and Ann McCracken, and William Steel Dickson, with pertinent quotes. Meanwhile, the republican tradition was articulated in a mural on Newington Avenue, North Belfast, that represented pikemen, lakes and mountains again, the republican phoenix, and portraits of Wolfe Tone, the McCrackens, and James Connolly. In other words, an unbroken link was posited between the United Irishmen, the revolutionary Irish Republican Brotherhood (which adopted the phoenix as a symbol of republican renaissance in the 1860s (Jarman 1997: 237), 1916, and the Troubles (by way of a plaque, erected on Easter Monday 1996, dedicated to "all those from the Greater Newington area who lost their lives as a result of the conflict in this country"). The same tradition featured in a wall painting by Síle na Gig (a women-only muralist group) that focused on women in South Link, Andersonstown: the image juxtaposed a mother and child during the Famine, Mary Spring-Rice and Mary Childers (gun-smugglers in 1914), and an IRA volunteer during the Troubles (Rolston 2003: 18).

The Easter Rising was commemorated in a series of murals featuring the Ballykissane tragedy (in which the first Irish volunteers taking part in the uprising were killed) (Figure 26, see Fulcrum), the women of 1916 (Cumann na mBan) (Figure 27, see Fulcrum), a "tribute to the heroes of 1916" (featuring an extract from the proclamation together with images of a volunteer and the dying Cú Chulainn) in Ludlow Square, New Lodge, and an ambitious reproduction of Walter Paget's "Birth of The Irish Republic" in Berwick Road, Ardoyne (Figure 28). A later IRA figure, Tom Williams (executed and buried in Crumlin Road jail for his role in the killing of an RUC officer in 1942), also appeared in republican murals (Figure 29, see Fulcrum). But it was the prison struggle of the 1970s and the Hunger Strikes that became the most familiar trope for republican muralists, particularly around anniversaries. Ciarán Nugent, the first republican prisoner to reject the criminalization policy by refusing to wear prison uniform, was represented in 2005 (Figure 30, see Fulcrum). And the image of Bobby Sands,

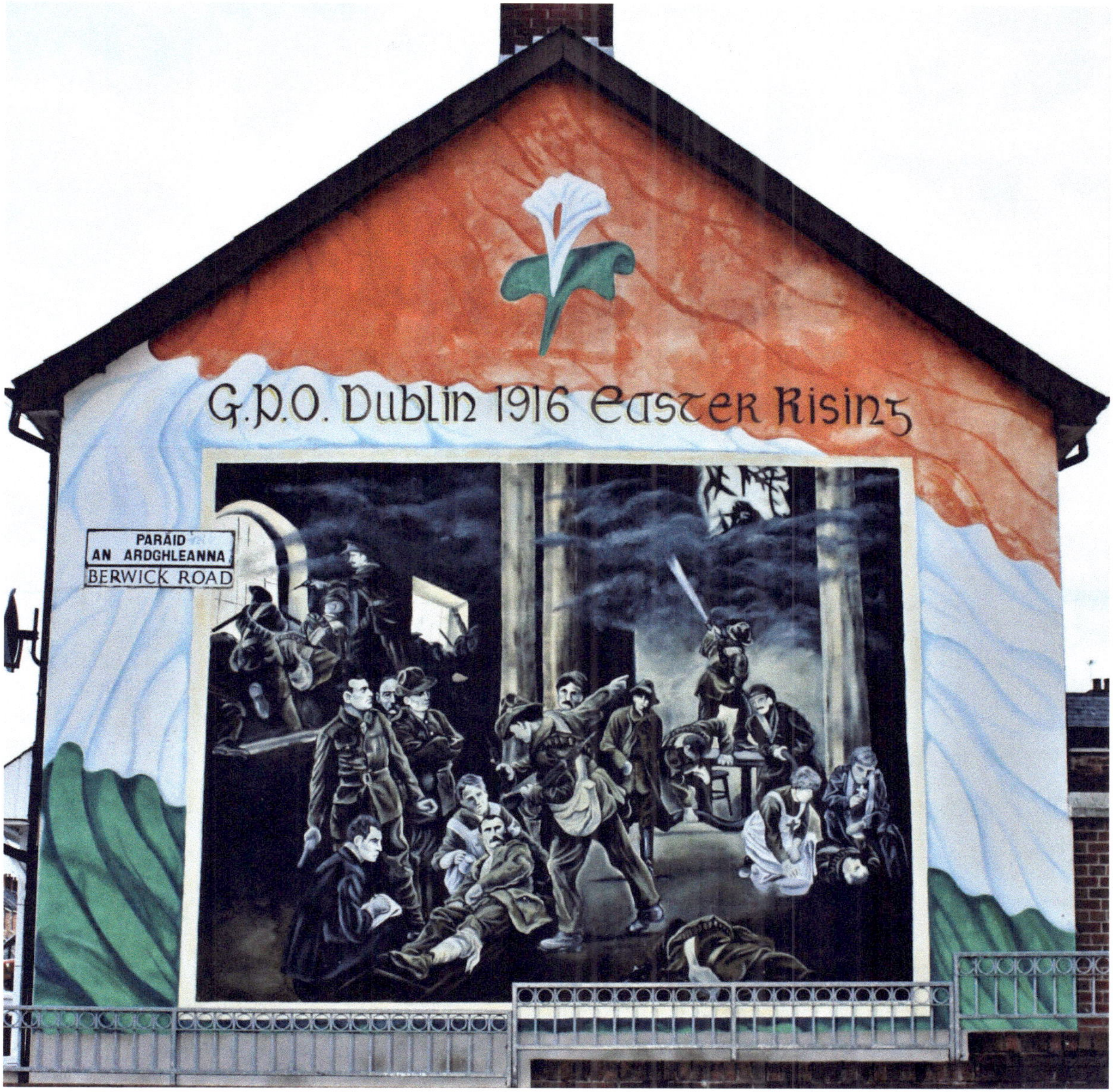

FIGURE 28 Birth of the Republic, Berwick Road, Ardoyne, North Belfast, 2002. Photo by Tony Crowley.

in a mural that was first painted on the side of the Sinn Féin offices on the Falls Road in 1989, was re-painted in 1995 (Figure 31, see Fulcrum); it took its iconic form in 2005 and was re-imaged in 2015 (it is probably the most photographed mural in Northern Ireland) (Figure 32). Other individual Hunger Strikers were also remembered, sometimes close to where they had lived: Joe McDonnell in Lenadoon (Figure 33, see Fulcrum), Kieran Doherty in Andersonstown (Figure 34, see Fulcrum), Raymond McCreesh in Camlough (Figure 35, see Fulcrum). Other memorials appeared throughout republican heartlands: Derrymen Mickey Devine in the Short Strand, East Belfast (Figure 36, see Fulcrum), and Patsy O'Hara in Andersonstown, West Belfast (Figure 37, see Fulcrum). More frequently, the Hunger Strikers were remembered collectively in a variety of formats. These included: a full

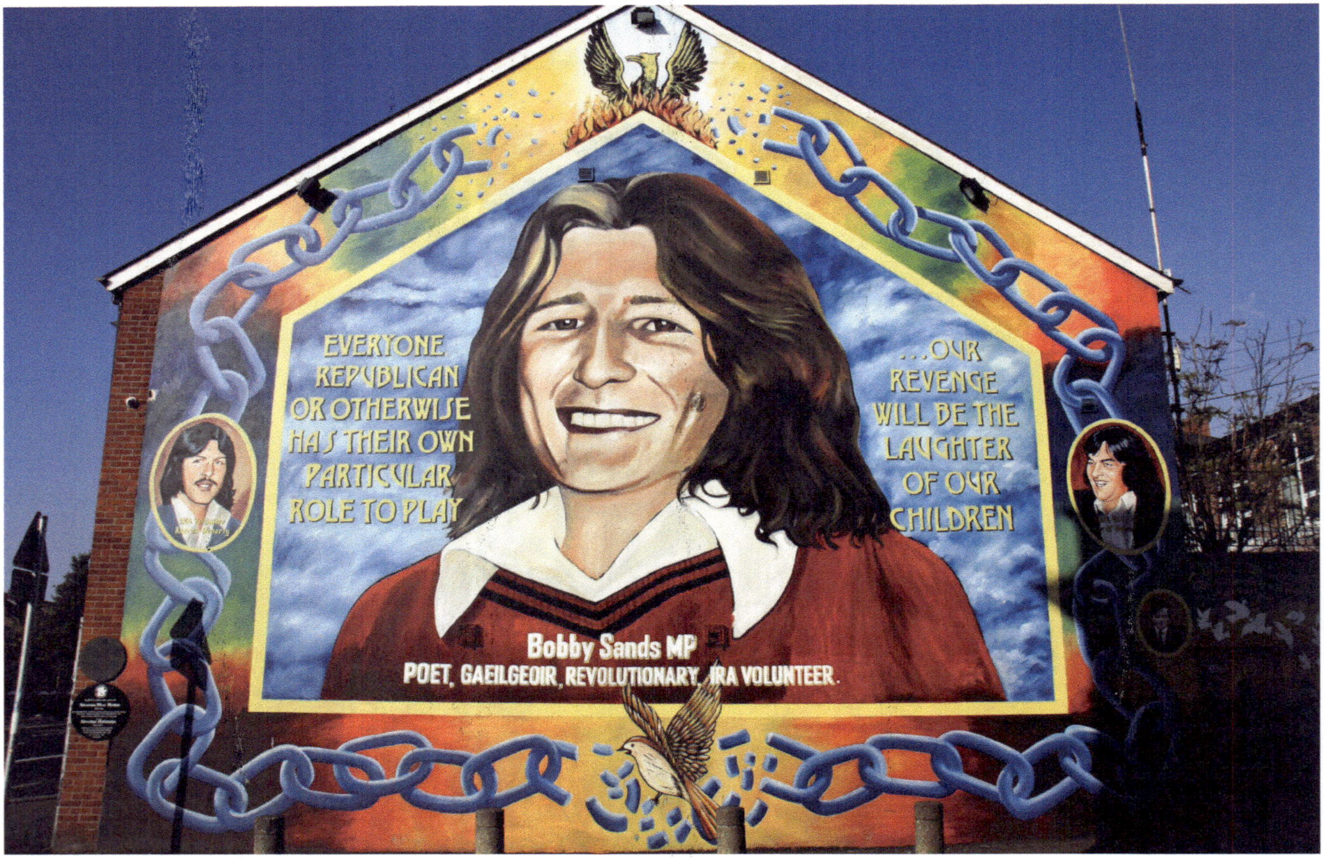

FIGURE 32 Everyone republican or otherwise, Sevastopol Street, Falls Road, West Belfast, 2015. Photo by Tony Crowley.

rendering of Sands's poem "The rhythm of time" (Figure 38, see Fulcrum); a vibrant reminder of the prisoners' roles as IRA volunteers (by way of the "comms" used by the prisoners and the external leadership) (Figure 39); the articulation of a claim for martyrdom ("no greater love") (Figure 40, see Fulcrum); and tributes to the prisoners as harbingers of peace (Figure 41) and freedom (Figure 42, see Fulcrum).[5] Commemoration of the ten dead men took place in nationalist and republican areas across Northern Ireland: in Belfast and Derry, of course, but also in smaller towns such as Armagh (Figure 43, see Fulcrum) and Lurgan (Figure 44, see Fulcrum).

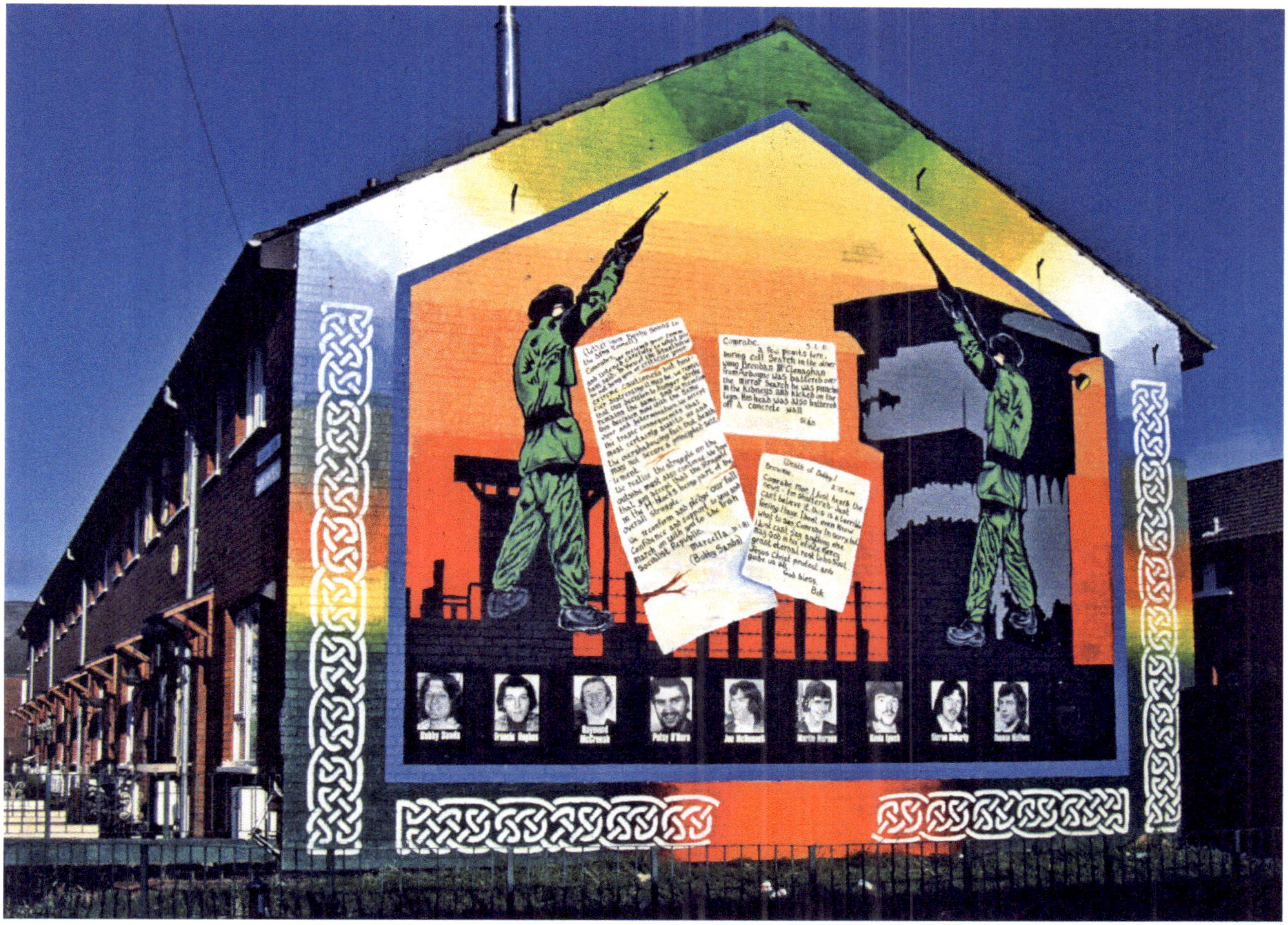

FIGURE 39 Comms, Ardoyne Avenue Ardoyne, North Belfast, 1998. Photo by Tony Crowley.

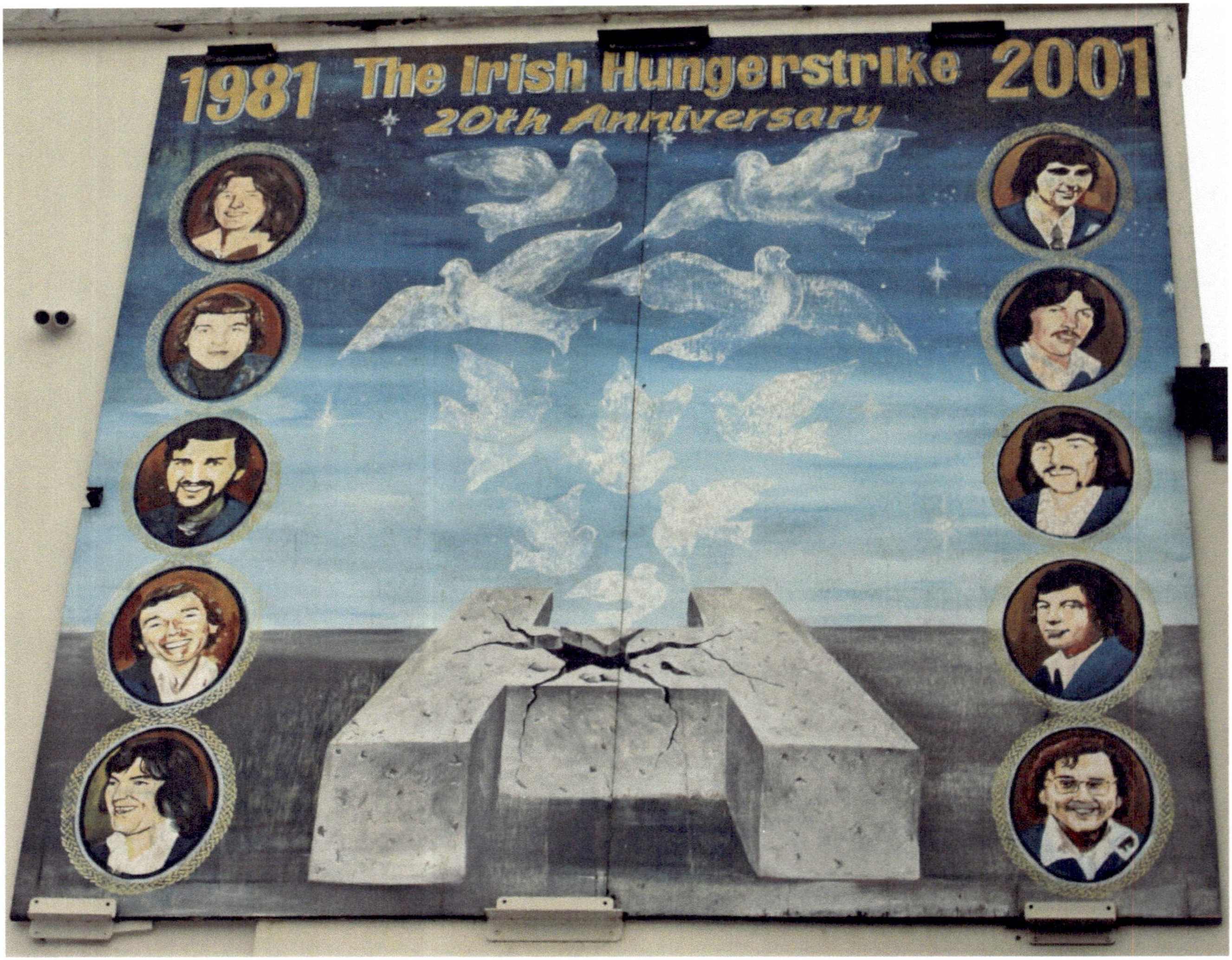

FIGURE 41 Hunger Strike 20th anniversary, Falls Road, Andersonstown, West Belfast, 2001. Photo by Tony Crowley.

As noted earlier, republican memory-making sought to inculcate the notion of an unbroken tradition, stretching from the United Irishmen to the Hunger Strikers. Yet in the 1994–2006 period, it also sought to remember the more recent dead (murals on both sides have very infrequently portrayed living figures). This was a relatively new emphasis and one that was first evident on a large scale not in murals, but in the construction of more durable memorials beyond their traditional location in graveyards.[6] Dedicated to individuals or local sections of the IRA, these were attempts to establish the narrative of the heroic republican dead. They appeared across Northern Ireland, in rural areas such as Crossmaglen (Figure 45, see Fulcrum) and Cappagh (Figure 46), in towns such as Coalisland (Figure 47, see Fulcrum) and Armagh (Figure 48, see Fulcrum) and of course in the larger urban areas (Figure 49), (Figure 50, see Fulcrum). Such physical memorials, erected by various republican groups, came in several forms, ranging from commemorative plaques (Figure 51) (Figure 52, see Fulcrum) to large-scale commemorative gardens (Figure 53) (Figure 54, see Fulcrum). Memory was, to coin a phrase, set in stone.[7]

Murals were not neglected in this grand effort at memorialization and from the late 1990s on, particularly in Belfast, a large number of images were painted that linked specific republican volunteers with particular locations (again, usually where they or their families had lived). Many of these murals were painted by Danny Devenny and his co-workers (Marty Lyons and Micky Doherty); they were interesting because they portrayed their subjects with faces uncovered and thus as recognizable individuals (in general, only the Hunger Strikers had previously been painted in this way). This "humanizing" of IRA volunteers as "ordinary" men and women marked an important shift (and one that was later copied by loyalist muralists—see **chapter five, fig. 99**), and the trope is evident in numerous murals from the early 2000s. In Ballymurphy, for example, IRA volunteers "Todler" Tolan, Michael Kane, James McGillen, and John Stone, were represented in a local safe house with two older women (named on a plaque as Kathleen McCullough and Elizabeth McGivern), drinking tea and eating sandwiches, rocket and launcher and rifles resting against the wall along with the utensils (Figure 55). The image was revised shortly afterwards: Toner's combat jacket was replaced by a suit and tie and his rifle disappeared (though the rocket launcher and rifles remained in the kitchen) (Figure 56, see Fulcrum).[8] Another Ballymurphy mural depicted IRA volunteers Jim Bryson and Paddy Mulvenna (both killed locally by the British Army) towering over the estate with trademark Lewis gun and jeep emblazoned with "Oglaigh na hÉireann" (de Baróid 2000: 122); again, both men were figured in civilian clothes (Figure 57).

Ballymurphy became the prime site of a collection of murals of this type, in which numerous IRA volunteers were depicted in dual fashion—on active service but also in "normal" roles and civilian dress—and the form was replicated elsewhere (Figure 58) (Figure 59, see Fulcrum) (Figure 60, see Fulcrum). In other cases, IRA involvement was indicated symbolically—by flags, beret, black gloves, and Easter lilies (Figure 61, see Fulcrum), a republican phoenix (Figure 62, see Fulcrum), or Mother Ireland (Figure 63, see Fulcrum)—with accompanying facial portraits and names. But if these murals constitute a form of "humanized" roll call, there were some instances in which names were not ascribed to the images of the volunteers. For example, a mural in Turf Lodge, West Belfast, was a riff on an image taken from the early 1980s ("You may kill the revolutionary but never the revolution"), in which the heroic socialist realist depiction of the revolutionaries, with combat fatigues and rifles,

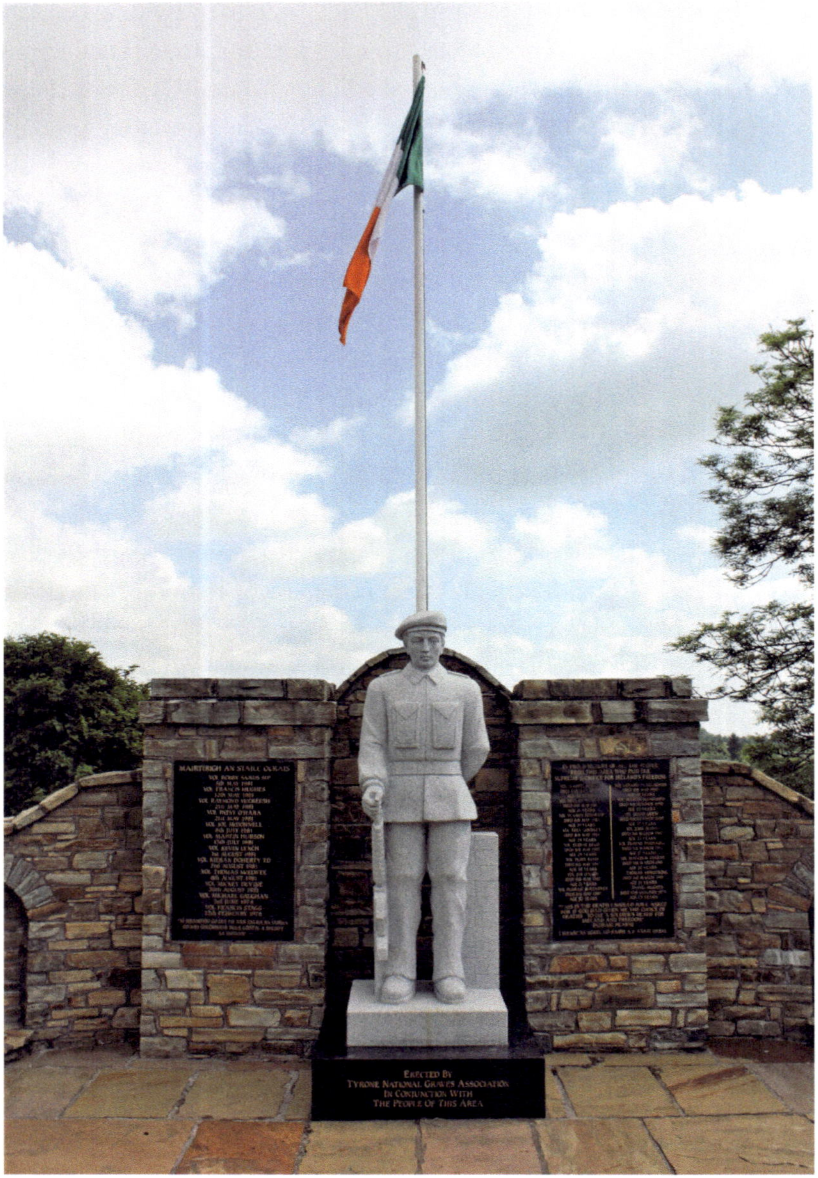

FIGURE 46 A soldier's death, Cappagh Road, Cappagh, 2001. Photo by Tony Crowley.

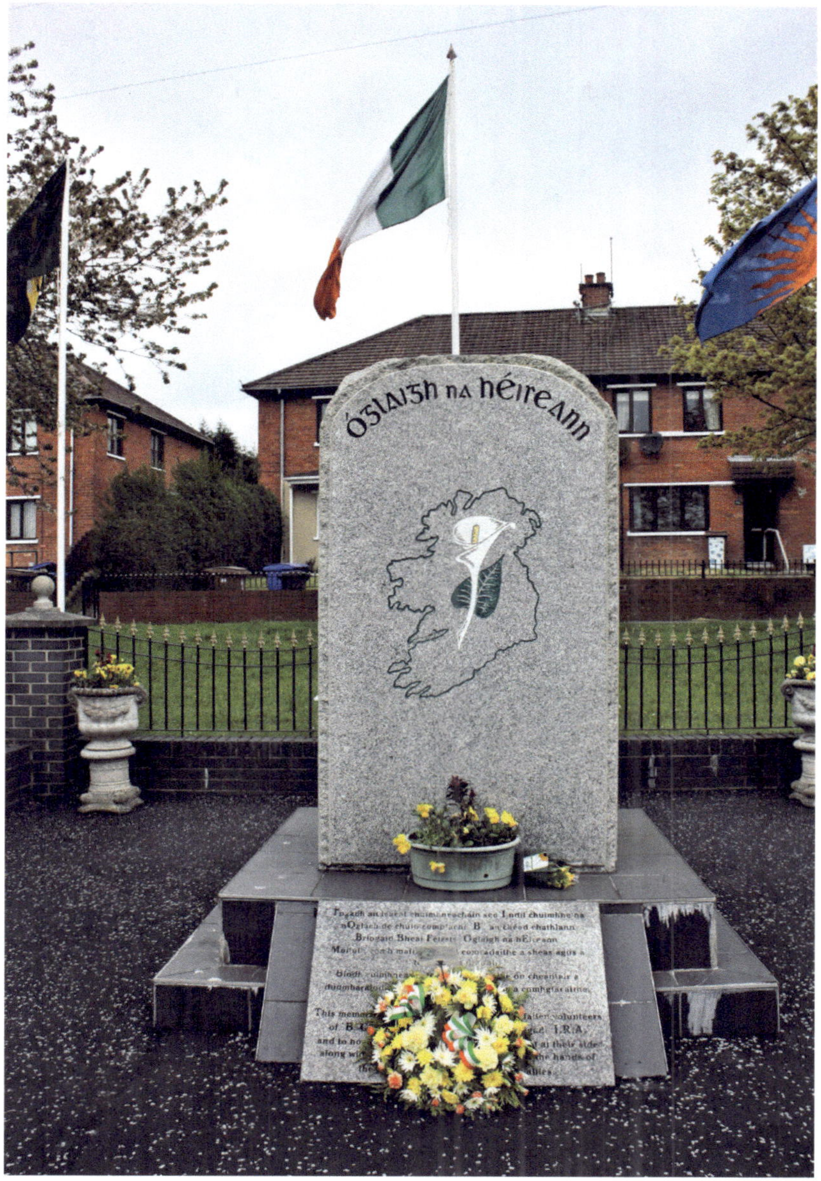

FIGURE 49 Óglaigh na hÉireann, Bingnian Drive, Andersonstown, West Belfast, 2003. Photo by Tony Crowley.

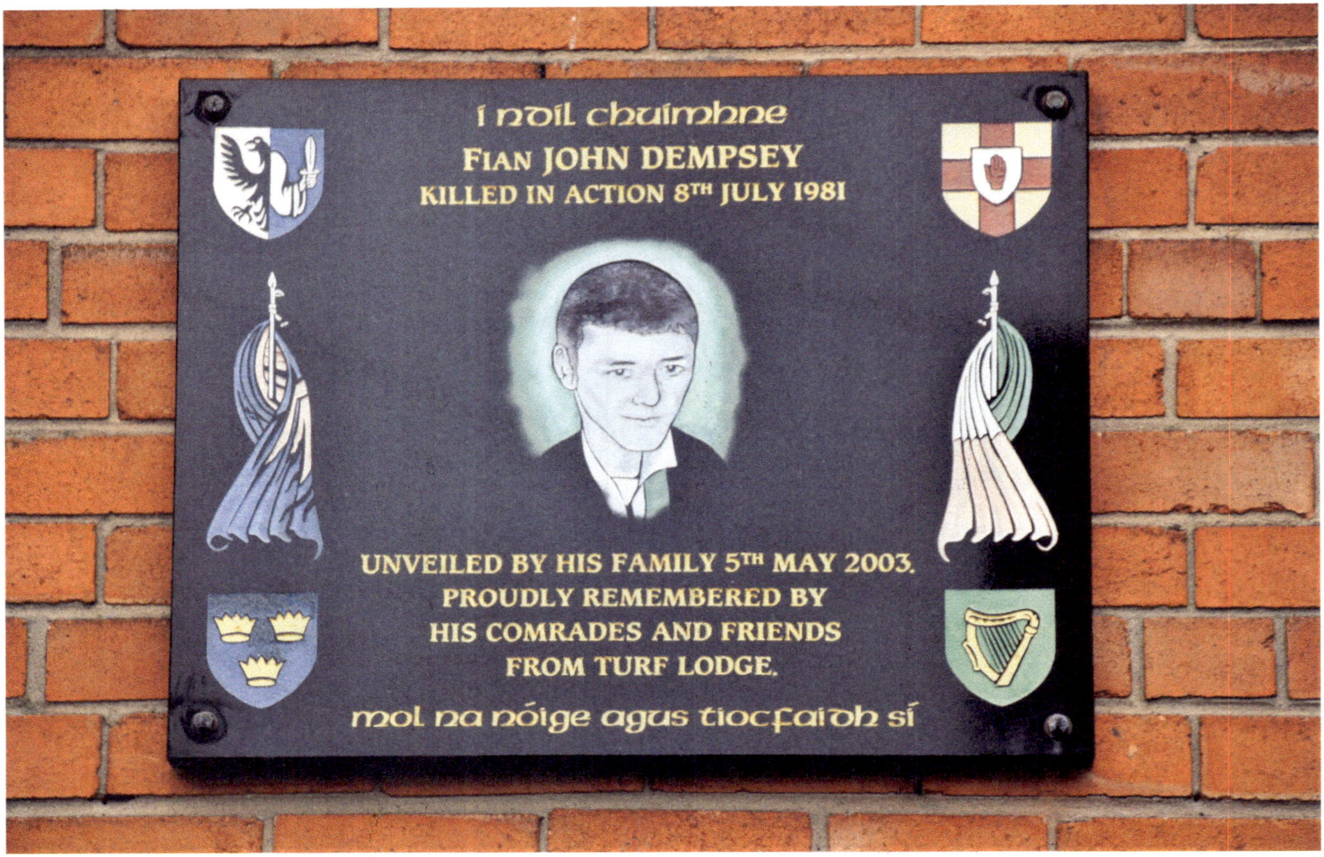

FIGURE 51 Fian John Dempsey, Divis Drive, Andersonstown, West Belfast, 2003. Photo by Tony Crowley.

is contrasted with the pen portraits of eleven local IRA volunteers (all of whom are wearing jackets and ties) (Figure 64, see Fulcrum). Another image, in the Markets, depicted three IRA volunteers (with rocket launchers and rifles) with seven pen portraits (Figure 65, see Fulcrum). While a mural on Glenalina Road, Ballymurphy, identified its protagonists on a small plaque rather than on the image itself (Figure 66, see Fulcrum). In these particular examples, the relationship between people, place, and memory in tight-knit, working-class, republican

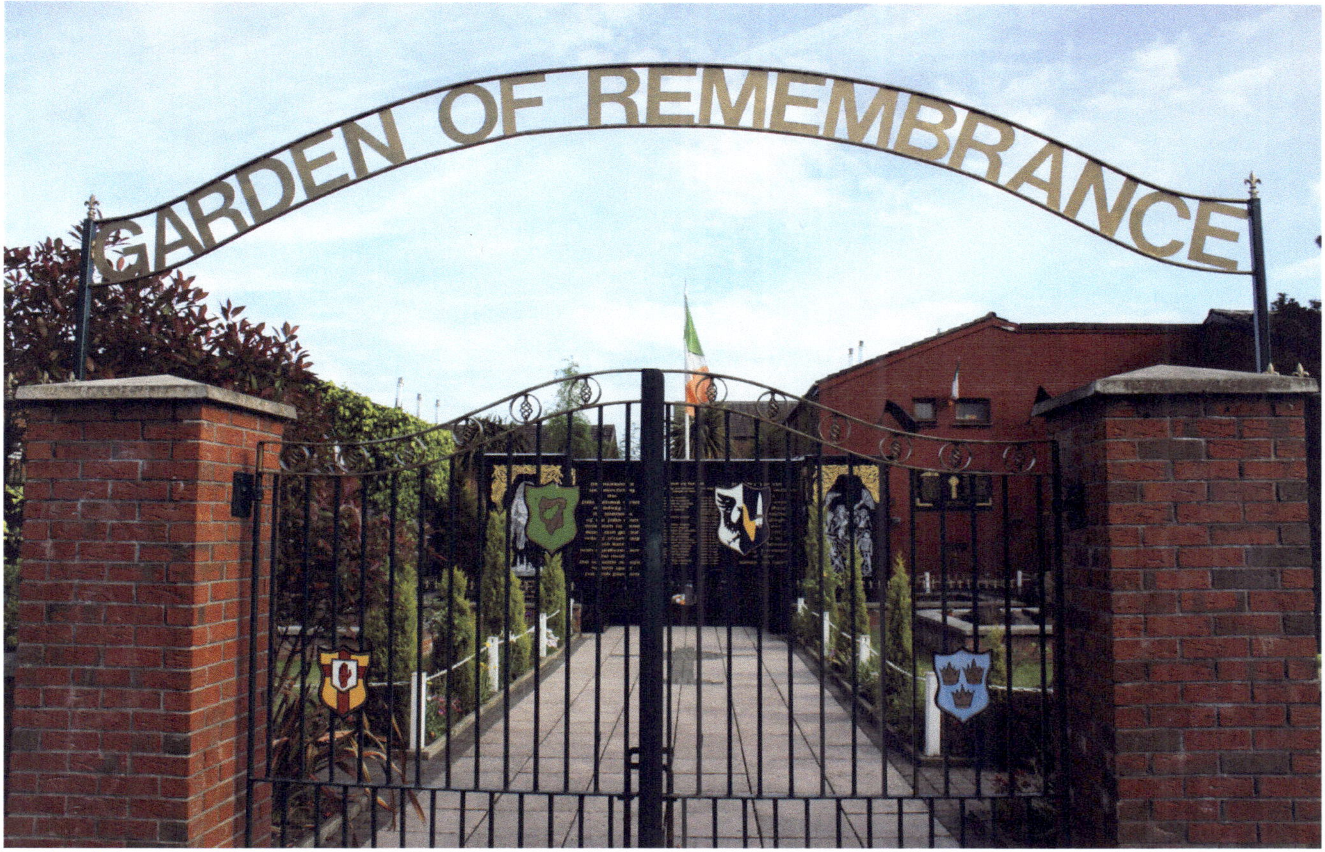

FIGURE 53 Garden of Remembrance, Falls Road, West Belfast, 2002. Photo by Tony Crowley.

communities is clear: no names were required on the mural since as neighbors, schoolfriends, and workmates, they were communally recognized. Implicit in this entire set of murals is the belief that the faces of IRA volunteers, as "ordinary people in extraordinary roles," belonged on the streets in which they were born, grew up, and sometimes died.[9]

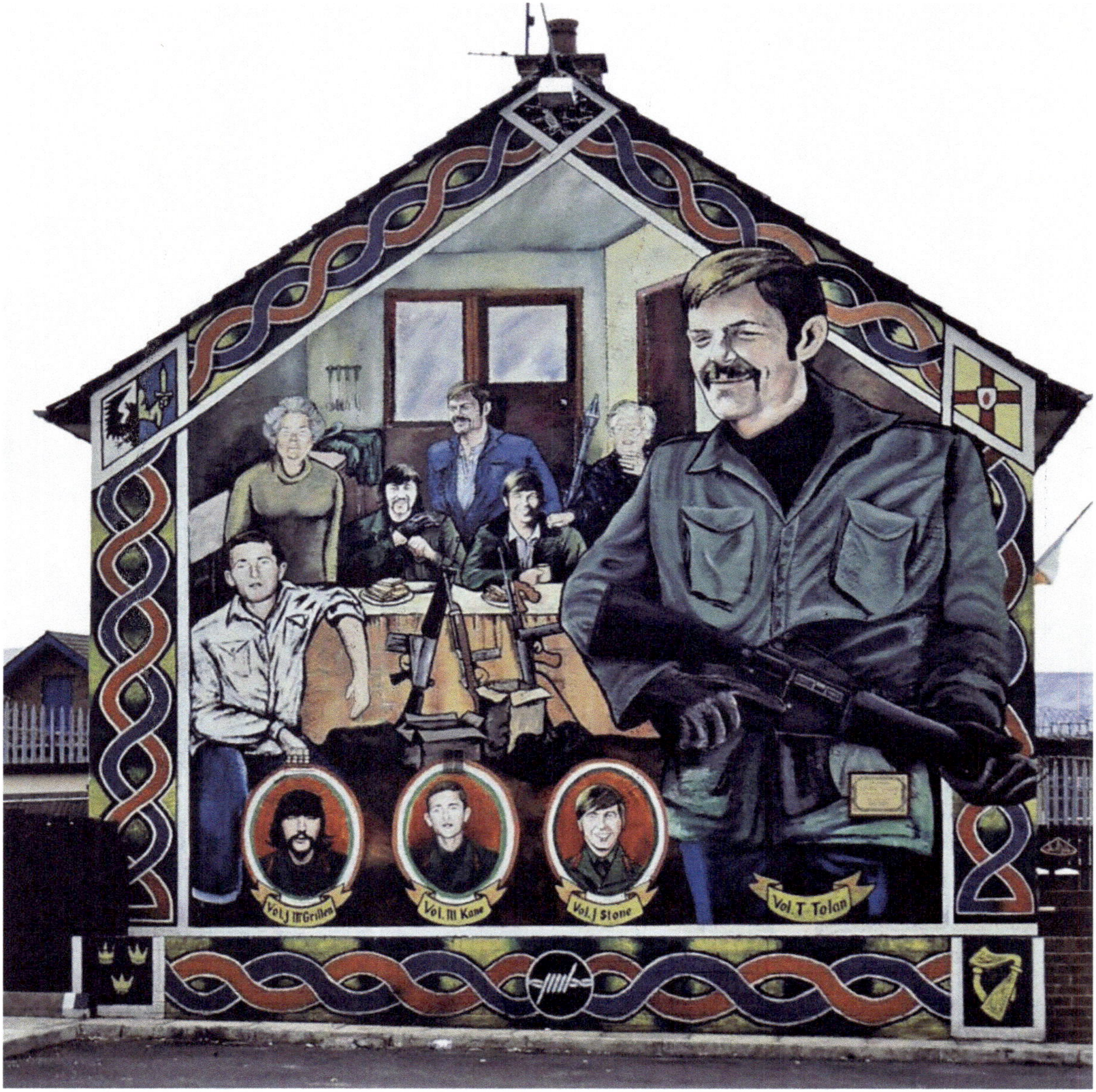

FIGURE 55 Safe house (i), Ballymurphy Crescent, Ballymurphy, West Belfast, 2002. Photo by Tony Crowley.

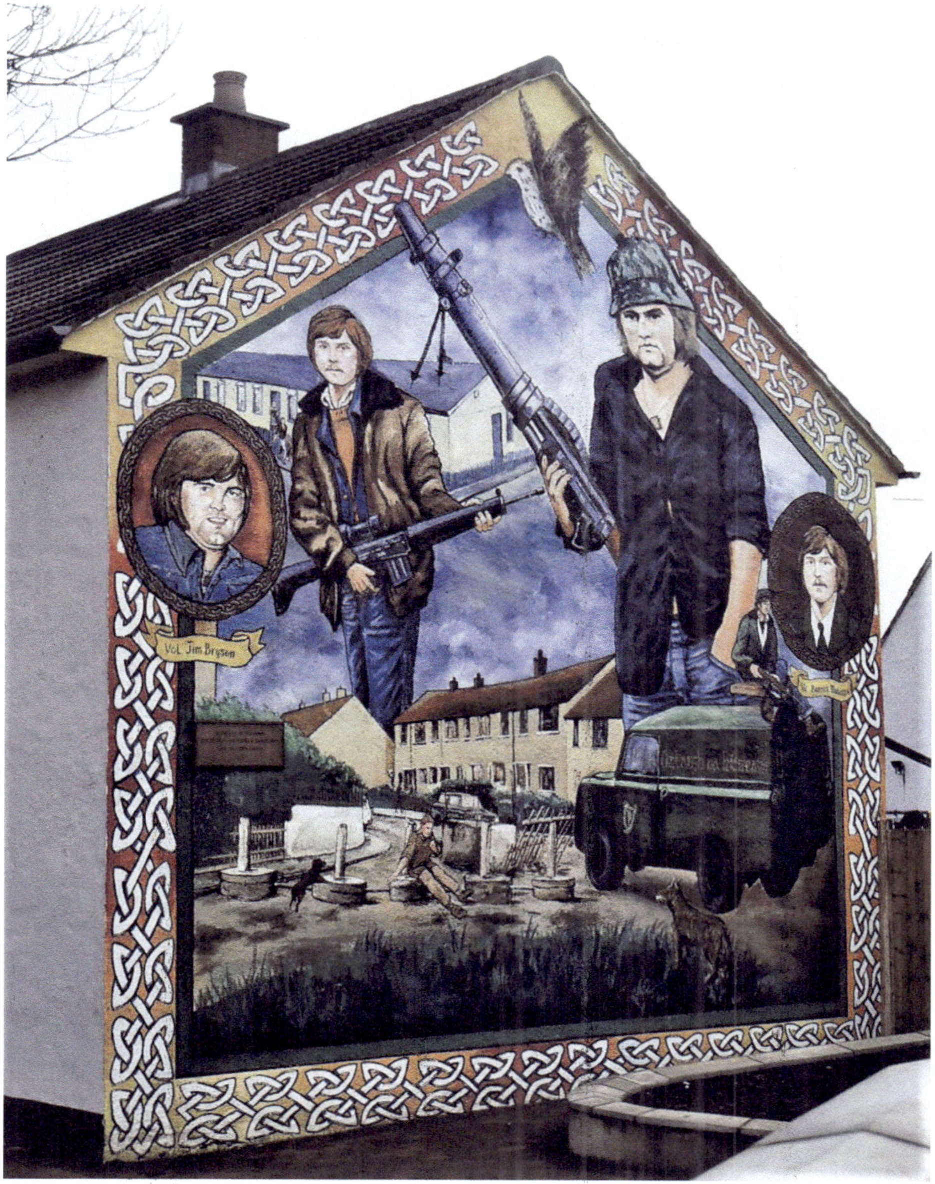

FIGURE 57 Bryson and Mulvenna, Ballymurphy Road, Ballymurphy, 2002. Photo by Tony Crowley.

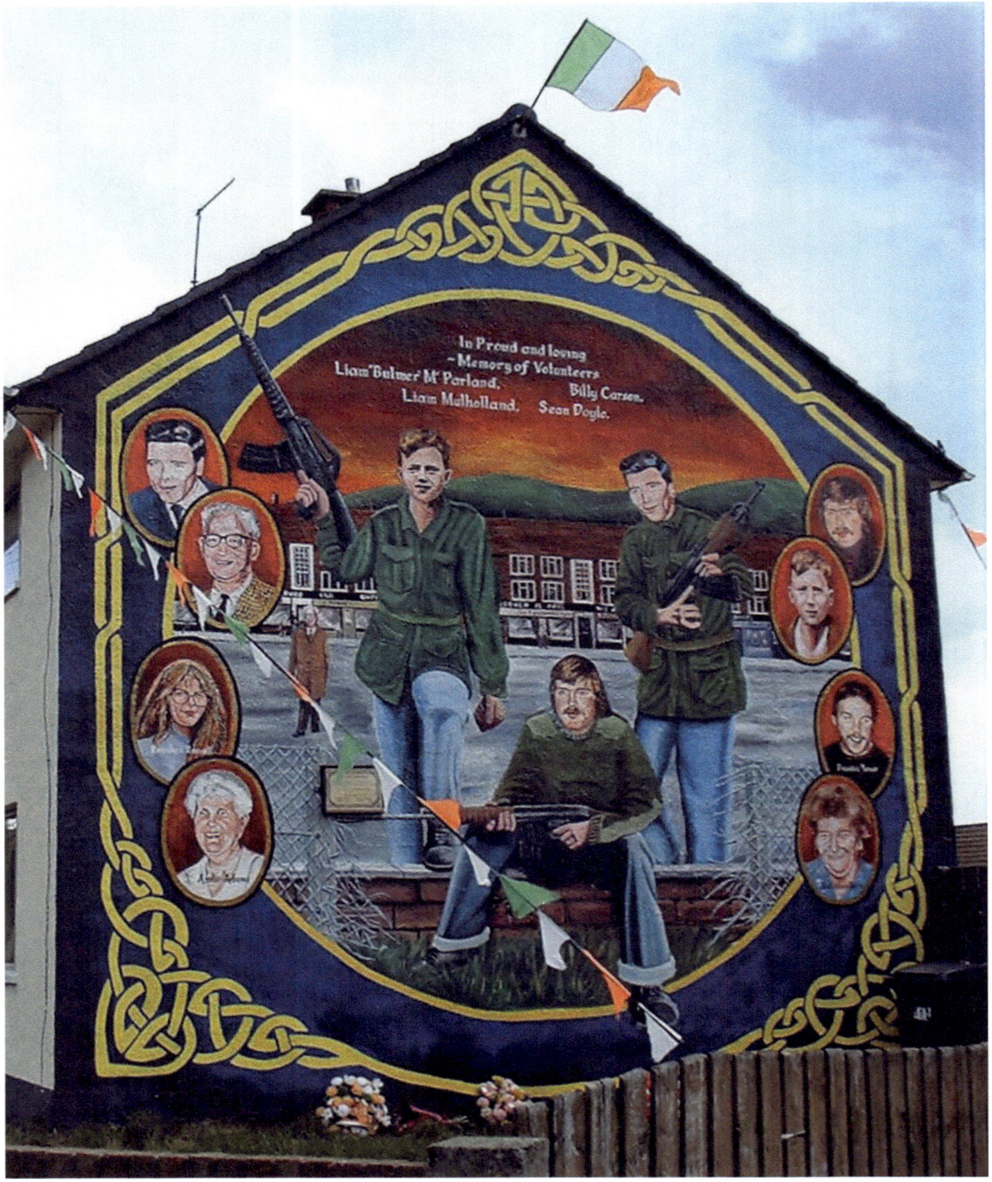

FIGURE 58 In proud and loving memory of volunteers, Glenalina Road/Whiterock Road, Ballymurphy, West Belfast, 2002. Photo by Tony Crowley.

4. WAR AND PEACE—AGAIN

The urge to memory evinced in republican murals is guided by the desire to revere or honor those who had fought, and sometimes died, for the cause; for that reason, memory frequently required that something be done. On occasion, the transaction was clear: "Honour Ireland's dead Wear an Easter lily" (Figure 67, see Fulcrum). In this case the exchange was relatively undemanding, but more frequently, the debt was implicit—that the living owed something to the dead, though what exactly was unclear. This was something of a double-edged sword for mainstream republicanism. On the one hand, it encouraged affiliation to the cause, by asserting in effect that "these people gave their lives, *therefore* we have to maintain the fight in order to honor their memory." But on the other hand, the memory of the dead and their sacrifice also prompted the more difficult question—"what was it, exactly, that the dead had died for, and had republicanism achieved their goal?" Sometimes this was rather abruptly put as an accusation: "Bobby Sands didn't die for X" (an end to collusion and the unionist veto, the disbanding of the RUC, the opening of all roads, power-sharing, a republican Deputy First Minister, and so on). But such a claim was ahistorical. Bobby Sands didn't die for any of those things precisely because he couldn't have, since the prison struggle wasn't about those issues. And as to what his position on those questions would have been—that is surely unknowable and only open to speculation.[10] Nonetheless, the objection raised a question that was asked throughout the republican movement and indeed beyond, and one that was embodied in the dead faces staring down from the walls: what had been achieved by twenty-five years of war?

As noted above, when republicans called their ceasefire in 1994, it was with the expectation that they would play a central role in an inclusive political process that would result in "a just and lasting settlement." Some seventeen months later, with little progress made towards such a process (and after the introduction of the British government's demand for IRA decommissioning as a pre-condition for talks), the IRA declared that it had returned to war at 6pm on February 9 1996; at 7pm it exploded a large bomb at London's Canary Wharf. Its statement asserted that "instead of embracing the peace process, the British Government acted in bad faith, with Mr. Major and the unionist leaders squandering this opportunity to resolve the conflict" (English 2003: 289). Later that year the IRA destroyed a large part of Manchester city center with a huge bomb, and exploded two bombs at Thiepval Barracks, the British Army headquarters in Northern Ireland. Though unionist (and some British) politicians seized on the resumption of war as a vindication of their scepticism towards republican intentions, the general reaction was one of dismay and renewed anxiety.

Republican resentment was reflected in the reappearance of murals that heralded, rather than commemorated, the IRA. The message, proclaimed in large graffiti on Welsh Street, the Markets, South Belfast, was that the IRA was undefeated (and back) (Figure 68, see Fulcrum). And the theme was reiterated in a series of militaristic images that appeared across Northern Ireland—for example, in Newry (Figure 69, see Fulcrum), Crossmaglen (Figure 70, see Fulcrum), and Belfast (Figure 71, see Fulcrum). Other republican groups also re-asserted their willingness to use violence (Figure 72, see Fulcrum), and the period saw the appearance of new organizations that challenged the primacy of Sinn Féin and the IRA as the main representatives of republicanism. Dismissed as "micro-groups" and, later, as "dissidents," political groups such as Republican Sinn Féin (RSF), the32 County Sovereignty Movement (32CSM), and the Republican Network for Unity (RNU), together with military formations such as the Continuity Irish Republican Army (CIRA), the Real IRA (RIRA), Óglaigh na hÉireann (ONH), and the New IRA, rejected the Peace Process and the role of Sinn Féin and the Provisional IRA within it.[11] Building on dissent within the republican movement with regard to an "internal settlement"—"Stormont Never! Never! Never!" (Figure 73, see Fulcrum)—and decommissioning—"Not an ounce Not a bullet Remember '69' Never again" (Figure 74, see Fulcrum)—groups such as the RIRA laid claim to republican tradition (including the Hunger Strikers) (Figure 75, see Fulcrum).[12] They also ridiculed Sinn Féin and the Provisional IRA—"?IRA" (Figure 76, see Fulcrum)—on the basis that rather than "Brits out," any settlement negotiated with the British and unionism would amount to a 'sell out" (Figure 77, see Fulcrum). Always sensitive to this accusation, mainstream republicanism responded by reiterating familiar slogans—"Ireland unfree will never be at peace"—or with assertions of the republican belief in "tiocfaidh ár lá": "Either ballot or gun Our day will come" (Figure 78, see Fulcrum). In this respect, Sinn Féin's success in the Northern Ireland Forum elections (they gained 15.5% of the vote on an abstentionist platform), helped to bolster their political confidence. Nonetheless, with the IRA back at war, and Sinn Féin barred from all-party talks, mainstream republicanism faced a conundrum. The murals that reflected the dominant feeling seemed almost plaintive: "War or peace? Britain has the choice!" (Figure 79, see Fulcrum) and "Who really wants peace?" (Figure 80, see Fulcrum). This latter mural, in particular, illustrated the difficulty for the republican leadership. In it the dove of peace (a badly drawn budgie—some murals really were poorly executed), was held down by a Union Jack ball and chain (inscribed with "British government" and the names of the unionist parties), while to the right the map of Ireland was overlaid with the insignia of the four ancient provinces (thus implying a United Ireland). In reality, for republicans, the issue was not whether there was any possibility of negotiating a United Ireland (to say nothing of a socialist republic), but finding an answer to a more complex question: "peace—but at what price?"

In May 1997, Sinn Féin won two parliamentary seats in the General Election (Gerry Adams in Belfast West and Martin McGuinness in Mid Ulster), and seventy-four seats in the local elections (with 17% of the vote). In July that year the IRA re-instated its ceasefire, and in September Sinn Féin signed up to the Mitchell principles (the first of which was a "total and absolute commitment… To democratic and exclusively peaceful means of resolving political issues" (Mitchell et al. 1996: np). But if this seemed like progress towards peace, the reality on the ground was once again violence and sectarian division. Nowhere was this more visible than in the bitter conflict that ran from 1995 to 2001 around Orange Order marches through nationalist and republican districts. The focus of the most contentious dispute was the route of the Orange march from Drumcree church to Portadown, though a relatively small number of other marches were likewise contentious, including a parade through the Lower Ormeau Road in South Belfast.[13] For the Orange Order, and indeed loyalism and unionism, the matter involved the traditional right to march wherever it saw fit, a right that they took to be guaranteed by the principle of freedom of assembly. For nationalist and republican residents, who saw the marches as triumphalist, degrading, and therefore unwanted, the issue was the right to go about their everyday business without interference (during contentious parades, residents were often barricaded into their own areas) (Figure 81, see Fulcrum). In all, it was a volatile mix of contentious questions around tradition, identity, respect and equality, which embodied the larger issues that lay at the core of the conflict. And, given that there was a clash of rights, the role of the State, specifically its enforcement agencies (the police and army), was central. Thus republicans and nationalists called for the State to uphold their right to refuse to allow marches through their areas unless the residents were consulted and gave their consent (Figure 82) (Figure 83, see Fulcrum) (Figure 84, see Fulcrum). When marches were forced through (as they were in Portadown in 1995–1997), nationalists and republicans took it as evidence that they were second-class citizens in an unreformed state ("A Protestant parliament for a Protestant people") (Figure 85, see Fulcrum). "Nothing has changed," the walls declared (Figure 86, see Fulcrum) (Figure 87). The dispute over marching seemed to crystallize many of the wider issues at stake at a crucial moment in the conflict, and it provoked vicious sectarian antagonism and widespread violence. On 12th July 1998, following a decision to ban the Drumcree march, the nadir was reached: three young Catholic boys were killed in a loyalist petrol bomb attack on their home in Ballymoney.

5. THE AGREEMENT AND AFTER

On Friday April 10 1998 (Good Friday), after two years of on–off talks between representatives of various strands of unionism, loyalism, nationalism, republicanism, and the British and Irish governments, the parties to the talks signed the binding, internationally ratified *Belfast [Good Friday] Agreement.* Despite republican opposition to the deal (the IRSP and RSF rejected it) (Figure 88, see Fulcrum), it was endorsed by two separate referenda, one in Northern Ireland, the other in the Republic of Ireland, on May 22 1998. Though the grim death toll of the Omagh bombing, carried out by the RIRA on August 15 that year, demonstrated the ongoing potential for violence and its devastating effects, the war was, to all intents and purposes, over.[14] The conflict, however, was not—and in a

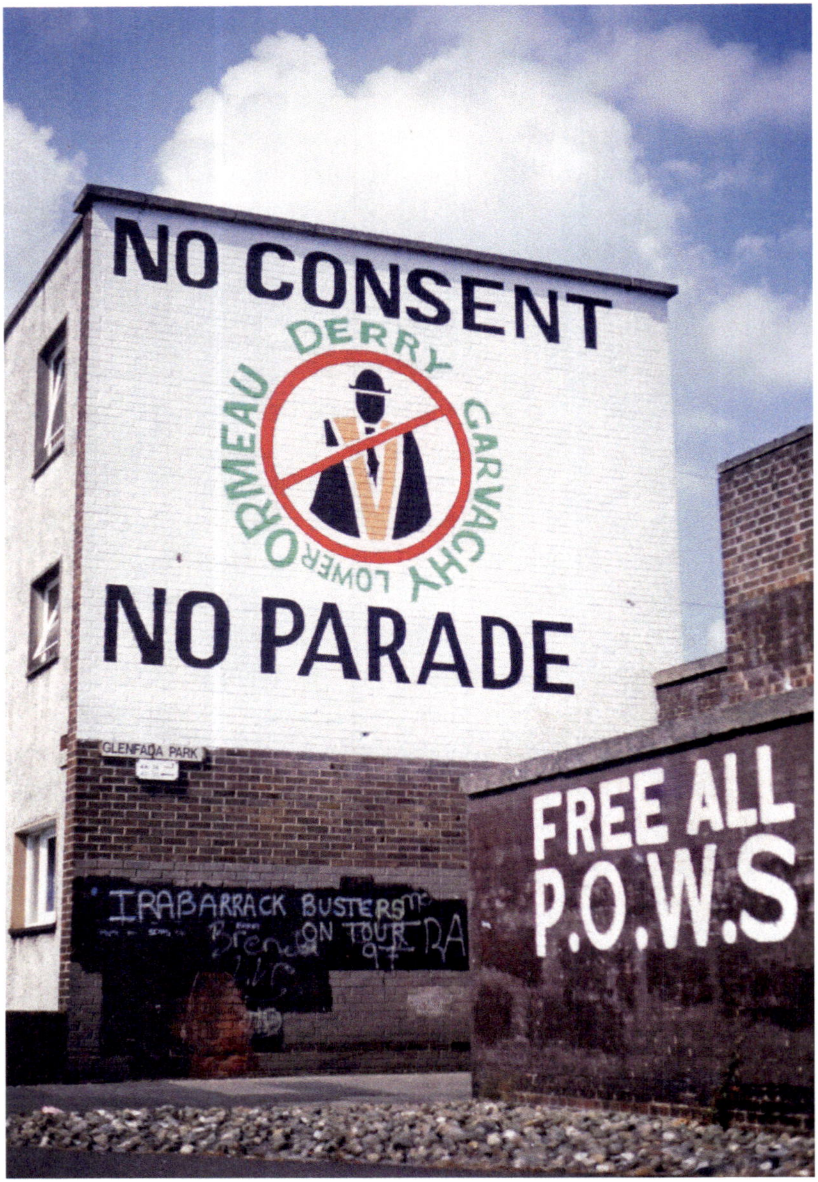

FIGURE 82 No consent no parade, Glenfada Park, Bogside, Derry, 1996. Photo by Tony Crowley.

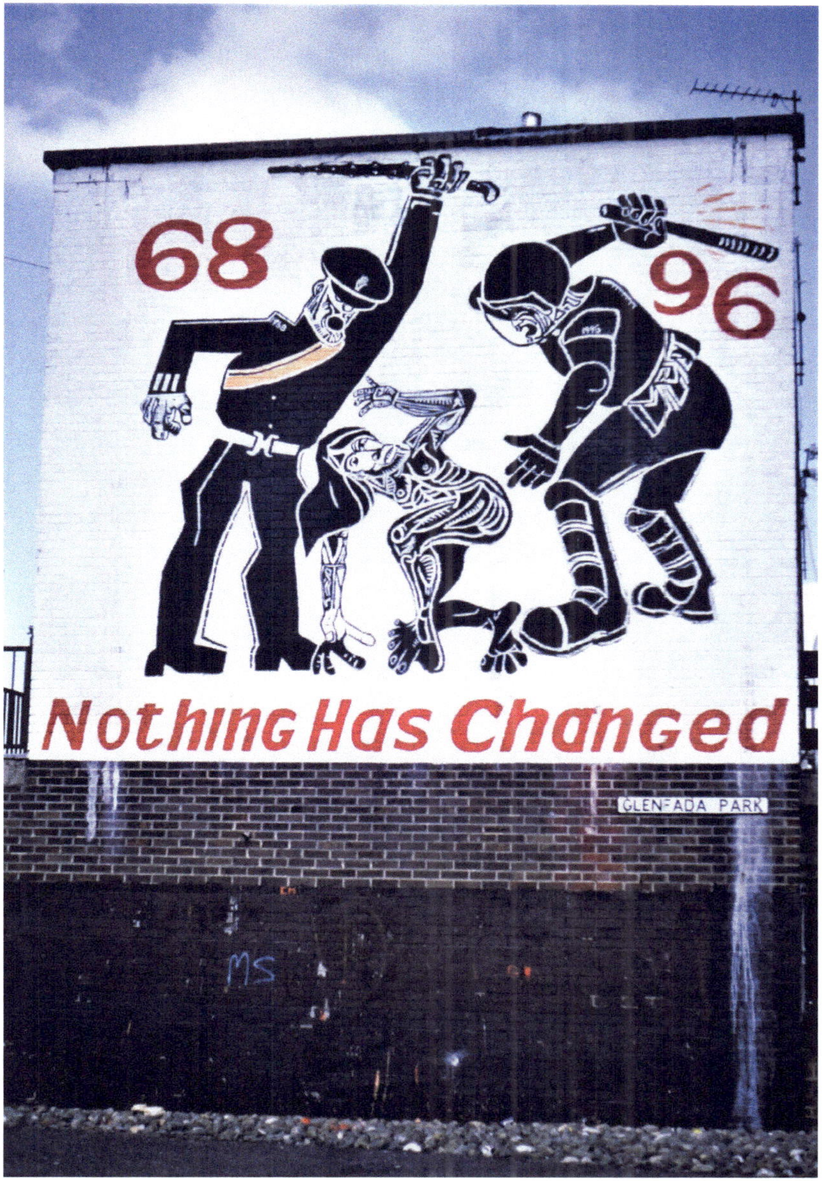

FIGURE 87 Nothing has changed, Glenfada Park, Derry, 1996. Photo by Tony Crowley.

divided, deeply sectarian and antagonistic society, it could not be otherwise. For although *The Belfast Agreement* produced a constitutional settlement and system of governance which brought the war between republicans and the British State to an end, the fundamental issues that concerned and divided nationalists/republicans and unionists/loyalists continued to play out.

There was, however, one central problem that united republicans and loyalists: the question of the prisoners—the men and women who had joined paramilitary organizations and used violence to pursue political ends. What was to happen to those who had committed the most terrible crimes, including, in some cases, multiple killings? From an orthodox legal perspective, the position was clear—once convicted, prisoners could only be released according to the rules that governed sentencing and parole. But this was not a normal law-and-order situation: as was generally acknowledged, it was highly unlikely, had the political circumstances been different, that many of the prisoners would have been involved in criminality.[15] Thus for republicans, it was simply an imperative that the prisoners should be released and, from the first ceasefire, there was a campaign that focused on this issue, in which murals were pivotal. The construction of the prisoners as "prisoners of war" (contrary to the policy of criminalization that the British had introduced in 1976), was central to the discursive strategy that underpinned these murals (Figure 89, see Fulcrum). Here, as in many of the prison murals, the effectiveness of the work lay in part in its location, with a list of prisoners from the local area figuring prominently; this trope was frequently combined with common features such as barbed wire, green ribbons, the dove of peace, images of Long Kesh, and the ubiquitous "Saoirse" (freedom) (Figure 90, see Fulcrum) (Figure 91, see Fulcrum) (Figure 92, see Fulcrum). As McConville has argued, the prisoners were fundamental to the forging of republican consent to *The Belfast Agreement* (McConville 2021), and it is clear that their release was seen as a key piece in the puzzle (Figure 93, see Fulcrum). Indeed, such was the importance of the prisoners that a complex mural representing their situation was painted in Ludlow Square, New Lodge, in 1997 (Figure 94). Composed around one of the original republican motifs painted in Beechmount in 1981 (hands bound by barbed wire), and a verse from Dylan's "Blowing in the wind," and topped by "Saoirse," "Free the prisoners," a green ribbon, and the dove of peace bearing keys, the mural represented the history of the republican prison campaign in a series of iconic images. Moving from the depiction of a Blanketman learning Irish, to a woman being strip-searched in Armagh jail, the mural reproduced posters from the H-Block and Hunger Strike campaigns, as well as images of women protesters, women banging bin-lids to announce the death of Bobby Sands, people being arrested, the Long Kesh compounds, familiar photographs of IRA volunteer Mairéad Farrell in and out of Armagh, and republican prisoners in an English jail campaigning for repatriation. Painted more than a quarter of a century ago, the significance of the topic is indicated by the fact that this is one of the few republican images to have survived to the present.

The issue of paramilitary prisoners was addressed in *The Belfast Agreement*, which provided for "an accelerated programme for the release of prisoners' belonging to organizations "maintaining a complete and

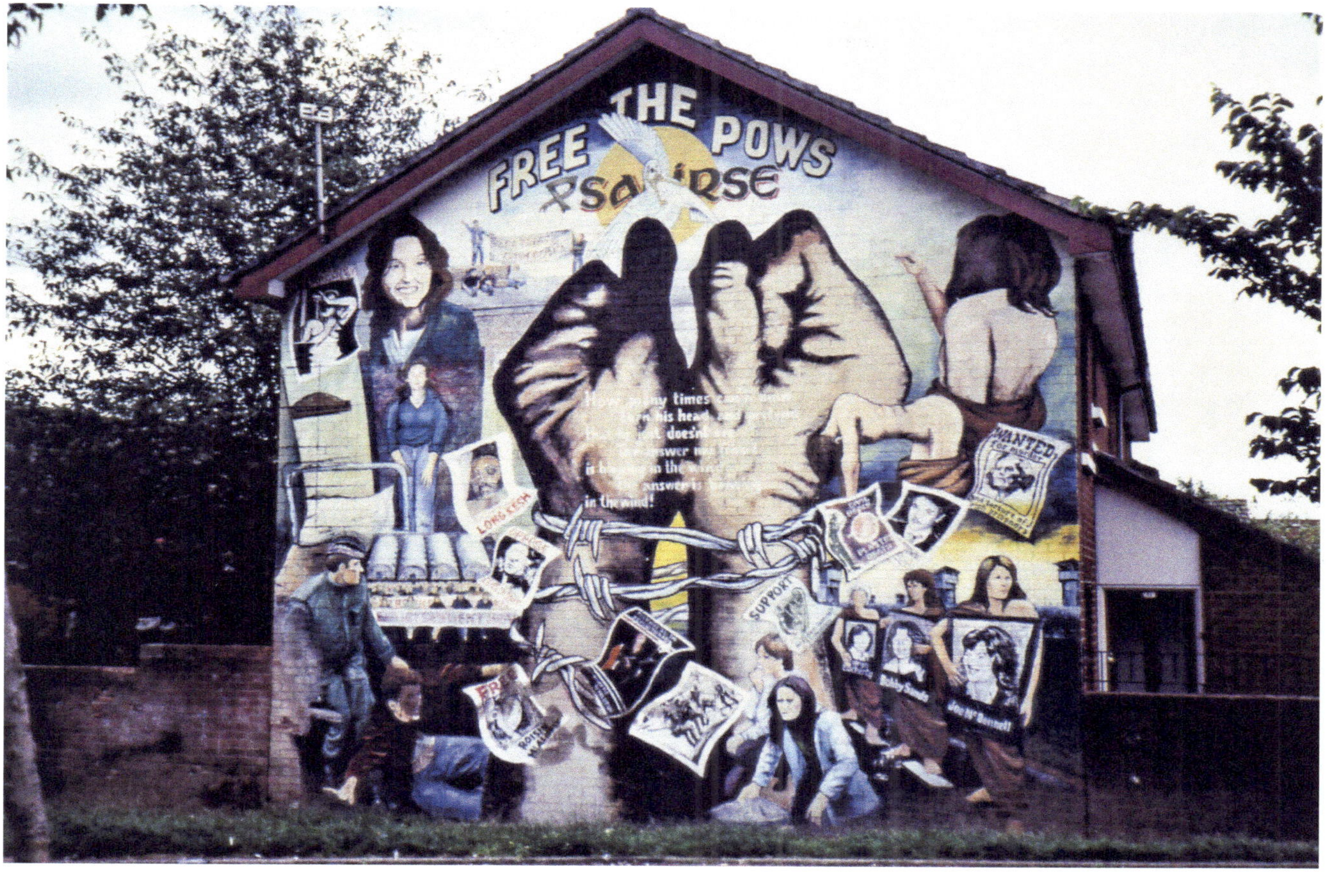

FIGURE 94 How many times, Ludlow Square/New Lodge Road, New Lodge, Belfast, 2007. Photo by Tony Crowley.

unequivocal ceasefire" (Northern Ireland Office 1998: 28); the last prisoners were released in 2000. But for republicans, another provision of the *Agreement* also carried symbolic and practical significance: the reform of policing. This was a sensitive issue for unionists (though not for all loyalists), but for republicans the RUC was a detested, corrupt organization whose history was one of sectarianism and collusion with loyalist paramilitaries. The contempt was made clear on the walls (Figure 95, see Fulcrum) (Figure 96, see Fulcrum), with particular attention drawn to specific events such as the deaths of children killed by plastic bullets fired by police officers (Figure 97, see Fulcrum). The republican demand was succinct: disband the RUC as an integral part of the Peace Process (Figure 98, see Fulcrum). The *Agreement* itself set up a "Commission on policing for Northern Ireland" with the aim of establishing a force that would "enjoy widespread support from, and is seen as an integral part of, the community as a whole" (Northern Ireland Office 1998: 25). The subsequent Patten Commission, *A New Beginning: Policing in Northern Ireland* (1999), made a series of recommendations, including: the renaming of the force as the "Police Service of Northern Ireland" (PSNI); new and accountable policing boards; an ombudsman and complaints tribunal; removal of symbols of Britishness; a new code of ethics and oath of office (based on human rights); and a 50–50 recruitment policy of Catholics and Protestants (Independent Commission on Policing for Northern Ireland 1999: 107–122). Despite considerable opposition within republicanism generally, Sinn Féin eventually accepted the reformed police service in 2007.

In *The Cure at Troy*, Seamus Heaney set out the grim effects of the war, but articulated an expression of hope:

> The innocent in gaols
> Beat on their bars together.
> A hunger-striker's father
> Stands in the graveyard dumb.
> The police widow in veils
> Faints at the funeral home.
>
> History says, *Don't hope*
> *On this side of the grave,*
> But then, once in a lifetime
> The longed-for tidal wave
> Of justice can rise up,
> And hope and history rhyme
> (Heaney 1990: 69, emphasis in original)

There might have been some who dreamt that post-*Agreement* Northern Ireland would fulfil some of the more outlandish predictions of reconciliation and progress made at the time. But as it turned out, in the mundanity of the conflict that persisted beyond the polite meaningless words and expressions of intent, hope and history didn't rhyme. Indeed for mainstream republicans, the period 1998–2006 was one of frustration, anger, and occasionally despair as unionists refused to implement the *Agreement* over the issue of IRA decommissioning. Predictably, Sinn Féin muralists expressed republican disaffection with the ongoing stalemate across a number of areas: principally, the unionist refusal to engage with the *Agreement*, but also ongoing disputes about marches, the slow implementation of the Patten report, and the lack of recognition of nationalist cultural activities (including funding for St Patrick's Day festivities) (Figure 99) (Figure 100, see Fulcrum) (Figure 101, see Fulcrum). But such was the nature of the on-off crisis, that Sinn Féin were always in danger of being outflanked by republicans opposed to what they regarded as the capitulation of decommissioning (Figure 102). Notably, when the IRA agreed to put its arms "beyond use" in August 2001 (the process was completed by 2005), there were no murals to celebrate the fact.

For Sinn Féin, the political imperative after the *Agreement*, was to become the largest party of nationalism by eclipsing the SDLP in national and local elections, and they achieved this aim relatively quickly and emphatically. Elections were always the occasion for murals and the images varied in their complexity, ranging from simple injunctions to vote in order "to keep the Orange Order out," "to strengthen the Peace Process" (a refrain heard

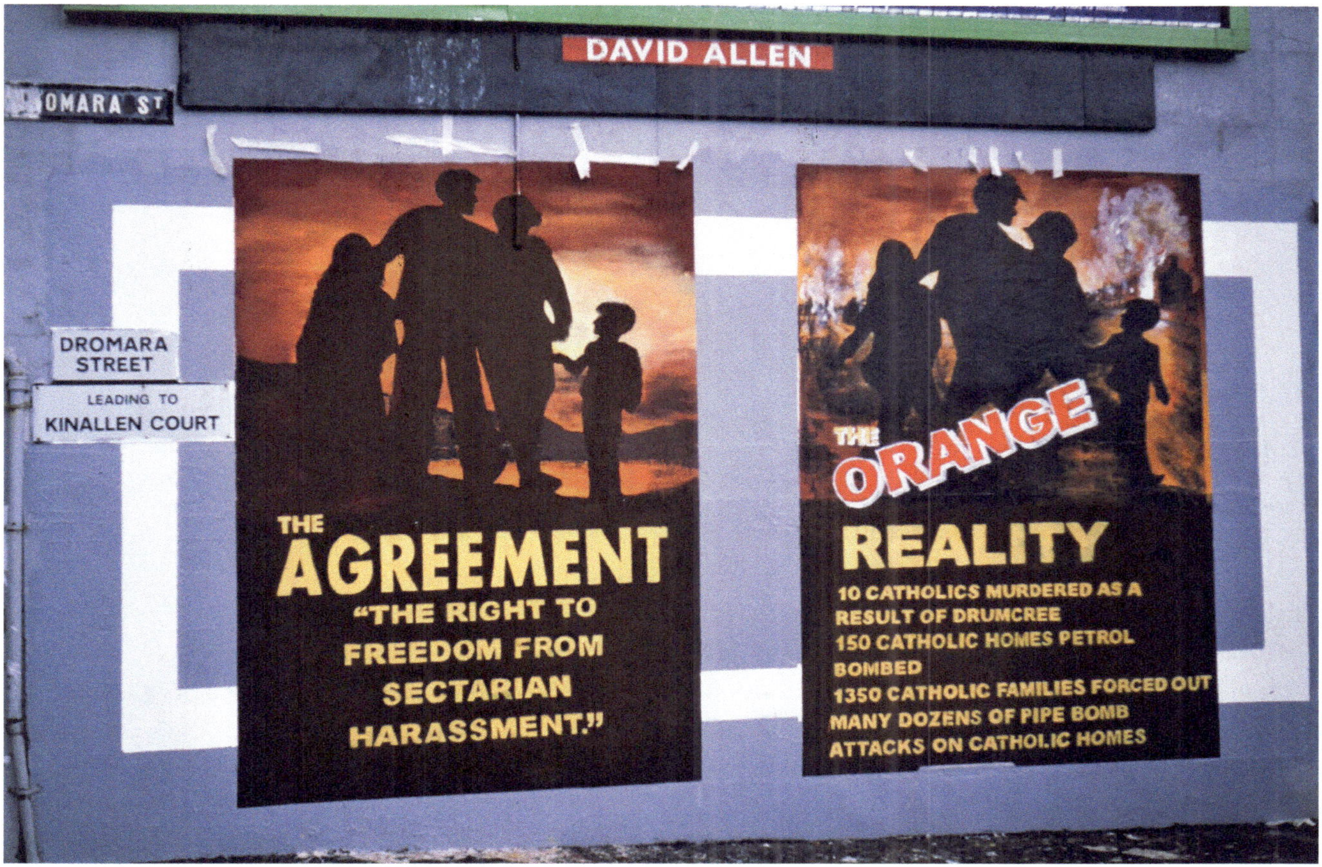

FIGURE 99 Agreement Reality, Dromara Street, Lower Ormeau Road, South Belfast, 2000. Photo by Tony Crowley.

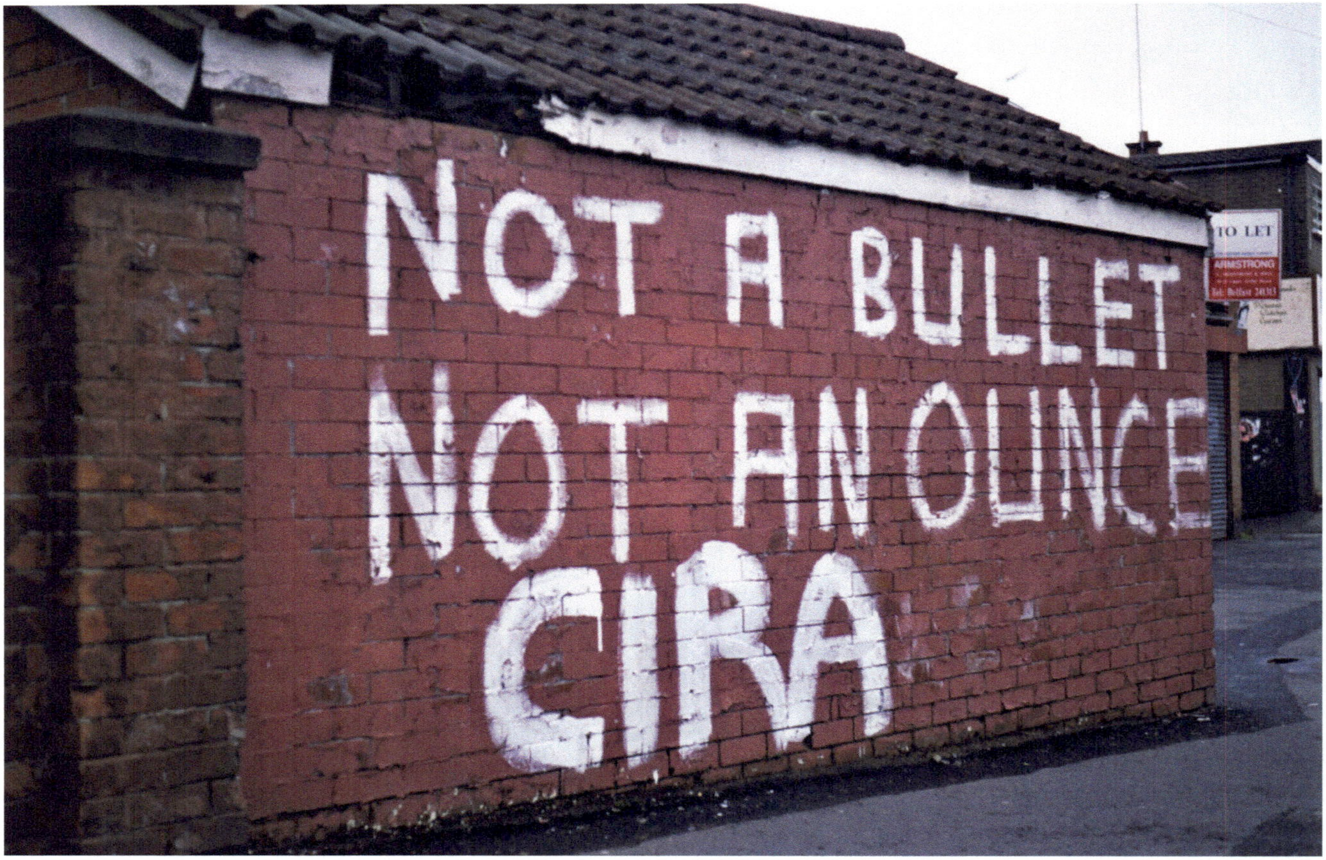

FIGURE 102 Not a bullet, Andersonstown Road, Andersonstown, West Belfast, 2001. Photo by Tony Crowley.

long after peace had been achieved), to build a New Ireland (using the phrase "ar aghaidh linn"—"let's go," rather than "tiocfaidh ár lá"), and on to complex exhortations that used popular culture (in the form of comic book characters) to mock opponents while pointing out the potential for political victory (Figure 103) (Figure 104, see Fulcrum) (Figure 105, see Fulcrum) (Figure 106, see Fulcrum). Yet consolidation of Sinn Féin's role as the leading voice of constitutional nationalism was not confined to electioneering, and in the post-*Agreement* years, the party sought to become the hegemonic social, cultural, and political force in its heartland areas and beyond. This is not to say that the party took direct control of all activities in those areas (a criticism frequently made), but that party loyalists often influenced or indeed directed organizations across the social field (from elected office

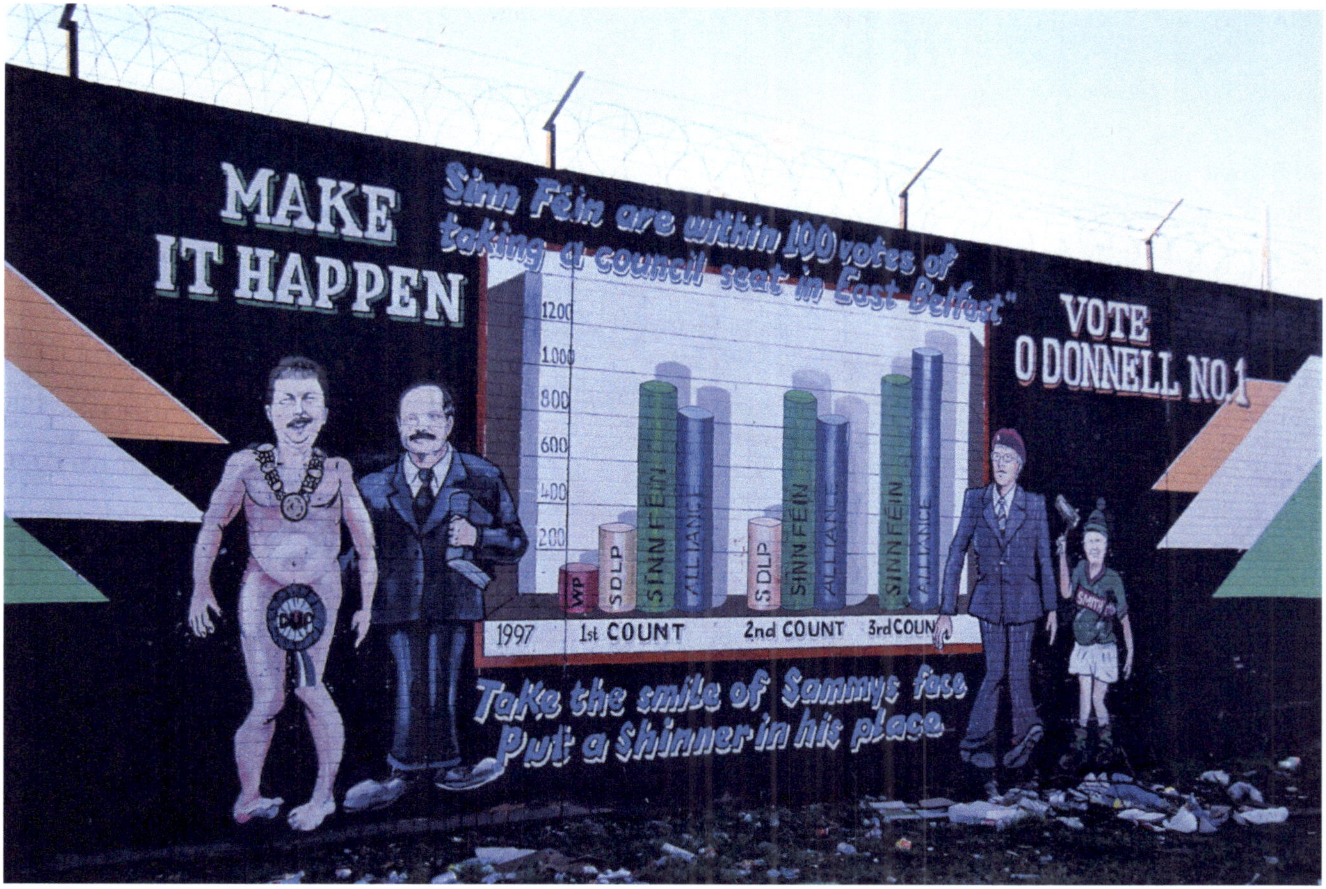

FIGURE 103 Make it happen, Mountpottinger Road, Short Strand, East Belfast, 2001. Photo by Tony Crowley.

to local community group), not least because they were prepared to put the work in. And in the construction of visible cultural hegemony, muralists played an important role.[16]

The forging of hegemony can be simple and direct, as well as subtle and complex; it involves the inculcation of values, ideas, norms, and practices. In essence, it is about the creation of a community with a broadly shared set of beliefs and attitudes that can translate into behavior and particular responses in specific historical circumstances. Such values and practices may exist latently within a community, but the key to hegemonic rule is to articulate them, to augment them, to disseminate them, and to bring people to the point at which they recognize that this is the sort of community that "we" are. In that sense, the post-ceasefire and post-*Agreement* years were crucial for republicans and nationalists since their communal identity was no longer defined by being simply against the British State and the effects of the State's war machine. In the new context, a developed form of republican and nationalist identity needed to be articulated distinctly—as a particular type of community that embodied a practical stance with regard to its historical situation. Murals were the main visual medium through which that identity was forged and represented.[17]

One significant development in this regard was the use of a boundary wall of Andrews flour mill on Divis Street (opposite Divis Tower, a structure that carried a British Army watchtower on its roof until 2005), as a canvas for murals. Though the first mural in 2000 was a 25-meter depiction of the distances at which plastic bullet victims had been killed (in contradiction of the rules for their use) (Figure 107, see Fulcrum), the wall quickly became (and remains) the site of murals that mainly, though not exclusively, articulate an internationalist outlook and sympathies.[18] This was not a new development, since as outlined in chapter two, republicans had sought to "internationalize the conflict" during the war. Post-war, however, the aim was different. There was still a desire to make links with radical causes around the world—for example, with the Palestinians (Figure 108), Aboriginal rights activists (Figure 109, see Fulcrum), the Cuban revolution (Figure 110, see Fulcrum), Catalunyan and Basque separatists (Figure 111, see Fulcrum) (Figure 112, see Fulcrum), the American Indian Movement (Figure 113, see Fulcrum), and freedom movements in general (Figure 114, see Fulcrum). But the international perspective in these murals has to be seen as more than simply an extension of provisional republicanism's wartime attempt to make common cause with other radical political and military resistance movements. For it is not obvious, to take one example, why the residents of New Lodge, an impoverished area in North Belfast, should take an interest in Australian Aboriginal land rights (Figure 115, see Fulcrum). The key to understanding such murals is to put them in the context of the republican attempt to forge cultural hegemony in their own areas. In essence, the murals reflect and shape political sentiment in nationalist and republican areas in the post-war period by enregistering them as radically engaged communities both at home and globally. This is not a misrepresentation of communal feelings and attitudes: it is hardly surprising that people who have lived through repression and deep poverty might feel empathy for others in a similar plight. But it is clear that murals formed part of an attempt to channel and organize political sentiments in specific ways. For those who viewed the images as part of their everyday experience, the murals implicitly (and sometimes explicitly) suggested that like others in the world, they had a just cause that was, is, and should be, fought for politically. For the increasing number of mural tourists (the International Wall has become one of Northern Ireland's main tourist sites) (Figure 116), the images characterized nationalist and republican areas as liberal, outward-looking, and welcoming. The visually striking image of Frederick Douglass, the escaped slave, abolitionist, and successful writer, illustrates the point: knowingly directed

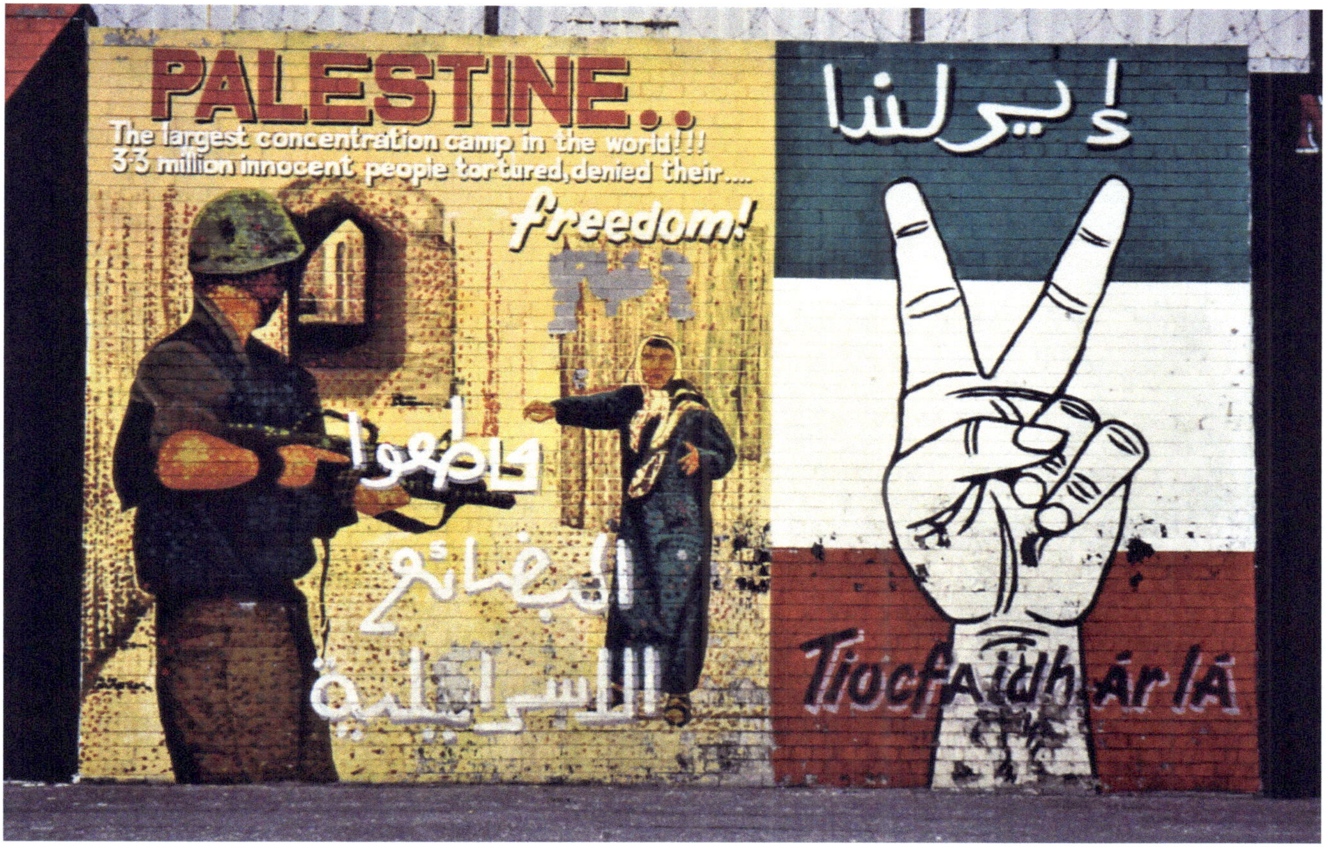

FIGURE 108 Palestine, International Wall, Divis Street, Lower Falls, 2002. Photo by Tony Crowley.

towards an American audience, the mural notes both the Irish welcome given to Douglass, and offers a self-aware acknowledgment of the historical involvement of the Irish in racism (Figure 117).

Some murals were closely associated with Sinn Féin (and the paintings themselves were frequently completed by a relatively small group of mainstream republican activists). Examples included an image of James Connolly sponsored by the party's Trade Union department (Figure 118), a memorial to the first member of the republican youth organization, Na Fianna Éireann, to die during the Troubles (Figure 119, see Fulcrum), and the campaign against collusion (Figure 120). Other murals were not directly associated with the party, though party members were often involved in community organizations that commissioned the images, such as the West Belfast Taxi

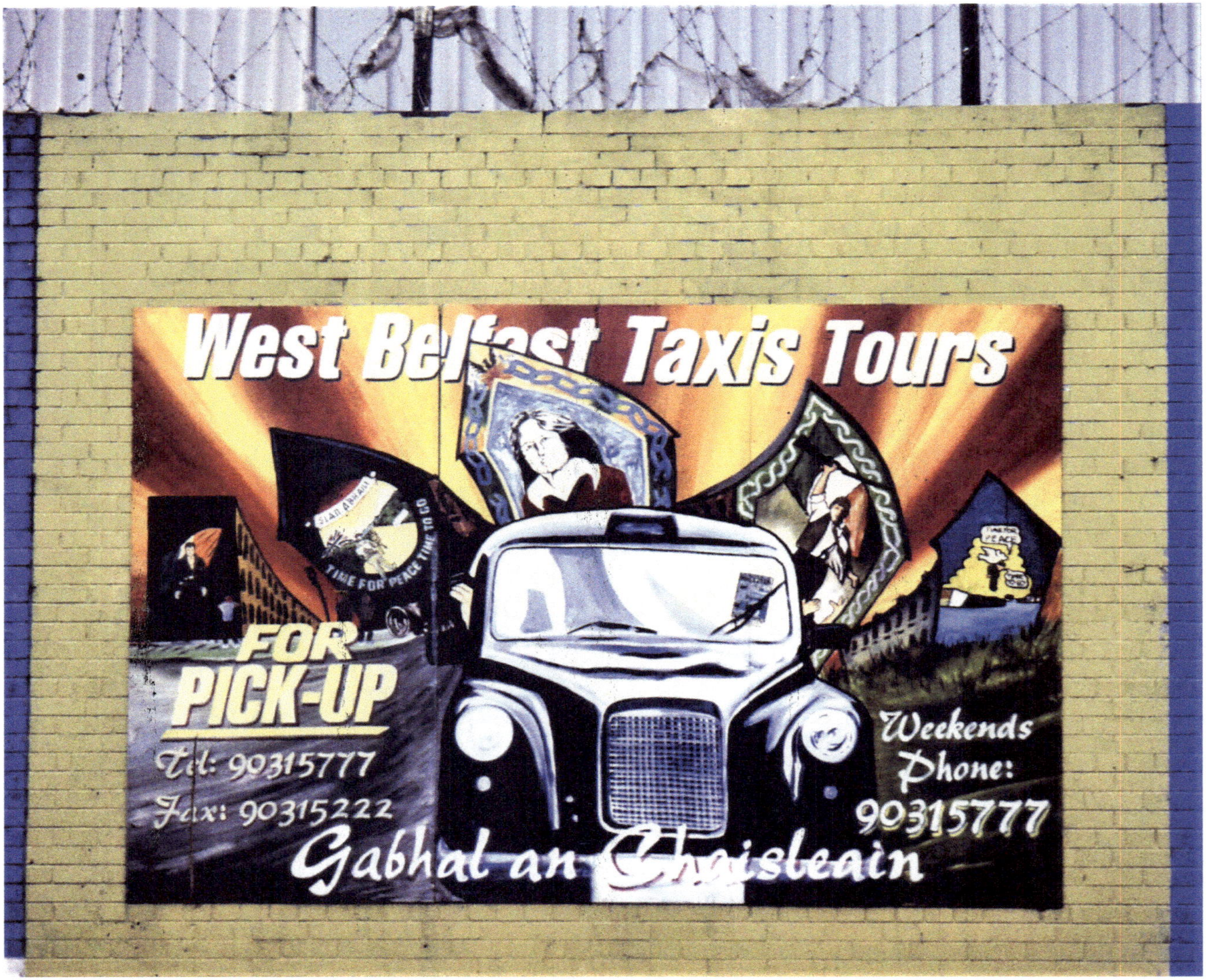

FIGURE 116 West Belfast taxi tours, International Wall, Divis Street, West Belfast, 2002. Photo by Tony Crowley.

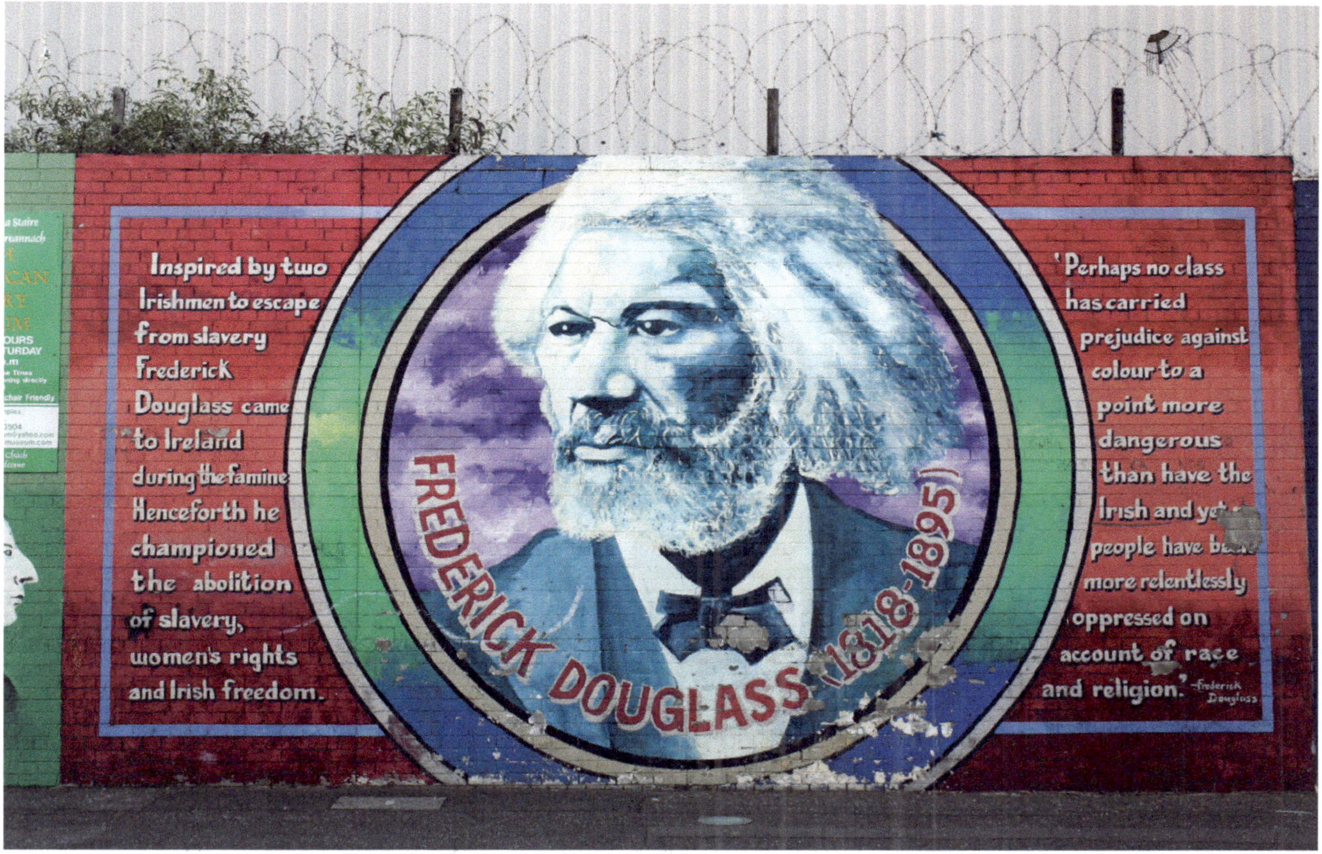

FIGURE 117 Frederick Douglass, International Wall, Divis Street, Lower Falls, West Belfast, 2006. Photo by Tony Crowley.

Association (Figure 121).[19] Memorials were interesting in this regard. As noted earlier in this chapter, republicans engaged in large-scale commemoration from the mid-1990s, but families and local communities also remembered through the walls (Figure 122). Likewise, Sinn Féin became involved in specific events such as the dreadful dispute involving Holy Cross schoolchildren (depicted in a mural that referenced Little Rock 1957) (Figure 123), and campaigns to investigate State killings during the war (Figure 124, see Fulcrum). But local community organizations also ran campaigns against social blights such as drug-dealing and joy-riding (Figure 125, see Fulcrum). And although the republican version of history was recorded (Figure 126, see Fulcrum), very specific forms of local history also made it onto the walls. These were often nostalgic in terms of content and tone

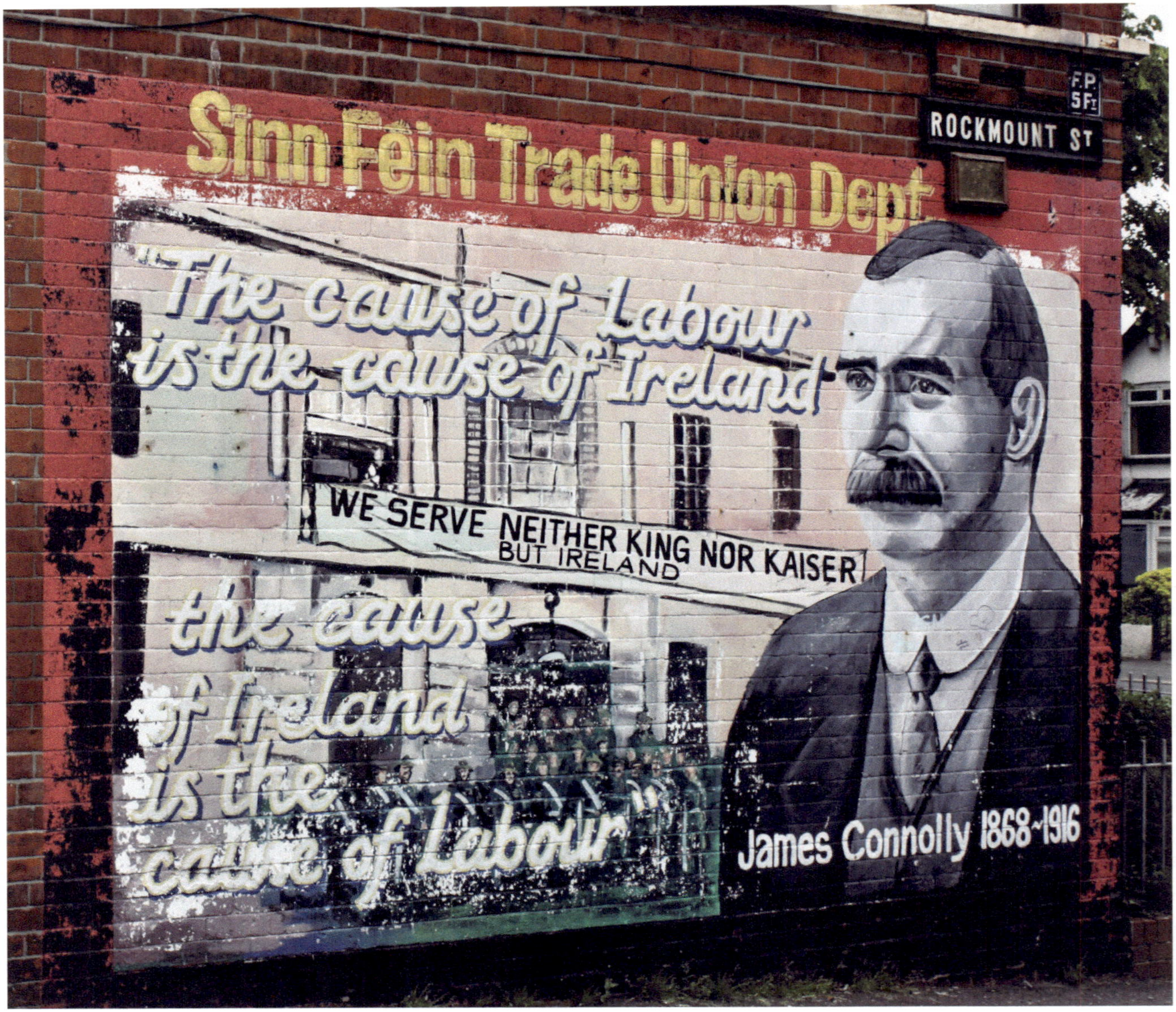

FIGURE 118 The cause of labour, Rockmount Street, St James, West Belfast, 1996. Photo by Tony Crowley.

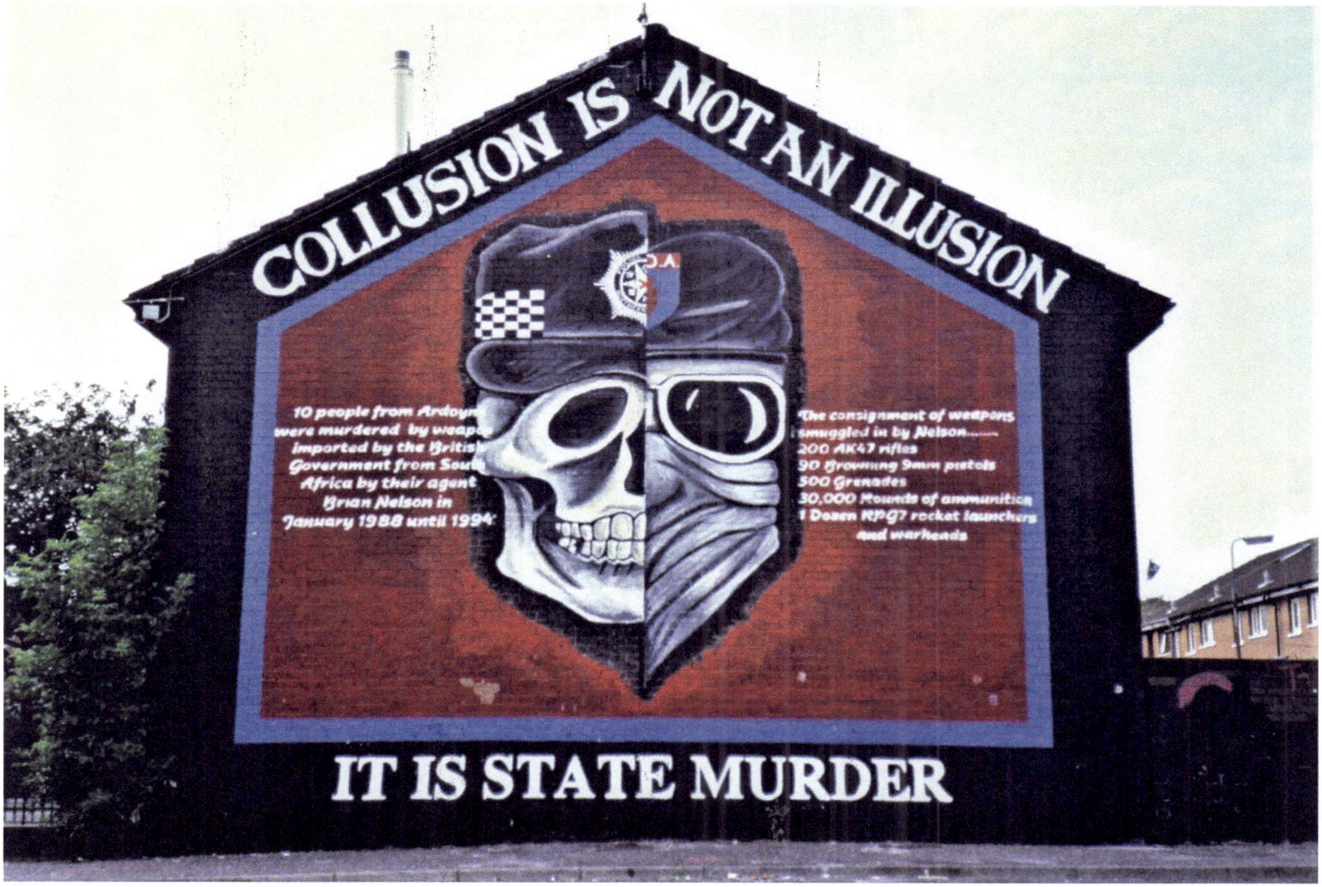

FIGURE 120 Collusion is not an illusion! Ardoyne Avenue, Ardoyne, North Belfast, 2001. Photo by Tony Crowley.

(Figure 127, see Fulcrum), although a pair of murals in New Lodge sharply made the point that past and present alike were typified by poverty and dispossession (Figure 128, see Fulcrum) (Figure 129, see Fulcrum).

There were other murals, too, which revealed the tensions and splits within the nationalist and republican constituencies, notwithstanding the Sinn Féin hegemony. In Derry, for example, along Rossville Street, the Bogside Artists (Kevin Hasson and William and Tom Kelly), painted twelve paintings ("The People's Gallery") between 1994 and 2008 (Figure 130, see Fulcrum) (Figure 131, see Fulcrum) (Figure 132, see Fulcrum). Maintaining that they were "not in anyone's employ," the artists asserted that they worked "independently

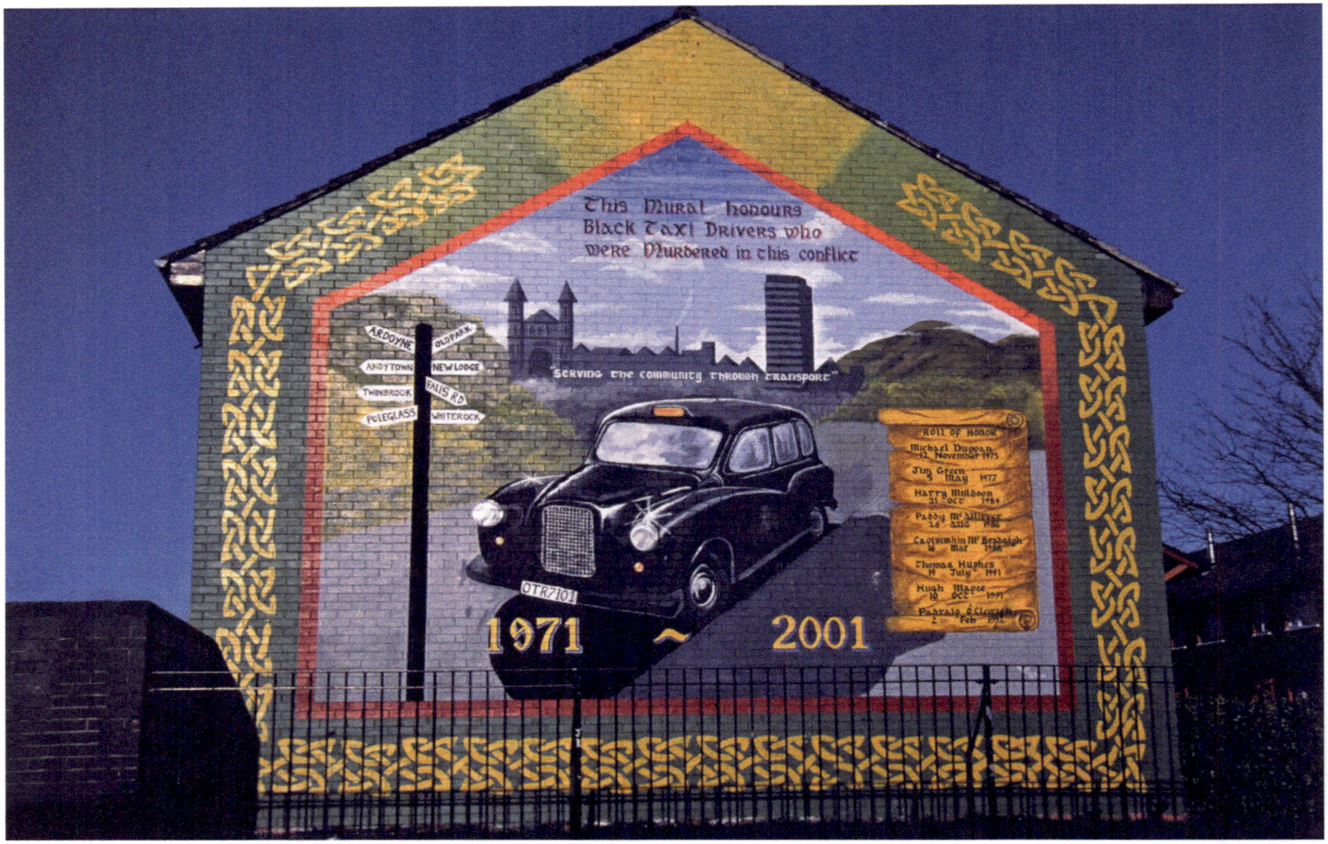

FIGURE 121 Black-taxi drivers, Ardoyne Avenue, Ardoyne, North Belfast, 2001. Photo by Tony Crowley.

and freely," avoided "images of combat, guns, murder and mayhem," painted murals that are "not a propaganda exercise for anybody or any organization," and tried to "tell the story of the Troubles" (Bogside Artists 2009: np).[20] Quite how it would be possible to pictorialize the story of the Troubles without images of violence and chaos is open to question (and in fact a number of the murals show the violence of the war—not least in the depiction of Bloody Sunday) (Figure 133, see Fulcrum). Nonetheless, the Bogside Artists remained resolutely non-affiliated, particularly in relation to the republican movement. A more complex and nuanced relationship existed between the broad Irish language movement (in the guise of a number of organizations) and republicanism (Crowley 2005: 192–197). Despite the impressive success of Irish language education, and

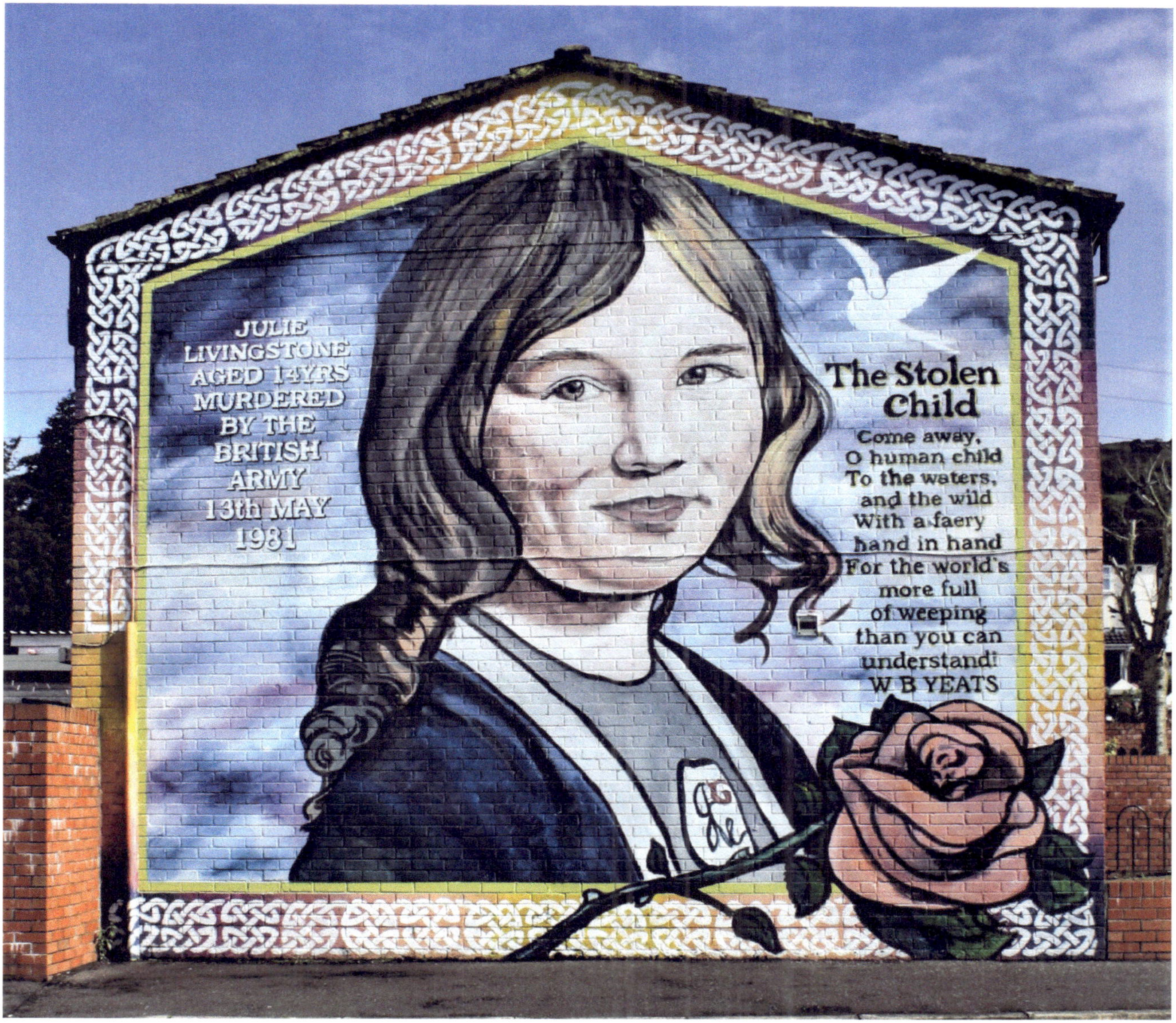

FIGURE 122 The stolen child, Glenveagh Drive, Suffolk, West Belfast, 2004. Photo by Tony Crowley.

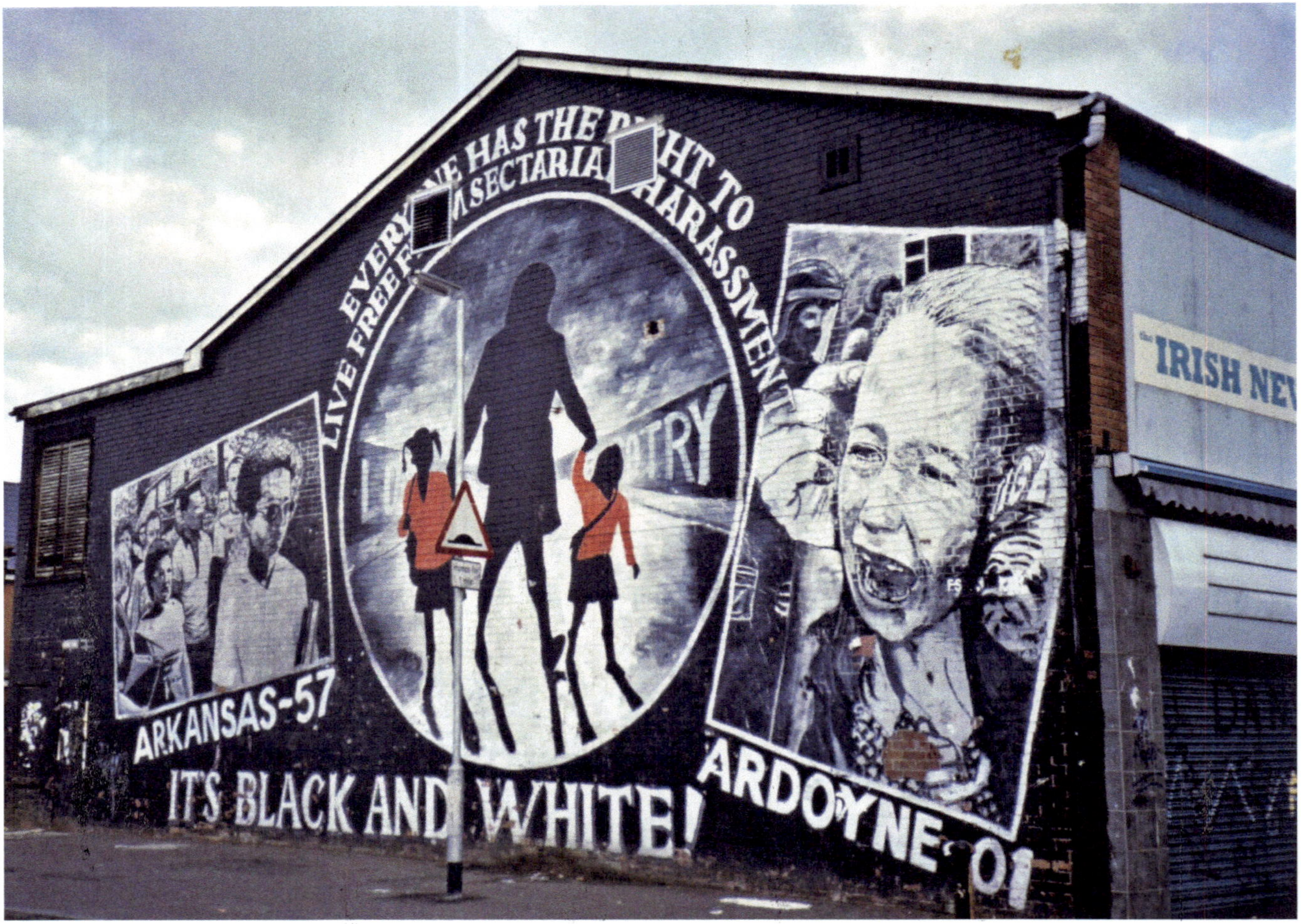

FIGURE 123 Sectarian harassment, Ardoyne Road, Ardoyne, North Belfast, 2001. Photo by Tony Crowley.

the ever-increasing visibility of an Gaeilge as a feature of everyday life in nationalist areas of Northern Ireland (Figure 134, see Fulcrum) (Figure 135, see Fulcrum), there was friction between those who saw the language as part of a specific political project, and those who regarded access to the language as a cultural right to which all and any were entitled (Figure 136). This was rarely a binary matter: there were republicans who regarded the language as apolitical, and Irish language activists who saw it as a key element of the republican struggle. Such debates served to counter the myth (perpetrated from within as well as without) of the nationalist and

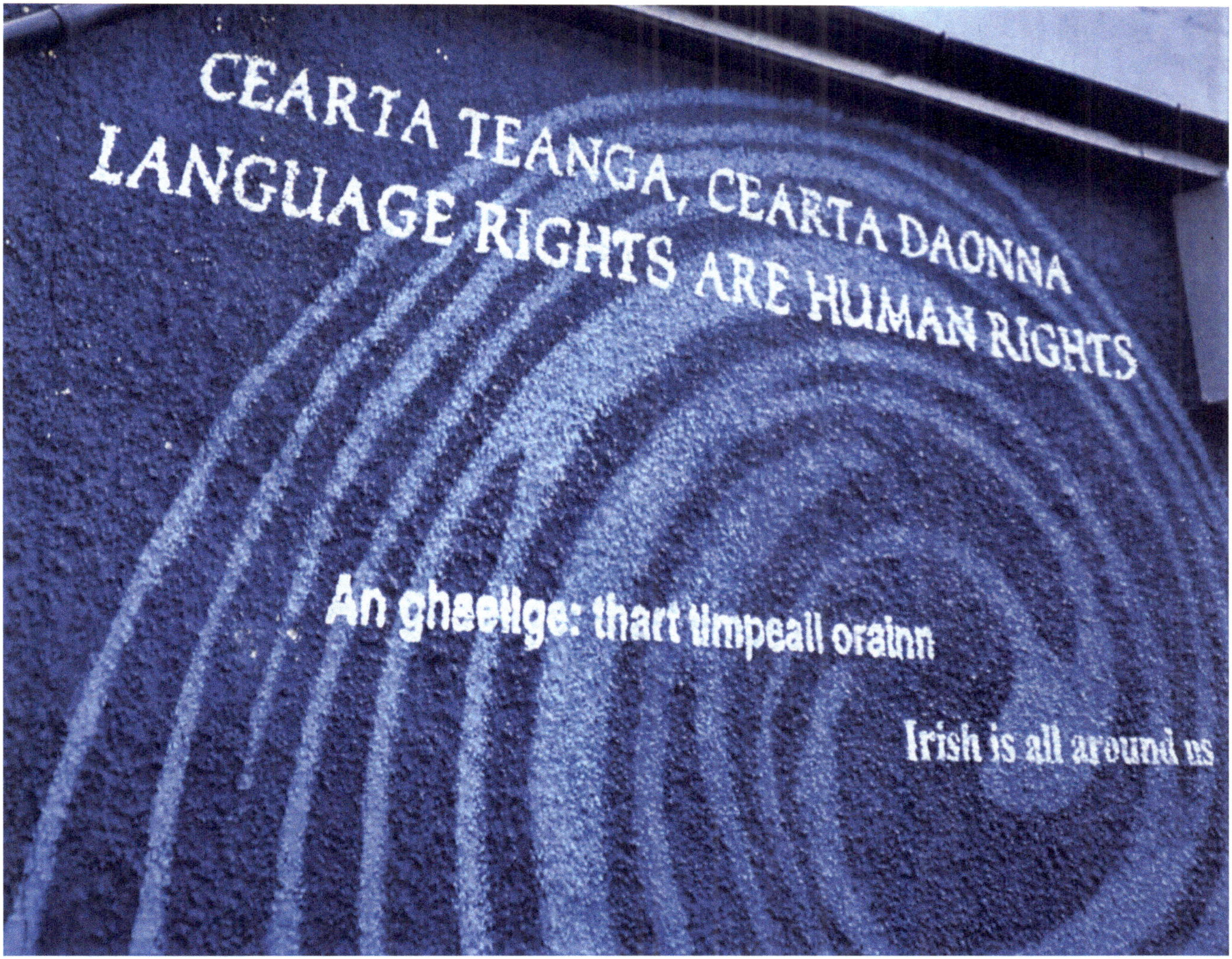

FIGURE 136 Cearta teanga Language rights, Brighton Street, West Belfast, 2000. Photo by Tony Crowley.

republican community as one unified and monolithic bloc. In reality, it was often anything but, and perhaps the clearest evidence of differences of opinion and principled division was the durability of anti-Peace Process republicanism in both political and military form (Figure 137) (Figure 138).

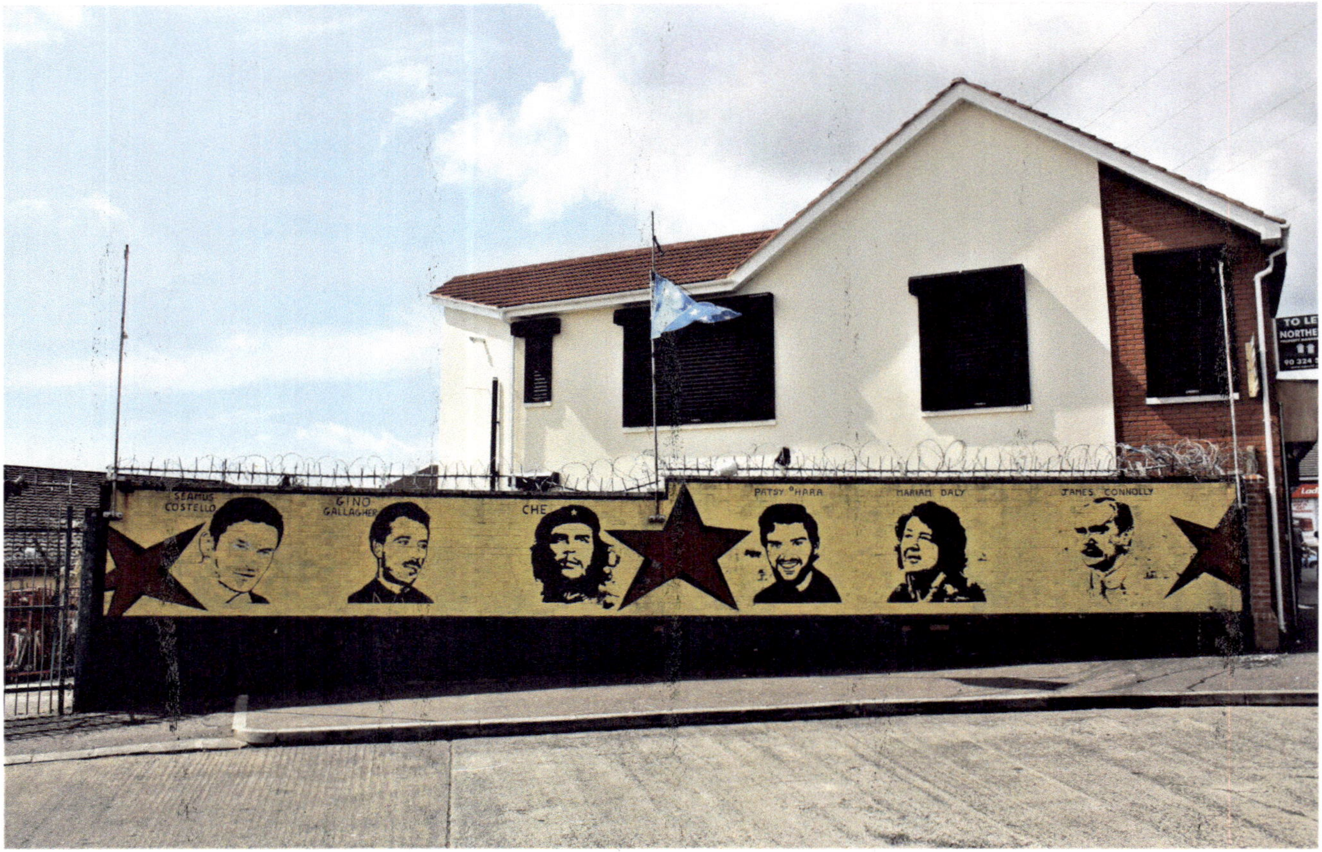

FIGURE 137 Revolutionaries, Divismore Crescent, Ballymurphy, West Belfast, 2006. Photo by Tony Crowley.

Writing in 2003, Bourke observed that "from the beginning, the settlement in Northern Ireland has stumbled from one crisis to the next as the representative institutions, intended to defuse the conflict, buckled under pressure from popular distrust" (Bourke 2003: 306). "Stumbling" is a generous way of putting it: the unpredictable staggering from one critical moment to another continued until 2006, the year in which Sinn Féin celebrated the 90th anniversary of Éirí Amach na Cásca (with a mural in the symbolically significant location of Beechmount that placed republican violence firmly, if heroically, in the past) (Figure 139). That same year, the party signed up to the *St Andrews Agreement*, which laid the basis for the restoration of the Northern Ireland executive in 2007 under a power-sharing arrangement between Sinn Féin and its

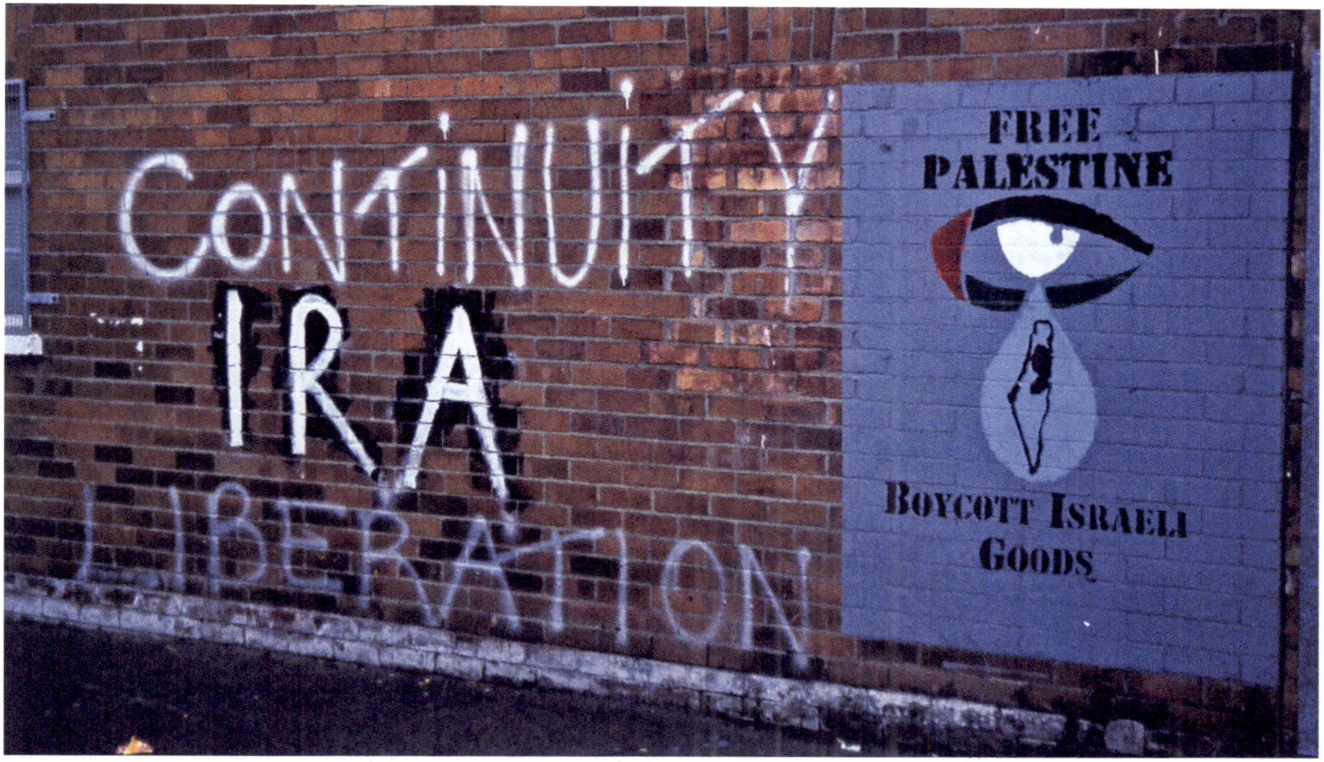

FIGURE 138 Continuity IRA, Iveagh Parade, Falls Road, West Belfast 2004. Photo by Tony Crowley.

arch-rival the Democratic Unionist Party (DUP). In May 2007 Ian Paisley became First Minister and Martin McGuinness the Deputy First Minister, and Sinn Féin nominated its elected representatives to the Policing Board. As with decommissioning, none of these politically significant developments were heralded by republican murals.

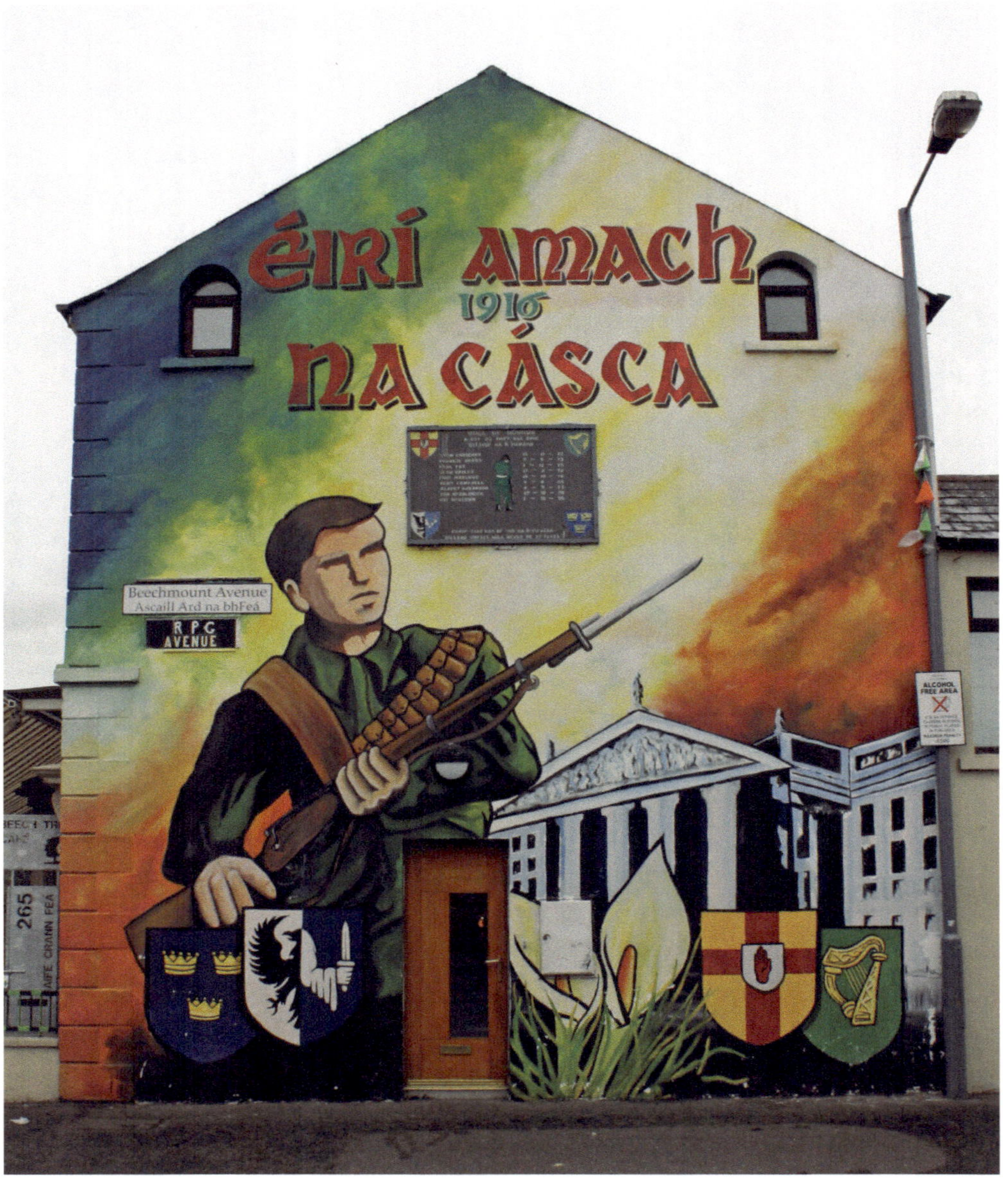

FIGURE 139 Eírí amach na Cásca, Beechmount Avenue/Ascaill Ard na bhFeá, Beechmount, West Belfast, 2006. Photo by Tony Crowley.

CHAPTER 5

Facing Out, Facing In: Peace, Negotiation, and Internecine Strife: Loyalist Murals 1994–2006

To access all images referenced in this chapter, please visit the open access version on Fulcrum at https://doi.org/10.3998/mpub.14527058.

> On behalf of the loyalist people on the Shankill Road we accept the unconditional surrender of the IRA.
> (Loyalist graffiti, Shankill Road, 1994) (Rolston 1998: 48)

1. RESPONDING TO CEASEFIRES

If the IRA ceasefire of August 31 1994 was a cause for both celebration and consternation in nationalist and republican areas of Northern Ireland, in unionist and loyalist communities the response was cautious and skeptical. Though UVF graffiti appeared on the Shankill almost immediately, accepting "the unconditional surrender of the IRA" (on nearby Crimea Street, the message was that "The IRA ran away in 69 The IRA surrendered in 94" Rolston 1998: 48), this was bravura and it masked anxiety about the future. As noted in chapter four, the *Downing Street Declaration* asserted a commitment to "uphold the democratic wish of the greater number of the people of Northern Ireland on the issue of whether they prefer to support the Union or a sovereign united Ireland" (*Downing Street Declaration* 1993: np). But the unionist and loyalist community was mistrustful and often openly hostile towards the political manoeuvring of their traditional opponents—the republican movement and the Irish government—and the intentions of their ostensible allies in the British State.

On the walls, one response was sardonicism. In loyalist West Belfast, for example, the republican epithet—"Britain out of Ireland 25 years Time to go"—was reversed in a graffiti-mural that appeared on Agnes Street: "'Irish out of Britain' Eire Bring your dole sponger's back home 25 years Time to go..." (Figure 1, see Fulcrum).[1] But the dominant theme of loyalist murals in the aftermath of the ceasefire was violence and the threat of violence. In one sense, this simply reflected contemporary reality. In 1993 loyalists killed forty-eight people ("most of whom were civilians, who did not play any part in hostilities"), against the thirty-eight killed by republicans, and "by the summer of 1994 loyalist paramilitaries were killing people in greater numbers than ever before" (Edwards 2017: 221–225). Predictably, therefore, there was no shortage of murals portraying the loyalist capacity for violence, particularly with reference to specific units within the organizations. "C Company," of the UFF's 2nd Belfast Battalion, based on the Lower Shankill estate in West Belfast and led by Johnny Adair, had a reputation as a "killing machine," which it proudly celebrated in commissioned murals. Thus, adopting a refrain from Tina Turner's "The Best," Adair's unit declared themselves "simply the best" (Figure 2), portrayed their willingness to use heavy weaponry (including rocket attacks on republican and nationalist targets such as Sinn Féin offices and The Rock pub on the Falls Road) (Figure 3, see Fulcrum), and threatened the Irish government (Figure 4, see Fulcrum).

Loyalist murals featuring hooded, armed men were commonplace from the post-ceasefire period through to *The Belfast Agreement* (1998) and indeed beyond. They appeared throughout Northern Ireland, and they referenced all of the main loyalist paramilitary organizations: the UDA/UFF, the UVF, and the RHC. The images took various forms and in a number of examples the armed men were accompanied by self-justificatory edicts. One mural, dedicated to the South Belfast "A" Battalion of the UFF, quoted from the medieval *Declaration of Arbroath* (1320): "It is not for glory we fight, nor riches, nor honours—but for freedom alone. Which no good man loses, but with his life" (Figure 5).[2] Another UFF/UDA/UYM mural, in East Belfast, asserted that "nothing great and durable can be created without the presence of an elite" (Figure 6, see Fulcrum). Others carried less self-aggrandizing messages. An image on the Woodstock Road, East Belfast, proclaimed the continuity of the UVF, from its foundation in 1912 to 1994; featuring armed men in firing positions around the UVF crest, it asserted that the organization was "still undefeated" (Figure 7). While a UVF mural on Percy Place on the Lower Shankill carried a significant communication for republicans (reinforced by a representation of an assassination team sledge-hammering its way into a house): "Compromise or conflict" (Figure 8).

The common thread in these and many other murals like them was the loyalist capacity and willingness to engage in violence. The threat could be represented figuratively, as in two images in the Lincoln Court and Bond Street areas of Londonderry that represented Cú Chulainn and the UFF as "champions of Ulster," and marauding Eddie the Trooper as the embodiment of justice ("we determine the guilty, we decide the punishment") (Figure 9) (Figure 10).[3] Other murals presented the threat more graphically: a paramilitary figure disconcertingly looking down a rifle at the viewer, and in the same area of The Village, South Belfast, a loyalist assassination squad leaving a car (Figure 11, see Fulcrum) (Figure 12, see Fulcrum). What is striking about such images is the apparent contradiction between the readiness to espouse violence, and the avowed intention of the political leadership of loyalism to renounce it. For at one and the same time, while murals such as those illustrated above were being painted, the Combined Loyalist Military Command declared a ceasefire (on October 13 1994) and expressed its deep regret for past violence and a fervent desire for peace. The announcement, in the historic location of Fernhill House, West Belfast (where Carson had reviewed the West Belfast UVF in 1914), was made by Gusty Spence, one of the founders of the UVF jailed for murder in the 1960s, and a key political figure within loyalism. Spence declared:

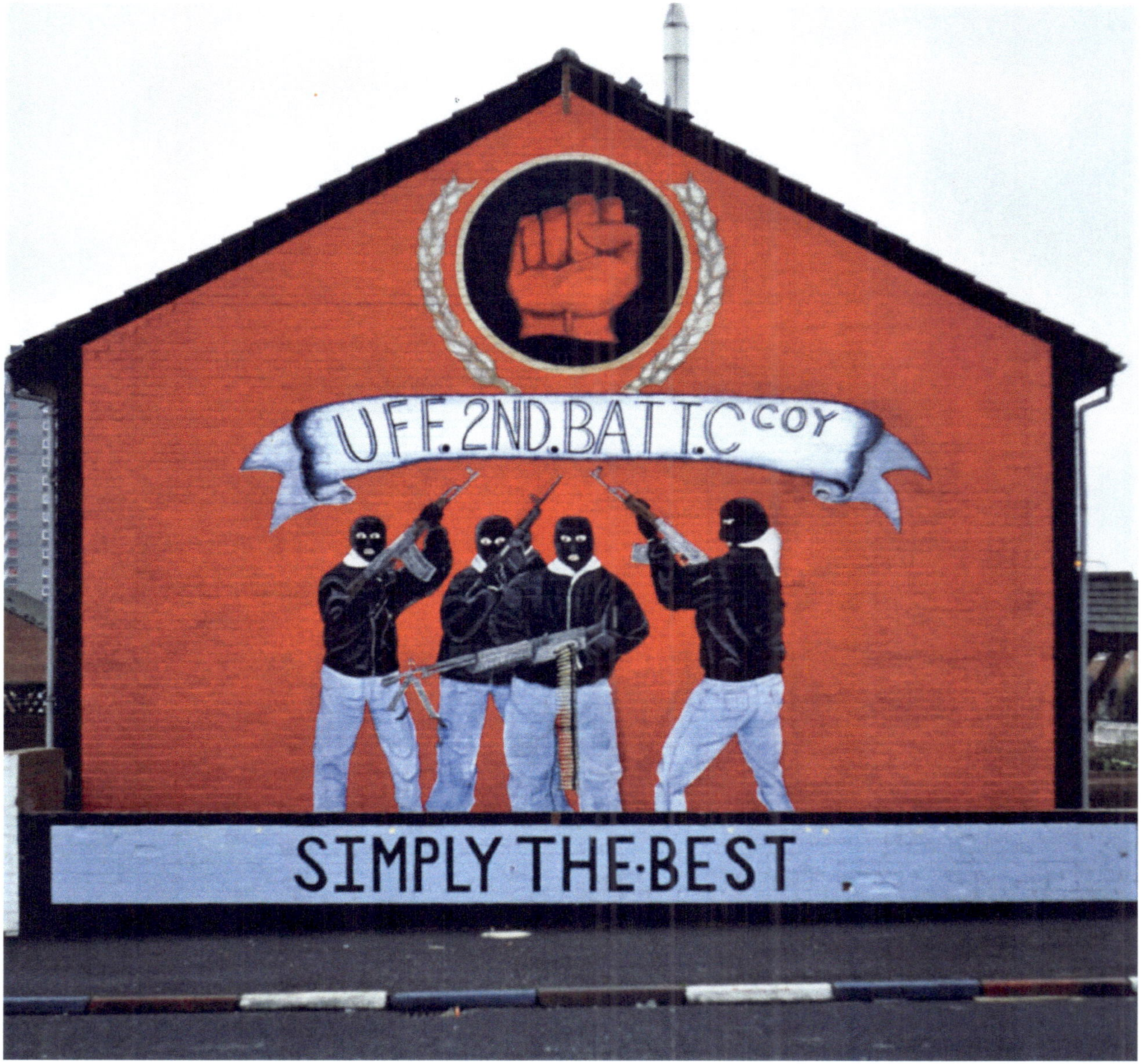

FIGURE 2 Simply the best, Dover Place, Lower Shankill, West Belfast, 1994. Photo by Tony Crowley.

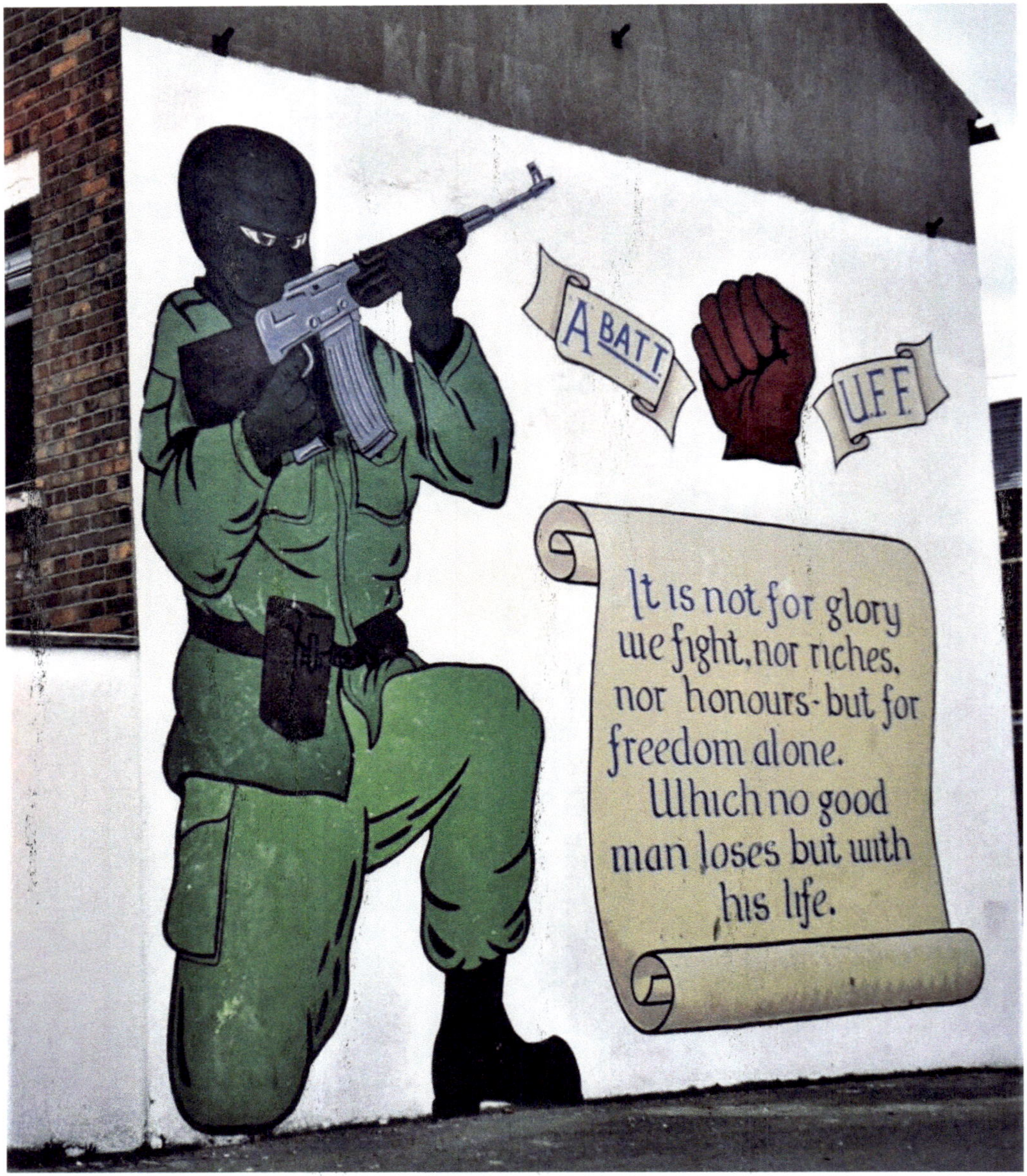

FIGURE 5 Not for glory, Roden Street, The Village, South Belfast, 1996. Photo by Tony Crowley.

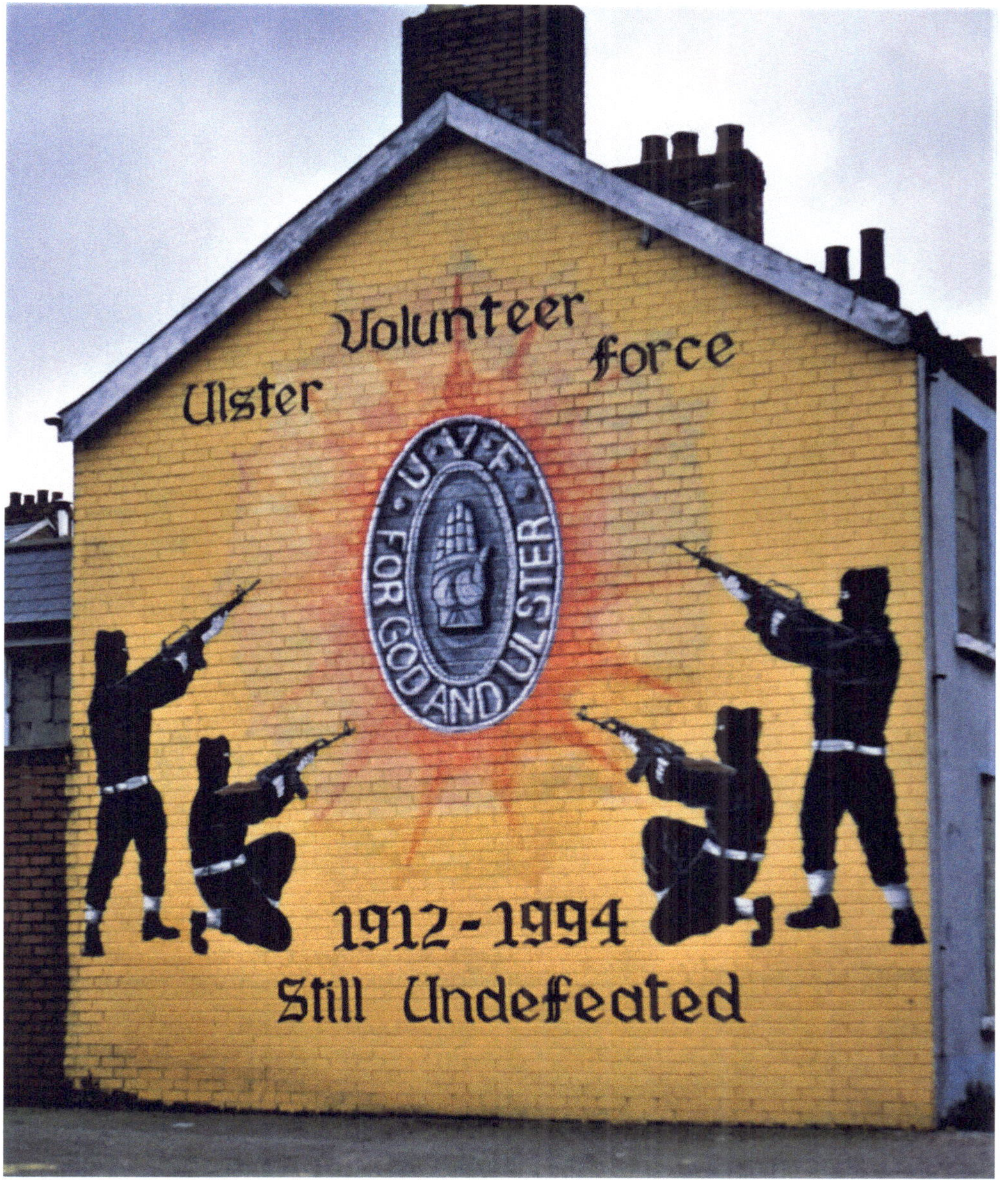

FIGURE 7 Still undefeated, Woodstock Road, East Belfast, 1994. Photo by Tony Crowley.

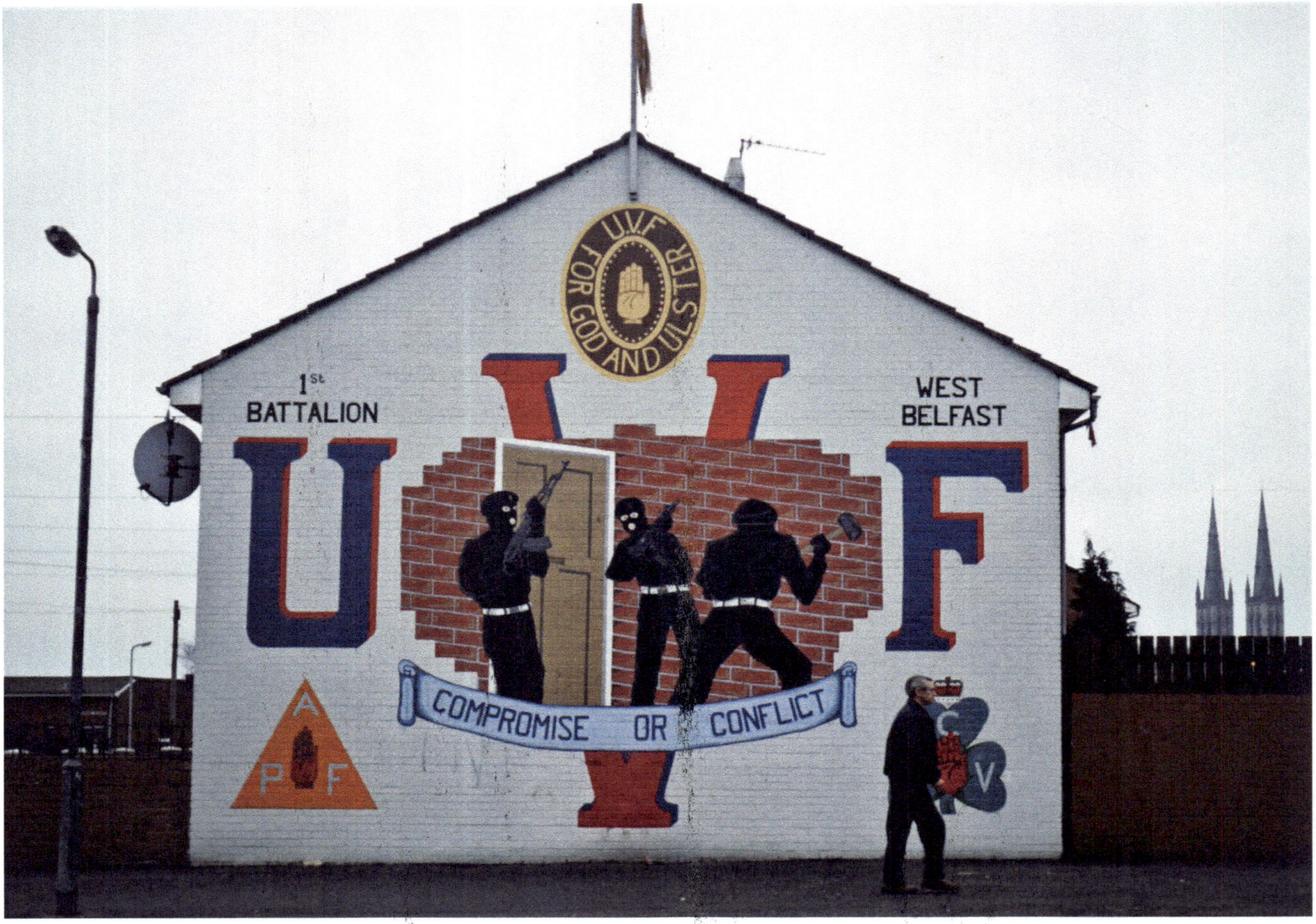

FIGURE 8 Compromise or conflict, Dover Place, Lower Shankill, West Belfast, 1998. Photo by Tony Crowley.

> In all sincerity, we offer to the loved ones of all innocent victims over the past twenty-five years, abject and true remorse. No words of ours will compensate for the intolerable suffering they have undergone during the conflict.
>
> Let us firmly resolve to respect our differing views of freedom, culture and aspiration and never again permit our political circumstances to degenerate into bloody warfare.
>
> We are on the threshold of a new and exciting beginning with our battles in the future being political battles, fought on the side of honesty, decency and democracy against the negativity of mistrust, misunderstanding and malevolence, so that, together, we can bring forth a wholesome society in which our children, and their children, will know the meaning of true peace. (Rowan 1995: 127)

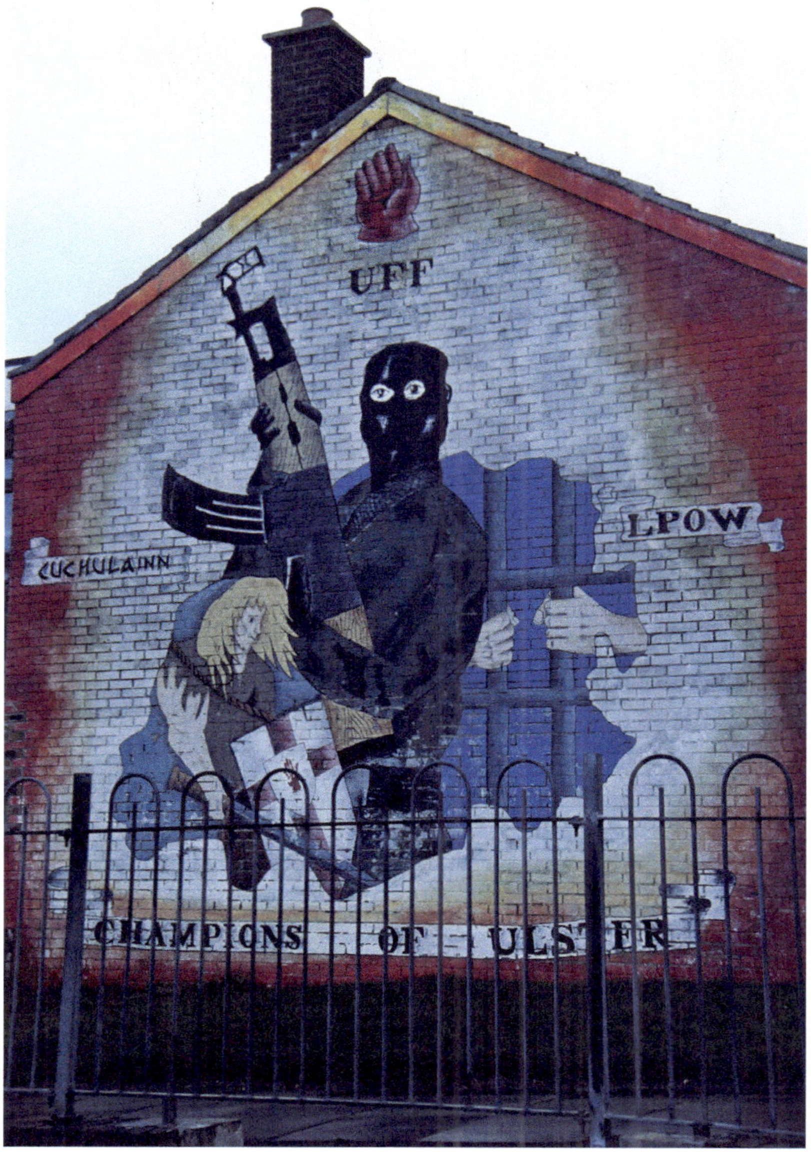

FIGURE 9 Champions of Ulster, Lincoln Court, Kilfennan, Londonderry, 1996. Photo by Tony Crowley.

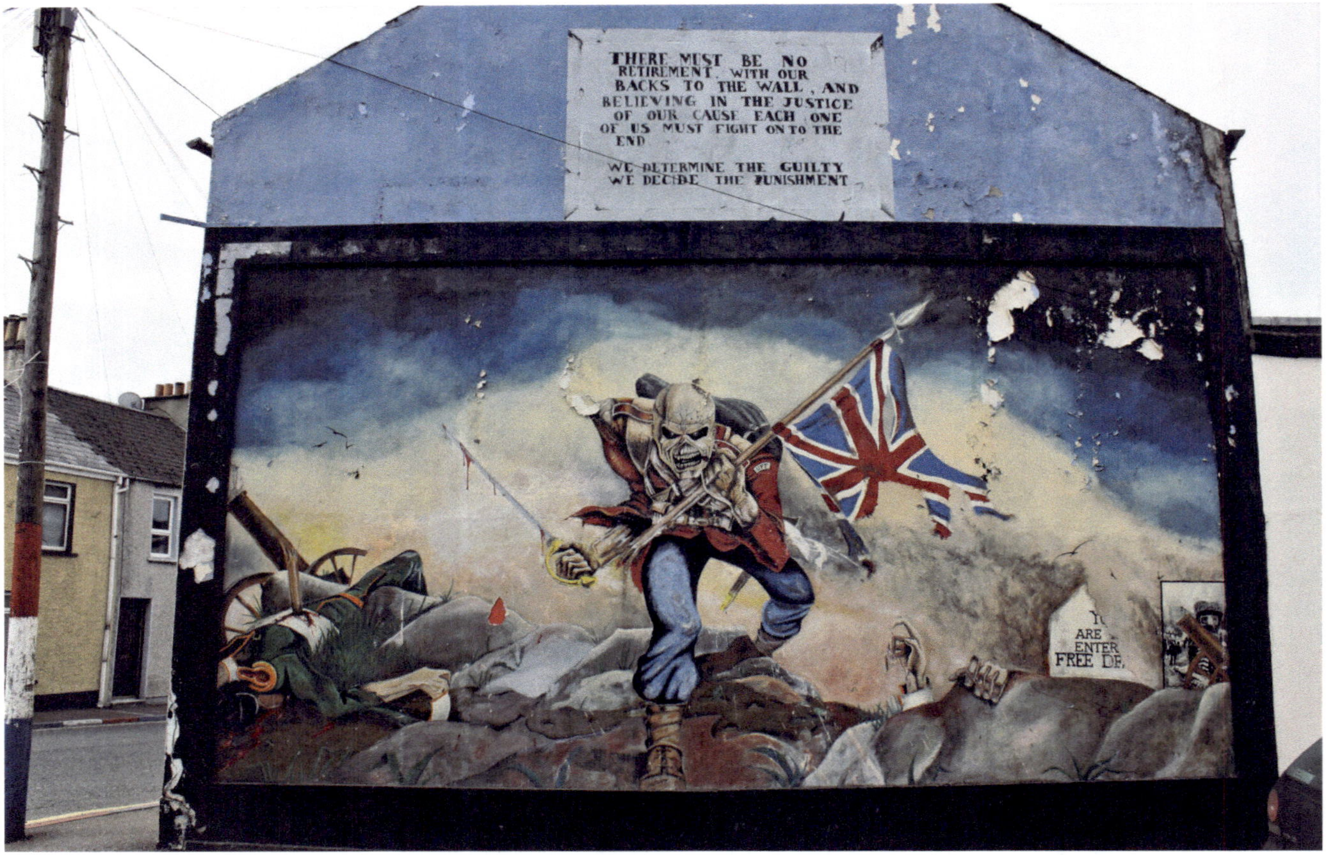

FIGURE 10 Eddie the judge, Bonds Place/Bonds Street, Londonderry, 1997. Photo by Tony Crowley.

The apparent discrepancy between what was appearing on the walls and what the political leadership was saying can be explained in part by the genuine uncertainty and apprehension as to whether the IRA had renounced the armed struggle permanently. This was encapsulated in a notable image on the Mount Vernon estate in North Belfast (a UVF stronghold); featuring two armed UVF volunteers, the mural declared that the UVF was "Prepared for peace Ready for war" (Figure 13). Though re-located (within feet of the original site), a version of this image remains in what is now one of the longest-lasting loyalist murals almost thirty years later (Figure 14).

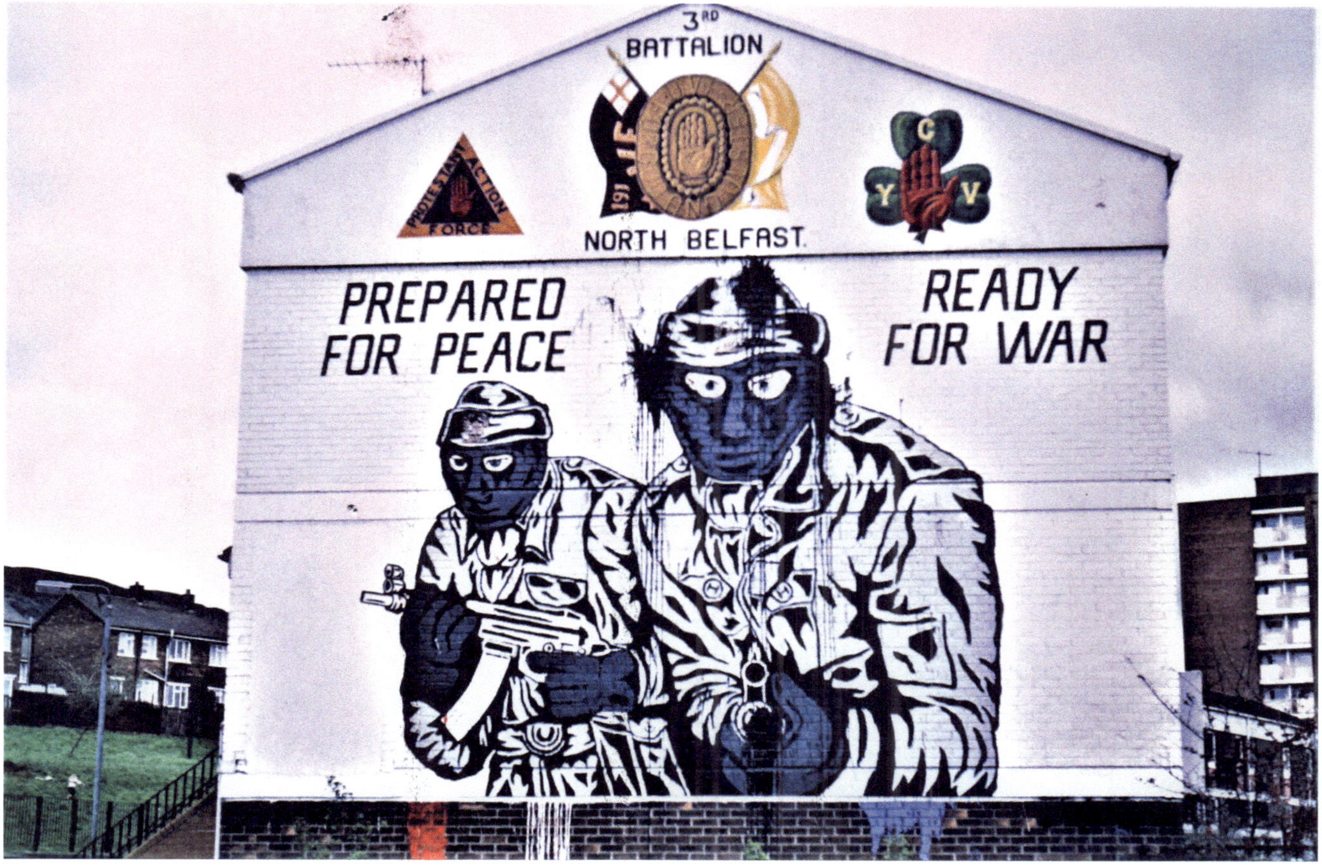

FIGURE 13 Prepared for peace ready for war, Mount Vernon Park, North Belfast, 1995. Photo by Tony Crowley.

As it turned out, the IRA went back to war in February 1996 (until July 1997) and the development was met with resignation—"The Provo's brought back their long war and took away our short peace" (Figure 15, see Fulcrum). And given the unpredictability of the situation, it is perhaps unsurprising that the loyalist paramilitary organizations also continued to announce their capabilities on the walls in murals that addressed republicans as well as their own communities. A second factor that explains the nature of the paramilitary murals was the ongoing tension within and between loyalist groups with regard to their participation in the Peace Process. There were displays of unity on the walls, including a mural that very unusually commemorated the

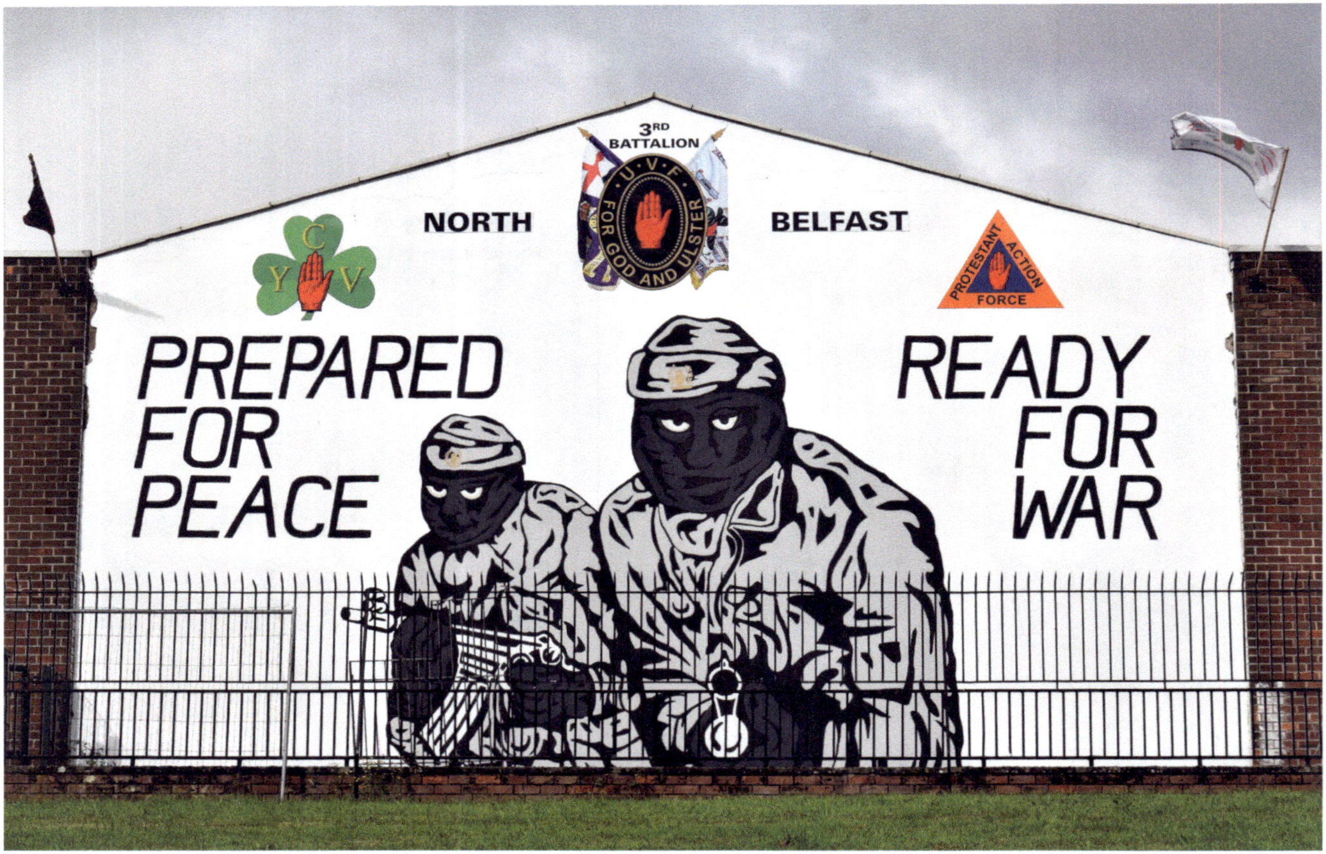

FIGURE 14 Prepared for peace ready for war, Mount Vernon Park, North Belfast, 2022. Photo by Tony Crowley.

dead of both main loyalist paramilitary organizations and linked them to the YCV and the First World War through the depiction of a poppy wreath (Figure 16, see Fulcrum). But there were many within loyalism who remained committed to the possibility of violence, not least because of the contentious but nonetheless common view that the loyalist onslaught of the early 1990s had been a factor in the changes in republican strategy (Taylor 2000: 134; McKay 2000: 101). This meant that there were divisions in the various organizations over the way forward, and these were often exacerbated by events on the ground, including the disputes around Orange Order marches, particularly the Drumcree conflict that took place in and around Portadown.

2. DRUMCREE AND ITS IMPLICATIONS

As noted in the previous chapter, the marching issue touched on many of the questions of identity and rights that lay at the core of the conflict. For unionists and loyalists, any attempt to curtail marching wherever and whenever was perceived as a fundamental assault on traditional symbolic practices and basic civil rights (Bryan 2000). Drumcree was specifically important in this regard because of the historical role of the area: the Orange Order was founded in 1795 in Loughall, a few miles away, and a celebration of the Battle of the Boyne took place at Drumcree church the same year. During periods of conflict (in the late nineteenth and early twentieth centuries in particular), the Drumcree march had been associated with violence (McKay 2000: 131–134). And this was exacerbated during the Troubles with the effective segregation of Portadown and the determination of the Orange Order to follow a route that went through the nationalist areas of Obins Street and the Garvaghy Road. Violent disorder erupted in the early 1970s, in 1985–1988 (after which Obins Street was closed to the marchers), and then again, on a large scale, in 1995–2001. In 1995 the march was eventually allowed through the Garvaghy Road, in silence, after consultation with local residents; at the end of the march the unionist leaders Ian Paisley and David Trimble joined hands in a display of triumphalism. In 1996 and 1997 the march was forced down the Garvaghy Road, against the wishes of the residents, following pressure from large numbers of loyalists gathered at Drumcree and the threat of violence from the Mid Ulster UVF (led by Billy Wright); this prompted widespread disorder in nationalist and republican areas throughout Northern Ireland. In 1998, after *The Belfast Agreement*, the Garvaghy Road was closed to the marchers, a decision that led to protests in loyalist areas across Northern Ireland, and a stand-off involving ten thousand loyalists and two thousand members of the security forces. As noted in chapter four, the confrontation was effectively brought to an end by the reaction to the murder of three young boys in a loyalist fire-bomb attack in Ballymoney. Though the conflict at Drumcree rumbled on to 2001 (and indeed is still marked annually), 1997 was the last time that the Orange Order was allowed to parade down the Garvaghy Road (Ryder and Kearney 2001).

The symbolic importance of Drumcree was outlined by Joel Patton, an Orangeman, loyalist activist, and founder of "the Spirit of Drumcree":

> It's about the survival of a culture, of an identity, of a way of life. It's about our ability to still hold on to parts of the country. The Ulster people have their backs to the wall. They're in retreat. They have been chased from a large part of the country and they feel that [Portadown], the citadel of Orangeism, where Orangeism was born 200 years ago, that is the place where they want to take their stand. Drumcree represents that… It's about the freedom of people to come from a church into a town, a Protestant town where they feel that they can express their culture in an open and free manner. They believe intensely that if it's taken away from them there, there isn't anywhere in Ulster that will be safe. (Taylor 2000: 239–240)

Given the nature and strength of feelings provoked by Drumcree and all it represented, it was inevitable that "the right to march" would be proclaimed widely on the walls. Images included the rhyming edicts delivered by the UDA/UFF on the Lower Shankill in 1996—"No more talk Time to walk" (Figure 17)—and in its South Belfast stronghold of Sandy Row—"UFF One Faith—One Crown We 'will' walk in Portadown" (Figure 18, see Fulcrum). While East Belfast loyalists expressed defiance: "Our message is simple; Where our music is welcome we will play it loud, Where our music is challenged we will play it louder" (Figure 19, see Fulcrum). A less strident but nonetheless clear mural appeared on the Lower Shankill estate in 2000. The image featured two Orangemen walking down Drumcree Road, towards Portadown, bearing banners: "We demand the right to march" and "Portadown District L.O.L. No. 1." To the right a UFF crest of star and clenched fist asserted that "Shankill Rd supports Drumcree," and next to it was the

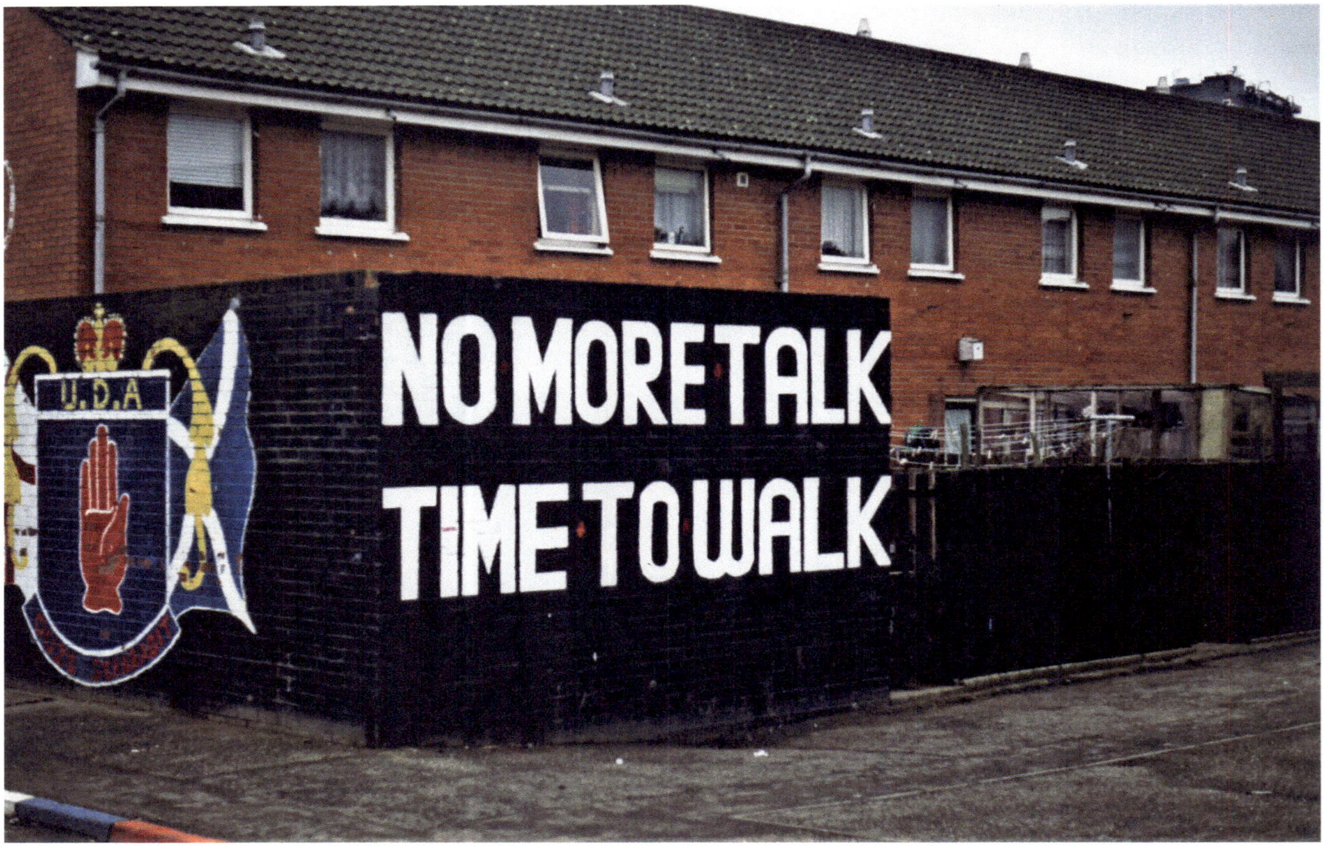

FIGURE 17 No more talk, Percy Place, Lower Shankill, West Belfast, 1996. Photo by Tony Crowley.

symbol of "the Spirit of Drumcree" group: Crown, Bible surrounded by an Orange sash in the form of a heart, and an adaptation of Martin Luther's protest against Papal authority—"Here we stand we can do no other" (Figure 20).[4]

As Patton's comments cited earlier reveal, what was at stake for unionists and loyalists ("the Ulster people" in Patton's tellingly exclusive phrase) at Drumcree could not have been more important. But it is clear that the conflict over the right to march down the Garvaghy Road, and all it implied, produced both unity and serious divisions within unionism generally but loyalism specifically. Such tensions were caused in part by a difference in the way in which Drumcree was pitched, since as Patton's framing made clear, for some

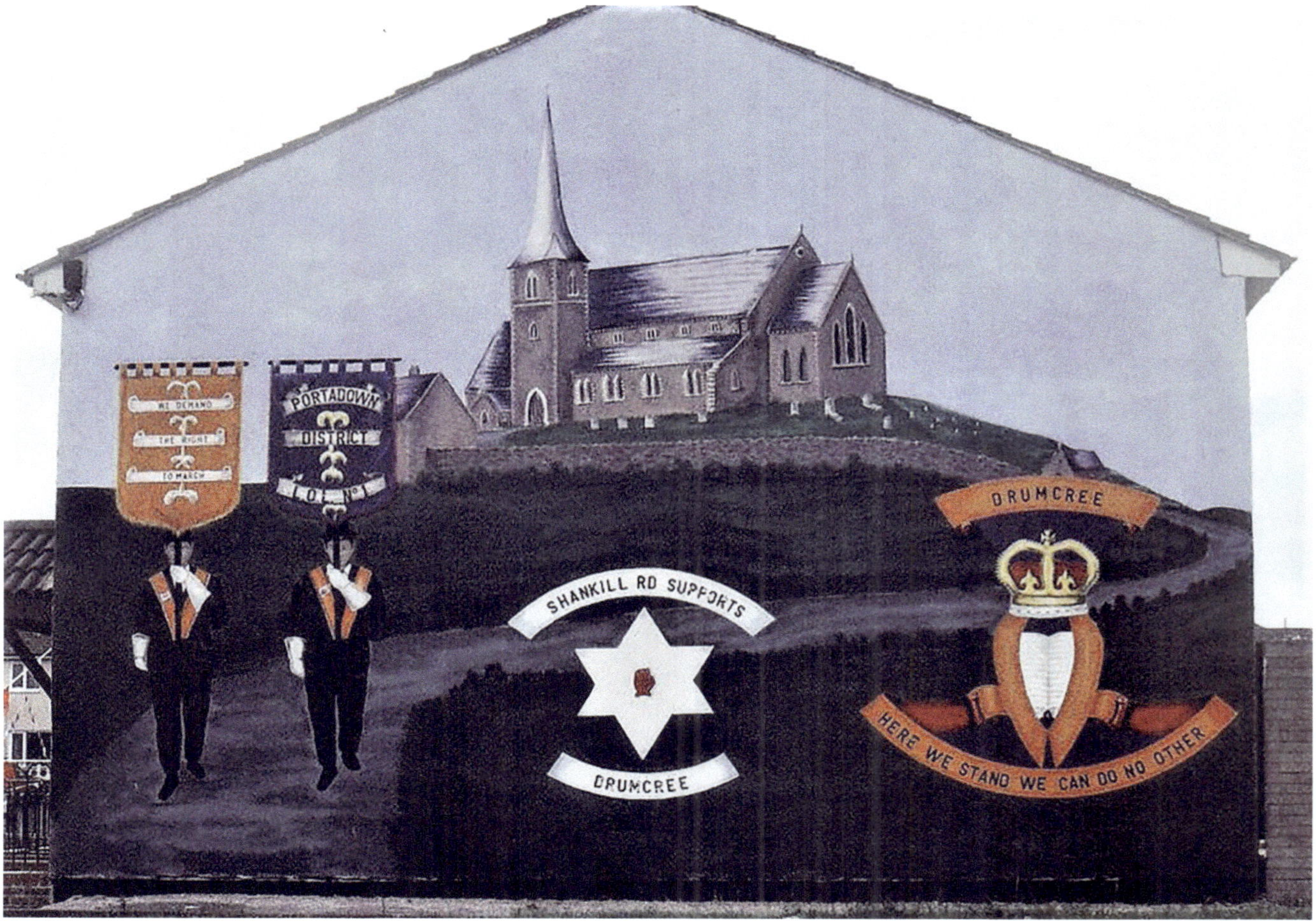

FIGURE 20 Drumcree, North Boundary Street, Lower Shankill, West Belfast, 2000. Photo by Tony Crowley.

participants, this was a question of culture, identity, and way of life, as opposed to the traditional unionist concerns that focused on constitutional status and civil liberties. Of course these two approaches are intertwined, but an emphasis on one rather than the other inflects arguments and the stances that derive from them in distinct ways. Given the weight accorded to cultural identity issues within particular loyalist circles, it is worth noting that they received support from the British far right, and this led to some disturbing images in a number of loyalist areas. An image on Sugarfield Street, off the Shankill in West Belfast, combined the Red Hand, the Northern Ireland flag, and a swastika flag (Figure 21). And graffiti references to white supremacist and neo-fascist organizations such as Combat 18, the British Movement, the British National

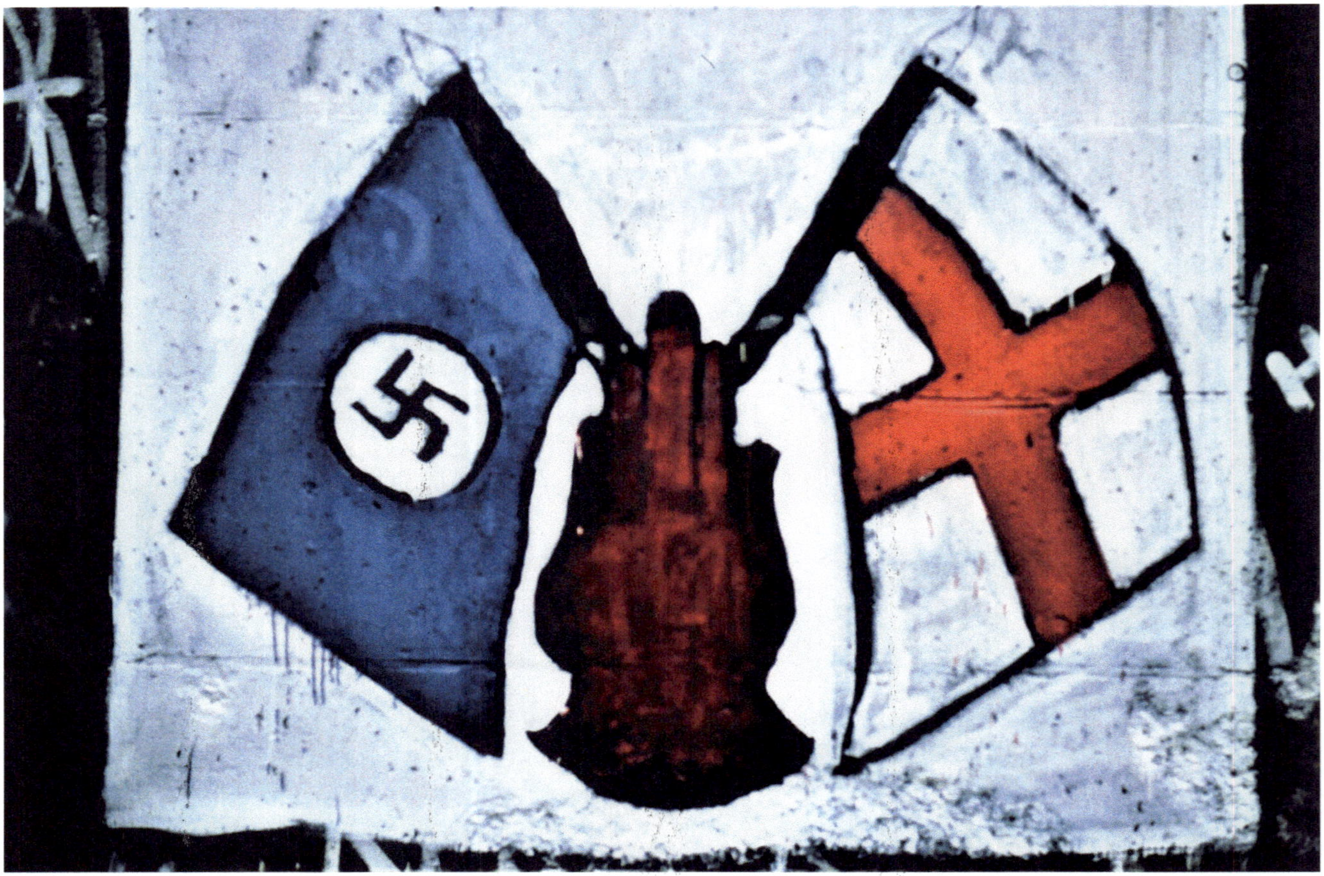

FIGURE 21 Swastika, Sugarfield Street, Upper Shankill, West Belfast, 1996. Photo by Tony Crowley.

Party, and the Ku Klux Klan, appeared in various locations in Belfast and Londonderry (Figure 22, see Fulcrum) (Figure 23, see Fulcrum) (Figure 24, see Fulcrum) (Figure 25, see Fulcrum). Needless to say, despite the purported concern of the far right for the loss of "the British way of life," Britain's role in the defeat of fascism in the Second World War meant that swastikas and all were not quite compatible with protestations of true Britishness, and they were often roundly condemned by many local residents and by the political leadership of loyalism. In specific areas such as the Lower Shankill and Rathcoole, however, the walls tended to reflect the political views of the leaders of particular paramilitary units (McKay 2000: 96). And expressions

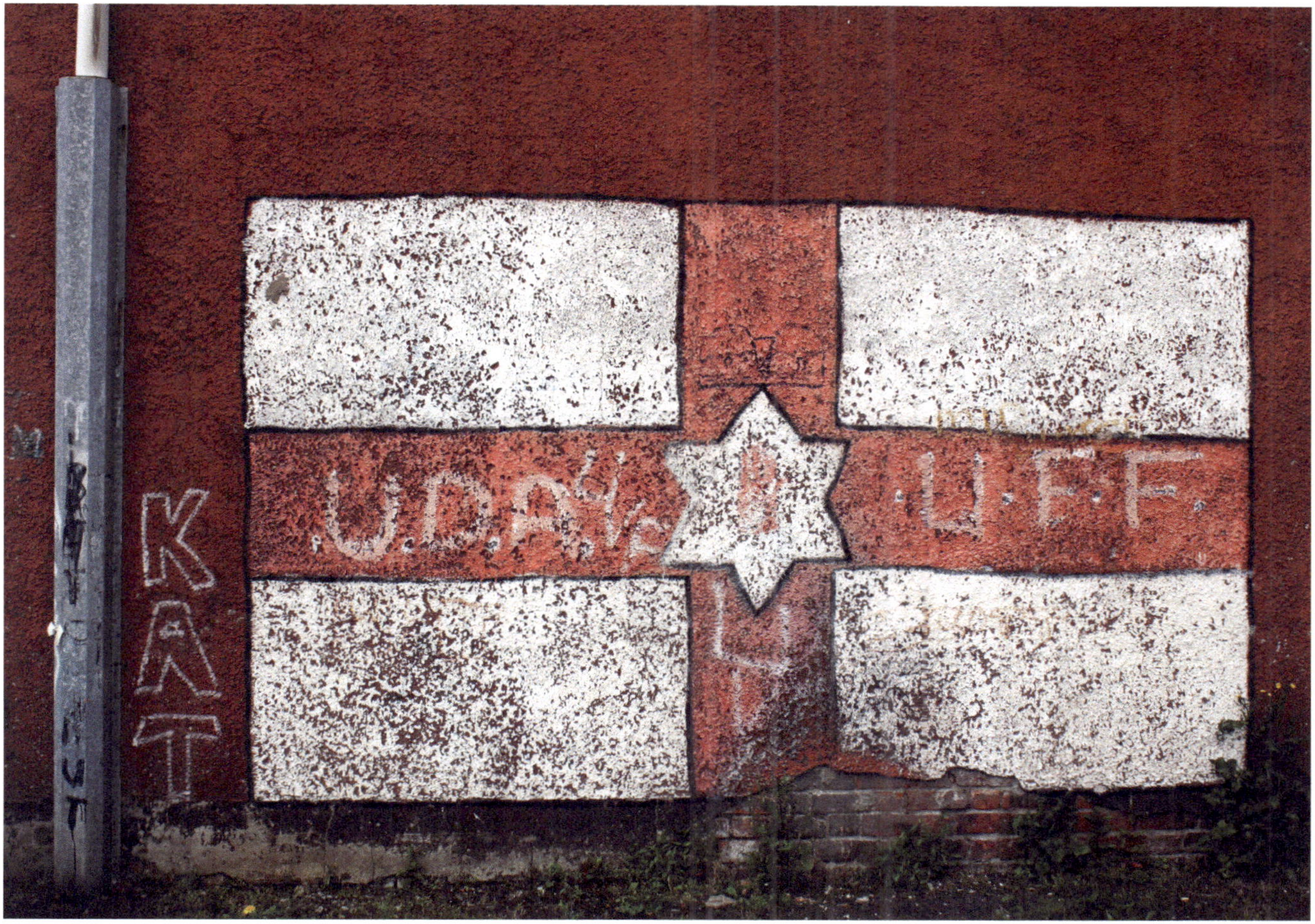

FIGURE 26 KAT, Boyne Court, South Belfast, 2004. Photo by Tony Crowley.

of naked sectarianism were hardly uncommon in loyalist areas. A mural on the Lower Shankill proclaimed that "There is no such thing as a nationalist area of Ulster Only areas temporarily occupied by nationalists," while the acronym "KAT" ("Kill all Taigs") appeared widely (Figure 26).[5]

The Drumcree crisis served to exacerbate tensions within loyalism towards the development of the Peace Process both before and after *The Belfast Agreement*. Nowhere is this more evident than in the emergence of the Loyalist Volunteer Force (LVF). During the 1996 Drumcree dispute, the Mid Ulster Brigade of the UVF defied the organization's Belfast leadership by breaking the ceasefire. In consequence, the Portadown unit of the Mid Ulster UVF were stood down and its leader, Billy Wright, was ordered to leave Northern Ireland. In response, Wright formed the LVF, a small splinter-group which killed fourteen people between 1996 and 1998 (almost all were randomly assassinated Catholic civilians) and developed close links with Johnny Adair's UDA C Company on the Lower Shankill. After Wright's killing by the INLA in the Maze prison in 1997, the LVF was involved in a feud with the UVF and played a role in the larger loyalist feud between elements of the UDA and UVF in 2000 (Figure 27, see Fulcrum). From one perspective, the LVF (the "Rat Pack") was a minor player in the war in Northern Ireland, though it commanded fierce loyalty within specific areas such as Portadown, Lurgan, and North Belfast. From a broader viewpoint, however, the influence of the LVF was indicative of the fractures within loyalism (and indeed unionism more broadly) with regard to the rapidly developing situation that followed the IRA ceasefires, the political negotiations that led end of the war, and the political settlement encapsulated in *The Belfast Agreement*.

3. POLITICS AND PRISONERS

Relations between mainstream unionism and the loyalist paramilitary groups and their political representatives during this period were strained at best. Though the working-class constituency from which paramilitaries were mostly drawn tended to vote for one or other of the unionist parties in elections, this was largely on the basis of a desire to maintain unionist dominance and to keep nationalists and republicans out (the practice of voting against "themmuns" is carried out on both sides). But loyalist paramilitary groups, and the political voices associated with them, had largely grown distrustful of the ways in which unionism had implicitly but consistently used the threat that paramilitaries posed, while publicly disdaining their organizations.[6] On occasion, the mistrust was manifest. When Ian Paisley, leader of the DUP, called on loyalist paramilitaries to disarm, the response was contemptuous: "If Ulster is sold out," a RHC mural demanded in Rathcoole, "why give up our guns Mr. Paisley?" (Figure 28, see Fulcrum). Another piece of graffiti drew a scornful historical contrast between Paisley's call for the decommissioning of loyalist weaponry and the formation of the UVF, gun-running and the role of Edward Carson: "UVF 1912 Clydevalley Carson Paisley 'Surrender guns' Some Carson" (Figure 29, see Fulcrum).

In order to challenge the dominant unionist parties, political parties associated with the paramilitaries had emerged in the late 1970s and early 1980s: the PUP (formed in 1979 and linked to the UVF and RHC) and the Ulster Democratic Party (UDP, established in 1981 and affiliated with the UDA).[7] The PUP and UDP were influential in persuading the loyalist paramilitaries to call a ceasefire in 1994 and on the basis of their performance in the Northern Ireland Forum poll in 1996, both parties were invited to the talks that led to *The Belfast Agreement*. As noted above, there was considerable scepticism towards the discussions with the British government and the "pan-nationalist front" (Figure 30, see Fulcrum)—"Ulster still says NO" was the refrain (Figure 31, see Fulcrum)—along with the determination to "Live free or like a freeman die not like a Fenian slave" (Figure 32, see Fulcrum). Nonetheless, loyalist paramilitarism, despite reservations and splits, supported the talks and indeed the eventual settlement ("Michael Stone Says YES," a banner in East Belfast proclaimed in the run-up to the referendum).[8] In the consequent elections to the Northern Ireland Assembly in 1998, and lacking the organizational resources of the larger parties, both the UDP and PUP resorted to the walls to get their message across in their strongholds. A UDP mural on Belle Vue Street, in the upper Shankill, was clear about the party's association with the UDA/UFF; it linked past (the Ulster Workers' Council (UWC) strike of 1974) and present (the loyalist prisoners) and focused on its *Common Sense* policy document (originally published in 1987 and revised in 1993) (Figure 33). A PUP mural was likewise unambiguous about its connection to the UVF/RHC; it also linked past and present (the formation of the YCV in 1912 and the UVF during the modern Troubles) and declared that it was "Still defending Ulster," promising that "We will always be ready" (Figure 34). In addition, it warned mainstream politicians: "To the politicians Words are not enough for the peace and freedom of the children and the people of Ulster 'Deeds and Actions.'" To the side, the mural called for a vote for the PUP, noting that "The PUP is about to bark." In fact, however, support for the political parties associated with the loyalist paramilitary groupings was the dog that didn't bark; the PUP gained only two seats in the Assembly elections, while the UDP ended up with none.[9]

Despite their differences, there was one issue that united loyalist paramilitary groups and their political representatives both before, during, and after the negotiations that led to the settlement—the highly contentious question of the release of paramilitary prisoners. This was a cause that loyalists shared with their republican counterparts, not least because on both sides of the political divide, the agreement of the prisoners was central to political progress (indeed on one occasion, Mo Mowlam, the British Minister for Northern Ireland, went to the Maze to meet IRA, UVF, and, particularly, UDA/UFF prisoners to "sell" the deal) (Woods 2006: 215). And yet despite this common cause, the prison issue was inflected differently for republicans and loyalists. For republicans, imprisonment was simply another example of the repressive apparatus of the British State with which they were at war, and thus the prison campaign was an extension of their armed struggle. For loyalists, however, imprisonment was particularly pointed because they asserted that they were fighting to maintain their constitutional status within the very state whose political and judicial system was responsible for jailing them.

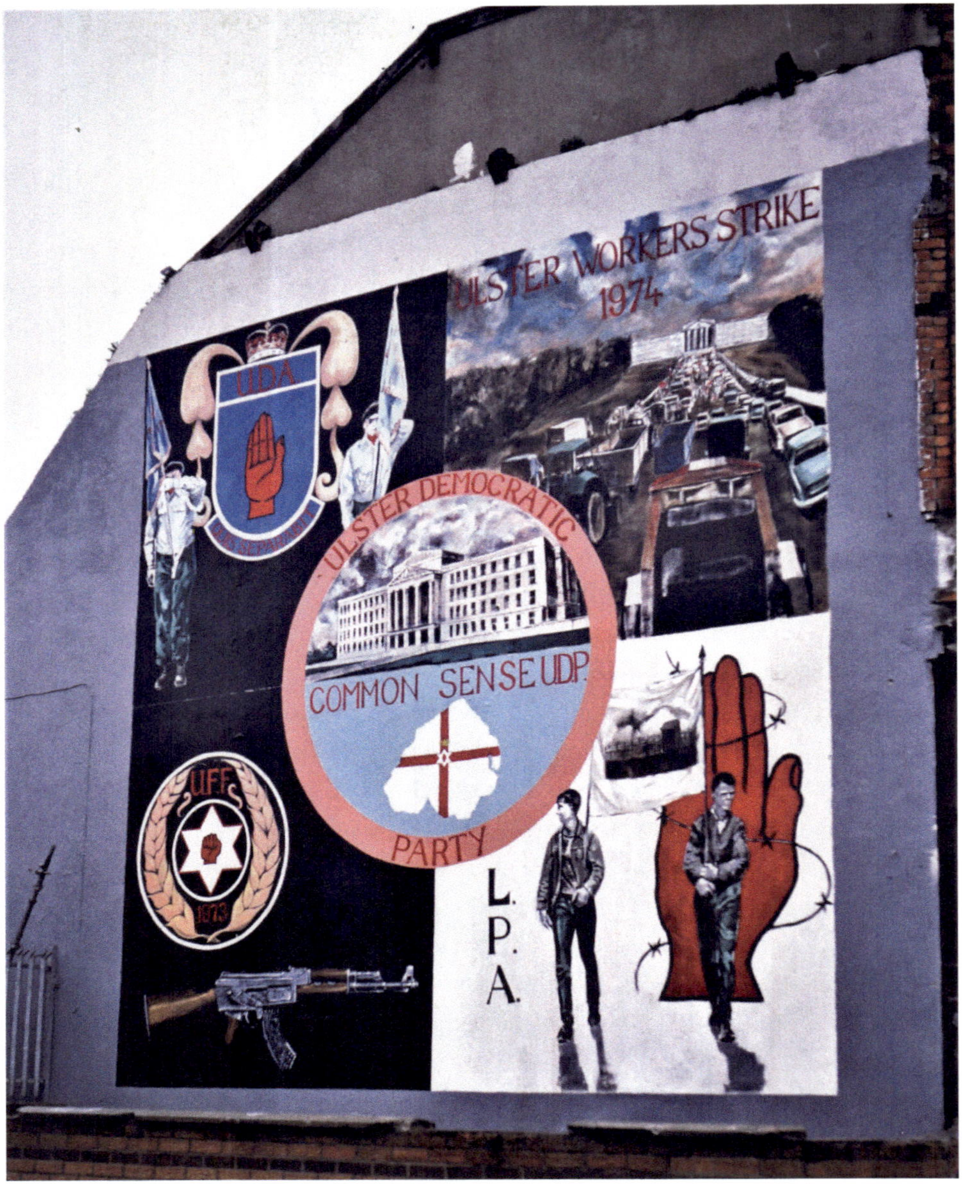

FIGURE 33 Common sense, Bellevue Street, Upper Shankill, West Belfast, 1998. Photo by Tony Crowley.

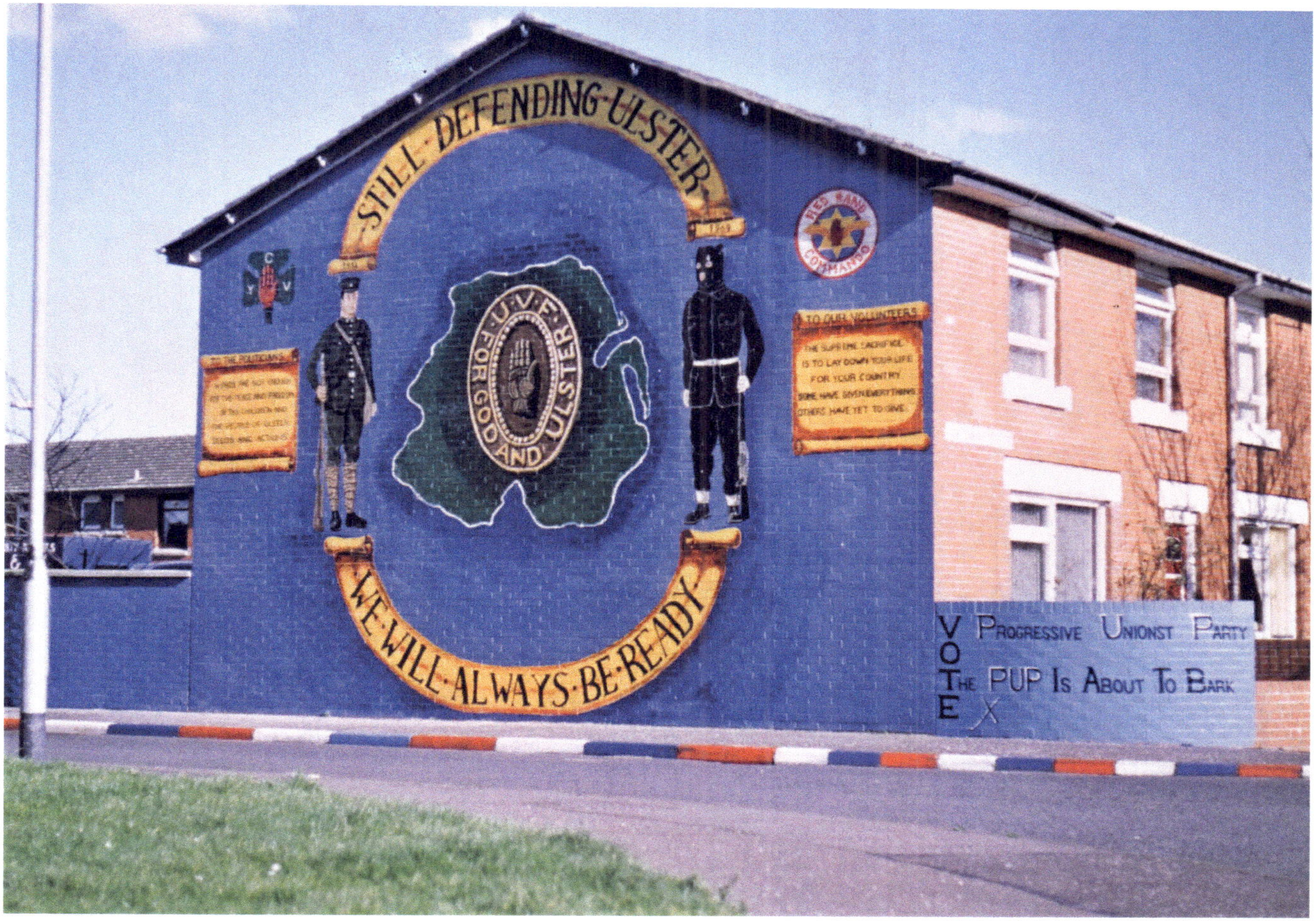

FIGURE 34 Still defending Ulster, Kenilworth Place/Newtownards Road, East Belfast, 1997. Photo by Tony Crowley.

As noted in the Introduction, one of the earliest prison murals appeared on Howard Street South in 1977, with the injunction to "Remember the loyalist prisoners' (and a reference to the Queen's Jubilee) (see **Introduction, fig. 21**). But the prison mural campaign intensified after the ceasefires in 1994 and featured a number of murals that appealed on behalf of loyalist prisoners in general, rather than those belonging to specific organizations (Figure 35) (Figure 36, see Fulcrum). More often than not, however, the murals were sponsored by the paramilitary groups to which the prisoners belonged (Figure 37) (Figure 38, see Fulcrum)

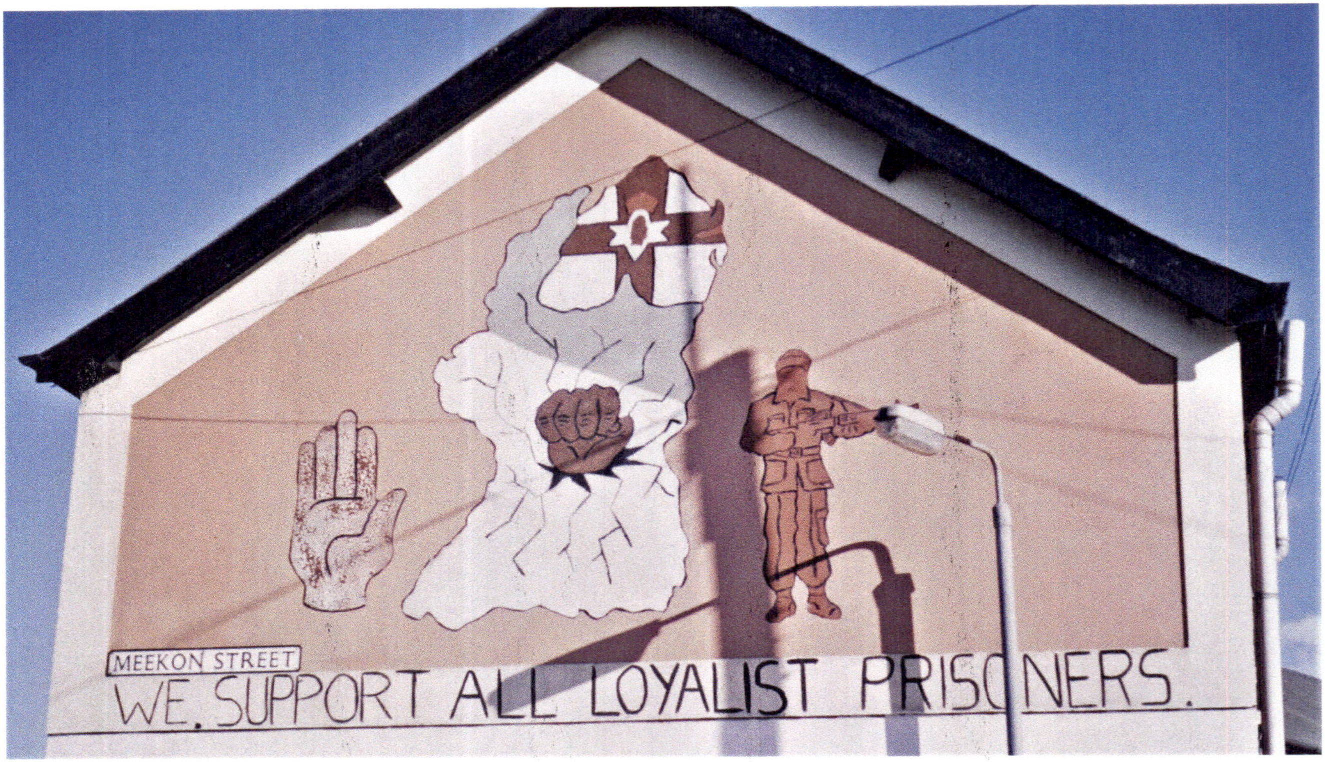

FIGURE 35 Support all loyalist prisoners, Meekon Street, East Belfast, 1996. Photo by Tony Crowley.

(Figure 39, see Fulcrum). And the murals were hardly reluctant to spell out the importance of the prisoners in the negotiations. One image demanded that the State "Release East Belfast's loyalist prisoners" in order to "Consolidate the peace" (Figure 40).

One UDA/UFF mural in Tullycarnet, South Belfast, which featured three high-powered weapons and a republican with a target on their head, declared that "We have achieved peace We have maintained peace—Now stop the injustice—Release our political hostages." (https://petermoloneycollection.com/2006/08/19/release-the-political-hostages/). The construction of the prisoners as hostages who required justice was developed in their figuration as "prisoners of war." This was a trope that republicans also used, but as noted above, its deployment was more complicated for loyalists, not least when it was coupled with the claim that

FIGURE 37 Send our prisoners home, Rydalmere Street/Donegall Road, South Belfast, 1996. Photo by Tony Crowley.

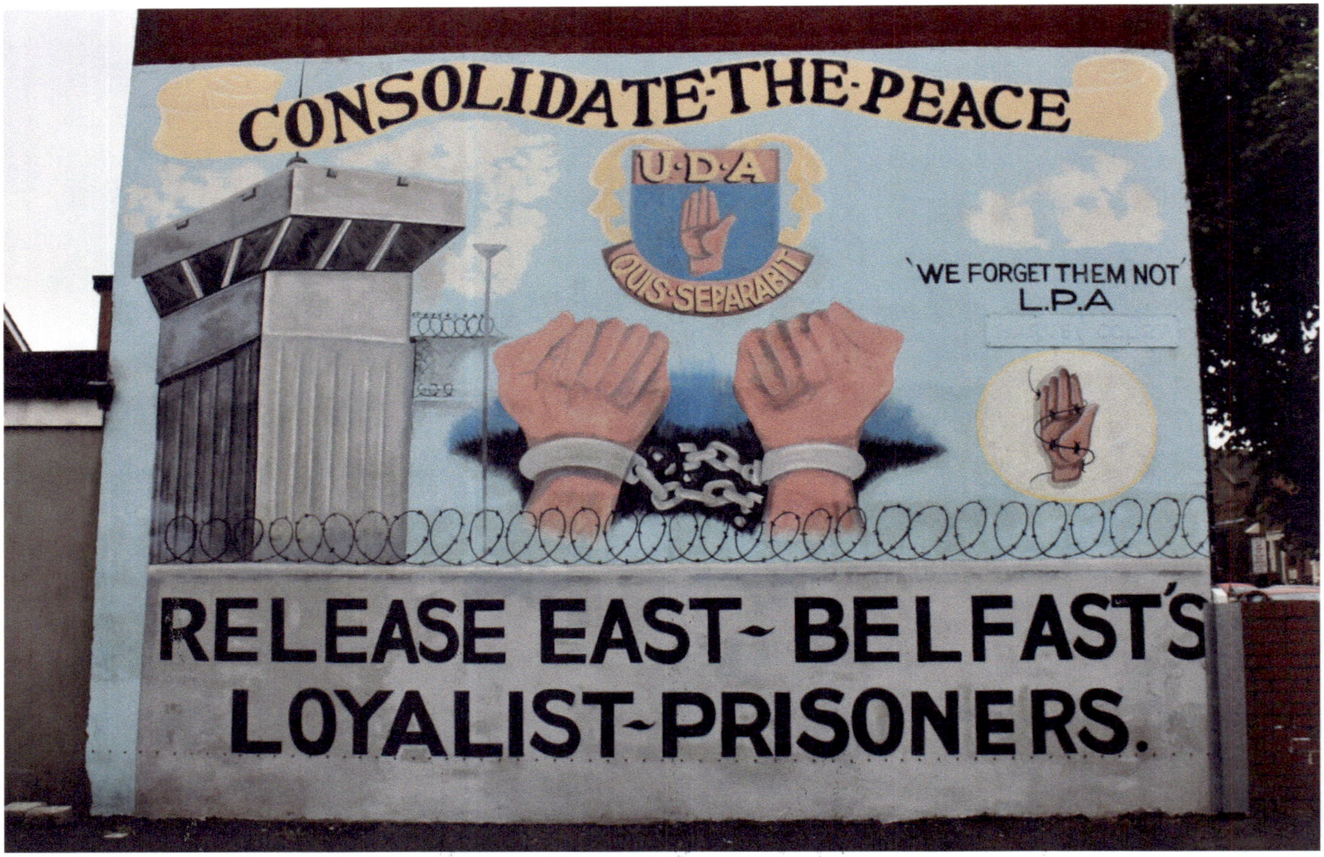

FIGURE 40 Consolidate the peace, Harvey Court, East Belfast, 1997. Photo by Tony Crowley.

with regard to the prisoners, "their only crime was loyalty" (Figure 41) (Figure 42, see Fulcrum). This plaint had appeared on a mural at Earl Street, North Belfast, in 1939 (see **chapter one, fig. 15**), in protest against the prosecution of loyalist rioters during the sectarian disturbances of 1935, but it undoubtedly referred back to the Home Rule Crisis and the loyalist revolt against the British State that began in 1912. The slogan captured the loyalist paramilitary conundrum—professing loyalty and allegiance to a monarch whose ministers directed a system of justice that categorized them as criminals and terrorists, and jailed them accordingly.

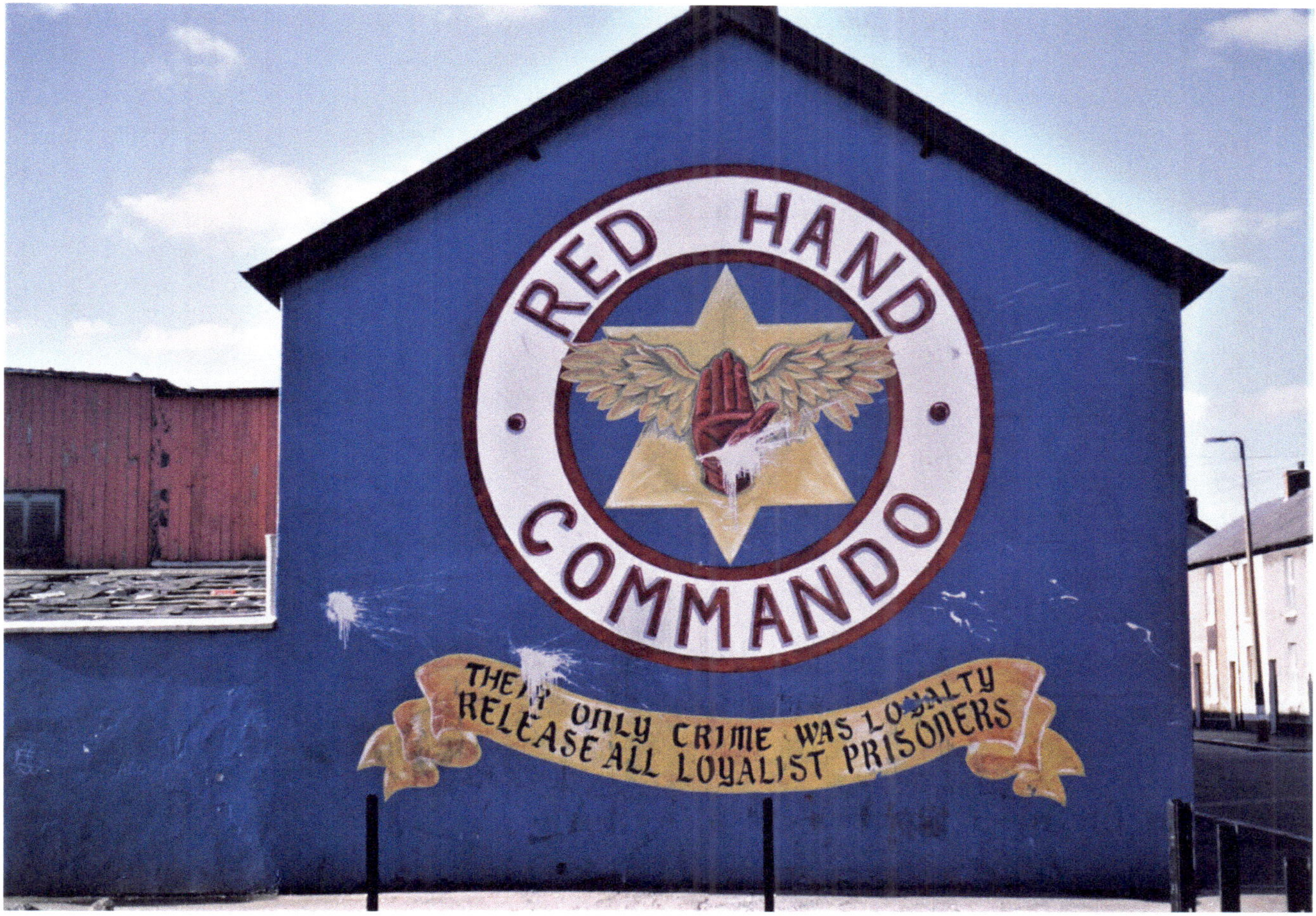

FIGURE 41 Their only crime was loyalty, Severn Street, East Belfast, 1996. Photo by Tony Crowley.

4. TRADITION AND INNOVATION

Many of the loyalist murals relating to prisoners manifested relatively innovative iconography (incorporating various symbols such as barbed wire, manacles, cell bars, watchtowers, and depictions of the H-blocks), though they were often dominated by the familiar crests, flags, guns, and paramilitary figures. There were, however, other aspects of unionist/loyalist tradition-making that continued much as they had for the previous ninety years or so.

For example, arches still featured as part of the July Twelfth celebrations, although they were less common than earlier in the century (arches decreased in number as bonfires grew in size). Most of the arches that were constructed conformed to tradition and were decorated with Orange lodge paraphernalia, references to King William, and the Union Jack and Northern Ireland flags (Figure 43, see Fulcrum), but there were others that were festooned with paramilitary symbols (Figure 44, see Fulcrum). Traditional murals on the other hand tended to draw on a stock of images that had been compiled earlier in the century and with which most people would be acquainted. Indeed, such is the integrity of everyday historico-semiotic knowledge in Northern Ireland that traditional murals often did not refer explicitly to an event such as the Battle of the Boyne to signify its importance, since they did not have to—the metonymic date (1690) sufficed to invoke a whole tradition (Figure 45, see Fulcrum). There were, however, the familiar images such as the depiction of King William in the Bobby Jackson mural in The Fountain, Londonderry, which appeared annually in the run up to the 12th July (see **chapter three, fig. 1**). And of course King William was portrayed in less and more accomplished fashion in unionist and loyalist areas across the length and breadth of Northern Ireland (Figure 46, see Fulcrum) (Figure 47). Likewise, the key historical moments at the beginning and end of the Siege of Derry—"the shutting of the gates" in December 1688 and "the breaking of the boom" and relief of the city in August 1689 (Figure 48) (Figure 49, see Fulcrum)—were represented in two striking images in the Bond Street area of Londonderry (both painted by "Attitude Artwork"—also responsible for "Eddie the Trooper" in Bond Street, see **fig. 10** above). And the names of the Apprentice Boys who closed and locked the gates against the Jacobite forces were recorded on a mural in the Old Warren area of Lisburn. Placing the gates over a representation of the crest of Londonderry, this image conjoined past and present with a reference to the Apprentice Boys parades that take place annually in August and December, and a red fist in barbed wire that represented loyalist prisoners (Figure 50). The December commemoration also features the burning of an effigy of Lieutenant-Colonel Robert Lundy, the Governor of Derry, who attempted to abandon the city at the height of the siege ("lundy" is the common term for "traitor" or "deceiver" in unionist and loyalist usage) (Figure 51, see Fulcrum).

Contemporary events also featured in the murals in representations of the monarchy (a theme that links to the early history of loyalist wall painting). The death of the Queen Mother was figured in 2002 (Figure 52, see Fulcrum), while the Golden Jubilee of Queen Elizabeth II was commemorated widely. The murals included a portrait of the Queen on the Rathcoole estate, flanked by the flags of the four countries of the United Kingdom and the crests of the UDA/UFF (Figure 53, see Fulcrum), and an image on the Shankill Road dedicated to "the 50th anniversary of the Accession" (Figure 54). This was a striking representation: along with the symbols of the four nations—thistle, rose, daffodil, and shamrock—and the Queen's title ("By the grace of God of the United Kingdom of Great Britain and Northern Ireland and our other realms and territories Queen, Head of the Commonwealth, Defender of the Faith"), the image depicted the sovereign, Windsor Castle, and the Sovereign's Orb (a symbol of divine and thus monarchical power—inaccurately figured here with a map of the Commonwealth). The lower

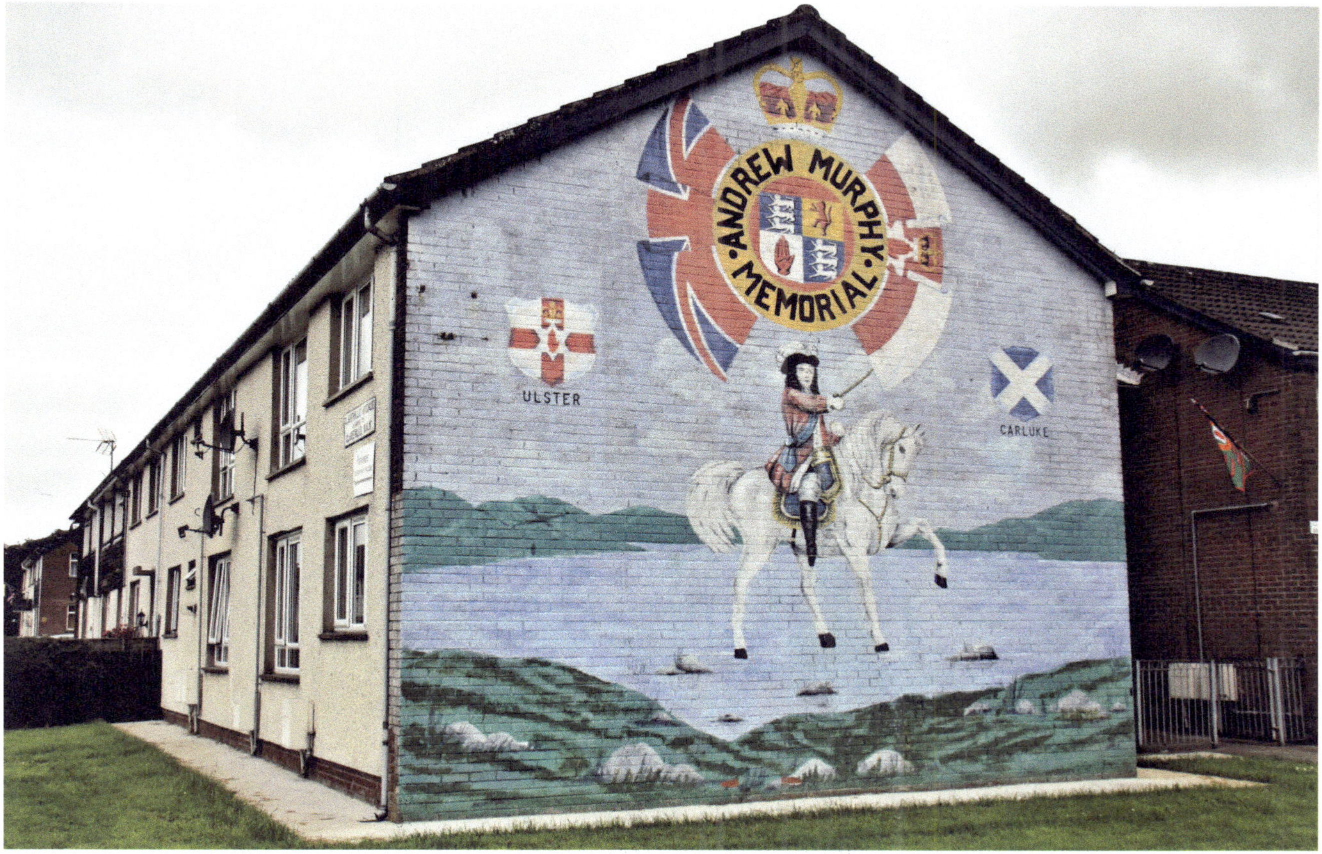

FIGURE 47 Andrew Murphy Memorial, Grange Drive, Ballyclare, 2014. Photo by Tony Crowley.

part of the mural presented the Royal Standard and Union Jack together with a declaration of loyalty: "We the British Subjects of Ulster pledge our allegiance to her sovereign Majesty Queen Elizabeth II now and forever The Heart of the Empire Ulster's loyal citizens." "The Heart of the Empire" was a historical reference to the Shankill that dates to the early twentieth century, but the discourse of Empire, largely banished from contemporary Britain, also appeared in a mural on the Westwinds estate, Newtownards, in 2006. Taking the form of an account of the composition of the Union Jack, the image represented the heyday of Empire: Britannia ruling the waves, *The Titanic*, Somme soldiers, Belfast City Hall, an (anachronistic) Harland and Wolff crane, and King George VI and the Queen Consort (later the Queen Mother) (Figure 55, see Fulcrum).[10]

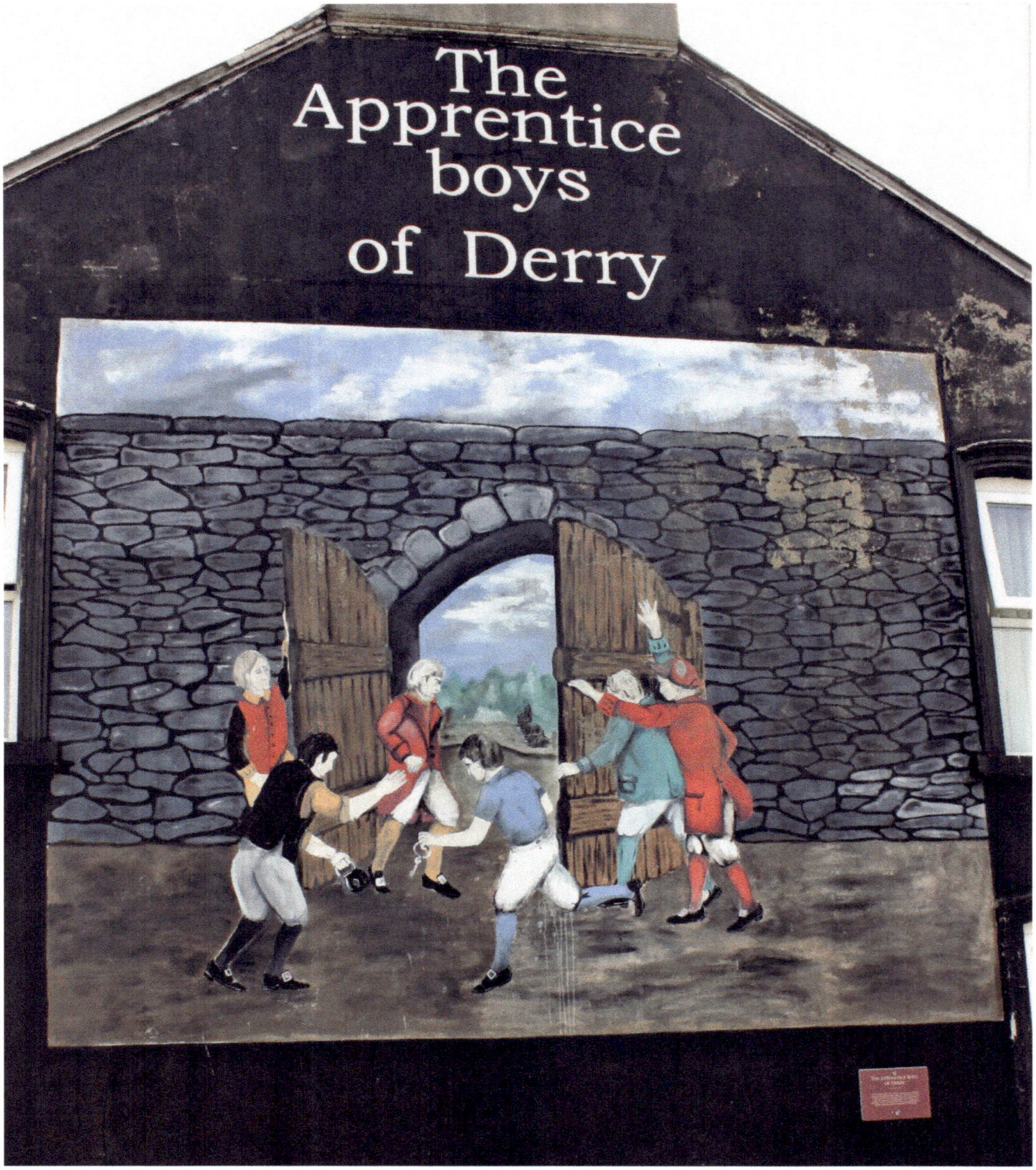

FIGURE 48 The Apprentice Boys, Emerson Street, Londonderry, 2006. Photo by Tony Crowley.

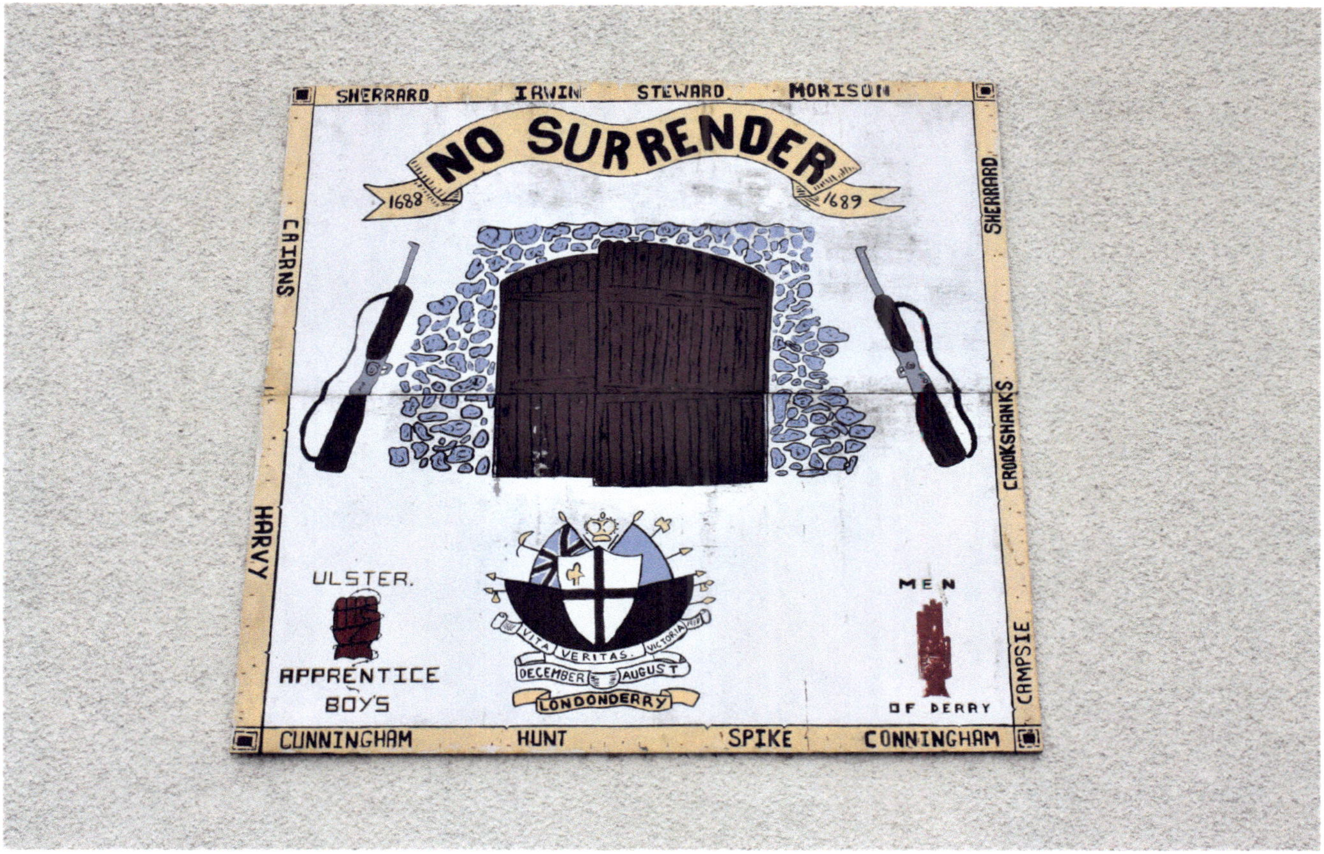

FIGURE 50 No surrender Men of Derry, Avonmore Park, Old Warren, Lisburn, 2000. Photo by Tony Crowley.

Loyalist murals were not, however, hide-bound by traditional themes, and by the 1990s they were playing with distinctive forms of affiliation, one of which was the representation of marching bands on the walls. Marching bands were not a new phenomenon; Jarman dates the practice to the very origins of Protestant parading in the late eighteenth century (Jarman 1997: 38). But as with any tradition, the elements were historically variable and the appearance of "blood and thunder bands" (also known as "Kick the Pope bands") has been described as "the most distinctive development in loyalist political culture since the 1960s" (Bryan 2000: 127). In fact most bands—usually consisting of members in quasi-martial dress playing side drums, flutes, and a huge bass drum—date from after the onset of the Troubles, but they quickly established themselves as an important factor in Ulster

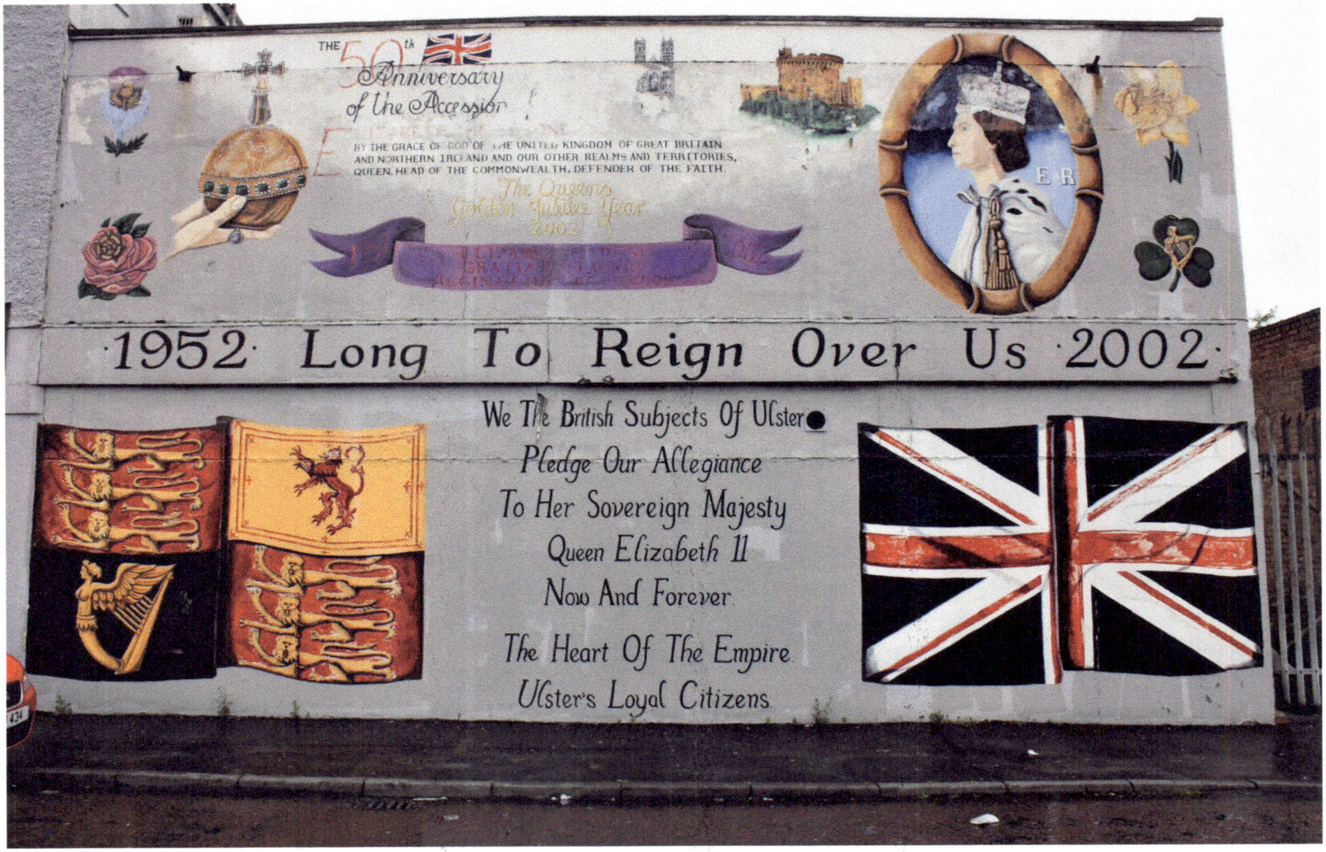

FIGURE 54 Long to reign over us, Argyle Street/Shankill Road, West Belfast, 2002. Photo by Tony Crowley.

Protestant identity, combining aspects of popular youth culture and traditional flute band practice (MacDonald 2010). Yet although the bands marched in Orange parades (notably the Twelfth), they were not usually connected directly to Orange institutions and there have been tensions between the urban, working-class, loud, and brash bands and the strict religious conformism of the Order with its strongholds in rural areas (Jarman 1997: 103; Bryan 2000: 127–129). As the band murals indicate, military regalia—crests, flags, and references to historical events—were used to convey their identity (Figure 56, see Fulcrum), and in some cases, the bands were more or less loosely connected to loyalist paramilitary organizations (Figure 57).

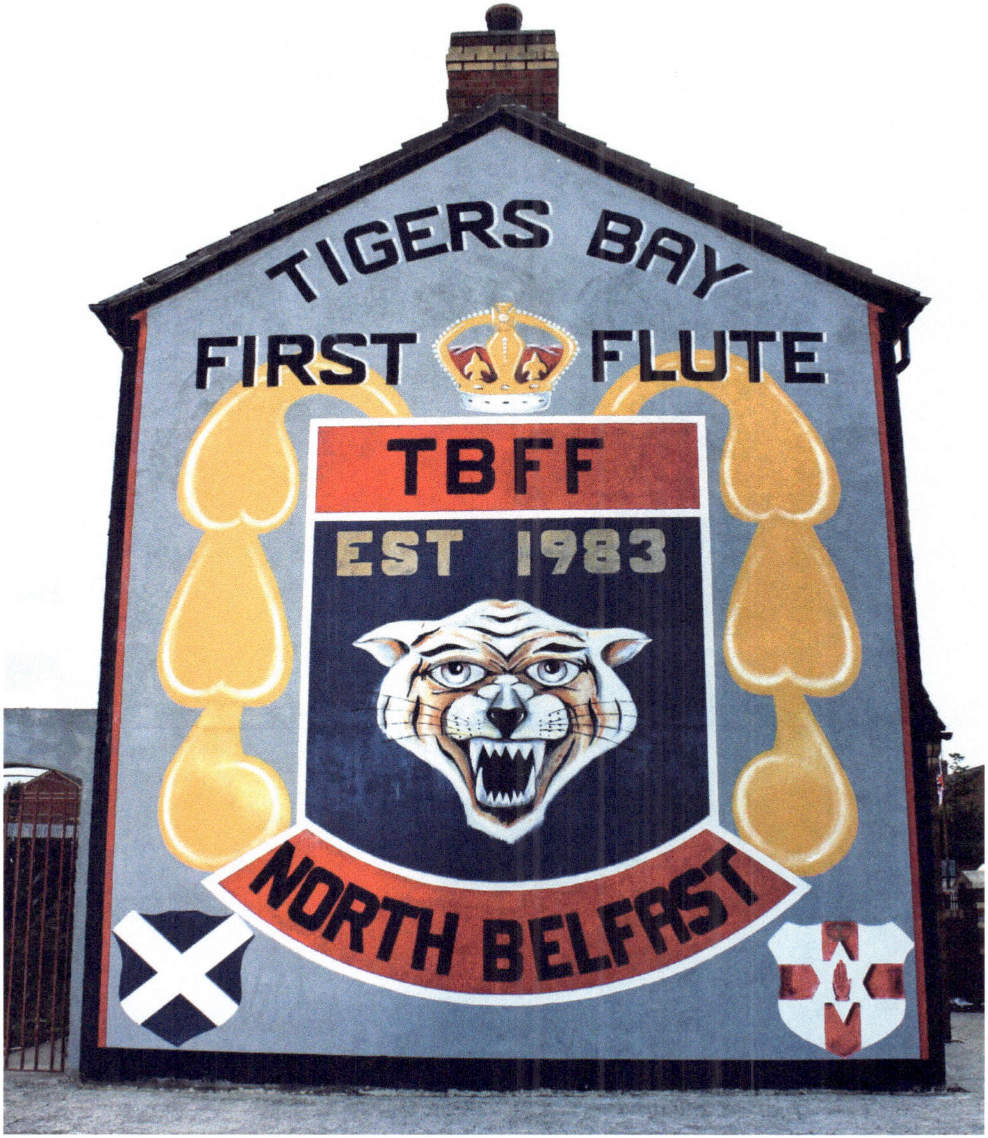

FIGURE 57 Tigers Bay First Flute, Mervue Street, Tigers Bay, North Belfast, 2005. Photo by Tony Crowley.

If the band murals were a relatively recent innovation within loyalist muralism, there were other developments that mirrored the changes taking place in the contemporary republican tradition in terms of a broadening of historical and cultural focus. For example, murals appeared that celebrated figures such as C.S. Lewis and George Best (both born in East Belfast) (Figure 58, see Fulcrum) (Figure 59, see Fulcrum), as well as aspects of local history such as the building of *The Titanic* (at the Harland and Wolff shipyard, also in East Belfast) (Figure 60, see Fulcrum). More significant, perhaps, was the treatment of Ulster-Scots history and culture in a series of murals in Londonderry and Belfast. Thus in murals entitled "from Pioneers to Presidents," Attitude Artwork represented the significance of the Ulster-Scots' influence in American history with portraits of, and pertinent quotes from, Presidents George Washington, James Buchanan, and Theodore Roosevelt. Washington's image was accompanied by his declaration that "if defeated everywhere else I will make my final stand for liberty with the Scotch-Irish (Ulster-Scots) of my native Virginia," with a note claiming that "history records that almost half of Washington's army were Ulster-Scots' (Figure 61). Buchanan's image, which originally appeared in Londonderry (Figure 62, see Fulcrum), was reproduced on Ainsworth Street in West Belfast and unveiled by the US Consul General; it quoted the President—"My Ulster blood is my most priceless heritage"—and noted that "250,000 Ulster-Scots emigrated to America in the 1700s" (Figure 63, see Fulcrum). While Roosevelt is cited as claiming that "my forefathers... were the men who had followed Cromwell and who shared in the defence of Derry and in the victories of Aughrim and the Boyne" (Figure 64, see Fulcrum). "Ulster sails west," a mural in Ballymoney that featured an emigrant ship, map of America, Presidential seal, and a pioneer, reinforced the message about the historical importance of the Ulster-Scots by quoting from President William McKinley: "they were the first to proclaim for freedom in these United States. Even before Lexington the Scotch Irish blood had been shed for American freedom" (Figure 65, see Fulcrum). And a mural in Bowtown, Newtownards, reminded "Uncle Sam" that "wherever there was fighting, or a wrong that needed righting," "the Ulster man was there" (Rolston 2013: 51).

Yet if the turn to America made sense in relation to the loyalist and unionist desire to garner support from a source usually associated with nationalism and republicanism, the prompt for the representation of Ulster-Scots culture, specifically Ulster-Scots language, lay closer to home. Provoked in part (though not entirely) by the raising of issues relating to the Irish language in the peace negotiations, Ulster-Scots was promoted as a historical vehicle of Ulster identity that required recognition. A mural on Templemore Street, East Belfast (see **Introduction, fig. 6**), promoted the case by celebrating "4000 years of Ulster Scots history and heritage Ulster & Scotland Shared language Shared literature Shared culture"; it advised "Dinnae houl yer wheest Houl yer ain" (Don't hold your tongue, Hold your own).[11] Given the perceived threat to unionist and loyalist identity, it is perhaps predictable that there was an urge to reach for the foundational past, as represented in a bold set of murals that appropriated Gaelic mythology. Cú Chulainn continued to appear, along with his companions in the Red Branch Knights (a band of warriors who defended Ulster during the reign of Conchobhar mac Nessa)

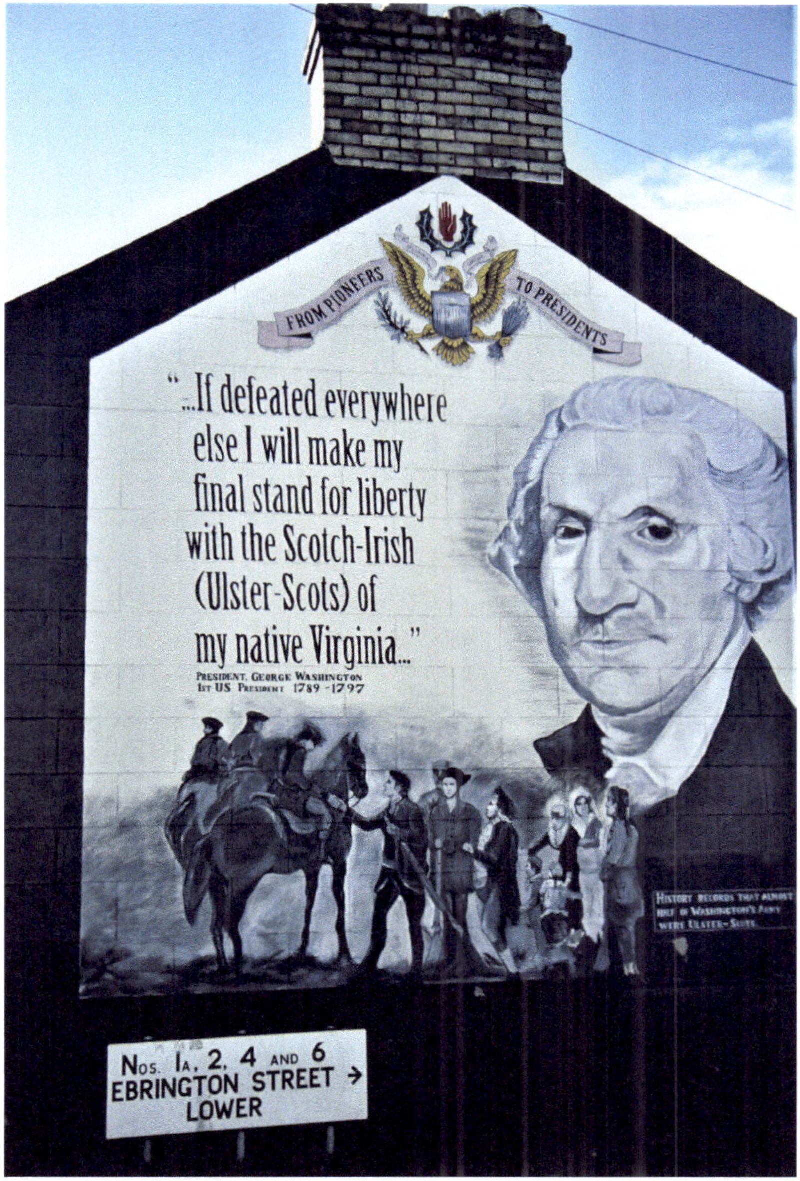

FIGURE 61 President George Washington, Ebrington Street Lower/Bonds Street, Londonderry, 1999. Photo by Tony Crowley.

who were linked to their contemporary counterparts, the RHC (https://muralsirlandedunord.over-blog.com/search/Red%20Branch/). Finn McCool (Fionn mac Cumhaill) also featured as a "defender of Ulster" (along with the UDA) (Figure 66, see Fulcrum). And the mythical origin of the Red Hand itself was presented in a later mural on the Newtownards Road, East Belfast, in gory style (Figure 67, see Fulcrum): "The strangest victory in all history: Heremon O'Neill racing a rival chieftain for possession of Ireland became the first man to touch its soil by cutting off his own hand and hurling it ashore! His sacrifice made Heremon the first king of Ulster, 1015 B.C." This was not the first or the last time in Irish history that blood, sacrifice, and territorial possession were linked.

Susan McKay's *The Protestants of Ulster* (2000) carried the sub-title "an unsettled people," and it provided an important account of a heterogeneous community divided in many ways—by class, education, geographic location, political outlook—but united in a shared sense of uncertainty about the future. The depth of that uncertainty varied, but loyalist murals often reflected, in a number of respects, the anxieties that existed before and after the signing of *The Belfast Agreement* (despite the fact, as noted previously, that the concord guaranteed the principle of consent and thus in effect copper-bottomed the union). One of the most important modes in which loyalist apprehension was represented was in the recourse to specific forms of social and individual commemoration. In one sense, of course, cultural memory had consistently been central to loyalist muralism from the inception of the tradition in the early twentieth century. But as noted in chapter three, mural-based commemoration intensified from the late 1980s in loyalist artworks. Again this replicated contemporary developments within republican practice, which is not to imply that loyalist artists were "copying" their republican counter-parts (or vice-versa), but that there was a general shift in the communal sensibility that the murals captured and conveyed. For better or worse, there was no escaping either the past, or the commemorated past.

Loyalist memory murals in the period from the 1994 ceasefires through to *The St Andrews Agreement* in 2006 can be considered as falling into two general categories. First, there were the murals that dealt with significant formative developments in Protestant/unionist/loyalist history. And within that category, there was also a specific set of murals that challenged what was perceived to be the dominant historical narratives of nationalism and republicanism. Second, there were the murals that addressed loyalist paramilitarism in general. And within that division, there was a group of murals that commemorated either individual figures or local units within the organizations. Of course this is a schematic account, since many of the murals slipped between these analytics and some functioned semiotically in multiple ways, but it is a helpful way of thinking about the large and increasing number of loyalist murals dedicated to memory that appeared from the mid-1990s on.

Within loyalism at this period there was a clear perception that their history and culture was misunderstood (together with an acknowledgment that republicans had become accomplished in presenting their own narrative). Thus the East Belfast Historical and Cultural Society (formed in 2002) observed that,

> our culture requires a higher and much more positive profile. We decided to demonstrate to all that as a community we have a rich and varied history and culture. A culture, which offends no one and a history, which demonstrates that we are not just implants who have no rights in our own country and a history of which we should feel very proud.

To that end,

> The Society decided to depict a small part of our history and culture in a montage of murals in Thorndyke Street in east Belfast… The murals tell a shortened history of our communities' history and culture. We are often accused of having no history, of having no culture; Thorndyke Street dispels that myth, which is pedalled by republicans. Education of our own and more importantly the wider community was one of the drivers behind the scheme. (East Belfast Historical and Cultural Society 2006: 1)

The result was a striking series of fifteen murals that filled a 130-foot-long arched wall on Thorndyke Street and covered key moments in Protestant/unionist/loyalist history from the seventeenth century to the present (Figure 68). The topics included (in order): "The Ulster Covenant"; "The folk come home & the Lord Protector of the Commonwealth" (Plantation and Cromwell); "The city is saved" (the Siege of Derry); "Civil and religious liberty for all" (the foundation of the Orange Order); "Better the grave than slavery" (the Home Rule Crisis); "Their sacrifice, our freedom" (the Somme); "The United Kingdom" (political composition and symbols); "Hitler attacks Belfast" (the 1941 Belfast blitz); "Defending the community" (early loyalist paramilitarism); "Unity-solidarity" (the UWC strike); "Their loyalty betrayed" (the disbandment of the B Specials and the UDR); "Out of the ashes, new life" (Cluan Place and sectarian conflict); "Britannia" (the history of the symbol and composition of the Union Jack); "The Commonwealth" (the history of the Commonwealth) and "In Flanders Fields" (Figure 69, see Fulcrum). The murals were accompanied by explanatory plaques and a booklet.[12]

If one of the goals of the East Belfast Historical and Cultural Society was to educate both its own community and the wider populace, one of the ways in which it did so was by challenging the historical account given by nationalism and republicanism. One example was the construction of the McCurrie–Neill Memorial Garden on the Lower Newtownards Road as a counter to the narrative of what republicans called "the defence of this area" in "the Battle of Saint Matthew's" (the Provisional IRA's first major engagement in the Troubles) in June 1970 (Figure 70, see Fulcrum). In the loyalist version, it was a "planned and unprovoked attack" by the IRA leading to "murder most foul" (Figure 71). Another example of this form of counter-memory was created slightly later by the West Belfast Athletic and Cultural Society in a mural that portrayed the effect of "30 years of indiscriminate slaughter by so-called non-sectarian Irish Freedom Fighters" (it was accompanied by a plaque listing those killed in the "Shankill atrocities"—"We will remember them always") (Figure 72). Likewise, in a further deployment of the discourse of

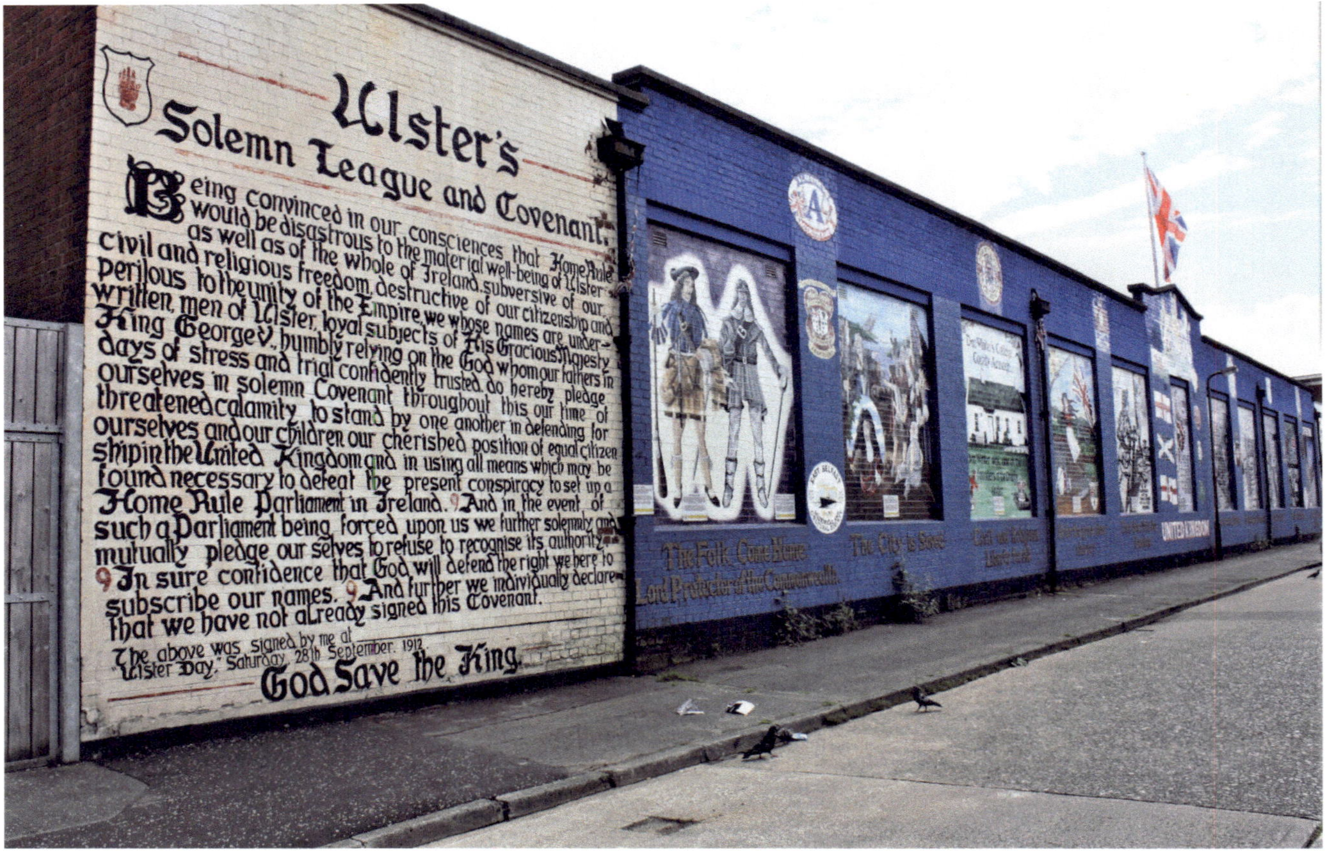

FIGURE 68 Our history and culture, Thorndyke Street, East Belfast, 2004. Photo by Tony Crowley.

grievance (often called "whataboutery" in Northern Ireland), a striking mural in Canada Street, East Belfast, again sponsored by the East Belfast Historical and Cultural Society, depicted "The untold story" of Protestant "refugees" fleeing "burning homes to live in the safety of Liverpool" in August 1971 (Figure 73, see Fulcrum).[13]

This explicit attempt to challenge republican narratives within the discourse of popular cultural history was notable, but it was also accompanied by a determination to foreground two of the most significant historical events in twentieth century loyalism against a backdrop of ongoing stalemate in the post-*Belfast Agreement* negotiations for the Stormont Assembly. The first was the revolt against Home Rule, which was represented in a series of murals that commemorated its 90th anniversary. The images, which mostly figured Carson, included the signing of the

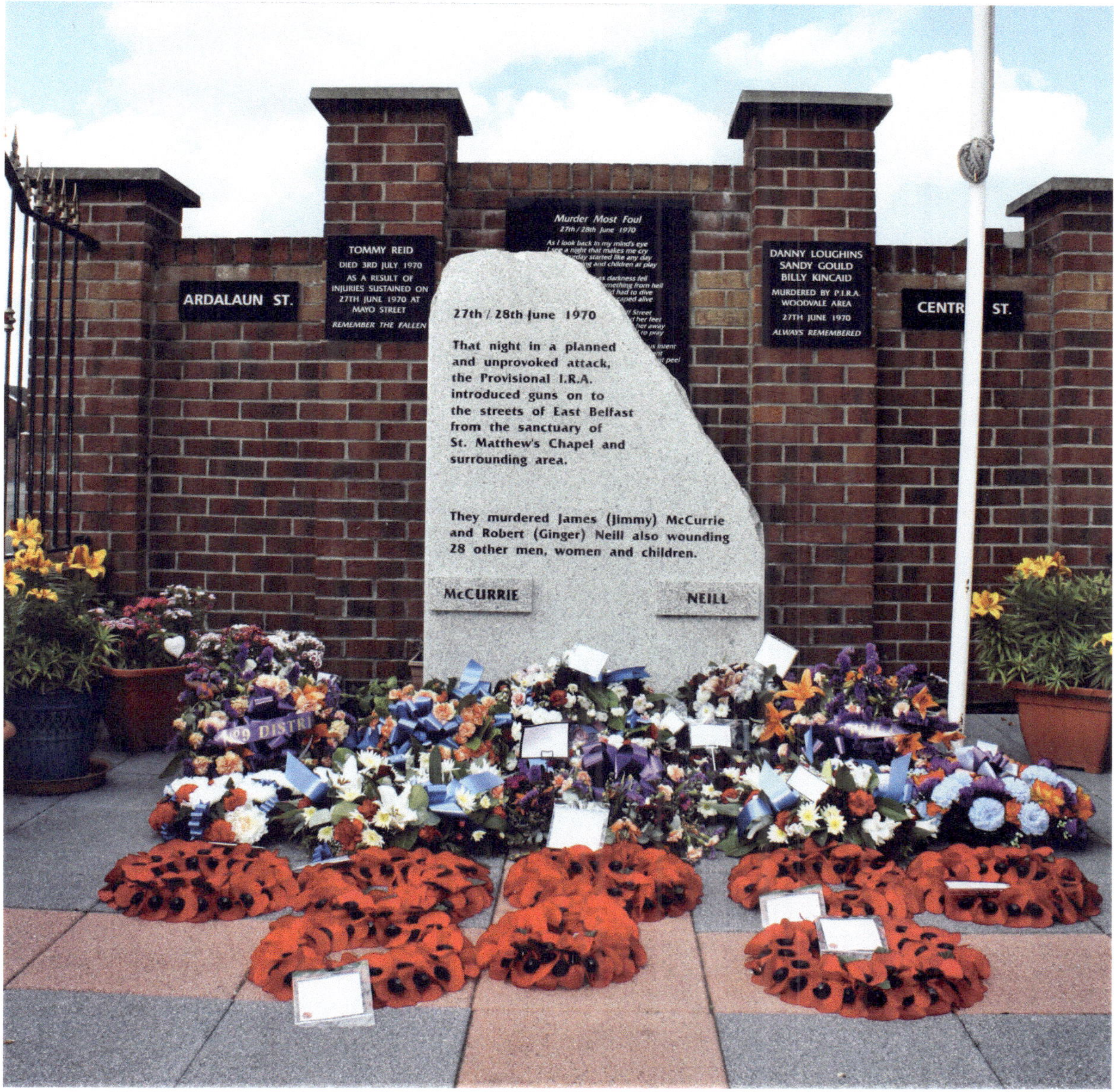

FIGURE 71 Unprovoked attack, Newtownards Road, East Belfast, 2003. Photo by Tony Crowley.

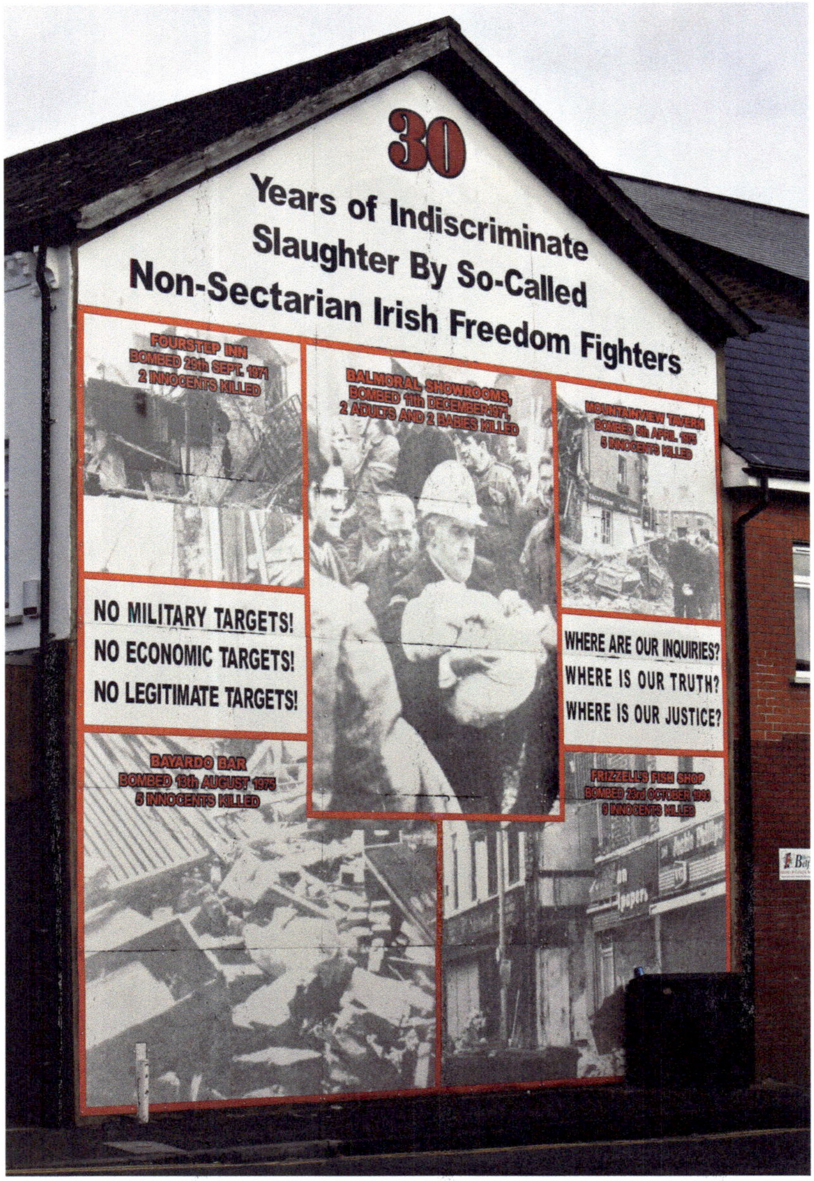

FIGURE 72 Indiscriminate slaughter, Dundee Street, Shankill Road, West Belfast, 2002. Photo by Tony Crowley.

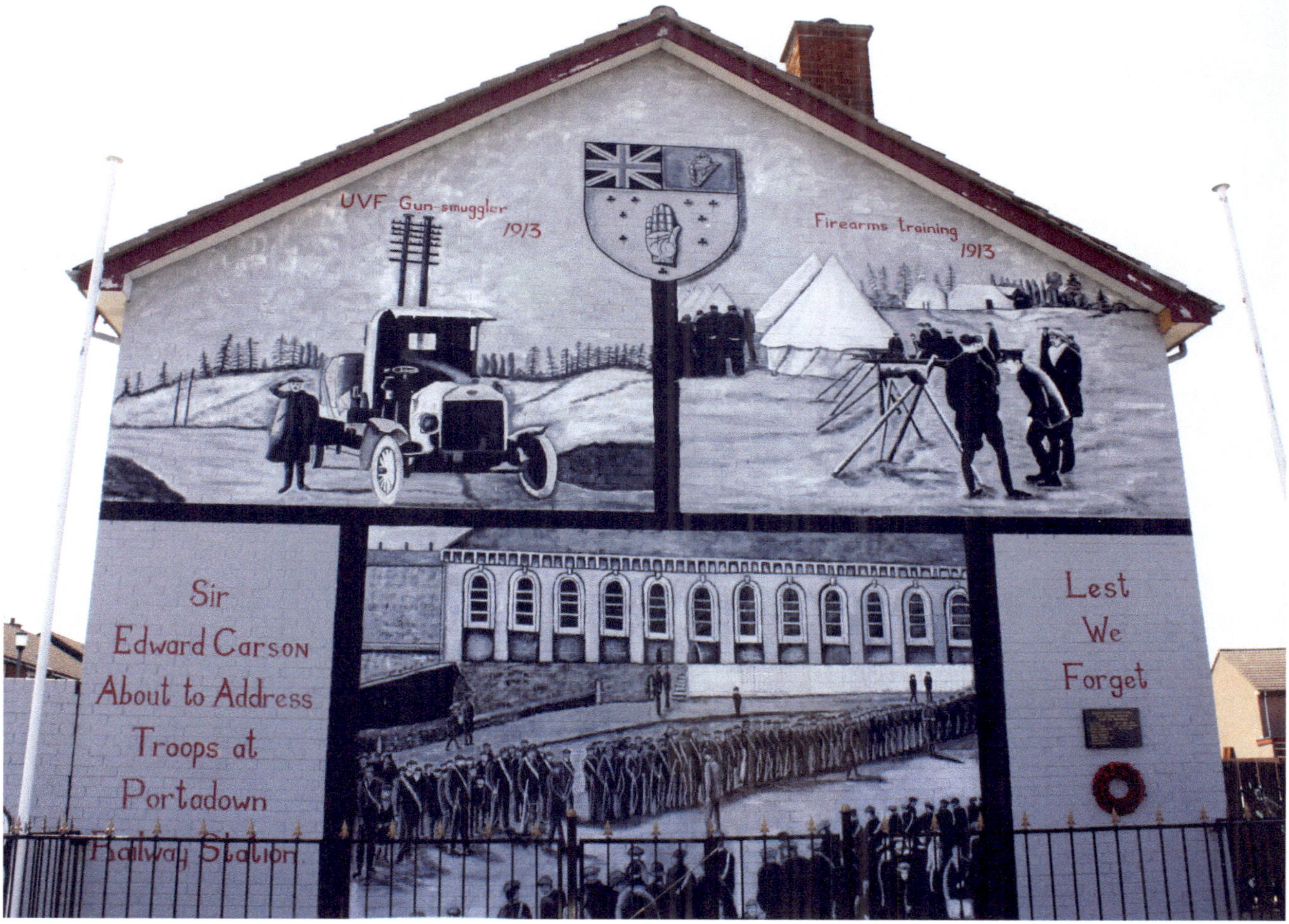

FIGURE 76 Carson at Portadown, Union Street, Portadown, 2006. Photo by Tony Crowley.

Covenant in 1912 (Figure 74, see Fulcrum), gun-running (Figure 75, see Fulcrum), and Carson inspecting Ulster Volunteers in Portadown and West Belfast (Figure 76). As with so many of the memory murals, there was a clear imperative to link the present with the past (and indeed the future). Thus an updated version of the 1914 postcard of an armed woman representing Ulster—"Deserted! Well I can stand alone" (see **chapter three, fig. 20**)—also featured a contemporary scene: "A Protestant farmer's wife guards her husband against sectarian attack from across

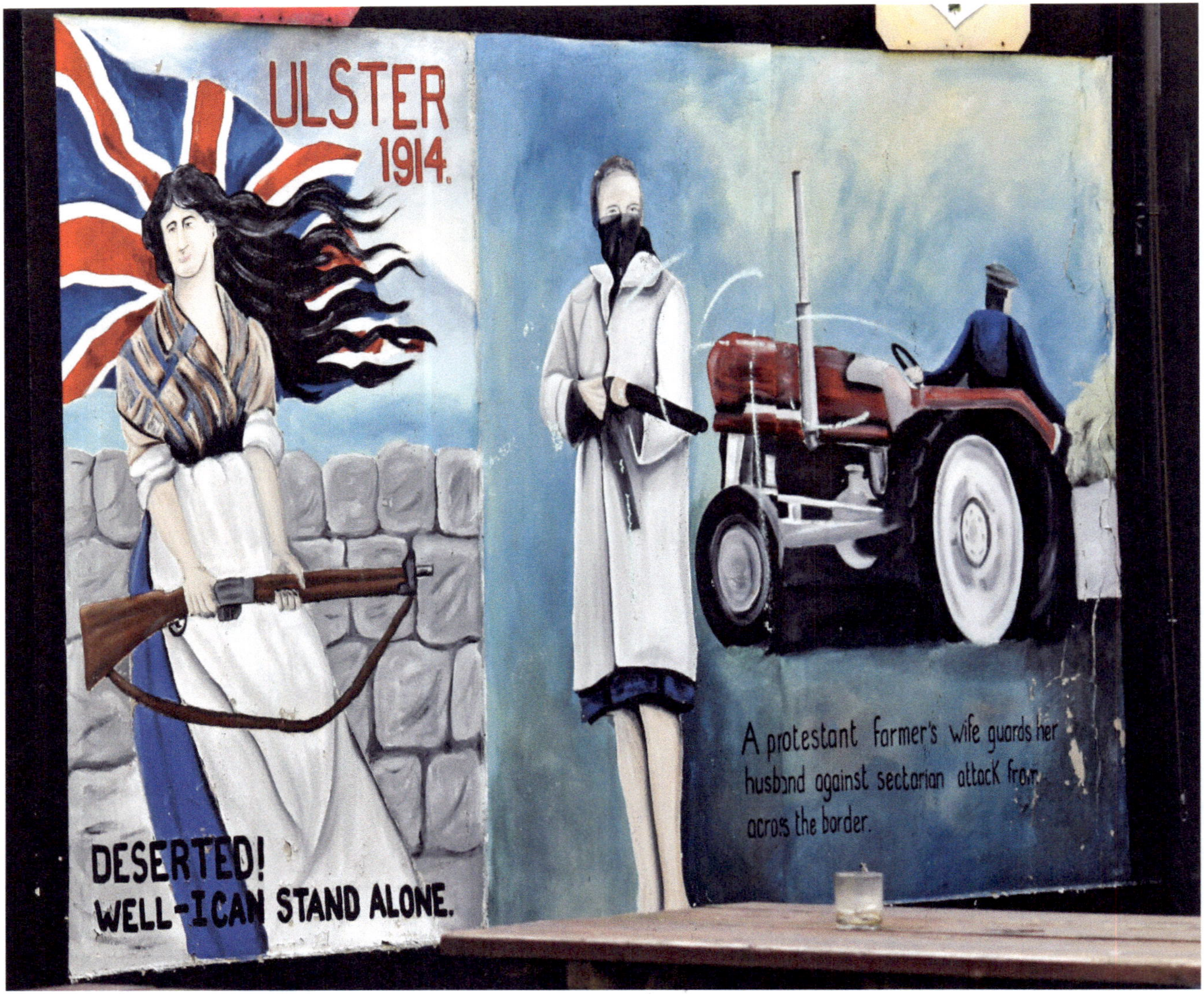

FIGURE 77 I can stand alone! Moscow Street/Shankill Road, West Belfast, 2002. Photo by Tony Crowley.

the border" (Figure 77). While a mural that remembered gun-running at Donaghadee in 1914 glossed the image with the comment: "Preparing to bear arms 1914 Prepared to bear arms 2004" (Figure 78, see Fulcrum).

The second important event commemorated in loyalist memory-murals was the Battle of the Somme, which began on the significant date of July 1 1916 (July 1 was the date of the Battle of the Boyne O.S.).[14] At the Somme, the 36th Ulster Division (largely composed of members of the UVF who had answered the call of the British State once the First World War was declared) suffered enormous casualties—some 5,500 in the first two days, including more than 2,000 fatalities. The attack, in which the Ulster Division were at the forefront, was a military disaster (Prior and Wilson 2005: 84–87), though also an occasion of formidable bravery (four Victoria Crosses were awarded to Ulster soldiers for their actions at the Somme). Given the nature of communications at the time, it took a while for news of the full extent of the carnage and its local implications to reach Northern Ireland. Early reports were wrongly confident: the war news in the *Belfast News-Letter* of July 7 was headed "Battle of the Somme. All still going well." But on the same page, the newspaper printed a "Message to the people of Ulster' from Carson that expressed "pride and admiration" for the soldiers of the Ulster Division who had made "the supreme sacrifice for the Empire of which they were so proud," and "sorrow and sadness at the loss of so many men who were to us personal friends and comrades" (*Belfast News-Letter* July 7 1916: 5). More importantly, the newspaper carried an eye-witness report (unsigned but later revealed to have been penned by Captain Wilfrid Spender of the Ulster Division's HQ staff) that began: "I am not an Ulsterman but yesterday, the 1st. July, as I followed their amazing attack, I felt that I would rather be an Ulsterman than anything else in the world." Recalling that the infantrymen "charged over the two front lines of enemy trenches, shouting 'No surrender, boys,'" and that "the Ulstermen were the target of the concentrated hostile guns and machine guns behind, and on both flanks," it was the conclusion of his piece that had powerful and long-lasting resonance:

> The Ulster Division has lost very heavily, and in doing so has sacrificed itself for the Empire. The Ulster Volunteer Force, from which the Division was made, has won a name which equals any in history. Their devotion, which no doubt has helped the advance elsewhere, deserves the gratitude of the British Empire. (*Belfast News-Letter* July 7 1916: 5).

Once articulated, the notion that the "blood sacrifice" of the 36th Ulster Division had created a debt that Britain needed to re-pay, soon became a tenet of political faith.[15]

As noted in chapter one, the actions of the 36th Ulster Division at the Somme were commemorated on the walls almost immediately with a mural in Ballymacarrett in 1917. By 1935 (a year of bitter sectarian violence), the *Belfast Newsletter* opined that the Somme ranked alongside Derry, Aughrim, and the Boyne as a loyalist touchstone, and a mural appeared in Coolfin Street, South Belfast, that incorporated a representation of James Prinsep Beadle's "Attack of the Ulster Division, 1 July 1916" (see **chapter one, fig. 9**). From the mid-1990s, however, depictions of the Somme and its significance became a central and repeated topic of loyalist muralism. The most popular image featured the 36th Ulster Division going over the top (Figure 79, see Fulcrum), though others focused on the VCs awarded to individual soldiers (four at the Somme, nine in all) (Figure 80). The imperative to remember "these men, and others like them" indicated another function of the First World War murals: the forging of the link between the UVF of 1912, the 36th Ulster Division, and the UVF that was formed in 1965 and fought in the Troubles (Taylor 2000: 34). The continuity was postulated in various ways. In some murals, the connection took the form of a connection between the YCV of 1912 and 1972 (the earlier YCV was a civic youth organization that merged with the UVF in 1914, its later counterpart was the youth wing of the UVF during the Troubles) (Figure 81). In others, the concatenation was implicit—usually by the juxtaposition of a memorial to dead (Troubles) volunteers and a First World War mural (Figure 82, see Fulcrum), or, less frequently, by the conjunction of specific individuals (one audacious mural linked a VC with a modern volunteer) (Figure 83, see Fulcrum). The political goal of the linkage was made clear by Billy Hutchinson, one of the founders of the later YCV: to create "an identity, a vision, and, above all, a historical lineage to Ulster's past crises… We saw ourselves as the inheritors of the UVF and YCV, which had fought against Home Rule and paid the ultimate sacrifice at the Somme" (Hutchinson 2020: 77). The political trajectory was outlined in a mural that moved from the formation of the Ulster Volunteers, to the Somme, to UVF volunteers on the Shankill in 1969, to the UVF and PUP "at the crossroads" of war and peace in 2002 (Figure 84).

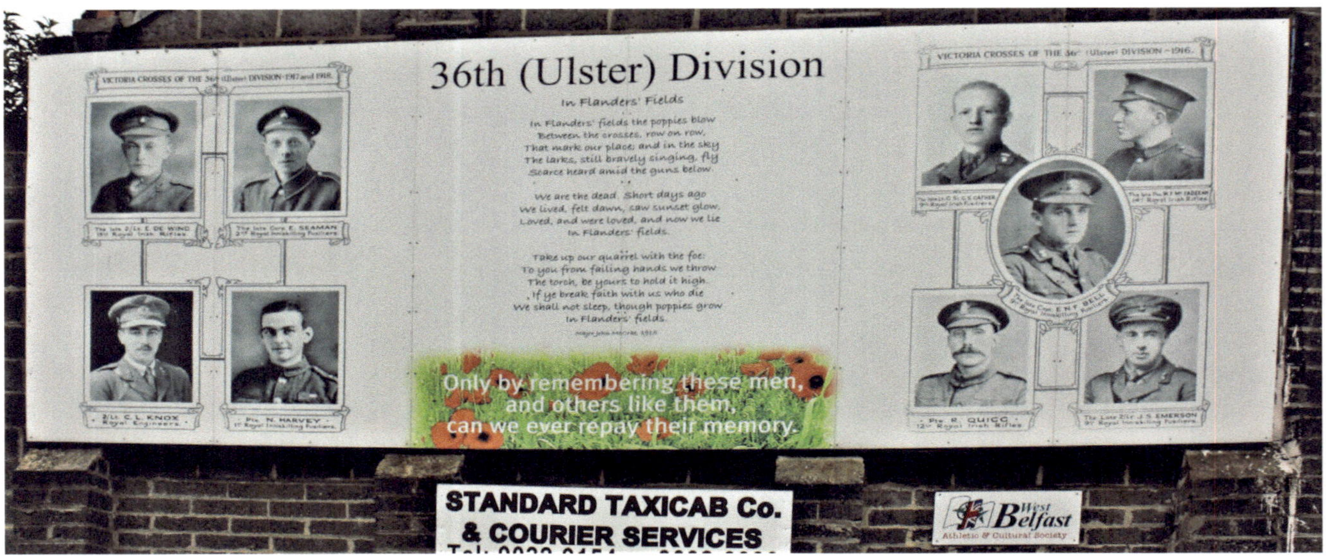

FIGURE 80 36th (Ulster) Division, Crimea Street/ Shankill Road, West Belfast, 2006. Photo by Tony Crowley.

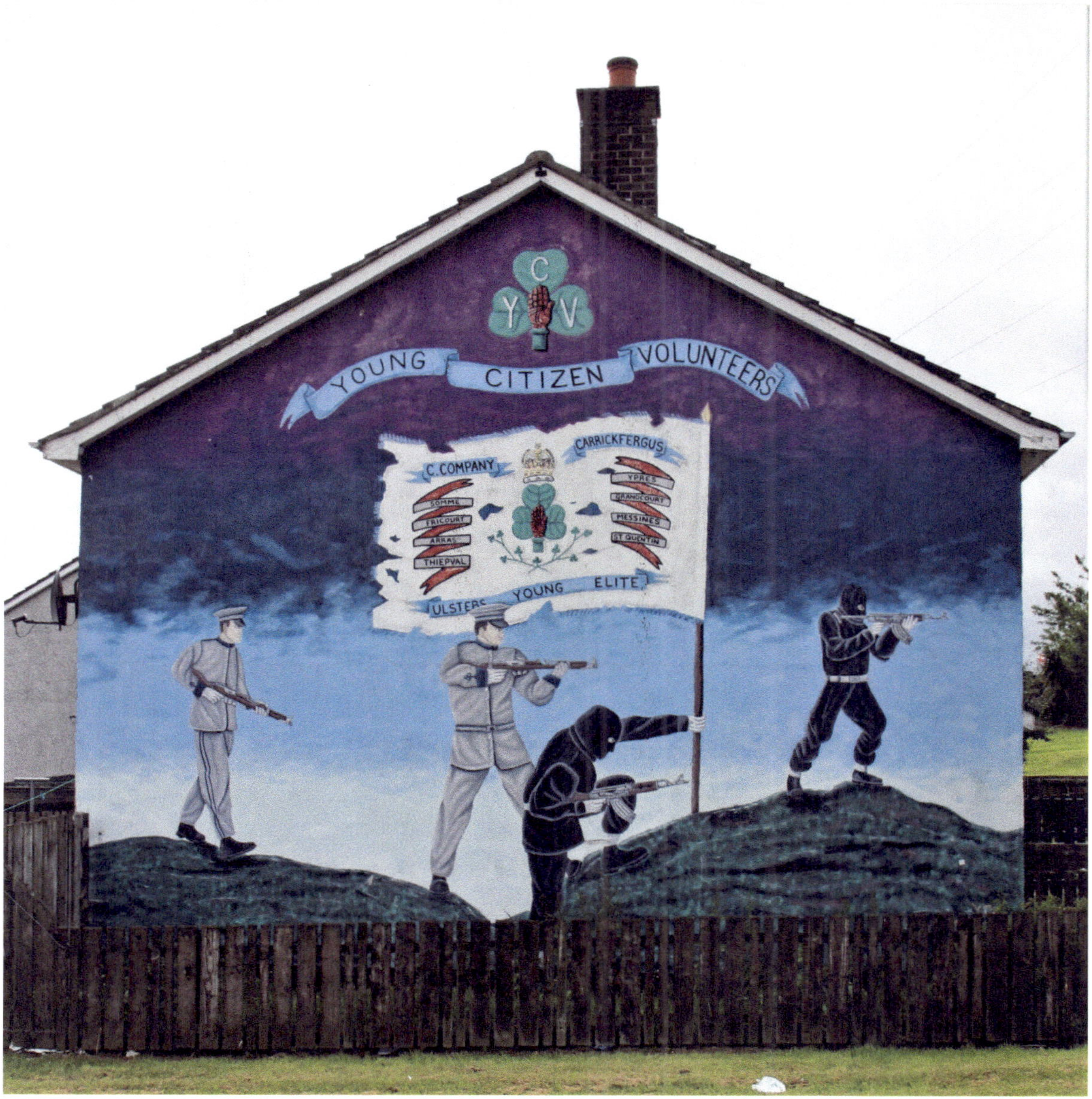

FIGURE 81 Young Citizen Volunteers, Castlemara Drive, Carrickfergus, 2002. Photo by Tony Crowley.

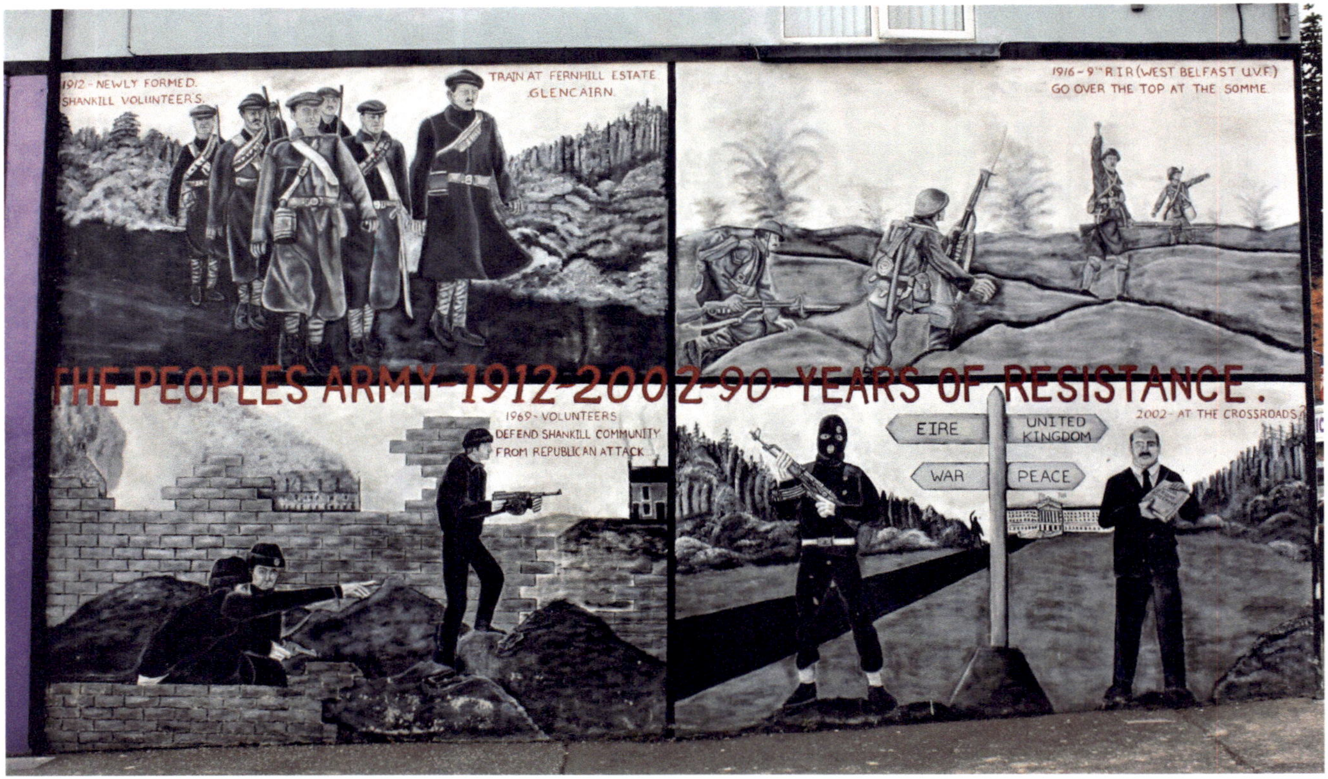

FIGURE 84 The people's army, Canmore Street/Shankill Road, West Belfast, 2002. Photo by Tony Crowley.

The requirement to remember was posited as a form of communal debt—"only by remembering these men... can we ever repay their memory"—and loyalist paramilitaries assertively commemorated their own dead. For the UVF, for example, the Woodvale area of North/West Belfast, particularly Disraeli Street, became a memorial gallery of volunteers who were: "murdered by cowards" (killed in a feud) (Figure 85, see Fulcrum); assassinated by the INLA (Figure 86, see Fulcrum); or executed by the Special Air Service (SAS) (Figure 87, see Fulcrum). The UDA's prime memory site was the Lower Shankill estate, where murals remembered its volunteers who were: "murdered by the enemies of Ulster" (the INLA) (Figure 88, see Fulcrum); "murdered by the UVF" (Figure 89, see Fulcrum); and in the case of Stephen McKeag, the UDA"s "Top Gun," killed by a drugs overdose (Figure 90, see Fulcrum). The commemoration of volunteers tended to align with the paramilitary group that dominated specific areas, though the demarcation was not strict: Stephen McCrea, of the RHC, featured on the Lower Shankill estate (Figure 91, see Fulcrum), whereas Duke Elliott, a founder member of the UDA—originally the Woodvale Defence Association—appeared on home territory in the Woodvale (Figure 92, see Fulcrum). Loyalist memorialization by murals became widespread throughout loyalist Northern Ireland: from Londonderry (Figure 93, see Fulcrum) to Antrim (Figure 94, see Fulcrum), to Portadown (Figure 95, see Fulcrum). It also began to take a permanent mode with the appearance of memorial gardens or enclosures (Figure 96) (Figure 97, see Fulcrum). In addition, however, and in a marked shift, memorials also began to refer to specific units within the paramilitary organizations. Though this was true of the UDA/UFF (Figure 98, see Fulcrum) it was particularly evident in a number of UVF murals at key locations around the Shankill Road (Figure 99) (Figure 100, see Fulcrum).

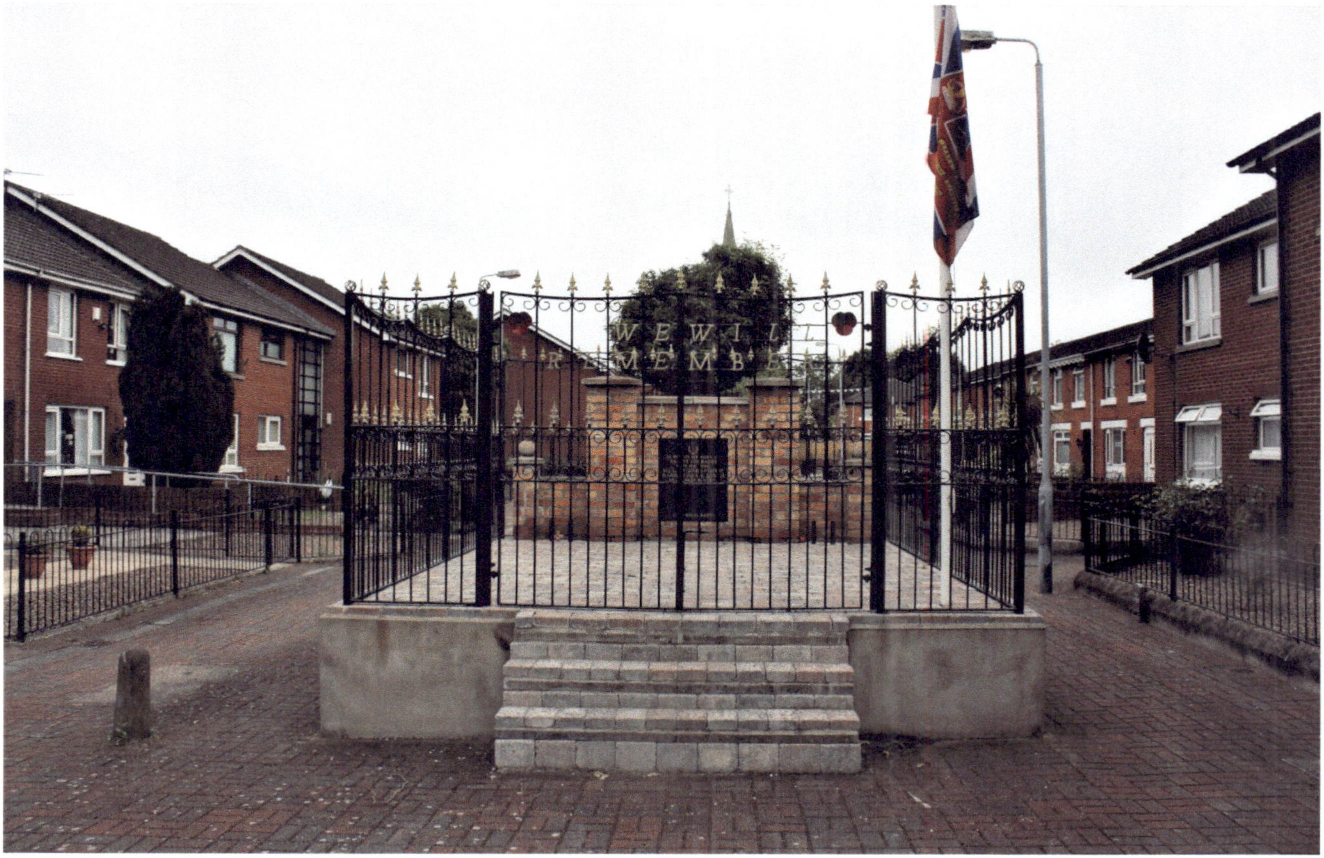

FIGURE 96 We will remember, Fraser Pass/ Ballymacarret Road, East Belfast, 2003. Photo by Tony Crowley.

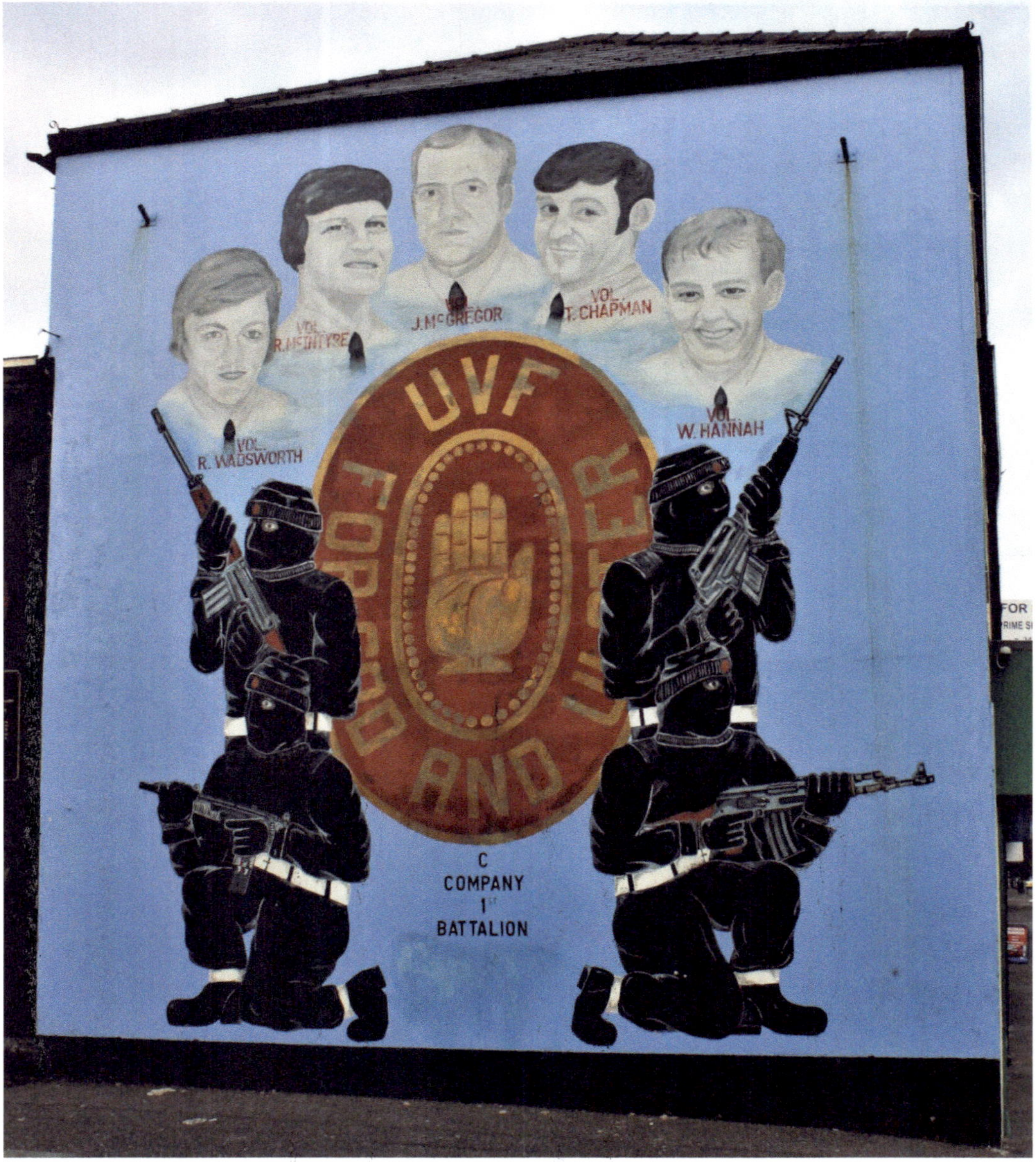

FIGURE 99 C Company 1st Battalion, Carnan Street, Shankill, West Belfast, 2005. Photo by Tony Crowley.

One of the most notable developments in loyalist muralism occurred in 2000 in and around the Lower Shankill estate, the stronghold of UDA "C" Company, headed by Johnny Adair. Adair, though once a supporter of the Peace Process, had become disillusioned with *The Belfast Agreement* and the political leadership of loyalism, which led him to ally with the LVF (the dissident group that had broken with the UVF over Drumcree). Adair imposed control through prodigious violence (despite the loyalist ceasefire), but also manifested his power culturally by commissioning a range of murals. Indeed the Lower Shankill estate was transformed into a gallery of images that included topics as varied as Eddie the Trooper (see **note 3**), Drumcree (see **fig. 24 above**), Cromwell (Figure 101), the ethnic cleansing of Protestants (Figure 102, see Fulcrum), the UDA Scottish Brigade (Figure 103, see Fulcrum), the history of the UDA (Figure 104, see Fulcrum), "loyalist martyr," Billy Wright (Figure 105, see Fulcrum), the links between Scotland and Ulster and the UFF (Figure 106, see Fulcrum), and Princess Diana, "Queen of Hearts" (Figure 107, see Fulcrum). A number of these murals were to have formed a centerpiece in a "loyalist day of culture" organized by Adair and C Company on August 19 2000. But during the UDA/UFF show of strength that began the day, Adair used the occasion to provoke the UVF by unfurling an LVF flag and attacking the Rex Bar, a UVF stronghold. The loyalist feud that followed was bitter indeed: families were driven from their homes and there were a number of killings. And of course the strife was played out on the walls in the form of defaced murals, accusations, and threats. As it turned out, however, Adair's attack on the UVF (and thereby on the Peace Process itself), was self-defeating. The UDA was torn apart by internal feuding, while Adair himself was jailed twice; on release in 2005, the UDA forced him into exile.

Like their republican counterparts, loyalist muralists hardly engaged with their enemies on the other side of the "Peace Line." On occasion there was graffiti that responded to specific events, such as the arrest of three republicans who had traveled to Colombia to train FARC (Fuerzas Armadas Revolucionarias de Colombia) guerrillas—"Farc off" (Figure 108, see Fulcrum). There was also a mural on the Lower Shankill estate that challenged the ambivalence of "The Sinn Féin commitment to the Peace Process" by detailing breaches such as the importation of arms, a Stormont spy ring, the training of FARC, and a republican break-in at police headquarters at Castlereagh (the mural depicted Gerry Adams as a politician and armed IRA volunteer) (Figure 109). In addition a mural in East Belfast detailed the unbalanced list of concessions given to republicans at the expense of loyalists (Figure 110, see Fulcrum). But in general, the focus of loyalist muralists was internal and their work between 1994 and 2006 reflected a set of complex and variable responses to the ceasefires, the political negotiations, *The Belfast Agreement*, and the Peace Process that followed it. In truth, although some loyalists engaged seriously and rigorously in politics as a way of creating a better society, many were confused by developments after 1994, some were dismayed, and others were fearful at the prospect of sharing power with people who they had long regarded as their most bitter enemies. In addition to which, the representatives of the political parties linked to loyalist paramilitarism, unlike their republican antagonists, did not have a significant electoral mandate and therefore had little influence within the new power-structures, nor did they have an international audience (despite the

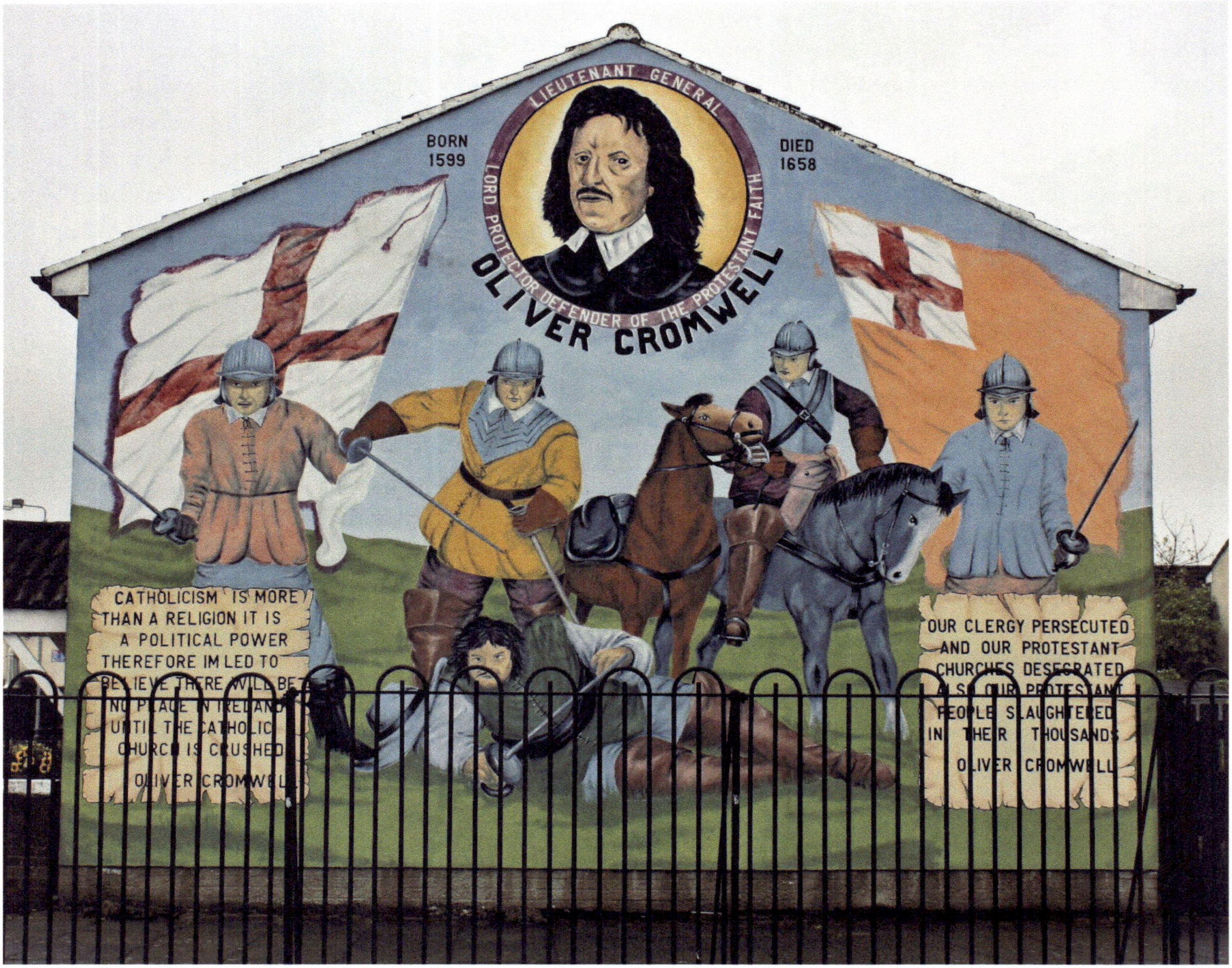

FIGURE 101 Oliver Cromwell, Shankill Parade, Lower Shankill, West Belfast, 2002. Photo by Tony Crowley.

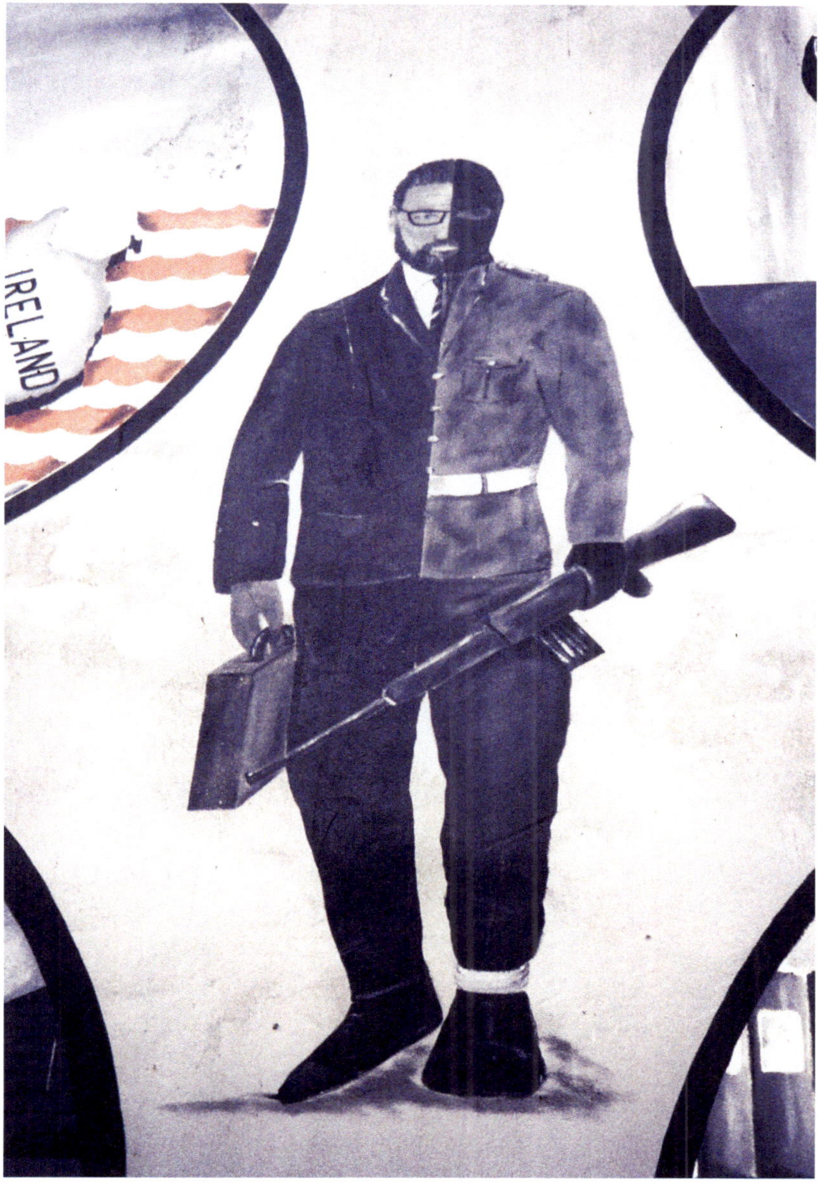

FIGURE 109 The Sinn Féin commitment to the Peace Process, Boundary Street, Shankill, West Belfast, 2003. Photo by Tony Crowley.

best efforts of the Ulster Scots muralists). What loyalism did have were paramilitary organizations that remained rooted in, and that continued to exert influence over, local communities across Northern Ireland.

Given the persistence of loyalist paramilitarism, together with the series of feuds that tore loyalist communities apart from 1999–2005 (between the UVF and the LVF in 1999–2001 and again in 2005, between the UVF and the UDA in 2000, and between various factions of the UDA in 2002–2003), it is unsurprising that at this particular time a large number of murals appeared which functioned as political territory markers within loyalist areas. Sometimes the markers were exclusive, signaling claims to undisputed control, sometimes they signified the dominance of one group, and on occasion they indicated that a number of political groupings existed within an area. Whatever their specific role, loyalist murals that featured armed men (and in one very unusual case, armed women) were painted abundantly across Northern Ireland. Strategically located, and often at the entrances to areas, the murals conveyed a clear message to republicans and nationalists, to State authorities, and indeed to the local inhabitants, that whatever developments were taking place at Stormont, and notwithstanding the efforts of the political leadership of loyalism, paramilitarism had not gone away. From Belfast to Bangor, Monkstown to Ballybeen, Rathcoole to Newtownards, Carrickfergus to Portadown, the threat of loyalist violence was made clear (Figure 111) (Figure 112). Yet although they were widespread, such images also represented a conundrum, given that in its own accounting, loyalism held that republicanism had been defeated and the Union secured. For if it were true, as a piece of loyalist graffiti claimed (Figure 113, see Fulcrum), that "peace was delivered" and, therefore, the police Historical Enquiries Team should "forget the past" (an astonishing injunction in Northern Ireland), then why were paramilitary groups still operational?[16] One answer was given in a UVF mural featuring the standard men with guns, which announced rather portentously, that "wheresoever, howsoever, or whenever we are called upon to make our exit, we shall do so as free men" (Figure 114, see Fulcrum). The problem was that as loyalism fractured between progressive elements that sought to make the peace work, and other factions that degenerated into criminal gangs, paramilitaries were not hastening towards the exit. Meanwhile, as noted at the end of the previous chapter, the political representatives of the vast majority of working-class loyalists, in the form of the DUP, agreed to enter government with the arch-enemy Sinn Féin. Like their republican counterparts, loyalist muralists passed up the opportunity to mark this momentous development on the walls.

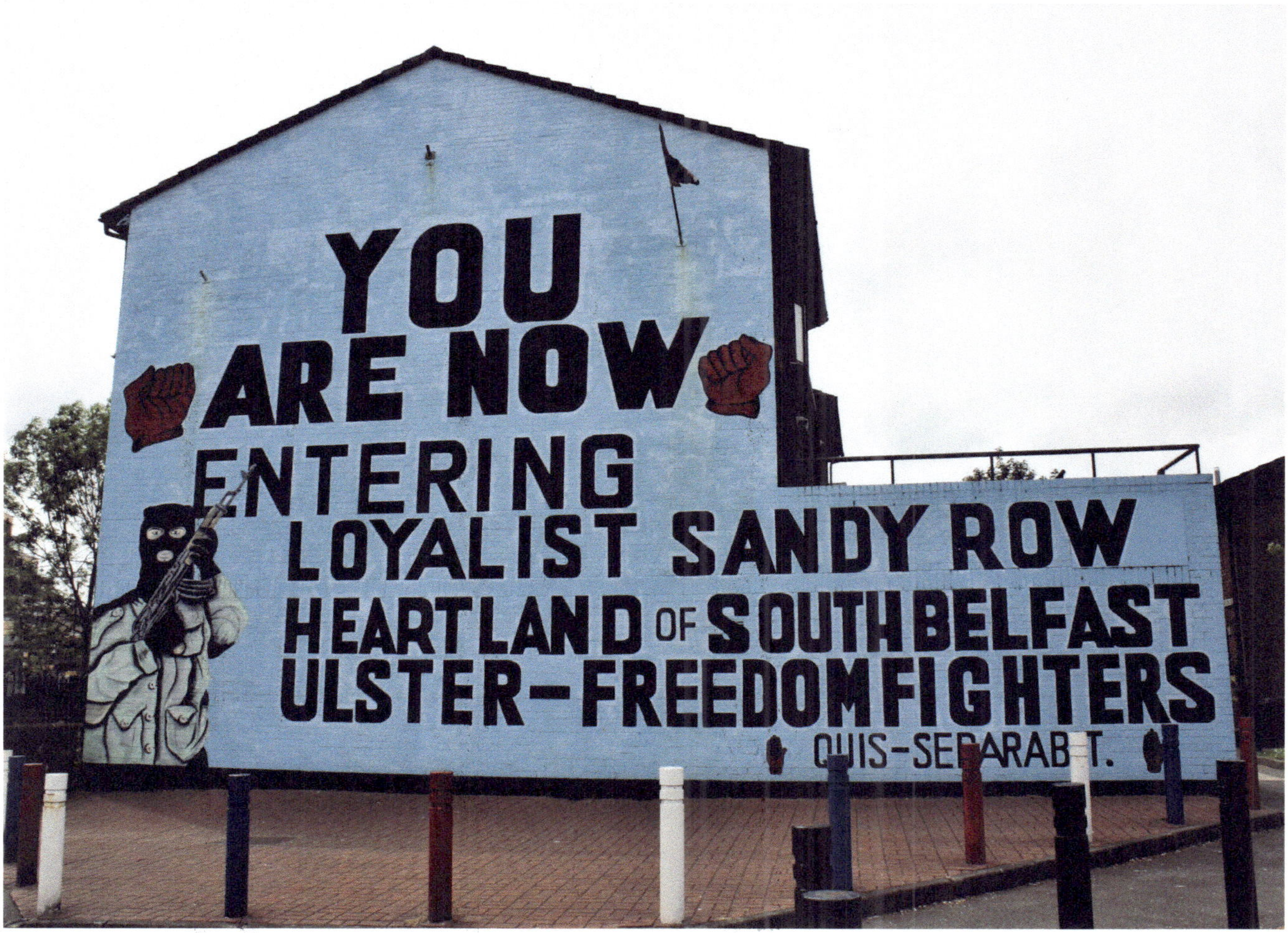

FIGURE 111 You are now entering loyalist Sandy Row, Linfield Road/Sandy Row, South Belfast, 2003. Photo by Tony Crowley.

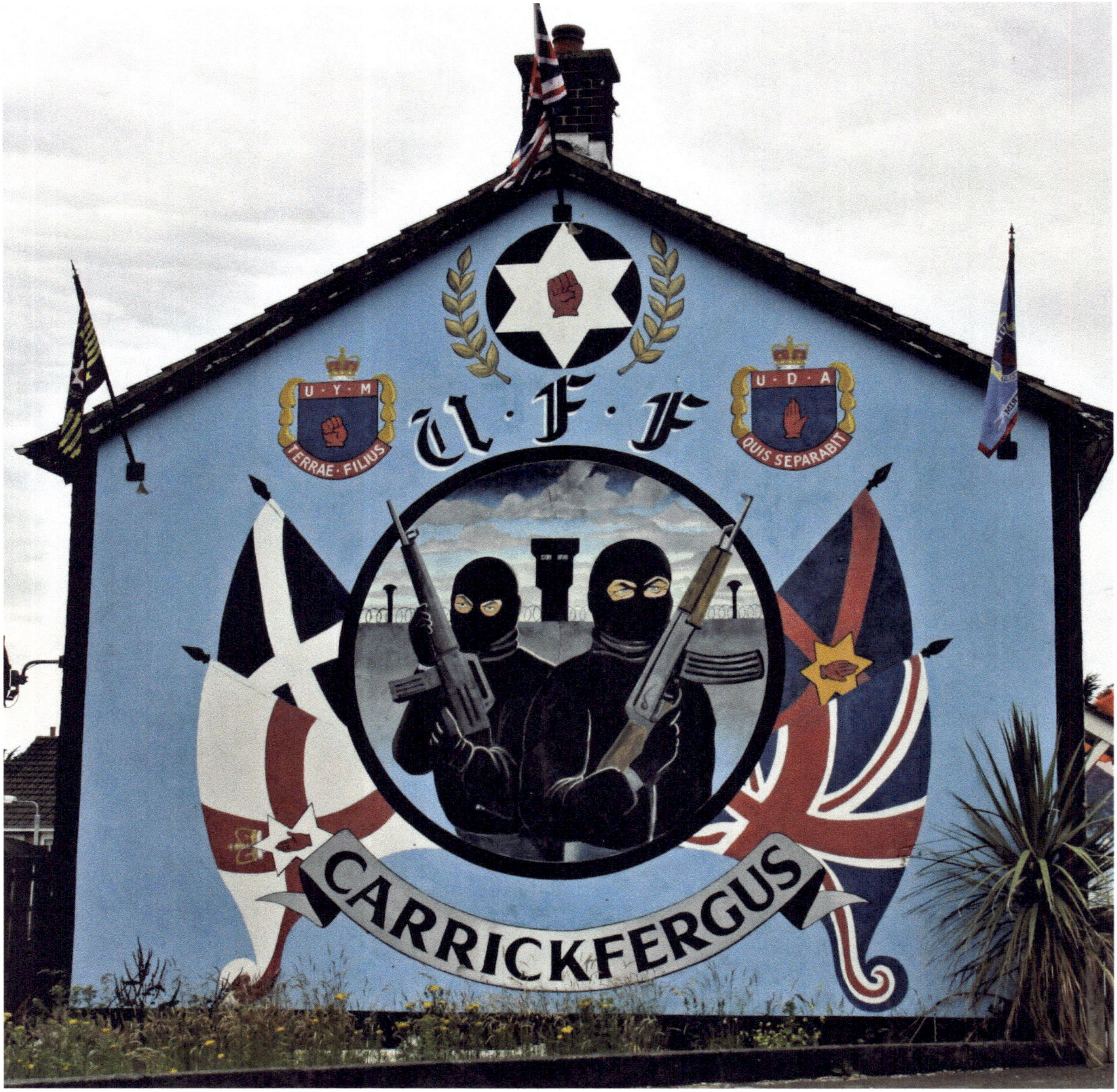

FIGURE 112 UFF Carrickfergus, Castlemara Drive, Carrickfergus, 2002. Photo by Tony Crowley.

CHAPTER 6

Managing History: Politics, Legacy, and Dissidence: Republican Murals 2007–2024

To access all images referenced in this chapter, please visit the open access version on Fulcrum at https://doi.org/10.3998/mpub.14527058.

> Understand the past— and build a better future le cheile. (Republican mural, Mountpottinger Road, Short Strand, 2010, Figure 1, see Fulcrum)

1. ALL CHANGE

In January 2007 the mainstream republican movement voted to accept the new policing arrangements in Northern Ireland, which meant that the principal unionist condition had been met for the establishment of a power-sharing executive. Following the March 2007 Northern Ireland Assembly election (in which the DUP and Sinn Féin were the largest parties, with thirty-six and twenty-eight seats respectively), an agreement was made to constitute an executive headed by First Minister Ian Paisley and Deputy First Minister Martin McGuinness (despite the titles, their roles had equal standing). Gerry Adams hailed the development by asserting that "the restoration of the political institutions, on 8 May, marks the beginning of a new era of politics on this island" (Rowan 2021: 220). To some sanguine commentators, this heralded at least the potential for "stable government," an opportunity for the "normal" politics of haggling over budgets, policies, and position. But in fact it was simply a prelude to a prolonged period of what the senior Belfast republican Jake Mac Siacais has called "an imperfect peace," characterized by a static imperative to preserve the "Peace Process" above all else:

> Keeping the process on the road at all costs and avoiding the recurring bouts of crisis at the heart of the process was the inevitable outcome of the very flaws inherent in a process which saw both governments and all the parties failing to comprehensively address the root causes of conflict.[1]

Consequently,

> What we have been bequeathed is a balkanised society. Its underlying dynamic is self-reinforcing and ensures that both the unionist and republican leaderships must constantly reassure their respective bases that they will remain vigilant in ensuring that the other will not be allowed to prevail. We live in a present haunted by an unresolved past. (Rowan 2021: 29)

Rather than "normal" politics, the devolved government in Northern Ireland has lurched from crisis to crisis and the "balkanisation" of Northern Ireland has led effectively to "power-division" rather than "power-sharing," with each bloc looking after the interests, or at least the perceived interests, of its base rather than society as a whole. The "perpetual crisis"[2] that affected the body politic took various forms, which included, among others, a disagreement about the future of the old Maze prison, the Flags Dispute, legacy issues, welfare reform, provisions for the Irish Language, the Renewable Heat Incentive scandal, Brexit, and the Northern Ireland Protocol. Such was the level of discord that two major initiatives were required to sustain the Assembly: the *Stormont House Agreement* in 2014 (which became in effect the *Fresh Start* plan in 2015) and the *New Decade, New Approach* agreement in 2020.[3] The Assembly functioned fitfully from 2007 to 2017, but as a result of a breakdown in relations between the DUP and Sinn Féin, it was suspended between 2017 and 2020. The *New Decade, New Approach* deal lasted from January 2020 to February 2022, at which point the Assembly ceased functioning again because of the withdrawal of the DUP on the basis of its objections to the Northern Ireland Protocol. As of February 2024, the Assembly has been restored, though it was immediately plunged into crisis as a result of criminal charges brought against the leader of the DUP.[4]

One of the difficult issues for all sides in Northern Ireland has been the legacy of the past. For if *The Belfast Agreement* brought an end to major violence (with the horrific exception of the Omagh bombing), the nature of the war, and the way in which it was conducted over a thirty-year period, meant that there were many issues that remained unresolved and many questions that were unanswered. It is a sign of the gravity of this issue that there have been three major sets of consultations, reports, and proposals on ways of "dealing with the past" (the ambiguity of the verb is telling—the *OED* defines "to deal with" as "to handle effectively, to take successful action in regard to" and "to administer, handle, dispose of"): the Eames/Bradley *Report of the Consultative Group on the Past* (2009), the Haas/O'Sullivan negotiations with the parties on "Contending with the Past" (2013), and *The Stormont House Agreement* (2014). In addition to which, the British government has unilaterally proposed legislation containing an effective amnesty—the *Northern Ireland Troubles (Legacy and Reconciliation) Bill* (2023)—an act that has achieved the rare success of uniting all sides in Northern Ireland. There is unanimous rejection, both by the political parties and civic society in general, of a law that appears to be incompatible with the obligations of international human rights law (to which the British government is a signatory) and, therefore, *The Belfast Agreement*.[5]

For republicans, legacy issues primarily related to the role of the British State either directly, through the actions of Crown Force personnel, or indirectly through collusion with loyalist paramilitarism. In both cases, the past bore down on the present because it demonstrated that the British State was not, nor could it ever be, a neutral player in Northern Ireland. But the past—specifically "the unresolved past"—was also a difficulty for mainstream republicans in another sense. For once Sinn Féin, as the chief representative of this strain of republicanism, adopted the route of constitutional nationalism within the constraints of the political system, it meant that its own political past could be used against it by its opponents within and without the republican tradition. Thus although the danger of violence by "dissident" republican groups reached its apogee in the late 1990s, dissenting organizations appeared from the late 2000s on, and part of their justification was precisely the failure of mainstream republicanism to achieve what they had set as their goal—a United Ireland (this was a particular point of contention in the celebrations around the centenary of the Easter Rising). In short, whether it was the bitterly unresolved issues relating to the war, or the ongoing but as yet unfulfilled task of unification, the past, which is not quite ever the past in Northern Ireland, continued to shape and influence the present.[6]

Mainstream republicanism became mired in the difficulties of power-sharing/division at Stormont, not least in attempting to manage the resentment of its own base—an anger that broke in 2017 and led to the withdrawal from Stormont. It was also engaged in dealing with the past in various ways, both in relation to the activities of the British State and its allies, but also in terms of recognizing and commemorating the role of the IRA and its volunteers (a good number of whom died between 2007 and 2022, including a number of senior figures—Brian Keenan, Martin McGuinness, and Bobby Storey among them).[7] And it was subject to political criticism from other republicans for its ongoing involvement in the "internal settlement" embodied in Stormont. And yet, one fact frames the period 2007–2022: the undoubted electoral and political success of Sinn Féin both in Northern Ireland and in the Republic of Ireland. In the 2020 General Election in the Republic, the party took the greatest number of first preference votes and emerged as the largest party in Dáil Éireann (they were excluded from government by a coalition of other parties). In the 2022 Northern Ireland Assembly election, Sinn Féin took the highest share of first preference votes (29%) and, with 27 out of 90 seats, became the largest party (they were excluded from taking the First Ministerial post by the DUP's withdrawal from Stormont over the Northern Ireland Protocol, though as of February 2024, Michelle O'Neill was appointed to the position). Led by two non-war generation women, the party was in a position that was unimaginable in 2007. Its confidence, bolstered by the changing demographics of Northern Ireland, led it to push hard for a poll on Irish unification. Whether such a poll is achievable is open to question; whether such a poll would be winnable, remains to be seen.

If the political fate of mainstream republicanism has been transformed during the "imperfect peace" of the past fifteen years, what of republican murals? The answer is that they reflected the complexity of the wide republican movement and its variable responses to the crisis-ridden politics of the period. Ranging from support for Sinn Féin (Figure 2) to calls for a return to armed struggle (Figure 3), from commemoration (Figure 4, see Fulcrum) to appeals to complete an unfinished history (Figure 5, see Fulcrum), from a coauthored representation of Guernica (by two leading artists—republican Danny Devenny and loyalist Mark Ervine) (Figure 6, see Fulcrum) to children's cartoons (Figure 7, see Fulcrum), republican muralists continued with some well-worn themes, but also began to explore different issues. In short, the murals recorded and embodied change.

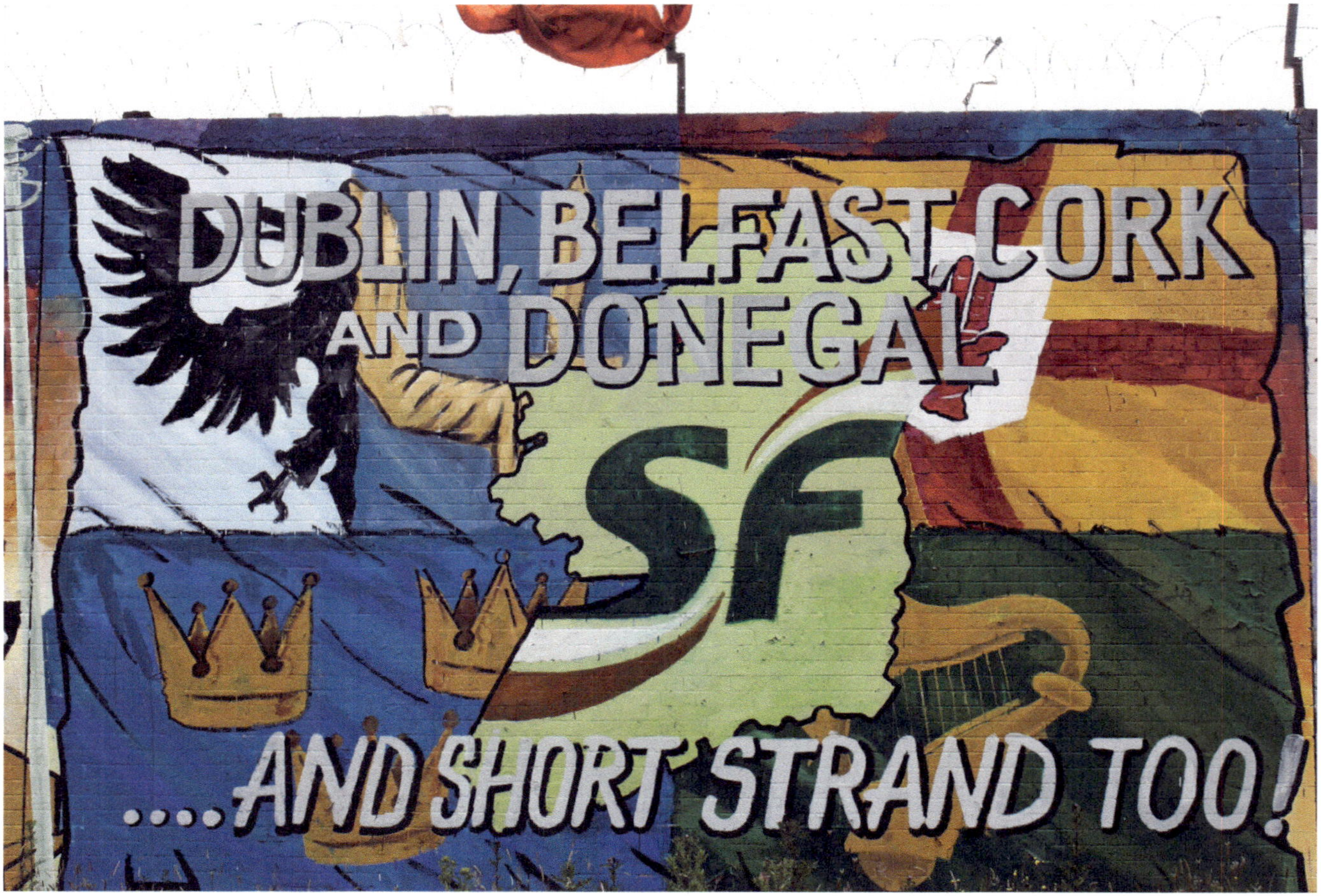

FIGURE 2 And Short Strand too! Mountpotinger Road, Short Strand, East Belfast, 2012. Photo by Tony Crowley.

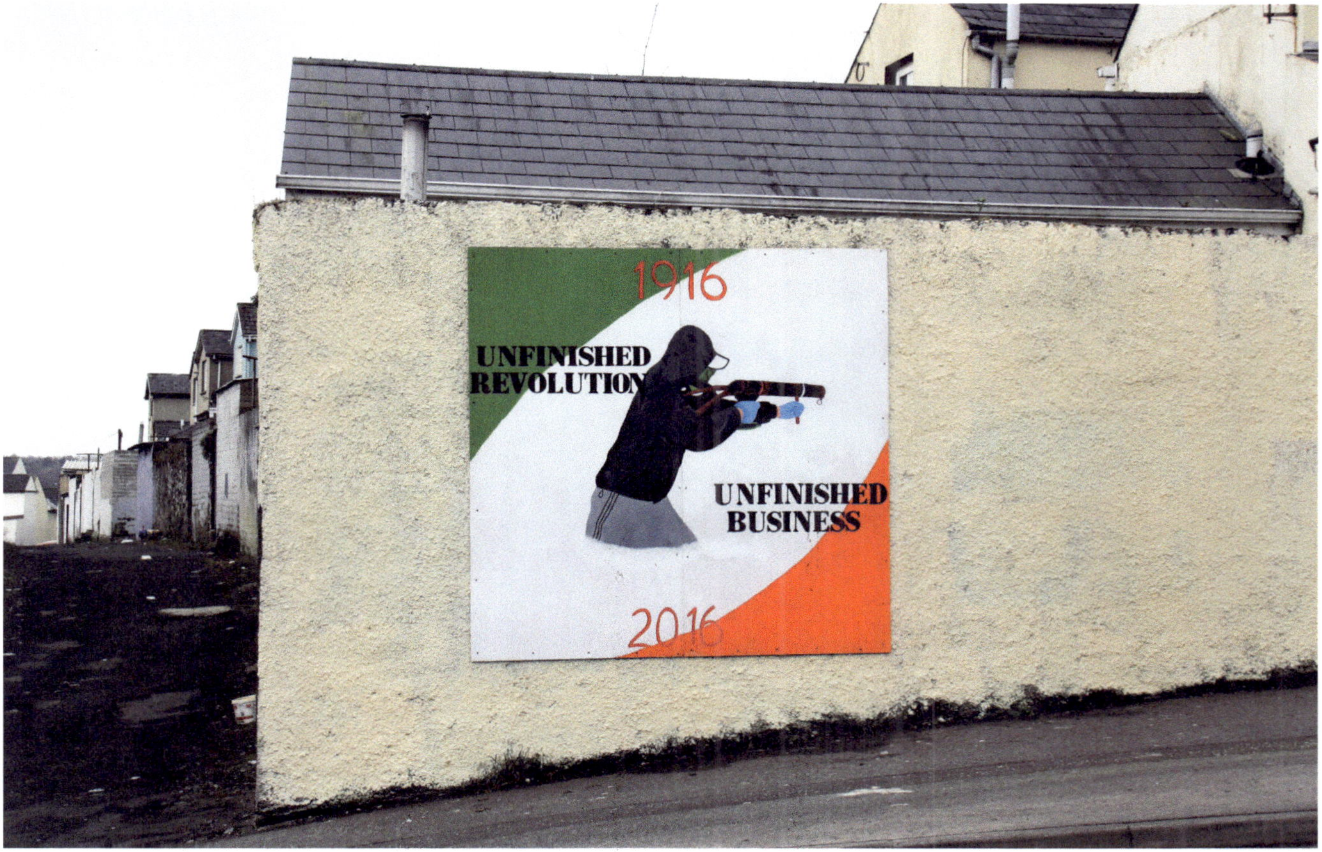

FIGURE 3 Unfinished revolution, Westland Street, Bogside, Derry, 2016. Photo by Tony Crowley.

2. FIGURING THE PAST

One of the dominant themes in republican murals of 2007–2024 has been the issue of the activities of the British State during the war, specifically those instances in which the police and/or the British Army were involved in the unjustified use of violence. Bloody Sunday, evidently, was the most egregious example, and the publication of the Saville Inquiry in 2010, which found the fourteen victims innocent of any wrongdoing, prompted an apology from the British Prime Minister. But the events in Derry had been foreshadowed by the Ballymurphy Massacre—a series of shootings by the same battalion of the Parachute Regiment that was involved in Bloody

Sunday: between August 9 and 11 1971, during the start of Internment, the paratroopers killed eleven civilians (including a woman and a priest who had gone to help one of the victims). As with Bloody Sunday, the Ballymurphy Massacre led to a sustained campaign, publicized on the walls, for independent investigation; the link between the events was signaled by the image of the priest waving a white handkerchief (Figure 8)—a reference to the iconic photograph of Fr. Edward Daly in the same position on Bloody Sunday (itself the subject of a Derry mural on the 50th anniversary) (Figure 9, see Fulcrum). Subject to obstruction (one mural represented Theresa Villers, the Northern Ireland Secretary, who denied demands for further investigation) (Figure 10, see Fulcrum), the Ballymurphy Massacre campaign demanded truth and justice (Figure 11). After new inquests were held, the coroner finally

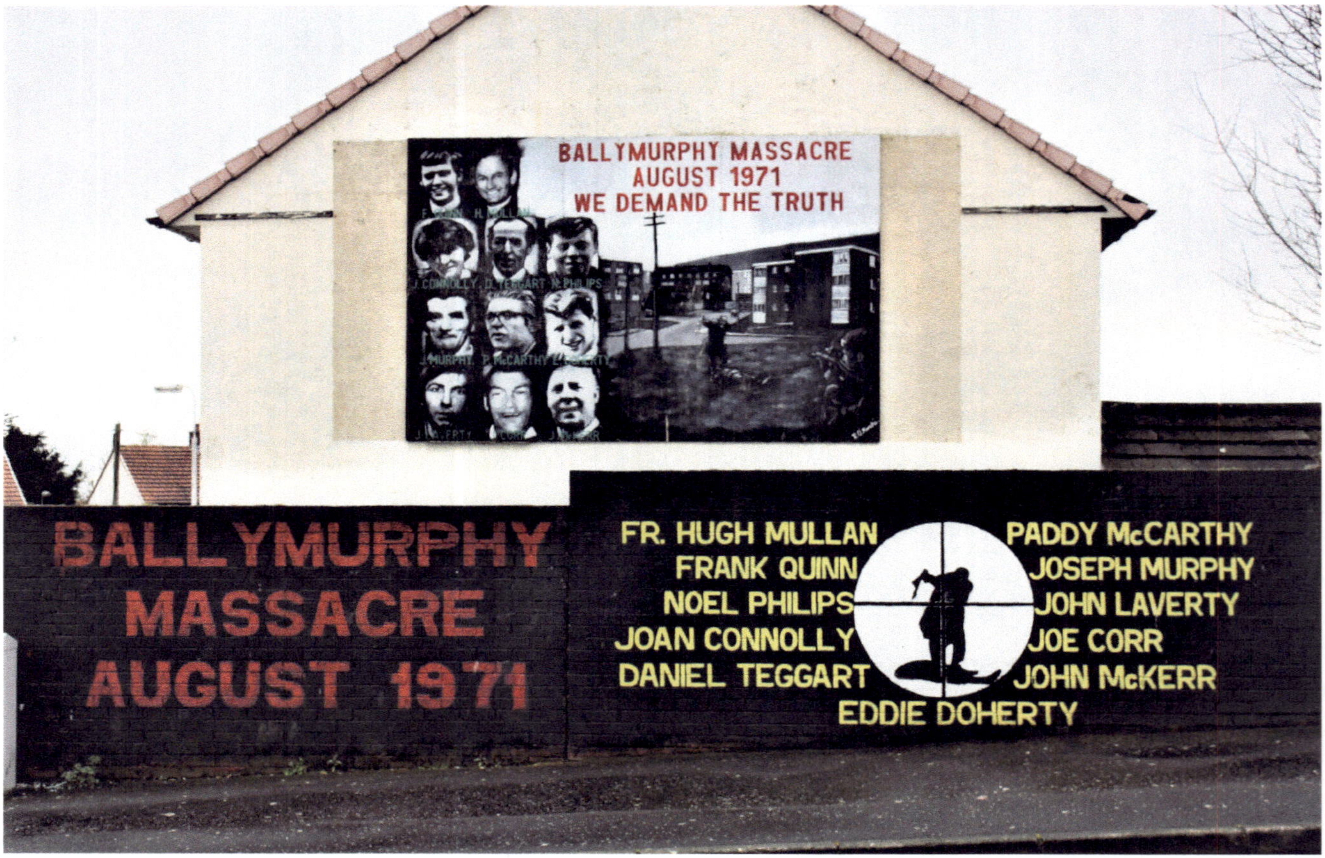

FIGURE 8 Ballymurphy Massacre, Divismore Way, Ballymurphy, West Belfast, 2009. Photo by Tony Crowley.

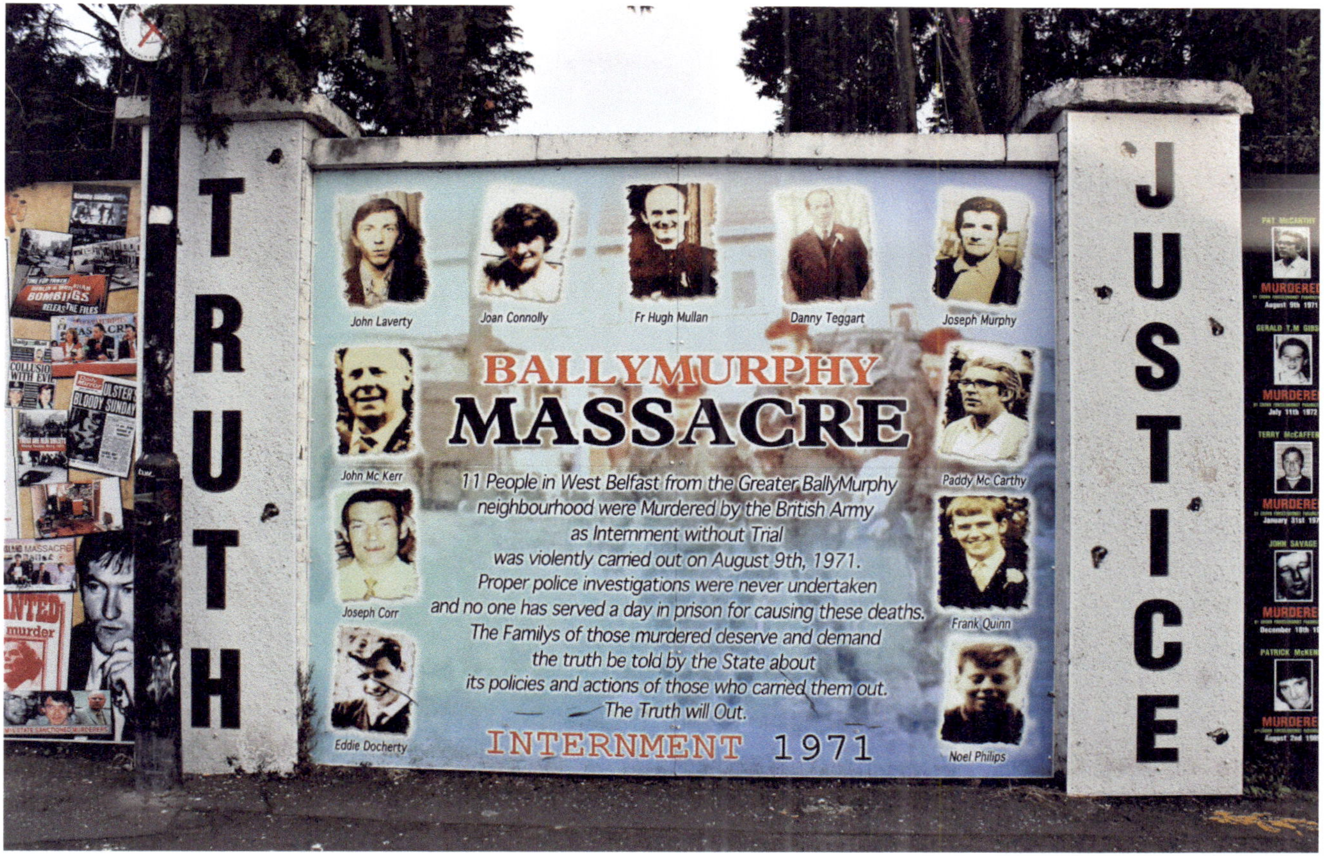

FIGURE 11 Truth, justice, Beechmount Avenue, Falls, West Belfast, 2010. Photo by Tony Crowley.

declared in 2021 that the victims were innocent and thus that the use of lethal force had been unjustified; oddly the British Prime Minister gave a private apology to the First and Deputy First Ministers (rather than to the families). In these instances, it took thirty-eight years and fifty years respectively for the British State to acknowledge and apologize for the most grievous abuse of its powers.

There were a number of republican campaigns that demanded the investigations of specific historical events, and again the murals played an important role in drawing attention to the issues. These included: the McGurk's Bar Massacre (on December 4 1971, the UVF bombed The Tramore Bar—known as McGurk's—and killed fifteen civilians; despite contemporary police and army reports of an IRA "own goal," a UVF bomber was convicted in 1976) (Figure 12, see Fulcrum); the Springhill Massacre (on July 9 1972, British Army snipers killed five civilians in the Springhill area of West Belfast, including a thirteen-year-old girl, two teenage boys, and another Catholic priest) (Figure 13, see Fulcrum); and the New Lodge Six Massacre (on the night of the February 3/4 1973, the British Army and loyalist gunmen killed three IRA volunteers and three civilians in the New Lodge area) (Figure 14, see Fulcrum). Other appeals included calls for the banning of plastic bullets (Figure 15, see Fulcrum) and for inquiries into the use of CR gas on republican prisoners during the burning of Long Kesh (Figure 16, see Fulcrum) and the killing of unarmed IRA volunteer Pearse Jordan (Figure 17, see Fulcrum). The most prominent and notable campaign, however, related to the killing of the lawyer Pat Finucane (Figure 18, see Fulcrum). Finucane was assassinated by the UFF, but it later became clear that there had been collusion between the loyalist paramilitaries and State Forces in the killing (the British Prime Minister acknowledged the fact of illegal collaboration and issued another apology, while refusing ongoing demands for a public inquiry). The case was significant because it acted as the focus for republican claims of extensive collusion between the British State (through British Army intelligence and police Special Branch) and loyalists. These claims formed the centerpoint of what became known as the "Collusion Wall" in Beechmount, West Belfast; it featured a summary history of the issue (Figure 19, see Fulcrum), extracts from various State-commissioned reports, and portraits of victims "Murdered by Crown Forces/Unionist Paramilitaries" (Figure 20, see Fulcrum). A mural on the International Wall proclaimed that "Collusion was not only not an illusion—It was the whole Goddamn institution."

In 2018 a mural appeared on the site of the old Andersonstown police station (now effectively a small dog-walking park and mural site); it announced that it was "Time for truth" and demanded "Fírinne anois Ceartas anois" (Truth now Justice now) (Figure 21, see Fulcrum). And yet notwithstanding the moral force of appeals for truth, there was a problem with the republican stance which others were not slow to point out—which is that republican appeals for the truth were uni-directional: the State and its allies were to unveil their secrets, while republicans, apparently, were to remain silent. Evidently the republican attitude could be justified in various ways: it focused properly on the incrimination of the State as an active participant in the "dirty war"; it channeled the pain and hurt of those who had been the victims of State and State-sponsored violence; it garnered support for the leading party of republicanism—Sinn Féin; and it protected those republicans who had committed acts for which they could still be prosecuted under existing legislation. And yet the simple demand that all other parties speak, while republicans, specifically members of the IRA, stay silent, was (and remains) problematic. At the very least, it adds to "the complex puzzle of conflict within which truth is often lost or buried" (Rowan 2015: 147), while courting the danger of claiming privileged rights for republicans.[8] In fact the mainstream republican movement was not entirely silent on past culpability. In 2002, on the 30th anniversary of Bloody Friday, the IRA expressed "sincere apologies and condolences" to non-combatants and their families, and in relation to those combatants who had died, it articulated a desire to "acknowledge the grief and pain of their relatives" (https://cain.ulster.ac.uk/events/peace/docs/ira160702.htm). In 2005 and 2007 respectively the IRA apologized for the inadvertent killings of fourteen-year-old Kathleen Feeney in the Brandywell, Derry, in 1973, and seventeen-month-old Angela Gallagher in Beechmount, Belfast, in 1971.[9] And the IRA also expressed regret for its role in hiding the bodies of "The Disappeared" (alleged informers whose corpses were secreted for decades), and attempted to recover the remains. Remorse did not extend to the killings of the informers in the first instance, however, nor did it extend to the brutal beating to death of Paul Quinn, allegedly at the hands of South Armagh republicans in 2007 (Figure 22, see Fulcrum). It wasn't that "sorry" was the hardest word for mainstream republicanism, but it was certainly complicated in terms of its implications and consequences.

There were no such complications in relation to the republican dead and, as traced in chapters two and four, they continued to be extensively commemorated and venerated on the walls and in formal memorial gardens. Referring to the Hunger Strikers, the widow of an RUC Inspector killed by the IRA claimed that "after they die, they will be forgotten, just as those policemen and soldiers who died are forgotten after a while, except by those who loved them" (Beresford 1987: 423). But that proved to be a considerable underestimation of the republican imperative to remember. The Hunger Strikers were commemorated collectively with new murals appearing around the anniversaries of their deaths (Figure 23) (Figure 24, see Fulcrum). And their status as touchstones of republican tradition was captured by an image on the International Wall that placed them centrally among imprisoned figures ranging from the United Irishmen (Wolfe Tone) through the Fenians (O'Donovan Rossa), 1916 (Connolly, Pearse, Markievicz), earlier Hunger Strikers (MacSwiney, Ashe, McCaughey, Stagg), and their contemporaries (Drumm, Farrell) (Figure 25, see Fulcrum). Other murals placed the ten dead men of 1981 specifically in the context of the twelve republicans who preceded them in Irish and British jails in the twentieth century (Figure 26, see Fulcrum), and, on the 40th anniversary, highlighted their rejection of the criminal status that the British State had imposed on them ("Ní coirpigh sinne! Éireannaigh sinne!"—We are not criminals We are Irishmen) (Figure 27, see Fulcrum). Yet as well as appearing as members of a tradition and a modern political movement, they were also represented as individuals with life histories (Kevin Lynch as a young All-Ireland hurler, for example) (Figure 28, see Fulcrum) or with something to say to the future ("After we are gone...") (Figure 29, see Fulcrum).

"Timeless memorials" is the name of a monumental mason's shop on the Falls Road, opposite Milltown cemetery (Figure 30, see Fulcrum), yet in terms of form and function, memorials were not timeless but historically specific and adapted to the location in which they were placed. For example, the construction of republican memorial gardens continued apace after 2007. In South Armagh, a large memorial to the South Armagh Brigade of the IRA was built at Tí Chulainn, Mullaghbawn, with Slieve Gullion as its beautiful backdrop (Figure 31). While in West Belfast, on Beechmount Avenue, a structure remembered a host of the dead of the "Lár na bhFál/Mid Falls" through a series of plaques and artworks: local men and women, POWs, members of Sinn Féin, Hunger Strikers, IRA volunteers, "innocent people from the area," and "the unsung heroes" (Figure 32, see Fulcrum). Similar sentiments, though from a very different ideological stance, were displayed in the nearby "Joe McElvey memorial garden" at the Workers' Party social club on the Grosvenor Road in West Belfast (Figure 33, see Fulcrum). While in Ardoyne, North Belfast,

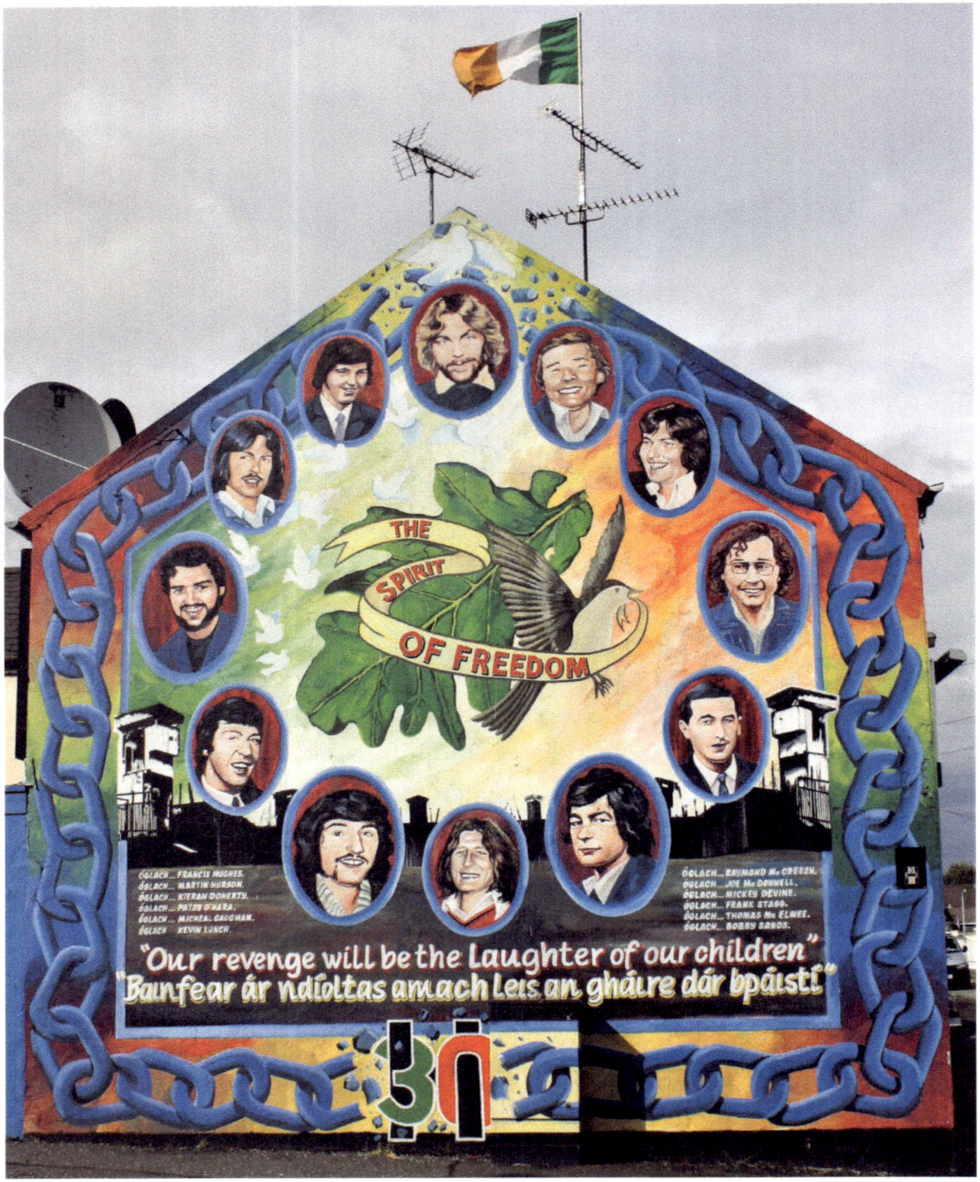

FIGURE 23 Spirit of freedom, Westland Street, Bogside, Derry, 2011. Photo by Tony Crowley.

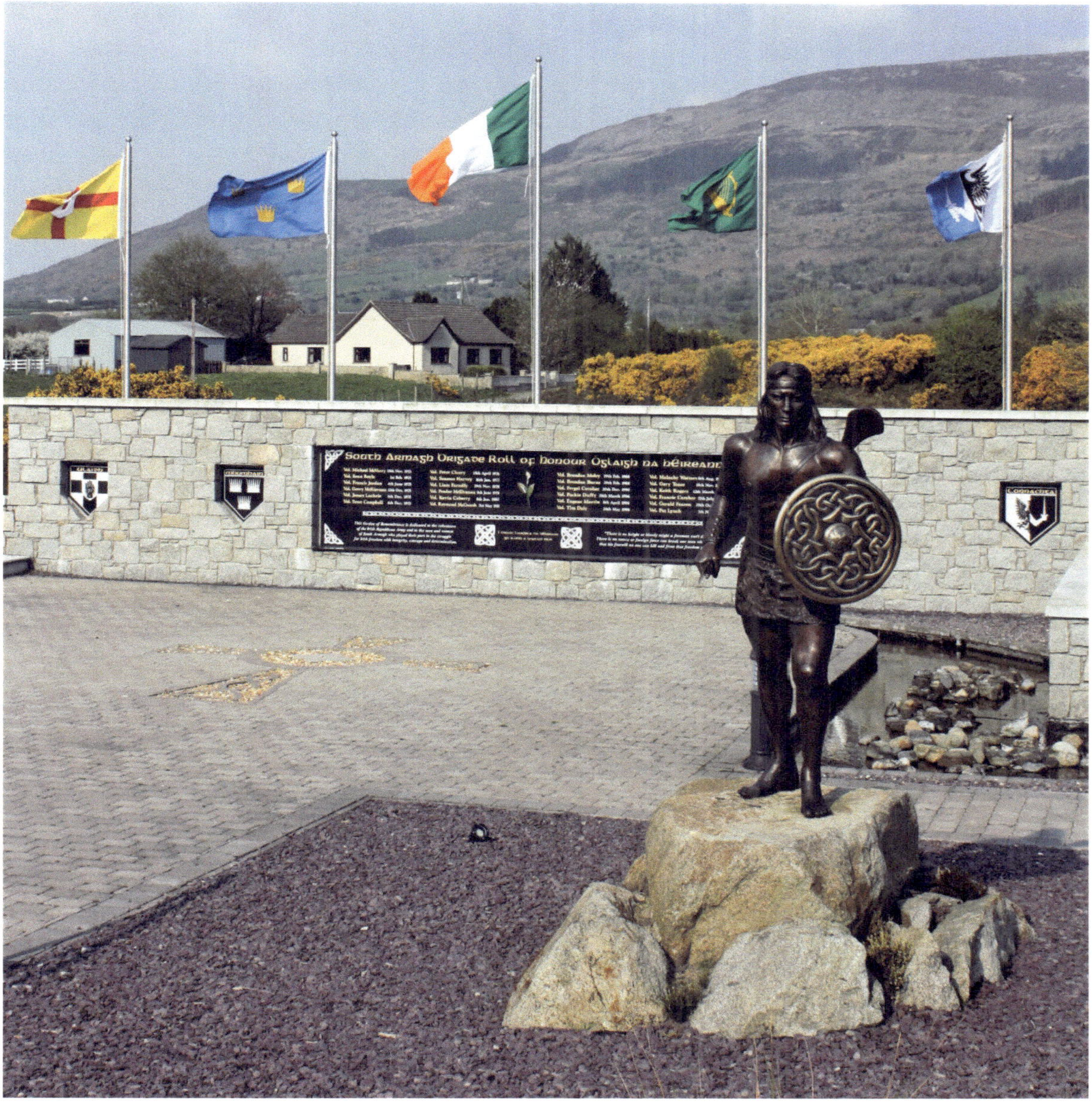

FIGURE 31 South Armagh Brigade, Mullaghbawn, South Armagh, 2010. Photo by Tony Crowley.

ten plaques on Herbert Street remembered local IRA volunteers and residents of the area, including the "1st victim of the present Troubles Sammy McLarnon RIP brutally murdered in his own home at 37 Herbert Street by the RUC on 15th Aug 1969" (Figure 34, see Fulcrum). This abundance of memory was exceeded, however, by the astonishing conversion of Ardilea Close into a shrine consisting of murals, photomontages, and artworks "in loving memory of all our dead"—ranging from the Hunger Strikers to "our friends and families" (Figure 35) (Figure 36, see Fulcrum)

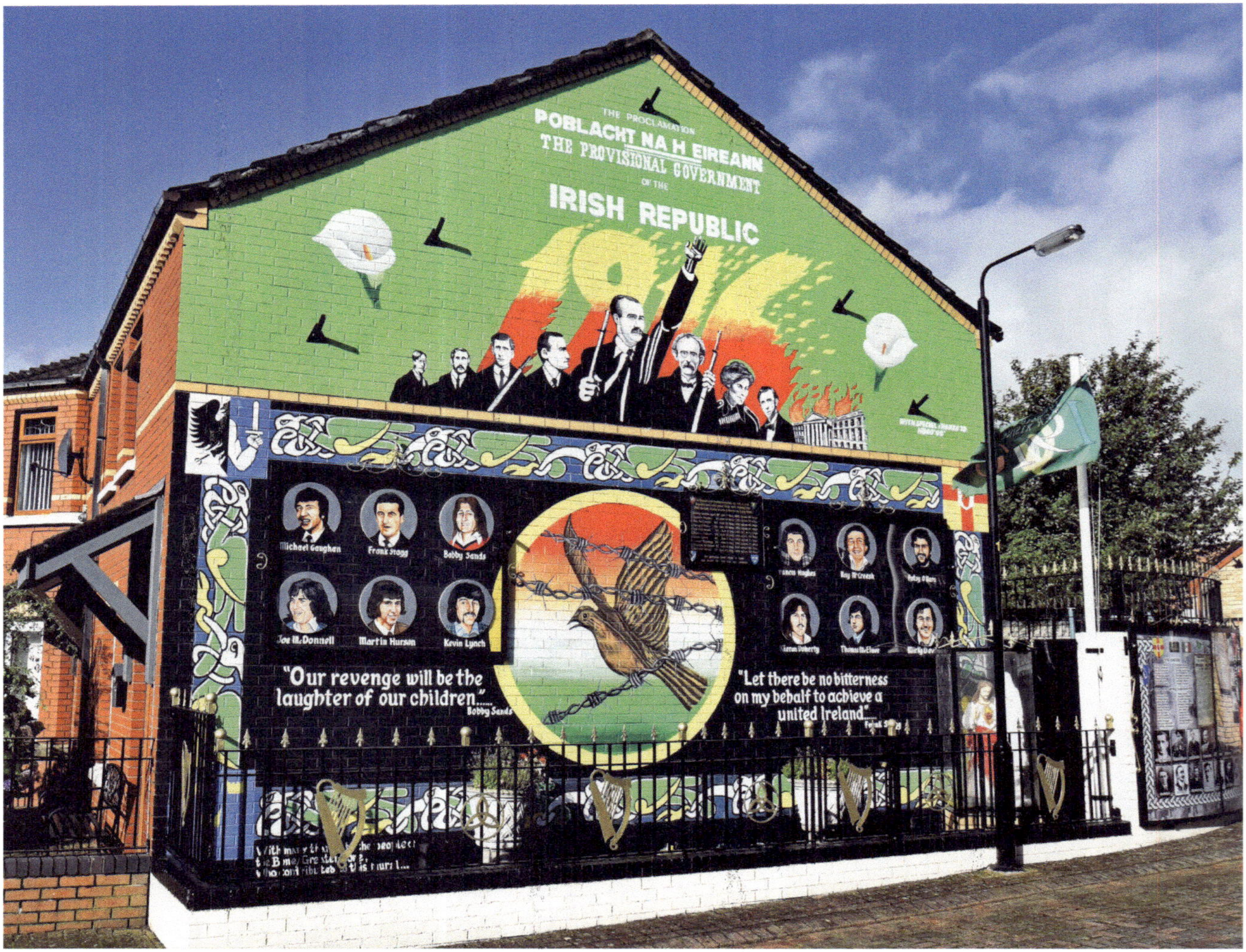

FIGURE 35 Let there be no bitterness, Ardilea Close, Ardoyne, North Belfast, 2018. Photo by Tony Crowley.

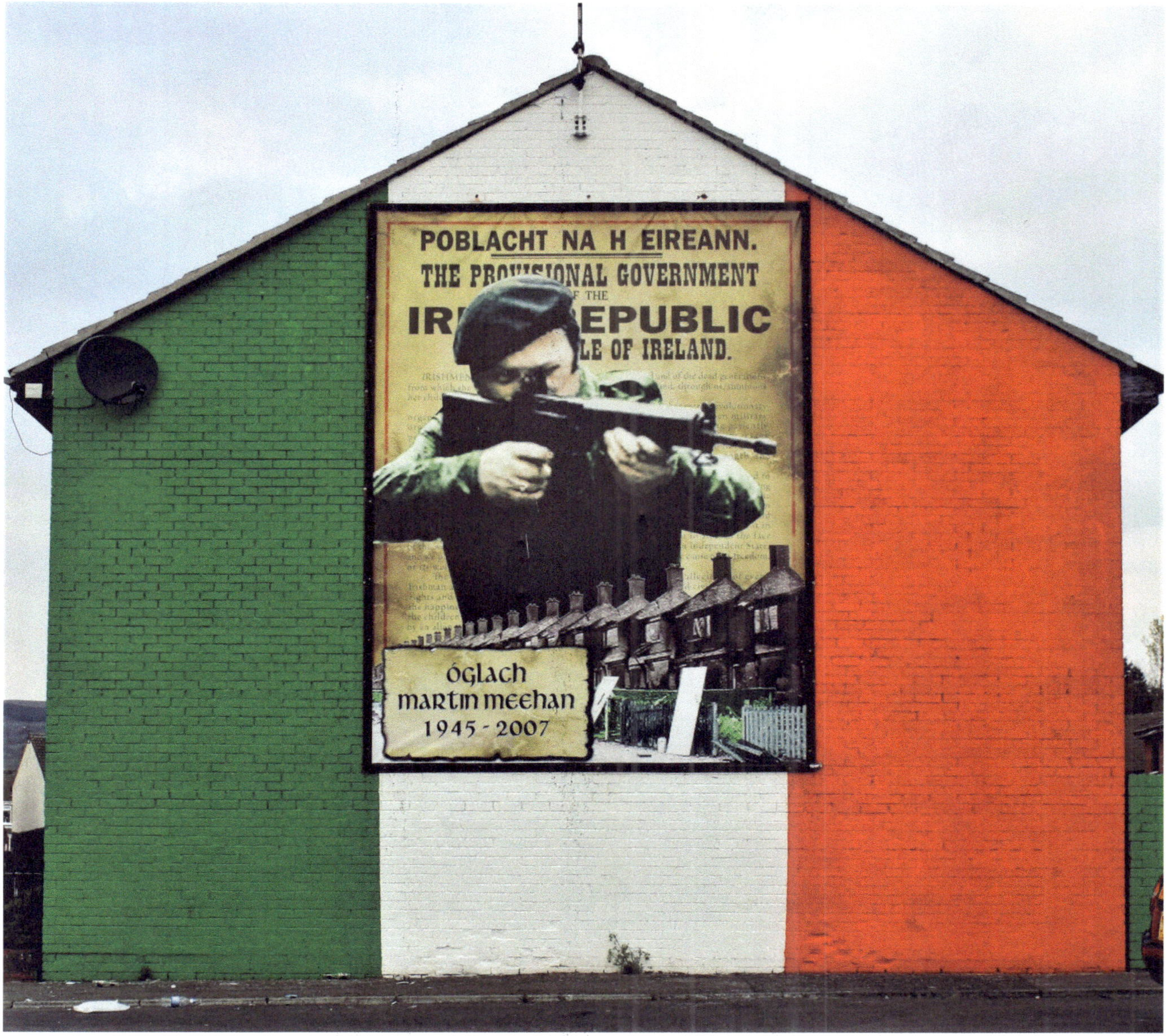

FIGURE 39 Óglach Martin Meehan, Ardoyne Avenue, Ardoyne, North Belfast, 2014. Photo by Tony Crowley.

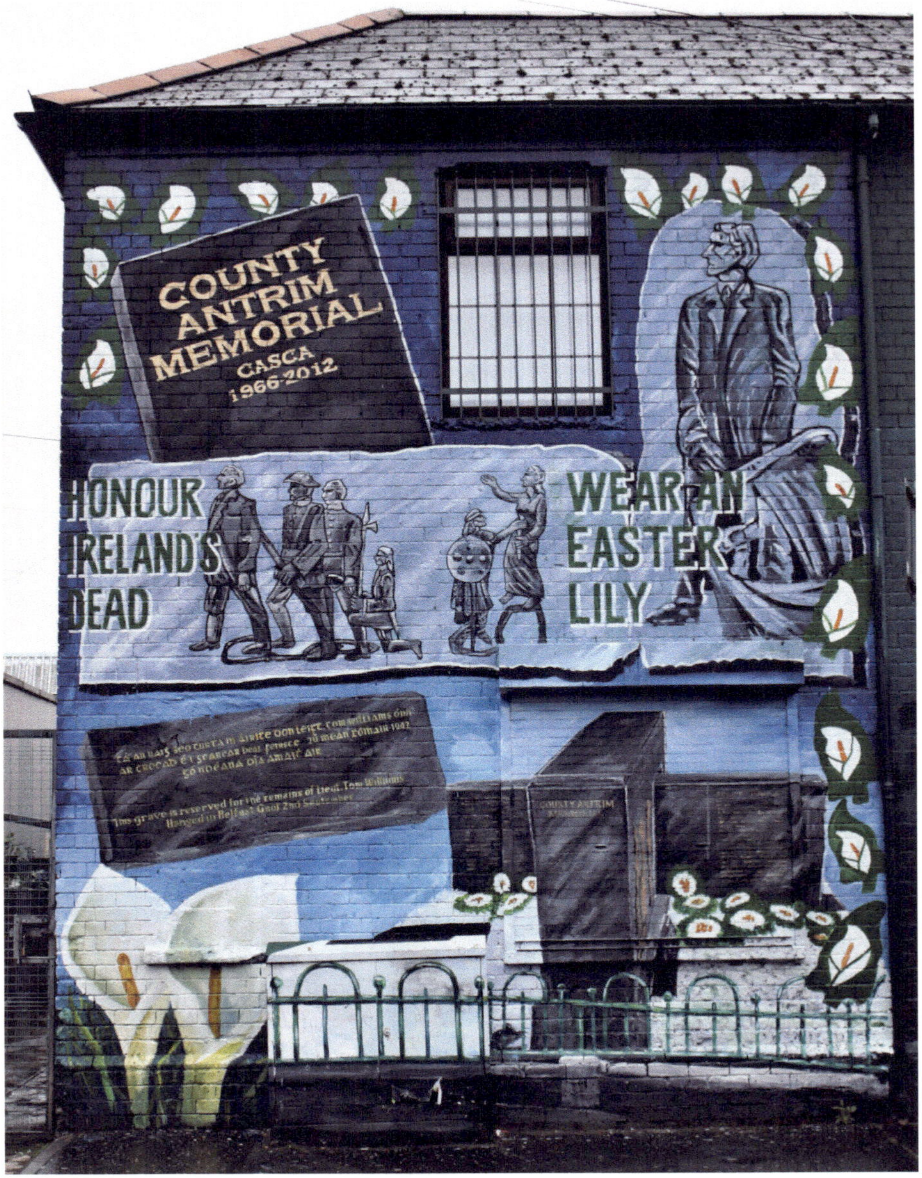

FIGURE 45 Honour Ireland's dead, Beechmount Avenue, Beechmount, West Belfast, 2012. Photo by Tony Crowley.

(Figure 37, see Fulcrum) (Figure 38, see Fulcrum). What is particularly notable about the displays of remembering in Herbert Street, Ardilea Close, and indeed a good many other locations, is that they are not situated on tourist routes, or even public through-roads (in fact both Herbert Street and Ardilea Close are cul-de-sacs): memory here is visual, communal, and profoundly local. What is also striking about republican remembrance is its ubiquity. From Belfast (Figure 39) to Tyrone (Figure 40, see Fulcrum), from Derry (Figure 41, see Fulcrum) to Armagh (Figure 42, see Fulcrum), republicanism remembered its men, women (Figure 43, see Fulcrum), and children (Figure 44, see Fulcrum). Across all tendencies of republicanism (of which there were a number, since it was never a unitary movement), the obligation was clear: "Honour Ireland's dead" (Figure 45).

3. 2016 AND ALL THAT HISTORY

Republicanism has a keen awareness of its own history and indeed a deep sense of the requirement to acknowledge its indebtedness to the past (as reflected in the establishment of the Eileen Hickey Iarsmalann na Staire Poblachtach Éireannach/Irish Republican History Museum in Conway Mill in 2007) (Figure 46, see Fulcrum).[10] The period 2007–2022 was particularly significant in this respect because it encompassed "the decade of centenaries," which is usually taken to begin with the centenary of the *Ulster Covenant* (1912) and end with the creation of the Irish Free State and Northern Ireland through Partition (1921/1922). It hardly needs stating that both sides celebrated their own anniversaries in their own ways, including, of course, on the walls. For republicans, the commemorations actually began with the centenary of the foundation of Na Fianna Éireann, a nationalist youth organization formed by Countess Markievicz in 1909 (Figure 47, see Fulcrum). But there were other significant debts that had to be recorded. The influence of James Connolly, for example, was highlighted by a number of murals, including one that advertised the James Connolly Visitor Centre on the Falls Road (opened in 2019) (Figure 48), and another that featured his activist daughter Nora Connolly (Figure 49, see Fulcrum). The foundation of Cumann na mBan in 2014 was also recorded (Figure 50) (Figure 51, see Fulcrum), with an emphasis on the involvement of women volunteers in both 1916 and the recent Troubles. Strikingly, these murals formed part of a series of images which portrayed the tradition of women's involvement in republicanism from the eighteenth century to the present. In these murals, which functioned as a corrective to an under-representation of women in previous work, women were figured as activists engaged explicitly in the dual strategy of violence and politics (Figure 52, see Fulcrum) (Figure 53, see Fulcrum) (Figure 54, see Fulcrum). One important mural in this re-writing of the republican story portrayed the frequently over-looked Hunger Strike in Armagh women's prison in 1980 (Figure 55, see Fulcrum).

There were other anniversaries or significant events that republican muralism focused on in the narrativization of their history. Individual figures were depicted, usually suffering the fate that republican activism frequently entailed in the twentieth century (imprisonment, death, or both): the execution of Roger Casement for

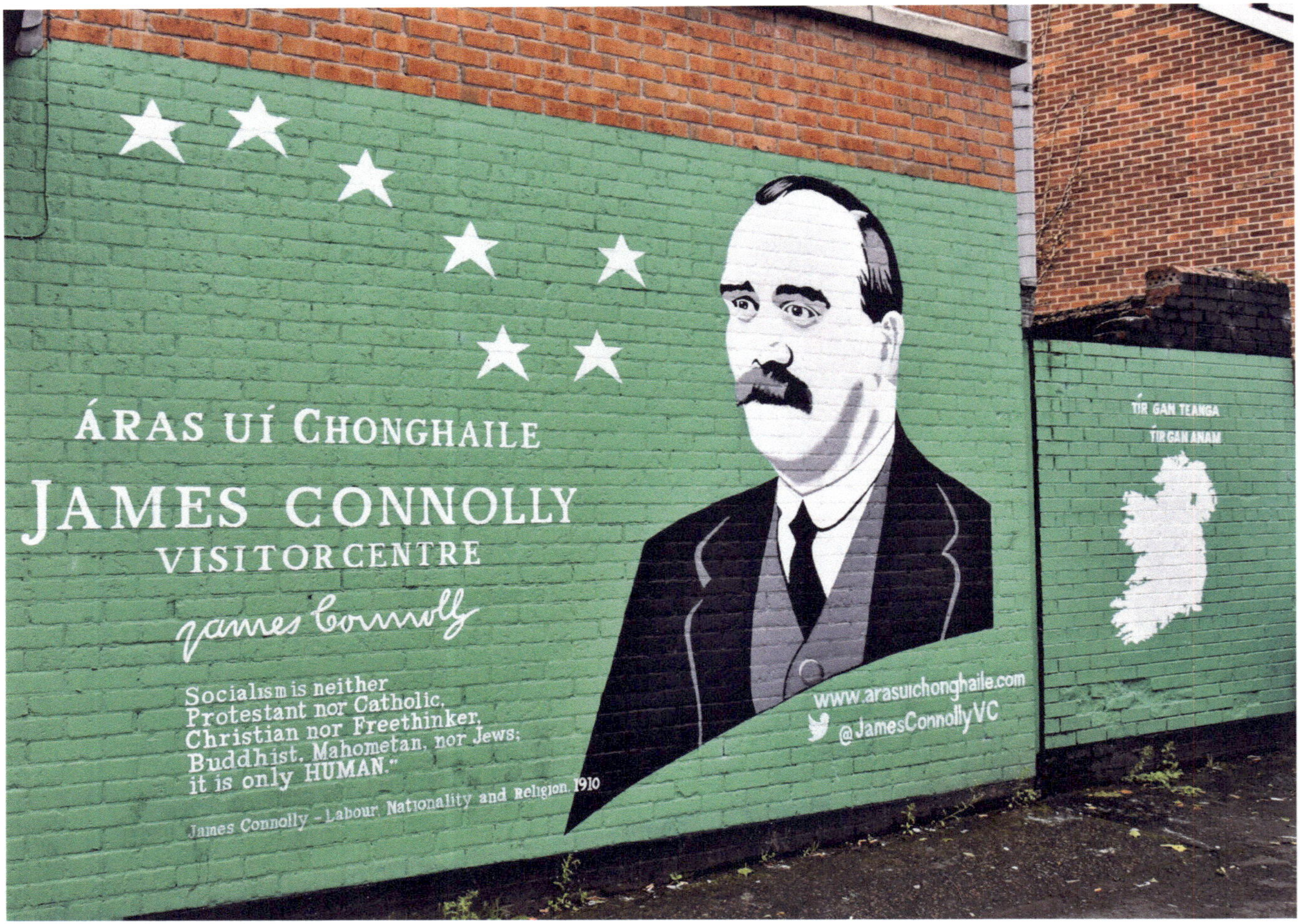

FIGURE 48 Áras uí Chonghaile, republican mural, Beechview Park, St James, West Belfast, 2020. Photo by Tony Crowley.

high treason in 1916 was the subject of one image (Figure 56, see Fulcrum), while Seán MacDiarmada, a signatory to the 1916 *Proclamation* executed by the British, featured in another (Figure 57, see Fulcrum). Other representations included Tomás Ághas (Thomas Ashe), the first twentieth-century Irish republican to die on Hunger Strike in 1917 (Figure 58, see Fulcrum), and Óglach Seán McCaughey, who died after an extended period of Blanket Protest, solitary confinement, and Hunger Strike, in Portlaoise prison in 1946 (Figure 59, see Fulcrum). A number of murals moved away from individuals and portrayed historical topics that had not often been represented in republican iconography. Examples were the formation of An Chéad Dáil (the First Dáil—the first government of

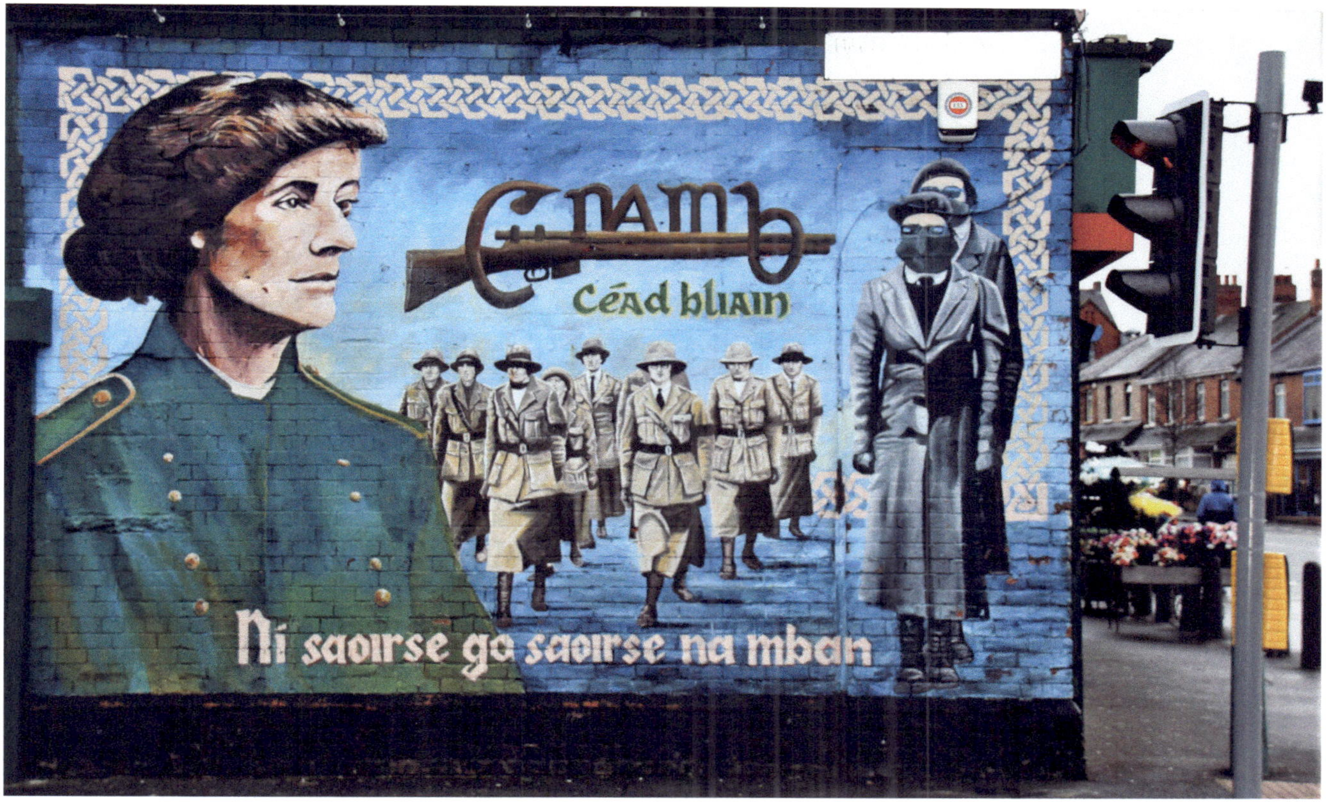

FIGURE 50 Cumann na mBan, Beechmount Avenue, Beechmount, West Belfast, 2014. Photo by Tony Crowley.

Independent Ireland, instituted while Ireland was still under British Rule) (Figure 60, see Fulcrum), and the Tan War 1919–1921 (also known as the Irish War of Independence), between republican and British forces (Figure 61, see Fulcrum). The violence of State forces in Belfast in the same period was also recorded in a representation of the brutal sectarianism that broke out repeatedly during and around Partition (together with the execution of the Sinn Féin Teachta Dála, Liam Mellows by the Free State government) (Figure 62, see Fulcrum).

If the walls were a prime location where the republican narrative was firmly and clearly established, there was one event that lay at the center of the story: the Easter Rising of 1916. Examples of complex and often sophisticated murals of the Rising abounded. At The Felons Club in West Belfast (founded as a social club for republican ex-prisoners), a revised version of a reproduction of Walter Paget's "Birth of the Republic" (1918) featured a scene inside the GPO, with leaders of the rebellion, the *Proclamation* and a republican phoenix rising (Figure 63). While at the junction of McQuillan Street and the Falls Road, Mo Chara's ambitious representation of a sweep

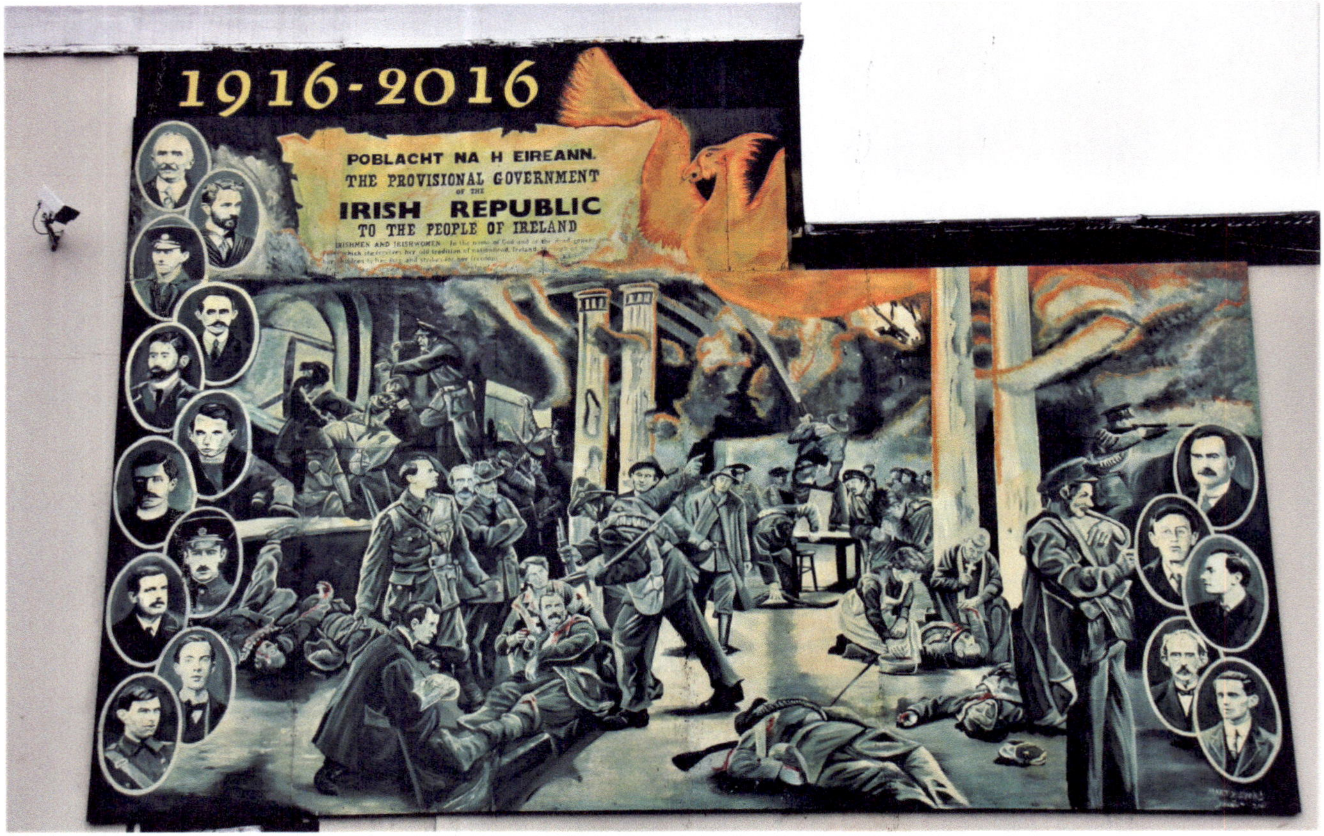

FIGURE 63 Phoenix rising, Lake Glen Road/Falls Road, Andersonstown, West Belfast, 2014. Photo by Tony Crowley.

of Irish history ranged from Cú Chulainn and Mother Ireland to the *Proclamation* and the burning of the GPO (Figure 64, see Fulcrum). Other images stressed the importance of the memory of 1916 (Figure 65, see Fulcrum), and the essential unity of the republican tradition—"unbowed, unbroken"—from 1916 to the Hunger Strikes to local republicans killed in the Troubles (Figure 66, see Fulcrum) (Figure 67, see Fulcrum). In Armagh, a mural of the *Proclamation*, with images of the leaders of the Rising and local republican dead, was contextualized by W.B. Yeats's poem "The Rose Tree" (and a rose tree) (Figure 68, see Fulcrum) (Figure 69, see Fulcrum). In Yeats's dialogue between Connolly and Pearse, the rose—Ireland—has to be nourished by the sacrifice of those who fight for it: "There's nothing but our own red blood/Can make a right Rose Tree." The call was echoed in Seán MacDiarmada's words in **fig. 64**—"we bleed that the nation may live."

Perhaps the most remarkable attempt to represent 1916 was the mainstream republican mural that stretched along the Divis Street section of the International Wall (more than two hundred feet) (Figure 70). Beginning with figures gathered from nationalist and republican tradition (Theobald Wolfe Tone, Betsy Gray, Henry Joy McCracken, Mary Anne McCracken, Robert Emmett, Anna Wheeler, James Fintan Lalor, Thomas Davis, John Mitchel, Michael Davitt, and John Devoy), the mural depicted events leading up to the Rising, with an emphasis on developments in the North. The images included: loyalist gun-running, Edward Carson, and the formation of the Ulster and Irish Volunteers; nationalist gun-running at Howth and the contribution of Cumann na mBan; Alice Milligan and Ethna Carberry (founders of the *Shan Van Vocht* newspaper, which published articles by Connolly), together with Belfast Cumann na mBan members, the Corr sisters; Seán MacDiarmada proselytizing in the Lower Falls with the aid of magic lantern shows; members of the Irish Volunteers and Cumann na mBan training in the Beechmount area; the Rising (with Belfast woman Winifred Carney inside the GPO) (Figure 71); and in an image that forged the continuity between past and present, a memorial stone to 1798, the *Proclamation*, the execution of Casement, Kilmainham jail (where the leaders of the Rising were executed), the prison protests of the 1970s (Frank Stagg, Michael Gaughan, Kieran Nugent and Mairéad Farrell), and the Hunger Strikers (Figure 72).

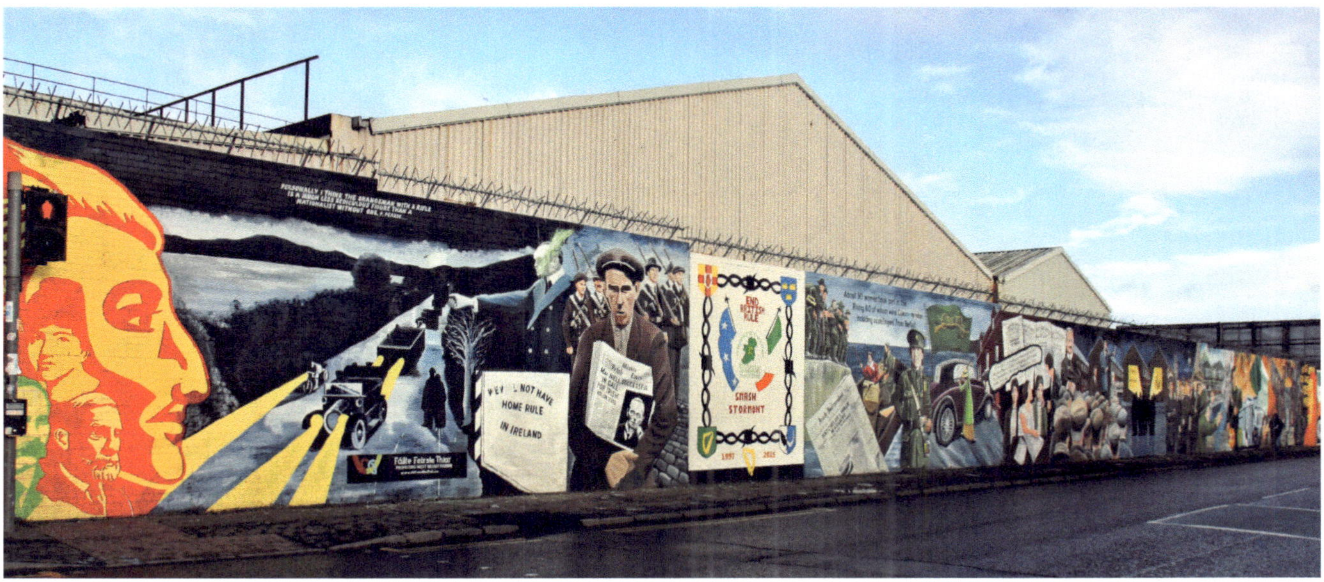

FIGURE 70 Republican history, International Wall, Divis Street, West Belfast, 2016. Photo by Tony Crowley.

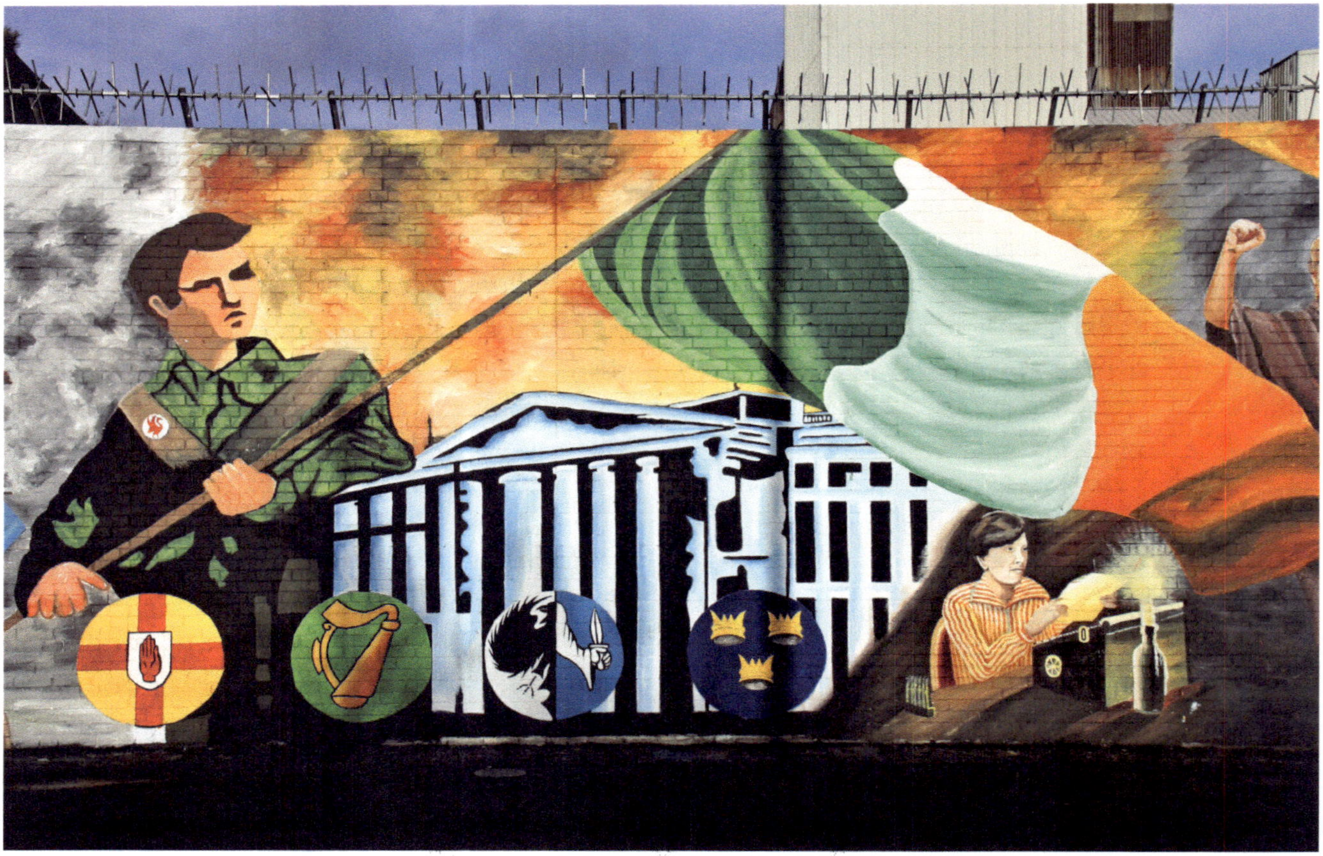

FIGURE 71 The GPO, International Wall, Divis Street, West Belfast, 2016. Photo by Tony Crowley.

Yet if this notable mural was an attempt to represent the unbroken continuity of republican tradition, its fate illustrated that this story was hardly uncontested. Objections were made to the depiction of Carson on the Falls, for example, and his image was vandalized a number of times. In addition, members of the 32CSM refused to remove one of their murals from the wall and thus the narrative was—literally—interrupted by an image that proclaimed the ongoing need to "Smash Stormont" (Figure 73). Likewise, the end of the mural was puzzling as it featured an image of Leonard Peltier, the imprisoned American Indian leader, with the words "And the world did gaze with deep amaze" (taken from the nationalist folksong *The Foggy Dew*) (Figure 74, see Fulcrum), next to an

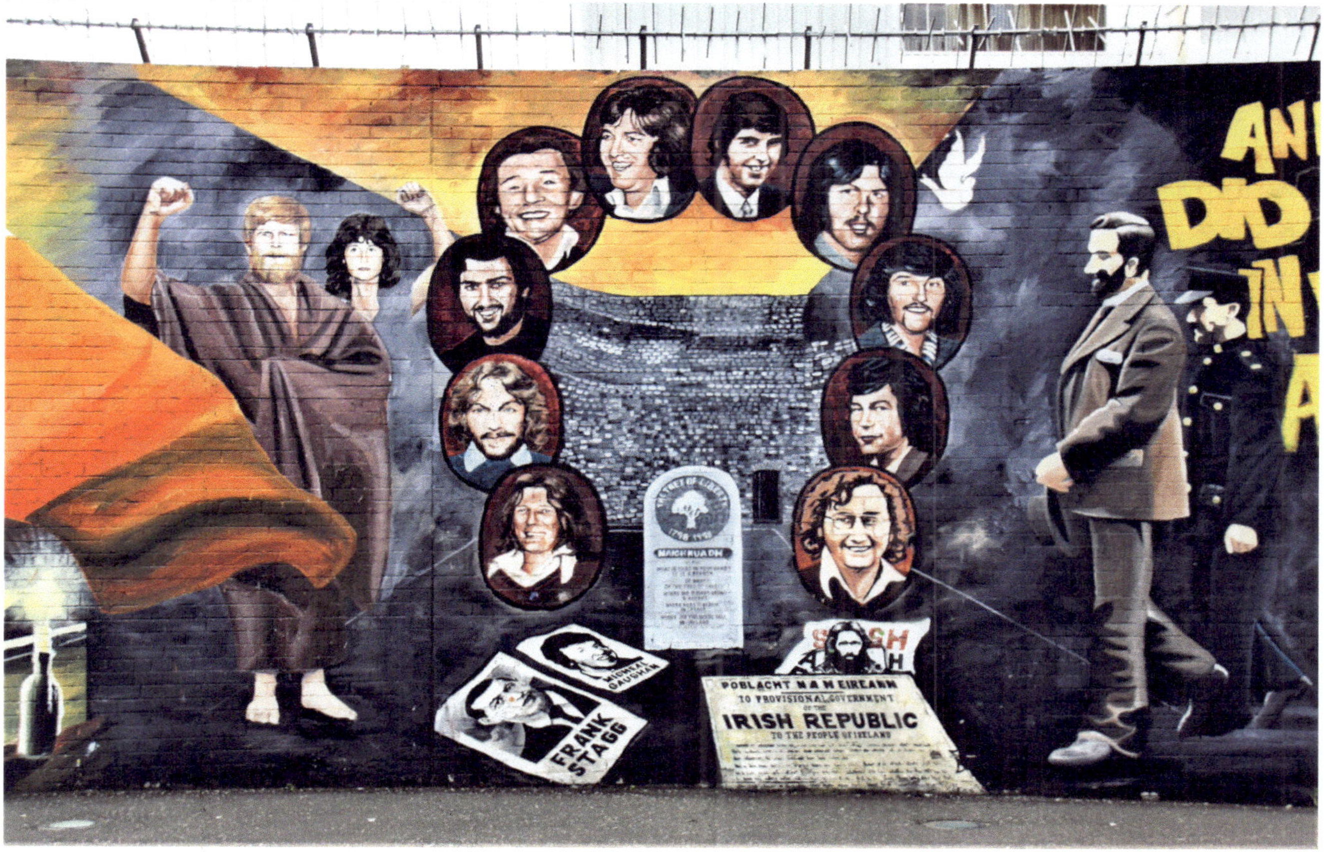

FIGURE 72 The tree of liberty, International Wall, Divis Street, West Belfast, 2016. Photo by Tony Crowley.

Irish Republican Prisoners Welfare Association (IRPWA) mural with the demand "Free all political prisoners" (Figure 75, see Fulcrum). The explanation for the discrepancy is that the end-space of the wall was taken by the IRPWA before the rival muralists could finish their mural with a host of other figures (ranging from Peltier to Du Bois, Gandhi to Angela Davies) and in the end only the image of Peltier, painted in the same format as Wolfe Tone, looked to the beginning of the mural.[11] Like their 32CSM counterparts, the IRPWA image-makers refused to take their mural down. The year 1916 may be a historical fact that can be commemorated, but its legacy is the subject of an ongoing debate.

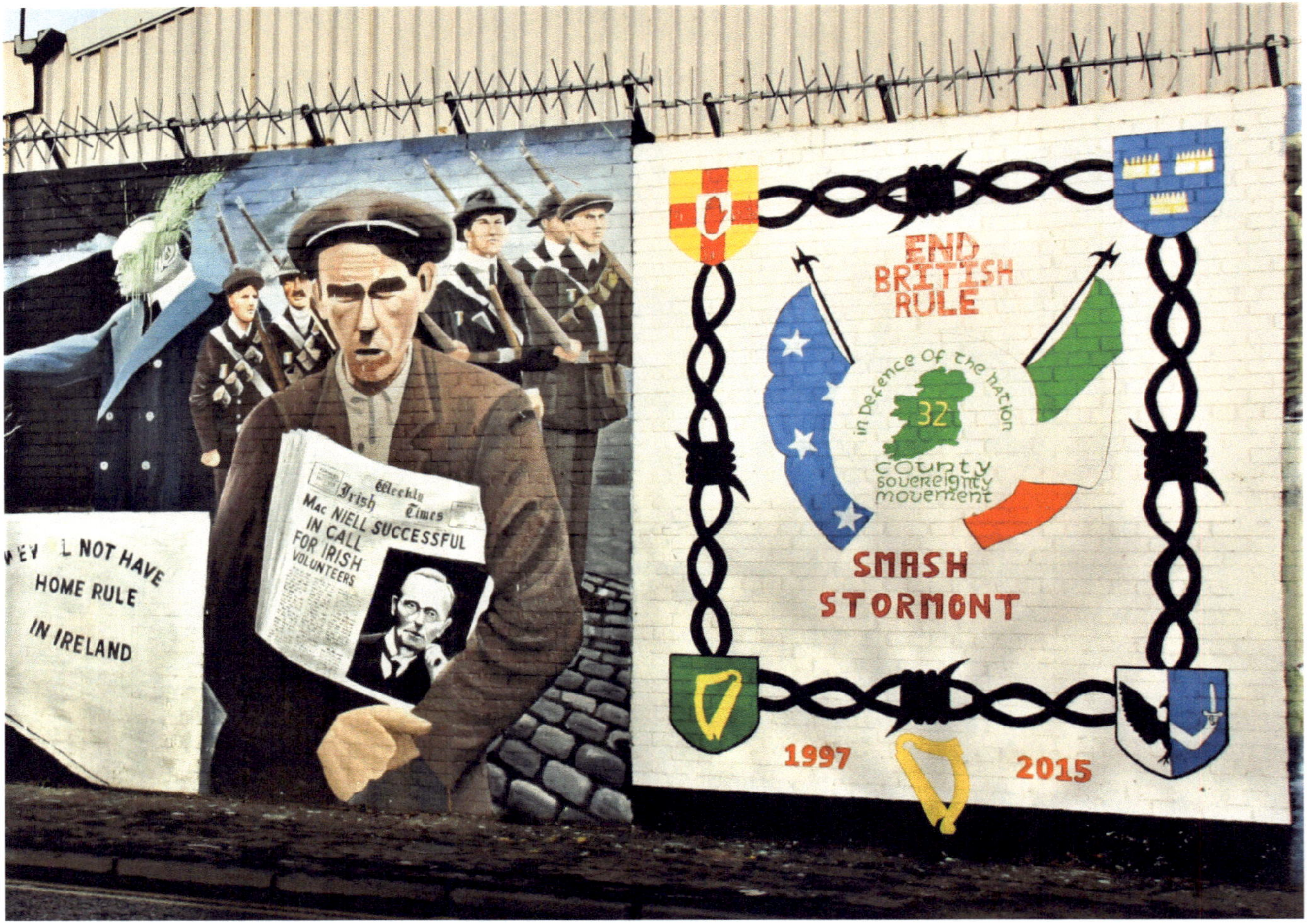

FIGURE 73 Smash Stormont, International Wall, Divis Street, West Belfast, 2015. Photo by Tony Crowley.

4. DISSIDENCE

The tactic of the 32CSM and the IRPWA in rejecting claims to cede space to the epic mural commemorating 1916 could be dismissed as petty obstructionism, but there is more to it than that. A mural on Mountpottinger Road, East Belfast, in 2010, celebrated the 40th anniversary of "The Battle of St Matthew's" with the message "Understand the past—and build a better future le cheile" (together) (see **fig. 1**). But understanding the past is hardly uncontentious, as the example of St Matthews illustrates (see **chapter five, figs 70, 71**), and the framing of the past is frequently tendentious (demonstrated in this example by the use of Irish, specifically the Irish name of the IRA—Óglaigh na hÉireann). In any case, the stubborn presence of the 32CSM and the IRPWA murals on the International Wall cannot be explained by arguments about the past (though interpretations of the past are partly what distinguish republican tendencies). Rather, they represent a specific standpoint towards the politics of the present. For, given that the 1916 mural considered in the previous section can be viewed as an attempt to establish a specific (read Sinn Féin) narrative of the past, the intercalating images function as a rejection of both the story itself but also, thereby, the trajectory of mainstream republicanism. They were not alone in this, and others were more explicit in their use of republican icons to offer comment (Figure 76). Given this, it is clear that while 2016 offered the possibility of organizing a grand-scale celebration of the Easter Rising (including marches and gatherings in republican areas across Northern Ireland), it was also problematic. For as republican critics noted, after all that happened—Irish Independence, Partition, the problematic history of both states on either side of the border, the collapse of Northern Ireland, the IRA's 'Long War' and the negotiation of the peace—the unification of Ireland, to say nothing of the achievement of a socialist Republic, remained unrealized and unrealizable without the agreement of a majority in Northern Ireland in a border poll to be held at the discretion of the British Secretary of State.

The republican organizations that rejected the Sinn Féin project were described both by their opponents and the media as "dissidents." This was, as noted in chapter four, a disputed label since those who were described as "dissidents" argued that they had not departed from republican orthodoxy and thus those who had (specifically Sinn Féin) were the real dissidents. Disputes over labels notwithstanding, there were various tendencies that were opposed to Sinn Féin's hegemony, though one lesson that they all recognized was the efficacy of the walls as a site of argument and contestation. Some older groups used murals to signal a continued presence. The Official Republican Movement, for example, whose military wing declared a ceasefire as far back as 1972 and eventually decommissioned in 2009, erected murals in memory of leading members (including an image that took back Joe McCann from the Provisionals—see **chapter 2 note 12**) (Figure 77, see Fulcrum), or events such as the Falls Curfew (Figure 78). The INLA, which had been engaged in armed struggle since 1974, declared a ceasefire in 1998 and also decommissioned in 2009, though it continued to promote itself (Figure 79, see Fulcrum). As with other republican groups, the INLA remembered its dead, including Hunger Strikers Patsy O'Hara (see **fig. 29**) and Mickey Devine (Figure 80) as well as other volunteers (Figure 81, see Fulcrum) (Figure 82, see Fulcrum). The IRSP, the political wing of the INLA, maintained its presence through social and political campaigns that highlighted the malign effects of British (Tory) rule and linked them to Partition (Figure 83, see Fulcrum) while also advertising its internationalism with a mural commemorating Castro (Figure 84, see Fulcrum). The party was also responsible for a re-imaging of the memorial mural to Miriam Daly on Oakman Street, Beechmount (see **chapter four, fig. 23**),

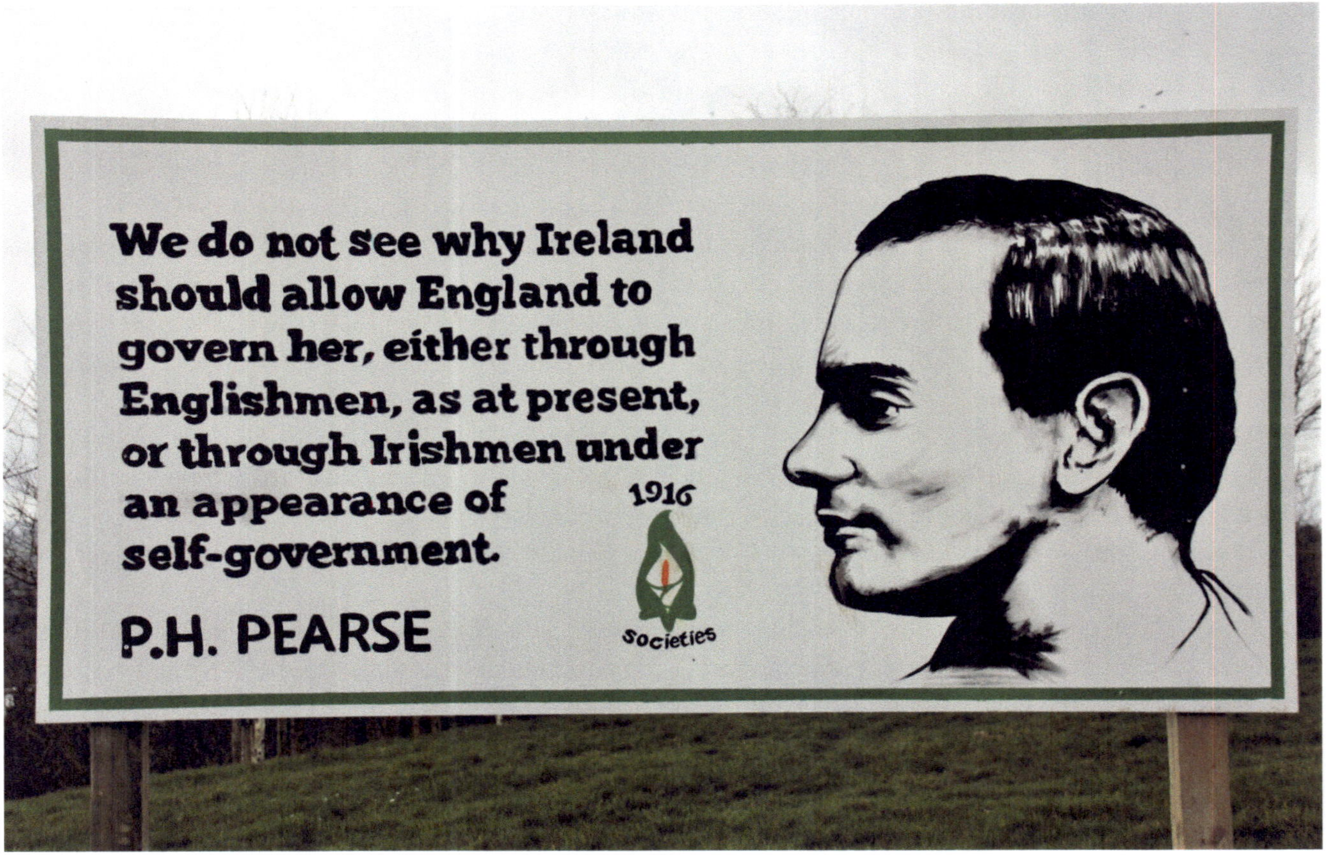

FIGURE 76 An appearance of self-government, Southway, Creggan, Derry, 2016. Photo by Tony Crowley.

which retained the message that "history is written by the winners" (Figure 85). This frequently cited quote is often misattributed (it is usually claimed to have been said by Winston Churchill, though its origins are unclear), but it is worth considering. It presumably refers to a post-conflict situation in which the victors' account becomes the dominant narrative. Yet in the case of this mural, its form, content, and function bear ironic witness to the fact that historiography is contested rather than settled. Indeed, from one perspective, the history of muralism in Northern Ireland evinces nothing less than the writing of history (or histories) by various parties. In that sense, the "history is written by the winners" claim is both curious and self-contradictory. Curious in that it appears to cede too much to "the winners," and self-contradictory in that historiography has been one of the functions of muralism since

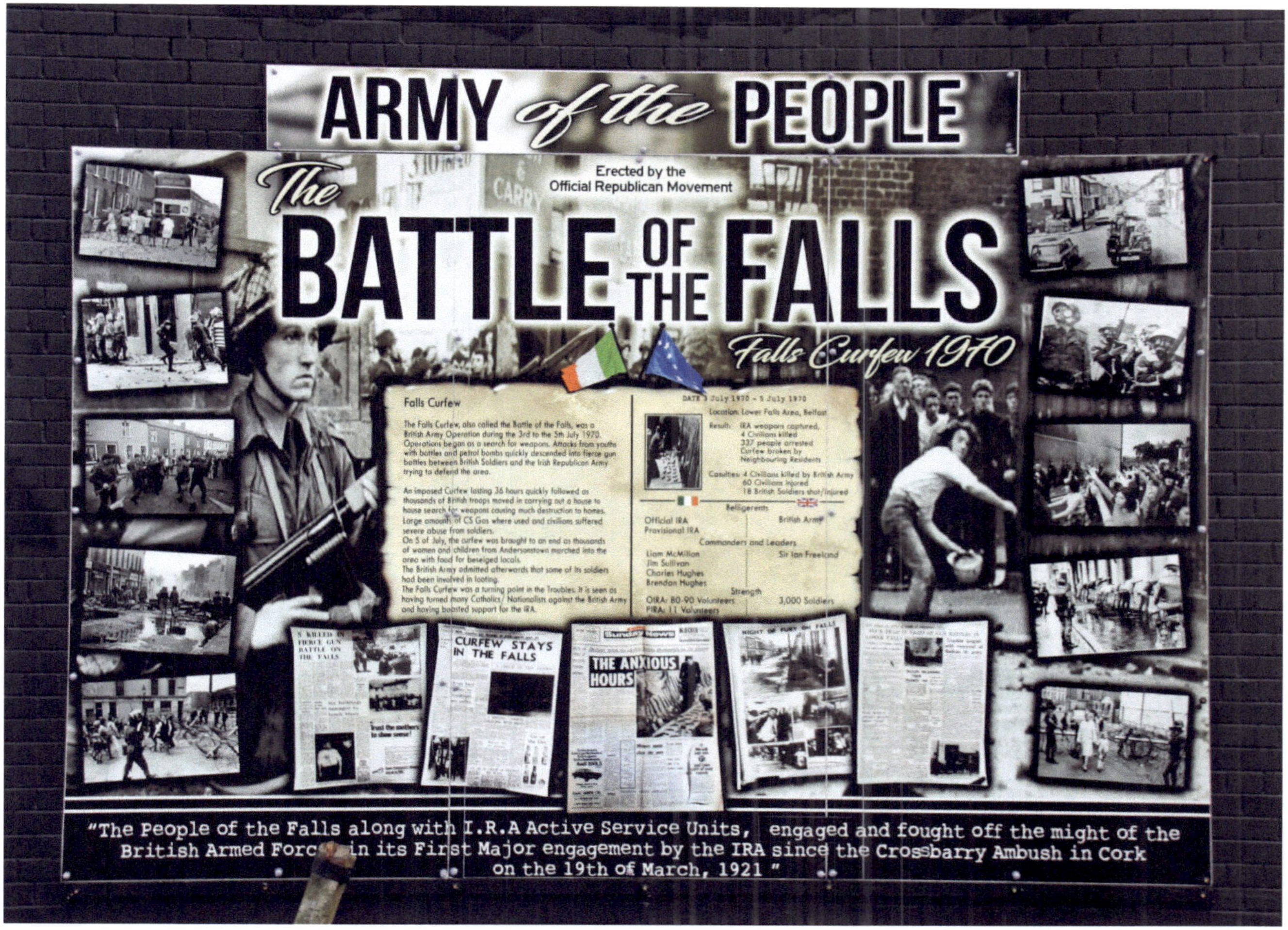

FIGURE 78 Battle of the Falls, International Wall, Northumberland Street, West Belfast, 2017. Photo by Tony Crowley.

its early twentieth-century origins. Besides which, deciding who "the winners" are in contemporary Northern Ireland is a complex issue open to question—as open to interpretation as history itself. None of which is to say that history-writing is an open playing field, since it is underpinned by power relations, questions of access, and issues of exclusion (not anyone can just paint anything on a wall). But to say that history is only written by the winners is to belie the active contestation of history that the murals embody.

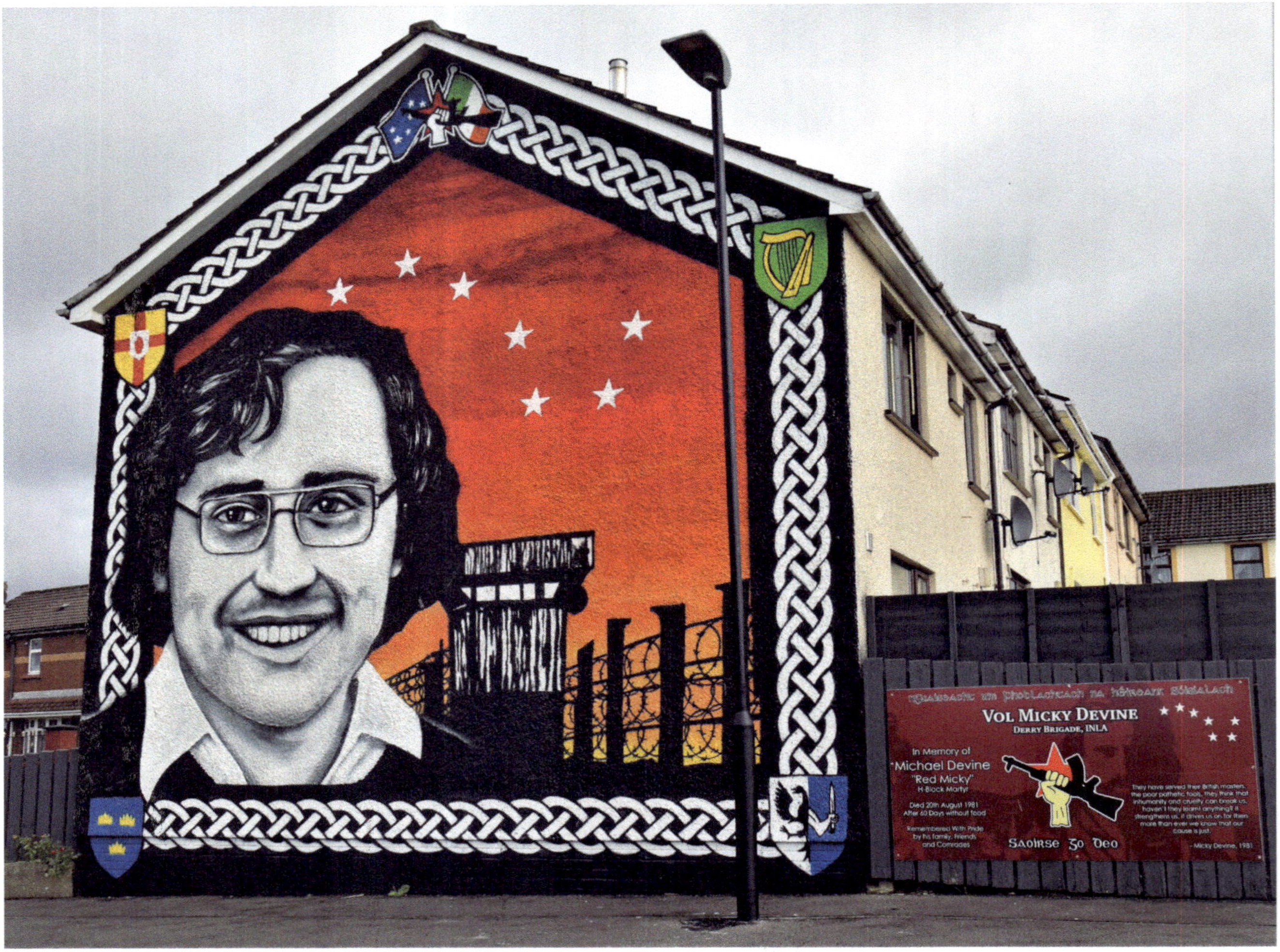

FIGURE 80 Volunteer Mickey Devine, Fern Road, Glengalliagh, Derry, 2021. Photo by Tony Crowley.

The origins of the Official Republican Movement and the IRSP/INLA lie in splits within republicanism over strategy and tactics: in 1969 the IRA split into Officials and Provisionals, and in 1974 the INLA/IRSP broke from the Officials. The organizations that have been called "dissident," however, date from more recent fissures within republicanism. The paramilitary Continuity IRA, and the linked political party, RSF, were formed in 1986 as a result of disagreement about the issue of electoral abstentionism. The CIRA became actively engaged in violence after

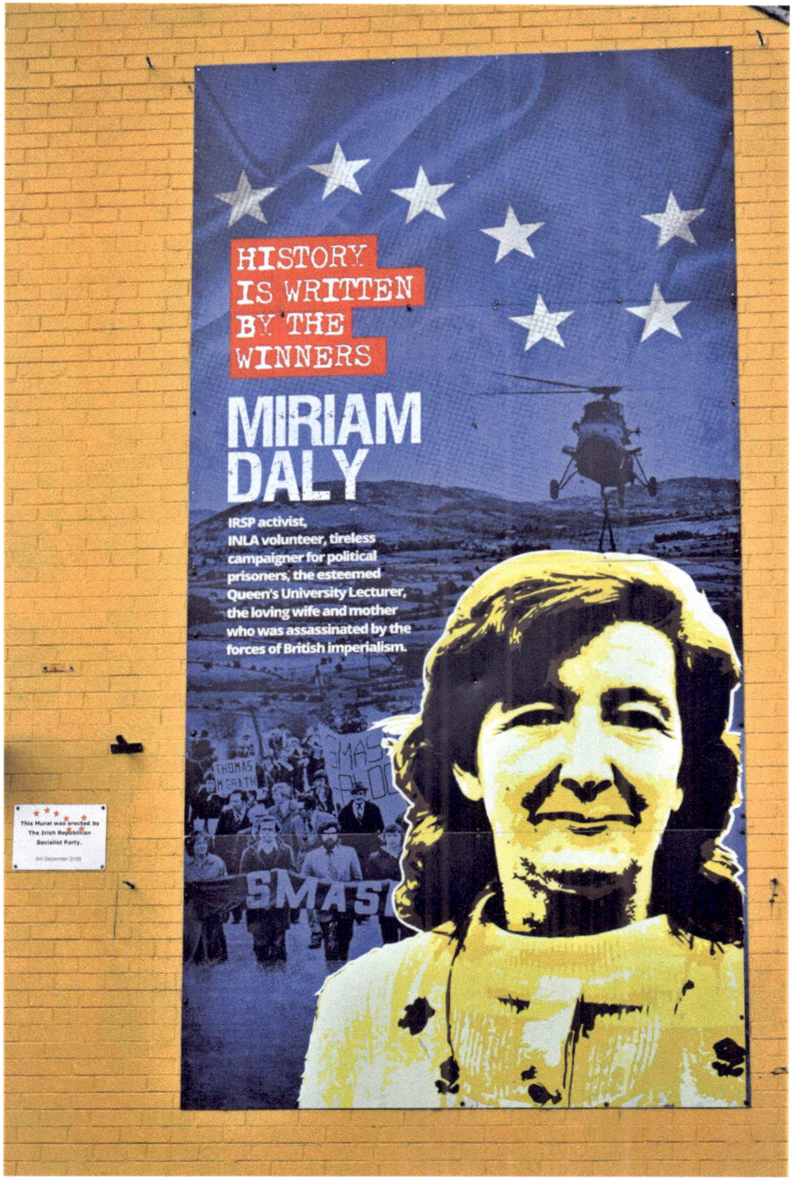

FIGURE 85 Miriam Daly, Oakman Street, Beechmount, West Belfast, 2016. Photo by Tony Crowley.

the first IRA ceasefire in 1994 and has carried out sporadic attacks since (including the killing of a police officer in 2009). Despite its logistical limitations, the CIRA maintains a forthright stance—"Not compromise" (Figure 86, see Fulcrum) and, together with RSF and associated groups such as Cumann na mBan and Na Fianna Éireann, claims fidelity to republican tradition (Figure 87, see Fulcrum). Another paramilitary group, the RIRA, formed in 1997 after the second IRA ceasefire, was responsible for the Omagh bombing in 1998 and, after a pause, a series of attacks in Britain and Northern Ireland, including the killing of two British soldiers at Massereene Barracks, Antrim, in 2009. Its support base was limited and geographically specific—the Red Rose symbol (see **fig. 69**) appeared in Creggan, Derry (Figure 88, see Fulcrum)—but an affiliated political group, the 32CSM, kept up a critical commentary on the Peace Process (Figure 89), including a response to Martin McGuinness's description of the RIRA killing of a policeman in 2009 as the work of "traitors to the island of Ireland" (Figure 90, see Fulcrum). In 2012 the RIRA merged with an independent republican group, Republican Action Against Drugs, and other smaller groups, to form the New IRA, which has carried out a sustained, if relatively low, level of violence (including the unintended killing of journalist Lyra McKee in Derry in 2019 and the shooting of a senior policeman in 2023).[12] Saoradh, a political party with links to the New IRA, attacked what it considered to be mainstream republican inconsistency with a mural that offered a "salute to the men and women of violence," and linked the leaders of the Easter uprising with contemporary armed volunteers (Figure 91). The same connection was made by another group associated with the New IRA (or IRA as it prefers to be known): on the side of the offices of the IRPWA a mural proclaimed the "Unfinished Revolution" with paramilitaries and an Easter lily (Figure 92). The (N) IRA itself echoed the discourse of the Provisional IRA with its iteration of the words used after the bombing of Brighton in 1984: "we only have to be lucky once" (Figure 93, see Fulcrum).[13]

Saoradh asserted its commitment to internationalism through references to the armed struggle of the Palestinians (Figure 94, see Fulcrum), but for most of the republican political groupings, the focus was closer to home. Éirígí, formed by a coalition of community and political activists who broke from Sinn Féin in 2006, campaigned on a number of social issues including the Irish language—"Tír gan teanga tír gan anam" (a country without a language is a country without a soul) (Figure 95, see Fulcrum). While the RNU, another group that split from Sinn Féin and was associated with the small paramilitary group ONH (on ceasefire since 2017), injected a rare moment of humor into an otherwise uncompromising mural portfolio with its parodic call for "More Blacks More gays More Irish" (Figure 96, see Fulcrum).[14] For the most part, however, the constant concern of most groups labelled "dissident" was the struggle against Sinn Fein's hegemony and its articulation of a particular narrative of republican tradition. The level of antagonism varied between outright hostility (Figure 97, see Fulcrum), the bitter disillusion of former comrades (Figure 98, see Fulcrum), and the attempt to appropriate figures usually associated with the IRA to the newer configurations (Figure 99, see Fulcrum).[15] On occasion the challenge to Sinn Féin was anonymous, though pointed, as in the caricature in Beechmount, West Belfast, of Martin McGuinness meeting the Queen (striding past gravestones marked "Ireland," "Palestine," "Afghanistan," and "Iraq," carrying

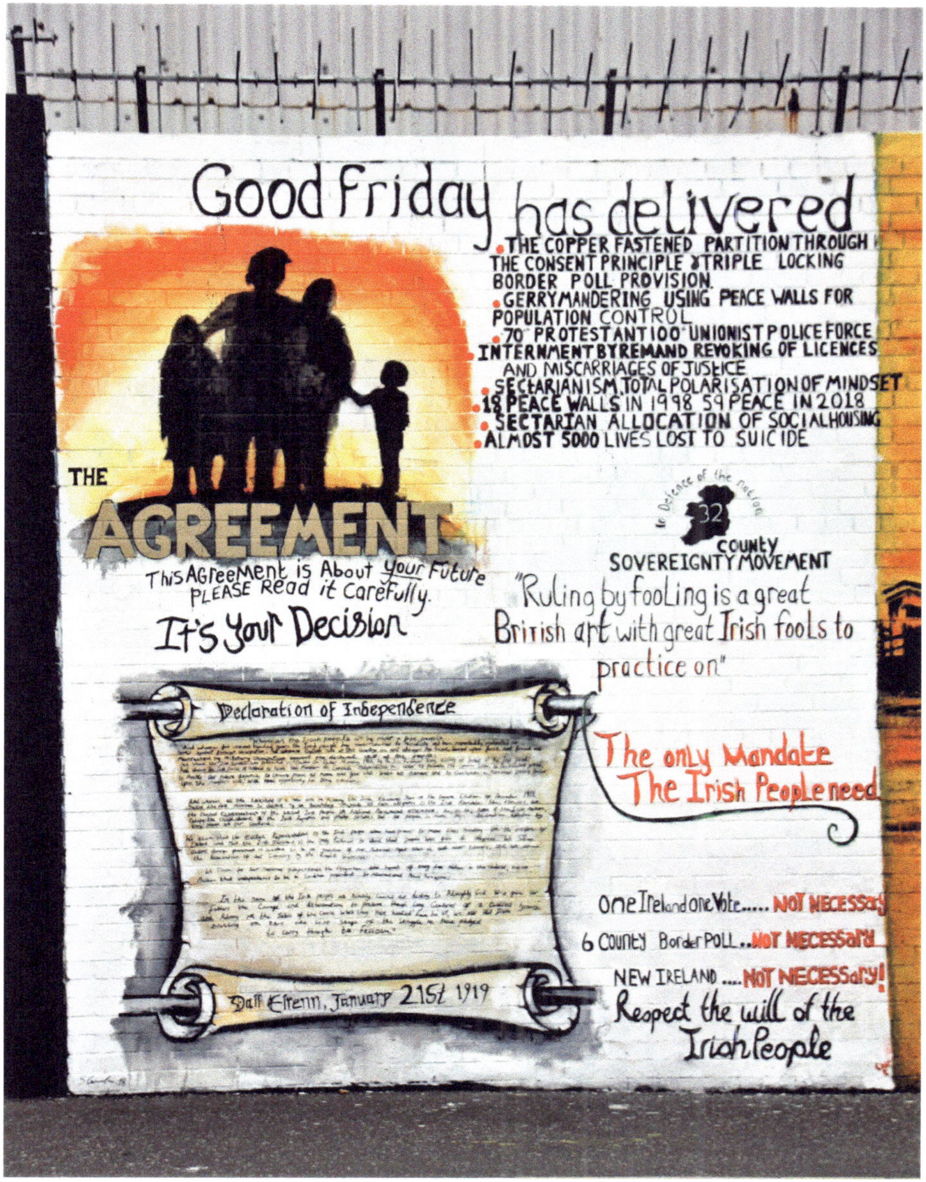

FIGURE 89 Good Friday has delivered, Divis Street, International Wall, West Belfast, 2020. Photo by Tony Crowley.

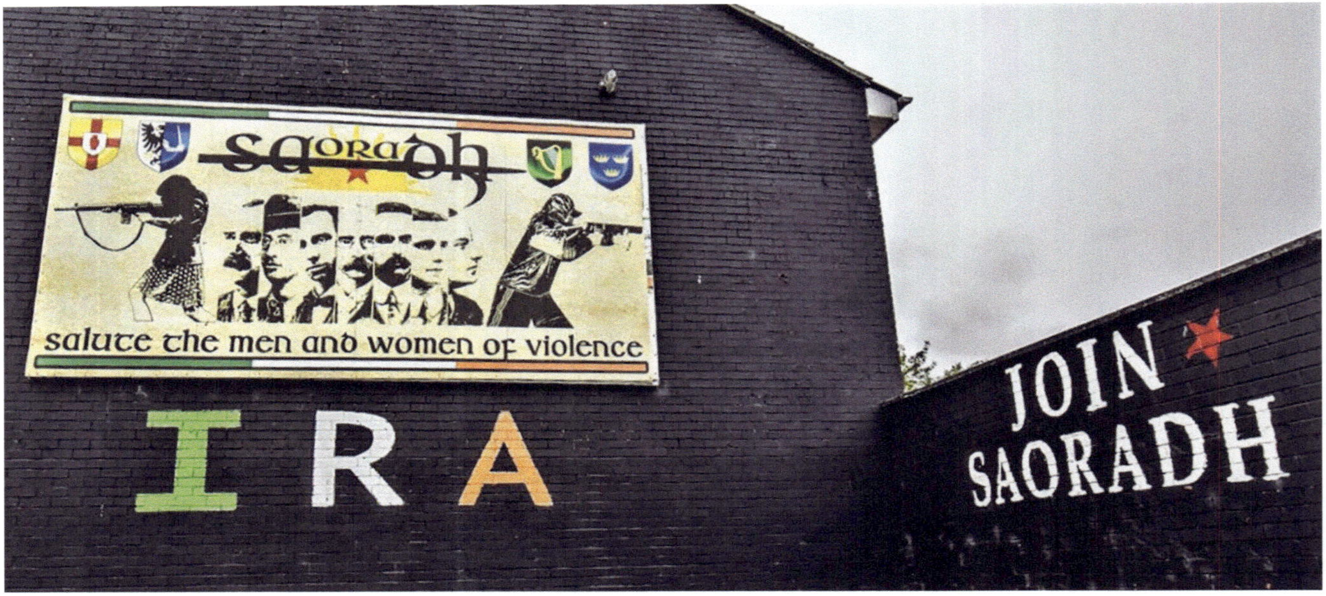

FIGURE 91 The men and women of violence, Ardoyne Avenue, Ardoyne, North Belfast, 2019. Photo by Tony Crowley.

an axe, and wearing a blood-stained Butcher's Apron—the republican term for the Union Jack) (Figure 100). An illustration of the political and cultural dominance that Sinn Féin exerts in republican areas is that the mural was censored shortly after it was painted, with the images of McGuinness, the Queen and the Irish gravestone painted out (Figure 101, see Fulcrum). To which a response was posted on an adjacent wall in short order, proclaiming that "Political dissent is not a crime!" It was a sentiment echoed in a quotation on a mural dedicated to Brendan (the Dark) Hughes, a life-long republican and IRA veteran who ended up fiercely opposed to Sinn Féin: "I don't mind being called a dissenter, I've been a dissenter all my life" (Figure 102, see Fulcrum).[16]

5. RE-IMAGING REPUBLICAN MURALS

In 2009 two murals appeared on Brompton Park in the republican heartland of Ardoyne, North Belfast (Figure 103, see Fulcrum and see **Introduction, fig. 13**), accompanied by two plaques. One plaque (see **Introduction, fig. 14**) announced that the murals were "Officially opened by the President of Ireland, Mary MacAleese" on June 19 2009 (MacAleese was born in Ardoyne). The other asserted that "This project has been funded through the Re-imaging Communities Programme which is supported by the Shared Communities

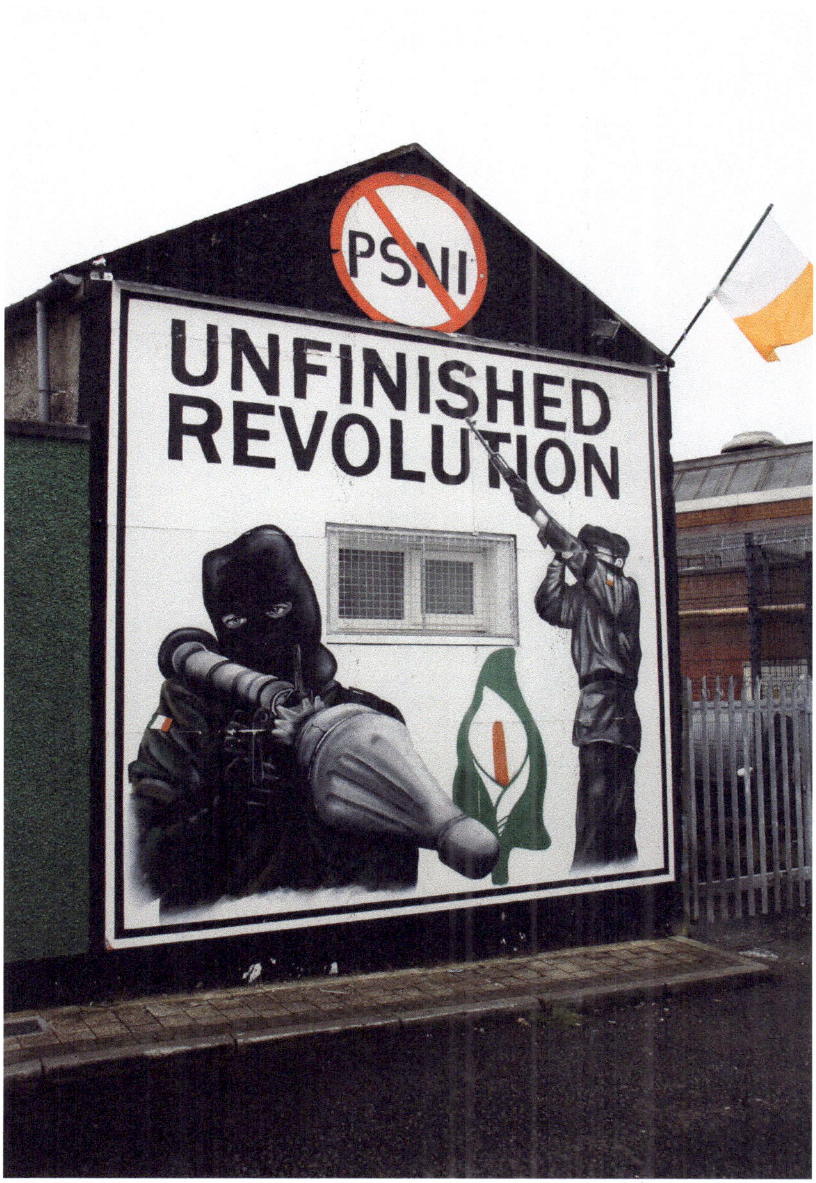

FIGURE 92 Unfinished revolution, Chamberlain Street, City Center, Derry, 2016. Photo by Tony Crowley.

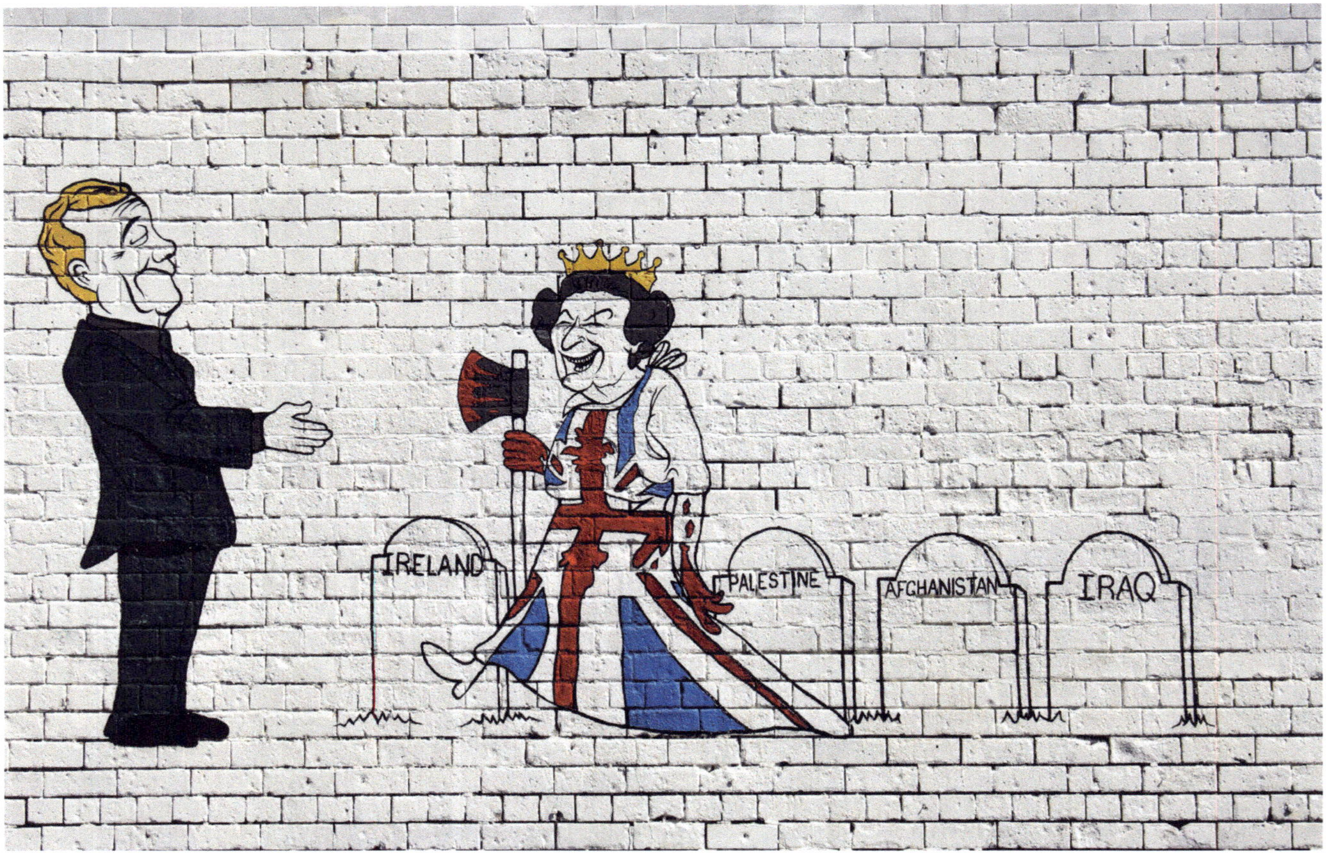

FIGURE 100 Martin McGuinness meets the Queen, Beechmount Avenue, Beechmount, West Belfast, 2016. Photo by Tony Crowley.

Consortium" with the aim of "Renewing Communities, Rebuilding Confidence, Reviving Hope, Restoring Pride." Sponsoring bodies include the British National Lottery, the Arts Council of Northern Ireland, the Department for Social Development, the Office of the First Minister and Deputy First Minister, and the International Fund for Ireland. The murals themselves were apolitical images of the Ardoyne Fleadh, and an abstract collage of children's faces. The appearance of these murals (and others like them in loyalist areas) was the result of the Re-imaging Communities Programme, established in 2006 to tackle the issue of "the public representation of community separation," in the form of "public symbolic displays, including marches, banners, flags, wall paintings, bunting, and painted kerbstones" (Dawson et al. 2009: vi–vii).[17] The explicit aim of the initiative was that of "converting and transforming these visible signs of sectarianism and inter-community separation," with the goal of encouraging "communities to reflect on and plan for ways of replacing divisive imagery with imagery that reflects communities in a more positive manner" (vii). Initially intended to last three years, with a budget of £3.3 million, and to cover 60–80 community-based schemes, the program exceeded expectations by funding 108 projects before its suspension in 2008. Further funding of £500,000 in December 2008 led to work on another 15 projects; after a pause between 2009 and 2012, the scheme was re-named "Building Peace through the Arts: Re-imaging Communities Programme" and ran from 2013 to 2015.

It is striking that republican engagement with the re-imaging schemes was extremely limited. Given the amount of money available, it might have been thought that republican muralists would welcome the possibility of additional funding (like their loyalist counterparts, no republican muralist was well paid for painting walls—if they were paid at all). But republicans largely shunned the re-imaging initiative for a number of reasons, but primarily because of their suspicion that State-funded programs would ultimately be designed to serve the interests of the State rather than the communities it professed to serve (such fears would have been confirmed by the claim in the 2009 report that "as a result of the projects many relationships between communities and the statutory sector were established or built upon"—links with the Housing Executive and the PSNI are specifically mentioned) (Dawson et al. 2009: xi). For many republican muralists, of various tendencies, and working in a number of different media ranging from traditional wall painting to digitally created images, the Statist re-imaging program represented a threat to the articulation of their narrative rather than an opportunity to move in a different direction at the behest of the State.[18]

In point of fact, mainstream republican muralists did engage in re-imaging, but not on the terms set out by others. Rather, their work contributed to the extension of political and cultural hegemony within republican areas that had developed from the beginning of the Peace Process in the late 1980s and early 1990s. They did so, however, in changed circumstances since, as noted above, Sinn Féin had not only become the main voice of constitutional nationalism, it was also on the way to becoming the largest political party at Stormont. This is not to say that traditional themes did not feature in republican work. As examined earlier in this chapter, republican centenaries were commemorated and cultural nationalist images were produced—including the stories of Niall of the Nine Hostages and Queen Macha in Armagh (Figure 104, see Fulcrum) and the Flight of the Earls in Ardoyne, North Belfast (Figure 105). Notwithstanding these examples, however, there was a clear departure in mainstream muralism towards a wider portfolio of interests and concerns. In one sense this reflects Sinn Fein's desire to put the war firmly in the past (while acknowledging its debt to the IRA and its volunteers) in order to consolidate its strengths and to move towards the future. Though whether the party, or those who represented it, were successful in this attempt is debatable; armed volunteers might no longer feature in mainstream republican

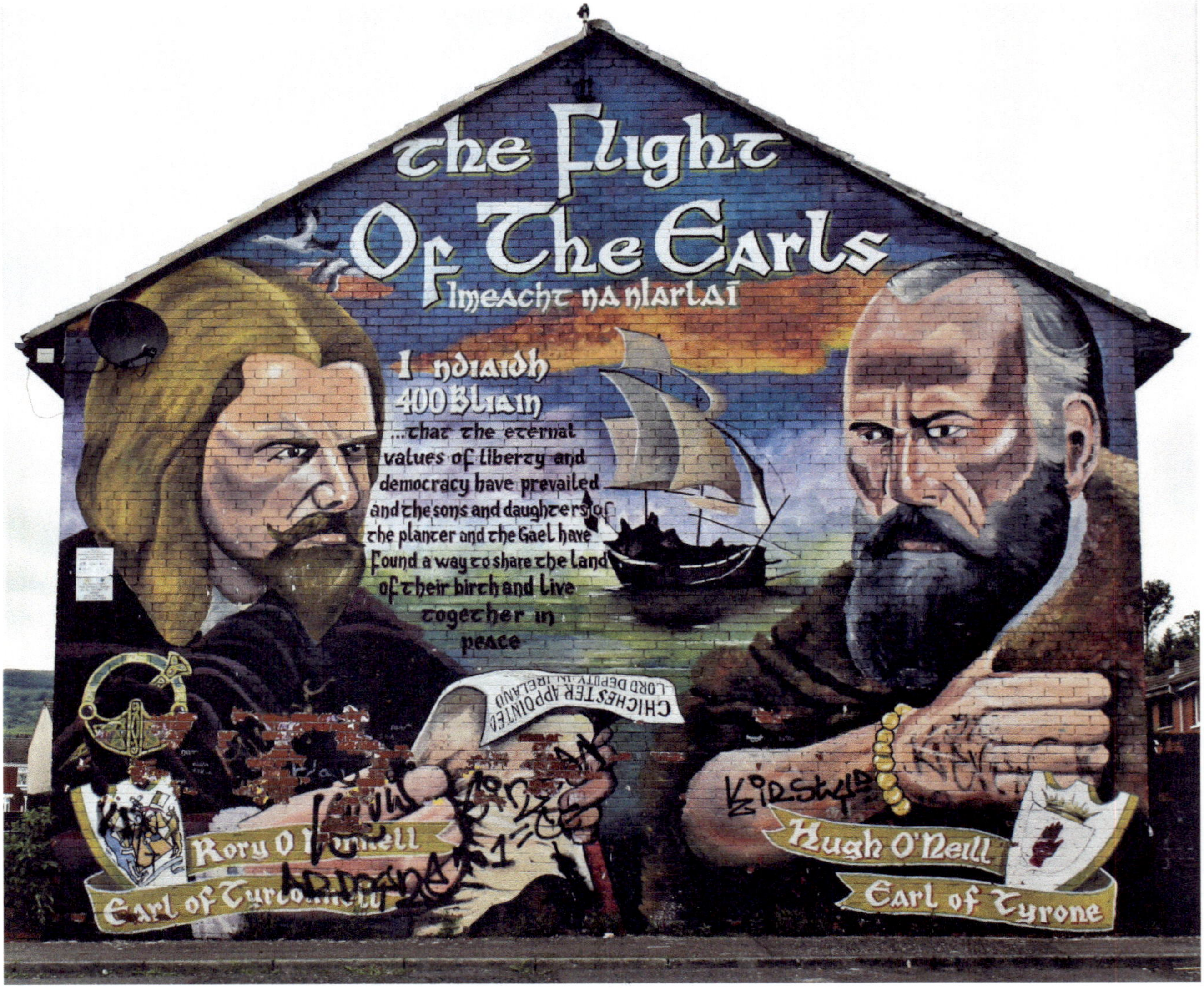

FIGURE 105 The Flight of the Earls, Ardoyne Avenue, Ardoyne, 2010. Photo by Tony Crowley.

murals, but for unionists and loyalists, every mural that commemorated a Hunger Striker or a dead volunteer was a sharp reminder of Sinn Féin's ties to the violence of the war period.

The shift in mainstream republican muralism, however, was clear and it was characterized principally by the representation of a set of concerns that mirrored the positioning of Sinn Féin as a center-left party (with purportedly radical allegiances). Whether such representations were compatible with the actual politics of Sinn Féin is beside the point: on the whole, though there were some exceptions, the murals reflected and disseminated rhetorical positions rather than practical politics. In a number of instances, the focus turned to the past for inspiration, with topics such as the cross-community Belfast dockers and carters' strike in 1907 (Rolston

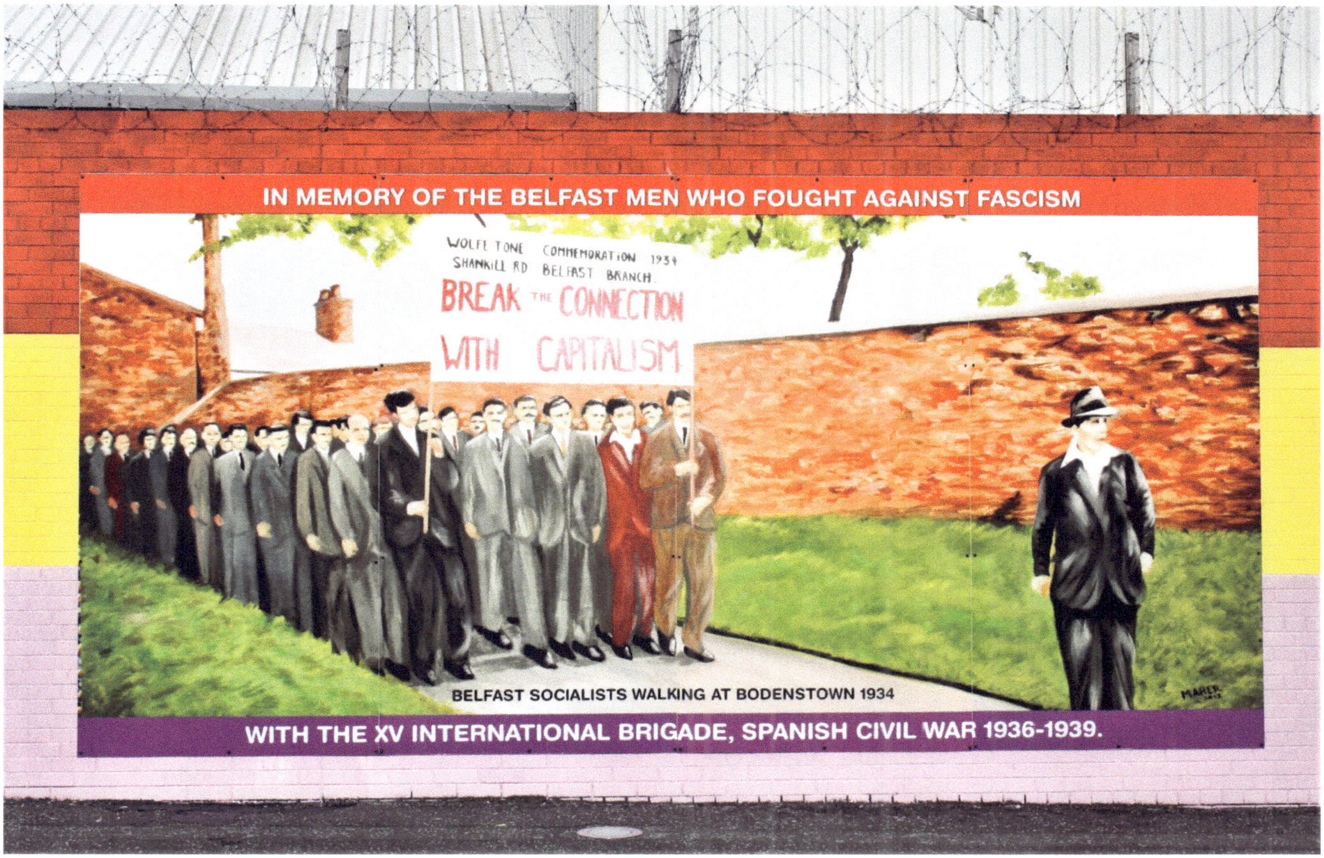

FIGURE 106 The International Brigade, International Wall, Northumberland Street, West Belfast, 2013. Photo by Tony Crowley.

2013: 14) and the volunteers (unionist and nationalist) who fought in the International Brigades in the Spanish Civil War. In an example of the complex dialogism of republican muralism, however, the mainstream republican mural hailing the International Brigade was answered by an image sponsored by Teach na Fáilte (affiliated with the IRSP). This work served as a reminder of the sectarianism that had long dogged republican efforts to forge working-class unity: a version of an iconic photograph, the Teach na Fáilte mural represented socialist marchers from the loyalist Shankill who were attacked by fellow republicans at the Wolfe Tone memorial at Bodenstown in 1934 (Figure 106). Other murals concentrated on contemporary issues, both global and local: human rights, capitalism, and the inequalities of climate change (Figure 107, see Fulcrum) (Figure 108, see Fulcrum) as well as the perennial housing crisis in Northern Ireland (Figure 109, see Fulcrum).[19]

6. A DIVERSE SCENE

The murals featured in **figures 106–109** were all sited on the two branches of the International Wall, which reflects its status as the locale on which leftist republican politics (of various tendencies) are articulated. As the name suggests, many of the political issues depicted on the wall relate to settings beyond Ireland, though some familiar affiliations were re-asserted both at this site and elsewhere.[20] Examples included support for Catalan and Basque independence (Figure 110, see Fulcrum) (Figure 111, see Fulcrum), the Cuban revolution (Figure 112, see Fulcrum), the Irish rebel Che Guevara (Figure 113, see Fulcrum), Mandela (Figure 114, see Fulcrum), the American Indian Movement (Peltier) (Figure 115, see Fulcrum), and opposition to American foreign policy (Rolston 2013: 30). Solidarity with the Palestinian cause has been a consistent theme in republican muralism, and numerous remarkable and striking images were painted across republican areas in Northern Ireland, usually during times of heightened crisis. The Israeli military offensives against Gaza in 2008 and 2014, for example, provoked a number of responses from leading republican muralists (including a version of the satirical cartoonist Carlos Latuff's "Do not disturb!") (Figure 116) (Figure 117, see Fulcrum) (Figure 118, see Fulcrum).[21] Again, however, what appears to be a set of murals supporting the same cause requires deciphering in order to reveal intra-republican politics. "Dissident" murals in North and West Belfast represented support for the armed struggle of the Palestinians and linked it to the situation in Ireland in order to challenge the dominant republican narrative (Figure 119). The representation of Leila Khaled in this mural is a coded way of asserting links between the (non-paramilitary) Socialist Republican Party Éirígí and the Popular Front for the Liberation of Palestine.[22] Other internationalist references were a little more obscure: even the most politically savvy inhabitants of West Belfast may have been stretched by the murals on the International wall that argued the case for "Tamil Eelam" and "Free West Papua" (Figure 120, see Fulcrum) (Figure 121, see Fulcrum).[23]

As argued in chapter four, murals serve to reflect and lead community sentiment in order to foster a type of political hegemony within a community and to give it an external identity. One example of the sort of values that

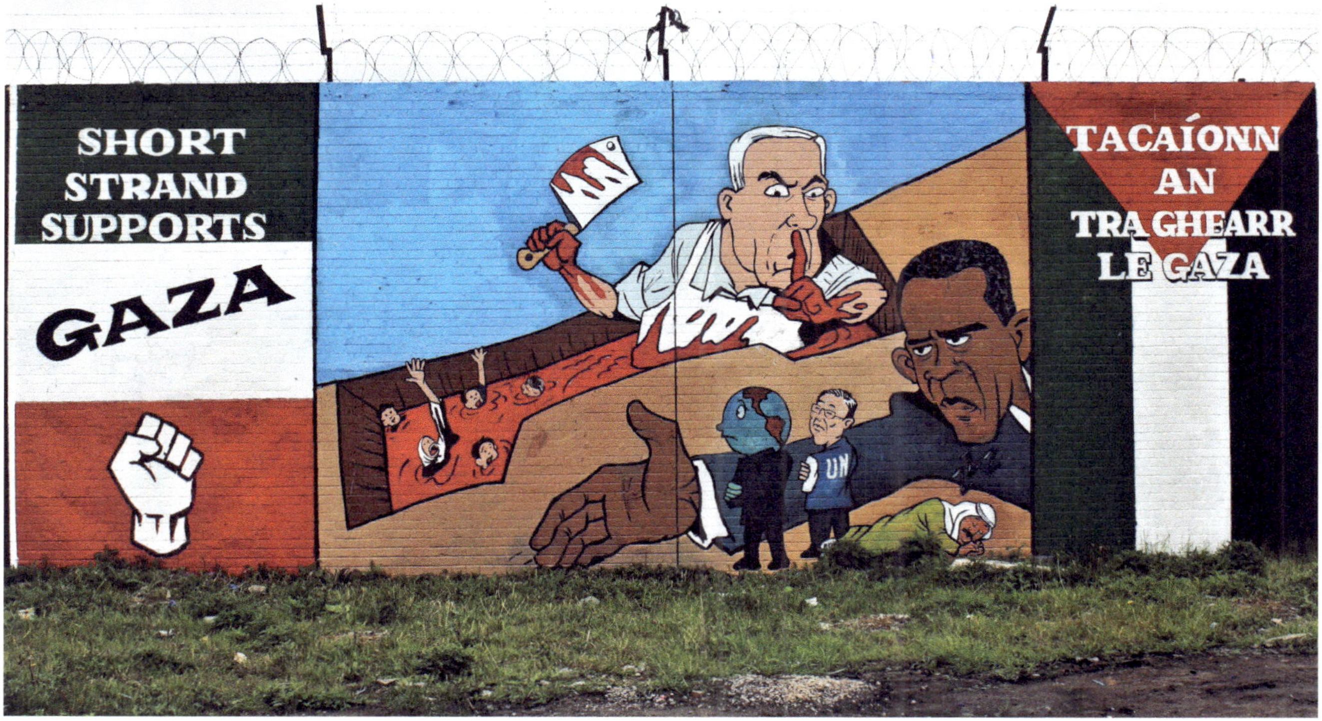

FIGURE 116 Short Strand supports Gaza, Mountpottinger Road, Short Strand, East Belfast, 2016. Photo by Tony Crowley.

were inculcated by the murals in this way was the promulgation of diversity in various forms. One significant mode of diversity was linguistic and cultural difference, marked by a multilingual street sign in the Markets area in South Belfast that featured English, Chinese, and Irish (Figure 122, see Fulcrum).[24] For nationalists and republicans, the most important form of linguistic diversity was of course the use of the Irish language, and numerous murals appeared in support of language organizations or initiatives. The argument for the language was made on traditional cultural nationalist grounds—"Tír gan teanga tír gan anam" (see **fig. 95**)—and by analogy—"Tá Fraincis ag na Francaigh Tá Gréigis ann sa Ghréig Tá Iodáils ag na hIodálaigh Bíodh Gaeilge ag na Gaeil" (It's French for the French Greek for the Greeks Italian for the Italians Let Irish be for the Irish) (Figure 123, see Fulcrum). And in locations around Northern Ireland, local groups made the language visible through basic language lessons on the walls (Figure 124, see Fulcrum). Campaigning groups, such as the Irish language umbrella group Pobal, which

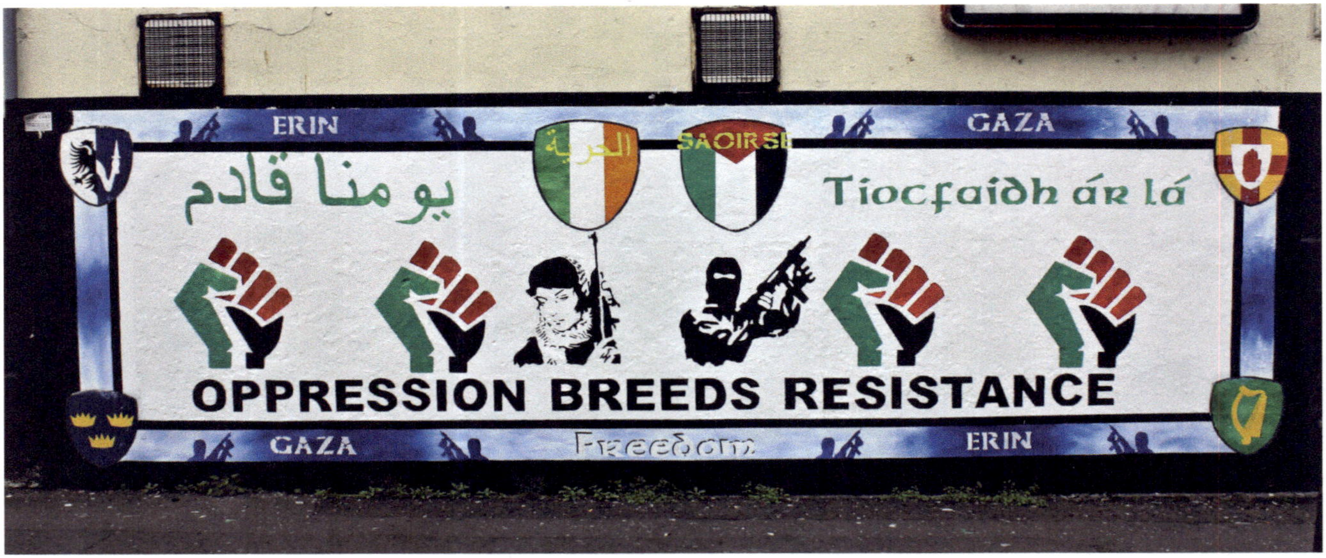

FIGURE 119 Oppression breeds resistance, McQuillan Street, Mid Falls, West Belfast, 2014. Photo by Tony Crowley.

commissioned murals around its base in West Belfast (Figure 125), fought for the introduction of Acht na Gaeilge/ An Irish Language Act (Figure 126, see Fulcrum) (a version of which—the *Identity and Language (Northern Ireland) Act*—was eventually passed in 2022 by the Westminster rather than Stormont parliament). The real success of a language, however, is not guaranteed by legislation but by its use in everyday practice, and in that sense at least, although the use of Irish is not as widely established as its proponents want, it has become part of daily life in nationalist and republican areas, particularly in relation to children's education. West Belfast is the acme in this respect and hosts six Irish medium nursery schools, five Irish medium primary schools, and the largest Irish medium secondary school in Ireland, Coláiste Feirste, together with an Irish language, culture, and arts center, Cultúrlann McAdam Ó Fiaich, an Irish language and business development agency, Forbairt Feirste, now located in Áras na bhFál, and a thriving Irish language radio station Radió Fáilte (Figure 127, see Fulcrum). In this area at least, Irish is a publicly practiced and visible medium of everyday life (Figure 128, see Fulcrum) and it has been officially recognized by Foras na Gaeilge as a Gaelphobal (Irish language network). Not the least remarkable aspect of the successful establishment of Irish has been its promotion in tourism (Figure 129, see Fulcrum); in this, as in other respects, republican West Belfast is presented as a very specific type of diverse, open, and welcoming community.

Murals have also functioned to support other forms of diversity within nationalist and republican areas of Northern Ireland. Anti-racism has been a common trope, based on the 1916 Proclamation's promise to "cherish all

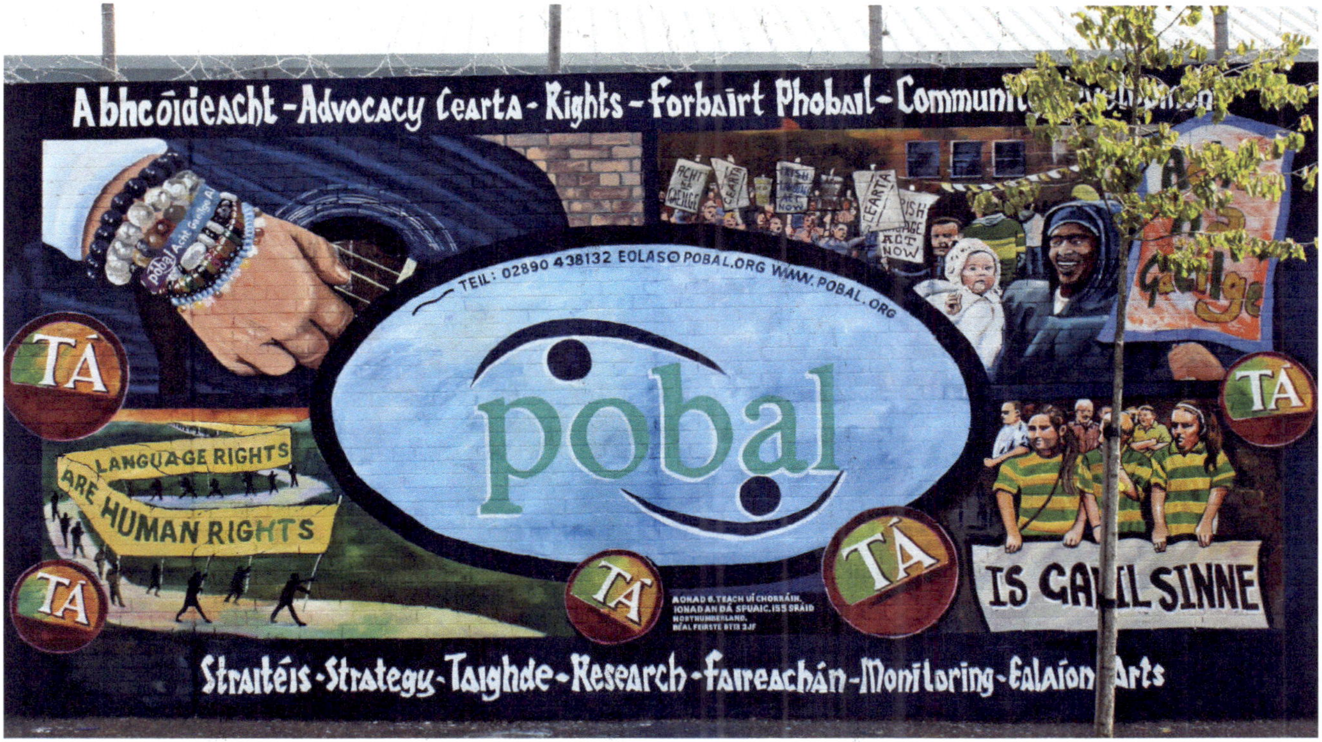

FIGURE 125 Pobal, International Wall, Northumberland Street, Lower Falls, West Belfast, 2012. Photo by Tony Crowley.

the children of the nation equally"—including "our Muslim brothers and sisters" (Figure 130, see Fulcrum). The focus has been wide-ranging—from anti-Irish and anti-Black racism in Britain in the mid-twentieth century (Figure 131, see Fulcrum), to anti-Roma and anti-Traveler sentiment (Figure 132), to the Black Lives Matter movement (Figure 133, see Fulcrum) and a complex and ambitious mural celebrating Black history—from Frederick Douglass to Angela Davis (Figure 134). In addition, the ongoing "refugee crisis" provoked a number of sympathetic murals (Figure 135, see Fulcrum), one of which drew a parallel between the Famine fugitives and contemporary refugees (Figure 136, see Fulcrum), while another pointed to the relation between the violence of Western capitalism and imperialism and the large numbers of people fleeing for their lives from Syria, Iraq, Aghanistan, and Libya (Figure 137).

In light of the number and range of murals in nationalist and republican areas, there was one mode of diversity that was only weakly represented: gender and sexuality. This is not to say that women did not feature on the walls, but when they did appear, it was, as indicated in section 3 above, primarily with regard to their roles as

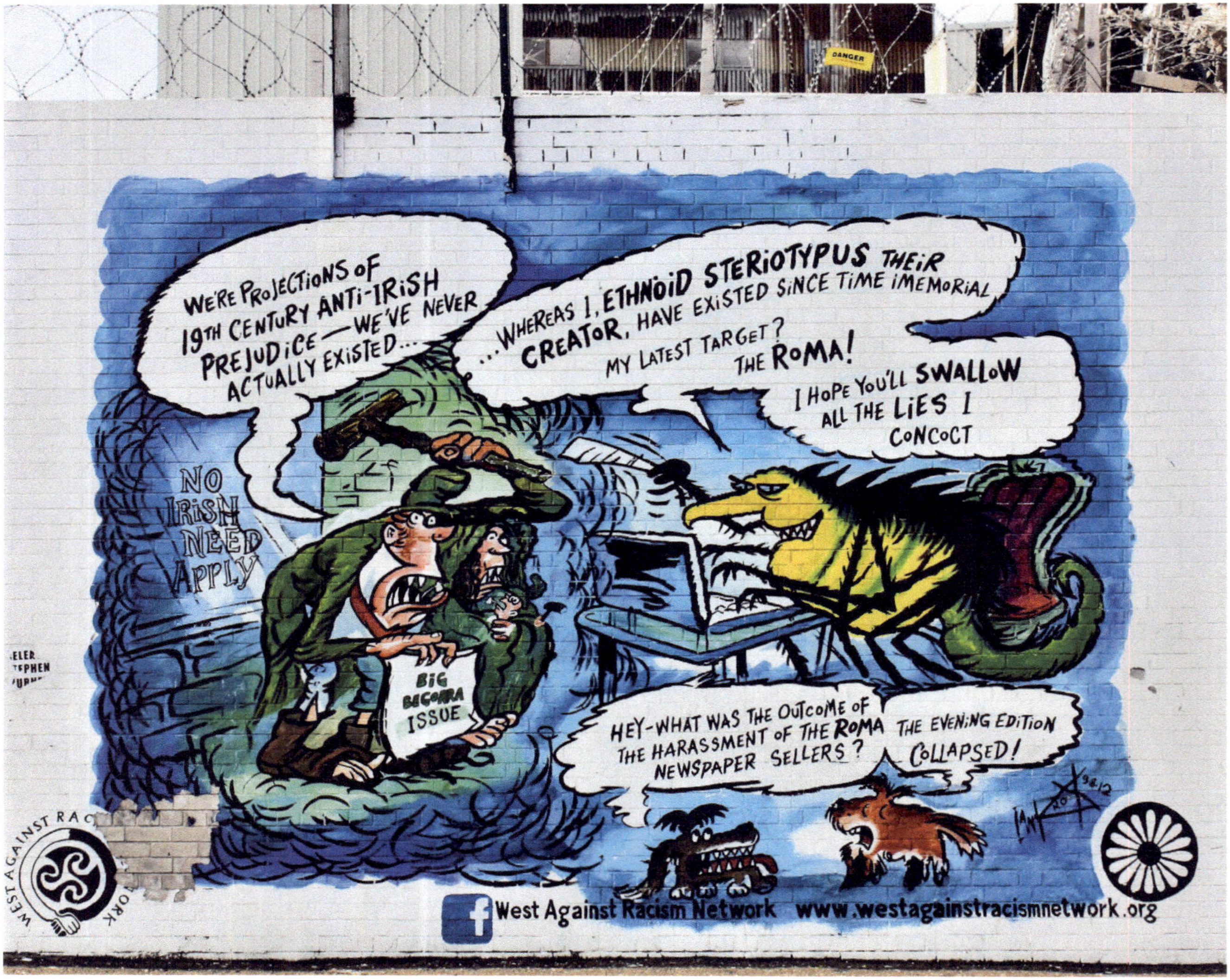

FIGURE 132 Ethnoid Steriotypus, International Wall, Divis Street, West Belfast, 2012. Photo by Tony Crowley.

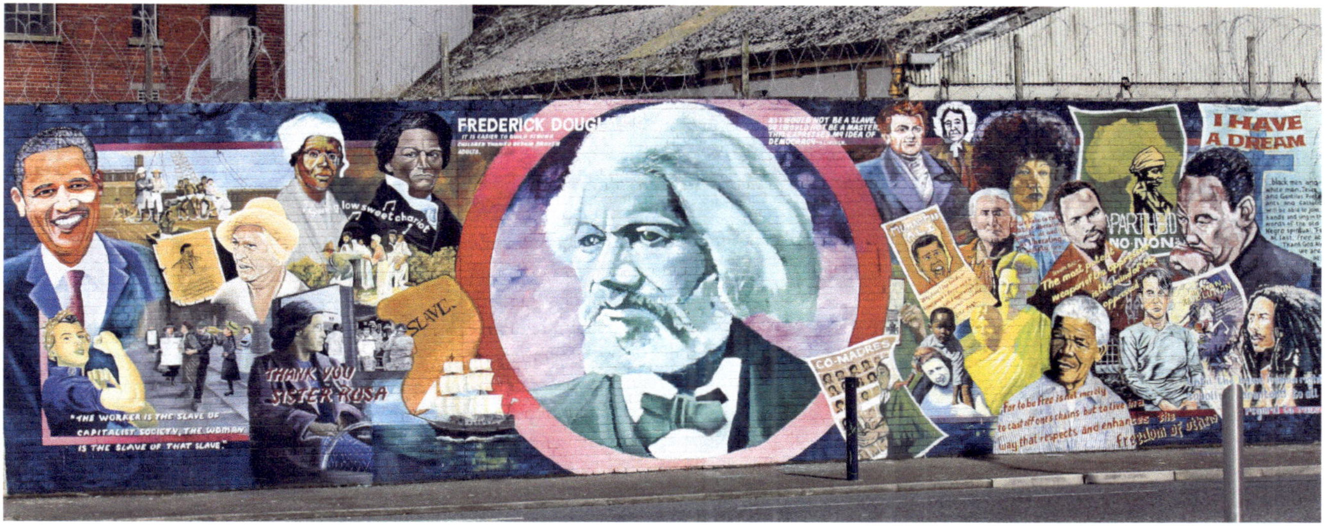

FIGURE 134 Black history, International Wall, Northumberland Street, West Belfast, 2020. Photo by Tony Crowley.

active republicans. There were in fact relatively few representations of women in non-republican roles. A mural in St James's, West Belfast, depicted "women of inspiration" such as Marie Curie and Rosa Parks (though the inclusion of IRA volunteer Mairéad Farrell alongside Mother Theresa raised a few eyebrows) (Figure 138, see Fulcrum). Women and children featured in murals at the Maureen Sheehan Health Centre in Divis, West Belfast, and at the Footprints Centre in Poleglass, outer West Belfast (dedicated to eradicating "the inequalities that impact upon the lives of women and children" (Figure 139, see Fulcrum). An image in the Markets, South Belfast, contrasted the traditional roles imposed on women in 1904 with the educated woman of 2004 (Figure 140, see Fulcrum), while an avowedly feminist image in the Bogside, Derry, declared that "Derry Women made more than shirts they made Communities" (a reference to the traditional employment of women in the city's shirt factories) and included a poster in favour of same-sex marriage (Figure 141). Derry also featured a number of murals celebrating International Women's Day—"100 years of struggle," "From petrol bombs to yarn bombs" (Figure 142, see Fulcrum). And a mural on the Peace Line interface at North Howard Street, Belfast, featured a demand for "Abortion rights now" (it was defaced almost as soon as it went up) (Figure 143, see Fulcrum). But these were the exceptions: in general, the men who dominated the mural scene were not painting women (with the caveats given above), and sisters were not doing it for themselves. As for sexuality, or at least non-hetero-normative sexuality, it was hardly mentioned at all. The shootings at a gay bar in Orlando, Florida, in 2016 prompted a number of supportive murals, including one on the International Wall next to an image of Connolly and the *Proclamation* (though it was unfortunately

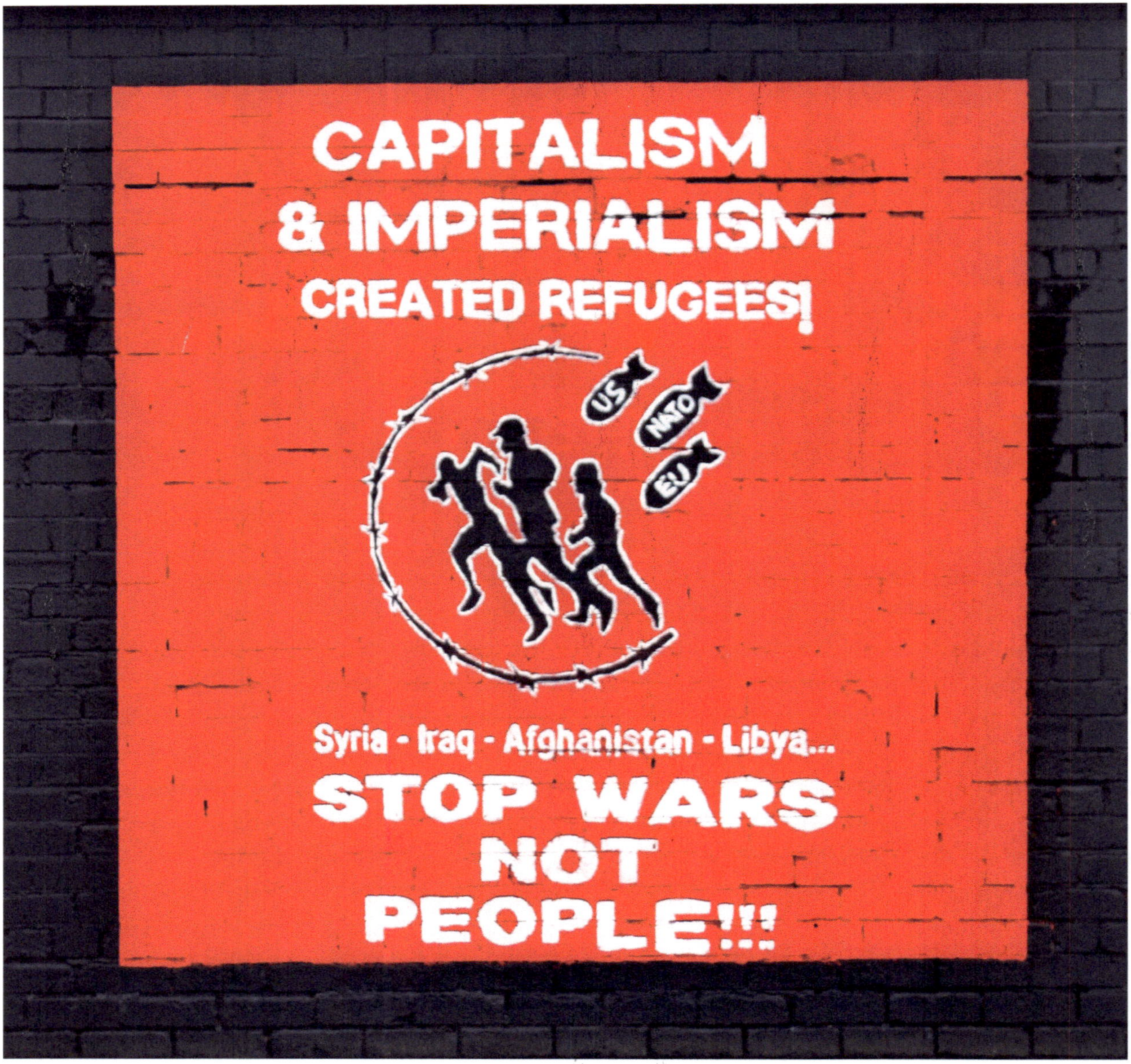

FIGURE 137 Stop wars not people, Beechmount Avenue, Beechmount, West Belfast, 2017. Photo by Tony Crowley.

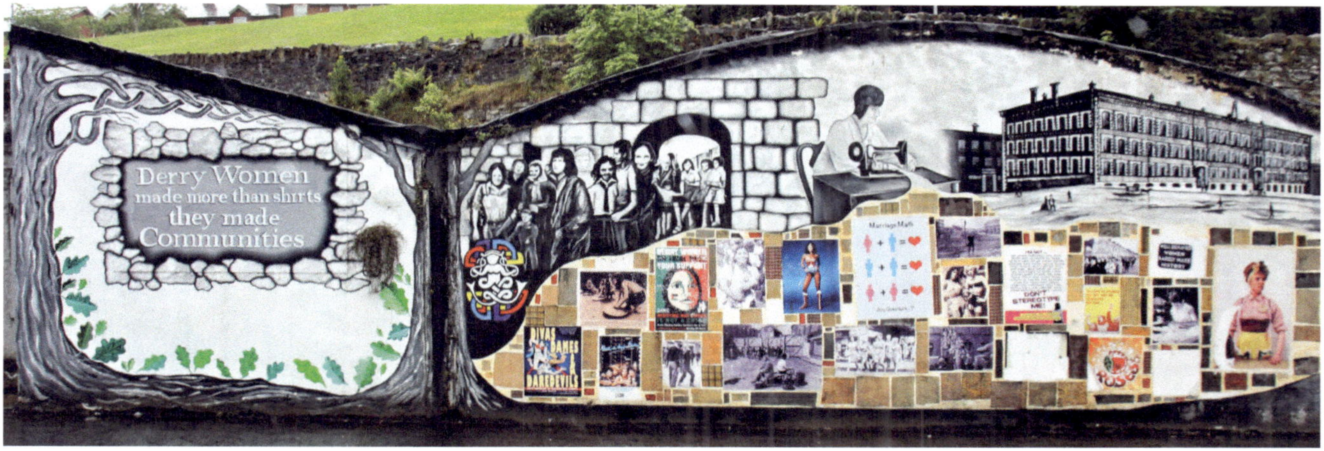

FIGURE 141 Derry women, Lecky Road, Brandywell, Derry, 2014. Photo by Tony Crowley.

sited below an advertisement for "paranormal tours" at "Belfast's infamous prison"—Crumlin Road gaol is now a tourist attraction) (Figure 144, see Fulcrum). But apart from that, there was very little attention paid on the walls to sexuality, despite the fact that social attitudes in this regard, particularly among the young, have shifted significantly in recent times. In this specific area then, despite its socially radical values and affiliations, republican muralism (which is not to say individual muralists) remained somewhat traditional in its stance.

7. COMMUNITY MURALS

The use of the category "community murals" is problematic because it suggests by implicit contrast that republican (and indeed loyalist) murals are not of and in their respective communities, but this is clearly not the case. Republican and loyalist muralists have typically been working-class men, rooted and living in their communities. Their murals undoubtedly often reflect the concerns and interests of political parties or paramilitary organizations, but while the images may be hegemonic—in attempting to direct or lead—it cannot be said that they are not linked to community concerns (which is not to say that the murals simply reflect those concerns, nor is it to claim that all members of a particular community agree with a mural or murals). Nevertheless, "community murals" makes sense as a category in that it refers to images that address specific problems or interests within a community, which may not have anything to do with the Troubles, the sectarian division in Northern Ireland, or the legacies of the past. Such murals were visible in republican and loyalist areas throughout the war, but it is unsurprising that their number increased significantly after the end of the violence. After all, from the beginning of muralism in Northern Ireland, painted walls had served as a model of relatively cheap, publicly visible, long-lasting, and easily renewable form of communication. In other words, murals had been made available as a genre for use by almost anyone who had the means and will to convert a blank wall into a message board.

The benefits of murals as a comparatively inexpensive medium of communication were all too clear to community groups, social activists, and local residents in working-class areas across Northern Ireland. Needless to say, the content and functions of these murals varied considerably. They were used to advertise services, to raise consciousness, to deter, to appeal, and to cajole. And they played a particular role in highlighting social problems that plagued working-class areas in particular, such as knife crime, alcohol and drug abuse, joy-riding, mental health issues, debt, and suicide (Figure 145, see Fulcrum) (Figure 146, see Fulcrum). It would be wrong, however, to think that the walls were simply sites of misery and suffering. Rather, local communities and institutions also used the walls to present positive messages, such as Yeats's maxim about education on St Patrick's College, North Belfast—"not the filling of a pail but the lighting of a fire" (Figure 147, see Fulcrum) or the advice "To find yourself, think for yourself," inscribed opposite Holy Cross Boys' Primary School in Ardoyne (together with images of Socrates, Plato, Aristotle, and J.S. Mill) (Figure 148, see Fulcrum). Murals also depicted local characters such as the legendary "Don Patricio" (Patrick O'Connell, who played for Belfast Celtic and managed Barcelona during the Spanish Civil War) (Figure 149, see Fulcrum) or the poet Patrick Fiacc, native of the Markets area in South Belfast (Figure 150, see Fulcrum). Other images, in a development that occurred across working-class communities, represented local history. In a series of six murals, for example, the Markets area was represented in a series of photographic collages (Figure 151, see Fulcrum) (and see **note 17**), while the same technique was used to depict the history of Springhill, Ballymurphy (Figure 152).[25] Local communities also used murals to express social solidarity such as support for the NHS during the Covid-19 pandemic (Figure 153, see Fulcrum) and the commemoration of Noah Donohoe, a teenage boy whose disappearance and death remains an unresolved mystery (both topics were the subject of murals in republican and loyalist communities) (Figure 154, see Fulcrum). Some murals celebrated local communities for their persistence, their success against the odds, and their resilience; a typical example was the toponymic image in Celtic design in Meenan Square, Derry, which simply and confidently announced "Bogside."

Though they have developed in any number of ways since the early 1980s, there is a sense in which it can be argued that murals in republican and nationalist areas have remained relatively constant. For then, as now, the walls were the canvas on which local people and organizations represented their issues, expressed their concerns, vented their anger, showed their confidence, demonstrated an understanding of their historical situation, and articulated their desires and goals. What changed, of course, was the material fact that at the inception of modern republican muralism, the dominant issue was the war—the fact of British troops on the ground and the IRA's struggle against them. In the beginning therefore, most of the murals were concerned with that historical

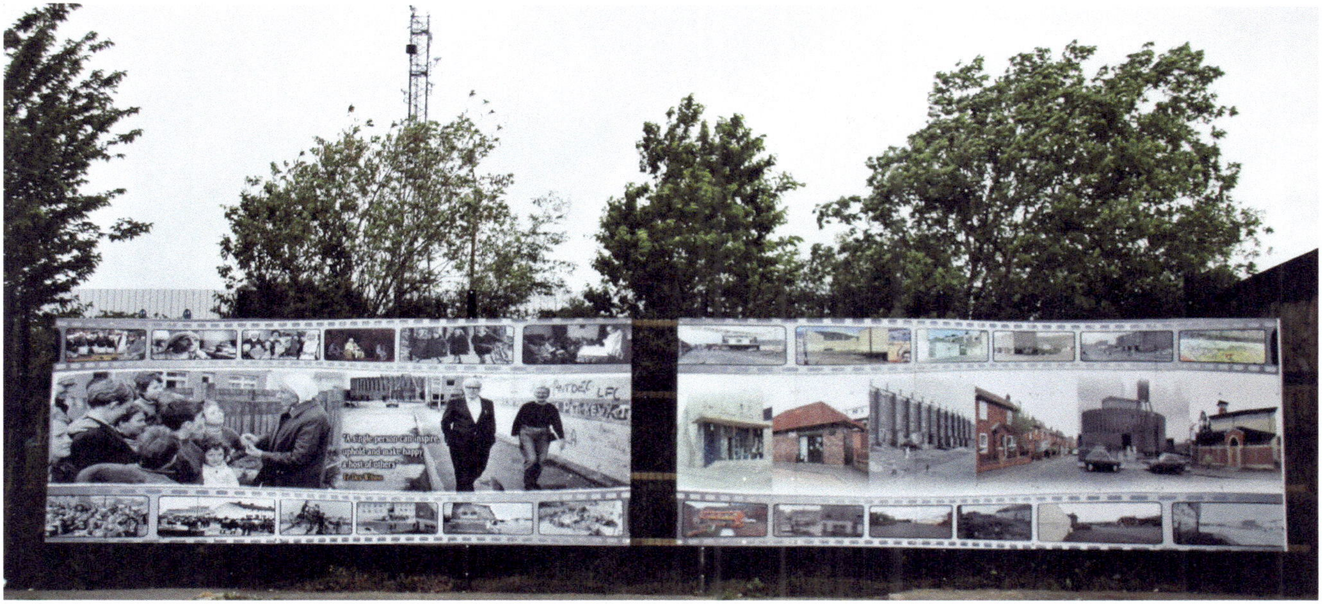

FIGURE 152 Springhill, Springhill Avenue, Ballymurphy, West Belfast, 2019. Photo by Tony Crowley.

problem. As circumstances changed, through the Peace Process and the settlement that it brought about, the murals (or at least the mainstream republican murals) shifted too. And as the conditions shifted again, the murals also adapted: some focused on the past, some were concerned with the ongoing questions of Partition and sectarianism, others turned to international issues, and an increasing number addressed the everyday questions that had remained the same throughout the war and the post-war periods: the injustice and inequality brought about by dispossession and poverty. In differing contexts, then, nationalist and republican murals continued to function as the medium through which history was reflected and refracted.

CHAPTER 7

The Problem of Change: Settlement, Uncertainty, and Fragmentation: Loyalist Murals 2007–2024

To access all images referenced in this chapter, please visit the open access version on Fulcrum at https://doi.org/10.3998/mpub.14527058.

> The prevention of the erosion of our identity is now our priority. (Loyalist mural, Movilla Road, Newtownards, 2022, Figure 1, see Fulcrum)

1. WINNING AND LOSING

The *Government of Ireland Act* passed through the British parliament in December 1920 and came into force in May 1921; the partition of Ireland that it enacted effectively created Northern Ireland as a State with a built-in unionist majority. *The Belfast Agreement* of 1998 copper-fastened the Union and established as a constitutional guarantee the right of the majority to maintain (or change) the status of Northern Ireland. Given these two historical facts, it might be thought that when the centenary of the formation of Northern Ireland took place in 2021 (following hard on the centennial commemoration of events such as the formation of the UVF and the Battle of the Somme), unionists and loyalists would celebrate with confidence and certainty. The reality was more complicated. There was a determination to remember and acclaim the past (Figure 2, see Fulcrum), and yet the prevailing sentiment among unionists and loyalists, particularly in the latter half of the decade of centenaries, was not happy remembrance but anxious resentment about the present and future role of Northern Ireland within the United Kingdom. There were a number of reasons for this, the most important of which arose from the Brexit debacle.

Following the Brexit referendum in 2016 (in which 56% of voters in Northern Ireland voted to remain), the British government decided to leave not just the EU but also the European Customs Union and the European Single Market.[1] This produced a problem, in that the Northern Ireland/Ireland border thereby became a customs and regulatory border between the EU and the UK. In order to avoid the difficulties that the creation of a hard border "on the island of Ireland" would entail, Theresa May's government proposed an "Irish backstop," which effectively meant that the UK, including Northern Ireland, would continue to have a common customs territory with the EU. Tory Brexiteer MPs, aided and abetted by their unionist counterparts in the DUP, voted this down, which led to the resignation of May and the election of Boris Johnson as Prime Minister. Despite explicitly promising the DUP party conference that there would be no border in the Irish sea, Johnson's government agreed the Northern Ireland Protocol (to the Brexit Withdrawal Agreement). Under the Protocol, the UK left the EU Customs Union, but Northern Ireland remained subject to EU Single Market regulations on goods. The hard border with the Irish Republic was thus avoided, but because Northern Ireland was an entry point into the Customs Union area, this meant that in effect there was a border in the Irish sea, in addition to which, disputes relating to a number of the Protocol regulations fell under the purview of the European Court (rather than the British legal system). For unionists the Protocol thus had clear constitutional implications; put simply, Northern Ireland was to be treated differently from the rest of the UK in terms of trade and law. Though the Protocol is subject to democratic review (in January 2025 the Protocol can be renewed or rejected by a majority vote in the Stormont Assembly), unionists and loyalists fiercely rejected its provisions. Street posters by the "East Belfast coalition" recorded the dominant anger: "Restore our place in the United Kingdom No EU law No EU court No EU checks End the Irish Sea border Nothing else will do" (Figure 3, see Fulcrum).[2] And an emphatic UVF mural, featuring two paramilitaries armed with automatic rifles, sent a clear message regarding the treachery of the government: "In war you can only be killed once. In politics, many times. Our British identity is non-negotiable!" (Figure 4).

It is worth re-stating that in none of the agreements that were introduced to try to make a success of the constitutional arrangements of *The Good Friday Agreement* (the *Saint Andrews Agreement*, 2006, the *Stormont House Agreement*, 2014, and *New Decade, New Approach*, 2020) was the future of Northern Ireland within the Union at stake or even discussed. And yet for unionists and loyalists, the Protocol was the culmination of a series of political and cultural setbacks that induced anxiety and resentment. Prominent among the issues that caused difficulties were the questions of symbolic recognition and the related question of the right to march. With regard to culture, the Flags Dispute of 2013 focused unionist and loyalist attention on what they considered to be the gradual erosion of the right to symbolize their identity—"They may have stole our banner But they will never steal our culture" (Figure 5, see Fulcrum).[3] This was exacerbated by attempts to curtail the building of bonfires to celebrate the 12th July (a bonfire in 2022 reached 202 feet in height; see **chapter one, fig. 2**), which was taken as "cultural oppression" and resisted with threats (Figure 6, see Fulcrum). Yet, as noted in earlier chapters, it was the refusal of the right to parade identity by marching wherever and whenever that provoked the most sustained protests. The most notable instance was the dispute that centered on a Parades Commission determination in July 2013 not to permit the return leg of the Ligoniel Orange parade to pass the Ardoyne shops on the Crumlin Road in North Belfast (behind which lies nationalist and republican Ardoyne). In response, a loyalist "civil rights" camp was set up at Twaddell Avenue, which lasted from July 2013 until October 2016 (Figure 7, see Fulcrum). With regard to cultural issues, a mural in Pitt Park, East Belfast, proclaimed in 2016 that "Culture threatens no one" (Figure 8). This wasn't quite consonant with loyalist opposition to an Irish language act, but in truth, as the Twaddell dispute demonstrated, in Northern Ireland symbolic capital is often scarcely distinguishable from

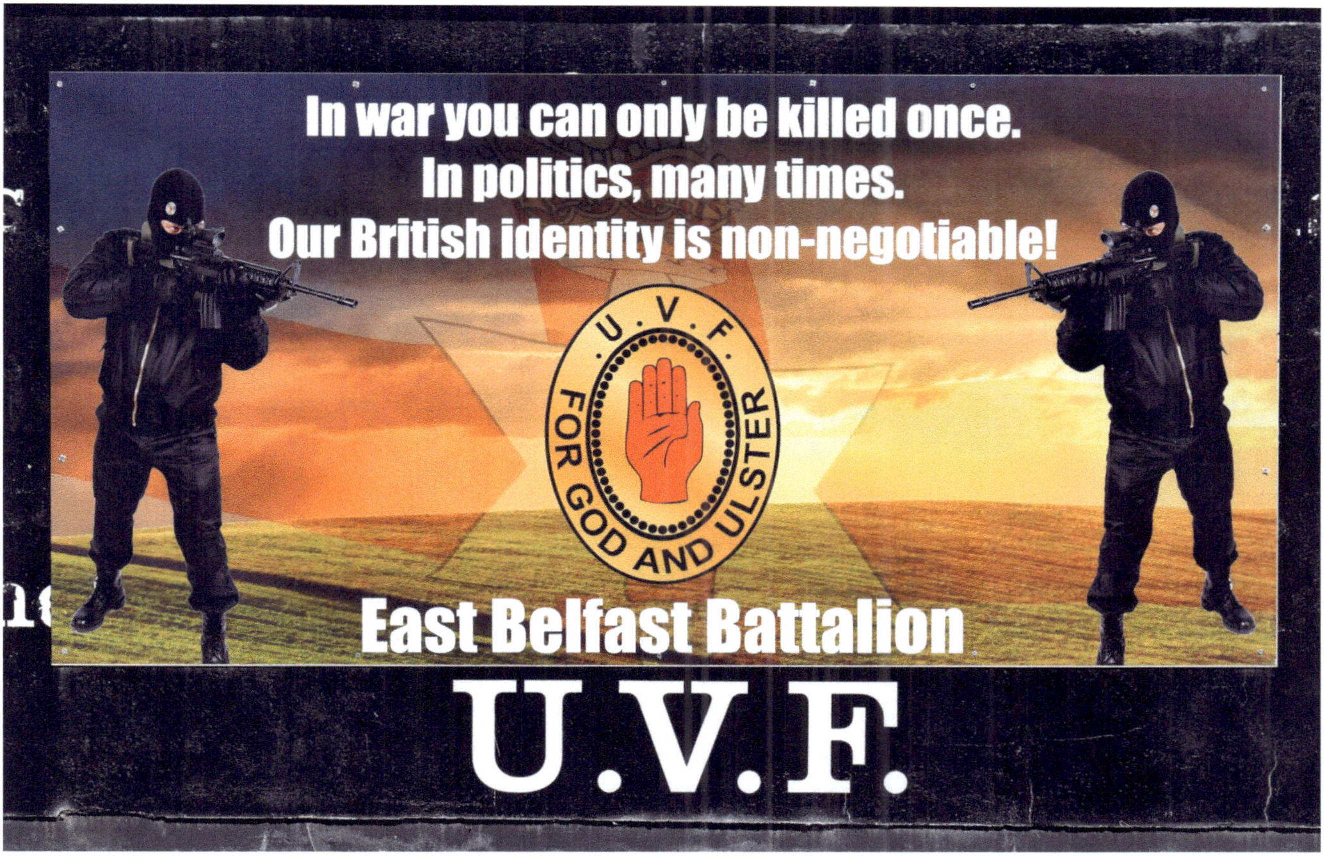

FIGURE 4 Non-negotiable, Carlingford Street, Willowfield, East Belfast, 2022. Photo by Tony Crowley.

political capital. As has been the case since the inception of the State, culture remains a realm in which fundamental issues of identity and belonging are played out and contested.

Unionist and loyalist unease had other causes too. As outlined in the previous chapter, 2007 saw mainstream republicanism accept the PSNI and enter into a power-sharing executive headed by its erstwhile sworn enemy, the Reverend Ian Paisley, the DUP leader. But thereafter the onward match of Sinn Féin continued unchecked. By 2022, Sinn Féin was the largest political party in both Dáil Éireann and, more significantly for its opponents, the Stormont Assembly. Under new (post-war) leadership, the republican movement potentially occupied a role that could not have been imagined in 2007 (the collapse of Stormont prevented Sinn Féin's Michelle O'Neill from taking the position until February 2024). Confident, supported by demographic change, and the beneficiary of the ever more bizarre behavior of the Tory government, Sinn Féin were able to argue for a border poll from a position

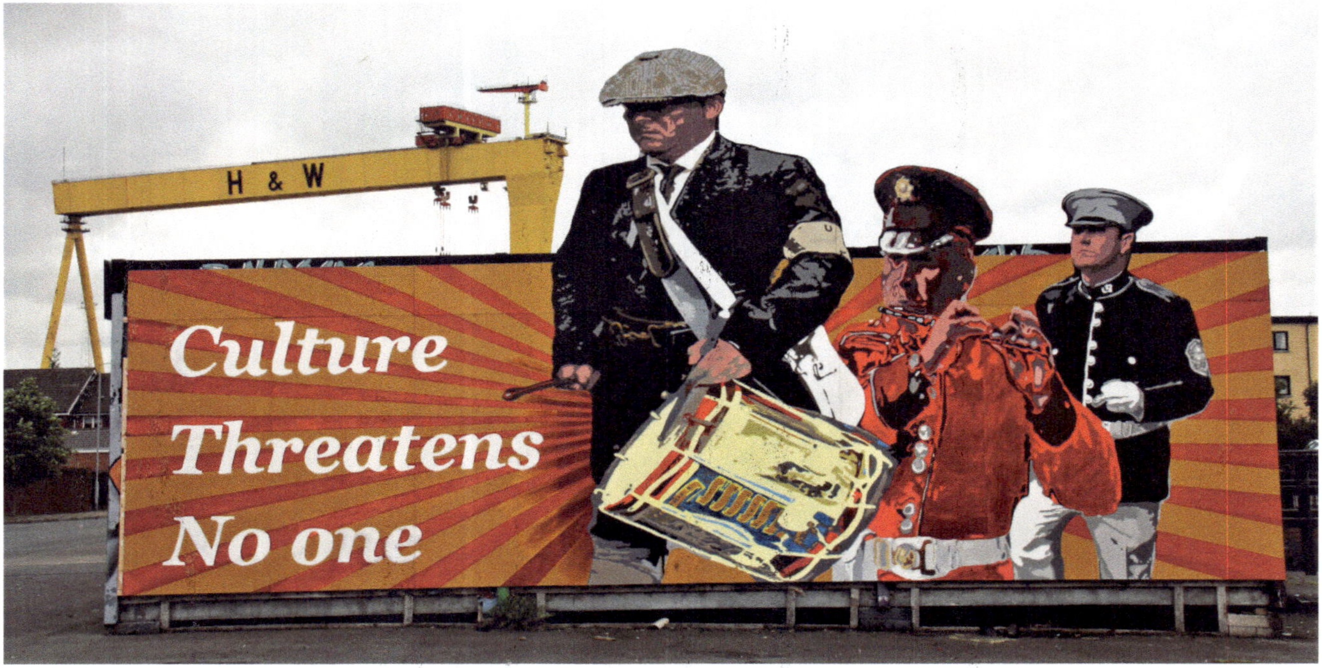

FIGURE 8 Culture threatens no one, Pitt Park, Newtownards Road, East Belfast, 2016. Photo by Tony Crowley.

of strength. Unionists and loyalists, by contrast, found themselves mired in a protracted and bitter dispute with the government at Westminster over the Protocol. In addition to which, the Queen, the embodiment of the Crown to which loyalty was professed, died on September 8 2022, an occasion that prompted an outpouring of adulation, devotion, and respect (Figure 9) (Figure 10, see Fulcrum) (Figure 11, see Fulcrum) (Figure 12, see Fulcrum) (Figure 13, see Fulcrum). The depth of the response also indicated a preoccupation with the future (a sentiment not shared by at least some republicans—within a few hours of the Queen's death, "Fuck the King" had appeared in the Brandywell in Derry) (Figure 14, see Fulcrum). Given the incertitude of the times, it is unsurprising that some elements of loyalism resorted to tropes that had first appeared during the Home Rule Crisis. As in the early twentieth century, the promise was made: "We will not be the generation to fail Ulster" (Figure 15). In Markethill, County Armagh, the argument was put simply: "The Northern Irish man and woman are born free and equal in dignity and rights to their English, Scottish and Welsh brothers and sisters" (Figure 16, see Fulcrum). Given the perceived infringement of that status by the Protocol, the message in the loyalist stronghold of Moygashel, and indeed across Northern Ireland's loyalist areas, was stark: a mural that reproduced the cover of the explanatory document to the 1998 *Belfast Agreement*, declared that it was "null and void" (Figure 17, see Fulcrum).

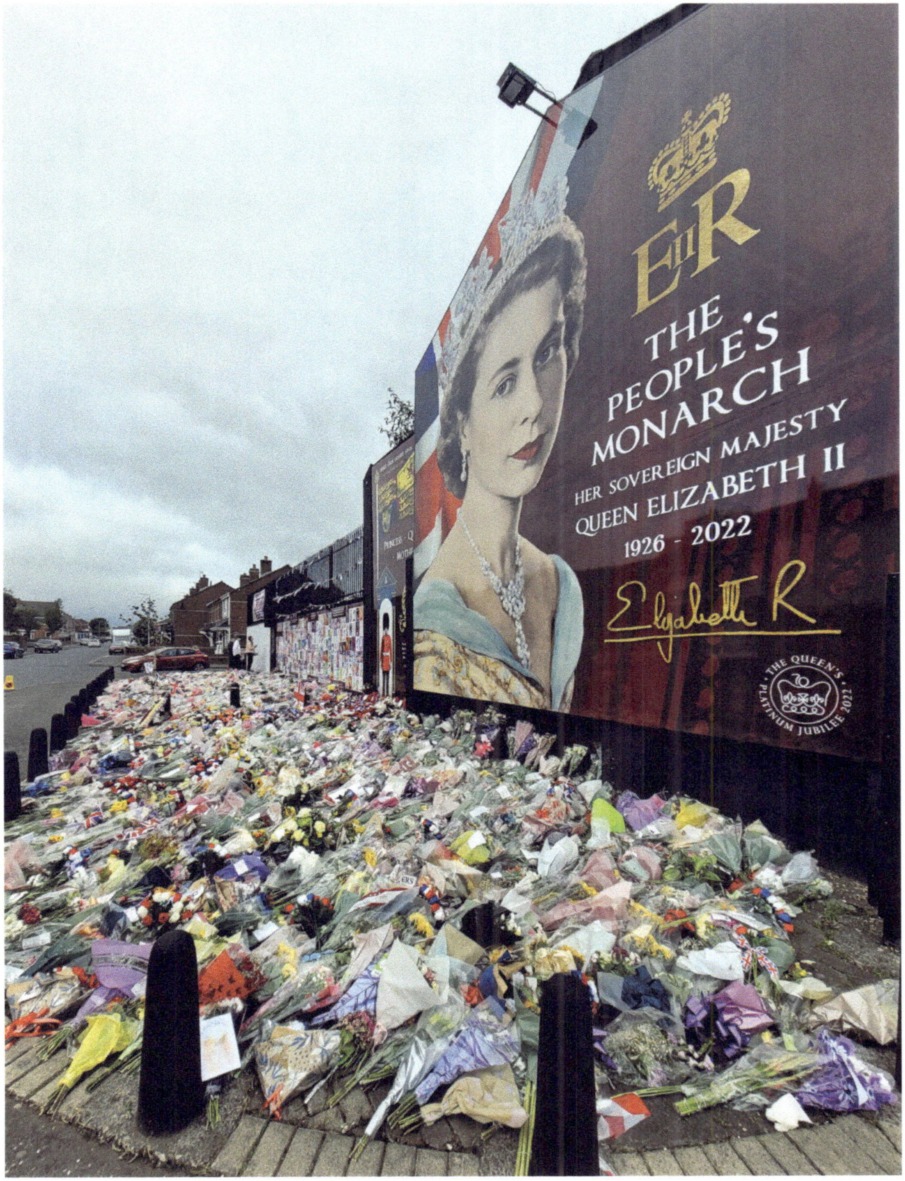

FIGURE 9 Her Sovereign Majesty, Crimea Street, Shankill, West Belfast, 2022. Photo by Tony Crowley.

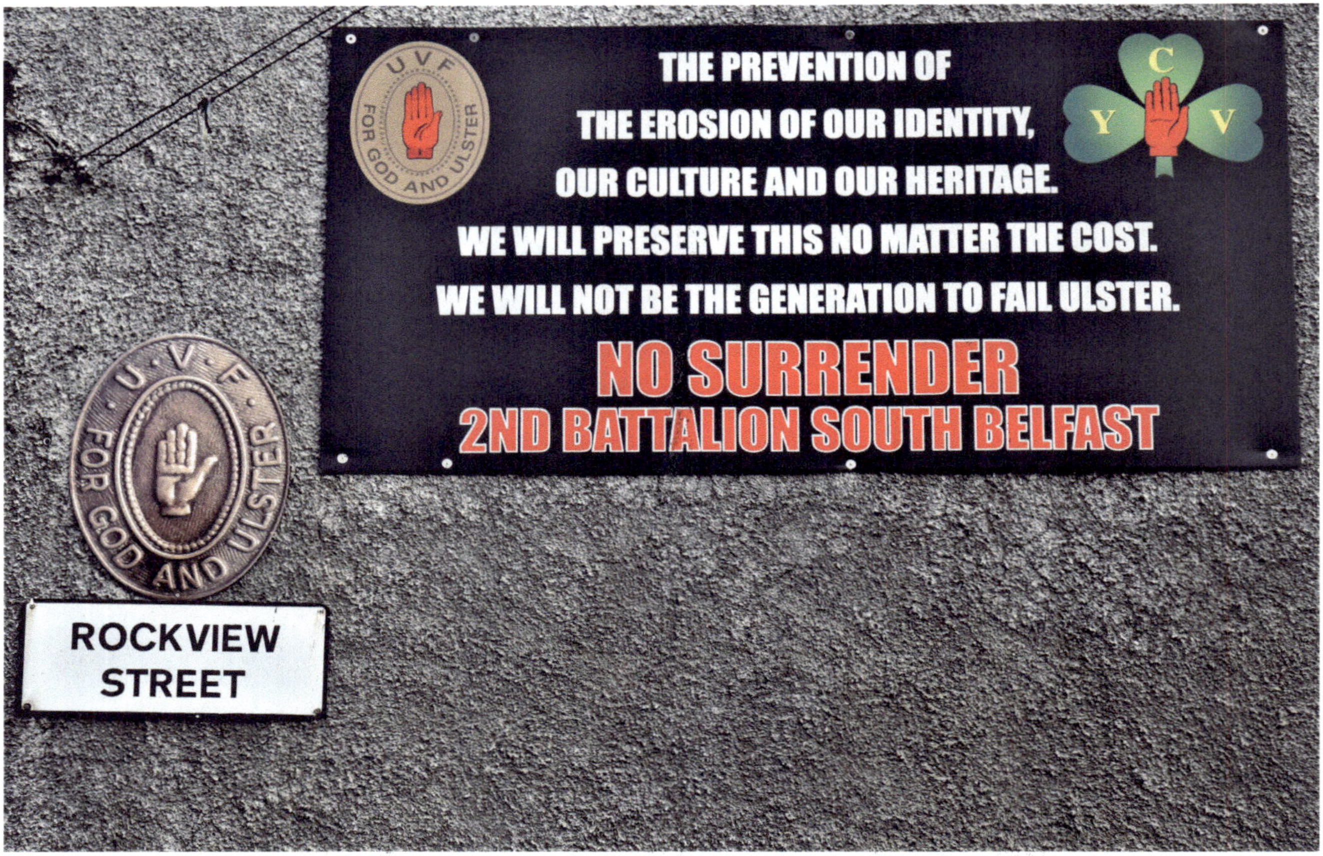

FIGURE 15 Not the generation to fail Ulster, Rockview Street, The Village, South Belfast, 2020. Photo by Tony Crowley.

2. RE-IMAGING LOYALIST MURALS

Unlike their republican counterparts, loyalists embraced the State's re-imaging program with enthusiasm, though there are two important caveats to this statement. First, as will be demonstrated later in the chapter, as well as re-imaging, there was a lot of new material that conformed to older conventions (particularly with regard to paramilitarism). And second, the involvement with State-sponsored re-imaging was largely, though not exclusively, confined to specific areas: the Lower Shankill, Tigers Bay, Sandy Row, and Lord Street—all in Belfast, and all dominated by the UDA.[4] The Lower Shankill was the primary re-imaging site, and there were good reasons for this, not least because, as discussed in chapter five, the Lower Shankill estate had been the location for a remarkable number of paramilitary murals commissioned by Johnny Adair's UDA C Company during loyalist feuding in the early

2000s. Following Adair's expulsion in 2003, and the re-imposition of the control of the central UDA leadership, the Shankill estate thus became a prime candidate for re-imaging as a way of signaling political change, including a clear commitment to the Peace Process. And from 2008 on, a number of murals were replaced with a variety of images (usually commissioned as a result of consultation between the local community, artists, and the Lower Shankill Community Association). Early examples, which appear not to have been part of the organized program, included two cultural murals—the myth of the origin of the Red Hand and Cú Chulainn (which replaced a UFF image and a portrait of UFF killer Steven McKeag respectively) (Figure 18) (Figure 19). Neither mural was particularly well executed, but the Cú Chulainn image was significant for the message painted on the side scroll:

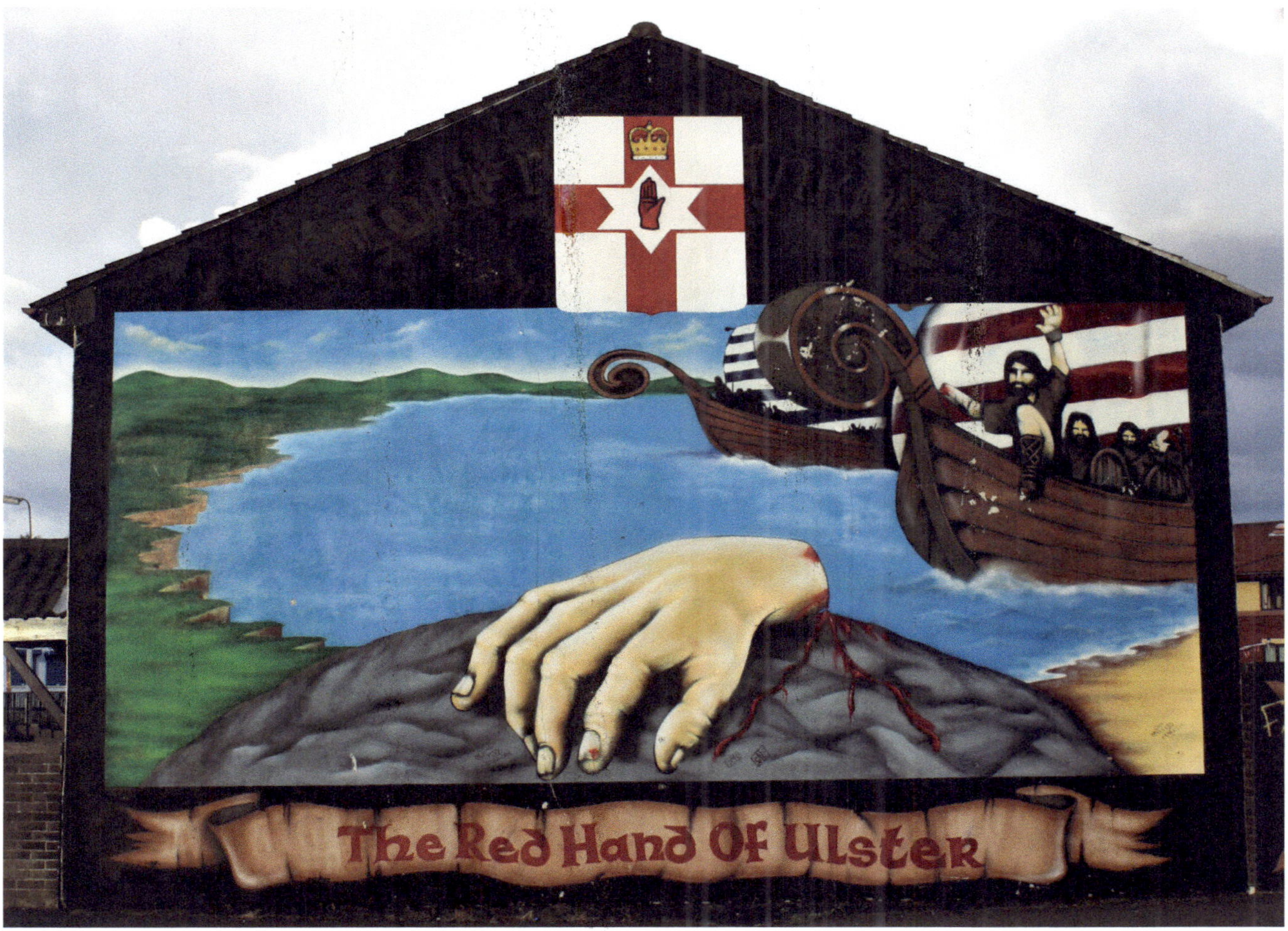

FIGURE 18 The Red Hand of Ulster, back Shankill Parade, Lower Shankill, West Belfast, 2008. Photo by Tony Crowley.

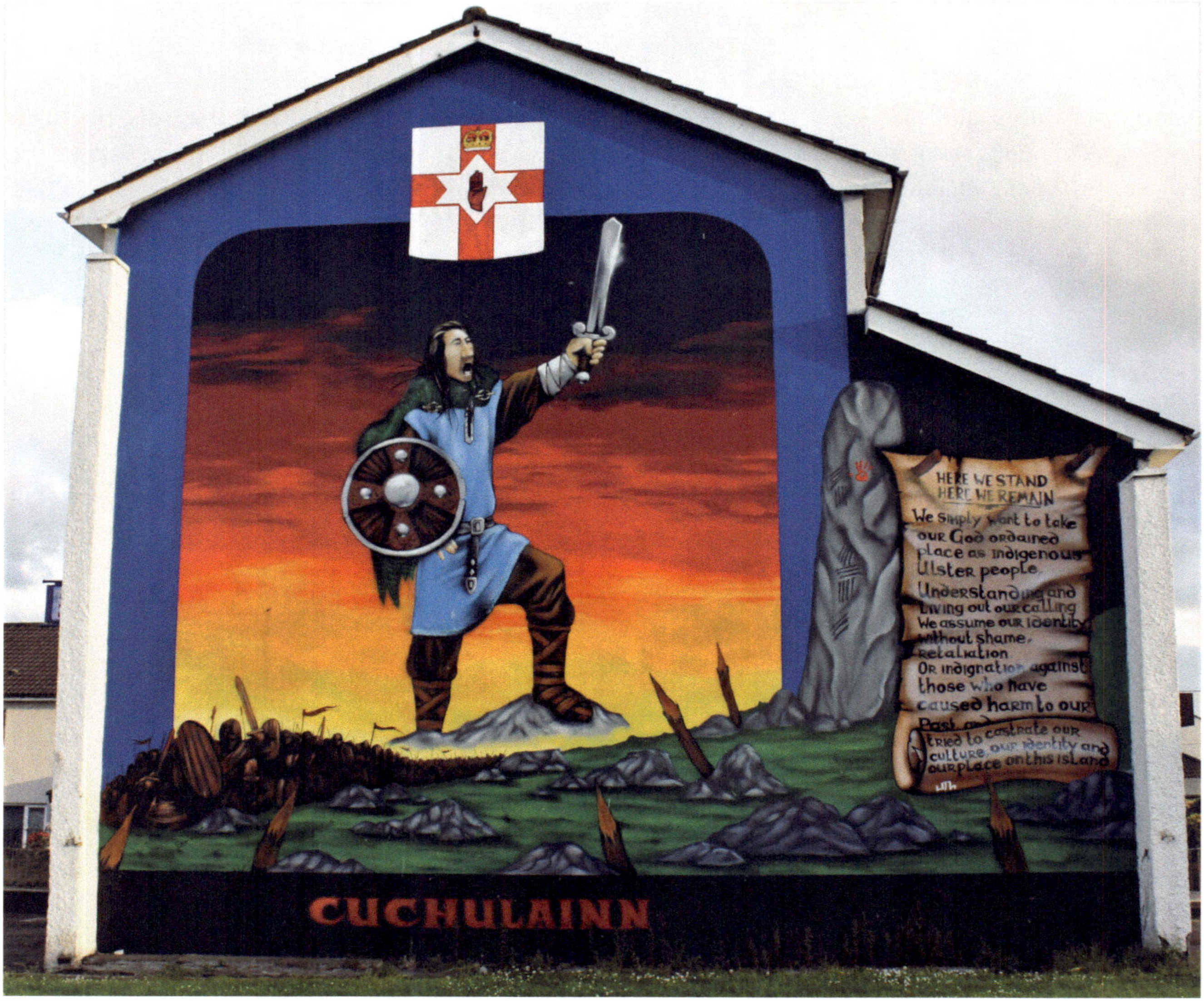

FIGURE 19 Cuchulainn, back Shankill Parade, Lower Shankill, West Belfast, 2008. Photo by Tony Crowley.

> Here we stand Here we remain We simply want to take our God ordained place as indigenous Ulster people. Understanding and living out our calling we assume our identity without shame, retaliation or indignation against those who have caused harm to our past and tried to castrate our culture, our identity, and our place on this island.

There are a number of striking features in this text: the claim to God-ordained indigeneity; the call to identity; the renouncing of threat against those who attempted emasculation; and the conflation of culture, identity, and place. In addition, "Here we stand" is a conscious echo of Martin Luther's cry "Hier stehe ich, Ich kann nich anders, Gott helfe mir" (Here I stand, I can do no other. God help me. Amen"), a phrase that formed part of one of the earliest official re-imaging murals in this area that featured Luther and the start of the Protestant Reformation.[5]

Across a number of years in the Lower Shankill estate, the re-imaging program commissioned various murals that explicitly sought not simply to replace paramilitary works, but also to draw attention to that fact through side panels that detailed the murals that had been removed. Among other themes, the new images—many of which were composed by the artist Lesley Cherry—depicted Human Rights ("Universal Human Rights") (Figure 20, see Fulcrum), local history ("Gold Rush") (Figure 21, see Fulcrum), sport ("Shankill Road Boxing") (Figure 22, see Fulcrum), inclusion ("Nothing about us without us is for us") (Figure 23, see Fulcrum), feminism ("The women's quilt") (Figure 24, see Fulcrum) and community politics ("Stop calling me resilient") (Figure 25, see Fulcrum) and "Never doubt" (Figure 26, see Fulcrum). They replaced, respectively, "UDA Scottish Brigade," "The Siege of Derry," "The persecution of the Protestant people," "The Malvern Arch," "Eddie," "Andrew Jackson," and "Ulster Scotland." Perhaps the best examples of the genre, with their accompanying explanatory panels, are "Shankill History A–Z," which displaced a Drumcree mural (Figure 27) (Figure 28, see Fulcrum) and "Remember Respect Resolution," which stood in for a mural that celebrated Cromwell (though in this case the mural was replaced by an abstract sculpture (Figure 29, see Fulcrum) (Figure 30, see Fulcrum).

Though focused on the Lower Shankill estate, the re-imaging scheme facilitated murals elsewhere in Belfast, as noted earlier. Thus the paramilitary tiger painted in 2000 at Cultra Street, Tigers Bay, in North Belfast (Figure 31), became a primary schoolchildren's tiger roaring for "community, pride and culture" (Figure 32). While in a striking example, the threatening paramilitary message at the entrance to Sandy Row—"You are now entering Loyalist Sandy Row" (a riff on the Bogside's "You are now entering Free Derry") (**chapter five, fig. 144**)—was transformed into an image of King Billy on the wall that stressed the multicultural nature of his forces ("Danish, English, Dutch, French Huguenots, Prussian, Scots, Irish, Swiss, Polish, Italian, Norwegian") (Figure 33). The accompanying plaque noted that replacement of the paramilitary mural "did not come easily to this community" and happened only after "long and detailed consultation." "The Loyalist community of Sandy Row is proud of its culture and heritage," it added, "and we believe that this new mural strengthens our identity

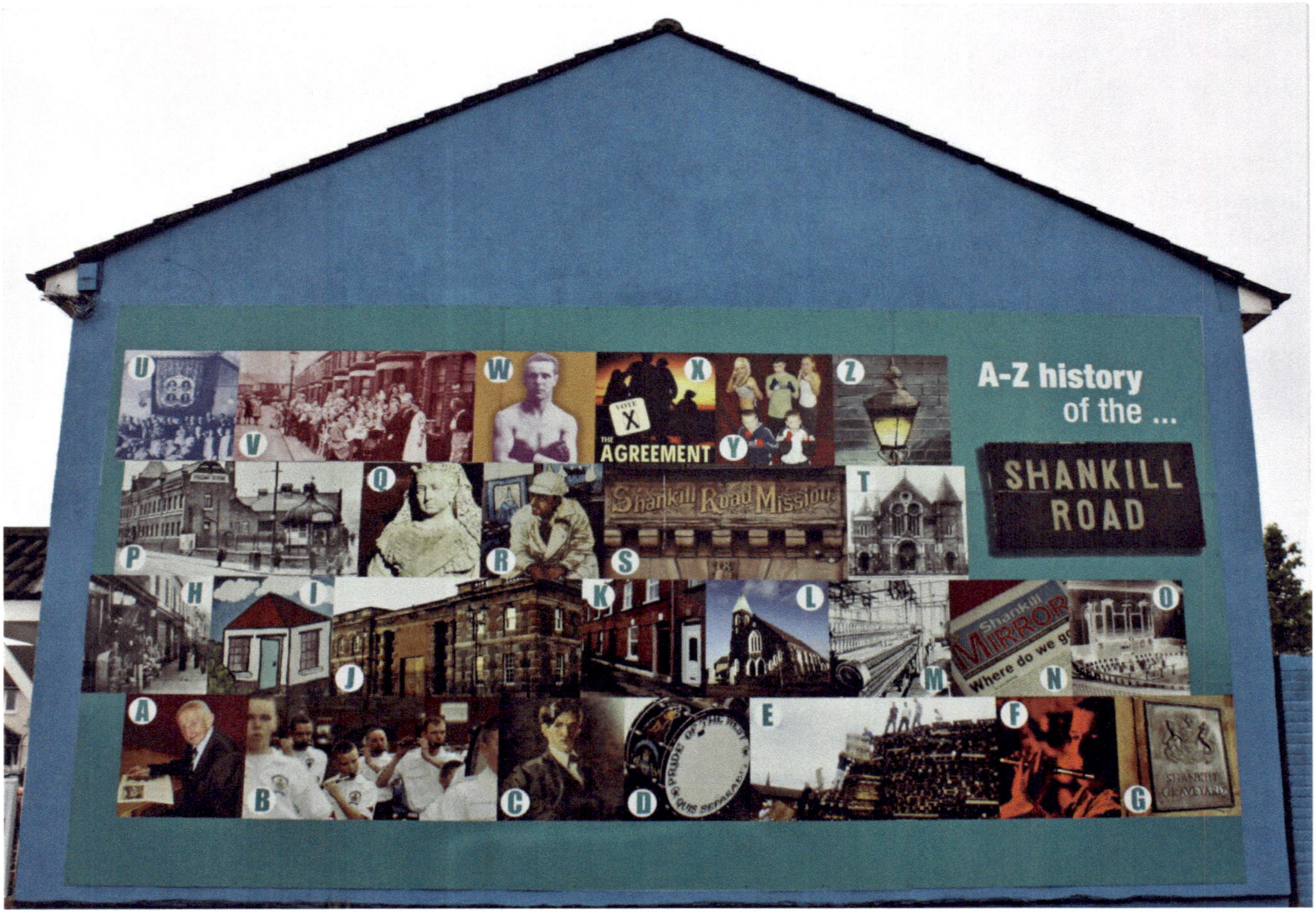

FIGURE 27 Shankill A–Z, North Boundary Street, Lower Shankill, West Belfast, 2009. Photo by Tony Crowley.

in a way that is shared, confident and open." In an interesting turn, a traditional image of King Billy was restored in The Village area of South Belfast, along with a plaque—"Streetscapes"—that gave a potted history of unionist/loyalist muralism since 1908 and described re-imaging as a process of eradicating "redundant sectarian imagery" in favor of "positive expressions of wider cultural celebration" (Figure 34). Other new images were not created as part of the formal re-imaging program, but they indicated a significant broadening within loyalist muralism. Murals depicting women appeared, for example, as in "Mother Daughter Sister" on Mervue Street in Tigers Bay (despite its figuration of women solely in terms of familial roles, the plaque beside the mural described it as "the

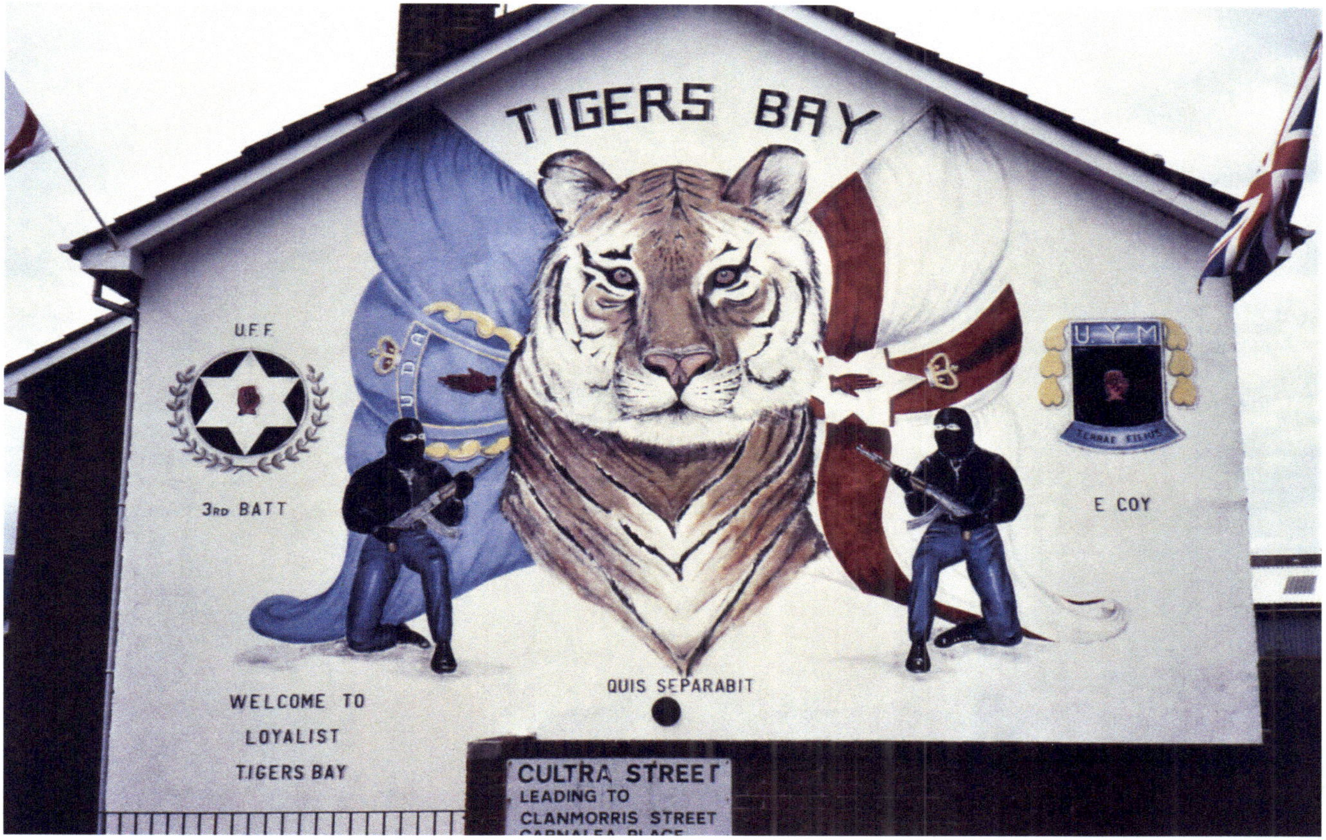

FIGURE 31 Paramilitary tiger, Cultra Street/North Queen Street, Belfast, 2000. Photo by Tony Crowley.

first of its kind to openly acknowledge the role of women within their community") (Figure 35, see Fulcrum).[6] "History girl," set against the Peace Line on Madrid Street, in East Belfast, featured the eponymous heroine alongside local images and quotes from working-class women recollecting their childhood (Figure 36, see Fulcrum). And women also appeared in a fascinating mural, again on Mervue Street, that addressed the period 1912–1918. As well as conventional references to First World War recruitment and the Battle of the Somme, the image highlighted the 1917 strike by Belfast shipyard workers for better terms and conditions, and, significantly, the entrance of women into the workforce during the war—as nurses, welders, and coal deliverers (Figure 37). Another mural, painted in Rathcoole in 2011 also depicted the crucial contribution of women to the war effort in its representation of a women munition worker: "On her their lives depend" (Figure 38, see Fulcrum).

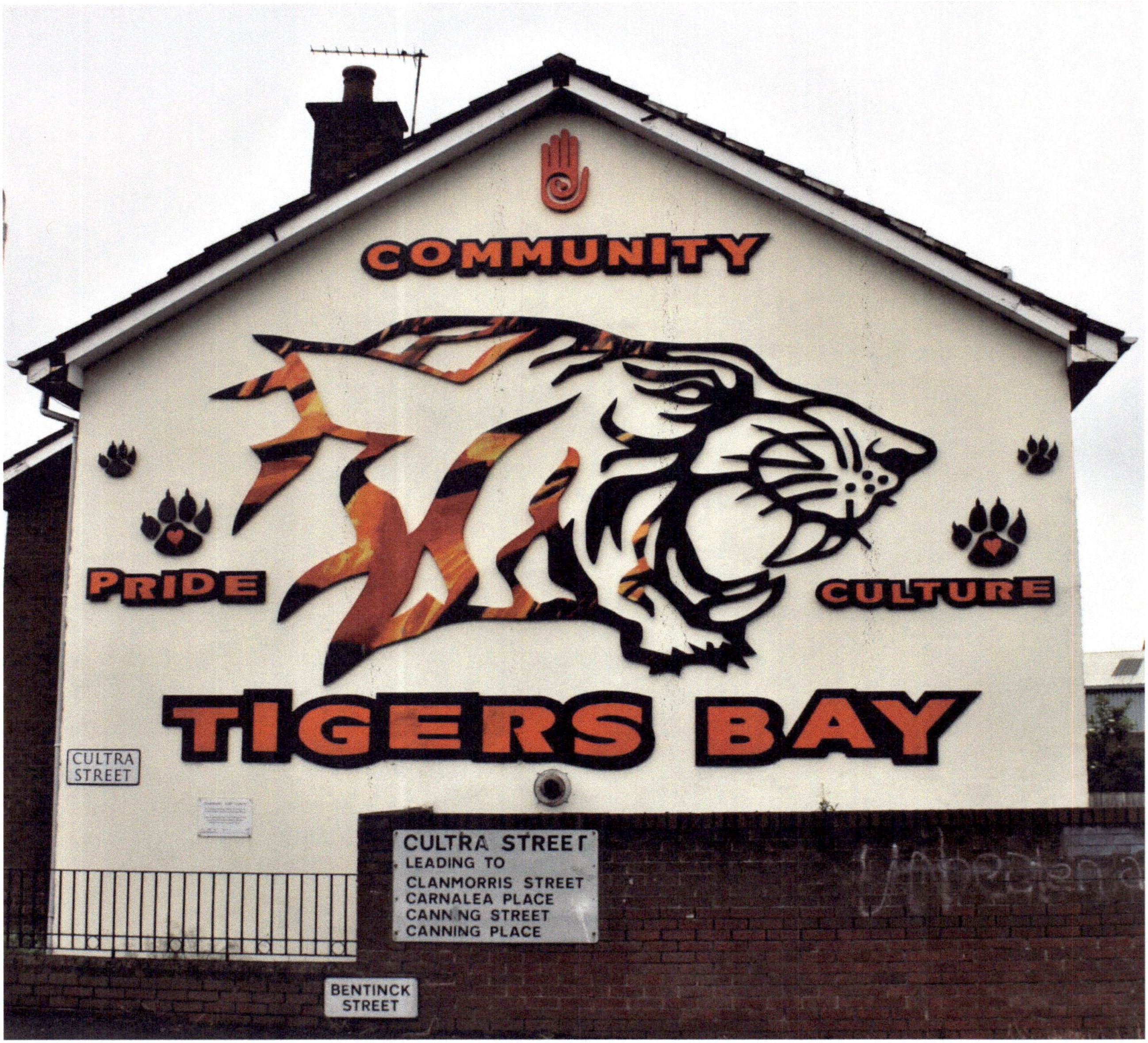

FIGURE 32 Community tiger, Cultra Street, Tigers Bay, North Belfast, 2009. Photo by Tony Crowley.

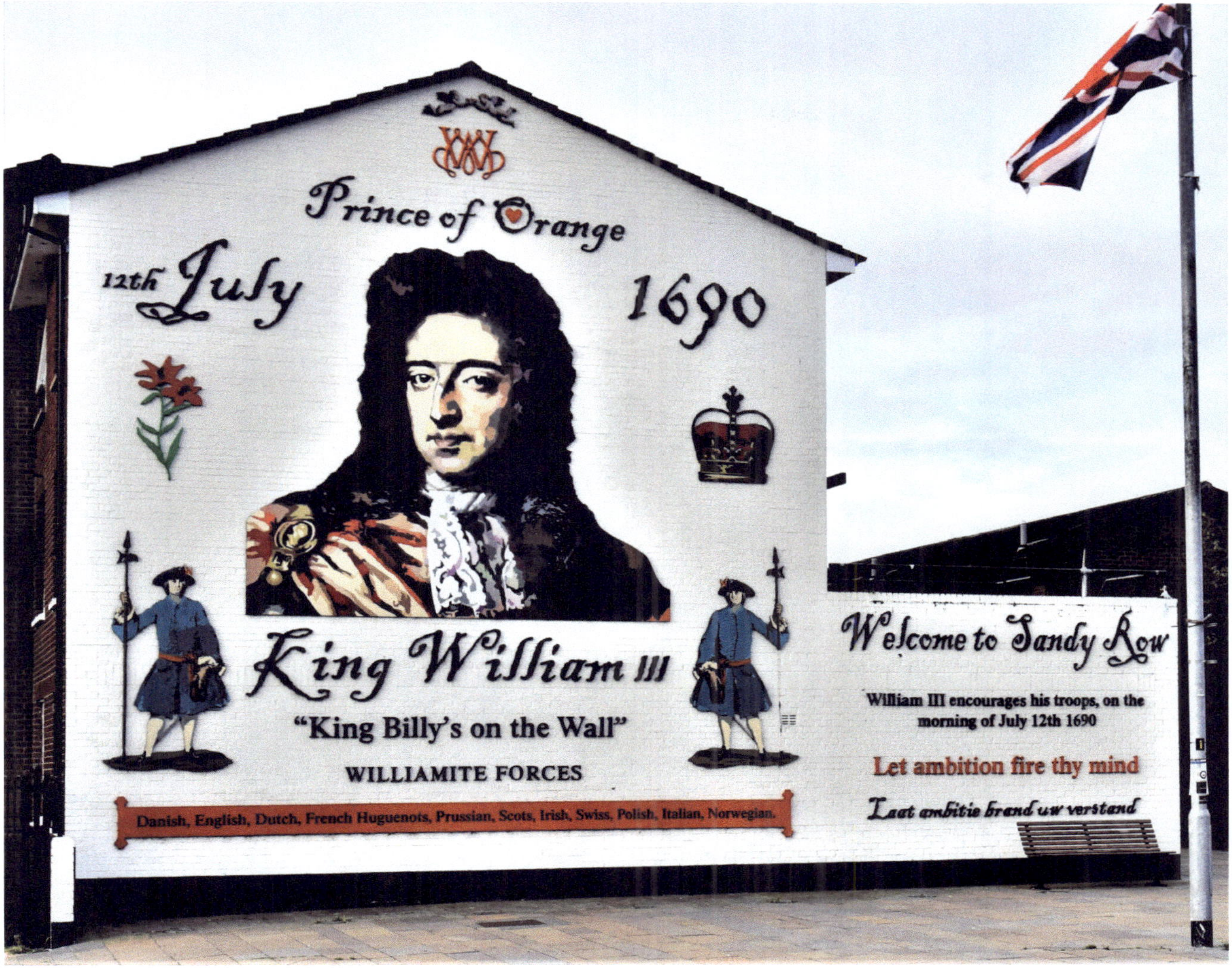

FIGURE 33 King Billy's on the wall, Sandy Row, South Belfast, 2020. Photo by Tony Crowley.

One final aspect of re-imaging took place on an important location: the Cupar Way Peace Line that divides the loyalist Shankill from the nationalist and republican Clonard and Falls. This particular Peace Line is a stark and grim piece of architecture—a wall topped with reinforced corrugated iron and wire netting that runs to sixty feet high in places (Figure 39, see Fulcrum). But in 2010–2012, community murals, sponsored by a variety

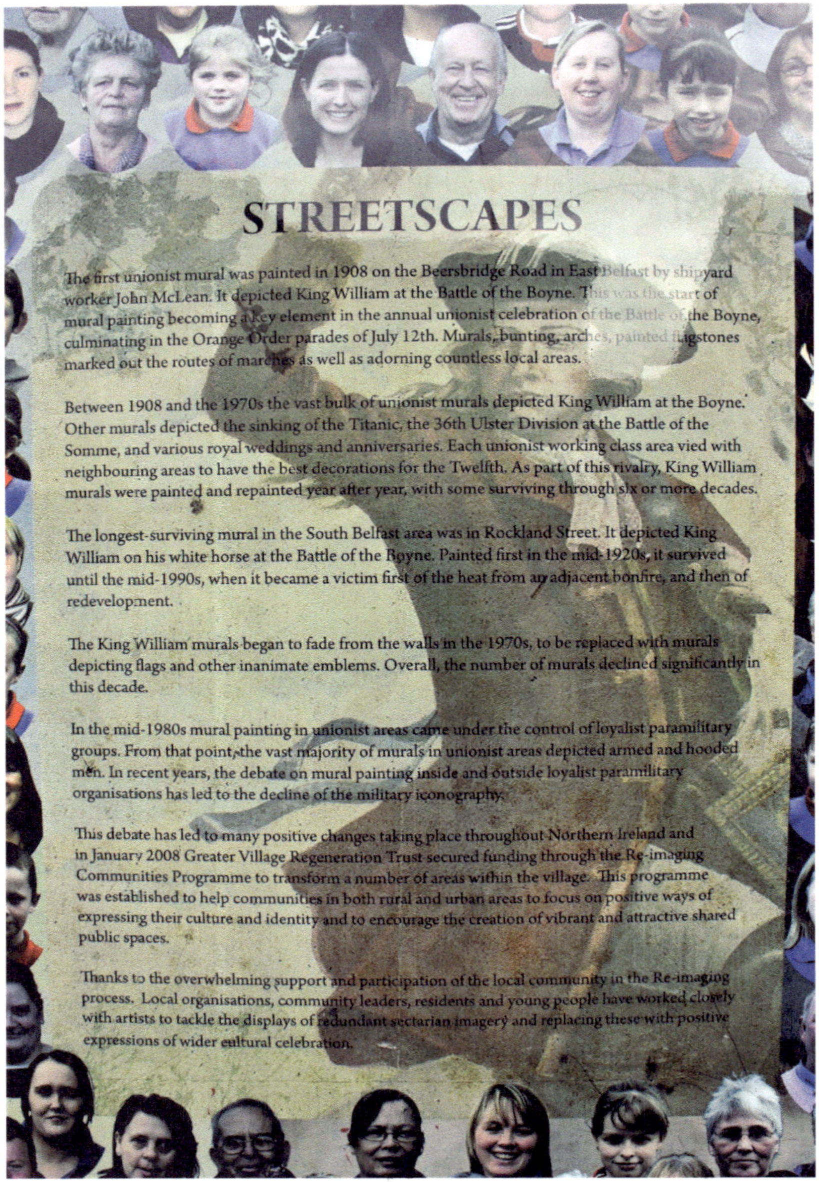

FIGURE 34 Streetscapes, Tavanagh Street, The Village, South Belfast, 2008. Photo by Tony Crowley.

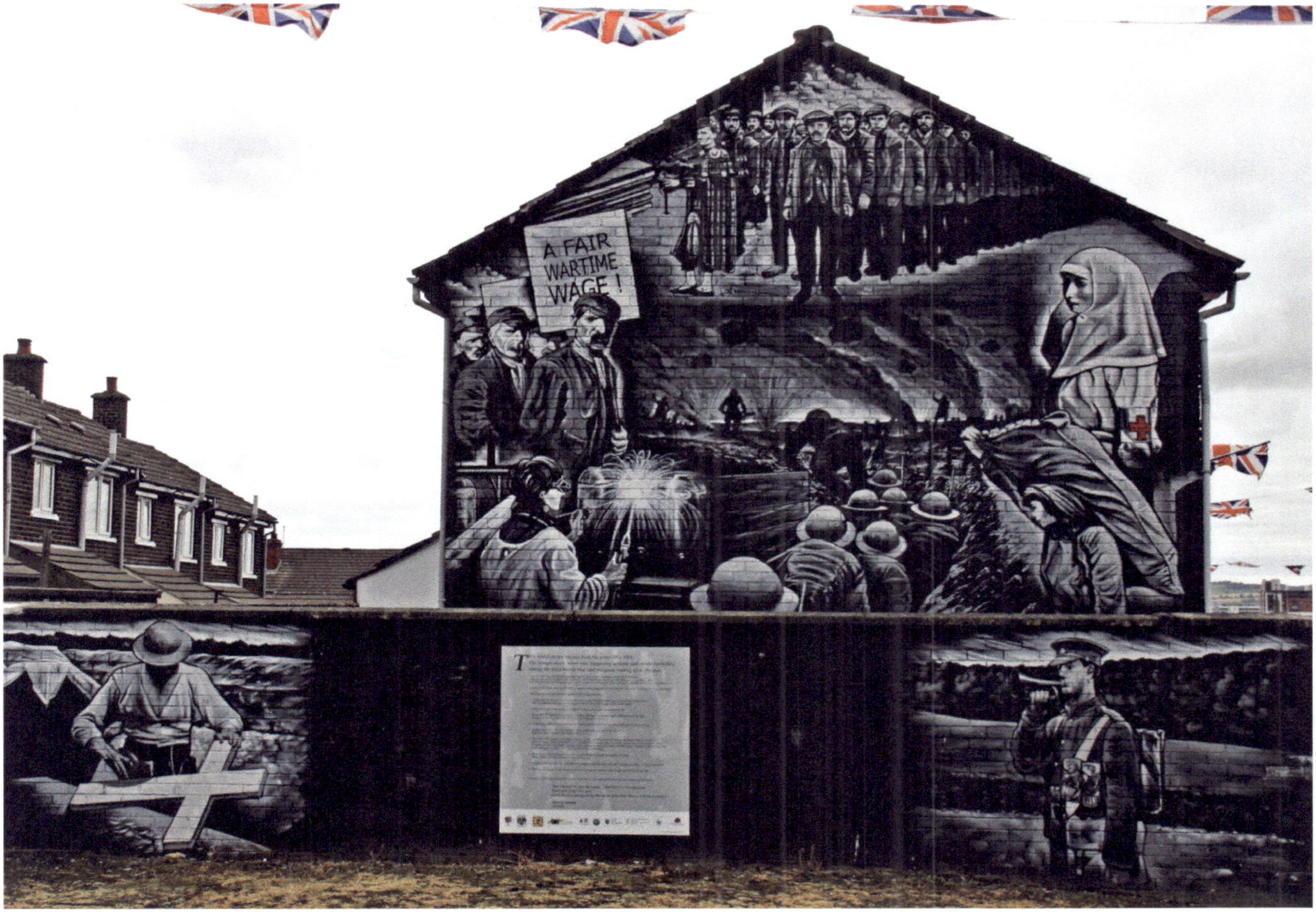

FIGURE 37 A fair wartime wage, Mervue Street, Tigers Bay, North Belfast, 2016. Photo by Tony Crowley.

of organizations, began to appear on the Shankill side of the wall (on the republican side the wall was almost entirely blank, though the Clonard memorial garden was built in Bombay Street against the Peace Line). Much of the mural work focused on themes that had become the staple of re-imaging—culture, identity, and local history. For example, a diptych, "Changing faces" featured a number of loyalist murals that have been "prevalent in the community for many years" but signaled the desire for transition with new images (that incorporated elements of the old): "times change, opinions soften, and people can begin to build a changing face" (Figure 40, see Fulcrum). Other attempts to show "The positive side of the Belfast Shankill Road Peace Wall" (Figure 41, see

Fulcrum) included spaces for poetry, the reflections of schoolchildren on "the other side of the wall," artworks that displayed the work and leisure activities of the Shankill, and a set of boards displaying local people's comments on their own history. Rita Duffy's *Banquet*, a piece of art designed to celebrate International Women's Day in 2011, was also moved to the Peace Line in 2012 (it was originally located on the Shankill) (Figure 42, see Fulcrum). A plaque detailed that the mural was the artist's response to research on the successful campaign for women's suffrage in Belfast and "change in the lives of women living in the Shankill throughout the 20th century." None of this re-imaging work was part of the State-sponsored program (though it was often funded directly or indirectly by State bodies). Indicatively, much of this work has been defaced or destroyed either by taggers, who have treated the Shankill side of the Peace Line as a canvas, or by the many tourists for whom the wall has become a stop-off "heritage" site on which to inscribe banal graffiti about peace, conflict, and being nice to each other ("Make tea not war") (Figure 43, see Fulcrum).[7]

3. FORMATIVE HISTORY

If loyalist engagement with re-imaging was significant, it was not at the expense of murals designed to address the formative history of Northern Ireland in the period 1912–1922 (not least because "the decade of centenaries" afforded the opportunity to celebrate the key events). As discussed in the previous chapter, republicans commemorated their own significant dates, but for loyalists the focus was on the *Ulster Covenant* (1912), the formation of the Ulster Volunteers and the UVF (1912 and 1913), and the event that dominated commemoration above all else, the Somme (July 1 1916). Thus the central role of Edward Carson (an iconic figure in loyalist murals since at least 1914—as noted in chapter one, the *Belfast News-Letter* had commented in that year on "cleverly-painted portraits of Edward Carson" on gable ends), was revisited in a series of images that highlighted his leadership of the anti-Home Rule movement with other figures such as James Craig and Fred Crawford (Figure 44, see Fulcrum). Murals addressed the signing of the *Covenant* (Carson was the first signatory on September 28 2012) (Figure 45), the fostering of the Ulster Volunteers (Figure 46, see Fulcrum) and the general set of developments that led to "the road to the Somme" (Figure 47, see Fulcrum) (Figure 48, see Fulcrum). Such is Carson's status, and such is the level of bitterness against the "Betrayal Act" of the Northern Ireland Protocol (Figure 49, see Fulcrum), that it is perhaps surprising that the words of his maiden speech to the House of Lords in 1921, denouncing Partition as the evitable consequence of Tory party politics, have not as yet featured in loyalist wall art.[8]

Other centenaries were commemorated on the walls, including the gun-running for the Ulster Volunteers in April 1914, which involved the *SS Clyde Valley* (re-named the *Mountjoy* for the purposes of the operation—the *Mountjoy* was the ship that broke the boom during the Siege of Derry in 1689). Murals celebrated

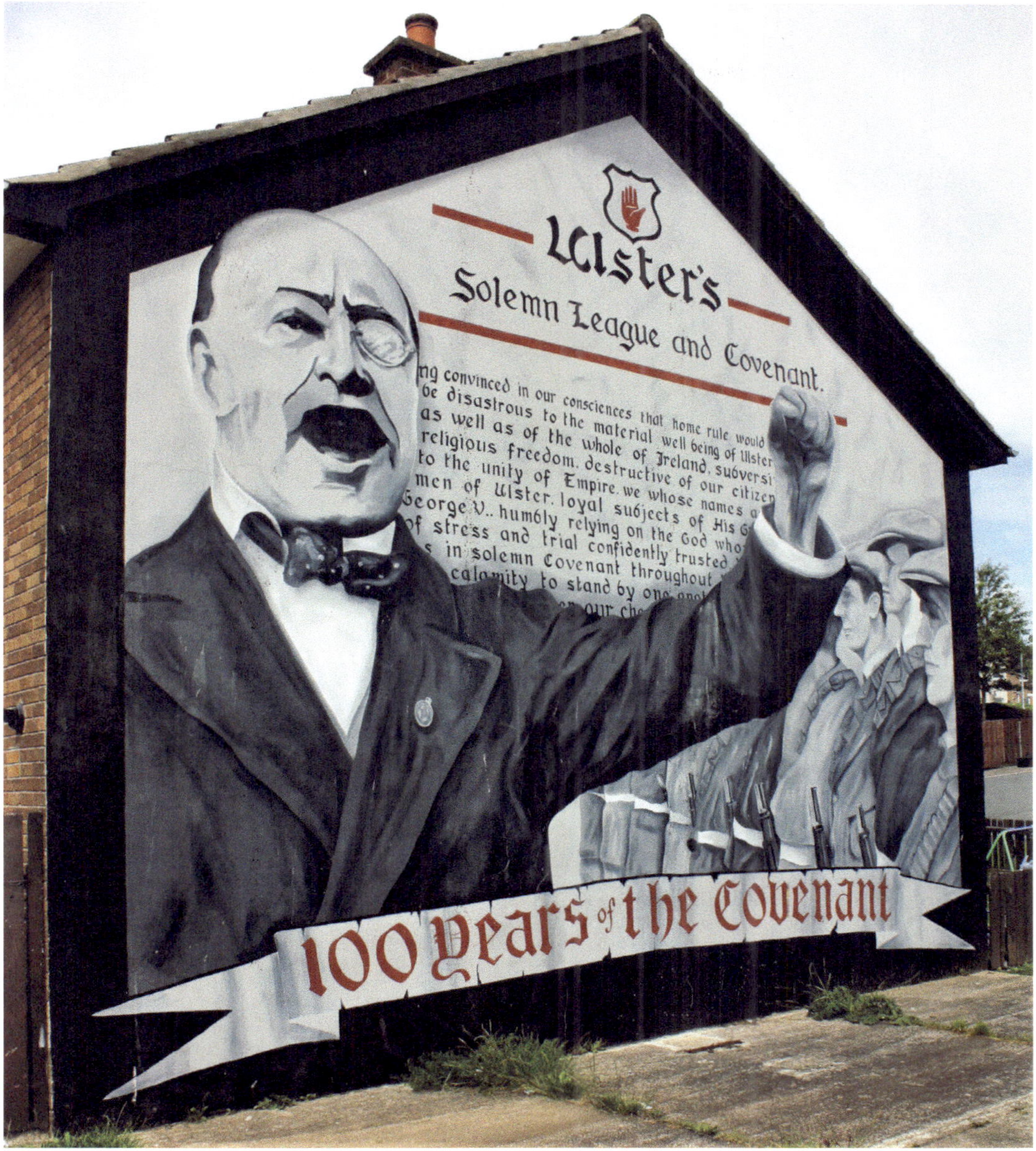

FIGURE 45 100 Years of the Covenant, Dean Park, Castlemara Estate, Carrickfergus, 2016. Photo by Tony Crowley.

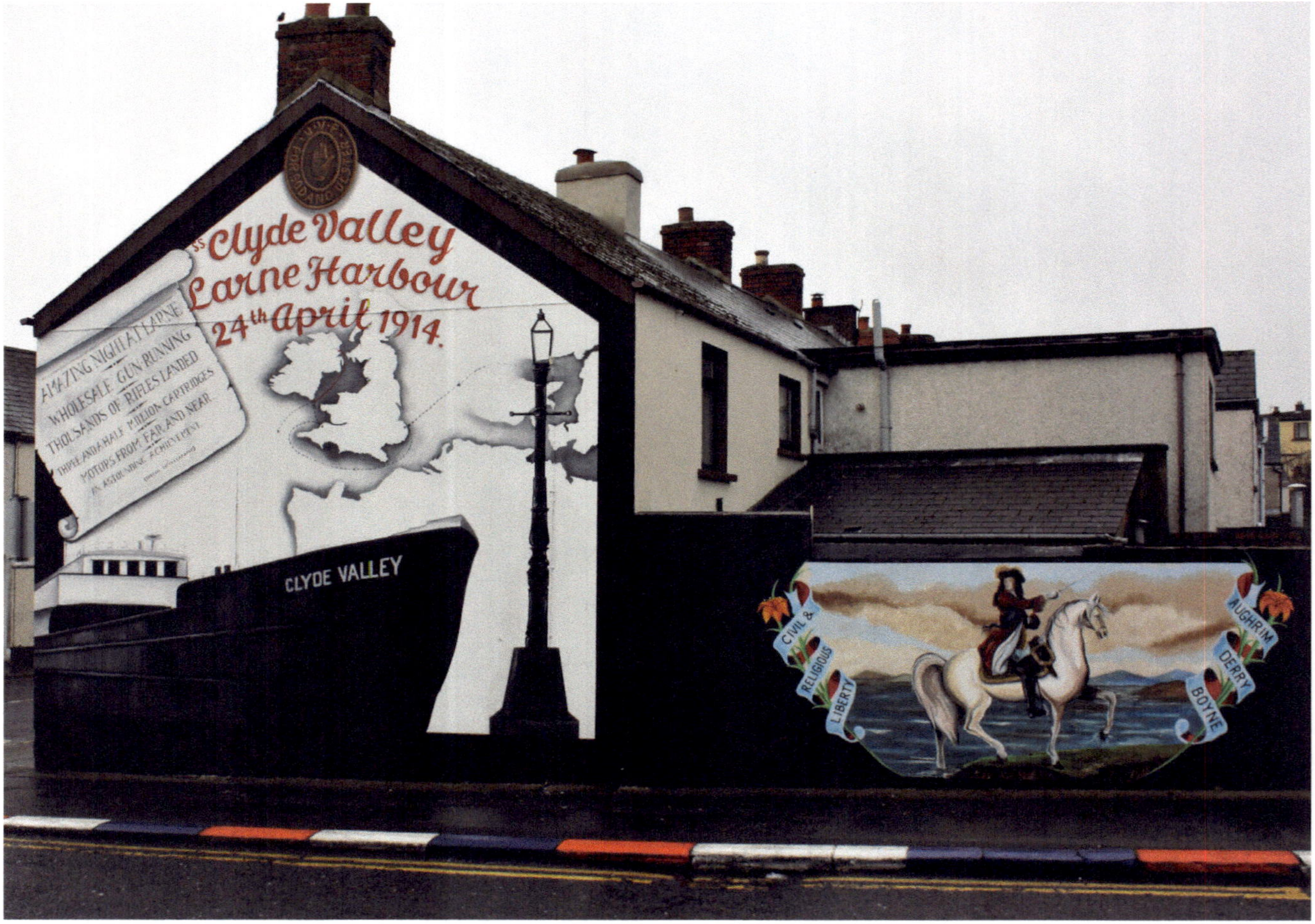

FIGURE 50 Clyde Valley, Herbert Avenue, Larne, 2014. Photo by Tony Crowley.

the landing of the weaponry at Larne, Bangor, and Donaghadee (Figure 50), as well as the innovative role of the UVF Motor Corps in transporting them (Figure 51, see Fulcrum)—the first time that motorized vehicles were used "on a large scale for a military-purpose, and with striking success" (Bardon 2005: 444). Yet although the *Covenant* and the formation and arming of the Ulster Volunteers were crucial events in unionist and loyalist history, the centenary of the Somme was the main concern of the commemorative muralists for the simple reason that the battle furnished "the central foundation myth of the Northern

Irish state" (Grayson and McGarry 2016: 1). Which is to say, as discussed in chapter five, the horrors of the Somme, specifically the sacrifice of a generation of Ulster's finest, were taken to have imposed a political and moral debt on Britain.[9] Given the uncertainty of the times after *The Good Friday Agreement* and all that followed, the 100th anniversary of the battle was evidently a good time to remind Britain of its obligations.

Representations of the battle varied, though they often included images of soldiers going over the top on the first day, as in a number of complex and sophisticated murals that appeared in loyalist areas across Northern Ireland. Many of these—in Portadown and Glengormely for example—were traditional murals (Figure 52) (Figure 53, see Fulcrum). Others—in Belfast and Larne—were digitally mastered before being placed on the wall (Figure 54, see Fulcrum) (Figure 55, see Fulcrum). In the digital images, the compositional technique allowed for innovation and creativity (in the Larne mural, for example, an image taken from Beadle's iconic painting "Battle of the Somme: Attack of the Ulster Division, 1 July 1916" was paired with a contemporary photograph of the trenches).[10] Somme murals did not shy away from the brutalities and consequences of the violence of war, though this was frequently represented allusively through the use of war poetry (the lines of John McCrae's "In Flanders fields" became a staple) (Figure 56) (Figure 57, see Fulcrum).[11] A number of the murals also alluded to the political allegiance of those who died (in **fig. 52** a number of the soldiers in the trench were wearing Orange sashes), while others were explicit about their political intentions ("to keep Ulster Free") and their identity ("part of Great Britain") (Figure 58, see Fulcrum).[12]

The focus of a number of First World War murals is the 36th Ulster Division, which was formed by the addition of thirteen battalions of mostly UVF men in addition to the existing regiments of the Royal Irish Fusiliers, the Royal Irish Rifles, and the Royal Inniskilling Fusiliers (Figure 59, see Fulcrum). Grayson and McGarry assert that commemoration of the 36th "has gradually come to displace King William and the battle of the Boyne as the pre-eminent focus of unionist historical memory" (Grayson and McGarry 2016: 3). This may be overstating the case, but it is clear that the losses of the 36th Division—estimated at more than 5,000 casualties, with 2,000 dead, on the first day of the Somme alone (Middlebrook 1971: 28)—are taken as testament to communal sacrifice. This is evinced in "36th Ulster Division," a mural which depicts a soldier, set against the Belfast hills, resting on arms reversed and bowing to a Cross and unnamed gravestones (with the exception of one—"Francis Lemon 1916"), with the anachronistic Harland and Wolff cranes symbolizing loyalist East Belfast (Figure 60, see Fulcrum). But individual losses were also acknowledged on the walls. The nine recipients of the Victoria Cross were hailed in one image (see **chapter five, fig. 80**), and Private William McFadzean, killed on the first day of the Somme, aged 20, was immortalized in numerous murals (and a loyalist folk song) (Figure 61, see Fulcrum). But the "ordinary dead" were remembered too—Private Robert Mussen in an alleyway on the Shankill, for example, and Sergeant Thomas Wortley in a housing estate in Carrickfergus (Figure 62, see

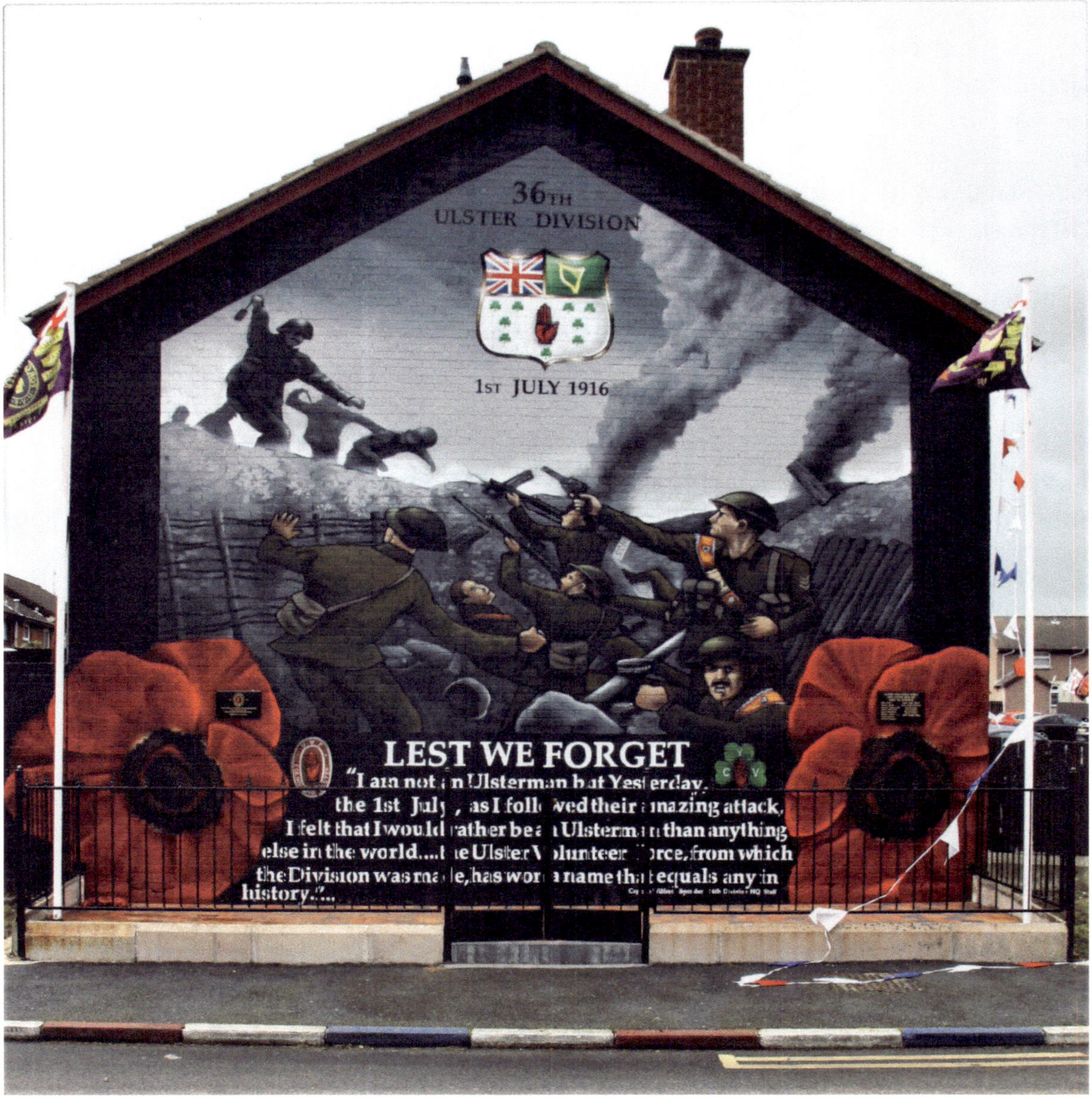

FIGURE 52 Somme attack, Union Street, Portadown, North Armagh, 2016. Photo by Tony Crowley.

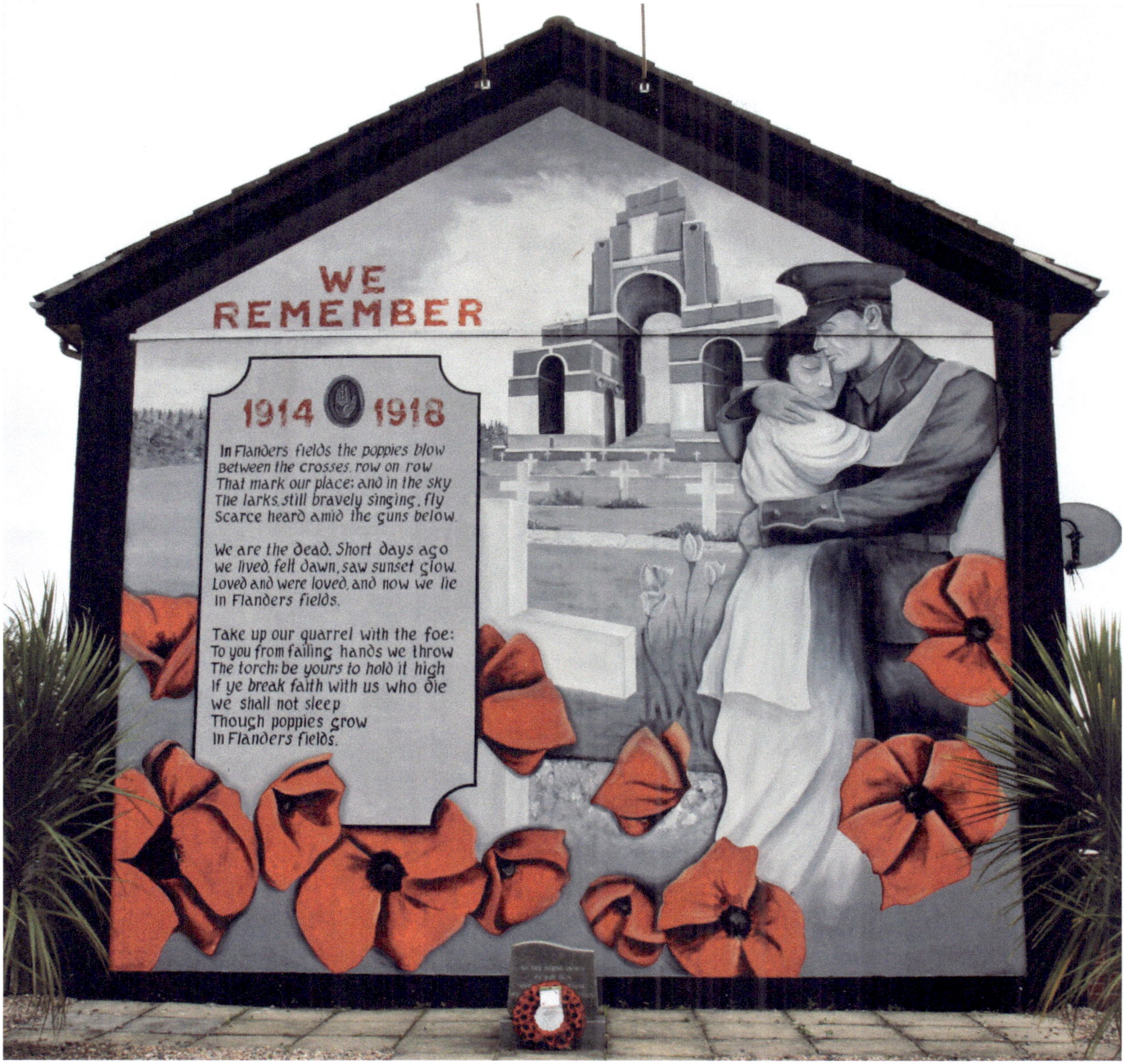

FIGURE 56 We remember, Cashel Court, Monkstown, 2014. Photo by Tony Crowley.

Fulcrum) (Figure 63, see Fulcrum). On occasion, though rarely, those who survived were also represented—as in Corporal Jim Donaghy's happy return to Drumahoe (Figure 64, see Fulcrum).

Evershed comments that "memory work is not simply about who should be 'remembered' and how; it forms part of a properly *political* conversation about the shaping of the social order" (Evershed 2016: 258). This is an important point and as the Somme murals discussed above indicate, the memory of the Somme is a way of asserting the legitimacy of an identity in a context in which it is perceived to be under threat. But if remembering is as much about the present as it is about the past, then shifts in patterns of remembrance intimate the possibility of social and historical change. A number of First World War murals are interesting in this respect; their significance is coded but nonetheless suggestive. In loyalist Highfield, West Belfast, for example, a Somme memorial mural in 2016, dedicated to "the memory and sacrifice of the West Belfast volunteers," bears a standard reference to the 32,186 "killed wounded missing" of the 36th Ulster Division. What makes it unusual is not simply the simultaneous numbering of the 37,761 dead of the 10th and 16th Irish Divisions, but the translation of the quote from the "Book of Lamentations" into Irish: "Is Úadair mo bhrón iad súid sileann na deora ó mo shúile" ("For these things do I weep My eyes flow with tears") (Figure 65). The fact that large numbers of Irish nationalists fought and died for Britain in the First World War has been subject in post-Partition Ireland to what F.X. Martin called—in 1967—"the 'Great Oblivion,' an example of national amnesia," though a more accurate description might be what Benier has termed "social forgetting" (Martin 1967: 68; Beiner 2018: 17–30). Yet if this awkward truth has caused difficulty for republicanism, with Sinn Féin taking part in Armistice Day commemorations in Belfast for the first time in 2013, a number of loyalist murals in Londonderry have used it to emphasize a common—if not yet shared—history. Painted in the car park of the International School for Peace Studies, in the Ebrington Centre which stands next to loyalist Bonds Place, two of these murals focus on "the costs of war" suffered by the "brothers-in-arms" of the 36th Ulster and the 10th and 16th Irish Divisions (Figure 66) (Figure 67, see Fulcrum). Another mural features the Battle of Messines (1917), in which the 16th and 36th fought alongside each other. It focuses on an incident in which the unionist soldier Private Meeke, of the Royal Inniskilling Fusiliers, was the main bearer in a stretcher party that brought back a wounded officer of the 16th Division, Willie Redmond, a Westminster Irish nationalist MP and brother of John Redmond, leader of the Irish Parliamentary Party in the House of Commons (Figure 68).[13] A final mural quotes Glen Barr, erstwhile UDA Brigadier, loyalist politician and community worker, on the lesson that the episode offered: "to embrace the story of Messines/Mesen and its spirit of brotherhood is to be freed from the slavery of bigotry and intolerance" (Figure 69, see Fulcrum).

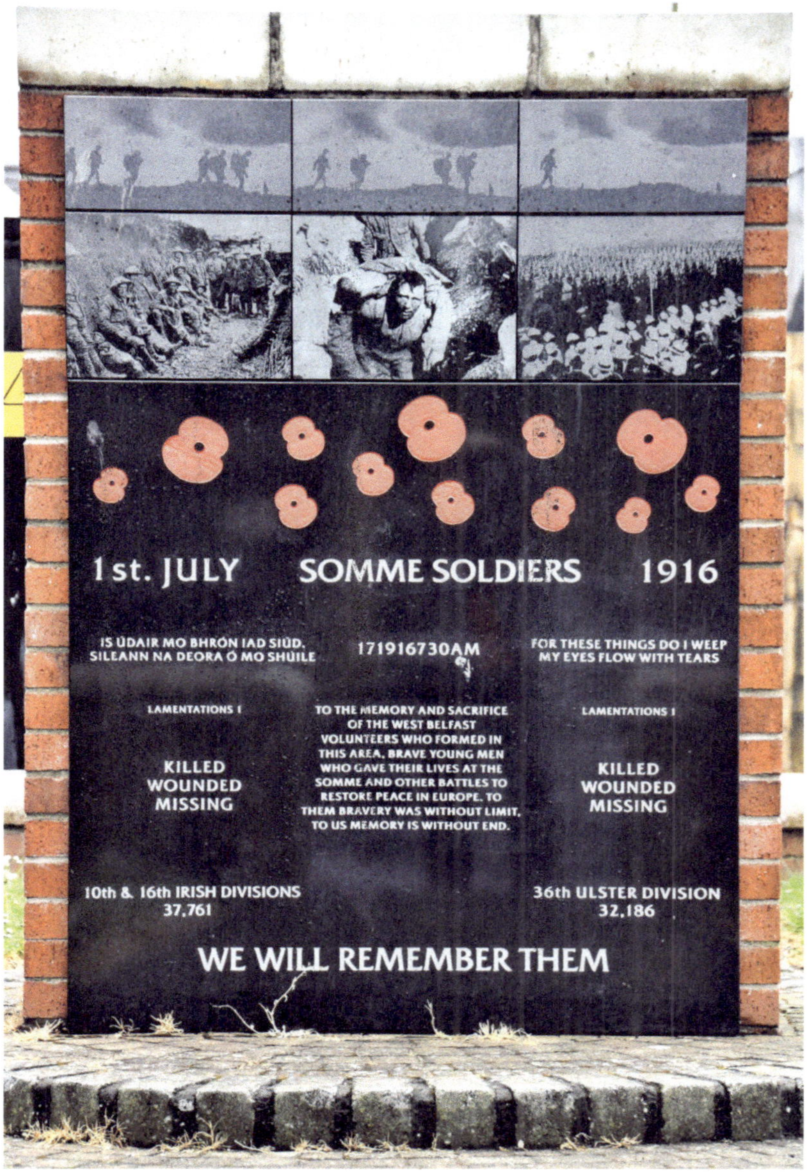

FIGURE 65 Somme soldiers, Black Mountain Way, Highfield, West Belfast, 2016. Photo by Tony Crowley.

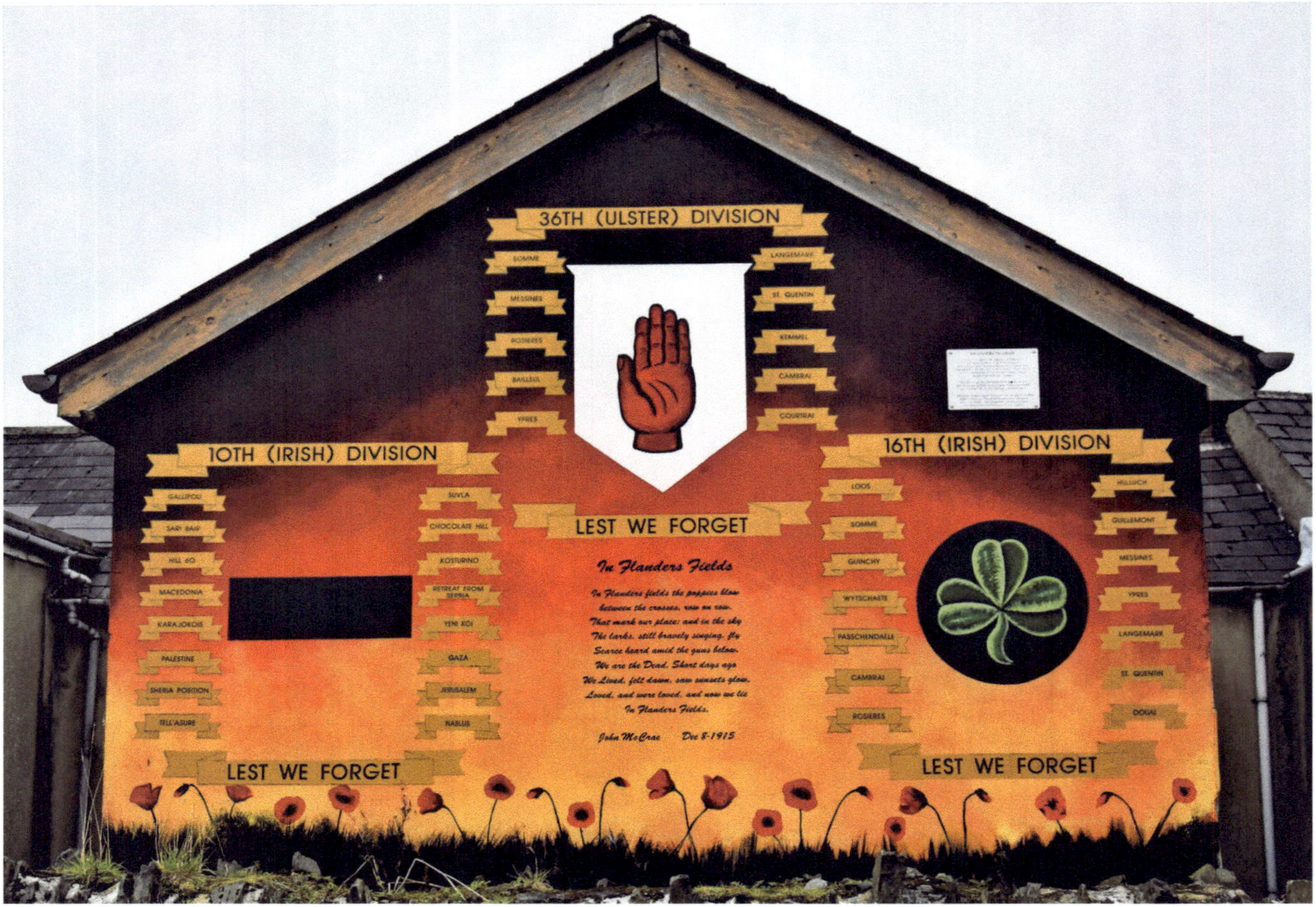

FIGURE 66 Brothers in arms, Ebrington Street, Londonderry, 2018. Photo by Tony Crowley.

4. REMEMBERING THE WAR(S)

The Highfield and Ebrington murals suggest a potential revision of the received history, but they are hardly typical. In general, the memory of the Somme and the First World War has been depicted on the walls as a way of asserting not simply loyalist identity, but also the putative connections between the actions of loyalists in the periods 1912–1918 and the recent Troubles. For many commentators this is a highly controversial linkage, and it has been fiercely contested, even by some within contemporary loyalism.[14] Nevertheless, this trope has featured in a number of murals and memorials, particularly, at least until relatively recently, those associated with the UVF. In some

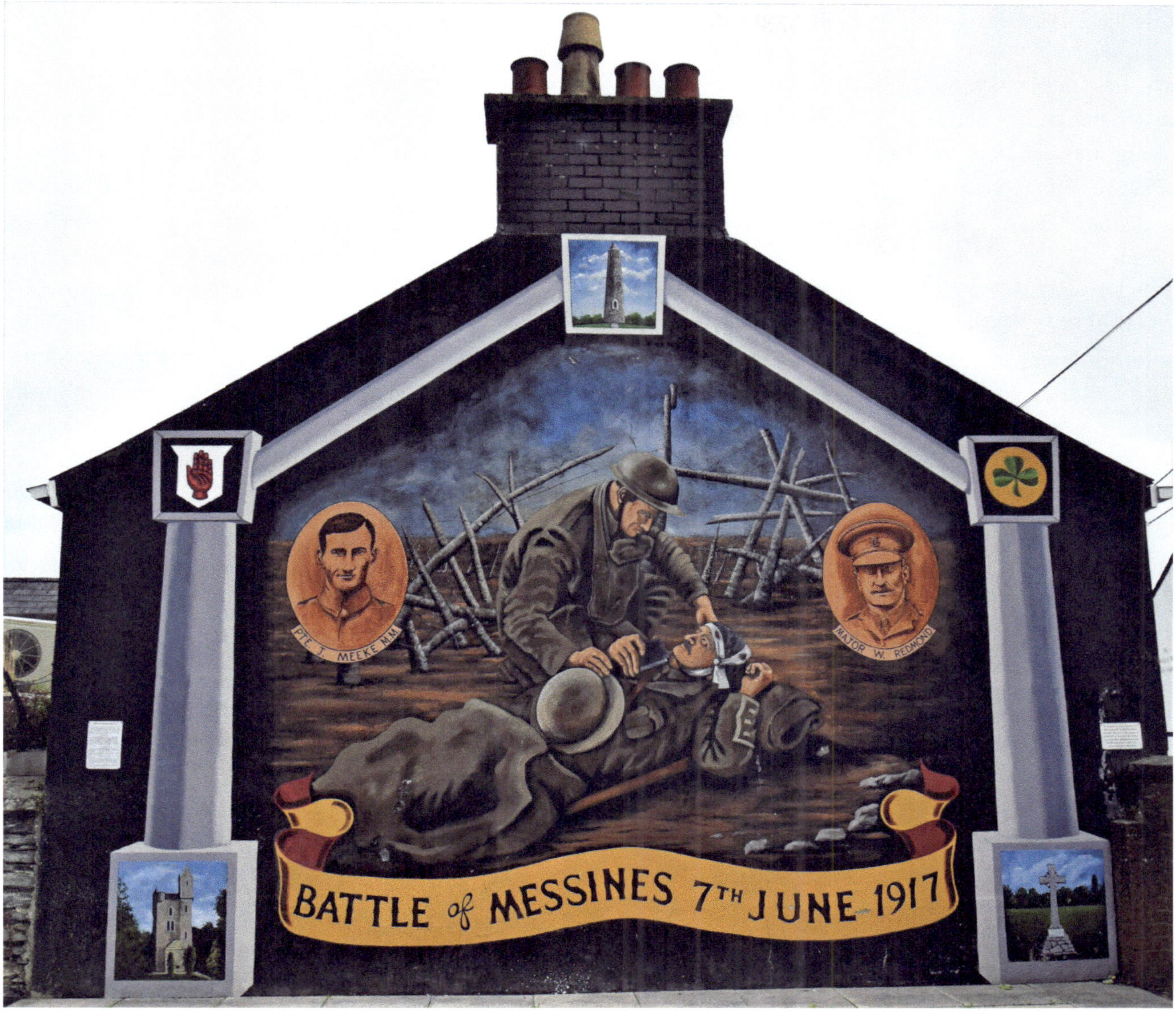

FIGURE 68 Battle of Messines, Ebrington Street, Londonderry, 2017. Photo by Tony Crowley.

examples, the link is explicit. Thus a mural on Glenwood Street, West Belfast, carried photographs that ranged from Carson's inspection of the West Belfast UVF through to contemporary UVF men bearing arms, underpinned by a field of poppies, tombstones, weapons then and now, quotations from Laurence Binyon's "For the fallen," and as a centerpiece, the UVF crest (Figure 70, see Fulcrum). While a memorial in Newtownards, in the form of a miniature version of the Thiepval monument to the missing of the Somme, bore a plaque that read: "In memory of all our fallen comrades both in the battle of the Somme and the fight against Republicanism From the officers and volunteers of the East Belfast Battalion [UVF]" (Figure 71). In other artworks, the connection was made by means of juxtaposition. A memorial in Ballybeen, South Belfast, for example, combined memorial stones to the 36th Ulster Division, the RHC ("to the memory of the brave men who made the ultimate sacrifice for their country) and the UVF ("to all the brave men who lost their lives fighting militant Republicanism") (Figure 72, see Fulcrum). Another example, in Sperrin Park, Londonderry, featured First World War imagery with poppies, the crests of the 10th Battalion Inniskilling Fusiliers, the 109th Brigade 36th (Ulster) Division, and the UVF. At the front of the image was a memorial stone: "In proud memory of our fallen comrades from the Nelson Drive Flute band Glorious on the graves of heroes Kindly upon all those who have suffered for the cause Thus will shine the dawn They gave their tomorrows for our today Lest we forget" (Figure 73, see Fulcrum). This mural offers a complex conflation of image and text across three wars—The First World War, Second World War ("Glorious on the graves of heroes" are Churchill's words) and the post-1969 conflict. The same commingling was used in an image on Carnan Street, West Belfast, dedicated to "C. Company 1st Belfast Battalion Ulster Volunteer Force," which brought together a depiction of soldiers going over the top, a "Roll of Honour" with the names of UVF volunteers killed since 1973, and lines from McCrae's "In Flanders Fields" (Figure 74, see Fulcrum).

The dominant message of these UVF murals is continuity, though as with the representation of all traditions, it is a construction based on selectivity. There is one feature of these images, however, which is indisputably linked to the First World War—the red poppy (originally an American symbol, it was taken up officially in Britain in 1921). The poppy has appeared on UVF memorial murals since at least the 1990s (Figure 75, see Fulcrum), and this contrasts notably with the absence of the symbol on UDA images. For the UDA the appeal to tradition is less straightforward, since its formation dates to no earlier than 1971 (Wood 2006: 3–4). In consequence, the invocation of continuity has taken a different form, as evinced by a number of more recent murals that refer to the creation of the Ulster Defence Union in 1893 (Figure 76).[15] This foundational link, usually implicit, though sometimes direct (Figure 77, see Fulcrum) was something of a leap (there is no reference to the UDU in either of the standard histories of the UDA (McDonald and Cusack 2004; Woods 2006), but it did have the singular advantage of placing the UDA in a loyalist tradition that pre-dated the UVF. In this regard, it is interesting to note that since around 2010, though more obviously in recent years, UDA muralists have also started to appropriate the poppy as a symbol of remembrance, a shift that reinforces a perceived reluctance to cede the loyalist past to the UVF (Figure 78, see Fulcrum).

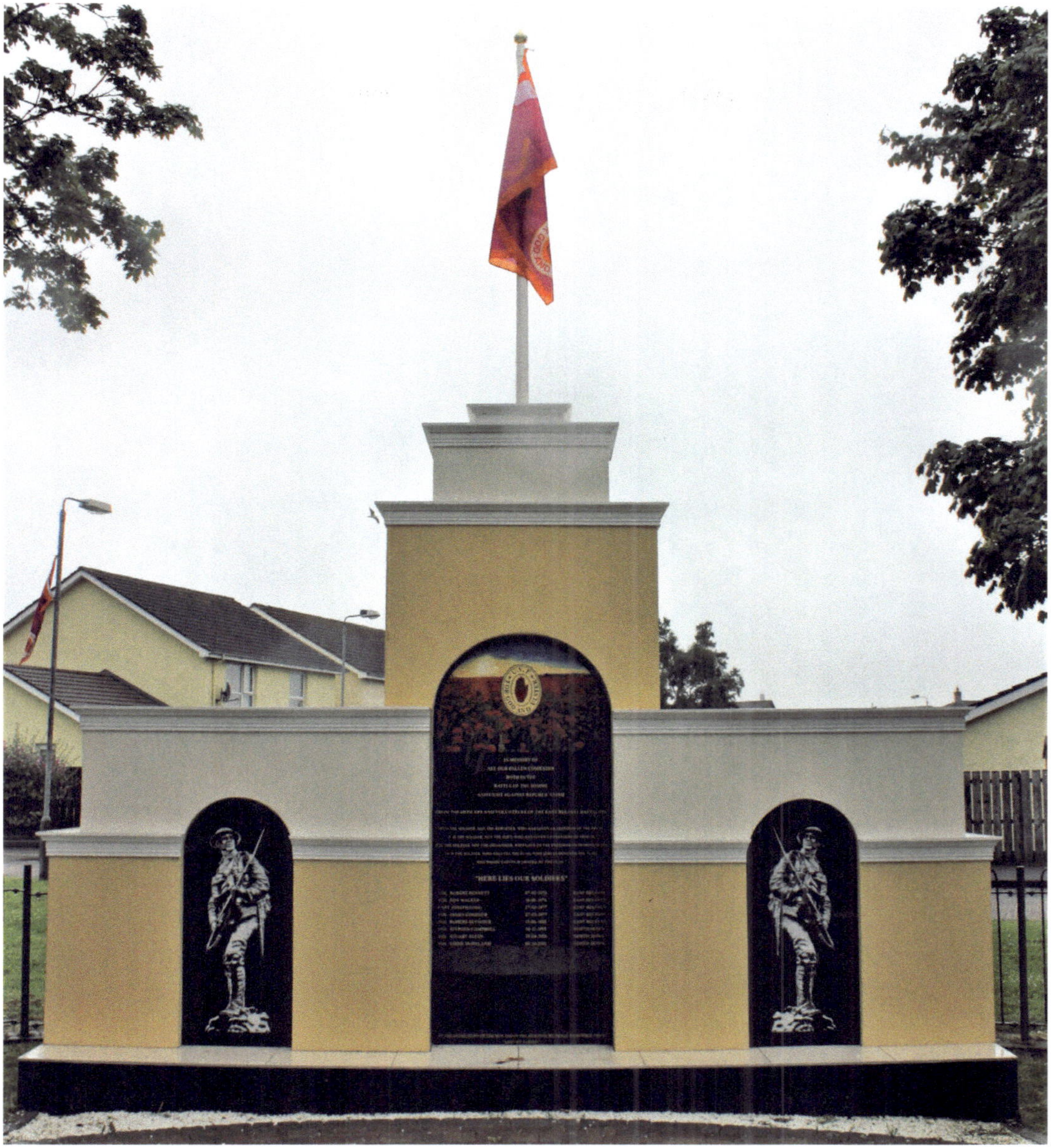

FIGURE 71 The fight against republicanism, Dakota Avenue, Newtownards 2013. Photo by Tony Crowley.

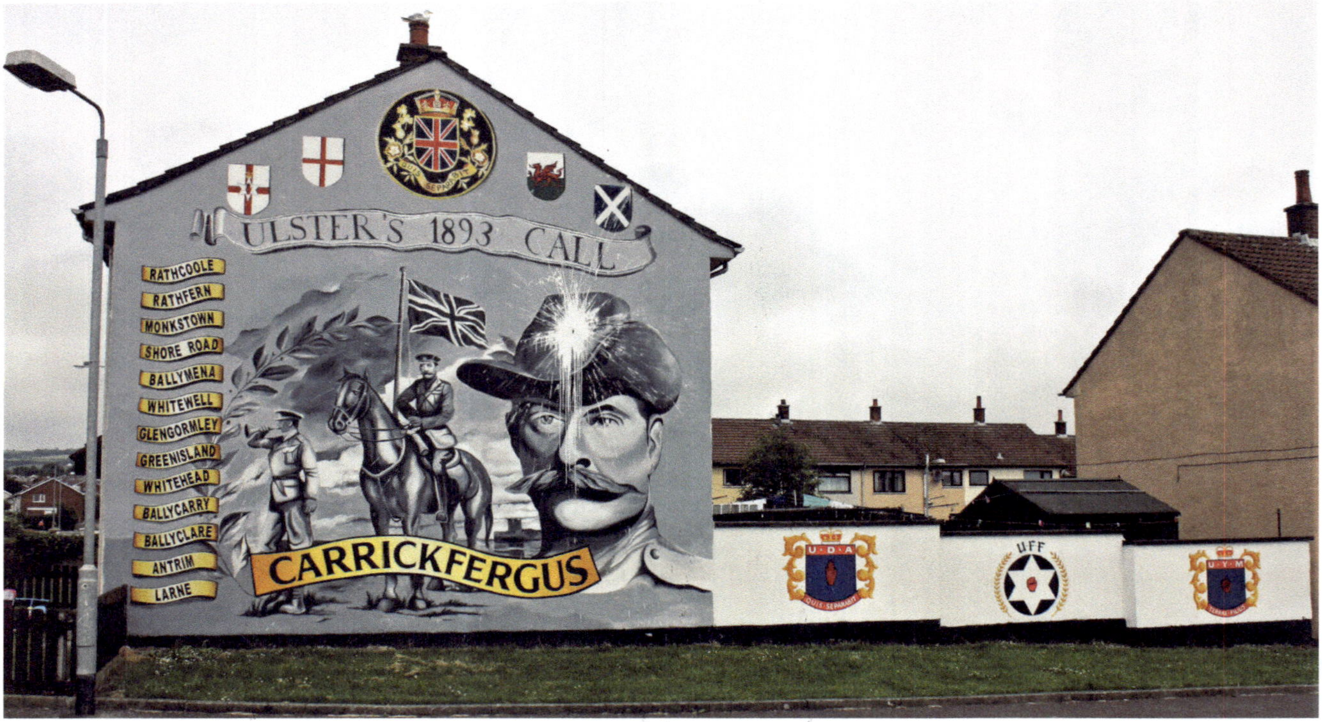

FIGURE 76 Ulster's Call, The Birches, Carrickfergus, 2013. Photo by Tony Crowley.

Some forms of loyalist commemoration focused exclusively on the recent Troubles. Unusually, and against the grain of factional remembrance, there are two examples of memorial gardens that are shared between the UVF and UDA: in Woodvale Court, North Belfast (though the stone refers to the UVF and the WDA—Woodvale Defence Association, an immediate pre-cursor to the UDA) (Figure 79, see Fulcrum) and on the Kilcooley estate in Bangor (where the stones remember the RHC, UDA, and UVF) (Figure 80, see Fulcrum). But these memorials do not reflect the dominant trend in loyalist paramilitary commemoration in which the imperative to remember tends to relate specifically to units or individuals within one of the organizations. A memorial at the Eastway social club on the Rathcoole estate, for example, was dedicated to South East Antrim UDA and UFF members "murdered by the enemies of Ulster" or killed "on active service" (a code that usually means killed in a premature bomb explosion) (Figure 81, see Fulcrum). Another memorial garden, at Kenbaan Street, East Belfast, listed the names of the "murdered and killed" members of the 4th Battalion, Castlereagh, UFF, UYM, and UDA (Figure 82, see Fulcrum). Individual UDA paramilitaries were also commemorated by murals (Figure 83, see Fulcrum), as were politico-military leaders (Figure 84). And a similar pattern appeared with the UVF. In the Loyalist Village area of South Belfast, the UVF remembered "fallen loved ones and friends… cruelly taken away by Republican scum" (Figure 85, see Fulcrum), while the East Belfast Brigade recalled "years of sacrifice" with an image of Long Kesh prison and a tombstone bearing the names of dead volunteers (Figure 86, see Fulcrum). Individual UVF volunteers were addressed (as were those of the RHC) (Figure 87, see Fulcrum) (Figure 88, see Fulcrum), and

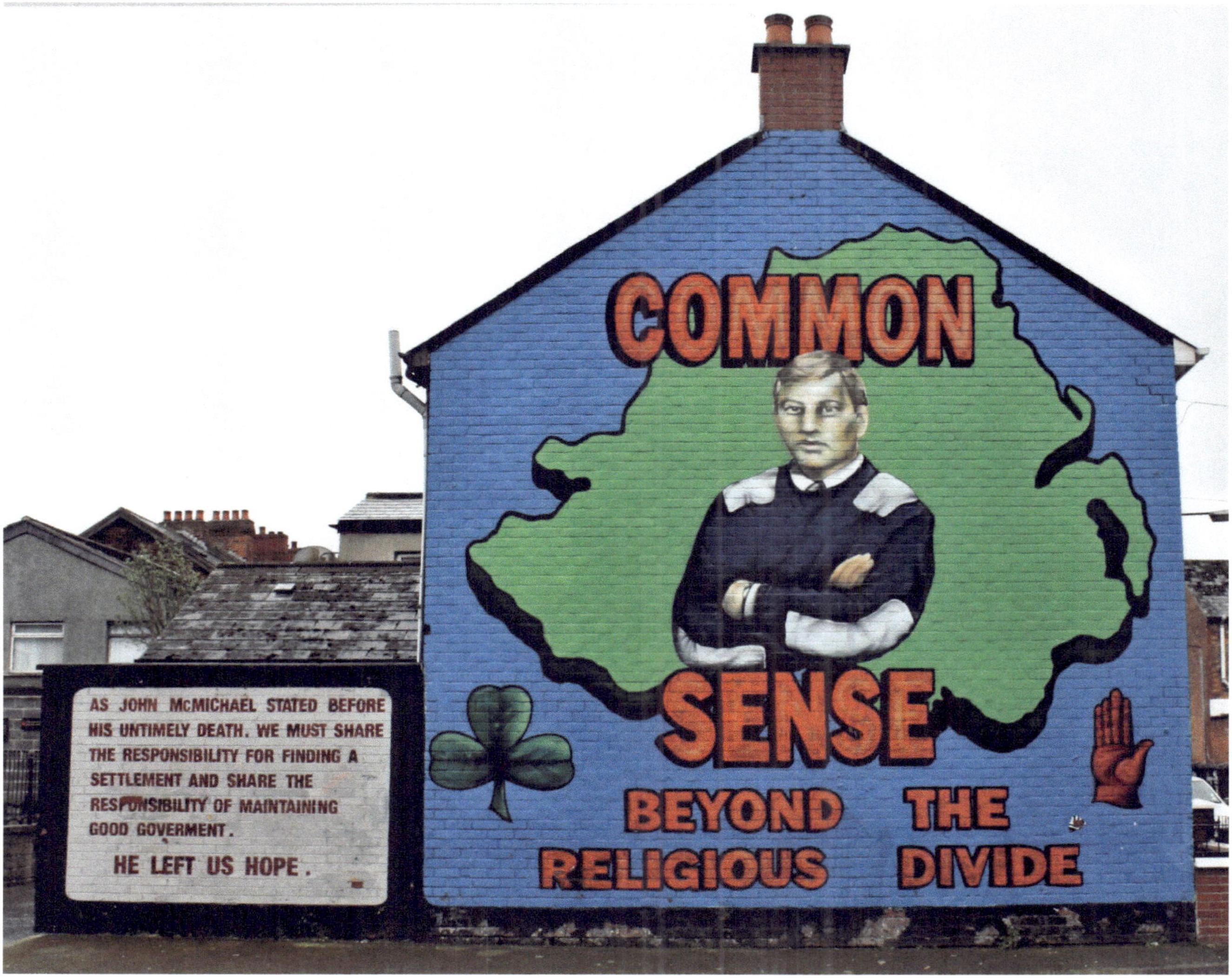

FIGURE 84 John McMichael, Lemberg Street, The Village, South Belfast, 2010. Photo by Tony Crowley.

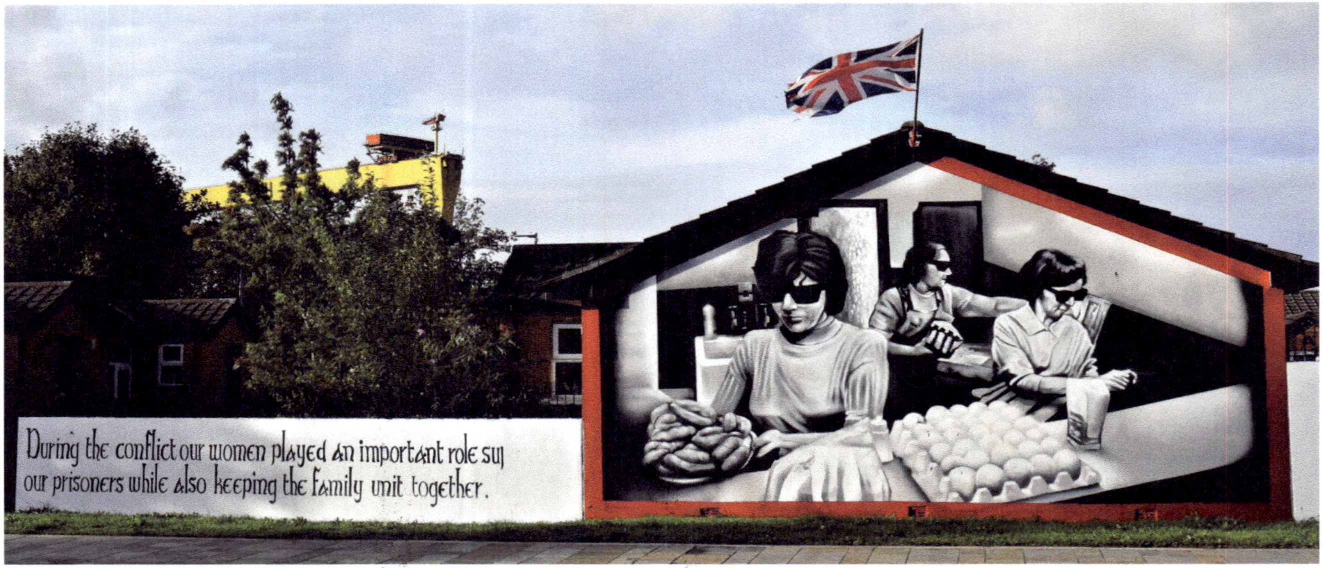

FIGURE 91 Women's role, Newtownards Road, East Belfast, 2022. Photo by Tony Crowley.

dead members of the political leadership of the PUP were heralded (Figure 89, see Fulcrum). In very recent times, the limits of war remembrance have been extended to include one group that had traditionally not featured at all: women. A poppy wreath on a First World War mural in East Belfast was dedicated to "East Belfast Battalion Women's Ulster Volunteer Force" (Figure 90, see Fulcrum). And a mural celebrating the 50th anniversary of the UDA represented women preparing food with a side caption that read: "During the conflict our women played an important role sup[porting] our prisoners while also keeping the family unit together" (Figure 91).[16]

5. MEN WITH GUNS

The 25th anniversary of *The Good Friday Agreement* occurred in 2023. Though the New IRA continues to pose a small threat, armed republicanism effectively disbanded in 2005 with the decommissioning of the IRA's arsenal (the INLA and Official IRA confirmed that they had disarmed in 2010). On the loyalist side, the Independent International Commission on Decommissioning reported that the UVF and UDA had decommissioned their weapons in 2009 and 2010 respectively (Independent International Commission on Decommissioning 2011: 10–12). Though the Commission issued caveats (primarily relating to the imprecision of fading memories, splits in organizations, the deaths of quartermasters, and deterioration of the ordnance), and notwithstanding the scepticism that has been expressed about the full extent of the materials that were destroyed, the official line was that guns had been taken out of Irish politics for good by 2010. Yet as the PUP politician Billy Hutchinson warned repeatedly during the disarmament process, eliminating an arsenal is important, but the real imperative is "to decommission the mindsets of the people who had the guns" (Hutchinson 2020: 230). Buying or making military equipment is always possible, given the right resources; convincing people that there is no place for guns and bombs is the difficult thing. And the need for persuasion persists. The most recent report of the Independent Reporting Commission (IRC), established in 2017 under the auspices of the *Fresh Start Agreement* (2015) to ascertain progress towards "the ending of paramilitarism 'once and for all,'" issued a frank warning: "the risks posed to society by the continuing existence of paramilitary groups and structures mean that paramilitarism remains a clear and present danger in and for Northern Ireland" (Independent Reporting Commission 2022: 15).[17]

In specific areas in Northern Ireland, mostly urban and working-class, the commission asserts that paramilitarism is "part of the fabric of daily life," though the circumstances are variable:

> Part of the complexity of the situation is that while at one level what is happening is coercive control, that is not the complete picture. It is also the case that in some areas the presence and involvement [of paramilitaries] are reflective of the wishes of cohorts of the community, with the groups involved being seen as in effect part of the so-called authority structure of that community. (19)

The existence of groups that reserve the right to resort to violence and constitute alternative power structures is a clear threat to the liberal democratic State, but there can be no doubt that such organizations persist. In point of fact, the IRC report presents a nuanced view of "the complex landscape" of paramilitarism. Evidently, one of the functions of paramilitary organizations can be to act "a cloak for overt criminality (such as extortion, drug dealing, threats, trade in counterfeit goods, money laundering, illegal money lending, sexual exploitation and other illegal activities)" (12). But there are also people who belong to paramilitary organizations for reasons related to "socio-economic disadvantage," and others who are "dormant" members with more or less formal affiliation (12). In addition, and importantly, there are those,

> who remain engaged in paramilitarism for political and identity reasons which reach back to the Troubles/conflict. These individuals, while remaining part of paramilitary structures, regard their primary motivation for continuing involvement as being driven by the needs and perspective of their community. This category also contains people, including at leadership level in some of the groups, who articulate a positive wish to see paramilitarism ended. (13)

The commission's commitment to abolishing paramilitarism is clear, but its report was also forthright in identifying the problems posed to that task by the "fractured nature of politics in the years since the Belfast/Good Friday Agreement," specifically the lack of a functioning government and the instability caused by the turbulence of the practical and political consequences of the Northern Ireland Protocol (13). Indeed a concise summary of the commission's findings would be that paramilitarism may take various forms—from outright criminality to paramilitaries who want to see the demise of their own organizations—but its roots lie deep in the soil of the divided State of Northern Ireland.

Though the commission's report concerns paramilitarism in general, there can be no doubt that its strictures apply to loyalist paramilitaries particularly. And as ever, the evidence can be found on the walls. Loyalist paramilitarism isn't hiding in plain sight, because it isn't hiding at all; its visible presence is registered in a number of modes in murals in loyalist areas, including self-celebration, territorial dominance, and readiness for violence. Thus various images laud loyalist organizations as communal defenders. In a complex collage on Disraeli Street in Woodvale, North Belfast, for example, the crests of the WDA/UFF/UYM/LPA are set against photographs of a UDA march in 1972, a previous mural, and a scene within Long Kesh, while to the left a UDA insignia lies against a Union Jack with images of memorial services; "Invictus (Undefeated)" sits above the mural's central message: "Defenders of our community since 1969" (Figure 92). And in a series of images at "Freedom Corner" on the Newtownards

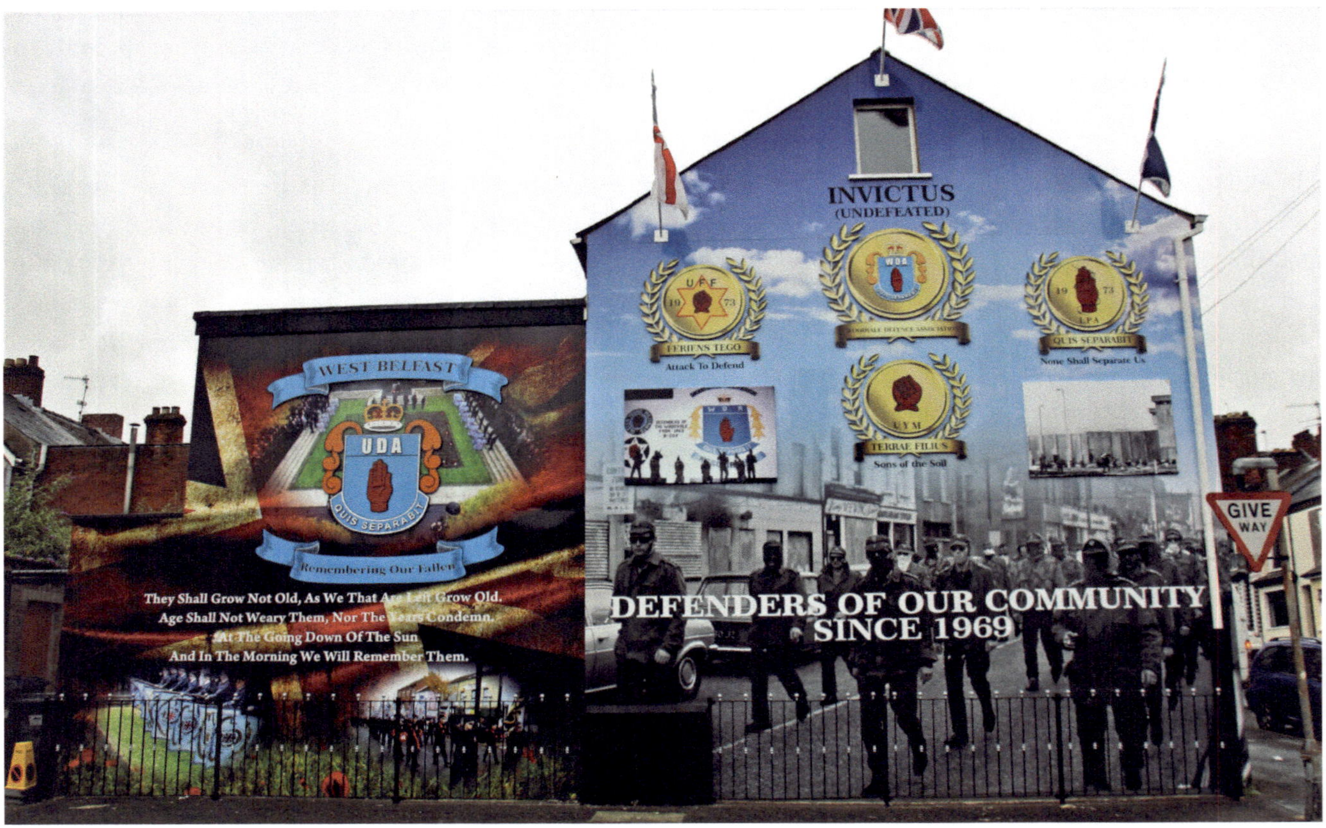

FIGURE 92 Invictus, Disraeli Street, Woodvale, North Belfast, 2017. Photo by Tony Crowley.

Road, East Belfast, re-painted three times since 2007, one mural commends the UDA and UFF as "Ulster's Present Defenders" (Figure 93, see Fulcrum). In the same vein, a mural at Highfield in West Belfast depicts two gunmen against the UDA badge with the slogan "Defending freedom from hate" (Figure 94, see Fulcrum). UVF and RHC murals conveyed the same message: loyalist paramilitaries had defended and would defend "the Protestant community" by fighting to "retain our Britishness" (Figure 95, see Fulcrum) (Figure 96). Occasionally murals appeared in apparently unlikely places—tucked away in cul-de-sacs for example—as in Ballyminetragh Gardens in Bangor, or Wellington Green, Larne (Figure 97, see Fulcrum) (Figure 98, see Fulcrum). In these instances, the images were primarily visible only to locals (or mural-hunters) but given their function—of signaling territorial control through the display of the organization and the area—their more familiar location is on prominent thoroughfares with high

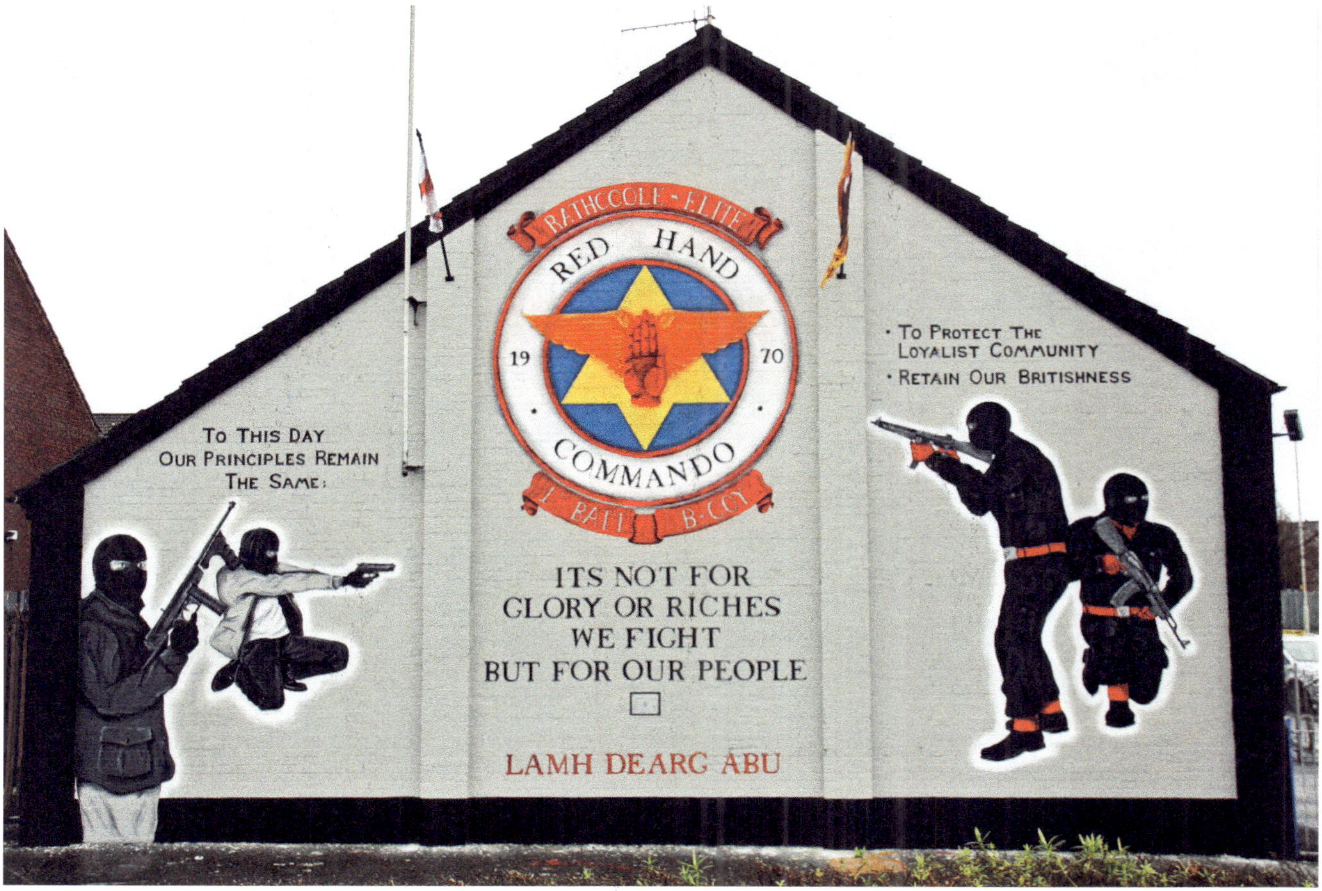

FIGURE 96 Retain our Britishness, Donardview Close, Rathcoole, Newtownabbey, 2016. Photo by Tony Crowley.

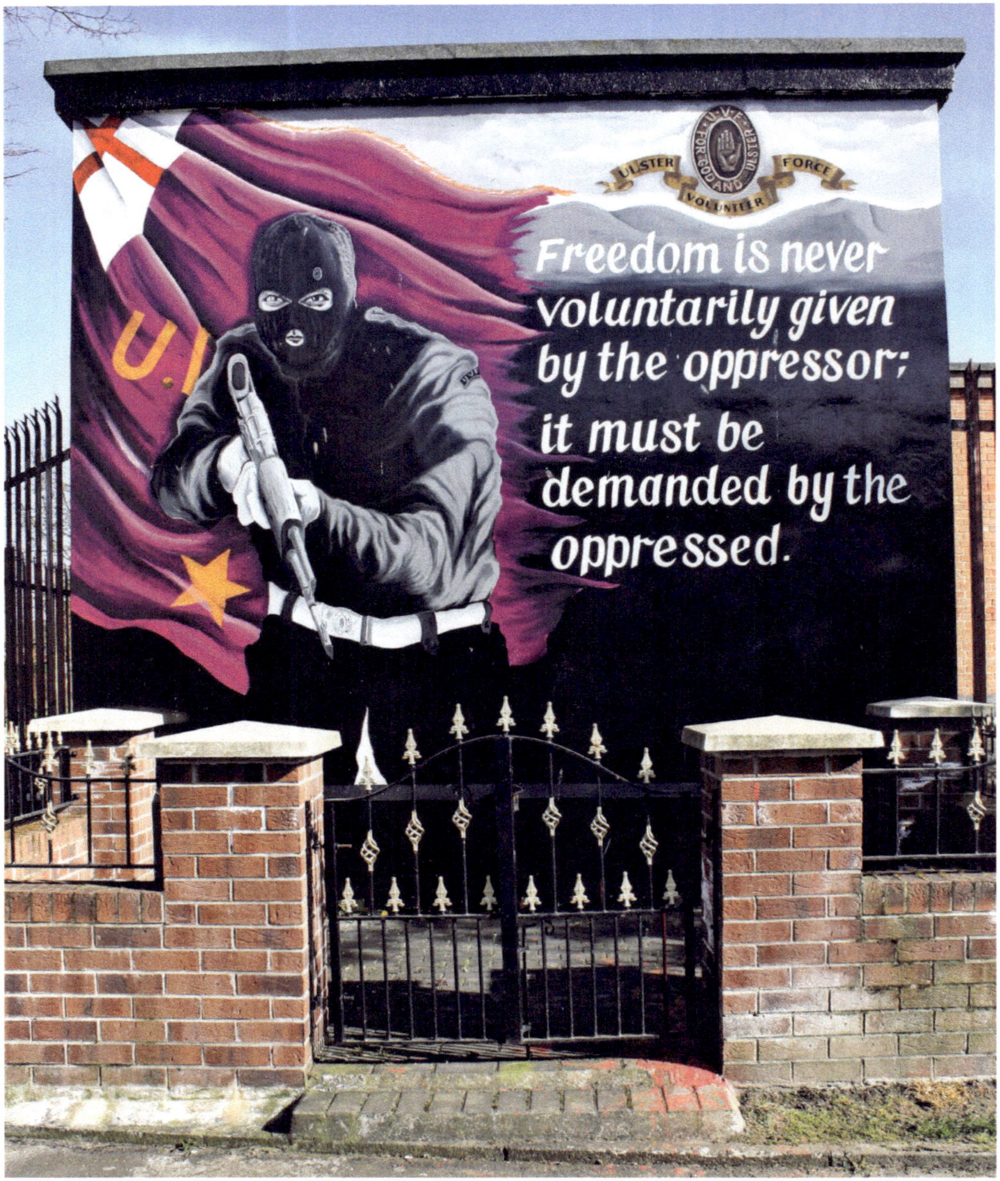

FIGURE 105 The oppressed, Inverwood Court, East Belfast, 2013. Photo by Tony Crowley.

visibility. This is particularly significant given the fragmentation of the loyalist organizations; the East Belfast UVF and the South East Antrim UDA, now operating in effect as autonomous groups, have frequently used murals to mark their areas of influence (Figure 99, see Fulcrum) (Figure 100, see Fulcrum) (Figure 101, see Fulcrum).

The readiness to resort to violence was a common theme in these murals, with the message reiterated that "Ulster's fighting men" (Figure 102, see Fulcrum) were ready to "lead the way," in the guise of the grim reaper (Figure 103, see Fulcrum) (Figure 104, see Fulcrum). The purported causes of this stance were variable. One mural painted loyalists as the dispossessed, with a quote from Martin Luther King's "Letter from Birmingham Jail": "freedom is never given voluntarily by the oppressor; it must be demanded by the oppressed" (Figure 105). Others cited the defense of rights (Figure 106, see Fulcrum), the menace of being forced to live in an Irish Republic (Figure 107), the right to self-defense (Figure 108, see Fulcrum), injustice (Figure 109, see Fulcrum), and the imposition of a border in the Irish

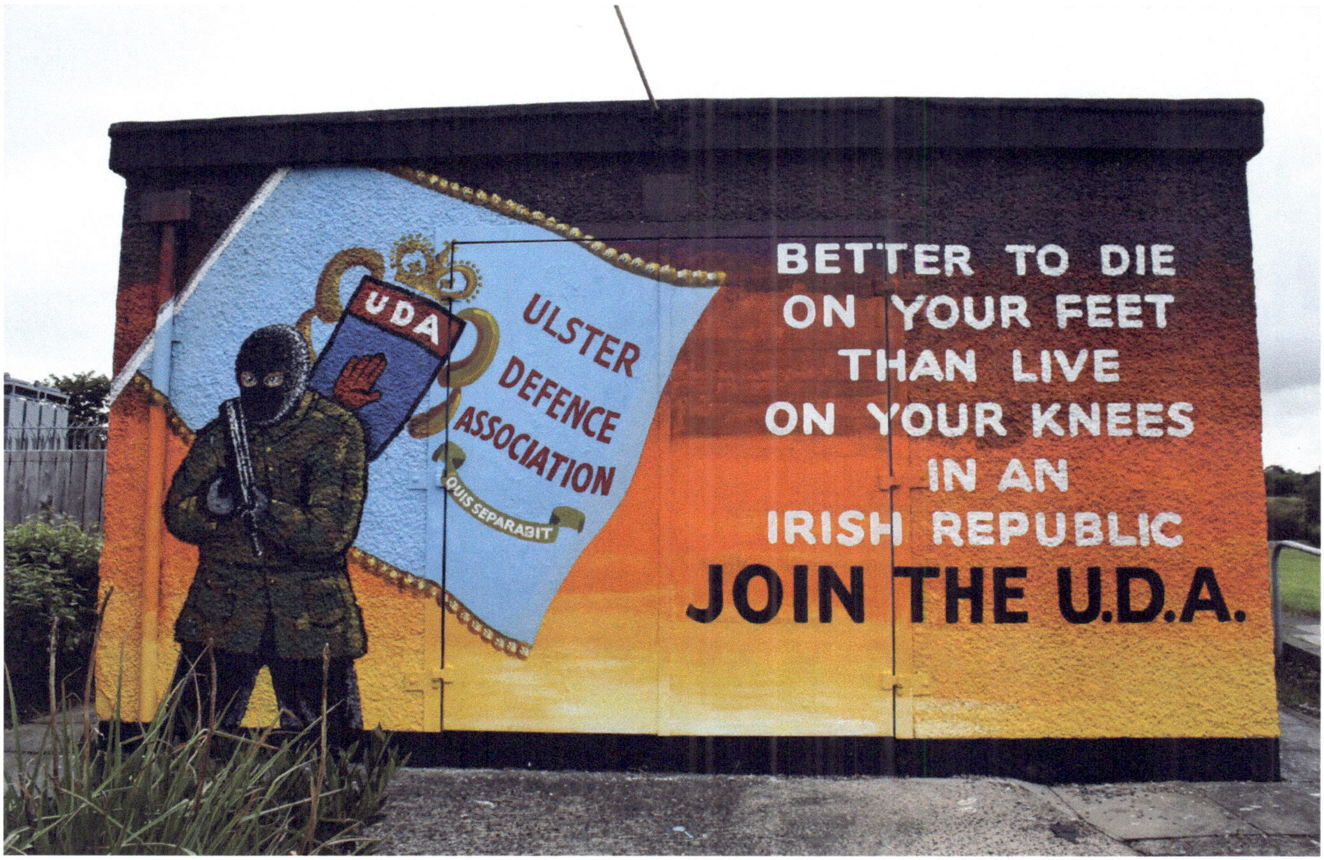

FIGURE 107 Better to die on your feet, Oakfield Drive, Glenfield, Carrickfergus, 2016. Photo by Tony Crowley.

sea as part of the Northern Ireland Protocol (Figure 110, see Fulcrum). A number of images were non-specific in relation to the danger, but explicit in terms of the threat that they heralded. An RHC image in Rathcoole, for example, warned "Don't play with our peace or attack our land" because "We await in the shadows" (Figure 111, see Fulcrum), while a UVF mural in the Shankill declared that "Our guns are silent and shall remain/But when needed we shall rise again" (Figure 112, see Fulcrum). The foundational principle invoked in these murals is that of "bearing arms for one's faith, community and country," described as "the highest obligation and privilege of citizenship" (Figure 113, see Fulcrum). But these words embody one of the recurrent conundrums of contemporary loyalism, since in a liberal democracy, the legitimate use of violence is the sole prerogative of the State. The difficulty is that the State, with whose war against republicanism loyalists once allied themselves, is now perceived to have abandoned loyalism. In 2021 a mural in Highfield, West Belfast, boasted of a century of "fighting a fascist republican enemy sponsored by

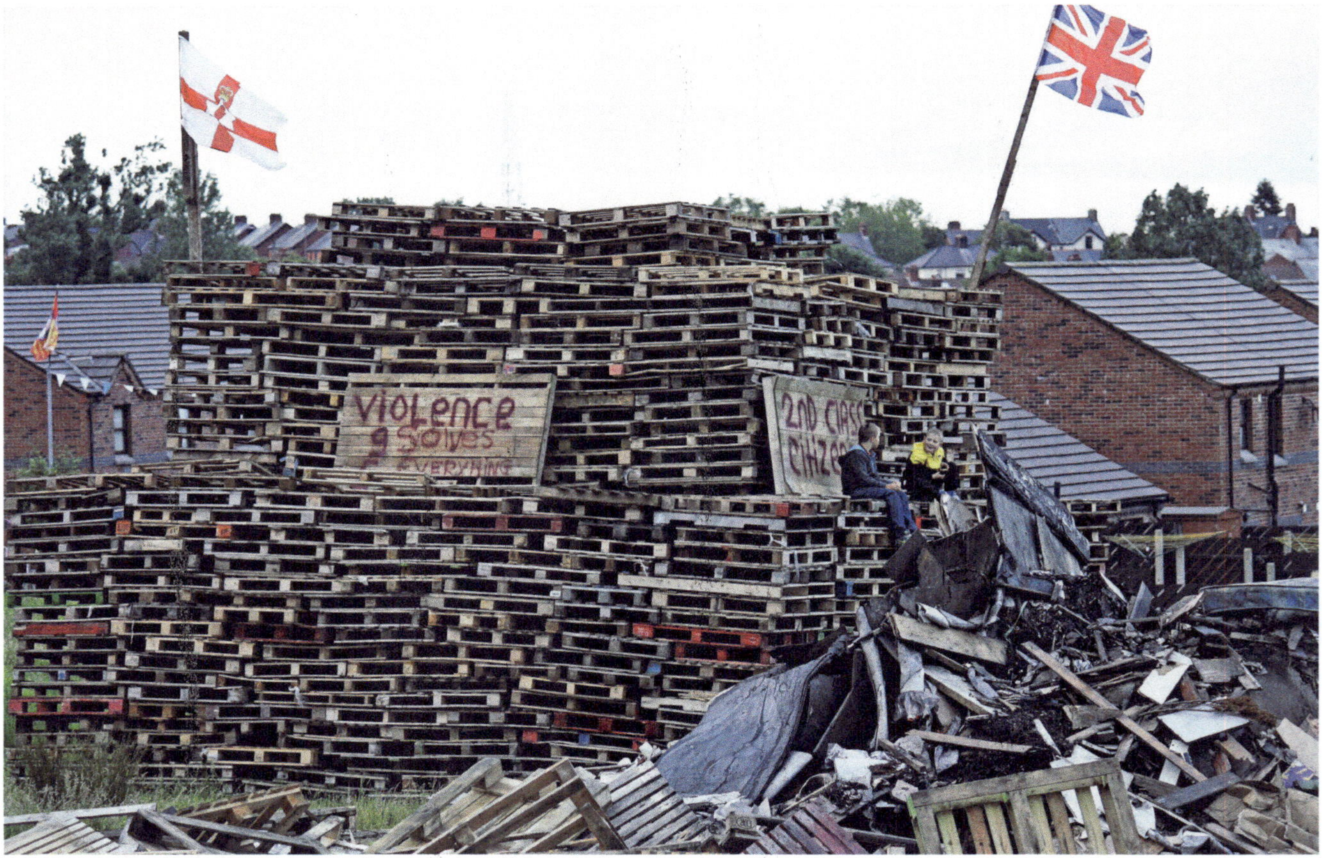

FIGURE 115 Violence solves everything, Glenbryn Park, Ardoyne, North Belfast, 2012. Photo by Tony Crowley.

the Irish state" (Figure 114, see Fulcrum). But not for the first time, loyalism's most dogged opponent appears to be the British government.

If this were a full representation of loyalist paramilitarism, the picture would be as bleak as the messages scrawled on a bonfire in Ardoyne in 2012: "2nd class citizens" and "Violence solves everything" (Figure 115). But as the IRC's 2022 report makes clear, the situation is more complicated. Although it is inviting ridicule to talk of "Peace, love & harmony," as featured in a mural of the PUP leader David Ervine in the Raven Club, East Belfast (no one who knew David Ervine would have described him as a hippie) (Figure 116, see Fulcrum), there are those

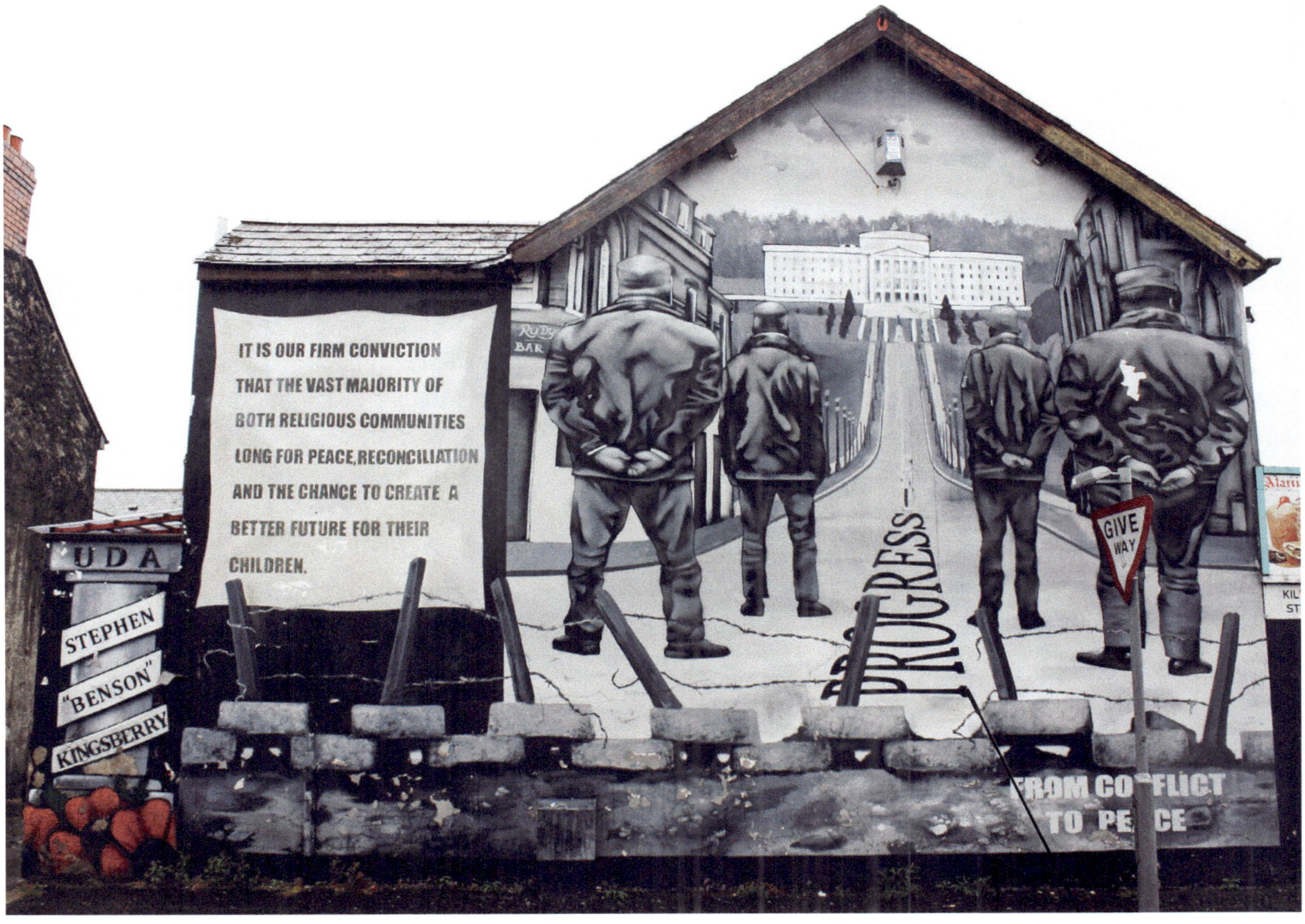

FIGURE 117 Progress, Kilburn Street, The Village, South Belfast, 2011. Photo by Tony Crowley.

within loyalist paramilitary organizations, or groups around them, who understand clearly the need for an alternative path. A UDA mural in Kilburn Street, South Belfast, for example, expressed "the firm conviction that the vast majority of both religious communities long for peace, reconciliation and the chance to create a better future for their children" (Figure 117). While a UVF mural in Carrickfergus asserted that "Progress requires inclusion" of the paramilitaries in the Peace Process (a point acknowledged by the IRC report) (Figure 118, see Fulcrum). In that regard, the activities of the Action for Community Transformation initiative (which began in 2008 as a conflict transformation program to facilitate the civilianization of the UVF and RHC) have been striking. They have instituted their own small museum, for example, and shown a determination to tell and explain "'our narrative—our journey' From the signing of the Covenant to the signing of the Belfast Agreement" (Figure 119, see Fulcrum). Loyalist paramilitaries are undoubtedly part of the problem in Northern Ireland, and some of the groupings have become little more than violent drug gangs with political cover, but as the IRC report insists, they also need to be part of the solution. As a side-image on a mural in The Village, South Belfast, observes: "Because loyalists have a past doesn't mean they shouldn't have a future" (Figure 120, see Fulcrum).

6. THE STRUGGLE FOR IDENTITY

An RHC mural in Rathcoole in 2016 declared the principles of the organization to be "To protect the loyalist community" and to "retain our Britishness" (see **fig. 96**), while a number of murals painted after the implementation of the Northern Irish Protocol have asserted that the prevention of the erosion of identity is now the priority for loyalism (see **figs 1, 4, 15**). But one of the most pressing questions for loyalists (and indeed the wider unionist community) is precisely what type of identity is to be preserved. This is a complex question, since as noted in chapter five, the Protestant/unionist/loyalist community is not unitary but heterogeneous and divided in all sorts of ways (it ranges from Creationists to secular socialists). It follows, therefore, that given the anxiety about the uncertain future, there is likely to be a struggle for what constitutes identity in and for this community. Aspects of this contest have been noted earlier in this chapter (see the discussion of re-imaging for example), but in this final section the main focus will be on the evidence provided by the walls for the ongoing debate about the nature, values, and aspirations of loyalism.

Evidently, one of the contributing factors in the construction of identity is communal memory, and this chapter has demonstrated the ways in which specific representations of particular events—the *Ulster Covenant* and the Somme for example—have molded an understanding of the past and present. But the memory of the violence of the recent past has also been subject to shaping through its representation in murals that aim to prevent forgetting. In a number of cases, including some that have been renewed, murals have drawn attention to IRA attacks, as in the images of "indiscriminate slaughter" on Dundee Street, West Belfast (Figure 121, see Fulcrum), "The dead cannot cry out" and "The price of peace is eternal vigilance" on Derwent Street, East Belfast (Figure 122, see Fulcrum) (Figure 123, see Fulcrum), and "the three Fusiliers" in Rathcoole (Figure 124, see Fulcrum). Other images, some of which have also been re-worked, have presented a loyalist version of the outbreak of the Troubles and the consequent disruption for the civilian population (see **chapter five, fig. 73**). Such images are significant in the cultural production of a political identity—a "we" that understands the recent past and its lessons for "us" in the present. None of which is to say that traditional images of the longer past have been neglected. King Billy and the Siege of Derry are both still celebrated on the walls, sometimes in beautiful form (Figure 125) (Figure 126, see Fulcrum), and the tradition of July 12th arches also appears to have re-emerged in specific locations (mostly beyond Belfast and Londonderry) (Figure 127, see Fulcrum) (Figure 128, see Fulcrum) (Figure 129, see Fulcrum).

But there are other currents flowing within loyalist communities, one of which is a concern for local history and thus local forms of identity (intra-communal identity in Northern Ireland can be intensely parochial, in both the positive and negative senses of that term). The "A–Z history of the Shankill" (see **fig. 27** above), is one example, and although this was a product of the re-imaging scheme, other manifestations of this interest were rooted in local communities and organizations. The slogan of the Shankill Historical Society was "Remembering the past with pride" (Figure 130, see Fulcrum) and one of a set of murals on the Donegall Road in South Belfast featured a photomontage that articulated the principle that underpinned this localism: "Sandy Row—Heritage—Culture—Identity" (together with the adage that "Today is yesterday's tomorrow") (Figure 131, see Fulcrum). The danger with such work is that it can veer into a form of nostalgia that obscures both poverty (through a focus on local "characters") (Figure 132, see Fulcrum) and the larger historical context of sectarianism (the "streets of dreams" for some might have been forbidden places of nightmare for others) (Figure 133, see Fulcrum). On the other hand, the advantage of much of this street art is that it draws attention to aspects of working-class history that are often ignored in histories of Northern Ireland such as the attachment to place. For example, a mural on the Bloomfield estate in Bangor, some twenty miles from Belfast, entitled "Bloomfield: a journey through time 1973–2018," featured scenes past and present from the Shankill Road and its environs in West Belfast (including two murals) (Figure 134). This might appear incongruous, but in actuality it reveals an important historical fact, because the estates in towns such as Bangor were built to house people who were removed from the Shankill during the slum clearances of the 1970s. And this in turn explains the close cultural and political ties between the working-class inhabitants of the estates and loyalist strongholds in Belfast.

Another fact addressed by local history murals is the centrality of labor to working-class life. In some examples, the image represents a traditional craftsman, such as the Lambeg drum maker in the extensive set of representations of life in Sandy Row painted in Stroud Street, South Belfast (Figure 135, see Fulcrum). But more often than not, the murals depict those archetypal figures of the working-class loyalist past: millers, dockers, and shipyard workers (particularly those who worked on the *SS Titanic*) (Figure 136) (Figure 137, see Fulcrum). It would be a mistake, however, to see murals that focus on loyalist local history as simply masculinist, since the opposite is true. Indeed "the thread of history" ties women into the texture of working-class life, as evinced in murals that showed

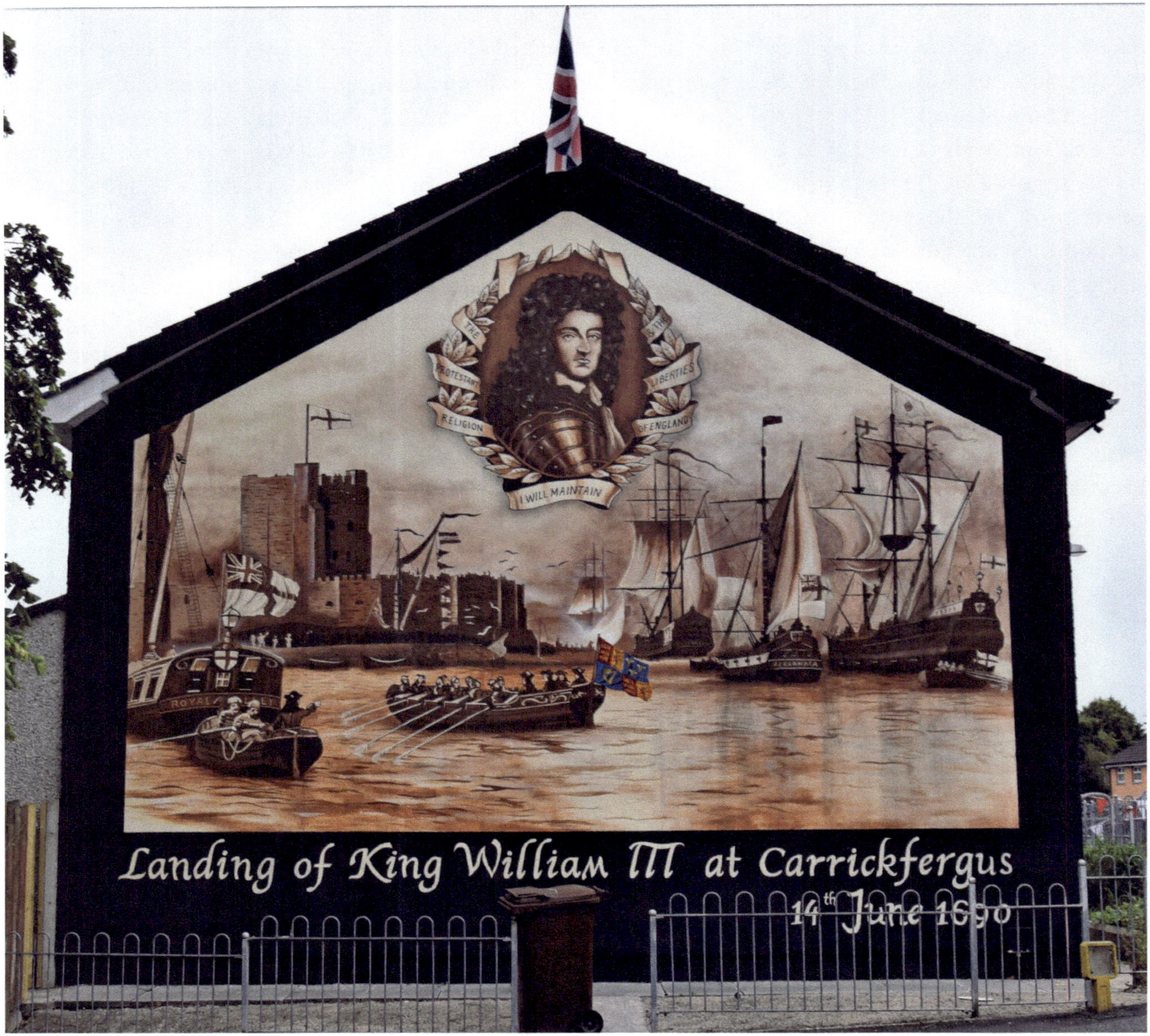

FIGURE 125 Landing of King William at Carrickfergus, Oakfield Drive, Glenfield, Carrickfergus, 2020. Photo by Tony Crowley.

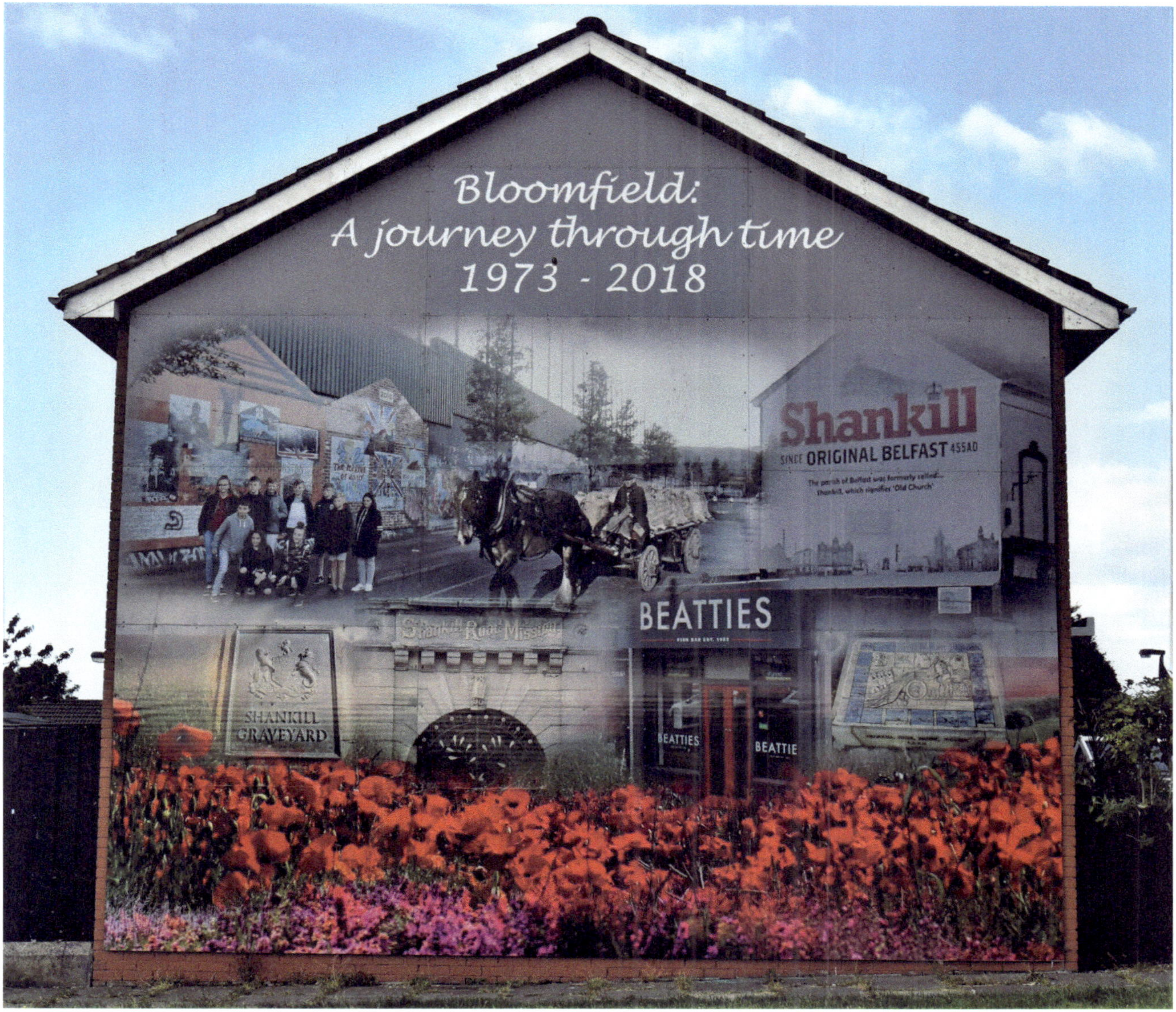

FIGURE 134 A journey through time, Ballyree Drive, Bloomfield, Bangor, 2018. Photo by Tony Crowley.

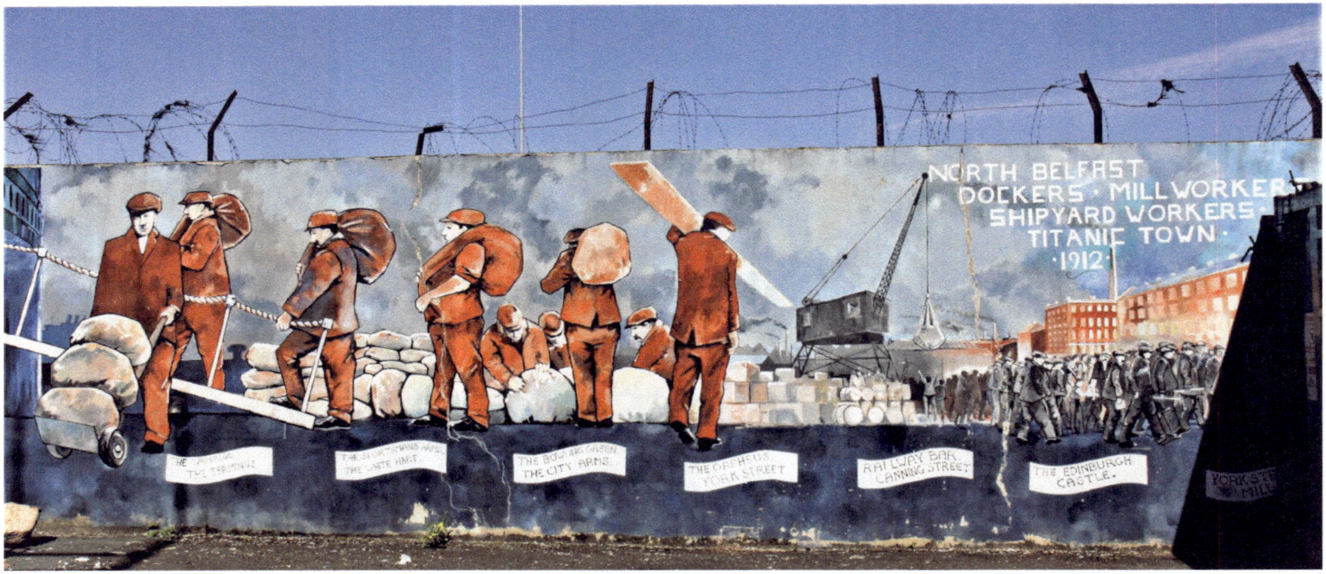

FIGURE 136 Titanic Town, St Vincent Street, North Belfast, 2012. Photo by Tony Crowley.

girls and women as "factory girls" (some of whom became weaver poets) (Figure 138) (Figure 139). Other murals linked to themes that had been represented in the re-imaging and related schemes (see section 2 above): suffragettism (Figure 140) (Figure 141, see Fulcrum), women's contribution to the war effort (First World War)—dedicated to "all the women of the Shankill" (Figure 142, see Fulcrum) - and a slightly odd depiction of "women through the ages" that ranged from Queen Victoria to female paramilitary auxiliaries (Figure 143, see Fulcrum).

As noted earlier, in 2014 a slogan on Linfield Road, Sandy Row, asserted that "they will never steal our culture" (**fig. 5**); in 2022 a mural in Rathcoole invoked "Respect Heritage Culture" (Figure 144, see Fulcrum). In both cases, the implication is that it is clear what constitutes loyalist culture, and it would certainly be easy enough to characterize it (and indeed to caricature it) with reference to a few dates, events, and practices. But like any other form of culture, loyalist cultural practice is differentiated rather than homogeneous. Of course there are mainstays—specific core political beliefs and the tropes that accompany them, and these have been clarified throughout this text and again in this chapter: "floreat Ultona" (Let Ulster flourish) (Figure 145, see Fulcrum).[18] But in reality there are distinct voices within loyalism and they are articulating specific and sometimes conflicting claims, ideals, and values. For example, like their nationalist and republican counterparts, loyalist communities are concerned about pressing social issues and they too resort to the walls to complain about the blight of drugs (Figure 146, see

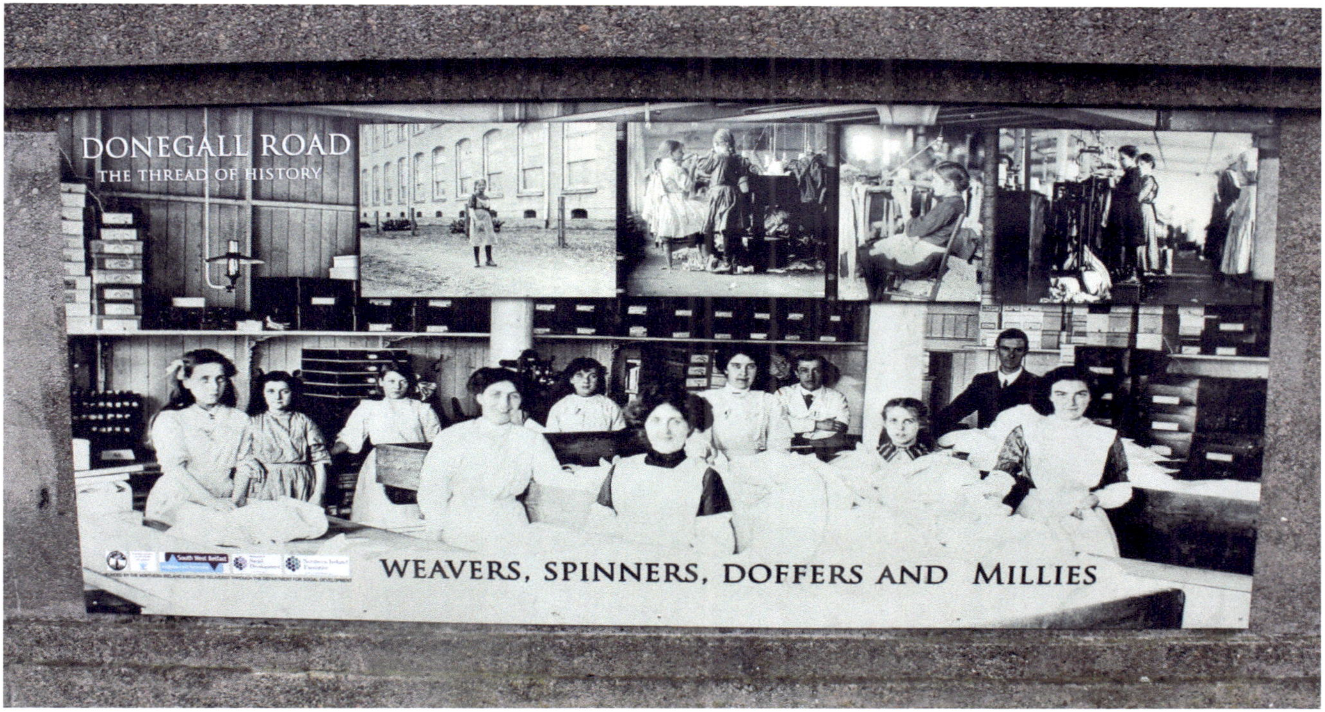

FIGURE 138 Mill workers, Donegall Road, The Village, South Belfast, 2014. Photo by Tony Crowley.

Fulcrum), the scourge of suicide and mental health issues (Figure 147, see Fulcrum), and the shortage of social housing (Figure 148, see Fulcrum); they also celebrate the NHS (Figure 149). And in the face of chronic scholastic under-achievement among Protestant working-class boys, there are murals that advocate education as the "passport to the future," the means to "dream seek achieve" (Figure 150, see Fulcrum) (Figure 151, see Fulcrum).[19] There is then a range of viewpoints within loyalism that constitutes a battle of social, political, and cultural ideas on a wide range of topics, not least that difficult, elusive, and complex question of identity.

There are voices within loyalism that see the cultural fact of Britishness (which is not the same as the political fact of being British) in simple terms. A mural in Portadown, for example, citing Thomas Carlyle, hails the centrality of Protestantism to British culture as one of the "three great elements of modern civilisation" (the others being gunpowder and printing) (Figure 152, see Fulcrum). This may be an accurate general claim in relation to post-Reformation British history, but it hardly fits with the reality of modern Britain with its many faiths (and, increasingly, none) and diverse identities. It would be difficult, for example, to find a mural elsewhere in Britain

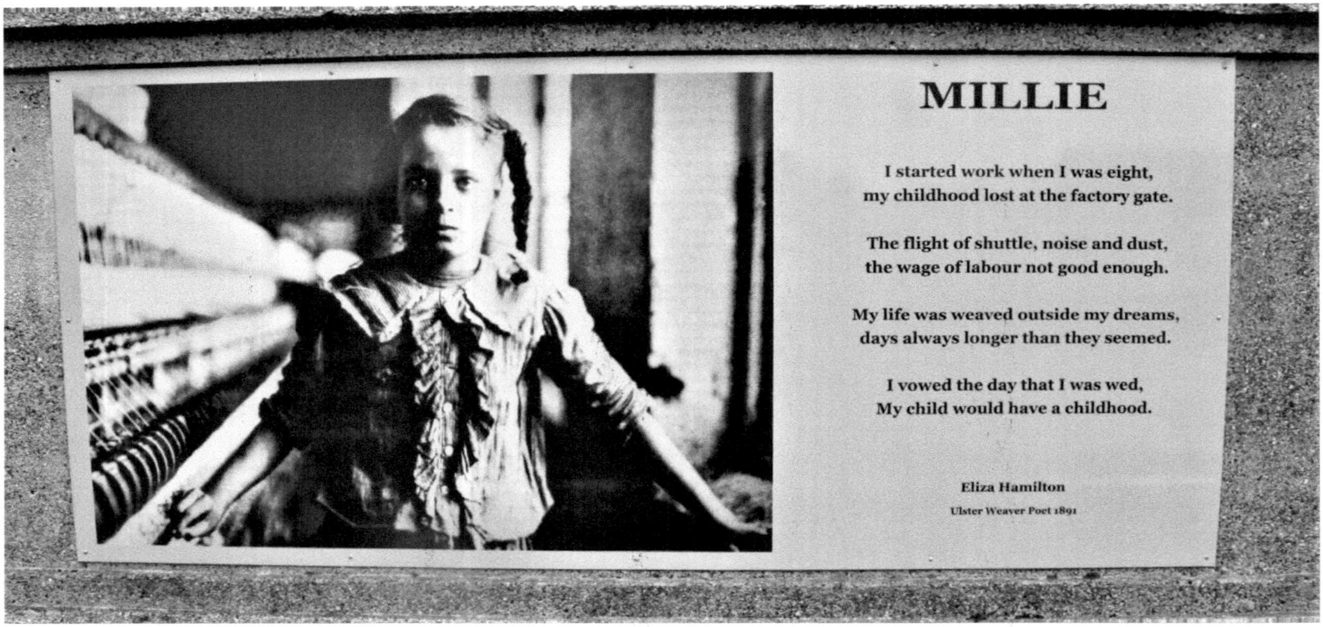

FIGURE 139 Millie, Donegall Road, The Village, South Belfast, 2014. Photo by Tony Crowley.

that argued for a leave vote in the Brexit referendum on the basis of a quotation from the Book of Revelations ("And I heard another voice from heaven, saying, Come out of her, my people, that ye be not partakers of her sins, and that ye receive not of her plagues") (Figure 153). In fact diversity is a problem for some within loyalism, and it is not hard to find indications of the same sort of racist and hypermasculine attitudes that were detailed in chapter five in warnings to landlords and housing agencies against placing "undesirables and immigrants" in houses that are to be "for locals only" (Figure 154, see Fulcrum), or the assertion that "real men 'take the knee'" only in order to fire their rifles (an image in Moygashel shows a British paratrooper kneeling to shoot—a coded reference to Bloody Sunday) (Figure 155, see Fulcrum). Elsewhere, an election poster in 2019 stated that "You can not be socialist and loyalist." As was intended, this provoked a deal of annoyance among those who consider themselves loyalist socialists, but the assertion itself may have been a response to an earlier mural at the Spectrum Centre at the top of the Shankill Road which announced that "Loyalist or racist You can't be both" (with accompanying image of a large boot squashing racism) (Figure 156). Both claims are of course affirmative rather than necessarily true or untrue, but they are signs of an ongoing and sometimes fiercely contested debate.

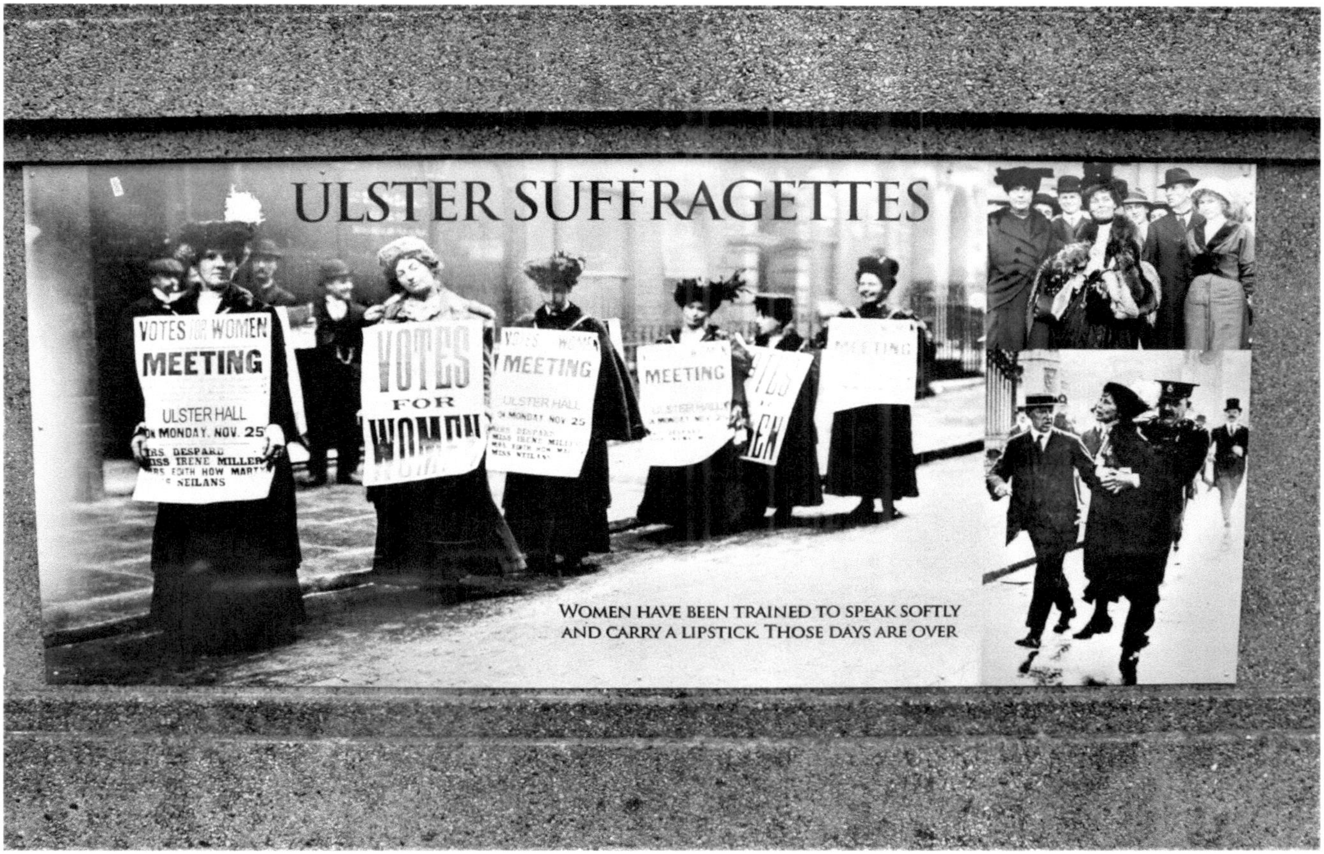

FIGURE 140 Those days are over, Donegall Road, The Village, South Belfast, 2014. Photo by Tony Crowley.

An indication of the nature of values and beliefs at stake in these arguments was given by a poster on a wall in the Grange Estate, Ballyclare in 2014 that addressed the abuse received by Portuguese workers living on the estate (Figure 157, see Fulcrum). The poster, headed by the flags of Portugal and Northern Ireland, and underpinned by the authority of "local community representatives" (including in all likelihood loyalist paramilitaries), appealed to local residents to stop the hostility towards the men, and to welcome them into the area. In an important sense, it is clear that the poster is a call for tolerance and recognition. And yet the terms of the appeal are revealing: these men are doing a necessary and specialist task; they are not taking local jobs; they are apolitical and areligious (Portugal is predominantly Catholic); they assimilate; they are hard-working, and they are

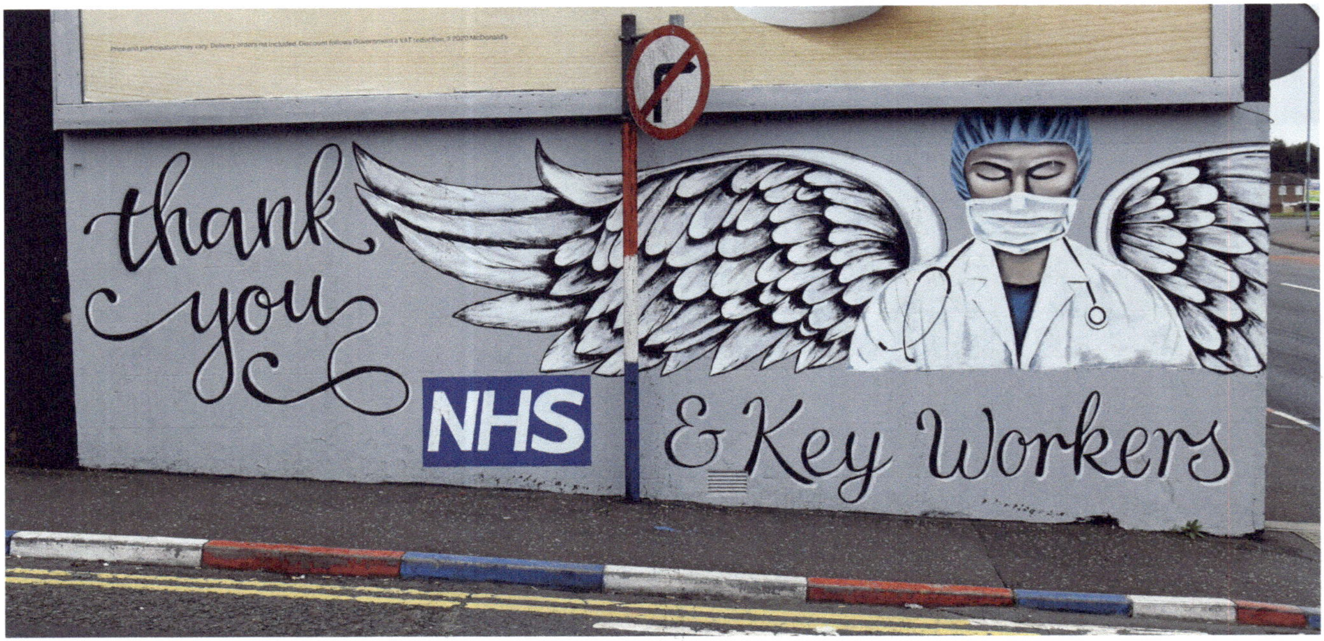

FIGURE 149 Thank you NHS and key workers, Bonds Place, Londonderry, 2020. Photo by Tony Crowley.

polite. In other words, they are model (temporary) workers and as such they can be welcomed. But what if they weren't good immigrants? A recent poster in Moygashel proclaimed that "It is not racist to protect your own community" (Figure 158, see Fulcrum), to which the response has to be that of course it is not necessarily racist to protect your own community; it just depends on what it is being protected against. Evidently, these indicators point to different views within loyalism towards a changing world that includes the embrace of diversity. A slightly gauche example of this process is an Orange Order mural in The Fountain, Londonderry, that depicted diverse members of the Order from the local area, Scotland, Ghana, and Canada (in Native American headdress)—presumably as a cipher for global Orangeism (Figure 159). But there are more interesting and nuanced attempts to treat this issue in two murals that form part of the educative project launched by the Action for Community Transformation initiative. One of these murals, on the loyalist side of the International Wall on Northumberland Street, pays tribute to "Kitchener's Own," specifically "foreign nationals" who fought alongside their British counterparts for King and Country in the First World War. Citing soldiers from across the Empire, the mural offers "special recognition to those within our community who are categorised as minorities but

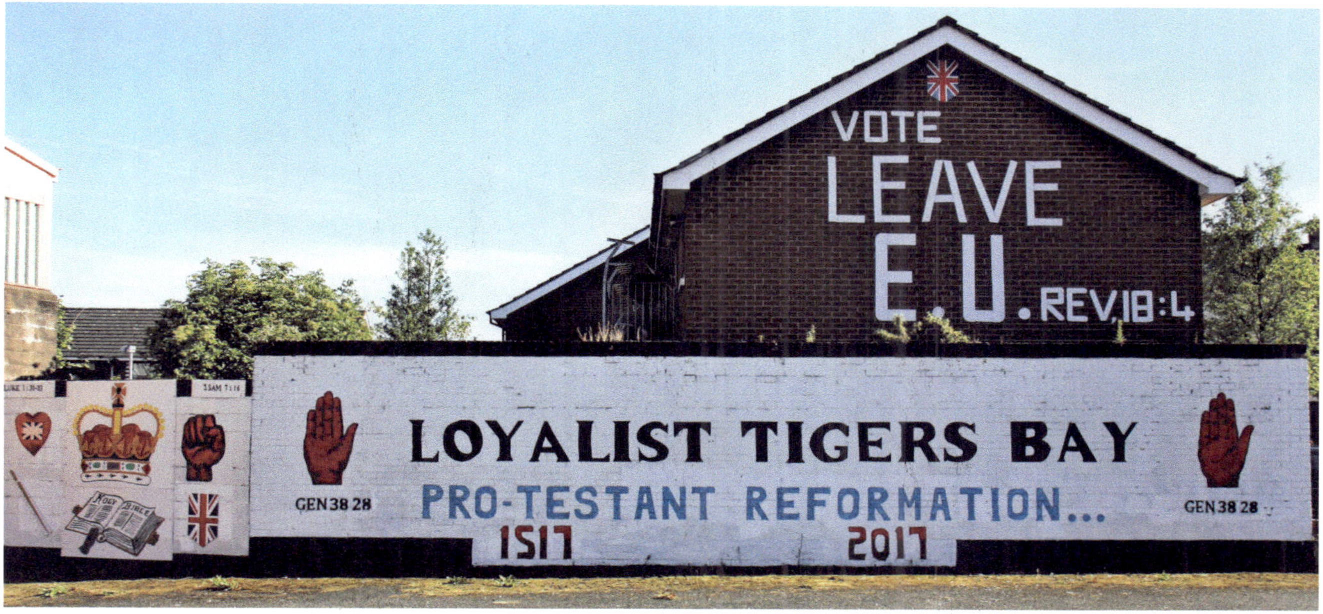

FIGURE 153 Vote leave, Limestone Road, Tigers Bay, North Belfast, 2017. Photo by Tony Crowley.

whose sacrifice was significant" (Figure 160). The second mural, in The Village, South Belfast, represents the Polish 303 Mazovian Squadron, which fought with the RAF in the Battle of Britain. The accompanying plaque notes that "many Polish servicemen remained in Great Britain and Ireland after the war, laying the foundations for a large Polish community that now (in Northern Ireland) numbers over 30,000. The Poles fought fiercely on all fronts for their freedom and ours, and their sacrifice should never be forgotten" (Figure 161, see Fulcrum). Of course it is right to point out again that both murals acknowledge only the good immigrants—those whose forebears fought for Britain—and it may be that the limited nature of the recognition reveals the state of the debate. But nevertheless, these works stand as attempts to address racial and ethnic diversity in areas that are solidly and unquestionably loyalist; if nothing else, and together with other images that focus on gender and class, they indicate that a debate has started within loyalism around identity and difference.

How that debate will turn out is unknown: the men with guns—past and present—are represented in many contemporary murals and one way and another they continue to exert their influence in the everyday life of a community that faces an uncertain and complicated future. Complicated because unionists and loyalists find themselves in an awkward and peculiar situation (again): fighting against the government of the United Kingdom

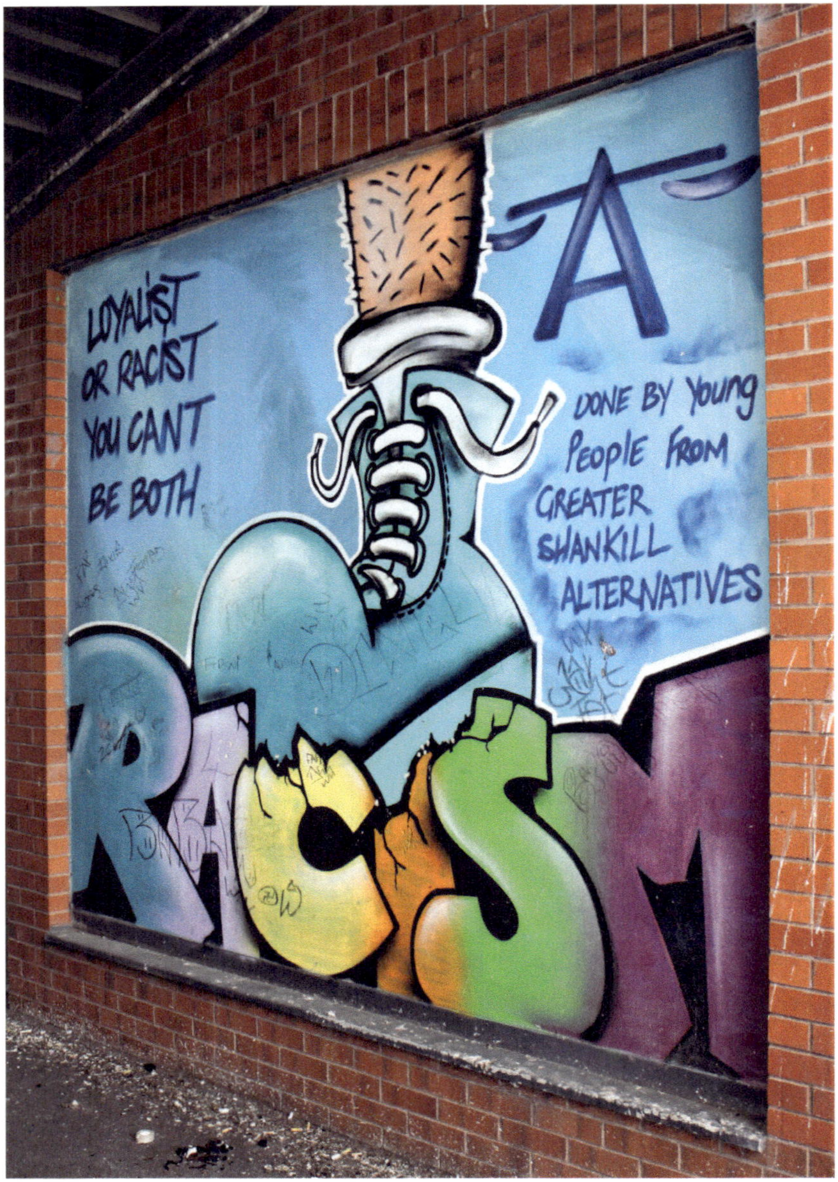

FIGURE 156 Loyalist or racist? Shankill Road, West Belfast, 2017. Photo by Tony Crowley.

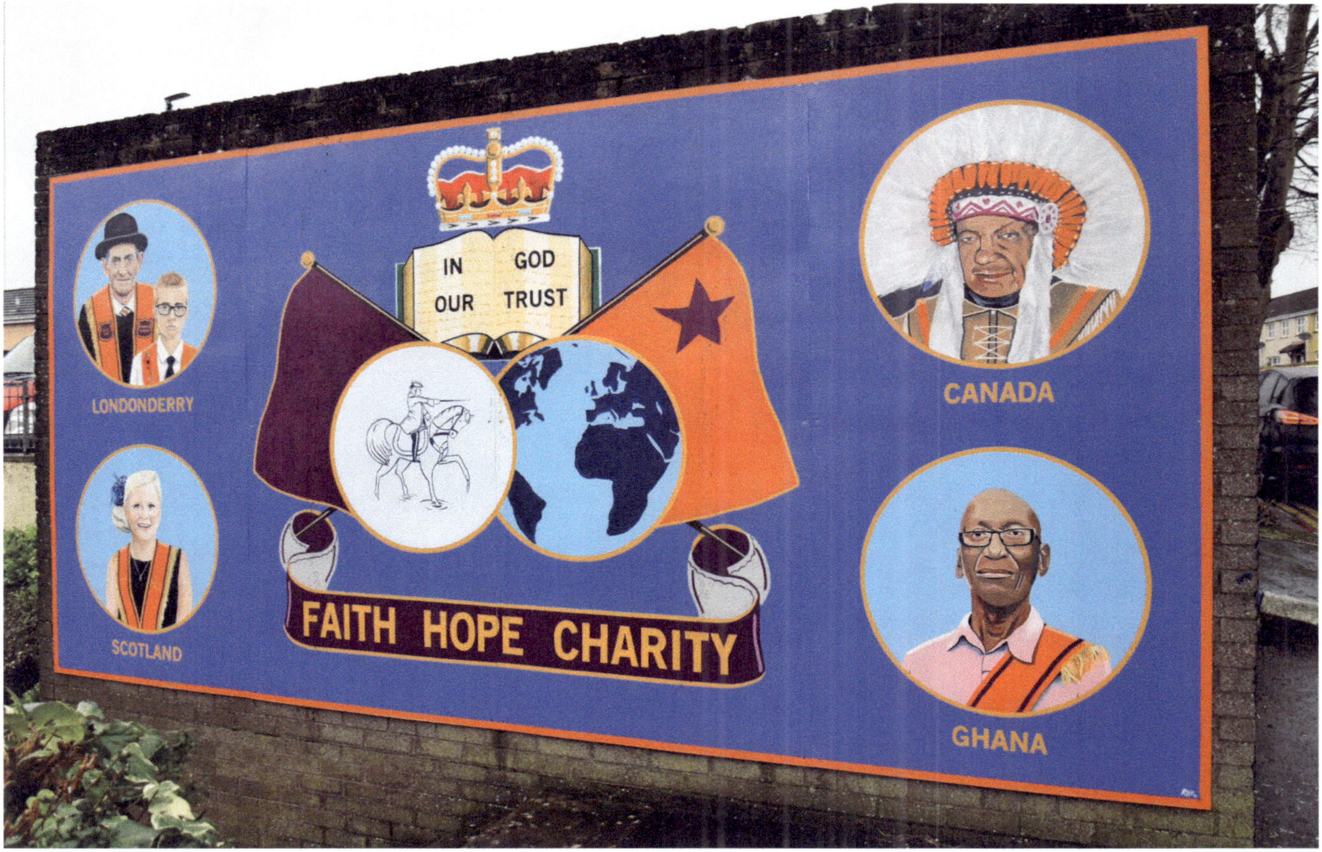

FIGURE 159 Global Orange, The Fountain, Londonderry, 2020. Photo by Tony Crowley.

because they do not believe its assurances and promises with regard to the Union. Whatever the future holds, and it is uncertain, if the history of muralism rendered in this book is any guide, it is more than likely that the walls will tell the story.

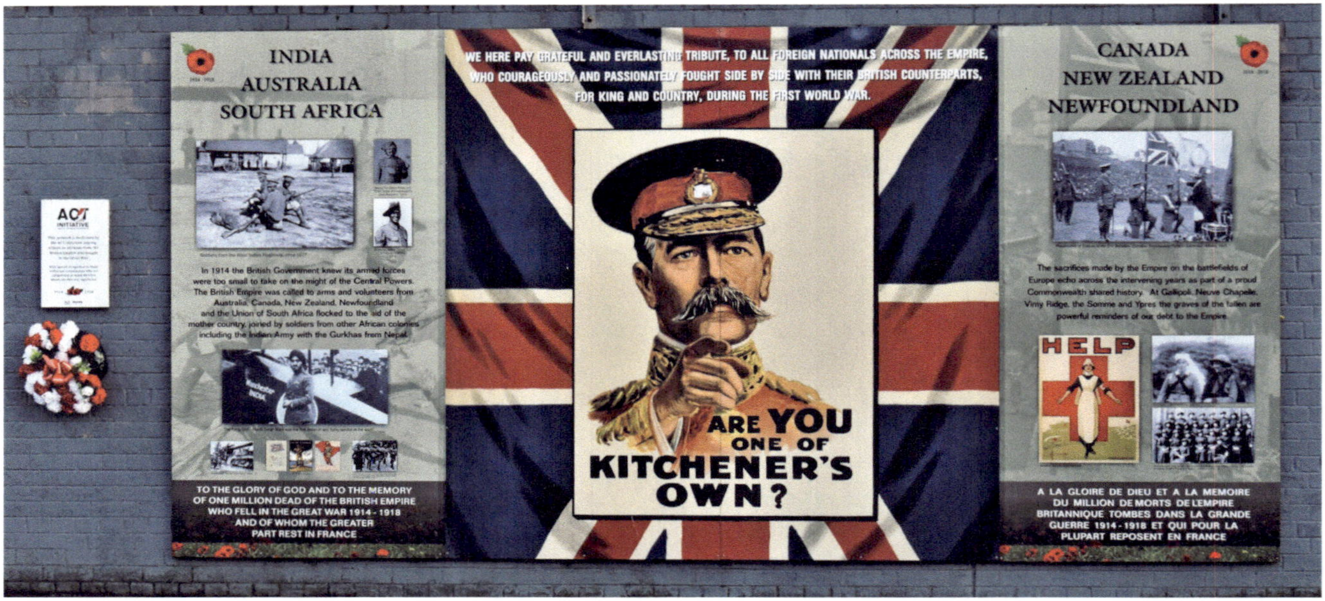

FIGURE 160 Kitchener's own, Northumberland Street, West Belfast, 2017. Photo by Tony Crowley.

CHAPTER 8
The End of Muralism?

To access all images referenced in this chapter, please visit the open access version on Fulcrum at https://doi.org/10.3998/mpub.14527058.

> The grievances of both communities are captured on infamous murals dotted throughout Belfast. Featuring free pick-ups from the city centre, your guide will take you through the narrow streets of Belfast and explain the stories behind every mural. ("Belfast political and mural tour," Taxi Tours Belfast, 2023)

Muralism in Northern Ireland is now more than a century old, and it surely stands as the longest continuing modern tradition of political wall art. It is a variable tradition in terms of range (everything from Gaelic mythology to contemporary housing issues), intensity (from the lull of the post-Second World War period to the current proliferation), and quality (from badly sketched animals to artwork of the highest level). But the determination to take to the walls to paint has been a constant of Northern Ireland's history, all the way from anti-Home Rule agitation in the pre-Partition period of the early twentieth century, to the nationalist led Stormont parliament of the present. And the questions with which I started this book, questions of authority and power, still apply: can anyone paint on a public wall? Can anyone paint anything on a public wall? Who gets to say?

Needless to say, the contemporary murals scene is vastly different from the situation in 1908, or 1981, or even 1998, in important ways. Today's muralists are not in danger, as they were during the war years, and they are freer to work with a variety of topics (though they are still subject to their commission, however loosely that is construed). Their subject matter is also distinct. Republican and loyalist murals may still present their different versions of history, manifest their political allegiances, and commemorate the dead. But the leading muralists on both sides now also work as freelancers and can be found painting all sorts of murals—to advertise local businesses, for example, or to support local community groups. There are other changes too. Technically, the older method of muralism involved an artist sizing up a wall, treating and preparing it, and then creating an image through the application of brushes dipped in paint. Over the past twenty years or so, however, digital technology has allowed for the appearance of a different type of mural altogether. Created on a computer, with the advantage of complex graphic design, and printed up on plastic sheets, these new murals are produced readymade, in pieces that are slotted together as they are fixed to the designated wall. These display boards are generally, though not exclusively, used by loyalists and "dissident" republicans (mainstream republican muralists still stick, for the most part, to paint on walls). Evidently this technological shift has had a significant effect on the form (from small to enormous images), content (digitization makes it possible to produce highly complicated collages and color schemes), and pace of production (a board can be designed and made in a couple of days if necessary) of contemporary murals. It is scarcely surprising to note that the traditional muralists reject the new medium, not simply because it threatens their livelihood (which it does), but also because they see it as aesthetically inferior (though there is evidently skill in the graphic design of many of the new works).

One of the most important shifts over the past twenty years or so has been in the audience of the murals. For, as demonstrated by the epigraph at the start of this chapter, muralism, particularly in Belfast and Derry/Londonderry, has become part of Northern Ireland's burgeoning tourist scene. Murals tours—by coach, taxi, and on foot—are enormously popular, particularly those coordinated by organizations that employ ex-combatants/prisoners as guides. In the summer months in particular, specific places such as the International Wall on Divis Street and Northumberland Street, are packed with visitors—British, European, Japanese, American… Even though these are relatively broad roads (despite what the advert says, not all of Belfast's streets are "narrow"), the crowds are considerable, as indeed are those that queue to photograph Free Derry Wall and to record the work of the Bogside Artists. There is much to be said for mural tourism—not least in that it generates money for the local economies and provides work for people who otherwise struggle to find it. It also allows people on both sides to present their narrative: the "Falls/Shankill Tour," hosted by Coiste (a republican ex-prisoners' organization), is divided into two parts: "on the nationalist leg of the tour, the visitor will see the world-famous International Wall with its political artworks, the Republican Memorial Garden and the world-famous mural of Bobby Sands. This tour tracks the course of the 'Peace Wall' and goes through Clonard with its famous Clonard Monastery Church and Bombay Street, the epicentre of events in 1969." After which, the group is handed over "to the loyalist tour guide who will bring it on to the Shankill Area, to hear the unionist/loyalist perspective on our past and visit local sites of interest" (https://www.coiste.ie/falls-shankill-tour/).

There are crass aspects to mural tourism as a number of critics have noted (McDowell 2008; Nagle 2011). After all, "dark tourism," of which mural tourism in Northern Ireland is a sub-genre, is usually predicated precisely on the fact that the sites visited have witnessed conflict, violence, and death. In Northern Ireland, as elsewhere, tourists pay at least in part for the voyeuristic frisson of wandering safely around areas in which tragedy was enacted relatively recently.[1] This can lead to some grotesque nonsense, as when the tourist buses pull up on Cupar Way, on the loyalist side of the huge "Peace Wall" that divides the loyalist Shankill from republican Clonard (see **chapter seven, fig. 39**). Armed with pens provided by the bus drivers, the tourists are invited to make their own contributions to the ongoing process of conflict resolution (Figure 1). Insights include: "Make tea not war" (see **chapter seven, fig. 43**), "Stop wars Stop walls" (Figure 2, see Fulcrum), "Erik just asks why??" (Figure 3,

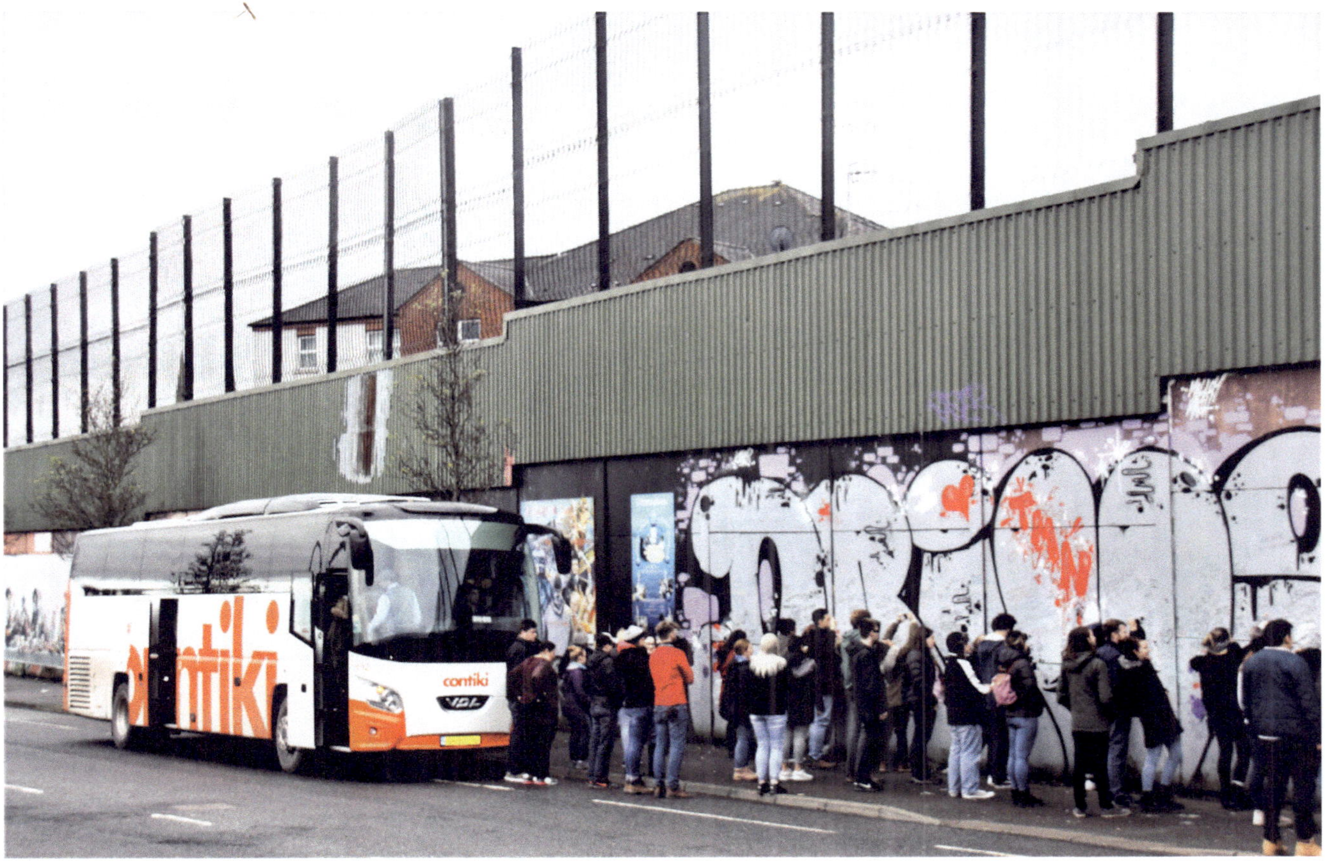

FIGURE 1 Tourist bus, Cupar Way, Shankill, West Belfast, 2018. Photo by Tony Crowley.

see Fulcrum) and “Stop writing ‘Peace’ Start drinking beer together and then fuck each other” (Figure 4, see Fulcrum). To all of which, there was one heart-felt response that undoubtedly reflected local opinion on both sides of the wall: “Fuck you and your patronising slogans” (Figure 5).

There have been other developments in muralism that are interesting and potentially significant. The first is the non-figurative form of tagging, a practice that originated in Philadelphia and flourished in New York in the late twentieth century (Ferrell 2016: xxx). In Belfast it started to appear extensively on the Cupar Way Peace Wall and around the northern boundary of Belfast city center more than a decade ago, though it is now visible all over the city. There are a number of leading individual figures or crews involved in the Belfast tagging scene

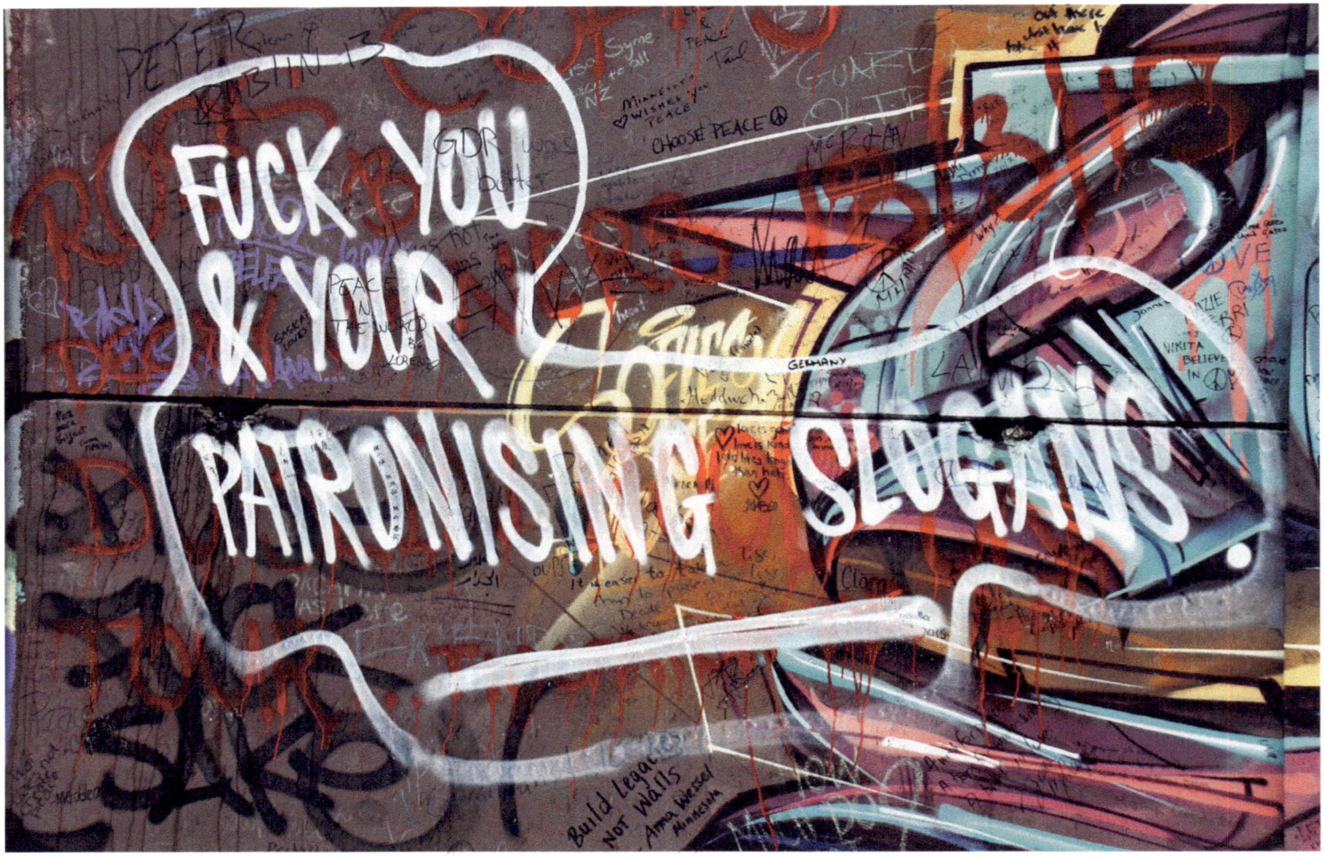

FIGURE 5 Patronising slogans, Peace Line, Cupar Way, Shankill, West Belfast, 2016. Photo by Tony Crowley.

(all of whom are anonymous and guard their identities carefully): NOTA, TMN, ANCO, RMS, 4FUN, MASH, GECO, EVOS (Figure 6, see Fulcrum) (Figure 7, see Fulcrum). One way of interpreting this work is to see it as what Raymond Williams called a "structure of feeling"—a clear, if not fully articulated, shift in ways of thinking, values, and attitudes, usually expressed in an emergent cultural practice. And this is borne out in the few publicly available interviews with the taggers, which evince a relatively common set of attitudes, influenced by post-punk, anarchism, and "straight edge" ethics and style. NOTA, for example, comments that "Being true to yourself is the only thing that counts! Fuck the rest" (NOTA 2012). From one perspective, this could be read simply as a type of anti-establishmentarianism (NOTA—"None of the above"), an individualist form of non-conformism (tags are, after all, frequently iterations of the same name over and over). None of the tagging work is explicitly political, at least in the sense that it makes no reference to the history of power relations and conflict that has characterized Northern Ireland since the inception of the State. And yet, placed within the historical context of the strict communalism of a sectarian society, it may be that the apparently apolitical stance of tagging is more interesting than first appears. For example, its refusal to engage with the binary, violent history of Belfast may represent a form of politics in and of itself. One thing is clear: tagging is resented by forces as diverse as Belfast city council, property owners, and traditional muralists, which may indicate no more than that this artistic practice simply fails to conform to the cultural and political genre of muralism that has long dominated in Northern Ireland.

The second new development in muralism—mostly, though not exclusively, in Belfast and Derry/Londonderry, has been the appearance of "street art," usually consisting of both figurative and abstract murals on a wide variety of topics. It is a form that critics have strictly separated from "tagging," as evinced by an account of Belfast city council's decision to create " 'street art walls' across the city in a bid to encourage 'safe and legal' art and cut down on illegal tagging." The basis of the decision was the recognition that "in many places, [street art] works have become tourist attractions and are creating a real sense of civic pride. However, the council also acknowledges the concern and frustration that particular types of graffiti such as tagging can cause to communities, and the cost of its removal" (Kenwood 2023). The categorization of "street art" as "safe and legal" is an interesting delineation that indicates the State's stance towards it. "Legal" of course simply means "permitted by the law," but in what sense is it "safe"? To what does the adjective refer—the location, the people who practice the form, the content?

There have always been "other" murals in Northern Ireland—images painted by community groups, for example, or even, in rare cases, by British soldiers within army barracks.[2] And of course there were the State "re-imaging" initiatives during 1977–1981 (see **chapter two**), 2006–2009, and 2013–2015 (see **Introduction** and **chapters six** and **seven**). But the relatively recent appearance of street art as an organized, funded, and widespread activity is unusual in two respects: it is, for the most part, not linked to groups rooted in local communities, and it is not funded directly by the State (though grants from state-funded artsbodies, as well as commercial sponsorship, underpin it). There are various organizations involved in this development, such as the path-breaking Cathedral Quarter Trust, Eastside Arts, and Seedhead Arts in Belfast.[3] And as a result of their activities over the past decade or so, street art has been popularized with events such as "Culture Night" and "Hit the North" (and to a lesser extent "Hit the East"), which have drawn enormous crowds to see work by local and international artists. Originating in a desire to re-generate the north of the city center, a neglected area that consists of demolition sites (cum car parks), or buildings marked for demolition, the aim of "Culture Night" and "Hit the North" has been to attract locals and tourists and to generate economic benefits. Much of the art is high-quality and reflects the status of the international street artists who are commissioned to paint on the boards, hoardings, and walls of what is still a relatively dingy and run-down area of the city. "Son of Protagoras," for example (Figure 8) was painted in 2014 in a courtyard on Talbot Street (opposite St Anne's Cathedral) by the French artist MTO.

Much of this new muralism in Belfast is now located in a small area of the northern city center bounded by North Street, Union Street, Kent Street, Library Street, and Little Donegall Street. The area is a mix of dereliction, gentrification, and student accommodation, and it features a number of counter-cultural bars and clubs (including Belfast's few LGBTQ+ venues). The new murals are stylistically eclectic and include examples of, among others, free style, pop art, cartoons, abstract art, surrealism, graffiti art, and figurative work (Figure 9) (Figure 10, see Fulcrum) (Figure 11,

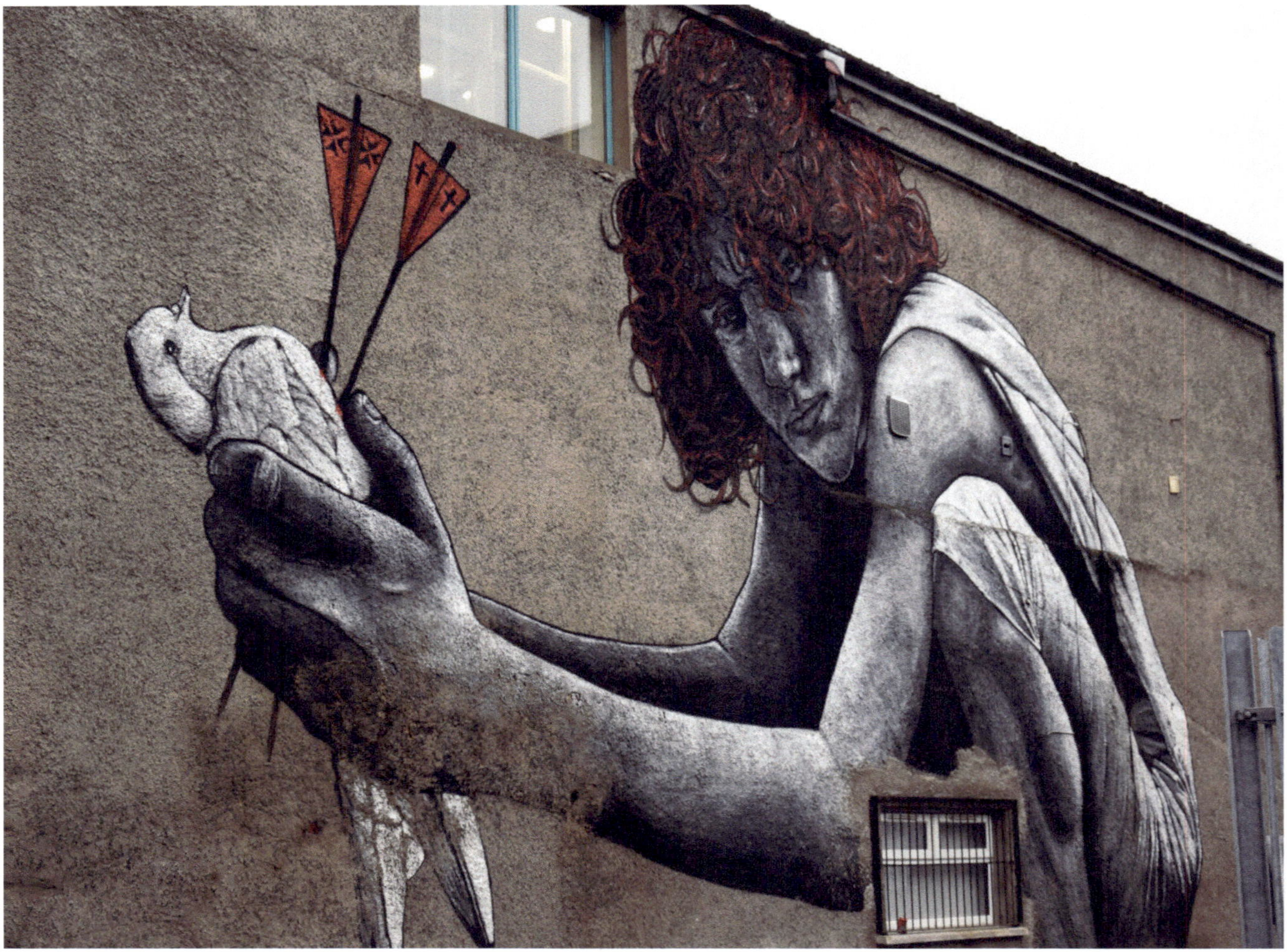

FIGURE 8 Son of Protagoras, Talbot Street, Belfast City Center, 2020. Photo by Tony Crowley.

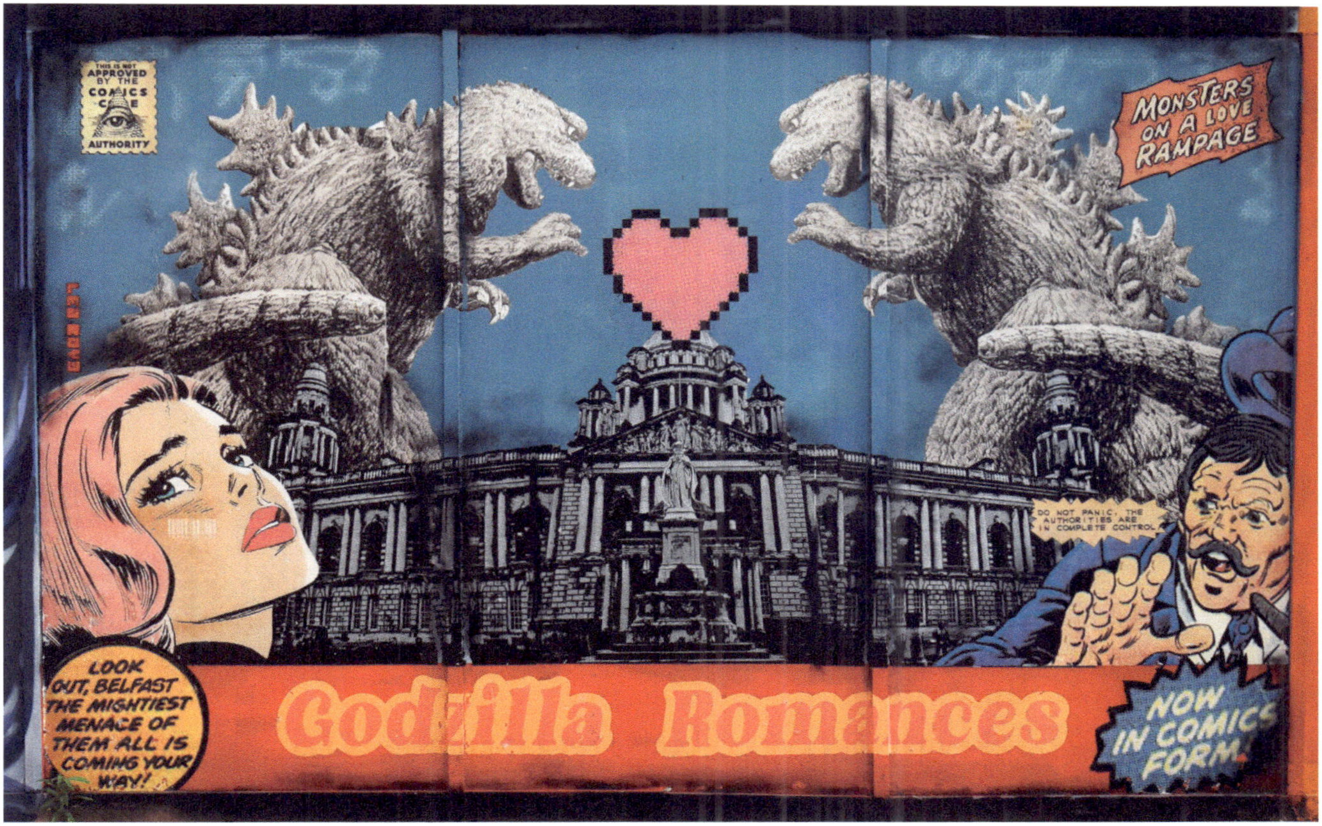

FIGURE 9 Godzilla romances, Kent Street, City Center, Belfast, 2023. Photo by Tony Crowley.

see Fulcrum) (Figure 12, see Fulcrum). Perhaps the most striking aspect of these murals, however, is the lack of overt reference to political issues. There are some exceptions, with murals indirectly citing feminism—"Girls just wanna… fun…damental rights" (Figure 13)—and diversity—"Together Show some love" (Figure 14, see Fulcrum). There is also a mural depicting Lyra McKee (a journalist accidentally shot and killed by the New IRA during rioting in Derry/Londonderry in 2019). And, uniquely, the 2023–2024 Israeli assault on Gaza has been marked by a Palestinian solidarity mural. But the Lyra mural makes only an allusion to the circumstances of her death by quoting from a letter to her younger self: "Here's to saying goodbye to bombs and bullets" (Figure 15). And the pro-Palestinian mural is relativized by the re-creation of the ironic "Give peas a chance" image produced next to it (featuring a tin of peas) (Figure 16, see Fulcrum). Other than these anomalies, the murals make no mention of the thirty-year war (1969–1998), nor indeed the continuing sectarian conflict that dominates Northern Ireland life. One way of accounting for

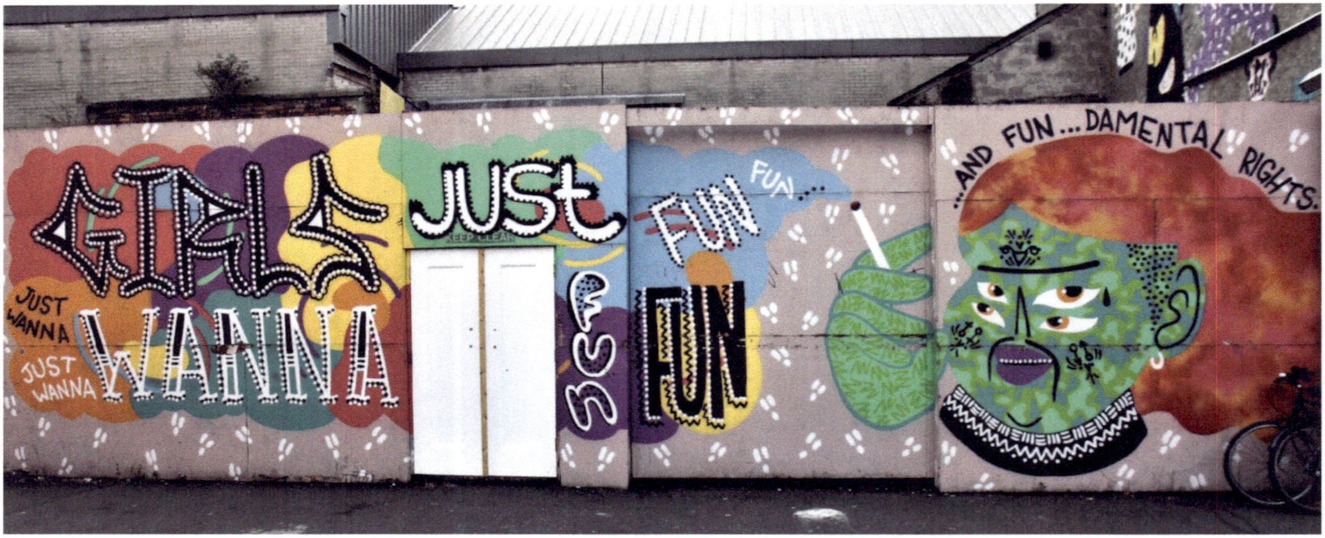

FIGURE 13 Girls just wanna, Union Street, Belfast City Center, 2018. Photo by Tony Crowley.

this apparently puzzling absence is to argue that, as with tagging, precisely because of the divided, sectarian nature of Northern Ireland, apolitical wall art of the type that adorns the northern edge of Belfast city center (and indeed parts of Derry/Londonderry), is political simply because it refuses to engage with the hegemonic order. In other words, not referring to Northern Ireland's bloody political history is a way of grappling with it. But the question bears analysis.

A couple of hundred yards away from the apolitical murals of Belfast city center lies the relatively new estate of Carrick Hill (formerly Unity flats, a republican enclave), at the entrance to which plaques remember dead IRA volunteers from the local area (Figure 17, see Fulcrum). They are a reminder, as has been demonstrated throughout this study, that Northern Ireland is a place characterized by a heightened sense of history, the past, and memory. Indeed the imperative to commemorate both grand historical events and individual people is ever-present on the walls: "remember," "lest we forget," "we shall remember," "in memory of," "i ndil chuimhne" (in loving memory). Given that, the lack of reference to the past in the new muralism is both striking and puzzling, and the claim that not alluding to history is a way of addressing it, is open to scepticism. There is another interpretation: that the new murals serve, unintentionally or not, the neo-liberal goal of creating a city center space that is made "safe" for consumerism and leisure, precisely through the erasure of history and politics, specifically the violence of the war and its legacy. In this sense, the ever-new, apolitical, images are part of the larger ahistorical vision embodied in the redevelopment of Belfast city center that has taken place since the 1990s, within which there is no room for

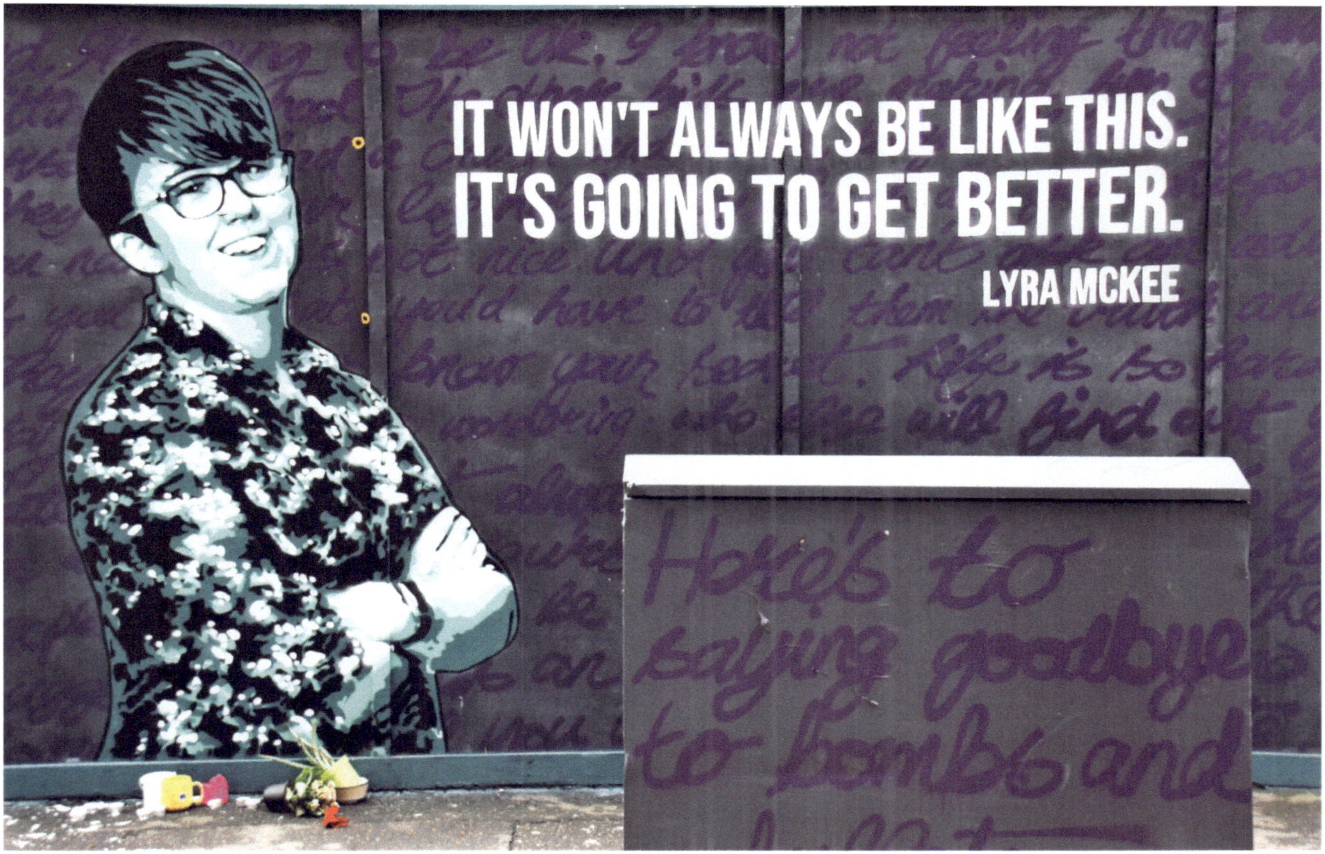

FIGURE 15 Lyra McKee, Kent Street, City Center, Belfast, 2019. Photo by Tony Crowley.

the past. This is remarkable, given that the city center was the site of considerable violence and destruction during the war. On Bloody Friday in 1972, for example, the IRA detonated 22 bombs, mostly car bombs, in a space of 80 minutes, killing nine people and wounding 130, many horribly. And that was but the worst example of a litany of violent events—bombings, fire-bombings, shootings—that occurred within the relatively small confines of the city center. A lot of history happened in this place, a lot of violent history. And yet there is little or no memory of it.[4] Instead, the dis-membered and mis-remembered city center has become an island of amnesia in a sea of bitter, complex, and difficult memory. The new muralism has played a role in that process, particularly in its location in an area that has only recently begun to be developed. Once fully gentrified and subject to "consumption-driven urban development" (Markusen and Schrock 2009: 344), it remains to be seen whether the northern city center will remain one of Belfast City Council's designated "safe and legal" spaces for street art.

It will be interesting to see what happens to the new murals. At the moment, they remain limited, for the most part, to the city centers of Belfast and Derry/Londonderry (as noted earlier, "Hit the East" in East Belfast, particularly around Laburnum Lane in Bloomfield, has also encouraged apolitical mural work, though that site is now subject to redevelopment). They have also been adopted in city and town centers throughout Northern Ireland as a relatively cheap form of advertisement (usually on the shutters that protect the premises when closed). Yet the new muralists, with very few exceptions, have not ventured into the republican and loyalist heartlands across Northern Ireland.[5] International artists (or at least non-local international artists) are not painting their stuff in Lenadoon or Rathcoole. The question arises then: do the new murals indicate the end of muralism in Northern Ireland? Or at least the end of political muralism of the type that has dominated the tradition traced in the historical account given in the previous chapters of this book? The answer to that question is—surely not. From the inception of the tradition in the early twentieth century, to the painting of the vast majority of murals that exist today, muralism in Northern Ireland has been the product of, and formed part of, a bitter, divided, and frequently violent social conflict. The walls were used to tell social stories before the war, during the war, and in the post-war period, and although the violence has largely ended, the conflict itself remains unresolved. Simply by dint of that fact, there is every reason to believe that political muralism will continue. Its form and content may change, as with all traditions, but its continuity seems assured.

At the beginning of my account of this history, I cited the artist Joseph Carey's appreciation of muralism in Northern Ireland in the *Northern Whig* in 1924: "I fancy the like of it is not to be seen elsewhere. Endless scribblings on blank walls you will find. But where else have whole gables been covered, turning the streets into a sort of al fresco art gallery?" (Carey: 1924: 6). For more than a century, the streets of Northern Ireland have been an alfresco political art gallery, the location of a sustained practice of muralism that continues to be intriguing, varied, and socially significant. Carey's question is a good one: where else indeed?

Notes

Introduction

1. *Le journal mural* was a wall newspaper produced by Atelier Populaire, a group of artists and art students, during the events of Paris 1968; it was over-sized in order to facilitate collective reading.

2. For an account of the experience of the dangerous politics of space, see Edwards 2017: 120–121.

3. For a semi-fictional account of British Army activity in Northern Ireland in the late 1970s, in which the purpose of British Army foot patrols in republican function is explained as "presence, deterrence and intel," see A.F.N. Clarke, *Contact* (Clarke 1984: 7). Ken Wharton's *A Long, Long War* contains a host of soldiers' testimonies describing the process of "reading the signs" (Wharton 2008).

4. The best detailed, though slightly out of date, guide to the bibliography of Northern Ireland can be found at the CAIN website (Conflict Archive on the Internet): https://cain.ulster.ac.uk/bibdbs/bibliography/index.html. The CAIN site is an invaluable source for materials related to Northern Ireland.

5. The image of the Warrenpoint mural was highly unusual in that it figured muralists at work. Painting murals was a dangerous business during the war and republican muralists in particular tended to be extremely reluctant to be photographed; it was not until a while after the first ceasefire that muralists began consistently to put their names to their work. For an account of the dangers of muralism, see Whelan 2011.

6. Mark Ervine, interview July 4 2013. Ervine, the son of the influential loyalist political leader David Ervine, is a prolific and accomplished (non-paramilitary) muralist.

7. The RUC was disbanded in 2001 and replaced by a new organization—the PSNI.

8. Thatcher's actual words, in a speech in the House of Commons on November 10 1981, were: "Northern Ireland is part of the United Kingdom; as much as my constituency is" (Thatcher's constituency was Finchley, North London).

9. One senior member of the republican movement described me as nothing more than "a fucking idiot with a camera," a phrase that may be epitaphial.

10. For a harrowing set of accounts which capture the misery and trauma of the violence and its consequences, see David McKittrick et al., *Lost Lives: The Stories of Men, Women and Children who Died as a Result of the Northern Ireland Troubles* (McKittrick et al. 1999) and Susan McKay's *Bear in Mind These Dead* (McKay 2008); Colin Davidson's portraits of victims in *Silent Testimony* (Davidson 2015) are likewise heart-wrenching.

11. The earliest rigorous (and often over-looked) academic research on murals, undertaken as part of a broader study, is Belinda Loftus's Ph.D. 1982 thesis, *Images in Conflict: Visual Imagery and the Troubles in Northern Ireland (1968–1981)*, which issued in two invaluable and pioneering studies, *Mirrors: William III and Mother Ireland* (1990) and *Mirrors: Orange and Green* (1994). The work of Bill Rolston is foundational for any serious study of the murals; as well as a panoply of important articles, it includes *Politics and Painting: Murals and Conflict in Northern Ireland* (1991); *Drawing Support: Murals in the North of Ireland* (1992); *Drawing Support 2: Murals of War and Peace* (1995); *Drawing Support 3: Murals and Transition in the North of Ireland* (2003); *Drawing Support 4: Murals and Conflict Transformation in Northern Ireland* (2013) and *Drawing Support 5: Murals, Memory and Identity in the North of Ireland* (2022). Rolston's contribution to various aspects of the history of Northern Ireland both during the war and in the transition to peace is peerless and like everyone else working in the field, I am indebted to him for his professional help and friendship. McCormick's archive is hosted

at the CAIN site, "Political Wall Murals in Northern Ireland" (https://cain.ulster.ac.uk/murals/index.html), which also includes a variety of other materials. The "Extramural Activity" site, maintained by Seosamh Mac Coille and Cahal Collie, is at https://extramuralactivity.com/; it contains prodigious historical detail for individual murals and now includes the important work of Peter Moloney, another veteran mural collector and historian of the Troubles, and a link to the site of republican muralist Gerard "Mo Chara" Kelly (https://gerardmocharakelly.wordpress.com/). Alain Miossec's "Murals Irlande du nord" can be found at https://muralsirlandedunord.over-blog.com/. Both the CAIN and "Extramural Activity" sites have maps of their murals. On a personal and intellectual level, I have never found the "mural hunters" of Northern Ireland to be anything other than non-competitive, intellectually generous, and personally kind, and I am deeply grateful for that. I also wish to acknowledge my gratitude to Phil Lismore, who gave me access to his own mural images at a later stage of my research.

12. Later, the Arts Council published, in the same series of "Troubles Archive Essays," Billy Hutchinson's *Transcendental Art* (2011), which addresses loyalist murals inside and outside prison; the pamphlet will be discussed in chapter three. The Ulster Museum's "The Troubles and Beyond" exhibition (which opened in 2018) features murals by Danny Devenny and Marty Lyons and Mark Ervine representing, respectively, republican and loyalist versions of Cú Chulainn (Figure 1, see Fulcrum).

13. The early history of the term is complicated. "Mural" is first recorded in English in the sixteenth century as an adjective, usually in the phrase "mural crown" or "crown mural," meaning a crown, garland, or wreath conferred by the Romans on the first soldier to scale the walls of a besieged town. The general sense of "pertaining in some way to a wall" ("placed, fixed, or executed on a wall") is a sixteenth-century development and it is not until the mid-nineteenth century that "mural painting," in the sense of "a painting executed directly on to a wall or ceiling," and the activity of such painting, first appears. "Mural" appears to be a shortened version of "mural painting" and is registered at the beginning of the twentieth century—at the same time as "muralist" (*Oxford English Dictionary* s.v. "mural" adj.1; n.1; n.2; "mural painting; "muralist").

14. There is no evidence at all that the Red Hand of Maltravieso is linked to either the red hand of the O'Neills nor indeed to the Red Hand of loyalism.

15. Guthrie gives an overview of various theories, but his claim as to the "ordinariness" of the wall paintings has been controversial (Guthrie 2006).

16. Defending murals painted by Shantallow Youth in Derry in 1990, against the depredations of priests and some local residents, the Sinn Féin strategist Eoghan Mac Cormaic made the claim that "the latest (some would say that it is in fact the oldest) uncensored 'media' is the wall mural" (Mac Cormaic 1990: 8). Putting aside the fallacious assertion that murals are not subject to censorship (by a variety of means), the claim is noteworthy for its acknowledgment of the long history of wall painting.

Chapter 1

1. The abbreviations PUL (Protestant Unionist Loyalist) and CNR (Catholic Nationalist Republican) have been adopted relatively recently to refer to the major divisions within Northern Ireland (during the war the dominant terms were nationalist and unionist). But the terms are problematic for two reasons: first, they make assumptions about the link between religion and political allegiance (there are Protestants who believe in a United Ireland and a Republic as the ideal form of political State, and nationalists who want a United Ireland but don't care what form the State takes). Second, they homogenize the communities to which they refer and thereby obscure important differences. In this regard, it is important to demarcate "unionist" from "loyalist," though in this case the distinction is not grounded in political belief (both pledge allegiance to the Crown) but primarily class. Since the start of the Troubles at least, "loyalist" has tended to be used of working-class unionists and their organizations, though as McKay notes, "it is also often paired with or even used as shorthand for 'paramilitaries'" (McKay 2021: 2). At the end of the nineteenth and in the early twentieth centuries, however, "loyalist" and "unionist" were used pretty much inter-changeably (though the inflection of class was always there).

2. For a sustained account of Gramsci's theory of hegemony, and its political significance, see Hall 2021 (originally published in 1988).

3. Another early example of political wall-writing is recorded in "Protestant graffiti" (https://digitalfilmarchive.net/media/protestant-graffiti-41). Dated "circa 1920," this short British Pathé film pans along a wall on which is written: "Derry says No Surrender. Britannia rules the waves."

4. The quotation, which introduces the film, is taken from the prologue to *Romeo and Juliet*: "Two households, both alike in dignity/(In fair Verona, where we lay our scene),/From ancient grudge break to new mutiny,/Where civil blood makes civil hands unclean" (Prologue ll.1–4).

5. Later murals reiterated the omission, focusing instead on the figure of William, though there were exceptions (Figure 2). The elision accentuates an odd aspect of the original painting, which is its failure to depict the vanquished Jacobites (the only two dead figures are Schomberg and a loyalist soldier). West's work is available at https://commons.wikimedia.org/wiki/File:William_III_at_the_Battle_of_the_Boyne.jpg.

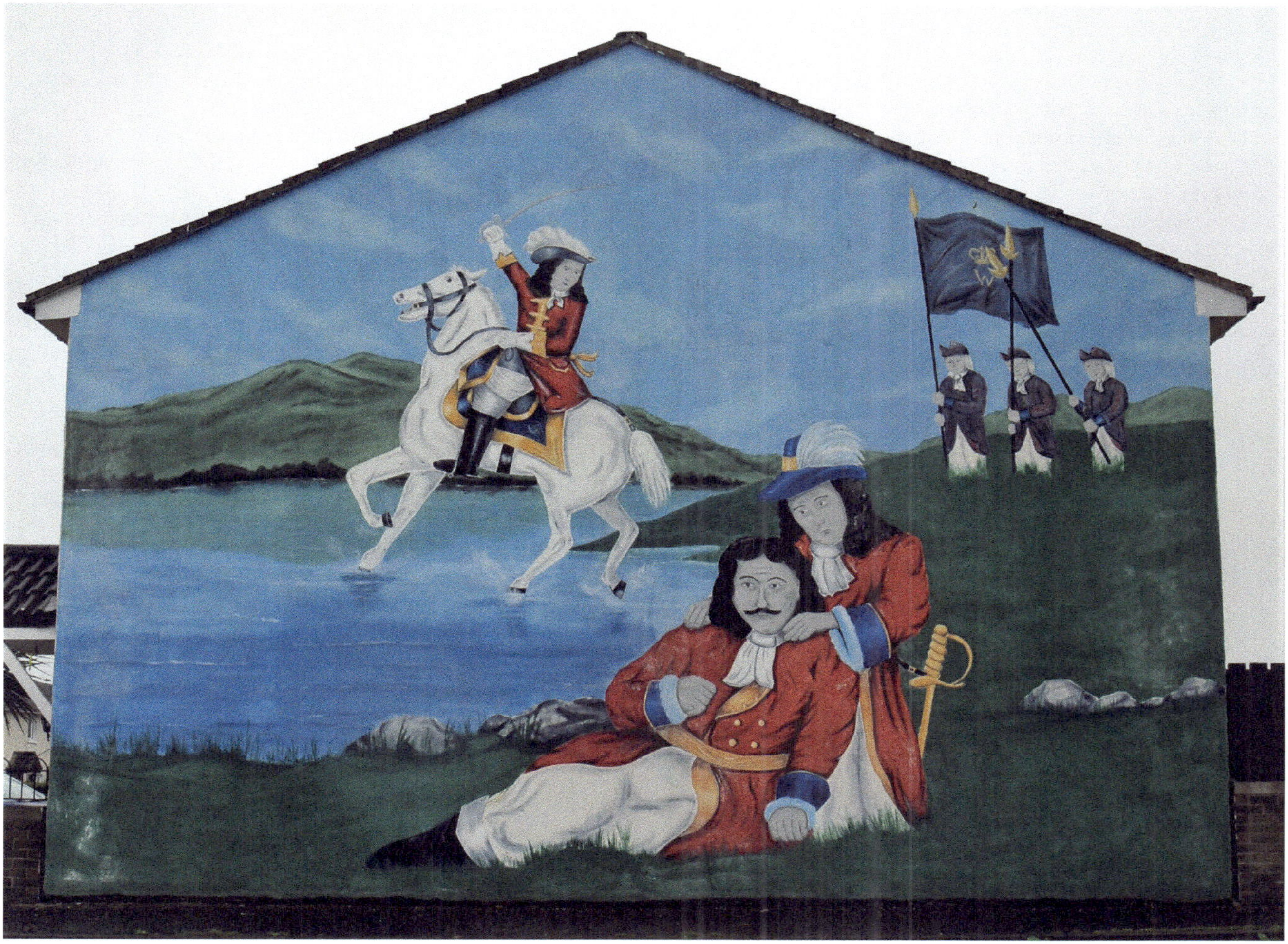

FIGURE 2 King William and the death of Schomberg, Shankill Parade, Lower Shankill, West Belfast, 2000. Photo by Tony Crowley.

6. In 1957 Helen Kerr interviewed Tommy Henderson for her undergraduate dissertation in a fine art degree (recently published as *Glorious Twelfth: A Folk Art Project*, Kerr 2023). Originally a study of wall paintings in Belfast, the text includes some wonderful sketches of murals and a number of rare photographs. Kerr notes that "Mr Henderson claims that he painted the first wall painting, some years before the First World War when he owned a house-painting business and paint shop in the Shankill Road area" (Kerr 2023: 13).

7. "The Carnan Roll of Honour" raises the issue of the durability of particular locations as "lieux de mémoire": in 2011 Carnan Street was the site of a roll of honor commemorating the dead of "C" Company UVF during the Troubles (see **chapter seven, fig. 74**).

8. Kipling's phrase "lest we forget," widely used in remembrance ceremonies, is adapted from the Book of Deuteronomy (4.9): "Only take heed to thyself, and keep thy soul diligently, lest thou forget the things which thine eyes have seen, and lest they depart from thy heart all the days of thy life: but teach them thy sons, and thy son's sons." "The captains and the kings" later became the title of a satirical folksong on British imperialism penned by Brendan Behan.

9. Though it has primarily been used for military or paramilitary purposes, the origin of the slogan is Biblical: "quis nos separabit a caritate Christi? tribulatio? an angustia? an persecutio? an fames? an nuditas? an periculum? an gladius?"; "Who shall separate us from the love of Christ? Shall tribulation, or distress, or persecution, or famine, or nakedness, or peril, or sword?" (Romans 8:35).

10. For remarkable footage of the Jackson murals a little later (1966), see "Derry City—1966 (The Fountain & The Bogside)," at https://www.facebook.com/Derryofthepast/videos/derry-city-1966-the-fountain-the-bogside-/1885347898183259/

11. I am indebted for the details of the history that follows to McBrinn's "Belfast's *other* murals" (McBrinn 1997).

12. Luke also painted murals in the Masonic Hall in Rosemary Street (1956) and in the Millfield Technical College (unfinished) (Hewitt 1978: 83, 104).

13. Conor (1881–1968) was born in Fortingale Street off the Shankill and his work focused primarily on depictions of Belfast working-class life; he was an Academician at the Ulster Academy of Arts and the Royal Hibernian Academy of Arts. For a discussion of Conor's work and its significance, see Wilson 1981 and Jonathan Bell 2002.

14. As observed in note 7, a specific lieu de mémoire can perdure over generations: a King Billy mural is displayed on the same wall today (Figure 3, see Fulcrum).

Chapter 2

1. Gaelic sports were elided on the basis of their association with Irish nationalism, rugby because it was a middle-class sport.

2. An early loyalist mural in Londonderry provided another example of how the walls were used to challenge. Underneath an image of a crown and harp with two Union Jacks, topped with the slogan "For God and Ulster," was the challenge: "No Surrender IRA name your day The B men are ready. 1688, 1690, 1920" (Figure 4, see Fulcrum).

3. In 1997, the Emmet memorial mural was re-created at the nearest available location to the original (Figure 5, see Fulcrum).

4. Given the political tendencies of both wings of Irish republicanism at the time of its painting, the image of Connolly suggests that this mural was probably the work of adherents to the Official (as opposed to Provisional) IRA.

5. Images of the "Provisionals" and "IRA 75" slogans are available at https://petermoloneycollection.wordpress.com/visual-history-2-the-catholic-insurgency/ and https://www.tate.org.uk/art/archive/items/tga-201020-3-24/atkinson-colour-photograph-of-a-wall-in-northern-ireland-painted-with-an-irish-flags-a.

6. "The five demands" were: the right not to wear a prison uniform; the right not to do prison work; the right of free association with other prisoners, and to organize educational and recreational pursuits; the right to one visit, one letter, and one parcel per week; full restoration of remission lost through the blanket/no wash protest.

7. Importantly, the conditions of imprisonment shaped the cultural revival itself. After 1976, non-conforming prisoners had no access to the arts and crafts workshops in which they had previously been so productive. Instead, they turned to music and, significantly, the Irish language; the revival of Irish that has become such a marked component of the cultural life of nationalist/republican communities in Northern Ireland, was generated in part within the "Jailtacht" (Crowley 2005: 194 ff.; Mac Giolla Chríost 2012).

8. For an account of mural painting in the prisons, particularly after the Hunger Strikes, see Rolston 2014. Interviews with Jake MacSiacais and Danny Devenny in July 2021 confirmed that there were various murals within Cage 11 and later the republican H-Block

compounds. They included depictions of Ériu, landscapes, Celtic designs (modelled on the work of Jim Fitzpatrick), Mao, Ho Chi Min, Che Guevara, Connolly, Pearse, Mandela, and other images related to South Africa and Palestine. There were also representations of musicians such as The Who and Hendrix.

9. The quote is wrongly ascribed to Bobby Sands on the mural. O'Casey and Ashe were friends and O'Casey's words are taken from *The Story of Thomas Ashe* (1917). Ashe died from the effects of force-feeding during a Hunger Strike for prisoner of war status.

10. Despite the fact that republican prisoners were fighting for rights that would extend to their loyalist counterparts, the loyalist response to the Hunger Strikes (at least outside the prison) was hostile; graffiti on Sandy Row declared: "Support the UVF Sands rot in hell" (Figure 6, see Fulcrum).

11. The image of the revolutionary appeared in Rossville Street, Derry, in 1982 (Figure 7) and in adapted form, in Turf Lodge, West Belfast, in 1999 (see **chapter four, fig. 64**); the accompanying slogan has been used repeatedly in republican murals.

12. Donnelly's photograph was originally published in 1971 in *The Daily Mirror, Life*, and, locally, in *The United Irishman* (the organ of Official Sinn Féin) and *An Phoblacht* (the organ of Provisional Sinn Féin) (Mulqueen and Smyth 2020); it features McCann in an engagement with British soldiers in the Markets area of Belfast on the night of internment—August 9 1971. Given that McCann

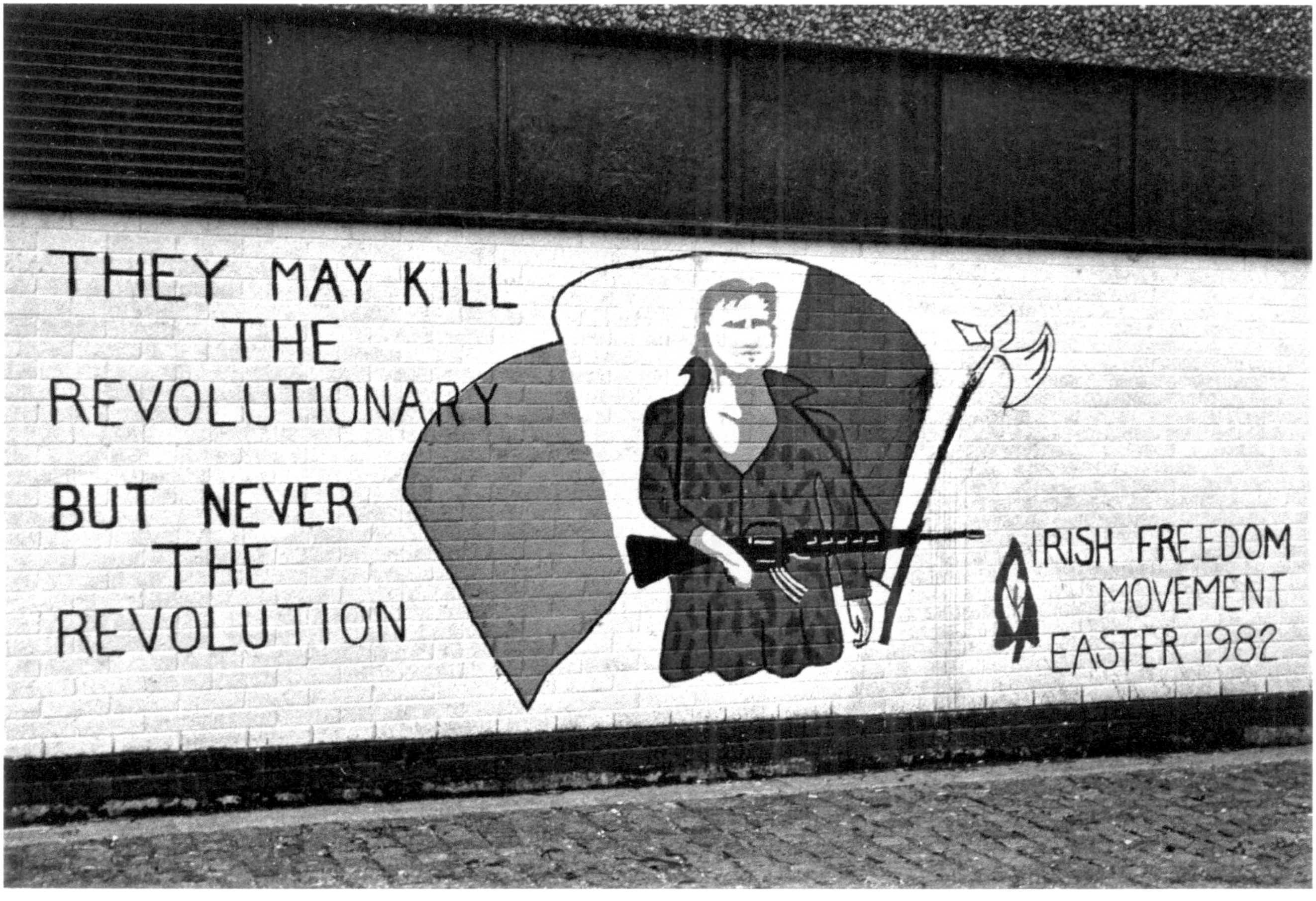

FIGURE 7 Irish Freedom Movement, Rossville St., Derry, 1982. Photo by Tony Crowley.

was a commander in the Official IRA (bitter rival of the Provisionals after the split in 1969), the use of the image in *An Phoblacht* has been described as a "cheeky piece of Provo journalistic piracy" (Smyth 2010: 57). By the 1980s, as is evident from the mural (in which the Starry Plough has been replaced by a Tricolor), the image had become an iconic representation of republican "Resistance."

13. The most famous public articulation of the policy was given by Danny Morrison, Director of Publicity for Sinn Féin, at the party's Ard Fheis in 1981: "Who here really believes we can win the war through the ballot box? But will anyone here object if, with a ballot paper in this hand and an Armalite in the other, we take power in Ireland?" (English 2005: 224).

14. SWAPO fought against the South African State in order to achieve liberation for South West Africa (originally a British mandate, but ceded to South Africa in 1948); South West Africa gained independence in 1990 and became Namibia.

15. The ascription of the coinage of the phrase to Bobby Sands is open to dispute, since as Mac Giolla Chríost points out, Gerry Adams referred to "Tiocfaidh ár lá" as common usage in Long Kesh in the 1970s (Mac Giolla Chríost 2012: 51–52). Ciarán Carson claims that "strictly speaking, 'tiocfaidh ár lá' is bad Irish, based on an English subtext" (or, in technical terms, an effect of superstrate English on substrate Irish) (Carson 1998: 41). But citing Ó Dónaill's *Foclóir Gaeilge—Béarla*, the standard Irish dictionary, Mac Giolla Chríost contends that the formulation is at least "grammatically acceptable" (Mac Giolla Chríost 2012: 51–52), even if "it is better to say /Beidh ár lá againn/ or /Beidh ár lá linn/" (120). Ironically, an English version of the phrase was used in Joyce's *Portrait of the Artist as a Young Man* (1916) by the Irish nationalist, Michael Davin, when he predicts to the somewhat skeptical Stephen Dedalus that "our day will come yet, believe me" (Joyce 1992: 220). The editor, Seamus Deane, characterizes this as "an old Fenian slogan" (317).

16. For an illuminating discussion of the use of Irish in the murals, see Mac Giolla Chríost 2012: 109–131.

17. The phrase "structure of feeling" was coined by Raymond Williams to refer to cultural artifacts that embody emergent and therefore non-hegemonic and not fully worked-out views, tendencies, and values Williams (1976: 128–135).

Chapter 3

1. The liberties afforded by the Glorious Revolution did not extend to Catholics. The *Act of Toleration* (1689) afforded freedom of worship to non-conformists (subject to Oaths of Allegiance and Supremacy); Catholic emancipation was achieved in 1829. Many of Burke's "*antient* indisputable laws and liberties" were in fact highly disputable and often not very ancient at all.

2. The flag of Northern Ireland, also known as the Ulster banner, consists of a red cross on a white background, at the center of which is a six-pointed star (representing the six counties of Ulster) with a Red Hand topped by a Crown. The flag was used for official purposes by the government of Northern Ireland from the coronation of Elizabeth II (1953) till the imposition of Direct Rule (1972); it continues to be flown by unionists and loyalists.

3. Long Kesh Detention Centre was a series of Second World War Nissen huts on the site of a disused RAF airfield near Lisburn, south of Belfast; it opened as an internment camp in 1971, with the first sentenced prisoners following in 1972. In 1976 eight "H-Blocks" (buildings in the shape of an "H") were added to the prison. Prisoners, both loyalist and republican, tend to refer to it as "Long Kesh"; the official name was "Her Majesty's Prison The Maze (Cellular)" (Graham and McDowell 2007: 343–368).

4. The whereabouts of the prison murals was the subject of some controversy. For a long period it appeared that they were in the custody of the Northern Ireland Prison Service, but it has been revealed that they are in curatorial holding at the Ulster Museum (personal communication, William Blair, Director Ulster Museum, January 12 2022).

5. The essay also appeared in 2012 on "longkeshinsideout.co.uk," a forum for former UVF and RHC prisoners.

6. For a discussion of Conor's account of early loyalist muralism, see the Introduction above.

7. A photograph of this mural is reproduced on the "longkeshinsideout.co.uk" site: https://www.flickr.com/photos/longkesh/page2. Sassoon's lines became a common refrain in UVF murals.

8. The Northern Ireland Assembly, initiated in 1982, was one of a series of failed interventions by the British State; it folded in 1986. The origin of the "blue skies of Ulster" quote is unclear; it is variously attributed to Edward Carson or to Ian Paisley himself.

9. *Ballymena Observer*, July 19 1984, p.2.

10. Militarily, the IRA came close to wiping out the British Cabinet, including the Prime Minister, in its attack on the Grand Hotel in Brighton in October 1984. Politically, Sinn Féin gained five seats in the Northern Ireland Assembly in 1982, won West Belfast in the General Election in 1983, and took fifty-nine local council seats in 1985.

11. A number of the "Shankill murals," though not all, were signed and dated by "Skilly."

12. Another mural, in Hopewell Crescent, on the other side of the Shankill Road, reiterated the theme. Incorporating the central icons of Crown, Bible, the Union Jack and Northern Ireland flag, together with the star and "1690," the mural bore a Biblical motto: "The throne is established by righteousness" (Proverbs 16: 12) (Figure 8, see Fulcrum).

13. As Terence Brown has shown, the rhetorical construction of Protestantism in Northern Ireland as a monolith elides important historical, doctrinal, and theological differences between distinct churches (Brown 1985). Contemporary Northern Irish Protestant denominations include the Presbyterians (consisting of the Presbyterians, the Reformed Presbyterians, and the Free Presbyterians), the Church of Ireland, Methodists, Baptists, Quakers, the Brethren, and the Assemblies of God. Suzanne McKay also examines a range of Protestant faiths and political standpoints in *Northern Protestants: An Unsettled People* (2000).

14. The origin of the Red Hand is the subject of popular legend: two chieftains raced to take possession of Ulster (the prize of the first to land) and in order to claim priority, one of the chieftains, Heremon O'Neill, chopped his hand off and threw it on to the land. Thereafter the Red Hand became the symbol of the O'Neills and Ulster itself. The myth was later depicted in murals on the Lower Shankill estate and on the Newtownards Road (see **chapter five, fig. 67** and **chapter seven, fig. 18**).

15. Prisoners were a perennial concern for the communities from which they were drawn, and indeed the paramilitary organizations to which they belonged. One of the earliest non-traditional loyalist murals was a call to "Remember the Loyalist prisoners" in 1977 (see **Introduction, fig. 22**).

16. The postcard image was reproduced as a mural repeatedly during later points of crisis for loyalism; see, for example, **chapter five, fig. 77**).

17. See, for example, the activities of Stephen McKeag, a UDA assassin from the Lower Shankill thought to have killed between twelve and thirty victims, many of whom were Catholic civilians (McDonald and Cusack 2004: 1–6). A mural painted on the Lower Shankill estate to commemorate McKeag has been renewed a number of times and remains today (Figure 9). For an in-depth analysis of the republican killing of an off-duty police officer, see Cobain 2020.

18. The two murals referenced in the Spike and Gerry mural confirm its UDA/UFF provenance. The mural on the far right is dedicated to the 2nd Battalion C Company Lower Shankill UDA/UFF/UYM (see **chapter five, fig. 2**). The mural to the center was painted on the Kentucky Fried Chicken outlet on the Shankill Road (opposite the estate) (Figure 10, see Fulcrum); after considerable controversy, and pressure from KFC, the mural was removed (http://news.bbc.co.uk/1/hi/northern_ireland/6136844.stm). The joke on "Jerry"/"Gerry" also works on another level, since "Jerry" was the term used in Britain to refer to the German enemy in the Second World War.

19. The links between these organizations are not entirely clear but commonly understood in the following terms: the YCV was the youth wing of the UVF, while the PAF was a cover name used by UVF members (usually in relation to killings committed by UVF members with which the organization did not want to be associated or had not sanctioned). The RHC was a highly secretive group linked to, but not under the command of, the UVF.

20. The reference to the UDF is significant (and relatively rare, though see **fig. 17** this chapter). In 1985 McMichael was instrumental in the formation of the UDF—a small group within the UDA selected for intensive training. A number of UDF members went on to become the leaders of the UDA when it was re-constituted in the late 1980s (Woods 2006: 123–124).

21. Areas such as The Village, Sandy Row, and Donegall Pass are either contiguous or in close proximity, and they are all fiercely loyalist. Yet each area has its own identity, sustained by history, cultural practices, demographics, and geographic location. Proximity and broad political allegiance does not preclude rivalry and sometimes antagonism. For a discussion of Donegall Pass and its relations with neighboring loyalist areas, see Holloway 1994a, 1994b. The same point can be made of republican areas: they may sit beside each other, but they maintain clear identities. The cultural and political importance of flute bands is discussed in chapter six.

22. The Battle of the Boyne was fought over and along the Boyne river, principally at Oldbridge, near Drogheda, County Meath, in what is now the Republic of Ireland. It took place on July 1 (Julian Calendar), and July 12 (Gregorian Calendar) (see chapter 5 note 14).

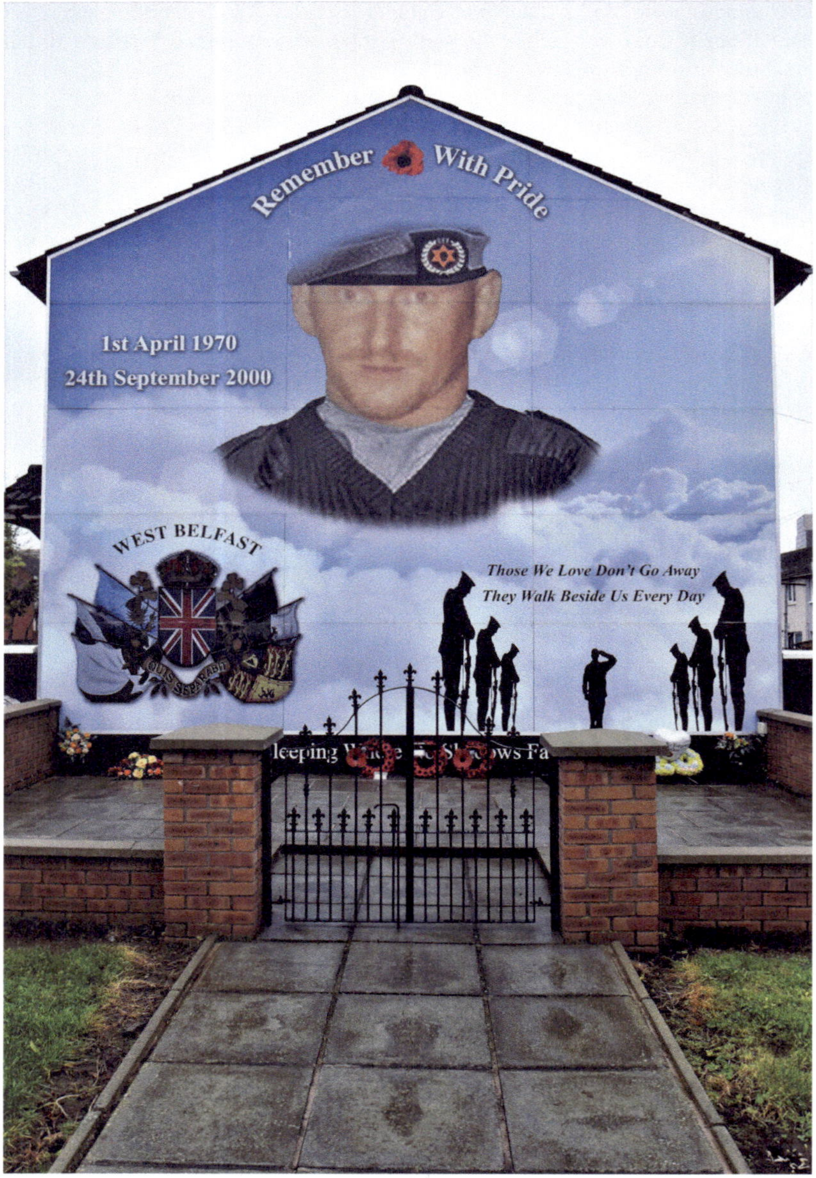

FIGURE 9 Stephen McKeag, Hopewell Crescent, Lower Shankill, West Belfast, 2021.

23. The killing of Robert Bradford was a very murky affair; it was investigated by Lyra McKee who was killed inadvertently by the New IRA in Derry 2019 during an attempt to assassinate PSNI officers (see **chapter eight, fig. 15**). McKee's account of the Bradford killing, *Angels with Blue Faces*, was published posthumously in 2019.

24. The crest of Londonderry/Derry has been the subject of historical contention. The red cross and sword on a white background is the arms of the city of London (to denote the establishment of Derry by the London guilds in 1613); below there is a keep and the figure of death; in the 1613 crest, the red cross bore a harp, but this was dropped in later versions and re-inserted by the city council only in 2002.

Chapter 4

1. If, as Raymond Williams claims, "culture is one of the two or three most complicated words in the English language" (Williams 1983: 87), then "dúchas" may be its counterpart in Irish. It has a variety of attested meanings, some of which, as with "culture," refer to both history and nature and appear to be conflicting: hereditary right or claim; birthright, heritage; ancestral estate, patrimony; native place or country, ancestral home; traditional connexion; kindred affection, natural affinity; heredity, innate quality, natural bent; natural, wild, state; wildness, madness; inherited, inherent, innate, native.

2. In the 1990s republican and nationalist areas saw the institution of a number of annual féilte and fleadhanna (festivals—usually involving music, dancing, sport, and general cultural activities) (Figure 11, see Fulcrum). The most successful, initiated in 1988, was the West Belfast Festival, later to become the annual Féile an Phobail, now the largest community arts festival in Ireland; the Féile staged a number of important intra- and inter-community debates in the post-war period.

3. The Mass Rock mural was updated in 1997 following a loyalist blockade and picket of Our Lady of Mercy Catholic Church in the loyalist stronghold of Harryville, Ballymena. The new mural drew attention to the links between past and present—"1696–[19]97 Penal Days in Ireland Harryv[ille]." Another elaborate version of the same image appeared at South Link in Andersonstown in 1996; entitled "Leathannta na Péindlithe" (Penal Times), it drew attention to the £25 reward for the discovery of a wolf or priest.

4. Heaney's poem, in fact, refers to the 1798 Rebellion rather than the Famine. The second "Gorta Mór" mural featured a composite of contemporary sketches, including "The ejectment of the Irish tenantry," from the *Illustrated London News*, December 16 1848, showing the consequences of the failure of the potato crop—eviction and emigration (Figure 12, see Fulcrum).

5. The "comms" were messages written on tiny bits of paper smuggled in and out of the prison; the "comms" featured in the mural are: the note from Sands to the IRA Army Council confirming the intention to proceed with the Hunger Strike; the note from the IRA Officer Commanding (Bik McFarlane) to Gerry Adams on the death of Sands; a note regarding the mistreatment of an Ardoyne prisoner (the mural is in Ardoyne). "Greater love hath no man" is a Biblical quotation: "Greater love hath no man than this, that a man lay down his life for his friends" (John 15: 13).

6. One of the most striking aspects of the murals is the fact that they are not designed to be preserved in perpetuity, indeed "most are expected to have a short life" (Jarman 1997: 212). Nevertheless, there are murals that have lasted for a considerable period of time. As noted earlier, the Famine mural on Lenadoon Avenue was painted in 1995 and the prison mural on Ludlow Square dates from 1996. On the loyalist side, the Bobby Jackson mural in The Fountain area dates to the 1920s, though in different forms and locations.

7. Other memorial modes included the naming of streets, buildings, and public parks (Figure 13, see Fulcrum). For a discussion of the politics of memorialization, see Viggiani 2014.

8. Later still (2014), the mural was re-composed. In this final version, the weapons and kitchen war-cabinet disappeared, replaced by a happy Tricolor-waving band underneath the republican phoenix and doves of peace; "working-class heroes" was added to the bottom of the image (Figure 14, see Fulcrum). As of March 2024, the mural had been painted over.

9. "Ordinary people in extraordinary roles" is, in fact, a quotation from a loyalist mural and was used to describe UVF volunteers (Figure 15, see Fulcrum). For a reading of the political significance of the Ballymurphy murals, see Crowley 2022.

10. Bobby Sands might have followed a number of his fellow prisoners in rejecting the Sinn Féin strategy as it developed before and after *The Good Friday Agreement*; he might also have followed some of his colleagues into the leadership of Sinn Féin. We simply don't know.

11. The term "dissident" was hotly disputed. See Crowley 2011 and McGlinchey 2019.

12. "Stormont Never! Never! Never!" was an ironic riff on Ian Paisley's address at the loyalist mass meeting to reject the *Anglo-Irish Agreement* in 1985; the speech ended: "Our answer to Dublin rule is: Never! Never! Never!" (Taylor 2000: 182).

13. Though the "Drumcree conflict" ran in effect from 1995 to 2001, its origins lie in restrictions imposed on the Orange Order's march in 1986; there is a token attempt on July 12th each year to march the "traditional" route. See chapter five for further discussion.

14. Twenty-nine people died as a result of the Omagh bombing, the highest single-incident death toll during the Troubles (though thirty-three people had been killed in the loyalist dual bombing of Dublin and Monaghan on May 17 1974). Though there have been sporadic incidents thereafter, Omagh signaled the end of large-scale republican violence for political purposes.

15. The Northern Ireland prison population, both before and after the Troubles, was small by international standards (Butler 2016: 341–343).

16. The Sinn Féin eclipse of the SDLP was relentless: in the 2001 and 2005 General Elections, Sinn Féin won 4 and 5 seats respectively, against the SDLP's 3 and 3. In elections to the Northern Ireland Assembly in 1998 and 2003, Sinn Féin took 18 and 24 seats, the SDLP 24 and 18. And in local elections in 2001 and 2005, Sinn Féin gained 108 seats (on 20.6% of the vote) and 126 (on 24.3%), the SDLP 117 (on 19.40%) and 110 (on 17.4%). Sinn Féin also took the SDLP's seat in the European Parliament Election of 2004. It is reported that Tony Blair told the SDLP leadership in 2000 their problem was that they lacked political leverage because they didn't have guns to decommission (Godson 2003: 6). It might be observed that they didn't have murals either.

17. There were other media of course. Sinn Féin continued to publish *An Phoblacht/Republican News* and became adept at using broadcast media; it also began to advertise professionally, and when social media platforms appeared in the early-to-mid-2000s, it very quickly became adept at making use of the opportunities they afforded.

18. The International Wall (sometimes called the Solidarity Wall) was initially confined to Divis Street, but as that space filled up, the longer stretch of wall on Northumberland Street (running from Divis Street to Beverly Street and divided by the Peace Line) also became a mural canvas.

19. Public transport routes were frequently disrupted in West Belfast during the Troubles. In response to which, a cheap, reliable, and popular alternative transport system was provided (on both the Falls and Shankill roads) by black taxis ("black hacks"), which operated in effect as buses that picked up and stopped on request. Taxi drivers were soft targets and a number of republican drivers were assassinated.

20. The full range of the Bogside Artists' work, including images and details of the historical events they depict, is available at: https://cain.ulster.ac.uk/bogsideartists/murals.htm

Chapter 5

1. The mockery here includes an allusion to an infamous comment by the British Prime Minister, Harold Wilson, in his denunciation of the UWC strike in 1974 that brought down the early attempt at power-sharing proposed in the *Sunningdale Agreement*. Wilson's words condemning the loyalist strikers were bitterly resented and long remembered: "purporting to act as though they were an elected government, spending their lives sponging on Westminster and British democracy and then systematically assaulting democratic methods. Who do these people think they are?" (Bew 1993: 86). *The Belfast Agreement* was described by the SDLP's Seamus Mallon as "*Sunningdale* for slow learners"; it was a sardonic but somewhat ahistorical quip (English 2003: 317).

2. The *Declaration of Arbroath* was written by Scottish nobles and addressed to Pope John XXII. Dismissing the Pope's excommunication of King Robert the First (of Scotland), for failing to meet the papal demand for a truce in the First Scottish War of Independence, the declaration asserted the antiquity of Scotland as an independent, sovereign state and rejected English rule (Cannon and Crowcroft

2015). First translated from the original Latin in the late seventeenth century, the *Declaration of Arbroath* is now frequently referred to as a Scottish declaration of independence; that makes its use in the context of a UFF mural significant, given the UDA's flirtation with the idea of independence for Ulster (McDonald and Cusack 2004: 105–106).

3. Eddie (Eddie the Head) is the mascot of Iron Maiden, the English heavy metal band; he features in various guises on their album covers and paraphernalia. In 1983 he was figured on the cover of the single "The Trooper" as a redcoat British soldier at the disastrous Charge of the Light Brigade (1854), during the Crimean War. The UDA/UFF adopted this representation of Eddie, in which the marauding trooper held UDA, UFF, or Union Jack flags, while in the background the grim reaper appeared standing over graves marked with the names of prominent republicans (some of whom were killed by loyalist paramilitaries). An entry into the search box in the Murals of Northern Ireland archive finds eleven Eddie murals—in Ballymena, East, South, and West Belfast, Carrickfergus, Larne, and Londonderry. The original loyalist Eddie may have been painted in the UDA compound within the Maze prison (Rolston 2013: 161–163).

4. A later (2009) mural on the estate depicted Luther's rebellion at the Diet of Worms (1521), one of the key initial events in the Reformation (Figure 16, see Fulcrum). Luther's famous declaration was: "Hier stehe, ich kann nicht anders; Gott helfe mir" (Here I stand, I can do no other; may God help me). In a small side panel, the text explained that "this wall was a site for local slogans and graffiti," whereas "the new mural depicting Martin Luther is both historic and symbolic for the Lower Shankill."

5. The issue of graffiti raises a significant question: given that it can be written by "any fucking idiot with a spray can" (as a leading loyalist once said to me), how representative is it of the feelings and views of the local community? This is a difficult issue. On the one hand, it is important not to over-interpret a single piece of graffiti, given the danger of idiots with spray cans. On the other hand, an accumulation of similar examples of graffiti suggests that they represent a viewpoint within a particular community (even if it is a sub-section of the group). Other factors also come into play: is the graffiti left on the wall, or scrubbed out, or mocked? Is it ascribed to a particular group, or simply anonymous? Similar questions also apply to murals, but given that murals (or at least most murals) require planning, time, and energy, they can't be treated with the same caution that an individual piece of graffiti merits.

6. Quoting his father, Billy Hutchinson, a UVF commander in Long Kesh and later PUP politician, made the point succinctly in his autobiography when referring to Ian Paisley MP, leader of the DUP: "my dad warned me to stay away, telling me that Paisley 'would fight to the last drop of everyone else's blood'" (Hutchinson 2020: 17). Elsewhere, he notes: "in what would become a recurring theme throughout the conflict, Ian Paisley seized on people's grief and anger to boost his own profile… Paisley was always there, manipulating the Protestant working class for his own agenda" (51).

7. The UDP and PUP occupied distinct positions on the political spectrum. Though the beliefs of individual leaders and members differ, the UDP was broadly center-right while the PUP was center-left; important PUP figures such as Billy Mitchell, David Ervine, and Billy Hutchinson described themselves as socialists. For a discussion of "Northern Ireland's lost opportunity"—"the frustrated promise of political Loyalism"—which focuses primarily on the UVF, RHC, and the PUP, see Novosel 2013.

8. As noted in the Introduction, Michael Stone was a loyalist hero on the basis of his one-man attack on the funeral of the three IRA volunteers killed by the SAS in Gibraltar 1988.

9. The UDP eventually folded in 2001 as a result of internal tensions and disagreement between the UDP and the UDA/UFF; it was superseded by the Ulster Political Research Group (which does not contest elections). The PUP continues to engage in electoral politics and although it lost its Assembly seat in 2007, it retains a limited presence on local councils. Its impact in working-class areas of Belfast and beyond remains significant, however, largely through its ACT initiative (Action for Community Transformation)—a loyalist conflict transformation campaign. The failure to translate what is often strong local support into electoral gains can be attributed to a range of causes—from a refusal to vote for parties associated with paramilitary violence (past and present), to the recognition that mainstream unionism is the only effective challenge at Westminster and the Stormont Assembly to nationalist and republican parties.

10. The Westwinds mural is a partial copy of an image that appeared in a remarkable representation of Protestant/unionist/loyalist history on Thorndyke Street (see the discussion later in this chapter).

11. For a discussion of the language politics of the 1990s, and the treatment of language in *The Belfast Agreement*, see Crowley 2005 chs. 7, 8; for an account of the political construction of Ulster-Scots, see Crowley 2006.

12. The "Out of the ashes" mural offers an interesting example of the self-referentiality of muralism; its depiction of Cluan Place, a small cul-de-sac that backs on to republican Short Strand (itself an enclave within loyalist East Belfast), includes a mural visible to none but the inhabitants of Cluan Place (Figure 17, see Fulcrum).

13. Though there was widespread civil unrest and rioting after the introduction of internment in 1971, there is little evidence that nationalists or republicans engaged in large-scale attacks against loyalist areas. But in the summer of 1971 supporters of the Orange Lodge in Liverpool did indeed offer shelter and respite from the general violence and chaos of the time to parties of women and children for short periods during the summer holidays, though the total numbers were less than one thousand (*The Liverpool Echo*, August 28 1971, p.1).

14. In 1750 the Calendar (New Style) Act was adopted and the Gregorian calendar (N.S.) replaced the Julian calendar (Old Style); the change was effected from 1752 and required an adjustment of eleven days (hence July 1 became July 12).

15. Spender, who won the Military Cross in the attack on Thiepval on the first day of the Somme offensive, was an Englishman (from Plymouth), but he was hardly a neutral observer. He was an anti-Home Rule campaigner, signed the *Ulster Covenant*, became an organizer for the Ulster Volunteers at Carson's behest, and served as a staff officer in the 36th Ulster Division. Spender's tribute to the Ulstermen at the Somme has featured frequently in UVF commemorative murals.

16. The Historical Enquiries Team was set up by the PSNI to investigate 3,235 unsolved killings that took place between 1969 and 1998; it had very limited success and was wound up in 2014.

Chapter 6

1. The concept of the "imperfect peace" appears to have been articulated by the Labour Secretary of State for Northern Ireland, Mo Mowlam, in 1999: "the peace we have now is imperfect, but better than none" (Rowan 2004: 159).

2. "Perpetual crisis" is Gerry Adams's phrase at another moment of breakdown in 2000; his comment that "no process can limp from crisis to crisis the way this one has," proved to be wholly inaccurate https://www.irishtimes.com/news/no-process-can-limp-from-crisis-to-crisis-says-adams-1.243023

3. For a discussion of the various initiatives that underpinned the stop-start functioning of government in Northern Ireland post-2007, see Rowan 2021.

4. It could be argued that in some areas, such as Education or Health, ministers have attempted to govern with a broad remit, within the limits set by the Westminster government. But politics in Northern Ireland remains stuck in a zero-sum game in which a gain on one side means a loss on the other. Given that, the basic rule of politics is to make sure that that you either win or make sure that you don't lose (hence zero change).

5. The legality of the Legacy Act has been challenged by various groups, including the Irish government. In February 2024, the High Court at Belfast found the bill to be in contravention of the European Convention on Human Rights. After the British General Election of July 2024, the new Labour government declared its intention to repeal the Act.

6. The point is an adaptation of the oft-quoted line in William Faulkner's *Requiem for a Nun* (1951): "The past is never dead. It's not even past" (Faulkner 1996: 85).

7. It is striking that none of these major figures within republicanism have figured in murals after their death.

8. Clearly, this is an enormously complex issue. Dawson 2007 provides a theoretical account of a number of questions that relate to the question of "making peace with the past." A more succinct, accessible and empathetic discussion of the issues can be found in the journalist Barney Rowan's "'The Troubles' with Truth," ch. 9 of *Unfinished Peace Thoughts on Northern Ireland's Unanswered Past* (Rowan 2015), and "The War of Lies and Truth," ch. 11 of *Living with Ghosts: The Inside Story of a Troubles Mind* (Rowan 2022).

9. Commemorative plaques were erected in the Brandywell and Beechmount; there was no reference to the IRA on the stones.

10. A new and expansive republican museum, the Roddy McCorley Republican Heritage Centre, opened in August 2023 at the Roddy McCorley Club at Moyard House on the Glen Road in West Belfast.

11. I am grateful to the republican muralist Danny Devenny for information with regard to the 1916 mural, which he composed and painted together with his co-workers Marty Lyons and Micky Docherty.

12. Lyra McKee's killing is an interesting case-study in the partial and functional nature of commemoration. There is a mural in Belfast City Center in her memory (see **chapter eight, fig. 15**), but in the place where she was killed, on Fanad Drive, Derry, there is nothing permanent to mark the location (flowers are left by her family and friends on the anniversary of her death). By contrast, at the corner from which the killer fired, there is a plaque to an unarmed IRA volunteer, Michael Quigley, killed by a British soldier in 1972 (Figure 18, see Fulcrum).

13. The full text of the IRA statement after Brighton read: "The IRA claims responsibility for the detonation of 100lb of gelignite in Brighton against the British cabinet and Tory warmongers. Thatcher will now realize that Britain cannot occupy our country, torture our prisoners and shoot our people in their own streets and get away with it. Today we were unlucky, but remember we only have to be lucky once, you will have to be lucky always. Give Ireland peace and there will be no war" (Carroll 2023: 227–228)

14. The reference is to the discriminatory notices placed in rental advertisements in Britain, in the 1950s and 1960s in particular, when West Indian and Irish immigrants sought work in British cities ("no Blacks, no Irish"). An anti-racism mural on the International Wall in 2010 also addressed this issue (see **chapter six, fig. 131**).

15. The mural in **fig. 98** was sponsored by members of D Company, 2nd Battalion, Belfast IRA, which was based in Lower Falls, Clonard and Divis; a number of the veterans of D Company reject the Peace Process and Sinn Féin's role in it.

16. Hughes was a leader of D Company and is venerated by his former comrades.

17. The Re-imaging Communities Programme built on an earlier scheme that ran in 2004–2005; funded by the Arts Council NI and Belfast City Council, the scheme had a budget of £2.4 million.

18. One republican area that did engage with the re-imaging scheme was the Markets in South Belfast. In 2008–2009 the artist Raymond Henshaw completed a series of six murals that were sponsored by the Arts Council; the murals took the form of collages of photographs with the topics "Portraits," "Social," "Bars," "Industry," "Sport and culture," and "Social History."

19. The shortage of acceptable housing, and the unfair allocation of the available stock for the purposes of gerrymandering, had been an issue in Northern Ireland since the inception of the State. In 1968 housing became one of the foremost concerns for the Northern Ireland Civil Rights Association; a CRA march in Derry in October 1968 was confronted brutally by the RUC in an attack that was televized world-wide. It was one of the events that marked the beginning of the Troubles.

20. For earlier examples of the internationalist strain in republican muralism, see **chapter four, section 5** above.

21. The most sustained and impressive mural display of republican solidarity with Palestine appeared on the International Wall in the first months of 2024 as a result of the Israeli war on Gaza. Led by republican muralists, but with the encouraged participation of anyone who wanted to contribute, a series of images that reproduced work by Palestinian artists relating to Gaza were painted along the length of the wall (Figure 19, see Fulcrum). For a visual account of the painting of the murals, see "Painting for Palestine," (https://www.facebook.com/groups/1331388700895445).

22. Leila Khaled, a member of the PFLP, was involved in aircraft hijackings in 1969 and 1970; the PFLP is a secular, socialist Palestinian group opposed to the Middle East "Peace Process" and its outcomes.

23. "Tamil Eelam" is the proposed Tamil State to be created in north and east of Sri Lanka; "Merdeka" ("independent, free") is the slogan of the Free Papua movement, which campaigns for freedom from Indonesian rule for West Papua.

24. South Belfast, specifically the area around Donegall Pass, has a small Chinese community. In the 2021 census, 4.6% of the population of Northern Ireland spoke as their primary tongue a language other than English, of which the pre-eminent were Polish (20,100 people), Lithuanian (9,000), Irish (6,000), Romanian (5,600), and Portuguese (5,000); 12.4% of the population "had some ability in the Irish language"; 10.4% "had some ability in the Ulster-Scots language" (Census 2021).

25. When photographing this mural, I was surprised, though pleased, to find that it used at least one photograph I had taken in the 1980s (it can be found in the Murals of Northern Ireland archive held at the Claremont Colleges Digital Library). There are numerous instances in which murals reference murals.

Chapter 7

1. In the referendum, 34% of unionists voted to remain, along with 88% of nationalists and 70% of those who considered themselves neither unionist nor nationalist (Garry 2016: 2). The overall figures were 55.8% remain and 44.2% leave (compared with the UK figures of 48.11% remain, 51.89% leave).

2. The text of the Protocol is available at "Protocol on Ireland/Northern Ireland," *Official Journal of the European Union*. Document 12020W/TXT (L 29/7). January 31 2020, https://eur-lex.europa.eu/legal-content/EN/TXT/HTML/?uri=CELEX:12020W/TXT&from=EN#d1e32-102-1. Downloaded January 31 2023.

3. On December 3 2012, Belfast City Council voted to curtail the flying of the Union flag at Belfast City Hall to the eighteen specified days per annum required by statute (it had flown every day since 1906). For a discussion of the decision and its repercussions, including prolonged social disorder, see Nolan et al. (2014).

4. There were examples of loyalist re-imaging outside Belfast, at Sperrin Park in Londonderry for instance, but these were the exceptions.

5. See chapter 5 note 4. The entry "Luther" in the MNI searchbox produces images of the father of Protestantism in housing estates in Lurgan 2009, Coleraine 2015, and Ballymena 2016.

6. By 2016 this mural had been displaced by an image featuring the flags of Scotland and Northern Ireland alongside the Union Jack. "Mother Daughter Sister" was also the title of a sculpture of a stylish working-class woman that appeared at the entrance to Sandy Row in 2015; it celebrated "the female culture and identity of Sandy Row and the generational contribution women have made to this community in the family and workplace."

7. See chapter eight for further discussion of the tourist phenomenon.

8. It should be remembered that for Irish unionists, Partition was a defeat: the least worst option. Carson's angry and pained words, delivered on December 14 1921, are pertinent to the recent relations between the DUP and their erstwhile friends in the Tory party: "I was a mere puppet in a political game. I was in earnest... What a fool I was. I was only a puppet, and so was Ulster, and so was Ireland, in the political game that was to get the Conservative Party into power. And of all the men in my experience that I think are the most loathsome it is those who will sell their friends for the purpose of conciliating their enemies, and, perhaps, still worse, the men who climb up a ladder into power of which even I may have been part of a humble rung, and then, when they have got into power, kick the ladder away without any concern for the pain, or injury, or mischief, or damage that they do to those who have helped them to gain power." The full text of the speech is available at https://api.parliament.uk/historic-hansard/lords/1921/dec/14/address-in-reply-to-his-majestys-most.

9. It is interesting to note that the Second World War is not perceived to have created a political and moral bond between unionism and the British State. This is reflected in the fact that there are relatively few murals that commemorate the Second World War (Figure 20, see Fulcrum); in those that do remember the war, the emphasis is usually placed on the Belfast Blitz (Figure 21, see Fulcrum). For a discussion of Northern Ireland in the Second World War see Barton 1995.

10. Beadle's painting was exhibited at the Royal Academy in 1917; it featured in murals from at least 1935 (see **chapter one, fig. 9**).

11. McCrae was a Canadian Medical Officer and Major who served with Allied forces during the war (including the Second Battle of Ypres); he died of pneumonia in 1918.

12. Focusing on the struggle for political identity, a mural in Lurgan in 2016 recalled the uncommemorated role of British soldiers from Ulster in the 1916 Easter Rising (Figure 22, see Fulcrum).

13. At the outbreak of the war, John Redmond called on the Irish Volunteers to enlist in the 10th and 16th (Irish) Divisions of the British Army in the hope that it would strengthen the case for Home Rule. This caused a split in the Volunteers, but Willie Redmond joined up and died from the wounds he suffered at Messines. His rescuer, Private Meeke, survived the war but died of TB in 1923; he was awarded the Military Medal.

14. As noted in chapter five, Billy Hutchinson is explicit about the connection between the "old" and the "new" UVF. But Evershed cites the objection of a former member of the PUP in this regard: "sordid, incestuous and squalid: that's how you would describe this forty years in Northern Ireland. There was nothing honourable about it, nothing honourable. In fact, it was disgusting. And it's got

nothing to do with the Ulster Volunteer Force who, number one, declared war on the British Army… and also the men who went to the Somme and fought at the Somme. It's a world of difference" (Evershed 2016: 256). In my own research I have found a range of opinions—from those who believe that the 1913 UVF and the 1965 UVF are the same organization, to those who believe that it is nigh on sacrilegious to link them.

15. The Ulster Defence Union was a unionist organization formed to resist the passing of Home Rule legislation in 1893; Colonel Saunderson (depicted in **fig. 76**) was one of the signatories of its manifesto (Jackson 1995: 116). The UDU motto, taken up by the UDA, was "Quis separabit" (see **chapter 1 note 9**). The first reference to the UDU appeared in a mural on the Lower Shankill estate in 2000 (**Introduction, fig. 18**).

16. This image is based on a photograph taken at the time which later featured in "Women through the ages" (**fig. 143**). The role of women in paramilitary organizations, loyalist and republican, is a very under-researched area. A number of women were convicted of terrorist offences, but other than that, our knowledge of the ways in which women supported and contributed to the functioning of paramilitarism is unclear. For an illuminating, if limited, account of women loyalist paramilitaries, see McEvoy 2009.

17. A report based on security force intelligence calculated that in 2020 there were approximately 12,500 loyalist paramilitaries in Northern Ireland (McKay 2021: 23).

18. "Floreat Ultona" was a catch-phrase current during the Home Rule period, though the Latin appears odd. "Ultonia" was the medieval Latin term for "Ulster" (derived from the Old Irish "Ulaid"); "Ultona" is not recorded.

19. In 2017, 36.6% of Protestant boys entitled to free school meals left with the minimal educational target of five GCSEs at grades A–C (Community Relations Council 2018: 163).

Chapter 8

1. The NPR write-up posted on the "Belfast Political Tours" site is headlined: "Tourists Can Now Experience Northern Ireland's Violent Political History" (https://www.npr.org/2017/11/17/564752434/tourists-can-now-experience-northern-irelands-violent-political-history). It is to be hoped that the headline is not true.

2. A number of photographs indicate that there were some murals within army barracks (see, for example, Wharton 2008: 386), but this is a completely unresearched field.

3. There is a growing street art scene in Derry/Londonderry, led by UV Arts and Peaball. My focus in the analysis that follows, however, will be Belfast, since the most significant developments are taking place there.

4. There is in fact a memorial to the dead in Belfast City Center; it sits on Victoria Street (opposite the Albert Clock). Sponsored by the Irish Congress of Trade Unions, and designed by the artist Robert Ballagh, it commemorates "Those Who Died from Violence from July 1969 to April 1976" and cites by anonymous number some 1,500 victims on a wall space of two square meters. Symptomatically, the effectively hidden memorial is neglected and frequently vandalized.

5. There are two exceptions on the Shankill and in Woodvale in loyalist West Belfast (Figure 23, see Fulcrum); there are various specific accounts that claim to explain the appearance of these images, none of which indicate that the new muralism is destined to make further inroads in these areas other than possibly for commercial purposes.

Bibliography

Abshire, Jean (2003) "Northern Ireland's Politics in Paint," *Peace Review*, 15.2, 149–161.

Alexander, Jeffrey (2004) "Toward a Theory of Cultural Trauma," in Alexander, Jeffrey C., Eyerman, Ron, Giesen, Bernard, Smelser, Neil J., and Sztompka, Piotr (eds), *Cultural Trauma and Collective Identity*, Berkeley: California University Press, 1–30.

Anderson, Tom and Bernard Conlon (2013) "In the Shadow of the Peace Walls: Art, Education, and Social Reconstruction in Northern Ireland," *Art Education*, 66.4, 36–42.

Anon (1990) "Shantallow youth statement," *2020 Vision Youth Bulletin*, 1, 6.

Anon (1991) "Writing on the wall," *Borderline*, 4.1, 9.

Anon (1992) "An seachtain," *Macha*, March, 3.

Anon [Culcavy Loyalist] (1993) "Letter to the Editor," *The Loyalist*, 3.5, 12.

Anon (1993) "Liverpool loyalists," *Combat*, November, 7.

Anon (1995) "Murals in Derry," *Fingerpost*, 11.3, 18–19.

Anon [An Súil Bui] (1995) "North Belfast murals: Best murals 1994–1995," *North Belfast Independent*, 1.1, 7.

Anon (1995) "Photographs (IRA members and murals)," *Communist Action*, 1, 22–23.

Anon (1995) "We shall remember," *Combat*, September, 6.

Anon (1995) "The Great Hunger and Ireland's War," *American Irish Newsletter*, 20.11, 7.

Anon (1996) "A mural to be proud of: Young Traveller women artists paint to raise awareness," *Women's News*, 79, 7.

Anon (1996) "We shall remember," *Combat*, September, 5.

Anon [An Súil Bui] (1996) "Mural mania sweeps Ardoyne," *North Belfast Independent*, 1.5, 8.

Anon [An Súil Bui] (1996) "The mystery continues," *North Belfast Independent*, 1.3.

Anon (1997) "Mural on a corned beef tin," *Fingerpost*, 16.1, 15.

Anon (1998) "Alliance delegation to visit Ballyduff," *City West News*, 11, 8.

Ardoyne Commemoration Project (2002) *Ardoyne: The Untold Truth*, Belfast: Beyond the Pale.

Arts Council Northern Ireland (n.d.) *Building Peace through the Arts—Re-Imaging Communities Programme Guidelines*, Belfast: Arts Council of Northern Ireland, www.artscouncil-ni.org/award/forms/re-image/Reimaging181109.doc

Arts Council Northern Ireland (2009) *Evaluation of the Re-Imaging Communities Programme*, Belfast: Independent Research Solutions.

Arts Council Northern Ireland (2016) *Evaluation of the Building Peace through the Arts: Re-Imaging Communities Programme*, Portadown: Wallace Consulting, http://www.artscouncil-ni.org/images/uploads/publications-documents/BPttA_Final_Programme_Evaluation.pdf

Assmann, Aleida (2011) *Cultural Memory and Western Civilisation: Functions, Media, Archives*, Cambridge: Cambridge University Press.

Barash, Jeffrey Andrew (2016) *Collective Memory and the Historical Past*, Chicago: University of Chicago Press.

Bardon, Jonathan (2005) *A History of Ulster*, Belfast: Blackstaff Press.

Barthel, Diane (1996) "Getting in Touch with History: The role of Historic Preservation in Shaping Collective Memories," *Qualitative Sociology*, 19.3, 345–364.

Barton, Brian (1995) *Northern Ireland in the Second World War*, Belfast: Ulster Historical Foundation.

BBC (1959) *Morning in the Streets* https://www.bbc.co.uk/iplayer/episode/b00d30nz/morning-in-the-streets

Beiner, Guy (2001) "The Invention of Tradition?" *History Review*, 12, 1–10.
Beiner, Guy (2007) "Between Trauma and Triumphalism: The Easter Rising, the Somme, and the Crux of Deep Memory in Modern Ireland," *Journal of British Studies*, 46.2, 366–389.
Beiner, Guy (2007) *Remembering the Year of the French: Irish Folk History and Social Memory*, Madison: Univeersity of Wisconsin Press.
Beiner, Guy (2018) *Forgetful Remembrance: Social Forgetting and Vernacular Historiography of a Rebellion in Ulster*, Oxford: Oxford University Press.
Belfast City Council (2009) *Belfast Journeys in Re-Imaging: Final Report*, Belfast: Belfast City Council.
Belfast Interface Project (2017) *Belfast Interfaces: Security Barriers and Defensive Use of Space*, Belfast: Belfast Interface Project.
Belfast Mural Guide (2014) Belfast: MSF Press.
Bell, Christine (2002) "Dealing With the Past in Northern Ireland," *Fordham International Law Journal*, 26.4, article 9, 1095–1147.
Bell, Jonathan (2002) *Conor: Drawing from Life*, Belfast: Appletree Press.
Bell, John, Neil Jarman, and Brian Harvey (2010) *Beyond Belfast: Contested Spaces in Urban, Rural and Cross-Border Settings*, Belfast: Community Relations Council and Rural Community Network.
Beresford, David (1987) *Ten Men Dead: The Story of the Irish Hunger Strike*, London: Grafton.
Beresford-Ellis, Peter (1993) "The preservation of the writing on the walls," *Irish Democrat*, January, 6.
Bew, Paul (1993) *Northern Ireland: A Chronology of the Troubles, 1968–1993*, Dublin: Gill & Macmillan.
Bew, Paul (2007) *Ireland: The Politics of Enmity 1789–2006*, Oxford: Oxford University Press.
Bhreathnach-Lynch, Sighle (1997) "The Easter Rising 1916: Constructing a Canon in Art & Artefacts," *History Ireland*, 5.1, 37–42.
Biggar, Nigel (ed.) (2014) *Burying the Past: Making Peace and Doing Justice after Civil Conflict*, Washington: Georgetown University Press.
Bloomfield, Sir Kenneth (1998) *We Will Remember Them*, Belfast: The Stationery Office.
Bogside Artists (1995) "We the accused," *Fingerpost*, 11.4, 15–17.
Bogside Artists (2009) *The People's Gallery*, Derry: Bogside Artists.
Borthwick, Stuart (2015) *The Writing on the Wall*, Liverpool: Bluecoat.
Borthwick, Stuart (2015) http://sluggerotoole.com/2015/12/19/the-mural-hunter-and-the-writing-on-the-wall/
Bourke, Richard (2012) *Peace in Ireland: The War of Ideas*, London: Pimlico.
Boyd, Andrew (1969) *Holy War in Belfast*, Tralee: Anvil Books.
Brady, Ciaran (1994) *Interpreting Irish History: The Debate on Historical Revisionism, 1938–1994*, Blackrock: Irish Academic Press.
Brady, Liam (1922) "Statement by witness: National and military activities, Derry, l914–1922," Dublin: Roinn Cosanta, 1922, https://www.militaryarchives.ie/collections/online-collections/bureau-of-military-history-1913-1921/reels/bmh/BMH.WS0676.pdf
Braun-Reinitz, Janet and Jane Weissman (2009) *On the Wall: Four Decades of Community Murals in New York City*, Jackson: University of Mississippi Press.
Brearton, Fran (1997) "Dancing unto death: Perceptions of the Somme, the Titanic and Ulster Protestantism," *The Irish Review*, 20.1, 89–103.
Bridgman, M. (2009) "Re-imaging communities," *ArtsHub*, February 26, http://www.artshub.co.uk/uk/news-article/opinions/visual-arts/re-imaging-communities-177113
Brown, Kris (2007) "'Our Father Organization': The Cult of the Somme and the Unionist 'Golden Age' in Modern Ulster Loyalist Commemoration," *The Round Table: Commemoration and Remembrance in the Commonwealth* 96. 393, 707–723.
Brown, Kris and Adrian Grant (2016) "A Lens Over Conflicted Memory: Surveying 'Troubles' Commemoration in Northern Ireland," *Irish Political Studies*, special issue, "Commemoration in Transition: Navigating Memory in Contested Societies," 31.1, 139–162.
Brown, Kris and Roger MacGinty (2003) "Public Attitudes toward Partisan and Neutral Symbols in Post-Agreement Northern Ireland," *Identities*, 10.1, 83–108.
Brown, Terence (1985) *The Whole Protestant Community: The Making of a Historical Myth*, Derry: Field Day.
Browne, Brendan Ciarán (2016) "Choreographed Segregation: Irish Republican Commemoration of the 1916 Easter Rising in 'Post-Conflict' Belfast," *Irish Political Studies*, special issue, "Commemoration in Transition: Navigating Memory in Contested Societies," 31.1, 101–121.

Brumm, Adam, Adhi Agus Oktaviana, Basran Burhan, Budianto Hakim, Rustan Lebe, Jian-xin Zhao, Priyatno Hadi Sulistyarto, Marlon Ririmasse, Shinatria Adhityatama, Iwan Sumantri, and Maxime Aubert (2021) "Oldest cave art found in Sulawesi," *Science Advances*, 7.3, https://www.science.org/doi/10.1126/sciadv.abd4648: eabd4648.

Bryan, Dominic (2000) *Orange Parades: The Politics of Ritual, Tradition and Control*, London: Pluto.

Bryan, Dominic and Gordon Gillespie (2000) *Transforming Conflict: Flags and Emblems*, Belfast: Institute of Irish Studies, Queen's University Belfast.

Bryan, Dominic and Gillian McIntosh (2005) "Sites of Creation and Contest in Northern Ireland," *SAIS Review of International Affairs*, 25.2, 127–137.

Bryan, Dominic and Gillian McIntosh (2005) "Symbols and Identity in 'New' Northern Ireland," in Paul Carmichael et al. (eds), *Devolution and Constitutional Change in Northern Ireland*, Manchester: Manchester University Press, 125–137.

Bryce, Ann (1991) "Rosemount Youth Club murals," *Fingerpost*, 5.2, 24–25.

Buckley, A. (1989) "'We're Trying to Find our Identity': Uses of History among Ulster Protestants," in E. Tonkin, M. McDonald, and M. Chapman (eds), *History and Ethnicity*, London: Routledge. 183–191.

Buckley, Anthony D. and Mary Catherine Kenney (1995) *Negotiating Identity: Rhetoric, Metaphor and Social Drama in Northern Ireland*, London: Smithsonian Institute Press.

Bulletin (Greater East Belfast Partnership) (1998) "Willowfield Murals," 10, 3.

Burke, Edmund (2009) *Reflections on the Revolution in France* [1790], ed. L.G. Mitchel, Oxford: Oxford University Press.

Burnhill, Eleanor (2007) "Weeds and wild flowers: Political tourism in west Belfast," *Edinburgh Review* 120.

Bush, Kenneth (2013) "The Politics of Post-Conflict Space: The Mysterious Case of Missing Graffiti in 'Post-Troubles' Northern Ireland," *Contemporary Politics*, 19:2, 167–189.

Butler, M. (2016) "Prisoners and Prison Life," in D. Healy (ed.), *The Routledge Handbook of Irish Criminology*, London: Taylor & Francis, 337–355.

Byers, E., S. Kelly, and K. Stevenson (2017). "'The North Remembers': The Uses and Abuses of the Middle Ages in Irish Political Culture, in B. Bildhauer and C. Jones (eds), *The Middle Ages in the Modern World* (Proceedings of the British Academy; Vol. 209), Oxford: Oxford University Press, 45–72.

Byrne, J. et al. (2012) *Attitudes to Peace Walls*, www.ark.ac.uk/peacewalls2012/

Cannon, John and Robert Crowcroft (2015) "Arbroath, declaration of," in *A Dictionary of British History* (3rd ed.), Oxford: Oxford University Press, https://www.oxfordreference.com/view/10.1093/acref/9780191758027.001.0001/acref-9780191758027-e-168?rskey=oWbC9d&result=1.

Carroll, Rory (2023) *Killing Thatcher: The IRA, the Manhunt and the Long War on the Crown* London: Mudlark.

Carson, Ciarán (1989) *Belfast Confetti*, Oldcastle: The Gallery Press.

Carson, Ciarán (1998) *The Star Factory*, London: Granta.

Casciani, D. (2000). "Painting politics in Northern Ireland," BBC News Online, http://news.bbc.co.uk/1/hi/northern_ireland/771314.stm

Case, H., and J.C. Payne (1962) "Tomb 100: The Decorated Tomb at Hierakonpolis," *Journal of Egyptian Archaeology*, 48, 5–18.

Catto, Mike (1977) "Notes from a Small War: Art and the Troubles," in Mike Catto (ed.), *Art in Ulster*, vol. 2, Belfast: Blackstaff Press, 125–144.

Causevic, Senija and Paul Lynch (2008) "Tourism development and contested communities: The issue of Belfast, Northern Ireland," *EspacesTemps.net*, Textuel, 21.10 http://espacestemps.net/document6443.html

Census 2021 (2022) *Main Statistics for Northern Ireland Statistical Bulletin—Language* (https://www.nisra.gov.uk/system/files/statistics/census-2021-main-statistics-for-northern-ireland-phase-1-statistical-bulletin-language.pdf) downloaded January 6 2023.

Clarke, A.F.N. (1984) *Contact*, London: Pan.

Cobain, Ian (2020) *Anatomy of a Killing*, London: Granta.

Collins, Jim and Adrian Kerr (2009) *Free Derry Wall*, Derry: Guildhall Press.

Commission for Victims and Survivors (2019) *Addressing the Legacy of Northern Ireland's Past*, Advice paper, https://www.cvsni.org/media/1970/jan-2019-addressing-the-legacy-of-northern-ireland-s-past-policy-advice-paper.pdf

Commission for Victims and Survivors. 2019. *Understanding Legacy*. https://www.cvsni.org/understanding-legacy/.

Commission on Flags, Identity, Culture and Tradition (2021) *Final Report*, Belfast: The Executive Office https://www.executiveoffice-ni.gov.uk/publications/commission-flags-identity-culture-and-tradition-final-report

Community Relations Council (2018) *Northern Ireland Peace Monitoring Report Number Five*, Belfast: CRC.

Confino, Alon (1997) "Collective Memory and Cultural History: Problems of Method," *American Historical Review*, 102.5, 1386–1403.

Connerton, Paul (1989) *How Societies Remember*, Cambridge: Cambridge University Press.

Connerton, Paul (2008) "Seven Types of Forgetting," *Memory Studies*, 1.1, 59–71.

Conrad, Kathryn (2007) "Widening the Frame: The Politics of Murals Photography in Northern Ireland," in Wanda Balzano, Anne Mulhall, and Moynagh Sullivan (eds), *Irish Postmodernisms and Popular Culture*, London: Palgrave Macmillan, 85–99.

Consultative Group on the Past (2009) *Report*, Belfast: Consultative Group on the Past.

Conway, Brian (2014) *Commemoration and Bloody Sunday: Pathways of Memory*, Basingstoke: Palgrave.

Conway, Jack. "Unbowed and Unbroken: A Conversation with Irish Republican Visual Artist Danny Devenny," *Radical History Review*, 106, 163–171.

Cook, William (2000) "The long drawn-out struggle," *New Statesman*, June 26, 43–45.

Cooper, Mickey, *Bishop Street and the Fountain: A Shared History*, Derry: Gasyard Heritage Centre, 2015.

Cooper, Graham and Doug Sargent (1979) *Painting the Town*, Oxford: Phaidon.

Coppock, Christopher (1983) "Editorial," *Circa*, 8, 3.

Coulter, Colin and Michael Murray (eds) (2008) *Northern Ireland after the Troubles: A Society in Transition*, Manchester: Manchester University Press.

Cox, M., A. Guelke, and F. Stephen (2000) *A Farewell to Arms? From "Long War' to Long Peace in Northern Ireland*, Manchester: Manchester University Press.

Craigavon, Lord (1934) "Rights of the minority," in *The Stormont Papers 50 Years of Parliamentary Debates Online* 16.34), 1095–1096, April 24 1934 http://www.ahds.ac.uk/stormontpapers/pageview.html?volumeno=16&pageno=109.

Crooke, Elizabeth (2016) "Artefacts as Agents for Change: Commemoration and Exchange via Material Culture," *Irish Political Studies*, special issue, "Commemoration in Transition: Navigating Memory in Contested Societies," 31.1, 85–100.

Crowley, Tony (2005) *Wars of Words: The Politics of Language in Ireland 1537–2004*, Oxford: Oxford University Press.

Crowley, Tony (2006) "The Political Production of a Language: The Case of Ulster-Scots," *Journal of Linguistic Anthropology*, 16.1, 23–35.

Crowley, Tony (2011) "'Dissident': An Essay in Historical Semiotics," Critical Quarterly, 53.2, 2011, 1–11.

Crowley, Tony (2011) "The Art of Memory: The Murals of Northern Ireland and the Management of History," *Field Day Review*, 7, 22–49.

Crowley, Tony (2015) "Hegemonic Shifts: The Latest from the Walls of Northern Ireland," *Estudios Irlandeses*, 10, 58–76.

Crowley, Tony (2015) "Digitising the murals of Northern Ireland (1979–2013): Images and interpretation," *Breac: A Digital Journal of Irish Studies*, Fall 2015, https://breac.nd.edu/articles/digitizing-the-murals-of-northern-ireland-1979-2013-images-and-interpretation/

Crowley, Tony (2018) "War and Art: The Murals of Northern Ireland," in Andrew McNeillie and James McNeillie (eds), *Dead groundi*, Thame: Clutag Press, 106–116.

Crowley, Tony (2020) "From Cultural Difference to Monoglossia: Herder's Language Trap," in Tan Ying Ying and Pritipuspa Mishra (eds), *Language, Nations and Multilingualism: Questioning the Herderian Ideal*, London: Routledge, 2020.

Crowley, Tony (2022) "Reading Republican Murals in Northern Ireland: Archiving and Meaning-Making," *Studi irlandesi. A Journal of Irish Studies*, 12, 87–117, https://oajournals.fupress.net/index.php/bsfm-sijis/article/view/13738/12760

Cusack, Jim and Henry McDonald (1997) *UVF*, Dublin: Poolbeg.

Darby, J. (1998) *Scorpions in a Bottle: Conflicting Cultures in Northern Ireland*, London: Minority Rights Publications.

Davidson, Colin (2015) *Silent Testimony*, Belfast: National Museums Northern Ireland.

Davies, Haydn (2015) *Northern Ireland Tragedy, Grief, and Humour*, Manchester: House of Heroes.

Davies, Lyell (2001) "Republican Murals, Identity and Communication in Northern Ireland," *Public Culture* 13.1, 155–158.

Davis, Whitney (1992) *Masking the Blow: The Scene of Representation in Late Prehistoric Egyptian Art*, Berkeley: University of California Press.

Dawson, Graham (2005) "Trauma, Place and the Politics of Memory: Bloody Sunday, Derry, 1972–2004," *History Workshop Journal*, 59, 151–178.

Dawson, Graham (2007) *Making Peace with the Past: Memories, Trauma and the Irish Troubles*, Manchester: Manchester University Press.

Dawson, Graham (2014) "The Desire for Justice, Psychic Reparation and the Politics of Memory in 'Post-Conflict' Northern Ireland," *Rethinking History: Historical Justice*, 18.2, 265–288.

Dawson, H, S. Dunn, and V. Morgan (2009) *Evaluation of the Re-imaging Communities Programme: A Report to the Arts Council of Northern Ireland, Belfast: Arts Council of Northern Ireland*, Belfast: Arts Council.

Deane, Seamus (1983) "The Artist and the Troubles," in Tim Pat Coogan (ed.), *Ireland and the Arts*, London: Namara Press, 42–50.

de Baróid, Ciarán (2000) *Ballymurphy and the Irish War*, revised ed., London: Pluto.

Doherty, Jeni (1995) "Book review: Seeing is believing," *Fingerpost*, 11.3, 17.

Dolan, Anne (2003) "An Army of Our Fenian Dead: Republicanism, Monuments and Commemoration," in Fearghal McGarry (ed.), *Republicanism in Modern Ireland*, Dublin: University College Dublin Press, 132–144.

Dowling, P.J. (1968) *The Hedge Schools of Ireland*, Cork: Mercier.

Downing Street Declaration (1993) "The Joint Declaration of 15 December 1993 (Downing St Declaration)," https://www.dfa.ie/media/dfa/alldfawebsitemedia/ourrolesandpolicies/northernireland/peace-process--joint-declaration-1993.pdf

Eames, Robin and Dennis Bradley (2009) *Report of the Consultative Group on the Past*, https://cain.ulster.ac.uk/victims/docs/consultative_group/cgp_230109_report.pdf

East Belfast Historical and Cultural Society (2006) *Thorndyke Street Murals East Belfast*, Belfast: East Belfast Historical and Cultural Society.

Edkins, Jenny (2003) "The Rush to Memory and the Rhetoric of War," *Journal of Political and Military Sociology*, 31.2, 231–250.

Edwards, Aaron (2008) "Drawing a Line Under the Past," *Peace Review*, 20:2, 209–217.

Edwards, Aaron (2012) "Fearful of the Past or 'Remembering the Future and Our Cause'? A Response to Cheryl Lawther," *Irish Political Studies*, 27:3, 457–470.

Edwards, Aaron (2015) "On the Obfuscation of the Past," *Peace Review*, 27:3, 354–362.

Edwards, Aaron (2017) *UVF Behind the Mask*, Dublin: Merrion Press.

Elliott, Marianne, *Hearthlands: A Memoir of the White City Housing Estate in Belfast*, Newtownards: Blackstaff Press.

English, Richard (2003) *Armed Struggle: The History of the IRA*, Oxford: Oxford University Press.

Evershed, Jonathan (2016) "Ghosts of the Somme," in Richard S. Grayson, and Fearghal McGarry (eds), *Remembering 1916: The Easter Rising, the Somme and the Politics of Memory in Ireland*, Cambridge: Cambridge University Press, 241–259.

Extramural Activity eds Seosamh Mac Coille and Cahal Collie (2011–present) http://extramuralactivity.com/

Faith and Politics Group (1998) *Remembrance and Forgetting: Building a Future in Northern Ireland*, Belfast: Community Relations Council.

Falconer, Alan D. and Joseph Liechty (eds) (1998) *Reconciling Memories*, Dublin: The Columba Press.

Faulkner, William (1996) *Requiem for a Nun*, London: Vintage.

Fay, Marie Therese, Mike Morrissey, and Marie Smyth (1997) *Mapping Troubles-Related Deaths in Northern Ireland*, Londonderry: INCORE.

Fay, Marie Therese, Mike Morrissey, and Marie Smyth (1999) *Northern Ireland's Troubles: The Human Costs*, London: Pluto.

Fentress, James and Chris Wickham (1992) *Social Memory*, Oxford: Blackwell.

Ferrell, Jeff (2016) "Foreword: Graffiti, Street Art and the Politics of Complexity," in Jeffrey Ian Ross, *Routledge Handbook of Graffiti and Street Art*, London: Routledge, xxx–xxxviii.

Fiacc, Padraic (2012) *Ruined Pages: New Selected Poems*, eds Gerald Dawe and Aodán Mac Póilin, Belfast: Lagan Press.

Filardo-Llamas, L. (2012) "To Live in the Heart (and Mind) of Others: The Construction of Memory in Northern Irish Commemorative Plaques," *Critical Approaches to Discourse Analysis Across Disciplines*, 5.2, 153–170.

Filardo-Llamas, L. and Jiménez González-Cascos (2014). "Memory and Identity in the Public Sphere: Northern Irish Murals," in Yusuf Kalyango, Jr and Monika Weronika Kopytowska (eds), *Why Discourse Matters: Negotiating Identity in the Mediatized World*, New York: Peter Lang, 57–73.

Finlayson, A. (1997) "The Problem of 'Culture' in Northern Ireland: A Critique of the Cultural Traditions Group," *The Irish Review*, 20, 76–88.

Finn, G (1997) "Qualitative Analysis of Murals in Northern Ireland: Paramilitary Justifications for Political Violence," in N. Hayes (ed.), *Doing Qualitative Analysis in Psychology*, Hove: Psychology Press, 143–178.

Folgarait, Leonard (1998) *Mural Painting and Social Revolution in Mexico, 1920–1940: Art of the New Order*, Cambridge: Cambridge University Press.

Forker, Martin and Jonathan McCormick (2009) "Walls of History: The Use of Mythomoteurs in Northern Ireland Murals," *Irish Studies Review*, 17.4, 423–465.

Gallagher, Carmel and Anne Hanratty (1989) "The War on the Walls," *Ulster Folklife*, 35, 100–108.

Gallaher, Carol and Peter Shirlow (2006) "The Geography of Loyalist Paramilitary Feuding in Belfast," *Space and Polity*, 10.2, 149–169.

Galvin, Patrick (1972) *Letter to a soldier on British soil*, Michigan: Red Hanrahan Press.

Garry, John (2016) "*The EU Referendum Vote in Northern Ireland: Implications for our Understanding of Citizens' Political Views and Behaviour*," Belfast: KESS.

Gilley, S.W. (1991) "Pearse's Sacrifice: Christ and Cuchulain Crucified and Risen in the Easter Rising, 1916," in S.W. Sykes (ed.), *Sacrifice and Redemption: Durham Essays in Theology*, Cambridge: Cambridge University Press.

Gillis, John (ed.) (1996) *Commemorations: The Politics of National Identity*, Princeton: Princeton University Press.

Goalwin, Gregory (2013) "The Art of War: Instability, Insecurity and Ideological Imagery in Northern Ireland's Political Murals, 1979–1998," *International Journal of Politics, Culture and Society*, 26, 189–215.

Goalwin, Gregory (2019) "The Curious Case of Cú Chulainn: Nationalism, Culture, and Meaning-Making in the Contested Symbols of Northern Ireland," *Studies in Ethnicity and Nationalism*, 19.3, 307–324.

Godson, Dean (2003) "Meeting of the extremes," *The Spectator*, 6.

Goldberg, David (1993) "Halcyon days," *Causeway*, Fall, 18–21.

Gordon, Lucy and Elaine McClure (eds) (1997) *Remembrance*, Lurgan: Ulster Society.

Gould, Mary Rachel and Rachel E. Silverman (2013) "Stumbling Upon History: Collective Memory and the Urban Landscape," *GeoJournal*, 78.791–801.

Goulding, Stephen and Amy McCroy (2020). "Representing the (Un)finished Revolution in Belfast's Political Murals," *Critical Discourse Studies*, 1–27.

Graff-McRae, Rebecca (2010) *Remembering and Forgetting 1916: Commemoration and Conflict in Post-Peace Process Ireland*, Dublin: Irish Academic Press.

Graham, Brian (1994) "No Place of the Mind: Contested Protestant Representations of Ulster," *Ecumene*, 1.3, 257–281.

Graham, Brian (2004) "The Past in the Present: The Shaping of Identity in Loyalist Ulster," *Terrorism and Political Violence*, 16.3, 483–500.

Graham, Brian and Sara McDowell (2007) "Meaning in the Maze: The Heritage of Long Kesh," *Cultural Geographies*, 14.3, 343–368.

Graham, Brian and Peter Shirlow (2002) "The Battle of the Somme in Ulster Memory and Identity," *Political Geography*, 21.7, 881–904.

Graham, Brian and Yvonne Whelan (2007) "The Legacies of the Dead: Commemorating the Troubles in Northern Ireland," *Environment and Planning D: Society and Space*, 25.3, 476–495.

Graham, Donald (1985) "The Politics of Graffiti," *Ireland Politics and Society*, 1.1, 91–98.

Grayson, Richard S. and Fearghal McGarry (2016) *Remembering 1916: The Easter Rising, the Somme and the Politics of Memory in Ireland*, Cambridge: Cambridge University Press.

Gutmann, Amy and Charles Taylor (1994) *Multiculturalism: Examining the Politics of Recognition*, Princeton: Princeton University Press.

Guthrie, R. Dale (2006) *The Nature of Paleolithic Art*, Chicago: Chicago University Press.

Hackett, Claire and Bill Rolston (2009) "The Burden of Memory: Victims, Storytelling and Resistance in Northern Ireland," *Memory Studies*, 2.3, 355–376.

Halbwachs, Maurice (1980) *The Collective Memory*, trans. Francis Ditter and Vida Yazdi Ditter, London: Harper.

Halbwachs, Maurice and L. Coser (1992) *On Collective Memory*, ed. and trans. Lewis A. Coser, Chicago: University of Chicago Press.

Hall, Stuart (2021) *The Hard Road to Renewal: Thatcherism and the Crisis of the Left*, London: Verso.

Halliday, Donna and Neil Ferguson (2016) "When Peace is Not Enough: The Flag Protests, the Politics of Identity and Belonging in East Belfast," *Irish Political Studies*, 31:4, 525–540.

Hamber, B. (ed.) (1998) *Past Imperfect: Dealing with the Past in Northern Ireland and Societies in Transition*, Derry/Londonderry: University of Ulster, INCORE.

Hartnett, Alexandra (2003) "Introducing King Nuadha: Mythology and Politics in the Belfast Murals," in Bettina Kimpton (ed.), *Proceedings of the Harvard Celtic Colloguium*, vol. XXIII, 133–148.

Hayton, D. (1990) "The Propaganda War," in W.A. Maguire (ed.), *Kings in Conflict: The Revolutionary War in Ireland and its Aftermath, 1689–1750*, Belfast: Blackstaff Press, 106–121.

Healing though Remembering (2002) *The Report of the Healing through Remembering Project*, Belfast: Healing through Remembering.

Healing though Remembering (2007) *"Storytelling" Audit: An audit of Personal Story, Narrative, and Testimony Initiatives Related to the Conflict in and about Northern Ireland*, Belfast: Healing through Remembering.

Heaney, Seamus (1990) *The Cure at Troy*, Derry: Field Day.

Hennessy, Tom and Robin Wilson (1997) *With All Due Respect: Pluralism and Parity of Esteem*, Belfast: Democratic Dialogue.

Hepburn, A.C. (1990) "The Belfast Riots of 1935," *Social History*, 15.1 75–96.

Hewitt, John, "Painting and Sculpture in Ulster," in Sam Hanna Bell, Nesca A. Robb and John Hewitt (eds), *The Arts in Ulster A Symposium* (London: Harrap, 1951), 69–95.

Hewitt, John, *John Luke 1906–1975*, n.p.: Arts Councils of Ireland, 1978.

Hewitt, John, "Conor's Art," in Judith C. Wilson (ed.), *Conor's Art 1881–1968*, Belfast: Blackstaff Blackstaff Press, 107–127.

Hewitt, John (1992) *The Collected Poems of John Hewitt*, ed. Frank Ormsby, Belfast: Blackstaff Press.

Hill, Andrew and Andrew White (2008) "The Flying of Israeli Flags in Northern Ireland," *Identities: Global Studies in Culture and Power*, 15, 31–50.

Hill, Andrew and Andrew White (2012) "Painting Peace? Murals and the Northern Ireland Peace Process," *Irish Political Studies*, 27.1, 71–88.

HMSO (1954) *The Flags and Emblems (Display) Act (Northern Ireland)*, Belfast: HMSO.

HMSO (1985) *Agreement between the Government of the United Kingdom of Great Britain and Northern Ireland and the Government of the Republic of Ireland*, London: HMSO.

Hocking, Bryanna (2012) "Beautiful Barriers: Art and Identity along a Belfast 'Peace' Wall," *Anthropology Matters*, 14.1, 1–12.

Hocking, Bryanna (2014). "Great Transformations: 'Re-casting' Derry's Diamond War Memorial for the Demands of a 'Shared' Future," *Canadian Journal of Irish Studies*, 38.1/2, 228–259.

Hocking, Bryanna (2015) *The Great Reimagining: Public Art, Urban Space, and the Symbolic Landscapes of a "New" Northern Ireland*, Oxford: Berghahn.

Hoffmann, D.L., C.D. Standish, M. García-Diez, P.B. Pettitt, J.A. Milton, J. Zilhão, J.J. Alcolea-González, P. Cantalejo-Duarte, H. Collado, R. de Balbín, M. Lorblanchet, J. Ramos-Muñoz, G.-Ch. Weniger, A.W.G. Pike (2018) "U-Th Dating of Carbonate Crusts Reveals Neandertal Origin of Iberian Cave Art," *Science*, 359.6378: 912–915.

Holloway, David (1994a) "Pass masters," *Fortnight*, 332, 40–41.

Holloway, David (1994b) "Territorial aspects of cultural identity: The Protestant community of Donegall Pass, Belfast," *Causeway*, 1.5, 9–12.

Hopkins, Stephen (2016) "'Our Whole History has been Ruined!' The 1981 Hunger Strike and the Politics of Republican Commemoration and Memory," in *Irish Political Studies*, special issue, "Commemoration in Transition: Navigating Memory in Contested Societies," 31.1, 44–46.

Hobsbawm, Eric and Terence Ranger (1983) *The Invention of Tradition*, Cambridge: Cambridge University Press.

House of Commons Northern Ireland Affairs Committee (2005) "Report, together with formal minutes," *Ways of Dealing with Northern Ireland's Past: Interim Report—Victims and Survivors*, vol. I, London: House of Commons.

House of Commons Northern Ireland Affairs Committee (2005) "Oral and written evidence," *Ways of Dealing with Northern Ireland's Past: Interim Report—Victims and Survivors*, vol. II, London: House of Commons.

Howe, Stephen (2011) "Memory and History in Northern Ireland," *History Workshop Journal*, 71, 219–231.

Hughes, Quentin (1964) *Seaport: Architecture and Townscape in Liverpool*, London: Lund Humphries.

Hutchinson, Billy (2011) *Transcendental Art: A Troubles Archive Essay*, Belfast: Northern Ireland Arts Council.

Hutchinson, Billy (2020) *My Life in Loyalism*, Newbridge: Merrion Press.

Hutton, Patrick H. (1993) *History as an Art of Memory*, Burlington, VT: University of Vermont.

Hutton, Patrick H. (2016) *The Memory Phenomenon in Contemporary Historical Writing: How the Interest in Memory has Influenced Our Understanding of History*, Basingstoke: Palgrave Macmillan.

Huyssen, A. (1995) *Twilight Memories: Marking Time in a Culture of Amnesia*, London: Routledge.

Independent Commission on Policing for Northern Ireland (1999) *A New Beginning: Policing in Northern Ireland*, Belfast: Stationery Office.

Independent International Commission on Decommissioning (2011) *Final Report of the Independent International Commission on Decommissioning* https://cain.ulster.ac.uk/events/peace/decommission/iicd040711.pdf

Independent Reporting Commission (2022) *Independent Reporting Commission Fifth Report*, London: HMSO https://www.ircommission.org/sites/irc/files/IRC%20Fifth%20Report%20-%20Web%20Accessible.pdf

Irish Republican Army (1994) "Ceasefire statement, 31 August 1994," https://cain.ulster.ac.uk/events/peace/docs/ira31894.htm.

Irish Republican Army (2002) "Statement of apology," https://cain.ulster.ac.uk/events/peace/docs/ira160702.htm

Jackson, Alvin (1992) "Irish Unionist Imagery, 1850–1920," in Eve Patten (ed.), *Returning to Ourselves: Second Volume of Papers from the John Hewitt Summer School*, Belfast: Lagan Press, 344–359.

Jackson, Alvin (1992) "Unionist Myths 1912–1985," *Past & Present*, 136.1, 164–185.

Jackson, Alvin (1995) *Colonel Edward Saunderson: Land and Loyalty in Victorian Ireland*, Oxford: Oxford University Press.

"James Ward ARCA," *Mapping the Practice and Profession of Sculpture in Britain and Ireland 1851–1951*, University of Glasgow History of Art and HATII, online database 2011 [http://sculpture.gla.ac.uk/view/person.php?id=msib3_1216216083.

Jankowitz, Sarah (2018) "The 'Hierarchy of Victims' in Northern Ireland: A Framework for Critical Analysis," *The International Journal of Transitional Justice*, 12.2, 216–236.

Jarman, Neil (1992) "Troubled Images: the Iconography of Loyalism," *Critique of Anthropology*, 12.2, 133–165.

Jarman, Neil (1996) "The Ambiguities of Peace: Republican and Loyalist Ceasefire Murals," *Causeway*, Spring, 23–27.

Jarman, Neil (1996) "Violent Men, Violent Land: Dramatising the Troubles and the Landscape of Ulster," *Journal of Material Culture*, 1.1, 39–61.

Jarman, Neil (1997) *Material Conflicts: Parades and Visual Displays in Northern Ireland*, Oxford: Berg.

Jarman, Neil (1998) "Material of Culture, Fabric of Identity," in Daniel Miller (ed.), *Material Cultures: Why Some Things Matter*, London: UCL Press, 121–145.

Jarman, Neil (1998) "Painting Landscapes: The Place of Murals in the Symbolic Construction of Urban Space," in A. Buckley (ed.), *Symbols in Northern Ireland*, Belfast: Institute of Irish Studies, 81–98.

Jarman, Neil (1999) "Commemorating 1916, Celebrating 1916: Parading and Painting in Belfast," in Susanne Küchler and Adrian Forty (eds), *The Art of Forgetting*, Oxford: Berg, 171–196.

Jarman, Neil (1999) *Displaying Faith: Orange, Green and Trade Union Banners in Northern Ireland*, Belfast: Institute of Irish Studies.

Jarman, Neil (2001) "Not an Inch," *Peace Review* 13.1, 35–41.

Jarman, Neil (2001) "The Orange Arch: Creating Tradition in Ulster," *Folklore*, 112:1, 1–21.

Jelin, E. (2003) "Contested Memories of Repression in the Southern Cone: Commemorations in a Comparative Perspective," in P. Gready (ed.), *Political Transition*, London: Pluto Press, 53–69.

Jelin, E. (2003) *State Repression and the Struggles for Memory*, London: Latin America Bureau.

Johnson, Nuala (2012) "The Contours of Memory in Post-Conflict Societies: Enacting Public Remembrance of the Bomb in Omagh, Northern Ireland," *Cultural Geographies*, 19.2, 237–258.

Johnston, E. (1970) "Folk Art in Ulster," *Architectural Review*, 148.884, 205–206.

Jones, M. (2004) "Mining Our Collective Memory: Beyond the Academic-Activist Divide in Black Studies," *Souls—A Critical Journal of Black Politics, Culture, and Society*, 6.3–4, 71–76.

Joyce, James (1992) *A Portrait of the Artist as a Young Man* [1916], ed. Seamus Deane, London: Penguin.

Kansteiner, Wulf (2002) "Finding Meaning in Memory: A Methodological Critique of Collective Memory Studies," *History and Theory*, 41, 179–197.

Kelly, James (1994) "'The Glorious and Immortal Memory': Commemoration and Protestant Identity in Ireland, 1660–1800," *Proceedings of the Royal Irish Academy*, 94C, 25–52.

Kenedy, Conor (1998) "Bombing Belfast," *City West News*, 12, 14.

Killen, John (1985) *John Bull's Famous Circus: Ulster History through the Postcard 1905–1985*, Dublin: O'Brien Press.

Kennedy, Dennis. "Spender, Sir Wilfrid Bliss," *Oxford Dictionary of National Biography* (online ed.), Oxford: Oxford University Press.

Kenwood, Michael (2023) "Belfast council to look at providing sites for street art in bid to cut down on illegal graffiti," *Belfast Telegraph*, https://www.belfasttelegraph.co.uk/news/northern-ireland/belfast-council-to-look-at-providing-sites-for-street-art-in-bid-to-cut-down-on-illegal-graffiti/a1691457567.html

Kerr, Helen (2023) *Glorious Twelfth: A Folk Art Project* [1958], Belfast: Beyond the Pale.

King, Guy (2003) "Murals in the Bogside 1969–1999," *The Local Historian*, 33.4, 226–243.

Kipling, Rudyard (1994) *Collected Poems of Rudyard Kipling*, London: Wordsworth.

Klein, Kerwin L. (2000) "On the Emergence of *Memory* in Historical Discourse," *Representations*, 69, 127–150.

Krzyzanowska, Natalia (2016) "The Discourse of Counter-Monuments: Semiotics of Material Commemoration in Contemporary Urban Spaces," *Social Semiotics*, 26.5, 465–485.

Larsson, Fredrika (2014) *Identities on the Walls: A Comparative Study of Loyalist and Republican Murals in Northern Ireland*. Lund University, Department of History, https://www.academia.edu/5457819/Identities_on_the_Walls_A_Comparative_Study_of_Loyalist_and_Republican_murals_in_Northern_IrelandLatimer

Latimer, Joanne (2011) "A project to replace infamous Belfast murals comes under fire: Something a can of paint can't fix?" *Macleans Magazine*, July 6 2011, http://www2.macleans.ca/2011/07/06/something-a-can-of-paint-can-fix/Leonard

Lawther, Cheryl (2011) "Unionism, Truth Recovery and the Fearful Past," *Irish Political Studies*, 26.3, 361–382.

Lawther, Cheryl (2012) "Unionism, Truth and the Challenge of the Past: A Response to Aaron Edwards," *Irish Political Studies*, 27.3, 471–478.

Leerssen, Joep (1996) *Remembrance and Imagination: Patterns in the Historical and Literary Representation of Ireland in the 19th Century*, Cork: Cork University Press.

Lefebvre, Henri, *The Production of Space*, trans. Donald Nicholson-Smith, Oxford: Blackwell, 1991.

Leonard, Jane (1996) "The Twinge of Memory: Armistice Day and Remembrance Sunday in Dublin since 1919," in Richard English and Graham Walker (eds), *Unionism in Modern Ireland: New Perspectives on Politics and Culture*, Basingstoke: Macmillan, 99–114.

Leonard, Jane, *The Culture of War Commemoration*, Dublin: Cultures of Ireland, 1996.

Leonard, Madeleine (2011) "A Tale of Two Cities: 'Authentic' Tourism in Belfast," *Irish Journal of Sociology*, 19.2, 111–126.

Lisle, Debbie (2006) "Local Symbols, Global Networks: Re-Reading the Murals of Belfast," *Alternatives*, 27–52.

Loftus, Belinda (1977) "Will the real King Billy please stand up?" *Fortnight*, 142, 8–9.

Loftus, Belinda (1981) "Mother Ireland and the Troubles: Artist, Model and Reality," *Circa*, 1, 9–13.

Loftus, Belinda (1982) *Images in Conflict: Visual Imagery and the Troubles In Northern Ireland (1968–1981)*, 4 vols, PhD, Keele University.
Loftus, Belinda (1983) "Loyalist Wall Paintings," *Circa*, 8, 10–14.
Loftus, Belinda (1983) "Photography, Art and Politics: How the English Make Pictures out of Northern Ireland's Troubles," *Circa*, 13, 10–14.
Loftus, Belinda (1986) "Matters of Life and Death: Protestant and Catholic Ways of Seeing Death in Northern Ireland," *Circa*, 26, 14–18.
Loftus, Belinda (1988) "In Search of a Useful Theory," *Circa*, 40, 17–23.
Loftus, Belinda (1990) *Mirrors: William III and Mother Ireland*, Dundrum: Picture Press.
Loftus, Belinda (1994) *Mirrors: Orange and Green*, Dundrum: Picture Press.
Longley, Edna (1991) "The Rising, the Somme and Irish Memory," in Máirín Ní Dhonnchadha and Theo Dorgan (eds), *Revising the Rising*, Derry: Field Day, 29–49.
Loughlin, James (2002) "Mobilising the Sacred Dead: Ulster Unionism, the Great War and the Politics of Remembrance," in Adrian Gregory and Senia Paseta (eds), *Ireland and the Great War: "A War to Unite Us All?"* Manchester: Manchester University Press, 133–154.
Lundy, Patricia and Mark McGovern (2001) "The Politics of Memory in Post-Conflict Northern Ireland," *Peace Review*, 13.1, 27–33.
Lundy, Patricia and Mark McGovern (2005) *Community, "Truth-telling" and Conflict Resolution: A Critical Evaluation of the Role of Community-based "Truth-telling" Processes for Post-Conflict Transition—A Case Study of the Ardoyne Commemoration Project*, Belfast: the authors.
Lundy, P. and M. McGovern, (2006) *A truth commission for Northern Ireland*, ARK Research Update (Belfast and Derry: ARK), http://www.ark.ac.uk/publications/updates/update46.pdf.
Lynch, Robert (2019) *The Partition of Ireland: 1918–1925*, Cambridge: Cambridge University Press.
Lyons, Laura and Mairead Keane (1992) "'At the End of the Day': An Interview with Mairead Keane, National Head of Sinn Fein Women's Department," *boundary 2*, 19.2, 260–286.
Mac Cormaic, Eoghan (1990) "Censorship and control," *Nuacht Sheantalaimh*, 7, 8.
MacDonagh, Oliver (1983) *States of Mind: A Study of Anglo-Irish Conflict 1780–1980,* London: Allen & Unwin.
MacDonald, Darach (2010) *Blood and Thunder: Inside an Ulster Protestant Band*, Cork: Mercier.
Mac Giolla Chriost, Diarmait (2012) *Jailtacht: The Irish Language, Symbolic Power and Political Violence in Northern Ireland, 1972–2008*, Cardiff: University of Wales Press.
Mac Siacais, Jake (2022) *Surfing into Life on a Bathboard: A Gaeilgeoir Republican's Pathway to an Imperfect Peace*, Belfast: Beyond the Pale.
Markusen, Ann and Greg Schrock (2009) "Consumption-Driven Urban Development," *Urban Geography*, 30:4, 344–367.
Marx, Karl (1977) *Karl Marx Selected Writings*, ed. D. McLellan, Oxford: Oxford University Press.
Mattar, Daniela Vicherat (2017) "Speaking Walls: Contentious Memories in Belfast's Murals," in S.H. Awad and B. Wagoner (eds), *Street Art of Resistance*, London: Palgrave, 179–200.
McAreavey, Naomi (2018) "Building Bridges? Remembering the 1641 Rebellion in Northern Ireland," *Memory Studies*, 11.1, 100–114.
McAtackney, Laura (2011) "Peace Maintenance and Political Messages: The Significance of Walls during and after the Northern Irish 'Troubles,'" *Journal of Social Archaeology*, 11.1, 77–98.
McAuley, James (2000) "Mobilising Ulster Unionism: New Directions or Old?" *Capital & Class*, 24.1, 37–64.
McAuley, James (2016) *Very British Rebels? The Culture and Politics of Ulster Loyalism*, London: Bloomsbury.
McAuley, James W. and Joe McCormack (1990) "The Hound of Ulster and the Re-Writing of Irish History," *Études Irlandaises*, 15.2, 149–164.
McAuley, James W. and Jonathan Tonge (2007) "'For God and for the Crown': Contemporary Political and Social Attitudes Among Orange Order Members in Northern Ireland." *Political Psychology*, 28.1: 33–52.
McCauley, Jim (2016) "Memory and Belonging in Ulster Loyalist Identity," *Irish Political Studies*, special issue, "Commemoration in Transition: Navigating Memory in Contested Societies," 31.1, 122–138.
McBride, Ian (1997) *The Siege of Derry in Ulster Protestant Mythology*, Dublin: Four Courts Press.
McBride, Ian (ed.) (2001) *History and Memory in Modern Ireland*, Cambridge: Cambridge University Press

McBride, Ian (2001) "Memory and National Identity in Modern Ireland," in Ian McBride (ed.), *History and Memory in Modern Ireland*, Cambridge: Cambridge University Press, 1–42.
McBride, Ian (2009) "What Was It About?" *Irish Review*, 40, 177–181.
McConville, Seán (2021) *Irish Political Prisoners 1960–2000 Braiding Rage and Sorrow*, London: Routledge.
McBrinn, Joseph (1997) "Belfast's *other* murals," *Causeway*, 4.2, 39–43.
McCormick, Jonathan (2019) *A Directory of the Murals of Northern Ireland*, https://cain.ulster.ac.uk/mccormick/index.html
McCormick, Jonathan and Neil Jarman, Neil (2005) "Death of a Mural," *Journal of Material Culture*, 10.1, 49–71.
McDonald, Henry (2019) *Two Souls*, Newbridge: Irish Academic Press.
McDonald, Henry and Jim Cusack (2004) *UDA Inside the Heart of Loyalist Terror*, Dublin: Penguin Ireland.
McDowell, Sara (2007) "Armalite, the ballot box and memorialization: Sinn Féin and the state in post-conflict Northern Ireland," *The Round Table*, 96:393, 725–738.
McDowell, Sara (2008) "Commemorating Dead 'Men': Gendering the Past and Present in Post-Conflict Northern Ireland," *Gender, Place and Culture*, 15.4, 335–354.
McDowell, Sara (2008) "Selling Conflict Heritage through Tourism in Peacetime Northern Ireland: Transforming Conflict or Exacerbating Difference?" *International Journal of Heritage Studies*, 14.5, 405–421.
McDowell, S. (2009) "Negotiating Places of Pain in Post-Conflict NI: Debating the Future of the Maze/Long Kesh," in W. Logan and K. Reeves (eds) *Places of Pain and Shame: Dealing with Difficult Heritage*, London: Routledge, 213–230.
McDowell, Sarah and Máire Braniff (2014) "A War by Other Means? Commemorating Conflict in the New Northern Ireland," in Sara McDowell and Máire Braniff (eds), *Commemoration as Conflict: Space, Memory and Identity in Peace Processes*, London: Palgrave Macmillan, 38–59.
McDowell, Sarah and Peter Shirlow (2011) "Geographies of Conflict and Post-Conflict in Northern Ireland," *Geography Compass*, 5.9, 700–709.
McDowell, Sara and Catherine Switze (2011) "Violence and the Vernacular: Conflict, Commemoration, and Rebuilding in the Urban Context," *Buildings & Landscapes: Journal of the Vernacular Architecture Forum*, 18.2, 82–104.
McEvoy, K. (2006). *Making Peace with the Past: Options for Truth Recovery in Northern Ireland*, Belfast: Healing Through Remembering.
McEvoy, K. and B. Gormally (2009) *Dealing with the Past in Northern Ireland "From Below,"* Belfast: Community Foundation for Northern Ireland.
McEvoy, L., K. McEvoy and K. McConnachie (2006) "Reconciliation as a Dirty Word: Conflict, Community Relations and Education in Northern Ireland," *Journal of International Affairs*, 60.1, 81–106.
McEvoy, S (2009) "Loyalist Women Paramilitaries in Northern Ireland: Beginning a Feminist Conversation about Conflict Resolution," *Security Studies*, 18, 262–286.
McGarry, John and Brendan O'Leary (1995) *Explaining Northern Ireland: Broken Images*, Oxford: Blackwell.
McGlinchey, Marisa (2019) *Unfinished Business: The Politics of "Dissident" Irish Republicanism*, Manchester: Manchester University Press.
McGrattan, Cillian (2013) *Memory, Politics, Identity: Haunted by History*, Basingstoke: Palgrave.
McGrattan, Cillian (2017) "'The Possibilities are Endless': Republican Strategy to Deal with the Past and Transitional Justice in Northern Ireland," in J Dudgeon, (ed.), *Legacy: What to do about the Past in Northern Ireland*, Belfast: Belfast Press.
McGrattan, Cillian and Stephen Hopkins (2017) "Memory in Post-Conflict Societies: From Contention to Integration? *Ethnopolitics*, 16:5, 488–499.
McGuigan, Noel (1983) "The Open Air Gallery of Political Art," *Circa*, 8, 15–18.
McKay, Susan (2000) *Northern Protestants: An Unsettled People*, Belfast: Blackstaff Press.
McKay, Susan (2008) *Bear in Mind these Dead*, London: Faber and Faber.
McKee, Brian (2020) *Ardoyne '69: Stories of Struggle and Hope*, Dublin: Red Stripe Press.
McKittrick, David, Seamus Kelters, Brian Feeney, and Chris Thornton (1999) *Lost Lives: The Stories of Men, Women and Children who Died as a Result of the Northern Ireland Troubles*, Edinburgh: Mainstream Publishing.

McQuaid, Sara Dybris (2015) "Parading Memory and Re-member-ing Conflict: Collective Memory in Transition in Northern Ireland," *International Journal of Politics, Culture, and Society*, 30.1, 23–41.

McQuaid, Sara Dybris (2016) "Passive Archives or Storages for Action? Storytelling Projects in Northern Ireland," *Irish Political Studies*, special issue, "Commemoration in Transition: Navigating Memory in Contested Societies," 31.1, 63–85.

McTigue, Eoghan (2004) *All Over Again*, Belfast: Belfast Exposed.

McVeigh, Robbie and Bill Rolston (2007) "From Good Friday to Good Relations: Sectarianism, Racism and the Northern Ireland State," *Race & Class*, 48.4, 1–23.

McWilliams, Joseph (1982) "Violence and Painting in Northern Ireland," *Circa*, 6–7.

Martin, F.X. (1967) "1916: Myth, Fact and Mystery," *Studia Hibernica*, 7, 7–126.

Melaugh, Eamon (2018) *Derry's Troubled Years*, Derry: Guildhall Press.

Middlebrook, Martin (1971) *The First Day on the Somme*, London: Allen Lane.

Middleton, D. and D. Edwards (1990) *Collective Remembering*, London: Sage.

Miossec, Alain (2024) *Murals irland du nord*, https://muralsirlandedunord.over-blog.com/

Misztal, B. (2003) *Theories of Social Remembering*, Maidenhead: Open University Press.

Mitchell, Audra and Liam Kelly (2011) "Peaceful Spaces? 'Walking' through the New Liminal Spaces of Peacebuilding and Development in North Belfast," *Alternatives: Global, Local, Political*, 36.4, 307–325.

Mitchell, Billy (2000) "Somme Commemoration Speech," Monkstown, June 25 2000, http://www.pup-ni.org.uk/articles/bm/somme.htm

Mitchell, Billy (2002) "Principles of loyalism: An internal discussion paper," http://www.pup-ni.org.uk/loyalism/principlesdocument.aspx

Mitchell, George, John de Chastelain, and Harri Holkeri (1996) *Report of the International Body on Arms Decommissioning*, https://cain.ulster.ac.uk/events/peace/docs/gm24196.htm

Moloney, Ed (2007) *A Secret History of the IRA*, 2nd ed., London: Penguin.

Moloney, Ed (2010) *Voices from the Grave: Two Men's War in Ireland*, London: Faber and Faber.

Moloney, Peter (2019) "Peter Moloney Collection," in *Extramural Activity*, eds Seosmah Mac Coille and Cahal Collie (2011–present) http://extramuralactivity.com/

Montgomery, Daniel J. (1998) "Memory and redemption," *Lion and Lamb*, 17, 12–14.

Moody, T.W. (1978) "Irish history and Irish mythology," *Hermathena*, 124, 6–24.

Morgan, H.J. (1993) "Deceptions of demons," *Fortnight*, 320, 34–36.

Morgan, Leo (1992) "Information on murals," *Fight Racism! Fight Imperialism!* 109, 15.

Morrissey, Mike and Marie Smyth (2002) *Northern Ireland after the Good Friday Agreement: Victims, Grievance and Blame*, London: Pluto.

Mulqueen, John and Jim Smyth (2020) "'The Che Guevara of the IRA': The Legend of 'Big' Joe McCann," *History Ireland*, 18.1, 46–47.

Murray, Lesley (2016) "Placing Murals in Belfast: Community, Negotiation and Change," in Cameron Cartiere and Martin Zebracki (eds), *The Everyday Practice of Public Art: Art, Space and Social Inclusion*, London, Routledge, 45–62.

Murphy, Joanne and Sara McDowell (2018) "Transitional Optics: Exploring Liminal Spaces after Conflict," *Urban Studies*, 56.12, 2499–2514.

Nagle, John (2008) "From Mourning to Melancholia? The Ambivalent Role of Commemoration in Facilitating Peace-Building in Northern Ireland," *Irish Journal of Anthropology*, 11, 1, 28–34.

Nagle, John (2011) "Between Trauma and Healing: Tourism and Neoliberal Peace-Building in Divided Societies," *Journeys*, 11.1, 29–46.

Nagle, John (2018) "Defying State Amnesia and Memory Wars: Non-Sectarian Memory Activism in Beirut and Belfast City Centres," *Social & Cultural Geography*, 21.3, 380–401.

Nevett, T.R. (1982) *Advertising in Britain: A History*, London: Heinemann.

Ní Dhonnchadha, Máirín and Theo Dorgan (eds) (1991) *Revising the Rising*, Derry: Field Day.

Nietzsche, Friedrich (1997) *Untimely Meditations*, Cambridge: Cambridge University Press.

Nolan, P., D. Bryan, C. Dwyer, K. Hayward, K. Radford, and P. Shirlow (2014) *The Flag Dispute: Anatomy of a Protest*, Belfast: Queen's University Belfast, http://www.qub.ac.uk/researchcentres/isctsj/filestore/Filetoupload,481119,en.pdf

Nora, Pierre (1989) "Between Memory and History: Les Lieux de Mémoire," *Representations*, 26, Special Issue: Memory and Counter-Memory, 7–24.

Nora, Pierre (1996) "Preface to English Language Edition: From *Lieux de memoire* to Realms of Memory," in Pierre Nora (ed.), *Realms of Memory: The Construction of the French Past*, Vol. I, *Conflicts and Divisions*, ed. Lawrence D. Kritzman, trans. Arthur Goldhammer, New York: Columbia University Press, ix–xv.

Nora, Pierre (1998) "The Era of Commemoration," in Pierre Nora (ed.), *Realms of Memory: The Construction of the French Past*, Vol. III, *Symbols*, ed. Lawrence D. Kritzman, trans. Arthur Goldhammer, New York: Columbia University Press, 609–638.

North Down Borough Council Arts Section (2009) *Art of Regeneration*, n.p.

Northern Ireland Executive (2000) *Draft Programme for Government 2000–2*, http://cain.ulst.ac.uk/issues/politics/programme/pfg2000/draftpfg.pdf p.9.

Northern Ireland Human Rights Commission (2013) *Dealing with Northern Ireland's Past: Towards a Transitional Justice Approach*, Belfast: Northern Ireland Human Rights Commission

Northern Ireland Office (1998) *The Agreement: Agreement Reached in the Multi-Party Negotiations*, Belfast and London: Northern Ireland Office.

Northern Ireland Office (2018) *Addressing the Legacy of Northern Ireland's Past, Consultation Paper* https://assets.publishing.service.gov.uk/government/uploads/system/uploads/attachment_data/file/709091/Consultation_Paper_Addressing_the_Legacy_of_Northern_Irelands_Past.pdf

Northern Ireland Office (2018) *Addressing the Legacy of Northern Ireland's Past*, Public Consultation (Easy Read) https://assets.publishing.service.gov.uk/government/uploads/system/uploads/attachment_data/file/706289/Addressing_the_Legacy_of_Northern_Ireland_s_Past_Easy_Read.pdf

Northern Ireland Office (2018) *Addressing the Legacy of Northern Ireland's Past*, Public Consultation (Summary *Document*) https://assets.publishing.service.gov.uk/government/uploads/system/uploads/attachment_data/file/706302/Addressing_the_Legacy_of_Northern_Ireland_s_Past_Summary_Document.pdf

Northern Ireland Office (2019) *Addressing the Legacy of Northern Ireland's Past, Analysis of the Consultation Responses* https://assets.publishing.service.gov.uk/government/uploads/system/uploads/attachment_data/file/836991/Addressing_the_Legacy_of_the_Past_-_Analysis_of_the_consultation_responses__2_.pdf

Northern Ireland Tourist Board (2009) *Murals*, https://www.discovernorthernireland.com/murals/

Northern Whig (1909) "Nationalist nightingales," July 31, 9.

Northern Whig (1922) "Pettigo revisited," December 8, 8.

NOTA (2012) "NOTA—None of the above," https://wecancreate.wordpress.com/tag/straight-edge/

Novick, Peter (2000) *The Holocaust and Collective Memory: The American Experience*, London: Bloomsbury.

Novosel, Tony (2013) *Northern Ireland's Lost Opportunity: The Frustrated Promise of Political Loyalism*, London: Pluto.

O'Callaghan, Margaret (2007) "From Casement Park to Toomebridge: The Commenoration of the Easter Rising of 1916 in Northern Ireland in 1966 in Political Context," 96–147, in Margaret O'Callaghan and Mary Daly (eds), *1916 in 1966: Commemorating the Easter Rising*, Dublin: Royal Irish Academy.

O'Callaghan, Margaret and Mary Daly (eds) (2007) *1916 in 1966: Commemorating the Easter Rising*, Dublin: Royal Irish Academy.

O'Connor, Ulick (1975) *A Terrible Beauty is Born: The Irish Troubles, 1912–1922*, London: Hamish Hamilton.

Office of the First Minister and Deputy First Minister (2005) *A Shared Future: Policy and Strategic Framework for Good Relations in Northern Ireland*, http://www.asharedfutureni.gov.uk/

Office of the First Minister and Deputy First Minister [of Northern Ireland] (2006) *A Shared Future: First Triennial Action Plan 2006–2009*, Belfast: Community Relations Unit, OFMDFM.

Officer, David and Graham Walker (2000) "Protestant Ulster: Ethno-History, Memory and Contemporary Prospects," *National Identities*, 2.3, 293–307.

O'Hearn, Dennis (2006) *Nothing but an Unfinished Song: Bobby Sands, the Hunger Striker who Ignited a Generation*, New York: Nation Books.

O'Leary, Philip (1983) "'What Stalked through the Post Office?' Pearse's Cú Chulainn," *Proceedings of the Harvard Celtic Colloquium*, 3, 21–38.

Olick, Jeffer K. (1999) "Genre Memories and Memory Genres: A Dialogical Analysis of May 8, 1945 Commemorations in the Federal Republic of Germany," *American Sociological Review*, 64: 381–402.

Olick, Jeffrey K. (2007) *The Politics of Regret: On Collective Memory and Historical Responsibility*, London: Routledge.

Olick, Jeffrey K. and Joyce Robbins (1998) "Social Memory Studies: From 'Collective Memory' to the Historical Sociology of Mnemonic Practices," *Annual Review of Sociology*, 24.1, 105–140.

O'Malley, Padraig (1990) *Biting at the Grave The Irish Hunger Strikes and the Politics of Despair*, Belfast: Blackstaff Press.

Owens, Gary (1999) "Constructing the Martyrs: The Manchester Executions and the Nationalist Imagination," in Lawrence McBride (ed.), *Images, Icons and the Irish Nationalist Imagination*, Dublin: Four Courts Press, 18–36.

Patterson, Glenn (1996) *Lapsed Protestant*, Dublin: New Island.

Pearse, Padraic (2013) *Collected Works of Padraic H. Pearse: Political Writings and Speeches* [1916] Dublin, Éire-Gael Society.

Perry, Roger (2015) *The Writing on the* Wall, London: Plain Crisp Books.

Pinkerton, Patrick (2012) "Resisting Memory: The Politics of Memorialisation in Post-Conflict Northern Ireland," *The British Journal of Politics and International Relations*, 14.1, 131–152.

Prince, Simon and Geoffrey Warner (2019) *Belfast and Derry in Revolt: A New History of the Start of the Troubles*, Dublin: Irish Academic Press.

Prior, Robin and Trevor Wilson (2005) *The Somme*, London: Yale University Press.

Purbrick, L. (2011) "The Last Murals of Long Kesh: Fragments of Political Imprisonment at the Maze Prison, Northern Ireland," in A. Myers and G. Moshenska (eds), *Archaeologies of Internment*, New York: Springer, 263–284.

Purbrick, Louise, Jim Aulich, and Graham Dawson, eds. (2007) *Contested Spaces: Sites, Representations and Histories of Conflict*, London: Palgrave Macmillan.

Rapp, M., and M. Rhomberg (2012) "Seeking a Neutral Identity in Northern Ireland's Political Wall Paintings," *Peace Review*, 24.4, 470–477.

Redmond, Andrea (1997) "Women claim the walls," *Women's News*, 83, 8.

Redpath, Jackie (1983) "No Murals Here," *Circa*, 8, 20–21.

Renan, Ernest (1992) *Qu'est-ce qu'une nation*? trans. Ethan Rundell, Paris: Presses-Pocket, http://ucparis.fr/files/9313/6549/9943/What_is_a_Nation.pdf

Robinson, Joseph (2020) "We have long memories in this area": Ulster Defence Regiment place-memory along the Irish border," *Memory Studies*, Online first, https://journals.sagepub.com/doi/pdf/10.1177/1750698020921455

Robinson, Joseph and Andrew McClelland (2020) "Troubling places: Walking the 'troubling remnants' of post-conflict space," *Area*, 52.3, 654–662.

Rodrigo, Esther (2010) "Painting History: Murals in Northern Ireland," in David Clarke and Rúben Jarazo Alvaréz (eds), *To Banish Ghost and Goblin: New Essays on Irish Culture*, La Coruña: Netbiblo, 111–121.

Rolston, Bill (1991) *Politics and Painting: Murals and Conflict in Northern Ireland*, London: Associated University Presses.

Rolston, Bill (1992) *Drawing Support Murals in the North of Ireland*, Belfast: Beyond the Pale.

Rolston, Bill (1995) "Selling Tourism in a Country at War," *Race and Class*, 37.1, 23–40.

Rolston, Bill (1995) *Drawing Support 2: Murals of War and Peace*, Belfast: Beyond the Pale.

Rolston, Bill (1996) "Culture, Conflict and Murals: The Irish Case," in, T. Ziff (ed.), *Distant Relations: Chicano, Irish, Mexican Art and Critical Writing*, New York: Smart Art Press, 192–199.

Rolston, Bill (1997) "From King Billy to Cú Chulainn: Loyalist and Republican Murals, Past, Present, and Future," Éire-Ireland, 33.1, 6–28.

Rolston, Bill (1998) "All in the Mind? Photographing the Border," *Éire-Ireland*, 33.3, 245–254.

Rolston, Bill (2003) "Changing the Political Landscape: Murals and Transition in Northern Ireland," *Irish Studies Review*, 11.1, 3–16.

Rolston, Bill (2003) *Drawing Support 3: Murals and Transition in the North of Ireland*, Belfast: Beyond the Pale.

Rolston, Bill (2003) "Signs of the Times: Murals and Political Transformation in Northern Ireland," in Rosa Gonzalez (ed.), *The Representation of Ireland/s: Images from Outside and from Within*, Barcelona: Promociones y Publicaciones Universitarias, 27–43.

Rolston, Bill (2004) "Visions or Nightmares? Murals and Imagining the Future in Northern Ireland," in B. Cliff and E. Walshe (eds), *Representing the Troubles: Texts and Images, 1970–2000*, Dublin: Four Courts Press, 117–128.

Rolston, Bill (2004) "The War of the Walls: Political Murals in Northern Ireland," *Museum International*, 223, 2004, 38–45.

Rolston, Bill (2009) "'The Brothers on the Walls': International Solidarity and Irish Political Murals," *Journal of Black Studies*, 39.3, 446–470.

Rolston, Bill (2010) "'Trying to Reach the Future through the Past': Murals and Memory in Northern Ireland," *Crime, Media, Culture*, 6.3, 285–307.

Rolston, Bill (2012) "Reimaging: Mural Painting and the State in Northern Ireland," *International Journal of Cultural Studies*, 15.5, 447–466.

Rolston, Bill (2013) *Drawing Support 4: Murals and Conflict Transformation in Northern Ireland*, Belfast: Beyond the Pale.

Rolston, Bill (2013) "Prison as a Liberated Zone: The Murals of Long Kesh, Northern Ireland," *State Crime*, 2.2, 149–172.

Rolston, Bill (2014) "Prison Murals in Northern Ireland: Art and Resistance," *Social Justice* March 31 2014; http://www.socialjusticejournal.org/?p=2173

Rolston, Bill (2017) "Women on the Walls: Representations of Women in Political Murals in Northern Ireland," *Crime Media Culture*, 14.3, 365–389.

Rolston, Bill (2019) "Prison murals, Northern Ireland," https://billrolston.weebly.com/prison-murals-northern-ireland.html

Rolston, Bill (2020) "Ambushed by Memory: Post-Conflict Popular Memorialisation in Northern Ireland," *International Journal of Transitional Justice*, 14, 320–339.

Rolston, Bill (2022) *Drawing Support 5: Murals, Memory and Identity in the North of Ireland*, Belfast: Beyond the Pale.

Rolston, B. and Laurence McKeown (2017) "Male Republican Prisoners in Northern Ireland: Resistance, Emotions and Homosociality," *State Crime Journal*, 6.2, 265–285.

Romens, A. (2007) *Re-Imaging Communities or Re-Imaging Heritage? A Look at Northern Ireland's Latest Transformation Program*, http://www.saic.edu/pdf/degrees/pdf_files/aap/2007_Anne_Romans.pdf.

Rowan, Brian (1995) *Behind the Lines: The Story of the IRA and Loyalist Ceasefires*, Belfast: Blackstaff Press.

Rowan, Brian (2015) *Unfinished Peace: Thoughts on Northern Ireland's Unanswered Past*, Newtownards: Colorpoint.

Rowan, Brian (2021) *Political Purgatory: The Battle to Save Stormont and the Play for a New Ireland*, Newbridge: Merrion Press.

Rowan, Brian (2022) *Living with Ghosts: The Inside Story of a Troubles Mind*, Newbridge: Merrion Press.

Ruane, Joseph and Jennifer Todd (1991) "Why Can't you Just Get Along with Each Other? Culture, Structure and the Northern Ireland Conflict," in Eamonn Hughes (ed.), *Culture and Politics in Northern Ireland, 1960–1990*, Milton Keynes: Open University Press, 27–43.

Ryder, Caroline. "Painting the Town: Militant Street Art in Northern Ireland," *Swindle Quarterly*, 2005: 79–91.

Ryder, Chris and Vincent Kearney (2001) *Drumcree: The Orange Order's Last Stand*, London: Methuen.

Saleeby-Mulligan, Deborah (2009) *Painting the Irish Conflict: The Belfast Murals of Gerard Mo chara Kelly*, Berlin: Lambert.

Samuel, Raphael (1989) *Patriotism: The Making and Unmaking of British National Identity*, London: Routledge.

Samuel, Raphael (1994) *Theatres of Memory*. Vol. 1, *Past and Present in Contemporary Culture*, London: Verso.

Samuel, Raphael and Paul Thompson (1990) *The Myths We Live By*, London: Routledge.

Sand, Shlomo (2009) *The Invention of the Jewish People*, trans. Yael Lotan, London: Verso.

Sands, Bobby (1981) *The Writings of Bobby Sands*, Dublin: Sinn Féin.

Santino, Jack (1999) "Public Protest and Popular Style: Resistance from the Right in Northern Ireland and South Boston," *American Anthropologist*, 101, 515–528.

Santino, Jack (2001) *Signs of War And Peace: Social Conflict and the use of Public Symbols in Northern Ireland*, Basingstoke: Palgrave.

Schwartz, Barry (1982) "The Social Context of Commemoration: A Study in Collective Memory," *Social Forces*, 61.2, 374–402.

Sharma, R.S. (2007) *India's Ancient Past*, New Delhi: Oxford University Press.

Sherrard, Paul (1991) "Bus shelter murals," *Fingerpost*, 5.2, 96–97.

Shirlow, P. and B. Murtagh (2006) *Belfast: Segregation, Violence and the City*, London: Pluto Press.

Shirlow, Peter, Jonathan Tonge, James McAuley, and Catherine McGlynn (2013) *Abandoning Historical Conflict? Former Political Prisoners and Reconciliation in Northern Ireland*, Manchester: Manchester University Press.

Silke, Andrew 2000) "The Impact of Paramilitary Vigilantism on Victims and Communities in Northern Ireland," *International Journal of Human Rights*, 4.1, 1–24.

Simms, John G. (1974) "Remembering 1690," *Studies*, 63.251, 231–242.

Simpson, Kirk (2009) *Truth Recovery in Northern Ireland: Critically Interpreting the Past*, Manchester: Manchester University Press.

Sinn Féin (1993) *John Hume/Gerry Adams Statement 25th September 1993*, https://www.sinnfein.ie/contents/15218

Skinner, Jonathan and Lee Jolliffe (2016) *Murals and Tourism: Heritage, Politics and Identity*, London: Routledge.

Sluka, Jeffrey A (1992) "The Politics of Painting: Political Murals in Northern Ireland," in C. Nordstrom and J. Martin (eds), *The Paths to Domination, Resistance and Terror*, Berkeley: University of California Press, 190–216.

Sluka, Jeffrey A. (1995) "Domination, Resistance and Political Culture in Northern Ireland's Catholic-Nationalist Ghettos," *Critique of Anthropology*, 15.1, 71–102.

Sluka, Jeffrey A. (1996) "The Writing's on the Wall: Peace Process Images, Symbols and Murals in Northern Ireland," *Critique of Anthropology*, 16.4, 381–394.

Smith, Jonathan (1984) "The Art of the Ghettoes," *New Society*, October 18, 104–105.

Smithey, Lee (2011) "Mitigating Murals and Loyalist Cultural Innovation," in Lee Smithey (ed.), *Unionists, Loyalists and Conflict Transformation in Northern Ireland*, Oxford: Oxford University Press, 78–115.

Smyth, Jim (2010) "The lost revolution: the story of the Official IRA and the Workers' Party", *History Ireland*, 18.1, 56–58.

Smyth, Jim (ed.) (2017) *Remembering the Troubles: Contesting the Recent Past in Northern Ireland*, Notre Dame: University of Notre Dame Press.

Smyth, Marie (1998) "Remembering in Northern Ireland: Victims, Perpetrators and Hierarchies of Pain and Responsibility," in Brandon Hamber (ed.), *Past Imperfect: Dealing with the Past in Northern Ireland and Societies in Transition*, Derry/Londonderry: INCORE, 31–49.

Smyth, Marie (2001) "Putting the Past in its Place: Issues of Victimhood and Reconciliation in Northern Ireland's Peace Process," in Nigel Biggar (ed.), *Burying the Past: Making Peace and Doing Justice after Civil Conflict*, Washington: Georgetown University Press, 125–154.

Smyth, Marie and Marie-Therese Fay (2000) *Personal Accounts from Northern Ireland's Troubles: Public Conflict, Private Loss*, London: Pluto Press.

Soja, Edward (1980) "The Socio-Spatial Dialectic," *Annals of the Association of American Geographers*, 70.2, 207–225.

Solleder, Stefan (2016) "Unfinished Artefacts: The Case of Northern Ireland Murals, *Continent*, 5.1, 61–77, http://www.continentcontinent.cc/index.php/continent/article/view/230

The Stormont House Agreement (2014) https://assets.publishing.service.gov.uk/government/uploads/system/uploads/attachment_data/file/706293/Stormont_House_Agreement.pdf

Sutton, Malcolm (1994) *Bear in Mind these Dead: An Index of Deaths from the Conflict in Ireland, 1969–1993*, Belfast: Beyond the Pale Publications.

Switzer, Catherine and Brian Graham (2009) "'From Thorn to Thorn': Commemorating the Royal Ulster Constabulary in Northern Ireland," *Social & Cultural Geography*, 10:2, 153–171.

Switzer, Catherine and Brian Graham (2010) "Ulster's Love in Letter'd Gold": The Battle of the Somme and the Ulster Memorial Tower, 1918–1935," *Journal of Historical Geography*, 36.2, 183–193.
Switzer, Catherine and Sara McDowell (2009) "Redrawing Cognitive Maps of Conflict: Lost Spaces and Forgetting in the Centre of Belfast," *Memory Studies*, 2.3, 337–353.
Taylor, Peter (1997) *Provos*, London: Bloomsbury.
Taylor, Peter (2000) *Loyalists*, London: Bloomsbury.
Thompson, Simon (2002) "Parity of Esteem and the Politics of Recognition," *Contemporary Political Theory*, 1.2, 203–220.
Tóbín, Colm (1994) *Bad Blood: A Walk along the Irish Border*, London: Vintage.
Todd, Jennifer (1987) "Two Traditions in Unionist Political Culture," *Irish Political Studies*, 2.1, 1–26.
Townsend, Charles (2021) *The Partition: Ireland Divided, 1885–1925*, London: Allen Lane.
Travers, Pauric (1990) "Our Fenian Dead: Glasnevin Cemetery and the Genesis of Republican Funerals," in James Kelly and Uáitéar Mac Gearailt (eds), *Dublin and Dubliners: Essays in the History and Literature of Dublin City*, Dublin: Helicon, 52–72.
Traynor, Kevin (2008) *Loyalist Murals of Northern Ireland*, Belfast: Ashling Photography.
Traynor, Kevin (2008) *Nationalist Murals of Northern Ireland*, Belfast: Ashling Photography.
Turpin, John (1994) "Cuchulainn Lives On," *Circa*, 69, 26–31.
Valensi, Lucette (2000) "Traumatic Events and Historical Consciousness: Who is in Charge?" in Joep Leerssen and Ann Rigney (eds), *Historians and Social Values*, Amsterdam: Amsterdam University Press, 185–195.
Vannais, Judy (2000) "Mainstreaming murals," *Fortnight*, 385, 21–22.
Vannais, Judy (2000) "Out of the shadows of the gunmen," *Fortnight*, 382, 21–23.
Vannais, Judy (2001) "Postcards from the Edge: Reading Political Murals in the North of Ireland," *Irish Political Studies*, 16.1, 133–160.
Viggiani, Elisabetta (2006) *Public Forms of Memorialisation to the Victims of the Northern Irish "Troubles" in the City of Belfast*, https://cain.ulster.ac.uk/viggiani/index.html.
Viggiani, Elisabetta (2014) *Talking Stones: The Politics of Memorialization in Post-Conflict Northern Ireland*, Oxford: Berghahn.
Walker, Brian (1996) *Dancing to History's Tune: History, Myth and Politics in Ireland*, Belfast: Institute of Irish Studies, Queen's University of Belfast.
Walker, Brian (2000) *Past and Present: History, Identity and Politics in Ireland*, Belfast: Institute of Irish Studies, Queen's University of Belfast.
Wang, Q. and J. Brockmeier (2002) "Autobiographical Remembering as Cultural Practice: Understanding the Interplay between Memory, Self and Culture," *Culture & Psychology*, 8.1, 45–64.
Ward, James (1909) *Fresco Painting Its Art and Technique*, London: Chapman Hall.
Watson, Julian (1983) "Brightening the Place up?" *Circa*, 8: 4–10.
Weedon, Chris and Glenn Jordan (2012) "Collective Memory: Theory and Politics," *Social Semiotics*, 22.2, 143–153.
Wertsch, James and Henry L. Roediger (2008) "Collective memory: Conceptual Foundations and Theoretical Approaches," *Memory*, 16.3, 318–326.
Wertsch, James and Henry L. Roediger (2008) "Creating a New Discipline of Memory Studies," *Memory Studies*, 1.1, 9–22.
Wharton, Ken (2008) *A Long Long War: Voices from the British Army in Northern Ireland 1969–1998*, Solihull: Helion & Company.
Whelan, Peadar (2011) "Art as Struggle: The Murals of West Belfast," *An Phoblacht*, June 16, 4.
White, Jerry (2016) "Forms of Secularism and Multiculturalism: Charles Taylor and Ireland," *Irish Studies Review*, 24:3, 327–350.
White, T.J. and Denis Marnane (2016) "The Politics of Remembrance: Commemorating 1916," in *Irish Political Studies*, special issue, "Commemoration in Transition: Navigating Memory in Contested Societies," 31.1, 29–43.
Wiedenhoft Murphy, W. (2010) "Touring the Troubles in West Belfast: Building Peace or Reproducing Conflict?" *Peace & Change*, 35.4, 537–560.
Williams, Raymond (1976) *Marxism and Literature*, Oxford: Oxford University Press.
Williams, Raymond (1983) *Keywords: A Vocabulary of Culture and Society*, London: Fontana.
Wilson, Des (1983) "The Painted Message," *Circa*, 8: 19–20.

Wilson, Judith (1981) *Conor 1881–1968*, Belfast: Blackstaff Press.

Wilson, Robin (2008) "From Violence to Intolerance: Ethno-Nationalism and the Crowding Out of Civic Life," in Christopher Farrington (ed.), *Global Change, Civil Society and the Northern Ireland Peace Process: Implementing the Political Settlement*, Basingstoke: Palgrave Macmillan, 199–213.

Wilson, J. and K. Stapleton (2005) "Voices of Commemoration: The Discourse of Celebration and Confrontation in Northern Ireland," *Text & Talk*, 25.5, 633–664.

Winter, Jay (1995) *Sites of Memory, Sites of Mourning: The Great War in European Cultural History*, Cambridge: Cambridge University Press.

Winter, Jay (2006) *Remembering War: The Great War between Memory and History in the Twentieth Century*, New Haven: Yale University Press.

Winter, Jay (2017) *War Beyond Words: Languages of Remembrance from the Great War to the Present*, Cambridge: Cambridge University Press.

Wolterstorff, Nicholas (2015) *Art Rethought: The Social Practices of Art*, Oxford: Oxford University Press.

Wood, Ian S (2006) *Crimes of Loyalty: A History of the UDA*, Edinburgh: Edinburgh University Press.

Woods, Oona (1995) *Seeing is Believing: Murals in Derry*, Derry: Guidhall Press.

Woods, Oona (2008) *Murals of Derry*, Derry: Guildhall Press.

Yates, Frances (1974) *The Art of Memory*, London: Routledge and Kegan Paul.

Zerubavel, Yael (1995) *Recovered Roots: Collective Memory and the Making of Israeli National Tradition*, Chicago: University of Chicago Press.

Zerubavel, E. (2003) *Time Maps: Collective Memory and the Social Shape of the Past*, Chicago: University of Chicago Press.